THE WILEY BICENTENNIAL—KNOWLEDGE FOR GENERATIONS

*E*ach generation has its unique needs and aspirations. When Charles Wiley first opened his small printing shop in lower Manhattan in 1807, it was a generation of boundless potential searching for an identity. And we were there, helping to define a new American literary tradition. Over half a century later, in the midst of the Second Industrial Revolution, it was a generation focused on building the future. Once again, we were there, supplying the critical scientific, technical, and engineering knowledge that helped frame the world. Throughout the 20th Century, and into the new millennium, nations began to reach out beyond their own borders and a new international community was born. Wiley was there, expanding its operations around the world to enable a global exchange of ideas, opinions, and know-how.

For 200 years, Wiley has been an integral part of each generation's journey, enabling the flow of information and understanding necessary to meet their needs and fulfill their aspirations. Today, bold new technologies are changing the way we live and learn. Wiley will be there, providing you the must-have knowledge you need to imagine new worlds, new possibilities, and new opportunities.

Generations come and go, but you can always count on Wiley to provide you the knowledge you need, when and where you need it!

WILLIAM J. PESCE
PRESIDENT AND CHIEF EXECUTIVE OFFICER

PETER BOOTH WILEY
CHAIRMAN OF THE BOARD

To our students

Fundamentals of Statistical Reasoning in Education

Second Edition

Theodore Coladarci
University of Maine

Casey D. Cobb
University of Connecticut

Edward W. Minium (deceased)
San Jose State University

Robert B. Clarke
San Jose State University

BICENTENNIAL
1807
WILEY
2007
BICENTENNIAL

John Wiley & Sons, Inc.

PUBLISHER	JAY O'CALLAGHAN
ACQUISITIONS EDITOR	ROBERT JOHNSTON
PRODUCTION EDITOR	ANDREA JUDA
MARKETING MANAGER	EMILY STREUTKER
MEDIA EDITOR	LAUREN SAPIRA
EDITORIAL ASSISTANT	EILEEN MCKEEVER
DESIGNER	MICHAEL ST. MARTINE
PRODUCTION SERVICES	JEANINE FURINO / GGS BOOK SERVICES
BICENTENNIAL LOGO DESIGN	RICHARD J. PACIFICO

This book was set in Times Ten Roman by GGS Book Services and printed and bound by R.R. Donnelley. The cover was printed by Lehigh.

This book is printed on acid free paper. ∞

To order books or for custormer service please, call 1-800-CALL WILEY (225-5945).

ISBN10: 0-470-08406-5
ISBN13: 978-0470-08406-9
Printed in the United States of America

10 9 8 7 6 5 4 3 2 1

PREFACE

Fundamentals of Statistical Reasoning in Education 2e, like the first edition, is written largely with students of education in mind. Accordingly, we draw primarily on examples and issues found in school settings, such as those having to do with instruction, learning, motivation, and assessment. Our emphasis on educational applications notwithstanding, we are confident that readers will find *Fundamentals 2e* of general relevance to other disciplines in the behavioral sciences as well.

Our overall objective is to provide clear and comfortable exposition, engaging examples, and a balanced presentation of technical considerations, all with a focus on conceptual development. Required mathematics call only for basic arithmetic and an elementary understanding of simple equations. For those who feel in need of a brushup, we provide a math review in Appendix A. Statistical procedures are illustrated in step-by-step fashion, and end-of-chapter problems give students ample opportunity for practice and self-assessment. (Answers to roughly half of these problems are found in Appendix B.) Almost all chapters include an illustrative case study, a suggested computer exercise for students using the companion *SPSS for Windows*, and a "Reading the Research" box showing how a particular concept or procedure appears in the research literature. The result is a text that should engage all students, whether they approach their first course in statistics with confidence or with apprehension.

Fundamentals 2e reflects several improvements over its predecessor:

- "Effect size" is presented as a general concept that can be expressed in various forms: a standardized mean difference (Chapters 5, 6, 14), the coefficient of determination (Chapter 7), and omega-squared (Chapters 14, 16).

- The presentation of the chi-square test of independence (Chapter 18) has been streamlined (but not at the expense of conceptual development).

- A new concluding chapter provides an overview of statistical power.

- All chapters have benefited from the careful editing expected of any new edition, along with helpful clarification or elaboration here and there.

Fundamentals 2e is still designed as a "one semester" book. We intentionally sidestep topics that few introductory courses cover (e.g., factorial analysis of variance, repeated measures analysis of variance, multiple regression). At the same time, we incorporate effect size and confidence intervals throughout, which today are regarded as essential to good statistical practice.

Instructor's Guide

A guide for instructors can be found on the Wiley Web site at www.wiley.com/college/coladarci. This guide contains:

- Suggestions for adapting *Fundamentals 2e* to one's course.
- Helpful Internet resources on statistics education.
- The remaining answers to end-of-chapter problems.
- Data sets for the suggested computer exercises.
- *SPSS* output, with commentary, for each chapter's suggested computer exercise.
- An extensive bank of multiple-choice items.
- Stand-alone examples of *SPSS* analyses with commentary (where instructors simply wish to show students the nature of *SPSS*).
- Supplemental material ("*FYI*") providing elaboration or further illustration of procedures and principles in the text (e.g., the derivation of a formula, the equivalence of the t test, and one-way ANOVA when $k = 2$).

Acknowledgments

The following reviewers gave invaluable feedback toward the preparation of *Fundamentals 1e* and/or *Fundamentals 2e*: Terry Ackerman, University of Illinois, Urbana; Deb Allen, University of Maine; Tasha Beretvas, University of Texas at Austin; Shelly Blozis, University of Texas at Austin; Elliot Bonem, Eastern Michigan State University; David L. Brunsma, University of Alabama in Huntsville; Daniel J. Calcagnettie, Fairleigh Dickinson University; David Chattin, St. Joseph's College; Grant Cioffi, University of New Hampshire; Stephen Cooper, Glendale Community College; Brian Doore, University of Maine; David X. Fitt, Temple University; Shawn Fitzgerald, Kent State University; Gary B. Forbach, Washburn University; Roger B. Frey, University of Maine; Jane Halpert, DePaul University; Larry V. Hedges, Northwestern University; Mark Hoyert, Indiana University Northwest; Jane Loeb, University of Illinois, Larry H. Ludlow, Boston College; David S. Malcolm, Fordham University; Terry Malcolm, Bloomfield College; Robert Markley, Fort Hayes State University; William Michael, University of Southern California; Wayne Mitchell, Southwest Missouri State University; David Mostofsky, Boston University; Ken Nishita, California State University at Monterey Bay; Robbie Pittman, Western Carolina University; Phillip A. Pratt, University of Maine; Katherine Prenovost, University of Kansas; Bruce G. Rogers, University of Northern Iowa; N. Clayton Silver, University of Nevada; Leighton E. Stamps, University of New Orleans; Irene Trenholme, Elmhurst College; Gail Weems, University of Memphis; Kelly Kandra, University of North Carolina at Chapel Hill; James R. Larson, Jr., University of

Illinois at Chicago; Julia Klausili, University of Texas at Dallas; Hiroko Arikawa, Forest Institute of Professional Psychology; James Petty, University of Tennessee at Martin; Martin R. Deschenes, College of William and Mary; Kathryn Oleson, Reed College; Ward Rodriguez, California State University, Easy Bay; Gail D. Hughes, University of Arkansas at Little Rock; and Lea Witta, University of Central Florida.

We wish to thank John Moody, Derry Cooperative School District (NH); Michael Middleton, University of New Hampshire; and Charlie DePascale, National Center for the Improvement of Educational Assessment, each of whom provided data sets for some of the case studies.

We are particularly grateful for the support and encouragement provided by Robert Johnston of John Wiley & Sons, and to Katie Melega, Jeanine Furino, and all others associated with this project.

Theodore Coladarci
Casey D. Cobb
Edward W. Minium
Robert B. Clarke

CONTENTS

CHAPTER 1

Introduction

An anonymous sage once defined a statistician as "one who collects data and draws confusions." Another declared that members of this tribe occupy themselves by "drawing mathematically precise lines from unwarranted assumptions to foregone conclusions." And then there is the legendary proclamation issued by the nineteenth-century British statesman Benjamin Disraeli: "There are three kinds of lies: lies, damned lies, and statistics."

Are such characterizations justified? Clearly we think not! Just as every barrel has its rotten apples, there are statisticians among us for whom these sentiments are quite accurate. But they are the exception, not the rule. While there are endless reasons explaining why statistics is sometimes viewed with skepticism (math anxiety? mistrust of the unfamiliar?), there is no doubt that when properly applied, statistical reasoning serves to illuminate, not obscure. In short, our objective in writing this book is to acquaint you with the proper applications of statistical reasoning. As a result, you will be a more informed and critical patron of the research you read; furthermore, you will be able to conduct basic statistical analyses to explore empirical questions of your own.

Statistics merely formalizes what humans do every day. Indeed, most of the fundamental concepts and procedures we discuss in this book have parallels in everyday life, if somewhat beneath the surface. You may notice that there are people of different ages ("variability") at Eric Clapton and Bob Dylan concerts. Because Maine summers are generally warm ("average"), you don't bring a down parka when you vacation there. Baby boomers, you observe, tend to drive Volvo station wagons ("correlation"). You believe that it is highly unlikely ("probability") that your professor will take attendance two days in a row, so you skip class the day after attendance was taken. Having talked for several minutes ("sample") with a person you just met, you conclude that you don't like him ("generalization," "inference"). After getting a disappointing meal at a popular restaurant, you wonder whether it was just an off night for the chef or the place actually has gone down hill ("statistical significance").

We could go on, but you get the point: whether you are formally crunching numbers or simply going about life, you employ—consciously or not—the fundamental concepts and principles underlying statistical reasoning.

So what does formal statistical reasoning entail? As can be seen from the two-part structure of this book, statistical reasoning has two general branches: descriptive statistics and inferential statistics.

1.2   *Descriptive Statistics*

Among first-year students who declare a major in education, what proportion are male? female? Do those proportions differ between elementary education and secondary education students? Upon graduation, how many obtain teaching positions? How many go on to graduate school in education? And what proportion end up doing something unrelated to education? These are examples of questions for which **descriptive statistics** can help to provide a meaningful and convenient way of characterizing and portraying important features of the data.[1] In the examples above, *frequencies* and *proportions* will help to do the job of statistical description.

> The purpose of descriptive statistics is to organize and summarize data so that the data are more readily comprehended.

What is the average age of undergraduate students attending American universities for each of the past 10 years? Has it been changing? How much? What about the Graduate Record Examination (GRE) scores of graduate students over the past decade? Has that average been changing? One way to show the change is to construct a graph portraying the average age or GRE score for each of the 10 years. These questions illustrate the use of *averages* and *graphs*, additional tools that arc hclpful for dcscribing data.

We will explore descriptive procedures in later chapters, but for the present let's consider the following situation. Professor Spector, your statistics instructor, has given a test of elementary mathematics on the first day of class. She arranges the test scores in order of magnitude, and she sees that the distance between highest and lowest scores is not great and that the class average is higher than normal. She is pleased because the general level of preparation seems to be good and the group is not exceedingly diverse in its skills, which should make her teaching job easier. And you are pleased, too, for you learn that your performance is better than that of 90% of the students in your class. This scenario illustrates the use of more tools of descriptive statistics: the *frequency distribution*, which shows the scores in ordered arrangement; the *percentile*, a way to describe the location of a person's score relative to that of others in a group; and the *range*, which measures the variability of scores.

Because they each pertain to a single variable—age, GRE scores, and so on—the preceding examples involve **univariate** procedures for describing data. But often researchers are interested in describing data involving two characteristics of a person (or object) simultaneously, which call for **bivariate** procedures. For example, if you had information on 25 people concerning how many friends each person has (popularity) and how outgoing each person is (extroversion), you

---

[1]We are purists with respect to the pronunciation of this important noun ("day-tuh") and its plural status. Regarding the latter, promise us that you will recoil whenever you hear an otherwise informed person utter, "The data is . . . ." Simply put, data *are*.

could begin to determine whether popularity and extroversion are related. Is popularity greater among people with higher levels of extroversion and, conversely, lower among people lower in extroversion? The *correlation coefficient* is a bivariate statistic that describes the nature and magnitude of such relationships, and a *scatterplot* is a helpful tool for graphically portraying these relationships.

Regardless of how you approach the task of describing data, never lose sight of the principle underlying the use of descriptive statistics: The purpose is to organize and summarize data so that the data are more readily comprehended. When the question "Should I use statistics?" comes up, ask "Would the story my data have to tell be clearer if I did?" *Don't proceed statistically unless the answer is "Yes!"*

1.3 Inferential Statistics

What is the attitude of taxpayers toward, say, the use of federal dollars to support private schools? As you can imagine, pollsters find it impossible to put such questions to *every* taxpayer in this country! Instead, they survey the attitudes of a random **sample** of taxpayers, and from that knowledge they estimate the attitudes of taxpayers as a whole—the **population**. Like any estimate, this outcome is subject to random "error" or **sampling variation**. That is, random samples of the same population don't yield identical outcomes. Fortunately, if the sample has been chosen properly, it is possible to determine the magnitude of error that is involved.

The second branch of statistical practice, known as **inferential statistics**, provides the basis for answering questions of this kind. These procedures allow one to account for chance error in drawing inferences about a larger group, the population, on the basis of examining only a sample of that group. A central distinction here is that between **statistic** and **parameter**. A statistic is a characteristic of a sample (e.g., the proportion of *polled* taxpayers who favor federal support of private schools), whereas a parameter is a characteristic of a population (the proportion of *all* taxpayers who favor such support). Thus, statistics are used to estimate, or make inferences about, parameters.

> *Inferential statistics* permit conclusions about a population, based on the characteristics of a sample of the population.

Another application of inferential statistics is particularly helpful for evaluating the outcome of an experiment. Does a new drug, Melo, reduce hyperactivity among children? Suppose that you select at random two groups of hyperactive children and prescribe the drug to one group. All children are subsequently observed the following week in their classrooms. From the outcome of this study, you find that, on average, there is less hyperactivity among children receiving the drug.

Now some of this difference between the two groups would be expected even if they were treated alike in all respects, because of chance factors involved in the random selection of groups. As a researcher, the question you face is whether the obtained difference is within the limits of chance sampling variation. If certain assumptions have been met, statistical theory can provide the basis for an answer. If you find that the obtained difference is larger than can be accounted for by chance alone, you will infer that other factors must be at work to influence hyperactivity (the drug being a strong candidate).

This application of inferential statistics also is helpful for evaluating the outcome of a correlational study. Returning to the preceding example concerning the relationship between popularity and extroversion, you would appraise the obtained correlation much as you would the obtained difference in the hyperactivity experiment: Is this correlation larger than what would be expected from chance sampling variation alone? If so, then the traits of popularity and extroversion may very well be related in the population.

1.4   *The Role of Statistics in Educational Research*

Statistics is neither a beginning nor an end. A problem begins with a question rooted in the substance of the matter under study. *Does* Melo reduce hyperactivity? *Is* popularity related to extroversion? Such questions are called **substantive questions**.[2] You carefully formulate the question, refine it, and decide on the appropriate methodology for exploring the question empirically (i.e., using data).

Now is the time for statistics to play a part. Let's say your study calls for averages (as in the case of the hyperactivity experiment). You calculate the average for each group and raise a **statistical question:** Are the two averages so different that sampling variation alone cannot account for the difference? Statistical questions differ from substantive questions in that the former are questions about a statistical index—in this case, the average. If, after applying the appropriate statistical procedures, you find that the two averages are so different that it is not reasonable to believe that chance alone could account for it, you have made a **statistical conclusion**—a conclusion about the statistical question you raised.

Now back to the substantive question. If certain assumptions have been met and the conditions of the study have been carefully arranged, you may be able to conclude that the drug *does* make a difference, at least within the limits tested in your investigation. This is your final conclusion, and it is a **substantive conclusion**. Although the substantive conclusion derives partly from the statistical conclusion, other factors must be considered. As a researcher, therefore, you must weigh both the statistical conclusion *and* the adequacy of your methodology in arriving at the substantive conclusion.

It is important to see that, although there is a close relationship between the substantive question and the statistical question, the two are not identical. You will recall that a statistical question always concerns a statistical property of the data (e.g., an average or a correlation). Often, alternative statistical questions can

---

[2]The substantive question also is called the research question.

be applied to explore the particular substantive question. For instance, one might ask whether the *proportion* of students with very high levels of hyperactivity differs beyond the limits of chance variation between the two conditions. In this case, the statistical question is about a different statistical index: the proportion rather than the average.

Thus, part of the task of mastering statistics is to learn how to choose among, and sometimes combine, different statistical approaches to a particular substantive question. When designing a study, the question as to what statistical analyses should be performed ought to be considered in the course of refining the substantive question and developing a plan for collecting relevant data.

To sum up, the use of statistical procedures is always a middle step; they are a technical means to a substantive end. The argument we have presented can be illustrated as follows:

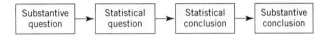

1.5   Variables and Their Measurement

Descriptive and inferential statistics are applied to **variables**.

> A *variable* is a characteristic (of a person, place, or thing) that takes on different values.

Variables in educational research often (but not always) reflect characteristics of *people*—academic achievement, age, leadership style, intelligence, educational attainment, beliefs and attitudes, and self-efficacy, to name a few. Two nonpeople examples of variables are school size and brand of computer software. Although simple, the defining characteristic of a variable—*something that varies*—is important to remember. A "variable" that doesn't vary sufficiently, as you will see later, will sabotage your statistical analysis every time![3]

Statistical analysis is not possible without numbers, and there cannot be numbers without **measurement**.

> *Measurement* is the process of assigning numbers to the characteristics you want to study.

For example, "20 years" may be the measurement for the characteristic, *age*, for a particular person; "115" may be that person's measurement for *intelligence*; on

---

[3]If this statement perplexes you, think through the difficulty of determining the relationship between, say, "school size" and "academic achievement" if *all* of the schools in your sample were an identical size.

a scale of 1 to 5, "3" may be the *sociability* measurement for this person; and since this hypothetical soul is female, perhaps she is assigned a value of "2" for *sex* (males being assigned "1").

But numbers can be deceptive. Even though these four characteristics—age, intelligence, sociability, and sex—all have been expressed in numerical form, the numbers differ considerably in their underlying properties. Consequently, these numbers also differ in how they should be interpreted and treated. We now turn to a more detailed consideration of a variable's properties and the corresponding implications for interpretation and treatment.

Qualitative versus Quantitative Variables

Values of **qualitative variables** (also known as **categorical variables**) differ in *kind* rather than in *amount*. Sex is a good example. Although males and females clearly are different in reproductive function (a qualitative distinction), it makes no sense to claim one group is either "less than" or "greater than" the other in this regard (a quantitative distinction).[4] And this is true even if the arbitrary measurements suggest otherwise! Other examples of qualitative variables are college major, marital status, political affiliation, county residence, and ethnicity.

In contrast, the numbers assigned to **quantitative variables** represent differing *quantities* of the characteristic. Age, intelligence, and sociability, which you saw above, are examples of quantitative variables: A 40-year-old is "older than" a 10-year-old; an IQ of 120 suggests "more intelligence" than an IQ of 90; and a child with a sociability rating of 5 presumably is more sociable than the child assigned a 4. Thus, the values of a quantitative variable differ in amount. As you will see shortly, however, the properties of quantitative variables can differ greatly.

Scales of Measurement

In 1946, Harvard psychologist S. S. Stevens wrote a seminal article on **scales of measurement**, in which he introduced a more elaborate scheme for classifying variables. Although there is considerable debate regarding the implications of his typology for statistical analysis (e.g., see Gaito, 1980; Stine, 1989), Stevens nonetheless provided a helpful framework for considering the nature of one's data. A variable, Stevens argued, rests on one of four scales: **nominal**, **ordinal**, **interval**, or **ratio**.

Nominal Scales   Values on a nominal scale merely "name" the category to which the object under study belongs. As such, interpretations must be limited to statements of kind rather than amount. (A qualitative variable thus represents a nominal scale.) Take ethnicity, for example, which a researcher may have coded

---

[4]Although males and females, on average, do differ *in amount* on any number of variables (e.g., height, strength, annual income), the scale in question is no longer sex. Rather, it is the scale of the other variable on which males and females are observed to differ.

1 = Italian, 2 = Irish, 3 = Asian, 4 = Hispanic, and 5 = African American.[5] It would be perfectly appropriate to conclude that, say, a person assigned "1" (Italian, we trust) is different from the person assigned "4" (Hispanic), but you cannot demand more of these data. For example, you could not claim that because $3 < 5$, Asian is "less than" African American; or that an Italian, when added to an Asian, begets an Hispanic (because $1 + 3 = 4$). The numbers don't mind, but it still makes no sense. The moral throughout this discussion is the same: One should remain forever mindful of the variable's underlying scale of measurement and the kinds of interpretations and operations that are sensible for that scale.

Ordinal Scales   Unlike nominal scales, values on an ordinal scale can be "ordered" to reflect differing degrees or amounts of the characteristic under study. For example, rank ordering students based on when they completed an in-class exam would reflect an ordinal scale, as would ranking runners according to when they crossed the finish line. You know that the person with the rank of 1 finished the exam sooner, or the race faster, than individuals receiving higher ranks.[6] But there is a limitation to this additional information: The only relation implied by ordinal values is "greater than" or "less than." One cannot say *how much* sooner the first student completed the exam compared to the third student, or that the difference in completion time between these two students is the same as that between the third and fourth students, or that the second-ranked student completed the exam in half the time of the fourth-ranked student. Ordinal information simply does not permit such interpretations.

Although rank order is the classic example of an ordinal scale, other examples frequently surface in educational research. Percentile ranks, which we take up in Chapter 2, fall on an ordinal scale: they express a person's performance relative to the performance of others (and little more). Likert-type items, which many educational researchers use for measuring attitudes, beliefs, and opinions (e.g., 1 = strongly disagree, 2 = disagree, and so on), are another example. Socioeconomic status, reflecting such factors as income, education, and occupation, often is expressed as a set of ordered categories (e.g., 1 = lower class, 2 = middle class, 3 = upper class) and, thus, qualifies as an ordinal scale.

Interval Scales   Values on an interval scale overcome the basic limitation of the ordinal scale by having "equal intervals." The 2-point difference between, say, 3 and 5 on an interval scale is the same—in terms of the underlying characteristic—as the difference between 7 and 9 or 24 and 26. Consider an ordinary Celsius thermometer: A drop in temperature from 30°C to 10°C is equivalent to a drop from 50°C to 30°C.

[5]Each individual must fall into only one category (i.e., the categories are *mutually exclusive*), and the five categories must represent all ethnicities among the study's participants (i.e., the categories are *exhaustive*).

[6]Although perhaps counterintuitive, the convention is to reserve *low* ranks (1, 2, etc.) for good performance (e.g., high scores, few errors, fast times).

The limitation of an interval scale, however, can be found in its **arbitrary zero**. In the case of the Celsius thermometer, for example, 0°C is arbitrarily set at the point at which water freezes (at sea level, no less). In contrast, the absence of heat (the temperature at which molecular activity ceases) is roughly −273°C. As a result, you could not claim that a 30°C day is three times as warm as a 10°C day. This would be the same as saying that column A in Figure 1.1 is three times as tall as column B. Statements involving ratios, like the preceding one, cannot be made from interval data.

What are examples of interval scales in educational research? Researchers typically regard composite measures of achievement, aptitude, personality, and attitude as interval scales. Although there is some debate as to whether such measures yield truly interval data, many researchers (ourselves included) are comfortable with the assumption that they do.

Ratio Scales   The final scale of measurement is the ratio scale. As you may suspect, it has the features of an interval scale *and* it permits ratio statements. This is because a ratio scale has an **absolute zero**. "Zero" weight, for example, represents an unequivocal absence of the characteristic being measured: *no* weight. Zip, nada, nothing. Consequently, you can say that a 230-pound linebacker weighs twice as much as a 115-pound jockey, a 30-year-old is three times the age of a 10-year-old, and the 25-foot sailboat *Adagio* is half the length of 50-foot *White Wings*—for weight, age, and length are all ratio scales.

In addition to physical measures (e.g., weight, height, distance, elapsed time), variables derived from *counting* also fall on a ratio scale. Examples include the number of errors a student makes on a reading comprehension task, the number of friends one reports having, the number of verbal reprimands a high school teacher issues during a lesson, or the number of students in a class, school, or district.

As with any scale, one must be careful when interpreting ratio scale data. Consider two vocabulary test scores of 10 and 20 (words correct). Does 20 reflect twice

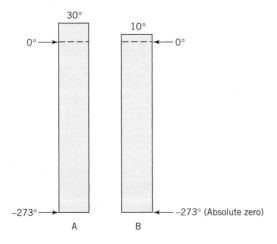

Figure 1.1   Comparison of 30° and 10° with the absolute zero on the Celsius scale.

the performance of 10? It does if one's interpretation is limited to performance on this particular test ("You knew twice as many words as I did"). However, it would be unjustifiable to conclude that the student scoring 20 has twice the *vocabulary* as the student scoring 10. Why? Because "0" on this test does not represent an absence of vocabulary; rather, it represents an absence of knowledge of the specific words on this test. Again, proper interpretation is critical with any measurement scale.

1.6   Some Tips on Studying Statistics

Is statistics a hard subject? It is and it isn't. Learning the "how" of statistics requires attention, care, and arithmetic accuracy, but it is not particularly difficult. Learning the "why" of statistics varies over a somewhat wider range of difficulty.

What is the expected reading rate for a book about statistics? Rate of reading and comprehension differ from person to person, of course, and a four-page assignment in mathematics may require more time than a four-page assignment in, say, history. Certainly, you should not expect to read a statistics text like a novel, or even like the usual history text. Some parts, like this chapter, will go faster; but others will require more concentration and several readings. In short, do not feel stupid or grow impatient if you can't race through a chapter and, instead, find that you need time for absorption and reflection. The formal logic of statistical inference, for example, is a new way of thinking for most people and requires some getting used to. Its newness can create difficulties for those who are not willing to slow down. As one of us was constantly reminded by his father, *"Festina lente!"*[7]

Many students expect difficulty in the area of mathematics. Ordinary arithmetic and some familiarity with the nature of equations are needed. Being able to see "what goes on" in an equation—to peek under the mathematical hood, so to speak—is necessary to understand what affects the statistic being calculated, and in what way. Such understanding also is helpful for spotting implausible results, which allows you to catch calculation errors when they first occur (rather than on an exam!). Appendix A is especially addressed to those who feel that their mathematics lies in the too-distant past to assure a sense of security. It contains a review of elementary mathematics of special relevance for study of this book. Not all these understandings are required at once, so there will be time to brush up in advance of need.

Questions and problems are included at the end of each chapter. You should work enough of these to feel comfortable with the material. They have been designed to give practice in how-to-do-it, in the exercise of critical evaluation, in development of the link between real problems and methodological approach, and in comprehension of statistical relationships. There is merit in giving some consideration to all questions and problems, even though your instructor may formally assign fewer of them.

A word also should be said about the cumulative nature of a course in elementary statistics: What is learned in earlier stages becomes the foundation for what

---

[7]"Make haste slowly!"

follows. Consequently, it is most important to keep up. If you have difficulty at some point, seek assistance from your instructor. Don't delay. Those who think matters may clear up if they wait may be right, but the risk is greater here—considerably so—than in courses covering material that is less interdependent. It can be like attempting to climb a ladder with some rungs missing or to understand an analogy when you don't know the meaning of all the words. Cramming, never very successful, is least so in statistics. Success in studying statistics depends on regular work, and, if this is done, relatively little is needed in the way of review before examination time.

Try constantly to "see the big picture." First, this pays off in computation. Look at the result of your calculation. *Does it make sense?* Be suspicious if you find the average to be 53 but most of the numbers are in the 60s and 70s. Remember, the eyeball is the statistician's most powerful tool. Second, because of the ladderlike nature of statistics, also try to relate what you are currently studying to concepts, principles, and techniques you learned earlier. Search for connections—they are there. When this kind of effort is made, you will find that statistics is less a collection of disparate techniques and more a concerted course of study. Happily, you also will find that it is easier to master!

Exercises

Identify, Define, or Explain

Terms and Concepts

descriptive statistics	substantive conclusion
univariate	variable
bivariate	measurement
sample	qualitative variable (or categorical variable)
population	quantitative variable
sampling variation	scales of measurement
inferential statistics	nominal scale
statistic	ordinal scale
parameter	interval scale
substantive question	ratio scale
statistical question	arbitrary zero
statistical conclusion	absolute zero

Questions and Problems

Note: Answers to starred (*) items are presented in Appendix B.

*1. Indicate which scale of measurement each of the following variables reflects:

   (a) the distance one can throw a shotput

   (b) urbanicity (where 1 = urban, 2 = suburban, 3 = rural)

   (c) school locker numbers

    (d) SAT score

    (e) type of extracurricular activity (e.g., debate team, field hockey, dance)

    (f) university ranking (in terms of library holdings)

    (g) class size

    (h) religious affiliation (1 = Protestant, 2 = Catholic, 3 = Jewish, etc.)

    (i) restaurant rating (* to ****)

    (j) astrological sign

    (k) miles per gallon

2. Which of the variables from Problem 1 are qualitative variables and which are quantitative variables?

3. For the three questions that follow, illustrate your reasoning with a variable from the list in Problem 1.

    (a) Can a ratio variable be reduced to an ordinal variable?

    (b) Can an ordinal variable be promoted to a ratio variable?

    (c) Can an ordinal variable be reduced to a nominal variable?

*4. Round the following numbers as specified (review Appendix A.7 if necessary):

    (a) to the nearest whole number: 8.545, −43.2, 123.01, .095

    (b) to the nearest tenth: 27.33, 1.9288, −.38, 4.9746

    (c) to the nearest hundredth: −31.519, 76.0048, .82951, 40.7442

5. In his travels, one of the authors once came upon a backroad sign announcing that a small town was just around the corner. The sign included the town's name, along with these facts:

Population	562
Feet above sea level	2150
Established	1951
TOTAL	4663

Drawing on what you have learned in this chapter, evaluate the meaning of "4663."

PART 1

Descriptive Statistics

CHAPTER 2

Frequency Distributions

2.1   Why Organize Data?

You perhaps are aware by now that in statistical analysis one deals with groups, often large groups, of observations. These observations, or data, occur in a variety of forms, as you saw in Chapter 1. They may be quantitative data such as test scores, socioeconomic status, or per-pupil expenditures, or they may be qualitative data as in the case of sex, ethnicity, or favorite tenor. Regardless of their origin or nature, data must be organized and summarized in order to make sense out of them. For taken as they come, data often present a confusing picture.

The most fundamental way of organizing and summarizing statistical data is to construct a **frequency distribution**. A frequency distribution displays the different values in a set of data and the frequency associated with each. This device can be used for qualitative and quantitative variables alike. In either case, a frequency distribution imposes order on an otherwise chaotic situation.

Most of this chapter is devoted to the construction of frequency distributions for quantitative variables, only because the procedure is more involved than that associated with qualitative variables (which we take up in the final section).

2.2   Frequency Distributions for Quantitative Variables

Imagine that one of your professors, Dr. Casteñeda, has scored a multiple-choice exam that he recently gave to the 50 students in your class. He now wants to get a sense of how his students did. Simply scanning the grade book, which results in the unwieldy display of scores in Table 2.1, is of limited help. How did the class do in general? Where do scores seem to cluster? How many students failed the test? Suppose that your score is 89—how did you do compared to your classmates? Such questions can be difficult to answer when the data appear "as they come."

The simplest way to see what the data are telling you is first to put the scores in order. To do so, Dr. Castcñeda locates the highest and lowest scores, and then he lists all *possible* scores (including these two extremes) in descending order. Among the data in Table 2.1, the highest score is 99 and the lowest is 51. The recorded sequence of possible scores is 99, 98, 97,..., 51, as shown in the "score" columns of Table 2.2.

Table 2.1   Scores from 50 Students on a Multiple-choice Examination

75	89	57	88	61
90	79	91	69	99
83	85	82	79	72
78	73	86	86	86
80	87	72	92	81
98	77	68	82	78
82	84	51	77	90
70	70	88	68	81
78	86	62	70	76
89	67	87	85	80

Now your instructor returns to the unordered collection of 50 scores and, taking them in the order shown in Table 2.1, tallies their **frequency** of occurrence, f, against the new (ordered) list. The result appears in the f columns of Table 2.2. As you see, a frequency distribution displays the scores and their frequency of occurrence in an ordered list.

Once the data have been organized in this way, which we call an **ungrouped-data frequency distribution**, a variety of interesting observations easily can be made. For example, although scores range from 51 to 99, Dr. Casteñeda sees that the bulk of scores lie between 67 and 92, with the distribution seeming to "peak"

Table 2.2   Scores from Table 2.1, Organized in Order of Magnitude with Frequencies (f)

Score	f	Score	f	Score	f
99	1	83	1	67	1
98	1	82	3	66	0
97	0	81	2	65	0
96	0	80	2	64	0
95	0	79	2	63	0
94	0	78	3	62	1
93	0	77	2	61	1
92	1	75	1	60	0
91	1	75	1	59	0
90	2	74	0	58	0
89	2	73	1	57	1
88	2	72	2	56	0
87	2	71	0	55	0
86	4	70	3	54	0
85	2	69	1	53	0
84	1	68	2	52	0
				51	1

at a score of 86 (not bad, he muses). There are two students whose scores stand out above the rest and four students who seem to be floundering. As for your score of 89, it falls above the peak of the distribution. Indeed, only six students scored higher.

2.3 Grouped Scores

Combining individual scores into groups of scores, or **class intervals**, makes it even easier to display the data and to grasp their meaning, particularly when scores range widely (as in Table 2.2). Such a distribution is called, not surprisingly, a **grouped-data frequency distribution**.

In Table 2.3, we show two ways of grouping Dr. Casteñeda's test data into class intervals. In one, the **interval width** (the number of score values in an interval) is 5, and in the other, the interval width is 3. We use the symbol "i" to represent interval width. Thus, $i = 5$ and $i = 3$ for the two frequency distributions in Table 2.3, respectively. The highest and lowest possible scores in an interval are known as the **score limits** of the interval (e.g., 95–99 in distribution A).

By comparing Tables 2.2 and 2.3, you see that frequencies for class intervals typically are larger than frequencies for individual score values. Consequently,

Table 2.3 Scores from Table 2.1, Converted to Grouped-Data Frequency Distributions with Differing Interval Width (i)

Distribution A: $i = 5$		Distribution B: $i = 3$	
Score Limits	f	**Score Limits**	f
95–99	2	96–98	2
90–94	4	93–95	0
85–89	12	90–92	4
80–84	9	87–89	6
75–79	9	84–86	7
70–74	6	81–83	6
65–69	4	78–80	7
60–64	2	75–77	4
55–59	1	72–74	3
50–54	1	69–71	4
	$n = 50$	66–68	3
		63–65	0
		60–62	2
		57–59	1
		54–56	0
		51–53	1
			$n = 50$

the former don't vary as irregularly as the latter. As a result, a grouped-data frequency distribution gives you a better overall picture of the data with a single glance: high and low scores, where the scores tend to cluster, and so forth. From distribution A in Table 2.3, for instance, you can see that scores tend to bunch up toward the upper end of the distribution and trail off in the lower end (easy exam? motivated students?). This is more difficult to discern from Table 2.2—and virtually impossible to apprehend from Table 2.1.

There are two cautionary notes you must bear in mind, however. First, some information inevitably is lost when scores are grouped. From distribution A in Table 2.3, for example, you have no idea *where* the two scores are in the interval 95–99. Are they both at one end of this interval, are both at the other end, or are they spread out? You cannot know unless you go back to the ungrouped data. Second, a set of individual scores does not yield a *single* set of grouped scores. Table 2.3 shows two different sets of grouped scores that may be formed from the same ungrouped data.

2.4   Some Guidelines for Forming Class Intervals

If a given set of individual scores can be grouped in more than one way, how do you decide what class intervals to use? Fortunately, there are some widely accepted conventions. The first two guidelines below should be followed closely; departures can result in very misleading impressions about the underlying shape of a distribution. In contrast, the remaining guidelines are rather arbitrary, and in special circumstances modifying one or more of them may produce a clearer presentation of the data. Artistry is knowing when to break the rules. Use of these conventions should be tempered with common sense and good judgment.

1. *All intervals should be of the same width.* This convention makes it easier to discern the overall pattern of the data. You may wish to modify this rule when several low scores are scattered across many intervals, in which case you could have an "open-ended" bottom interval (e.g., "<50"), along with the corresponding frequency. (This modification also can be applied to the *top* interval.)

2. *Intervals should be continuous throughout the distribution.* In distribution B of Table 2.3, there are no scores in interval 93–95. To omit this interval and "close ranks" would create a misleading impression.

3. *The interval containing the highest score value should be placed at the top.* This convention saves the trouble of learning how to read each new table when you come to it.

4. *There should be between 10 and 20 intervals.* For any set of scores, fewer intervals result in a greater interval width, i, and more information therefore is lost. (Imagine how uninformative a *single* class interval—for the entire set of scores—would be.) Many intervals, in contrast, result in greater complexity and, when carried to the extreme, defeat the purpose of forming intervals in

the first place.[1] This is where "artistry" is particularly relevant: Whether you select $i = 10$, 20, or any other value should depend on your judgment of the interval width that most illuminates your data. Of the two distributions in Table 2.3, for example, we prefer distribution A because the underlying shape of the distribution of frequencies is more evident with a quick glance and there are no empty intervals (i.e., $f = 0$).

5. *Select an odd (not even) value for the interval width.* As you will see in Chapter 3, an odd interval width gives you the convenience of working with an **interval midpoint** that does not require an additional digit. If you begin with whole numbers, this means that your interval midpoints also will be whole numbers.

6. *The lower score limits should be multiples of the interval width.* This convention also makes construction and interpretation easier.

2.5 Constructing a Grouped-Data Frequency Distribution

With these guidelines in mind, you are ready to translate a set of scores to a grouped-data frequency distribution. We illustrate this procedure by walking through our steps in constructing distribution A in Table 2.3.

Step 1 *Find the value of the lowest score and the highest score.* For our data, the values are 51 and 99, respectively.

Step 2 *Find the "range" of scores by subtracting the lowest score from the highest.* Simple: $99 - 51 = 48$.

Step 3 *Divide the range by 10 and by 20 to see what interval widths are acceptable; choose a convenient width.* Dividing by 10 gives us 4.8, which we round to 5, and dividing by 20 gives us 2.4, which we round to 3. We go with $i = 5$. (In Table 2.3, for illustrative purposes we present a frequency distribution based on *both* values of i. In practice, of course, one frequency distribution will do!)

Step 4 *Determine the lowest class interval.* Our lowest score is 51, so we select 50 for the beginning point of the lowest interval (it is a multiple of our interval width, i). Because $i = 5$, we add 4 (i.e., $5 - 1$) to this point to obtain our lowest class interval: 50–54. (If we had added 5, we would have an interval width of 6. Remember: i reflects the *number* of score values in a class interval, not the difference between the score limits.)

Step 5 *List all class intervals, placing the interval containing the highest score at the top.* We make sure that our intervals are continuous and of the same width: 50–54, 55–59, ..., 95–99.

[1]In some instances it *is* preferable to have no class interval at all ($i = 1$), as when the range of numbers is limited. Imagine, for example, that you are constructing a frequency distribution for the variable *number of children in household*.

Table 2.4   The Tally System for
Determining Frequencies

Score Limits	Tally	f
95–99	II	2
90–94	IIII	4
85–89	HHH HHH II	12
80–84	HHH IIII	9
75–79	HHH IIII	9
70–74	HHH I	6
65–69	IIII	4
60–64	II	2
55–59	I	1
50–54	I	1
		$n = 50$

Step 6   *Using the tally system, enter the raw scores in the appropriate class inter-*
vals. We illustrate the tally system in Table 2.4 (although tallies typically
are not included in the final frequency distribution).

Step 7   *Convert each tally to a frequency.* The frequency associated with a class
interval is denoted by f. The total number of scores, n, appears at the
bottom of the frequencies column. This, of course, should equal the sum
of all frequencies.

Interval width and score limits are always carried out to the same degree of accuracy as the original scores. For instance, Dr. Casteñeda's test scores are whole

Table 2.5   Grouped-
Data Frequency
Distribution for GPA

GPA	f
3.80–3.99	2
3.60–3.79	3
3.40–3.59	4
3.20–3.39	6
3.00–3.19	5
2.80–2.99	9
2.60–2.79	7
2.40–2.59	2
2.20–2.39	3
2.00–2.19	3
1.80–1.99	1
1.60–1.79	1
	$n = 46$

numbers, so the interval width and score limits for each of the intervals also are whole numbers. Suppose you wish to construct a frequency distribution of the grade point averages (GPAs), accurate to *two decimal places*, for students in a college fraternity. Table 2.5 shows a frequency distribution that might result. Note that $i = .20$ and that the score limits are shown to two decimal places.

2.6   The Relative Frequency Distribution

A researcher receives 45 of the surveys she recently mailed to a sample of teenagers. Is that a large number of returns? It is if she initially sent out 50 surveys—it's 90% of the total possible. But if she had mailed her survey to 1500 teenagers, 45 amounts to only 3%. For some purposes, the most relevant question is "How many?", whereas for others it is "What **proportion**?" or, equivalently, "What **percentage**?" And in many instances, it is important to know the answer to *both* questions.

The **absolute frequency** (f) for each class interval in a frequency distribution can easily be translated to a **relative frequency** by converting the absolute frequency to a proportion or percentage of the total number of cases. This results in a **relative frequency distribution**.

> A relative frequency distribution shows the scores and the proportion or percentage of the total number of cases that the scores represent.

To obtain the proportion of cases for each class interval in Table 2.6, we divided the interval's frequency by the total number of cases—that is, f/n. Proportions are expressed as a decimal fraction, or parts relative to one. A percentage, parts relative to $100,^2$ simply is a proportion multiplied by 100: (f/n)100. You need not carry out this

Table 2.6   Relative Frequency Distribution

Score Limits	f	Proportion	Percentage (%)
95–99	2	.04	4
90–94	4	.08	8
85–89	12	.24	24
80–84	9	.18	18
75–79	9	.18	18
70–74	6	.12	12
65–69	4	.08	8
60–64	2	.04	4
55–59	1	.02	2
50–54	1	.02	2
	$n = 50$		

---

[2]*Percent* comes from the Latin *per centum* ("by the hundred").

Table 2.7   Comparing Two Relative Frequency Distributions

Score Limits	Section 1		Section 2	
	f	%	f	%
95–99	2	4	2	10
90–94	4	8	3	15
85–89	12	24	5	25
80–84	9	18	4	20
75–79	9	18	3	15
70–74	6	12	1	5
65–69	4	8	1	5
60–64	2	4	1	5
55–59	1	2		
50–54	1	2		
	$n = 50$		$n = 20$	

second calculation: Simply move the proportion's decimal point two places to the right and—voilà!—you have a percentage. The common symbol for a percentage is %.

From Table 2.6, you see that the proportion of test scores falling in the interval 85–89 is .24 (12/50), which is equivalent to 24%—roughly one-quarter of the class. In the final presentation of relative frequencies, there often is little point in retaining more than hundredths for proportions or whole numbers for percentages.[3] There are some exceptions, however—perhaps the scores number in the several hundred, or perhaps you find yourself faced with exceedingly small values, such as a proportion of .004 (or the percentage equivalent, .4%).

Relative frequencies are particularly helpful when comparing two or more frequency distributions having different n's. Table 2.7 shows the distribution of test scores from Dr. Casteñeda's class ($n = 50$) alongside the distribution for the evening section he teaches ($n = 20$). As you can see, comparing frequencies is not easy. But conversion to relative frequencies puts both distributions on the same basis, and meaningful comparison is easier.

2.7   *Exact Limits*

So far, we have used as the limits of a particular class interval the highest and lowest scores that one *can actually obtain* that still fall in the interval. These, as you know, are the score limits of the interval, and for most purposes they will suffice. But as we will show, on some occasions it is useful to think in terms of **exact limits**[4]

---

[3]You should not be alarmed when the sum of the proportions (or percentages) occasionally departs slightly from 1.00 (or 100%). Provided you have not miscalculated, this minor inaccuracy simply reflects the rounding error that this convention can introduce.

[4]Exact limits also are referred to as the *real* or *true* limits of a class interval.

Figure 2.1 The exact limits of the score 87.

rather than score limits. The notion of exact limits is easily understood once you look more closely at the meaning of a specific score.

Consider three possible adjacent scores on Dr. Casteñeda's test: 86, 87, 88. The score of 87 is assumed to represent a level of knowledge *closer* to 87 than that indicated by a score of 86 or 88. Consequently, the score of 87 may be treated as actually extending from 86.5 to 87.5. This interpretation of a score is illustrated in Figure 2.1. *The limits of a score are considered to extend from one-half of the smallest unit of measurement below the value of the score to one-half of a unit above.*[5] If you were measuring to the nearest tenth of an inch, the range represented by a score of 2.3 in. is 2.3 ± .05 in., or from 2.25 in. to 2.35 in. If you were weighing coal (for reasons we cannot imagine) and you wished to measure to the nearest 10 pounds, a weight of 780 lb represents 780 ± 5 lb, or from 775 to 785 lb.

Now, consider the class interval 85–89. Since a score of 85 extends down to 84.5 and a score of 89 extends up to 89.5, the interval 85–89 may be treated as including everything between the *exact limits* of 84.5 and 89.5. Look ahead to Table 2.8 to see the exact limits for the complete distribution of Dr. Casteñeda's test scores. Notice that the lower exact limit of the class interval serves at the same time as the upper exact limit of the interval immediately below, and the upper exact limit of the class interval also is the lower exact limit of the interval immediately above. No one can ever fall right on an exact limit because every score here is reported as a whole number. It is as though there are boundaries of no thickness separating the intervals.

Table 2.8 Cumulative Frequencies and Percentages for a Grouped Frequency Distribution, with Exact Limits

Score Limits	Exact Limits	f	Cum. f	Cum. %
95–99	94.5–99.5	2	50	100
90–94	89.5–94.5	4	48	96
85–89	84.5–89.5	12	44	88
80–84	79.5–84.5	9	32	64
75–79	74.5–79.5	9	23	46
70–74	69.5–74.5	6	14	28
65–69	64.5–69.5	4	8	16
60–64	59.5–64.5	2	4	8
55–59	54.5–59.5	1	2	4
50–54	49.5–54.5	1	1	2
		$n = 50$		

[5]Age is the only common exception: when a person says she is 25, she typically means that her age is between 25.0 and 26.0.

Decimals need not cause alarm. Consider, for instance, the interval 2.60–2.79 in Table 2.5. A GPA of 2.60 includes everything between 2.595 and 2.605, and one of 2.79 includes GPAs from 2.785 to 2.795. Thus, the exact limits of the corresponding class interval are 2.595 to 2.795.

2.8   *The Cumulative Percentage Frequency Distribution*

It often is useful to know the percentage of cases *falling below* a particular point in a distribution: What percentage of Dr. Casteñeda's class falls below a score of 80? On a statewide achievement test, what percentage of eighth-grade students fell below "proficient"? At your university, what percentage of prospective teachers fell below the cutoff score when they took the teacher certification test? Questions of this kind are most easily answered when the distribution is cast in **cumulative percentage** form.

A **cumulative percentage frequency distribution** shows the percentage of cases that falls below the *upper exact limit* of each class interval.

Staying with Dr. Casteñeda, we present in Table 2.8 the cumulative percentage frequency distribution for his test scores. The procedure for constructing such a frequency distribution is easy:

Step 1   Construct a grouped-data frequency distribution, as described above. (We include exact limits in Table 2.8 for easy reference.)

Step 2   Determine the **cumulative frequencies**. The cumulative frequency for an interval is the total frequency *below the upper exact limit* of the interval, and it is noted in the column headed "Cum. *f.*" Begin at the bottom by entering 1 for the single case in the interval 50–54. This indicates that one case falls below the upper exact limit of 54.5. As you move up into the next interval, 55–59, you pick up an additional case, giving a cumulative frequency of 2 below its upper limit of 59.5. You continue to work your way up to the top by adding the frequency of each class interval to the cumulative frequency for the interval immediately below. As a check, the cumulative frequency for the uppermost class interval should equal *n*, the total number of cases.

Step 3   Convert each cumulative frequency to a cumulative percentage by dividing the former by *n* and moving the decimal two places to the right.[6] Cumulative percentages appear in the column headed "Cum. %."

The cumulative percentage is the percentage of cases falling below the *upper* exact limit of a particular interval of scores. For example, 64% of Dr. Casteñeda's students had scores below 84.5, and 46% scored below 79.5. Like any descriptive statistic, cumulative percentages are helpful for communicating the nature of your

---

[6]If you choose to leave the decimal point alone, you have a cumulative *proportion* instead of a cumulative *percentage*. Six of one, half a dozen of the other....

data. If Dr. Casteñeda's grading criteria are such that a score of 80 represents the bottom of the B range, then you see from Table 2.8 that fewer than half of his students (46%) received lower than a B on this exam. And the middle point of this set of scores—a cumulative percentage of 50%—lies somewhere within the exact limits of the class interval 80–84. (Do you see why?)

2.9   Percentile Ranks

Percentile ranks are closely related to our discussion of the cumulative percentage frequency distribution, and they are widely used in educational and psychological assessment to report the standing of an individual relative to the performance of a known group. A percentile rank is *the percentage of cases* falling below a given score point. If, in some distribution, 75% of the cases are below the score point 43, then this score is said to carry a percentile rank of 75. Stated another way, the score of 43 is equal to the 75th percentile. And you can say the converse as well: the 75th percentile is a score of 43.

Percentile ranks are often represented in symbolic form. For example, the 75th percentile is written as P_{75}, where the symbol P stands for "percentile" and the subscript indicates the percentile rank. Thus, $P_{75} = 43$ (and vice versa).

The 25th, 50th, and 75th percentiles in a distribution are called, respectively, the first, second, and third **quartiles;** they are denoted by Q_1, Q_2, and Q_3. Each quartile refers to a *specific score point* (e.g., $Q_3 = 43$ in the example above), although in practice you often will see reference made to the *group of scores* that a particular quartile marks off. The "bottom quartile," for instance, is the group of scores falling below the first quartile (Q_1)—that is, the lowest 25% of scores in a distribution. (See "Reading the Research: Quartiles.")

Calculating Percentile Ranks

Technically, a percentile rank is the percentage of cases falling below *the midpoint* of the score in question. Remember from Section 2.7 that, for any given score, half of the score's frequency falls above its "midpoint" and half below (again, we're speaking technically here). This said, only three steps are required to calculate the percentile rank for a given score.

Let's say you wish to determine the percentile rank for the score 86 in Table 2.9:

1 *Take half of the frequency, f/2, associated with the score in question.*
Four students obtained a score of 86 (i.e., $f = 4$), so the value you want is $f/2 = 4/2 = 2$.

2 *Add f/2 to the Cum. f for the score below the score in question.*
The score below 86 is 85, for which Cum. $f = 34$. Add $34 + 2$, which gives you 36.

3 *Divide this sum by n and multiply by 100.*
Easy: $(36/50)100 = 72$.

Table 2.9   Ungrouped Frequency Distribution with Percentile Ranks

Score	f	Cum. f	Percentile Rank	Calculations
99	1	50	99	$(.5 + 49)/50 \times 100$
98	1	49	97	$(.5 + 48)/50 \times 100$
92	1	48	95	$(.5 + 47)/50 \times 100$
91	1	47	93	$(.5 + 46)/50 \times 100$
90	2	46	90	$(1 + 44)/50 \times 100$
89	2	44	86	$(1 + 42)/50 \times 100$
88	2	42	82	$(1 + 40)/50 \times 100$
87	2	40	78	$(1 + 38)/50 \times 100$
86	4	38	72	$(2 + 34)/50 \times 100$
85	2	34	66	$(1 + 32)/50 \times 100$
84	1	32	63	$(.5 + 31)/50 \times 100$
83	1	31	61	$(.5 + 30)/50 \times 100$
82	3	30	57	$(1.5 + 27)/50 \times 100$
81	2	27	52	$(1 + 25)/50 \times 100$
80	2	25	48	$(1 + 23)/50 \times 100$
79	2	23	44	$(1 + 21)/50 \times 100$
78	3	21	39	$(1.5 + 18)/50 \times 100$
77	2	18	34	$(1 + 16)/50 \times 100$
76	1	16	34	$(.5 + 15)/50 \times 100$
75	1	15	29	$(.5 + 14)/50 \times 100$
73	1	14	27	$(.5 + 13)/50 \times 100$
72	2	13	24	$(1 + 11)/50 \times 100$
70	3	11	19	$(1.5 + 8)/50 \times 100$
69	1	8	15	$(.5 + 7)/50 \times 100$
68	2	7	12	$(1 + 5)/50 \times 100$
67	1	5	9	$(.5 + 4)/50 \times 100$
62	1	4	7	$(.5 + 3)/50 \times 100$
61	1	3	5	$(.5 + 2)/50 \times 100$
57	1	2	3	$(.5 + 1)/50 \times 100$
51	1	1	1	$(.5 + 0)/50 \times 100$

In this distribution, then, a score of 86 is equal to the 72nd percentile ($86 = P_{72}$). That is, 72% of the cases fall below the score point 86 (and 28% fall above).

For illustrative purposes only, we provide the calculations for each percentile in Table 2.9. The general formula for determining percentile ranks for scores in an ungrouped frequency distribution is given in Formula (2.1).

Percentile Rank
(ungrouped frequency distribution)

$$P = \left(\frac{f/2 + \text{Cum. } f(\text{below})}{n} \right) 100 \qquad (2.1)$$

Here, f is the frequency of the score in question, "Cum. f (below)" is the cumulative frequency for the score appearing immediately *below* the score in question, and n is the total number of scores in the distribution.

As a rule, statistical software does not provide percentile ranks for each score in an ungrouped frequency distribution, but Formula (2.1) easily can be applied if one desires the percentile rank for select scores.[7] Although cumulative percentages (which *are* routinely reported by statistical software) are not identical to percentile ranks, they can be used if an approximation will suffice.

Cautions Regarding Percentile Ranks

Be cautious when interpreting percentile ranks. First, do not confuse percentile ranks, which reflect *relative* performance, with "percentage correct," which reflects *absolute* performance. Consider the student who gets few answers correct on an exceedingly difficult test but nonetheless outscores most of his classmates: he would have a *low* percentage correct but a *high* percentile. Conversely, low percentiles do not necessarily indicate a poor showing in terms of percentage correct.

Second, percentile ranks always are based on a specific group and, therefore, must be interpreted with that group in mind. If you are the lone math major in your statistics class and you score at the 99th percentile on the first exam, there is little cause for celebration. But if you are the only *non*math major in the class and obtain this score, then let the party begin!

There is a third caution about the use of percentiles, which involves an appreciation of the "normal curve" and the noninterval nature of the percentile scale. We wait until Chapter 6 (Section 6.10) to apprise you of this additional caveat.

2.10 Frequency Distributions for Qualitative Variables

As we stated at the beginning of this chapter, frequency distributions also can be constructed for qualitative variables. Imagine you want to know what reward strategies preschool teachers use for encouraging good behavior in their students. You identify a sample of 30 such teachers and ask each to indicate his or her *primary* reward strategy. (Although teachers use multiple strategies, you want to know the dominant one.) You find that all teachers report one of three primary strategies for rewarding good behavior: granting privileges, giving out stickers, and providing verbal praise.

We trust you would agree that "dominant reward strategy" is a qualitative, or nominal, variable: Privileges, stickers, and verbal praise differ in kind and not in

---

[7]When data are grouped, as in Table 2.8, it is not possible to directly determine percentiles. Rather, one must "interpolate" the percentile rank (the details of which go beyond our intentions here). With small samples or large interval widths, the resulting estimates can be rather imprecise.

Table 2.10   Frequency Distribution for a
Qualitative (Nominal) Variable

Dominant Reward Strategy	f	%
Verbal praise	21	70
Stickers	6	20
Privileges	3	10
	$n = 30$	

amount. To assemble the resulting data in a frequency distribution, such as the one that appears in Table 2.10, follow two simple steps:

Step 1   List the categories that make up the variable. To avoid the appearance of bias, arrange this list either alphabetically or by descending magnitude of frequency (as in Table 2.10).

Step 2   Record the frequency, f, associated with each category and, if you wish, the corresponding percentage. Report the total number of cases, n, at the bottom of the frequencies column.

Question: Would it be appropriate to include *cumulative* frequencies and percentages in this frequency distribution? Of course not, for it makes no sense to talk about a teacher "falling below" stickers or any other category of this qualitative variable (just as in Chapter 1 it made no sense to claim that Asian is "less than" African American). Cumulative indices imply an underlying continuum of scores and therefore are reserved for variables that are at least ordinal.

2.11   Summary

It is difficult for data to tell their story until they have been organized in some fashion. Frequency distributions make the meaning of data more easily grasped. Frequency distributions can show both the absolute frequency (how many?) and the relative frequency (what proportion or percentage?) associated with a score, class interval, or category. For quantitative variables, the cumulative percentage frequency distribution presents the percentage of cases that fall below a score or class interval. This kind of frequency distribution also permits the identification of percentiles and percentile ranks.

Reading the Research: Quartiles

As you saw in Section 2.9, quartiles refer to any of the three values (Q_1, Q_2, and Q_3) that separate a frequency distribution into four equal groups. In practice, however, the term *quartile* often is used to designate any one of the resulting four groups rather than the three score points. For example, consider the use of the quartile in the following summary of a study on kindergartners:

Children's performance in reading, mathematics, and general knowledge increases with the level of their mothers' education. Kindergartners whose mothers have more education are more likely to score in the highest quartile in reading, mathematics, and general knowledge. However, some children whose mothers have less than a high school education also score in the highest quartile. (West et al., 2000, p. 15)

Kindergartners who scored "in the highest quartile" tested better than 75% of all kindergartners. Put another way, children in the highest quartile scored in the top 25%, which is why this quartile often is called the "top quartile." However named, this group of scores falls beyond Q_3.

Source: West, J., Denton, K., & Germino-Hausken, E. (2000). *America's kindergartners: Findings from the Early Childhood Longitudinal Study, Kindergarten Class of 1998–99.* National Center for Education Statistics. U.S. Department of Education. ERIC Reproduction Document Number 438 089.

Case Study: A Tale of Two Cities

We obtained a large data set that contained 2000–2001 academic year information on virtually every public school in California—in this case, over 7300 schools. This gave us access to more than 80 pieces of information (or variables) for each school, including enrollment, grade levels served, percentage of teachers fully certified, and percentage of students eligible for federal lunch subsidies. Central to this data file is an Academic Performance Index (API) by which schools were assessed and ranked by the state in 2000. The API is actually a composite of test scores in different subjects across grade levels, but it generally can be viewed as an overall test score for each school. This index ranges from 200 to 1000.

For this case study, we compared the public high schools of two large California school districts: San Diego City Unified and San Francisco Unified. Although there were many variables to consider, we examined only two: the API score and the percentage of staff fully certified to teach.

We start with the variable named FULLCERT, which represents the percentage of staff at each school who are fully certified by state requirements. Using our statistical software, we obtained frequency distributions on FULLCERT for all high schools in both districts.[8] The results of this ungrouped frequency distribution are seen in Table 2.11.

---

[8]As they say in the trade, we "ran frequencies" on FULLCERT.

Table 2.11   Ungrouped Frequency Distributions for 2000–2001
FULLCERT Scores: San Francisco and San Diego City District
High Schools

	Score	f	%	Cum. %
San Francisco	100	1	6.25	100.00
	96	1	6.25	93.75
	95	1	6.25	87.50
	91	2	12.50	81.25
	89	1	6.25	68.75
	87	1	6.25	62.50
	84	2	12.50	56.25
	81	1	6.25	43.75
	78	1	6.25	37.50
	72	1	6.25	31.25
	68	1	6.25	25.00
	61	2	12.50	18.75
	46	1	6.25	6.25
		$n = 16$		
San Diego City	100	3	16.67	100.00
	99	5	27.78	83.33
	98	4	22.22	55.56
	96	1	5.56	33.33
	95	1	5.56	27.78
	94	1	5.56	22.22
	93	1	5.56	16.67
	92	2	11.11	11.11
		$n = 18$		

We can learn much from Table 2.11. For instance, we can see that one San Francisco high school employed a fully certified teaching staff. We also know, from the cumulative percentage column, that one-third (33.33%) of the staffs in San Diego were 96% fully certified or less. Simple arithmetic therefore tells us that two-thirds (100.00 − 33.33) of the San Diego staffs were at least 98% fully certified.

The output in Table 2.11 is informative, but perhaps it would be easier to interpret as a *grouped* frequency distribution. Table 2.12 displays the grouped frequency distributions that we created manually. (Notice that we elected to use a class interval of 10 due to the relatively low number of scores here.) Table 2.12 depicts a clearer picture of the distribution of scores for both districts. San Diego's public high schools appear to have higher qualified staffs, at least by state credentialing standards. All 18 schools maintain staffs that are at least 90% fully certified. In contrast, only 5 of San Francisco's 16 schools, roughly 31%, fall in this category.

Table 2.12   Grouped Frequency Distributions for 2000–2001 FULLCERT Scores: San Francisco and San Diego City District High Schools

Score Limits	San Francisco			San Diego City		
	f	%	Cum. %	f	%	Cum. %
91–100	5	31.25	100.00	18	100.00	100.00
81–90	5	31.25	68.75	0	0.00	0.00
71–80	2	12.50	37.50	0	0.00	0.00
61–70	3	18.75	25.00	0	0.00	0.00
51–60	0	0.00	6.25	0	0.00	0.00
41–50	1	6.25	6.25	0	0.00	0.00
	$n = 16$			$n = 18$		

Next we compared the two districts in terms of their schools' API scores. Again, we used the grouped frequency distribution to better understand these data. Look at the distribution in Table 2.13: The scores are fairly spread out for both districts, although it seems that San Diego is home to more higher scoring schools overall. Indeed, the cumulative percentages at the 600–699 interval tell us that a third of the San Diego high schools scored above 699—compared to one-quarter of San Francisco's schools. San Francisco, however, lays claim to the highest API score (falling somewhere between 900 and 999, right?).

To this point, our analysis of the FULLCERT and API variables seems to suggest that higher test scores are associated with a more qualified teaching staff. Although this may be the case, we cannot know for sure by way of this analysis. To be sure, such a conclusion calls for *bivariate* procedures, which we take up in Chapter 7.

Table 2.13   Grouped Frequency Distributions for 2000–2001 API Scores: San Francisco and San Diego City Districts

Score Limits	San Francisco			San Diego City		
	f	%	Cum. %	f	%	Cum. %
900–999	1	6.25	100.00	0	0.00	100.00
800–899	0	0.00	93.75	1	5.56	100.00
700–799	3	18.75	93.75	5	27.78	94.45
600–699	3	18.75	75.00	6	33.33	66.67
500–599	4	25.00	56.25	3	16.67	33.34
400–499	5	31.25	31.25	3	16.67	16.67
	$n = 16$			$n = 18$		

Table 2.14   Ungrouped Frequency
Distributions for 2000–2001 API Scores:
California High Schools

Score	f	%	Cum. %
969	1	0.1	100.0
933	1	0.1	99.9
922	1	0.1	99.8
912	1	0.1	99.6
907	1	0.1	99.5
895	2	0.2	99.4
•	•	•	•
•	•	•	•
•	•	•	•
361	1	0.1	0.4
356	2	0.1	0.2
339	1	0.1	0.1
	$n = 854$		

Finally, what about the San Francisco school that scored so high? (Credit Lowell High School with an impressive API score of 933.) It must be one of the highest scoring schools in the state. To find out just where this school stands relative to *all* high schools in the state, we returned to our original data set and ran frequencies on the API variable for the 854 high schools in California. We present a portion of that output in Table 2.14. Look for an API score of 933. Using the cumulative percentage column, you can see that Lowell High scored higher than 99.8 percent of all high schools in the state. In fact, only one school scored higher.

Suggested Computer Exercises

The **sophomores** data file contains information on 521 tenth graders from a large suburban public school. The information in the file includes student ID, gender, scores on state-administered tenth-grade mathematics and reading exams, scores on an eighth-grade national standardized mathematics exam, and whether or not the student enrolled in an algebra course during the eighth grade.

1. The test scores represented by the READING variable are on a scale ranging from 200 to 300 points.

(a) Generate a frequency distribution for READING.

(b) Find the cumulative percentage for each of the following scores: 226, 262, and 280.

(c) Approximately one-tenth of the cases fall at or below which score?

(d) What score, roughly speaking, separates the top half from the bottom half of students?

2. Determine the proportion of females in the sophomore class.

Exercises

Identify, Define, or Explain

Terms and Concepts

frequency distribution (ungrouped and grouped)
frequency
grouped scores
class intervals
interval width
score limits
interval midpoint
proportion
percentage

absolute frequency
relative frequency
relative frequency distribution
exact limits
cumulative percentage
cumulative frequency
cumulative percentage frequency distribution
percentile rank
quartile

Symbols

f n i Cum. f Cum. % P_{25} Q_1, Q_2, Q_3

Questions and Problems

Note: Answers to starred (*) items are presented in Appendix B.

1. List the objectionable features of this set of class intervals (score limits) for a hypothetical frequency distribution:

Score Limits
25–30
30–40
40–45
50–60
60–65

2. Comment on the following statement: "The rules for constructing frequency distributions have been carefully developed *and should be strictly adhered to*."

*3. The lowest and highest scores are given below for different sets of scores. In each case, the scores are to be grouped into class intervals. For each, give (1) the range, (2) your choice of class interval width, (3) the score limits for the lowest interval, and (4) the score limits for the highest interval (do this directly *without* listing any of the intervals between the lowest and the highest):

(a) 24, 70

(b) 27, 101

(c) 56, 69

(d) 187, 821

(e) 6.3, 21.9

(f) 1.27, 3.47

(g) 36, 62

4. For each of the following intervals, give (1) the interval width, (2) the exact limits of the interval, and (3) the score limits and exact limits of the next higher interval (assume the scores are rounded to the nearest whole number or decimal place indicated unless otherwise specified):

(a) 10–14

(b) 20–39

(c) 2.50–2.74

(d) 1.0–1.9

(e) 30–40 (accurate to the nearest 10)

*5. Convert the following proportions to percents (to the same degree of accuracy):

(a) .26

(b) .05

(c) .004

(d) .555

(e) .79

6. Convert the following percents to proportions (again, to the same degree of accuracy):

(a) 42%

(b) 6.6%

(c) 43.7%

(d) 78%

(e) .8%

*7. Thirty prospective teachers take a standards-based teacher competency test. The results are as follows (each score reflects the percentage of standards for which the prospective teacher demonstrates proficiency):

81	91	89	81	79	82
70	92	80	64	73	86
87	72	74	75	90	85
83	82	79	82	78	96
77	85	83	87	88	80

Because the range of these 30 scores is $96 - 64 = 32$, plausible values of i are 2 or 3.

(a) How did we get these two values of i?

(b) Construct a frequency distribution with $i = 3$ and 63–65 as the lowest interval; include score limits and exact limits, frequencies, percentages, cumulative frequencies, and cumulative percentages.

(c) Construct a frequency distribution with $i = 2$ and 64–65 as the lowest interval; include percentages, cumulative frequencies, and cumulative percentages.

(d) Which frequency distribution do you prefer—one based on $i = 2$ or $i = 3$? Why?

8. The following is the cumulative frequency distribution for 30 scores on a "test anxiety" survey.

Test Anxiety	f	Cum. f	Cum. %	Percentile Rank
79	1			
73	1			
70	1			
67	1			
66	1			
64	1			
63	2			
62	2			
61	3			
60	4			
59	2			
58	2			
57	2			
56	1			
55	1			
53	1			
52	1			
49	1			
45	1			
39	1			

(a) Fill in the three blank columns (round the cumulative percentages to the nearest whole number).

(b) Find the cumulative percentage and percentile ranks for each of the following scores: 67, 57, and 49.

(c) Roughly two-thirds of the cases fall at or below which score?

(d) One-fifth of the cases fall at or below which score?

(e) Between what two scores is the "middle" of this distribution?

9. Suppose that the racial/ethnic breakdown of participants in your investigation is as follows: African American, $n = 25$; White, $n = 90$; Asian, $n = 42$; Hispanic, $n = 15$; "other," $n = 10$. Construct a frequency distribution for these data.

*10. Imagine you wanted to compare the frequency distributions for males and females separately (on some variable), and there are considerably more females than males. Which would you concentrate on—the original frequencies or the relative frequencies? Why? Provide an illustration to support your reasoning.

11. Provide the exact limits for the data we presented earlier in Table 2.5:

GPA	f	Exact Limits
3.80–3.99	2	
3.60–3.79	3	
3.40–3.59	4	
3.20–3.39	6	
3.00–3.19	5	
2.80–2.99	9	
2.60–2.79	7	
2.40–2.59	2	
2.20–2.39	3	
2.00–2.19	3	
1.80–1.99	1	
1.60–1.79	1	

*12. Imagine the data below are the GPAs for a sample of 60 sophomores at your university. Prepare a relative frequency distribution (use proportions), using an interval width of .30 and .90–1.19 as the score limits for the lowest interval.

3.08	1.81	3.63	2.52	2.97	3.48	1.00	2.70	2.95	3.29
1.40	2.39	4.00	2.69	2.92	3.34	3.00	3.37	3.01	2.11
2.36	3.23	2.99	2.61	3.02	3.27	2.65	3.89	1.60	2.31
3.93	2.98	3.59	3.04	2.88	3.76	2.28	3.25	3.14	2.85
3.45	3.20	1.94	3.80	2.58	3.26	2.06	3.99	3.06	2.40
2.44	2.81	3.68	3.03	3.30	3.54	3.39	3.10	3.18	2.74

13. The following scores were obtained by middle-level students on an "educational aspirations" assessment:

41	33	18	41	36	50	27	34	36	36
36	36	39	33	40	48	29	41	28	39
30	44	41	39	45	30	36	27	21	46
40	47	46	47	35	24	32	46	33	39
33	45	39	31	37	46	34	18	30	35
27	42	27	31	33	44	39	36	24	27
30	24	22	33	36	54	54	46	32	33
24	24	36	35	42	22	42	45	27	41

Construct a frequency distribution using an interval width of 3 and 18–20 as the score limits for the lowest interval. Convert the frequencies to relative frequencies (use proportions).

*14. Construct a relative frequency distribution (use proportions) from the scores in Problem 13 using an interval width of 5 and 15–19 as the lowest interval. Compare the result with the distribution obtained in Problem 13. From this example, what would you say are the advantages of sometimes using a larger interval size and thus fewer intervals?

CHAPTER 3

Graphic Representation

3.1   Why Graph Data?

The tabular representation of data, as you saw in Chapter 2, reveals the nature and meaning of data more clearly than when data are presented in an unorganized as-they-come manner. This is equally true—arguably more so—with the *graphic* representation of data. Although based entirely on the tabled data, a graph often makes vivid what a table can only hint at. A picture, indeed, can be worth a thousand words (or numbers).

There are many kinds of graphs, and books are available that describe graphic representation in variety and at length. We consider here only graphic representations of frequency distributions because of their prominence in educational research. We begin by considering the bar chart, which is used for graphing qualitative data, and the histogram and the frequency polygon, which are used for graphing quantitative data. We conclude with a presentation of the box plot, an additional method for graphing quantitative data.

3.2   Graphing Qualitative Data: The Bar Chart

Let's return to the data from Table 2.10, which pertain to the reward strategies used by preschool teachers. Figure 3.1 presents a **bar chart** for these data. A bar chart has two axes, one horizontal and the other vertical. The categories of the variable are arranged along the horizontal axis, either alphabetically or by frequency magnitude. Frequencies, either absolute (f) or relative (%), appear along the vertical axis. A rectangle, or bar, of uniform width is placed above each category, and its height corresponds to the frequency associated with the category. Gaps appear between the bars to signify the categorical nature of the data. Beyond the need to label the axes clearly and provide an informative title, that's about it.[1]

---

[1]The *pie chart* is a popular alternative to the bar chart, particularly in the print media. Named for obvious reasons, it presents each category's frequency as a proportion of a circle. To construct a pie chart accurately, all you need is a compass, a protractor, and the knowledge that a circle comprises 360 degrees.

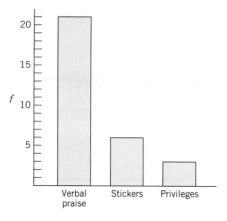

Figure 3.1   Bar chart, using data from Table 2.10.

3.3   *Graphing Quantitative Data: The Histogram*

The concept of a bar chart easily can be generalized to quantitative data, in which case you have a **histogram**. Although the basic idea is the same, a histogram is a bit more involved, so we will take more time describing this graph.

Consider Figure 3.2, which is a histogram of the data appearing in Table 3.1 (which we suspect you may recognize). This histogram consists of a series of bars of uniform width, each one representing the frequency associated with a particular class interval. As with the bar chart, either absolute or relative frequencies may be used on the vertical axis of a histogram, as long as the axis is labeled accordingly. Unlike the bar chart, the bars of a histogram are contiguous—their boundaries touch—to capture the quantitative nature of the data. (The exception occurs when

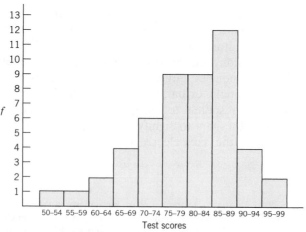

Figure 3.2   Histogram, using data from Table 3.1.

Table 3.1   Test Scores

Score Limits	Exact Limits	Midpoint	f
(100–104)	(99.5–104.5)	(102)	
95–99	94.5–99.5	97	2
90–94	89.5–94.5	92	4
85–89	84.5–89.5	87	12
80–84	79.5–84.5	82	9
75–79	74.5–79.5	77	9
70–74	69.5–74.5	72	6
65–69	64.5–69.5	67	4
60–64	59.5–64.5	62	2
55–59	54.5–59.5	57	1
50–54	49.5–54.5	52	1
(45–49)	(44.5–49.5)	(47)	
			$n = 50$

an *ordinal* variable is graphed, in which case the convention is to provide gaps between bars to communicate the "discontinuity" between values.) Values along the horizontal axis, the class intervals, are ordered left to right from smallest to the largest.

Figure 3.2, like Table 3.1, shows that scores range from class intervals 50–54 to 95–99, and, furthermore, that the greatest number of scores fall in the interval 85–89. This histogram also communicates the underlying shape of the distribution—more scores at the upper end, fewer at the lower end. Although the latter observation also can be made from Table 3.1, such observations are more immediate with a well-constructed histogram.

Labeling Class Intervals

No single convention exists for labeling the class intervals along the horizontal axis of a histogram. Figure 3.3 illustrates four common ways for handling this chore. Using the exact limits (Figure 3.3a) is technically the most accurate of the four, but it's also the most cumbersome. The midpoints provide the simplest approach (Figure 3.3b), but the underlying class intervals are not easily identified. In our view, the score limits provide the best balance between accuracy and convenience (Figures 3.3c and 3.3d). Of the two examples here, we prefer Figure 3.3d because it's simpler. The choice, however, is yours. All we ask is that you are clear and consistent with whichever method you use.

The Scale of the Histogram

How should you decide on the relative lengths of the horizontal and vertical axes? This is an important question, for different relative lengths will give different visual

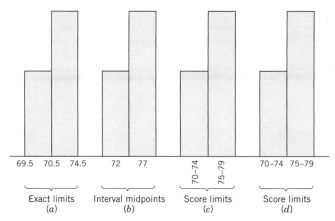

| Exact limits (a) | Interval midpoints (b) | Score limits (c) | Score limits (d) |

Figure 3.3   Four methods for labeling class intervals.

impressions of the same data. Indeed, armed with this knowledge, an unprincipled person easily can distort the visual impression of the data by intentionally manipulating the length of one axis relative to the length of the other.

Consider Figures 3.4a and 3.4b, which illustrate two alternatives to Figure 3.2. The impression from Figure 3.4a is that the distribution of scores is relatively flat, whereas Figure 3.4b communicates a decidedly narrow and peaked distribution. The data are identical, of course—the graphs differ only in the way we set up the two axes. By stretching or shrinking the range of scores (horizontal axis), or increasing or decreasing the range of frequencies (vertical axis), we can create any impression we want.

By the way, you sometimes will find this same devious tactic applied to the construction of "trend" graphs, where the horizontal axis is some unit of time (e.g., 1900, 1910, 1920, etc.) and the vertical axis is some statistic (e.g., in a given decade, the percentage of career-bound women who selected the profession of teaching). If you wish to make any decline look precipitous, or any increase look astronomical, simply shrink the length of the horizontal axis and stretch the vertical axis. The result can be so breathtaking that such a creation has been called a "gee-whiz!" graph (Huff, 1954).

How, then, should one proceed? The rule of thumb is that the vertical axis should be roughly three-quarters the length of the horizontal. (Width and height are measured from the span of the graphed data, not the borders of the graph.) Where possible, the vertical axis should include the frequency of zero. If this is awkward, as it is when the obtained frequencies are large, one should at least have a range of frequencies sufficient to avoid a misleading graph. In this case, it is good practice to indicate a clear "break" in the vertical axis sufficient to catch the reader's eye (see Figure 3.5). In short, let your conscience be your guide when you construct a histogram—and be equally alert when you examine one!

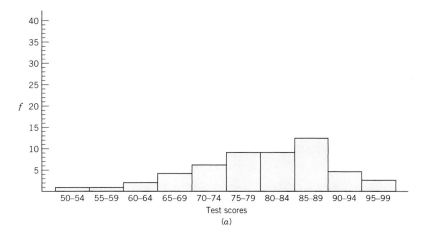

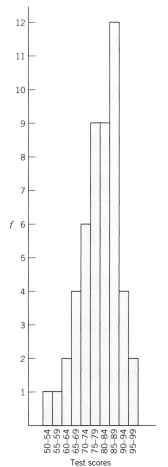

Figure 3.4 Effects of changing scale of axes (data from Table 3.1).

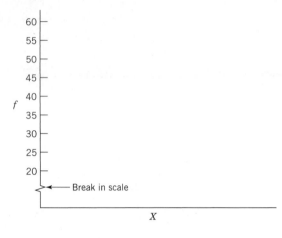

Figure 3.5   Where there is no frequency of zero: illustrating a break in the vertical axis.

3.4   *The Frequency Polygon*

A **frequency polygon** is another way to graph a frequency distribution. It makes use of *interval midpoints*, which we introduced to you in Chapter 2. The midpoint of an interval may be found by locating the point halfway between the interval's score limits (you can use the exact limits, if you prefer). In Table 3.1, the midpoint 97 is easily obtained by taking the difference between the two score limits $(99 - 95 = 4)$, dividing by $2 (4/2 = 2)$, and adding the result to the lower score limit $(95 + 2 = 97)$. To test our promise that you will get the same result, take a minute and calculate the midpoint using the *exact limits* of this interval $(94.5 - 99.5)$.

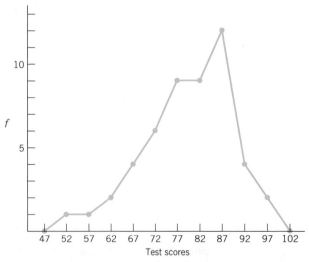

Figure 3.6   Frequency polygon, using data from Table 3.1.

In Figure 3.6, we present the Table 3.1 data in a frequency polygon. To construct this type of graph, proceed as you would with a histogram but label the horizontal axis with the *midpoints* of the class intervals. Plot a point above each midpoint, at a height corresponding to the frequency associated with the midpoint's class interval. Then connect the points with straight lines. If nothing further is done, the graph will not touch the horizontal axis. To "ground" the graph, identify the two class intervals that fall immediately outside the lowest and highest intervals having data. (We show these in parentheses in Table 3.1.) The midpoints at these intervals, plotted at zero frequency, are then connected to the graph. We show the plotted points in Figure 3.6 for illustrative purposes; normally, only the lines appear in the final graph. As with the histogram, either absolute or relative frequency may be represented in a frequency polygon.

By comparing Figures 3.2 and 3.6, you should be able to see a principal attraction of the frequency polygon: it is smoother in shape because the sharp corners of the histogram's rectangles have been eliminated. Consequently, a frequency polygon brings you that much closer to the underlying shape of a distribution.

3.5   *Comparing Different Distributions*

Comparison of two or more frequency distributions often is made easier by using graphic methods, particularly the frequency polygon. When distributions are based on unequal numbers of cases, comparison is infinitely easier when *relative frequencies* are used. Figure 3.7 compares the test scores from the two sections taught by Dr. Casteñeda (Table 2.7). Looking at Figure 3.7, you easily see that scores for

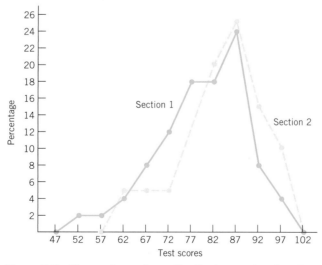

Figure 3.7   Comparison of two distributions, using data from Table 2.7.

Section 2 (the evening section) are somewhat better, and the range of scores is less, than for Section 1. (Why that might be, we leave to your imagination.)

3.6   *Relative Frequency and Proportional Area*

In histograms and frequency polygons, you saw that the *height* of the graph corresponds to frequency. Now you will see that the *area* under the graph can also represent frequency. *Interpreting area as frequency will become more and more important as you progress through the chapters of this book.*

To illustrate the relationship between area and frequency—or, more precisely, between **proportional area** and **relative frequency**—we will use this simple distribution:[2]

Score Limits	*f*	Proportion
12–14	2	.10
9–11	6	.30
6–8	8	.40
3–5	4	.20
	n = 20	

Suppose that on a very large piece of paper, you constructed a histogram for this distribution so that each interval is 3 in. wide and each unit of frequency on the vertical axis is equal to 1 in. This is represented, albeit in reduced scale, in Figure 3.8. The area for each bar can be obtained by multiplying its width (3 in.) by its height. Furthermore, the proportional area for each bar can be determined by dividing the area for that bar by the total area under the entire histogram (all the bars combined, or 60 square in.). The area results are as follows:

Score Limits	*f*	Area (W × H)	Proportional Area
12–14	2	3 × 2 = 6	6/60 = .10
9–11	6	3 × 6 = 18	18/60 = .30
6–8	8	3 × 8 = 24	24/60 = .40
3–5	4	3 × 4 = 12	12/60 = .20
		Total: 60 sq. in.	Total: 1.00

[2]In practice, of course, you rarely would use so few intervals.

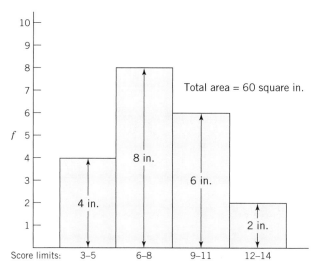

Figure 3.8   Histogram for frequency distribution in Section 3.6; dimensions given for bars.

Notice that the proportional areas are identical to the relative frequencies given in the table. The first relative frequency for one or more class intervals, then, must equal the proportion of area under the histogram included in those intervals. For example, the relative frequency with which individuals fall below the class interval 9–11 is .20 + .40 = .60. This is equal to the proportion of area below the interval 9–11 in Figure 3.8. The same would be true regardless of the scales used in constructing the histogram—*provided the bars are of equal width.* Indeed, this is why we stipulated earlier in this chapter that the bars of histograms (and bar charts) must be of uniform width.

We have used the histogram for considering the relationship between relative frequency and area because the procedure for obtaining the area of a rectangle is straightforward. However, what is true for a histogram also is true for smooth frequency curves of the sort you will encounter in subsequent chapters. This is so because the area under any smooth curve can be closely approximated by a histogram with many very narrow bars. We show this in Figure 3.9 for a **normal curve**—a distribution shape central to statistical work, and soon to be a close friend.

The proportion of area under a frequency curve between any two score points is equal to the relative frequency of cases between those points.

Figure 3.9 illustrates this principle. Because .34 (or 34%) of the total *area* falls between scores 50 and 60, .34 (or 34%) of the *cases* must have scores between 50 and 60. *Harness this principle, for it applies to much of the statistical reasoning to follow.*

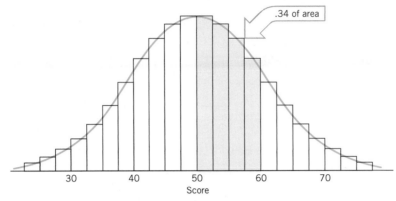

Figure 3.9 Normal curve with a histogram superimposed.

3.7 *Characteristics of Frequency Distributions*

Inspection of a carefully constructed, well-labeled histogram or frequency polygon can tell you much about the key characteristics of a set of data. Several of these characteristics are examined in detail in the next few chapters, and we will revisit them throughout the remainder of the text. Let's see what they are.

Central Tendency

Where on the score scale is the center of the distribution located? Around what score point do scores cluster? Both questions deal with the characteristic, **central tendency**. Two distributions that differ with regard to central tendency are shown in Figure 3.10*a*. You see that the scores for one distribution are generally higher on the horizontal axis—further to the right—than scores for the other. (Thus, when comparing the two distributions in Figure 3.7, you in part were making an observation regarding their central tendencies.) In the next chapter, you will encounter several commonly used measures of central tendency.

Variability

Do scores cluster closely about their central point, or do they spread out along the horizontal axis? This question concerns the **variability** of scores in a distribution. (Thus, you also were making an observation regarding the variability of the two distributions in Figure 3.7.) Figure 3.10*b* shows two distributions that differ in variability. We take up measures of variability in Chapter 5.

Shape

What is the shape of the distribution? Do scores fall in the bell-shaped fashion that we call the normal curve, or are they distributed in some other manner? Certain

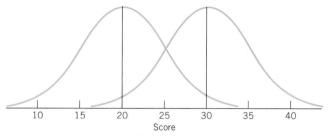

(a) Distributions that differ with regard to central tendency

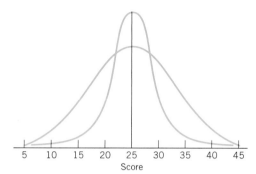

(b) Distributions that differ with regard to variability

Figure 3.10 Shapes of frequency distributions: differences in central tendency and variabilty.

shapes of frequency distributions occur with some regularity in educational research. Figure 3.11 illustrates several of these shapes, which we briefly comment on next. We will say more about the shapes of distributions in Chapter 4.

Normal Distribution   The **normal distribution** (Figure 3.11a)—the proverbial "bell-shaped curve"—tends to characterize the distributions of many physical (e.g., height), psychoeducational (e.g., aptitude), and psychomotor (e.g., muscular strength) variables. Nature indeed appears to love the normal curve! Contrary to some claims, however, it is not true that a normal distribution will result for *any* variable simply by collecting enough data. Some variables simply are nonnormal (e.g., annual income, scores on an easy test)—a fact that gobs of data won't change. Nonetheless, the normal distribution is of great importance in statistical inference, and you will hear much about it in subsequent chapters.

Bimodal Distribution   A **bimodal distribution** (Figure 3.11b) is rather like two normal distributions placed on the same scale, slightly offset. The two humps of a bimodal distribution indicate two locations of central tendency, and they could be telling you that there are two groups in the sample. For example, a bimodal distribution might obtain if you gave males and females a test of physical

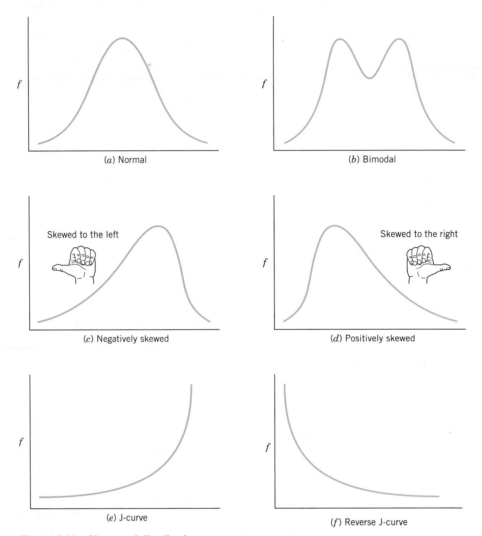

Figure 3.11   Shapes of distributions.

strength. When a bimodal distribution is obtained unexpectedly, the immediate task is to uncover *why*.

   Skewed Distribution   Figures 3.11*c* and 3.11*d* each show a **skewed distribution**, where the bulk of scores favor one side of the distribution or the other. When the scores trail off to the right you have a **positive skew**, and when they trail off to the left you have a **negative skew**.[3] An exceedingly difficult test will

---

[3]This nomenclature reflects the theoretical number scale, which ranges infinitely from negative numbers (left) to positive numbers (right).

produce a positively skewed distribution, for example, whereas a very easy test will result in a negative skew.

The nomenclature of skewed distributions is easy to remember by visualizing a closed fist with the thumb sticking out, as shown in Figures 3.11*c* and 3.11*d*. If the fist represents the bulk of the scores and the thumb the tail of the distribution, then the thumb points to the direction of the skew. Thus, direction of skew reflects the minority out in the tail of the distribution, not the masses toward the other end. (The chief executive officers of major corporations—a miniscule minority of wage earners, to be sure—*skew* the distribution of income in this country.)

J-Shaped Distribution   A J-shaped distribution (or **J-curve**) is an extreme form of negative skew—so much so that the upper end of the distribution does not return to the horizontal scale (hence, resembling the letter J). Most scores are at "ceiling"—the maximum score possible. For example, if you give an eighth-grade vocabulary test to college seniors, the resulting distribution should resemble Figure 3.11*e*: the vast majority of seniors would know most of the words (although, alas, there would be exceptions).

You are correct if you're thinking that the opposite distribution must be possible—where scores pile up at the lowest point on the scale (e.g., no errors, none correct, quick response). This distribution often is called, predictably, a **reverse J-curve** (Figure 3.11*f*).

3.8   The Box Plot

The **box plot** is a convenient method for graphing quantitative data (see Reading the Research: Box Plots). Like histograms and frequency polygons, a box plot conveys important information about a distribution, particularly in terms of central tendency, variability, and shape.

In Figure 3.12, we present the box plot for the distribution of scores from Table 2.9. This device derives its name from the "box" in the middle, which represents the middle 50% of scores: The box extends from the 25th percentile (or Q_1, the first quartile) to the 75th percentile (or Q_3, the third quartile). The line you see running through the box is the "median" score, which is equal to the 50th percentile (Q_2): half of the scores fall below, half of the scores fall above. (You'll hear more about the median in the next chapter.) The "whiskers" that are affixed to the box show the range of scores,[4] although it is common practice to limit each whisker to 1.5 times the difference between Q_3 and Q_1. If a score is more extreme than this, then the score appears as a separate data point beyond the whisker.

[4]For this reason, such a graph also is called a *box-and-whiskers plot.* For convenience, we use the shorter name.

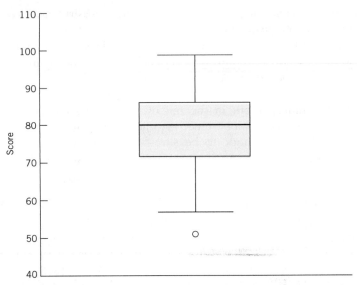

Figure 3.12   Box plot for frequency distribution in Table 2.9.

Figure 3.12 shows that the middle 50% of scores in this distribution fall between roughly 72 and 86, with a median score around 80. The whiskers extend from 99 to 57, with a lone low score of 51. That this score stands out so vividly ilustrates another strength of the box plot: identifying extreme scores, or outliers.

Sometimes an author chooses to arrange a box plot horizontally, as we have done in Figure 3.13. From a quick inspection, you can see that the information

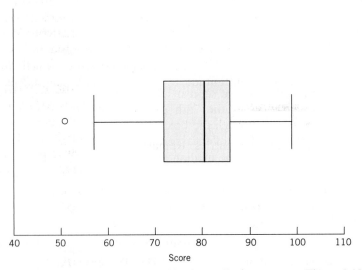

Figure 3.13   Box plot arranged horizontally (compare to Figure 3.12).

conveyed in this figure is identical to that in Figure 3.12. Thus, the difference between the two formats is entirely aesthetic.

3.9   Summary

Although a frequency distribution is useful for seeing important features of a set of data, graphic representation often makes it even easier. The bar chart is a popular way to graph qualitative data, and the histogram and frequency polygon are two ways to graph quantitative data.

In the histogram, the frequency for each class interval is represented by the height of a bar constructed over the score limits of the interval. In the frequency polygon, a point is plotted above the interval's midpoint at a height equal to the corresponding frequency; the points are then connected by straight lines. Comparisons among two or more distributions can be made easier by the application of graphic methods, particularly the frequency polygon. Use of relative frequencies here will avoid problems associated with an unequal number of cases.

Among the guidelines for constructing graphic representations are the following: Scores usually are represented along the horizontal axis and frequencies (or relative frequencies) along the vertical axis; scales should be selected so that the graph is somewhat wider than tall; and axes should be labeled and an informative title included. But there is no such thing as *the* graph of a set of data. Somewhat different pictures can result from grouping the scores in different ways and using different scales on the two axes. Your objective always is to communicate the data clearly, accurately, and impartially.

Although frequency is represented by height in a histogram or frequency polygon, you also should think of it in terms of the area under the graph. The relative frequency between any two score points equals the proportion of total area between those points, an important relationship that we will return to in work yet to come.

Finally, it will prove useful to describe a frequency distribution in terms of three key characteristics: central tendency, variability, and shape. In the next chapters we will treat these characteristics in detail.

Reading the Research: Box Plots

One of the more effective means for comparing frequency distributions is by way of side-by-side box plots. The accompanying figure, which appeared in Linn (2000), displays the eighth-grade results on an international mathematics exam for seven countries. The vertical axis represents student scores, ranging from 300 to 900, on the math assessment that was administered for the 1995 Third International Math and Science Study (TIMSS). The horizontal axis presents a select group of participating countries. Remarking on the graph, the author concluded: "Although the distributions for Japan and Korea are substantially higher than the distribution for the U.S., there is a large spread in all countries" (p. 10). Notice how these box plots reveal important information about central tendency ("substantially higher") and variability ("large spread") and, moreover, how the side-by-side presentation facilitates comparison of the seven countries.

To be sure, students from Japan and Korea tested better than students from the remaining countries. But it would be interesting to see how the Japanese and Koreans stacked up against an American performance standard, such as the *proficient* level on the National Assessment of Educational Progress (NAEP) exam.[5] In this spirit, Linn superimposed on his figure the approximated cut-score for the NAEP *proficient* designation (horizontal line). The resulting image shows that, by the American standard, "substantially more than a quarter of the students in Japan and Korea would fail" (p. 10).

Overall, these box plots illustrate the marked variability in student performance within each country, as well as the considerable overlap in student performance across countries (despite popular claims to the contrary). One final comment: You may have noticed that Linn chose to anchor his whiskers at the 5th and 95th percentiles, a practice you occasionally will encounter in the literature.

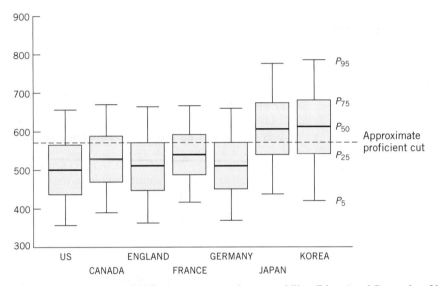

Source: Figure 7 in Linn, R. L. (2000). Assessments and accountability. *Educational Researcher, 29*(2), 4–16. Copyright © 2000 by the American Educational Research Association; reproduced with permission from the publisher.

Case Study: Boxes and Whiskers and Histograms, Oh My!

We obtained a data set from an urban high school in a southwestern state. The set contains various demographic and academic information on 358 juniors.

For this case study, we looked at how students performed on the *Stanford 9* mathematics and reading comprehension tests. After examining the overall results

[5]The NAEP is an achievement test regularly administered to a national sample of students in the United States. "Proficient" performance is where the student has "demonstrated competency over challenging subject matter, including subject-matter knowledge, application of such knowledge to real-world situations, and analytical skills appropriate to the subject matter" (http://nces.ed.gov/nationsreportcard/mathematics/achieve.asp).

for each subject area, we compared the performance of males and females. What we learned here we learned largely from graphic representations of frequency distributions.

We began by constructing a histogram for each set of scores, and then we examined their distributional characteristics (Figures 3.14*a* and *b*). The histogram for mathematics scores appears decidedly more peaked than that for reading comprehension scores, which takes on more of a bell shape. In terms of variability, scores in reading comprehension are slightly more dispersed than scores in mathematics. (Imagine taking the palm of your hand and pressing down on the top of Figure 3.14*a*. The compressed version likely would look similar to Figure 3.14*b*.) We also noticed a few extraordinarily high scores on both exams. (More on these later.) Finally, we detected a slight positive skew in Figure 3.14*a*. This suggests that, for these students at least, the mathematics test was a bit more challenging than the reading comprehension test.

An inspection of the box plots placed underneath the histograms confirms some of our earlier findings (see Figures 3.14*c* and *d*). As you see, we decided to present each box plot horizontally rather than vertically. (Recall from Section 3.8 that the small points extending beyond the ends of the whiskers signify extreme scores in the distribution. Do you see how these scores match up with the short bars in the tails of the histograms?) A comparison of the box lengths in Figures 3.14*c* and *d* indicates, as we found above, that mathematics scores are more bunched together (less spread out) than reading comprehension scores. In other words, the middle 50% of scores in the mathematics distribution lies within a smaller range (roughly between 670 and 700) than the middle 50% of scores in the reading comprehension distribution (roughly between 655 and 705). These different patterns of variability suggest that test performance, at least for this group of juniors, varies more so in reading comprehension than in mathematics. A possible explanation for this is that most math skills tend to be learned and practiced in school. In contrast, many reading skills often are acquired outside of school. Given that some students read a lot and others very little, it is not surprising that students' reading comprehension test performance varies as well.

Placed side-by-side (or, if horizontal, one above the other), box plots are effective tools for comparing the characteristics of two or more distributions. In Figures 3.15*a* and 3.15*b*, we used box plots to compare the test performance of males and females. For both reading comprehension and math, male and female distributions are similar in terms of central tendency, variability, and shape. We notice two subtle differences, however. First, female scores (in both subjects) cluster more closely, which we see by the relatively shorter box lengths for the female data. Male scores are slightly more spread out. Second, for each comparison, the boxes do not line up perfectly. In Figure 3.15*a*, the box for the male distribution sits a bit to the right (toward higher scores), whereas the opposite is true in Figure 3.15*b*. This perhaps is indicative of a modest gender difference in test performance in these two subjects, one favoring males and the other favoring females. (However, the considerable overlap between the two box plots in each subject would stop us from simplistically concluding that "males scored better in

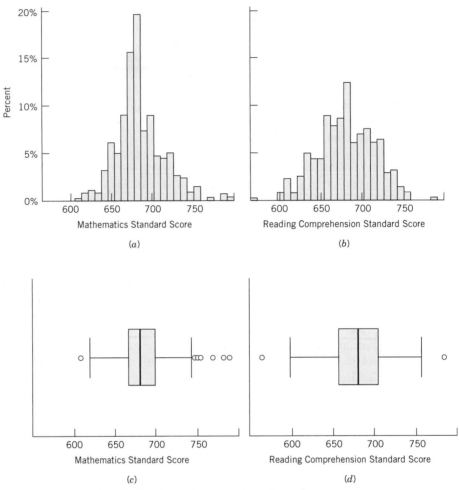

Figure 3.14 Graphic distributions of math and reading scores.

mathematics" and "females scored better in reading comprehension." Clearly, there are many exceptions to the rule.)

The box plots helped us make comparative judgments about the overall performance between males and females. We decided to look more closely at these distributions to make additional comparisons. Specifically, we compared high-scoring males and females on the reading comprehension exam by inspecting the upper tail of each histogram. Figures 3.16a and b present histograms of reading comprehension scores for females and males, respectively. We arbitrarily chose a score of 720 or above to designate a "high-scoring" region. (You'll notice that, for each histogram, we isolated the bars that fell into this region.) A comparison of the two regions indicates that a greater proportion of females scored 720 or higher on the reading comprehension exam. We already would have suspected this by

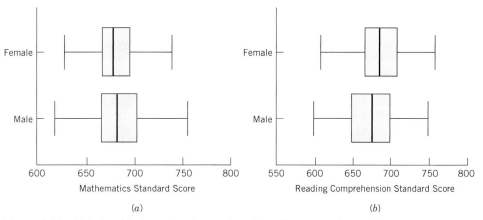

Figure 3.15   Side-by-side box plots for math and reading scores by gender.

comparing the upper whiskers of the box plots in Figure 3.15b, but the histograms provide greater specificity. In rough terms, the percentages (or areas) represented by the five isolated bars in Figure 3.16a sum to 12.5% (6% + 1% + 1% + 2.5% + 2%), whereas the four isolated bars in Figure 3.16b sum to 8% (2.5% + 4% + 1% + .5%). Thus, there is an additional 4.5% of women (12.5% − 8%) in the high-scoring region of the distribution of reading comprehension scores. Whether or not this difference is important or meaningful, of course, depends on how school officials use these test results. For example, if this school gave an award of some kind to the highest achieving students on this particular exam, a disproportionate number of the recipients would be female.

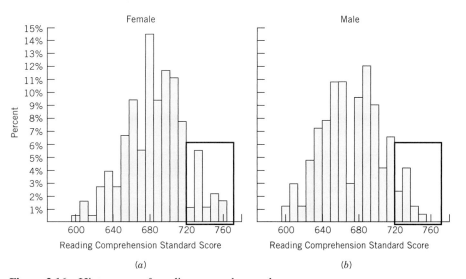

Figure 3.16   Histograms of reading scores by gender.

Suggested Computer Exercises

The **sophomores** data file contains information on 521 tenth graders from a large suburban public school. The information in the file includes student ID, gender, cumulative grade point average (CGPA), scores on state-administered tenth-grade mathematics and reading exams, scores on an eighth-grade national standardized mathematics exam, and whether or not the student enrolled in an algebra course during the eighth grade.

1. Generate a histogram for CGPA, and then address the following:

    (a) Describe the distribution of scores in terms of central tendency, variability, and shape.

    (b) Assume that a symmetric distribution of CPGA is indicative of "grading on the curve." Does this distribution suggest to you that teachers at this school subscribe to such a philosophy? Do you find any evidence to support claims of "grade inflation" at this school?

2. Generate side-by-side box plots to compare the CGPA distributions of students who enrolled in algebra in the eighth grade and those who did not. Comment on which group maintained higher CGPAs.

Exercises

Identify, Define, or Explain

Terms and Concepts

bar chart
histogram
frequency polygon
proportional area
relative frequency
normal curve
central tendency
variability

normal distribution
bimodal distribution
skewed distribution
positive skew
negative skew
J-curve
reverse J-curve
box plot

Questions and Problems

Note: Answers to starred (*) items are presented in Appendix B.

*1. Why might a statistically knowledgeable person prefer to inspect a frequency distribution rather than a graph? What would be an argument against this position?

2. Describe the similarities and differences between a bar chart and a histogram.

*3. Give the midpoints of each of the following intervals (assume the scores are rounded to the nearest whole number or decimal place indicated unless otherwise specified):

   (a) 10–14

   (b) 200–399

   (c) 2.50–2.74

   (d) 3.00–3.19

   (e) 30–40 (accurate to the nearest 10)

*4. Following the guidelines presented in this chapter, construct a histogram (using frequencies) to exhibit the distribution of test scores obtained in Problem 7 of Chapter 2. (Be sure to provide clear labels for the two axes and a title.)

5. Convert the histogram in the previous problem to a frequency polygon.

6. Suppose that in Problems 4 and 5 you had used percentages along the vertical axis instead of frequencies. What would be different about the new graphs, and what would be the same?

7. Construct a histogram based on the GPA data in Table 2.5.

*8. Convert the histogram in the preceding problem to a frequency polygon.

9. Construct a graph of the race/ethnicity breakdown from Problem 9 in Chapter 2.

10. How would you advise a friend who wishes to construct a frequency polygon for the race/ethnicity data in the preceding problem?

*11. Indicate the probable shape of each of the following distributions:

   (a) heights of a large sample of 25-year-olds

   (b) scores on the same math test taken by 30 fifth graders and 30 ninth graders (combined into a single frequency distribution)

   (c) verbal aptitude of high school students

   (d) SAT scores for students admitted to a very selective university

   (e) age of freshmen in American universities

   (f) alcohol consumption in a sample of 16-year-olds (number of drinks per week)

12. Suppose you obtained the following data after asking 30 rural children and 60 urban children to complete an "environmental awareness" survey:

Environmental Awareness Score	Rural Children f	Urban Children f
65–69	2	2
60–64	3	0
55–59	4	1
50–54	5	3
45–49	6	4
40–44	4	7
35–39	2	10
30–34	2	12
25–29	1	9
20–24	0	6
15–19	1	4
10–14	0	2
	$n = 30$	$n = 60$

   (a) Plot the relative frequency polygons for the two sets of data so that their distributions can be compared. (Be sure to provide clear labels for the two axes and a title.)

   (b) What conclusions do you draw from these two distributions?

*13. When should a graph be large? When would a small graph be acceptable?

CHAPTER 4

Central Tendency

4.1   The Concept of Central Tendency

The "average" arguably is the statistical concept most familiar to the layperson. What is the starting salary of software engineers? How tall are fashion models? What is the surf temperature in Anguilla? The average is omnipresent in the field of education as well. What leadership style predominates among school principals? How do home-schooled students perform on college entrance examinations? What is the general level of educational aspiration among children growing up in rural communities? An average lies behind each of these questions, and, as such, it communicates in a broad brushstroke what is "typical" or "representative" of a set of observations.

Average is an informal and, as you will see, somewhat imprecise term for **measure of central tendency**. In this chapter, we consider three measures of central tendency frequently used in education: the mode, median, and arithmetic mean. It is important for you to understand how their properties differ and, in turn, how these differences determine proper interpretation and use.

4.2   The Mode

The simplest measure of central tendency is the **mode**, and it requires only that one knows how to count.

> The mode is the score that occurs with the greatest frequency.

Look back to Table 2.2 and scan the frequency columns. The score 86 carries the greatest frequency and therefore is the mode—the **modal score**—for this distribution. Or examine the graph of spelling test scores shown in Figure 4.1. The mode is the score that corresponds to the highest point on the curve—in this case, a score of 18. You now realize why the two-humped distribution in Figure 3.11*b* is called a **bimodal** distribution.[1]

---

[1]The two peaks do not have to be of *identical* height for a distribution to qualify as bimodal.

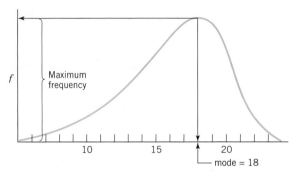

Figure 4.1   Distribution of spelling test scores, showing the mode.

Because of its mathematical primitiveness, the mode is of little use in statistical inference. However, do not undersell its importance, for the mode can be quite helpful as a descriptive device. Moreover, the mode is the *only* appropriate measure of central tendency for nominal, or qualitative, variables. Therefore, use the mode when you report central tendency for such measures as marital status, ethnicity, and college major.

4.3   *The Median*

The **median**, which we briefly introduced in the last chapter, has a somewhat different definition.

> The median, *Mdn*, is the middle score when the observations are arranged in order of magnitude, so that an equal number of scores falls below and above.

Consider the five scores:

$$8, 10, 11, 13, 15$$
$$\uparrow$$
$$Mdn$$

The halfway point is 11—two scores fall below and two fall above—so the median score is 11. When there is an even number of scores, simply take the midpoint between the two middle scores. Let's add a sixth score to the five above:

$$8, 10, 11, 13, 15, 16$$
$$\uparrow$$
$$Mdn$$

The two middle scores are now 11 and 13, and the midpoint between them is 12—the median for this distribution. What if the two middle scores are the same, as in the following distribution?

$$8, 10, 13, 13, 15, 16$$
$$\uparrow$$
$$Mdn$$

The halfway point is between 13 and 13 (as odd as this sounds), so the median score is 13. From these examples, you see that the median sometimes corresponds to an actual score and sometimes not. It doesn't matter, as long as the median divides the distribution equally.

The median has an important property that makes it a particularly attractive measure of central tendency for certain distributions. Because it is defined as the middle score in a distribution, *the median responds to how many scores lie above and below it, not how far away the scores are.* Suppose you took our original five scores and changed the highest to 150:

$$8, 10, 11, 13, 150$$
$$\uparrow$$
$$Mdn$$

The median is unaffected by this change, for the number of scores relative to the original median remains the same. The median's insensitivity to extreme scores is a decided advantage when you want to describe the central tendency of markedly skewed distributions.

Given the median's definition, the median score also divides a frequency curve into two equal *areas.* This follows from the relationship between relative frequency and area, which we considered earlier (Section 3.6). This property is shown in Figure 4.2.

The median is an appropriate measure of central tendency if the variable's scale of measurement is at least ordinal. For example, it would make little sense to report that "political science" is the median *college major*, "Franco-American" is the median *demographic group*, or "cafe latte" is the median *preferred beverage*.

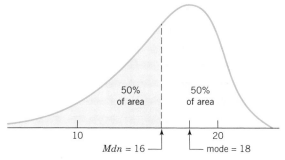

Figure 4.2 Distribution of spelling test scores, showing the mode and median, *Mdn.*

Each of these variables represents a nominal scale and, therefore, lacks an underlying continuum of values that the median (but not the mode) requires.

4.4   *The Arithmetic Mean*

The proverbial person-on-the-street typically says "average" when referring to the arithmetic mean. Unfortunately, people often use "average" to refer to *any* measure of central tendency, despite the profound differences among the three definitions. This invites confusion and misinterpretation—and sometimes deceit. Therefore, we encourage you to exorcise the term *average* from your vocabulary and, instead, use the precise term for the particular measure of central tendency that you are considering. (And insist that others do the same!)

For brevity, the arithmetic mean usually is referred to as the **mean**, a practice we will follow. The mean is represented by the symbol $\overline{X}$ ("X-bar").[2]

> The arithmetic mean, $\overline{X}$, is the sum of all scores divided by the number of scores.

Even though you have computed the mean since grade school, we need to introduce additional symbols before this definition can be expressed as a formula. It is common to use the capital letter X to stand for each value in a particular set of observations. For example, the scores 4, 5, 15 can be represented like this:

$$X : 4, 5, 15$$

So far, so good. Next is the symbol for the *number* of observations: n. In the present case, you have $n = 3$ scores.

Last but surely not least, a symbol is needed to denote the operation of *summation*. This is found in the capital Greek letter sigma, Σ. Read Σ as "the sum of (whatever follows)." When placed before the three scores above, Σ commands that you sum them: $\Sigma(4, 5, 15) = 4 + 5 + 15 = 24$. If we let X represent these three scores, then $\Sigma X = 24$.

You now have all you need to understand the formula for the mean:

Arithmetic mean

$$\overline{X} = \frac{\Sigma X}{n} \tag{4.1}$$

The mean of our three scores is $(4 + 5 + 15)/3 = 24/3 = 8$.

---

[2]Although $\overline{X}$ is common in statistics textbooks, the symbol M is used in the many educational research journals that follow the *Publication Manual of the American Psychological Association*. In such journals, *Mdn* is used for the median and "mode" for the mode.

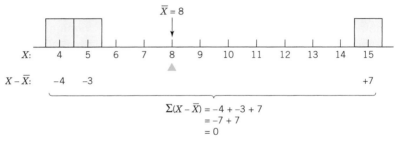

Figure 4.3 The mean as balance point (▲).

The mean is the **balance point** of a distribution, and the common analogy is the seesaw from the days of your youth. If you imagine a seesaw with the scores spread along the board according to their values, the mean corresponds to the position of the balance point. This is shown in Figure 4.3. As with the seesaw, if one score is shifted, the balance point also must change. If we change 15 to 12, the point of balance is now 7 ($\overline{X} = 7$); change 15 to 6 and the balance point shifts to 5 ($\overline{X} = 5$).

Unlike the median or mode, then, *the mean is responsive to the exact position, or magnitude, of each score in the distribution.* This responsiveness follows from an important principle:

> The sum of the deviations of scores from the mean always equals zero. That is, $\Sigma(X - \overline{X}) = 0$.

In other words, if you determine how different each score is from the mean, the sum of the *negative* deviations will equal the sum of *positive* deviations. Consequently, the total of all deviations is zero.

Look again at Figure 4.3, where a deviation is provided for each of the three scores. The deviation, $X - \overline{X}$, is obtained by subtracting the mean from the score. For $X = 4$, the deviation is $4 - 8 = -4$. That is, this score falls 4 points below the mean. For $X = 5$, the deviation is $5 - 8 = -3$; and for $X = 15$, it is $15 - 8 = +7$. Note that the negative deviations sum to -7, exactly balancing the positive deviation of $+7$. Thus, the principle that the deviations sum to zero is satisfied:

$$\Sigma(X - \overline{X}) = (-4) + (-3) + (+7) = 0$$

Because deviations sum to zero, the mean has an **algebraic property** that both the median and mode lack. Therefore, the mean is prominent in formulas that call for a measure of central tendency, as you will see in subsequent chapters.

What about scale of measurement? Clearly, it generally is nonsensical to compute the mean for a nominal variable.[3] In fact, from a strictly theoretical standpoint,

---

[3]An exception to this statement would be computing the mean for a dichotomous (two-value) variable. Say you code your research participants as either 0 (male) or 1 (female). The mean of all the 0s and 1s would be equal, quite conveniently, to the proportion of your sample that is female. (Do you see why?)

an interval scale is required for computing the mean. There is considerable debate, however, as to how strict one must be in practice. Consequently, it is commonplace to find published articles that report a mean on say, a five-point Likert-type variable.

Combining Means

One sometimes needs to compute an overall mean—a **grand mean**—from means based on separate groups. We will adopt common practice here and use subscripts to denote group membership. Suppose that you have data on two groups, with $\bar{X}_1 = 10$ and $\bar{X}_2 = 30$. Is the grand mean $(10 + 30)/2 = 20$? In other words, can you simply compute the mean of the two means? Yes, but *only if each group has the same n* (that is, $n_1 = n_2$). But what if $n_1 = 100$ and $n_2 = 5$? You perhaps are thinking that the overall mean should be much closer to 10 (the mean of the much larger group) than to 30. And you would be correct. To compute a grand mean, for which we introduce the symbol $\bar{\bar{X}}$, you must "weight" the two means by their respective n's. Specifically:

Grand mean

$$\bar{\bar{X}} = \frac{(n_1\bar{X}_1) + (n_2\bar{X}_2)}{n_1 + n_2}$$

(4.2)

If $n_1 = 100$ and $n_2 = 5$ for the two means above, the numerator of this formula is $(100)(10) + (5)(30) = 1000 + 150 = 1150$. Divide this value by $100 + 5 = 105$ and you have the grand mean: $\bar{\bar{X}} = 1150/105 = 10.95$. With almost all of the 105 students coming from the first group, you should not be surprised that $\bar{\bar{X}}$ is so much closer to $\bar{X}_1$ than $\bar{X}_2$. Indeed, $\bar{\bar{X}}$ is within one point of $\bar{X}_1$—quite different from the outcome had you simply split the difference between the two means.

4.5   *Central Tendency and Distribution Symmetry*

From the differences in their definitions, the values of the mean, median, and mode likely will differ in a given distribution.

In a perfectly *symmetrical distribution*, one-half of the distribution is the mirror image of the other. If such a distribution were a paper cutout, there would be perfect overlap if you folded the paper in half. In this case, the mean and median will be the same value: the middle score also is the algebraic balance point. What about the mode? In a *normal distribution*, as in Figure 4.4a, the mode shares the value of the mean and median. In a perfectly normal distribution, then, $\bar{X} = Mdn = \text{mode}$. But for reasons that should be apparent, this condition does not hold for the equally symmetrical *bimodal distribution*. Although the mean and median are the same, they are flanked by two modes (see Figure 4.4b).

By revisiting the defining characteristics of the mean, median, and mode, you perhaps can predict their relative locations in *skewed distributions*. Consider

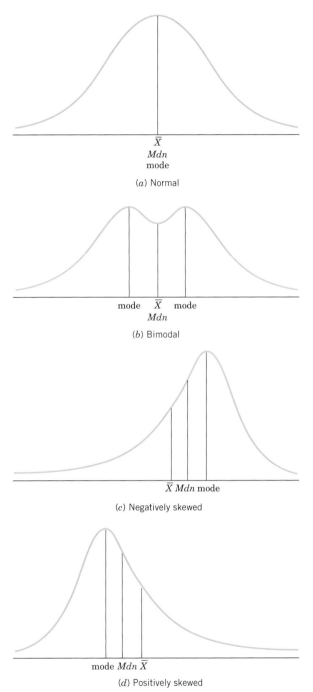

Figure 4.4 The relative positioning of $\overline{X}$, *Mdn*, and mode in various distributions (approximate).

Figure 4.4*c*, which is a *negatively* skewed distribution. Because the mode corresponds to the most frequently obtained score, it appears under the highest point of the distribution. But because the median reflects area—an equal proportion of scores falling above and below—it must sit to the left of the mode to satisfy this condition (see Figure 4.2). Regardless of distribution shape, the median always is the middle score. As for the mean, it is "pulled" by the extreme scores in the left tail of the distribution (because the mean is the balance point) and, consequently, appears to the left of the median. In negatively skewed distributions, then, $\overline{X} < Mdn <$ mode. Using the same logic, you can appreciate what prevails in a *positively* skewed distribution (Figure 4.4*d*): mode $< Mdn < \overline{X}$. As a result, the relative location of measures of central tendency (particularly the mean and median) may be used for making judgments about both the presence of skewness and its direction. Although there is no substitute for examining a frequency distribution or histogram, you have good reason to suspect skew if you obtain appreciably different measures of central tendency.

4.6   *Which Measure of Central Tendency to Use?*

Our discussion would suggest that it is of value to calculate more than one measure of central tendency (unless you are dealing with qualitative data, in which case only the mode is reported). Each measure tells you something different about a distribution's central tendency. To understand your data more fully, inspect them all. And to summarize your data more accurately, report more than one measure when your data depart from normality. As a striking example, consider the "average" net worth of U.S. households (in 2004) according to the Federal Reserve Board: $Mdn = \$93,100$ whereas $\overline{X} = \$448,200$. Any measure of central tendency includes the billionaires and paupers alike, but the billionaire's statistical tug on the mean is clearly evident. In this case, reporting both statistics paints a more complete picture than providing either statistic alone.

Having said this, we must acknowledge that it is the mean, not the median or the mode, that assumes prominence in formulas calling for a measure of central tendency. It also is the measure of choice in statistical inference. The preference for the mean is based on two general properties that it enjoys: mathematical tractability and sampling stability.

Mathematical Tractability

The mean responds to arithmetic and algebraic manipulation in ways that the median and mode do not. Consequently, it fits in more easily with important statistical formulas and procedures. You will find again and again that the mean is incorporated in other statistical procedures, either explicitly or implicitly. Indeed, when further statistical work is to be done, the mean will almost always be the most useful measure.

Sampling Stability

Suppose you collected test scores from four randomly selected groups of students in a large class and then determined the mean, median, and mode for each group. You probably would find minor differences among the four means, greater differences among the four medians, and quite a bit of difference among the four modes. That is, the mean would be the most *stable* of the three measures of central tendency—it would evidence the least "sampling variation." This observed trend is of great importance in statistical inference, where samples are used to make inferences about populations.

4.7   Summary

Three measures of central tendency are commonly encountered in the research literature: mode, median, and mean. They are summary figures that describe the location of scores in quantitative terms. The mode states what score occurs most frequently; the median gives the score that divides the distribution into halves; and the mean gives the score that is the balance point of the distribution (the value that the layperson usually thinks of as "the average"). Given their definitions, these three measures respond differently to the location of scores in a distribution and, consequently, may have different values in the same distribution. This is particularly true with nonnormal distributions.

The mode is the only appropriate measure of central tendency for qualitative, or nominal, variables. For describing other variables, all three measures are important to consider. However, because the mean has superior mathematical tractability and stability, it typically is the preferred measure of central tendency in statistical formulas and procedures.

Reading the Research: The Mean

Mean scores are often used to make performance comparisons between groups. For instance, Bol and Hacker (2001) compared the final exam scores of a group of graduate students who took practice tests prior to the final exam to another group who underwent the customary teacher-led review. These researchers concluded that "students who took the practice tests scored lower than the students who had a more traditional type of review ($Ms = 32.80$ and 37.65, respectively)" (p. 140). Notice the authors' reliance on mean scores in determining which group "scored lower." Also notice the use of M (rather than $\overline{X}$) for signifying the mean.

Source: Bol, L., & Hacker, D. J. (2001). A comparison of the effects of practice tests and traditional review on performance and calibration. *The Journal of Experimental Education, 69*(2), 133–151.

Case Study: Choosing the Middle Ground

As you have learned in this chapter, measures of central tendency are useful in describing what is typical or representative of a set of observations. For this case study, we illustrate the use of the mean, median, and mode in summarizing the

Table 4.1   Measures of Central Tendency for
ENROLL, ELL, and MEALS: California
Elementary Schools 2000–2001 ($n = 4779$)

	ENROLL	ELL (%)	MEALS (%)
$\overline{X}$	439.51	25.15	51.77
Mdn	417.00	18.00	53.00
mode	458.00	1.00	100.00

enrollment characteristics of California elementary schools. With nearly 5000 elementary schools to deal with, these descriptive statistics are a virtual must!

We return to the large database of California schools that we used in the Chapter 2 case study. Using our statistical software, we computed the mean, median, and mode for three elementary school variables: student enrollment (ENROLL), percentage of English language learners (ELL),[4] and percentage of students eligible for free or reduced-priced lunch (MEALS). The results are displayed in Table 4.1.

Let's first look at the figures for ENROLL. The mean enrollment for California elementary schools in 2000–2001 was roughly 440 students, the median enrollment was 417, and the modal enrollment was 458. Although each measure of central tendency is correct in its own right, there is some disagreement among them. Is one of these indicators better than the others? That is, does one more appropriately represent the "typical" size of a California elementary school? You have already learned in Section 4.2 that the mode is best reserved for qualitative or nominal variables. Because ENROLL is a quantitative variable, this leaves us with the mean ($\overline{X} = 440$) and median (*Mdn* = 417). The relatively larger mean raises the suspicion of a positively skewed distribution (as in Figure 4.4*d*), a hunch that is confirmed by the histogram in Figure 4.5. Because the mean is sensitive to extreme scores—the scores in the right tail of Figure 4.5—the median score probably is more representative of typical enrollment.

In some instances, the choice of central tendency measure (or any statistic, for that matter) can have a direct influence on education policy. For example, suppose California was considering legislation that required the state to provide technical assistance to elementary schools that served a significant proportion of ELL students. Further, suppose that this legislation made eligible those schools that enrolled a percentage of ELL students who fell above the "state *average*." If legislators interpreted "average" as the arithmetic mean of ELL (25.15), then all schools that enrolled more than roughly 25% ELL students would be eligible. Having examined the frequency distribution for ELL (not shown here), we know that approximately 40% of California elementary schools would be eligible for assistance using this interpretation of "average."

However, if legislators interpreted "average" as the *median* ELL (18.00), then half, or 50%, of the schools would receive assistance. The additional 10% of

[4]For these students, English is not their native language.

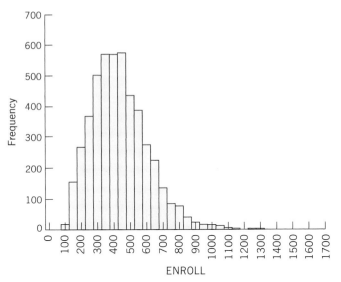

Figure 4.5 Enrollments of 2000–2001 California elementary schools ($n = 4779$).

schools that would be served are shown in the histogram in Figure 4.6.[5] This percentage difference can also be expressed in terms of number of schools: 10% of 4799 is roughly 480 schools. Thus, an additional 480 schools would receive support if the median, rather than the mean, were used as the measure of central tendency. Given the skewness in the ELL distribution, the median arguably would be the more equitable measure to use in this context.

We now move on to describe the last of our three variables: MEALS. Table 4.1 shows that the mean and median for MEALS are fairly close in value; neither has a descriptive advantage over the other. Even though the mode is best used with qualitative variables, it is difficult to avoid noticing that the most frequently occurring MEALS score for California elementary schools is 100%. Although a telling figure, this can be misleading as an indicator of central tendency. The histogram for MEALS in Figure 4.7 shows why.[6] To be sure, after inspecting the histogram, it seems that no measure of central tendency seems to work very well with this somewhat flat, or "rectangular," distribution. A school with 20% MEALS is nearly as common as a school with 50% or 90%.

---

[5]You may have noticed the contradiction between Table 4.1, which shows the modal ELL as 1.00, and Figure 4.6, where the modal ELL is 5.00. This is explained by the fact that these histograms are based on grouped data, a feature not altogether obvious when bars are labeled by midpoints. The most frequently occurring *score* in the distribution is 1.00. The frequently occurring *range of score* is around 5.00 (technically, between 2.50 and 7.50).

[6]In this case, the misleading nature of the mode could also be attributed to the degree of precision intrinsic to this variable, which is measured in hundredths of a percent. With so many possible unique values, it is no wonder that the mode misinforms us here.

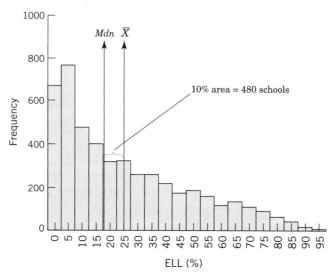

Figure 4.6   Percentages of ELL students in 2000–2001 California elementary schools ($n = 4779$).

We have described enrollment characteristics of California elementary schools via the mean, median, and mode. This case study has demonstrated the practical use of measures of central tendency, and it has shown that their interpretations should be made in light of the shape and variability of the underlying distribution.

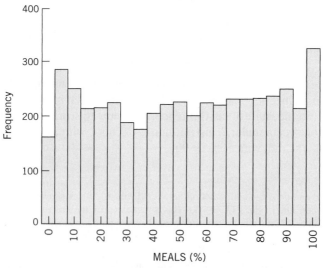

Figure 4.7   Percentages of students eligible for free or reduced-priced lunch in 2000–2001 California elementary schools ($n = 4779$).

Suggested Computer Exercises

Use the **sophomores** data file to address the following tasks and questions.

1. Generate a histogram for CGPA and use it to estimate the mean, median, and mode. Mark your estimates on the graph.
2. Obtain the actual median and mode for CGPA by way of a frequency distribution.

3. Which measure of central tendency do you think best captures the typical CGPA in this sophomore class? Explain.
4. Obtain the mean, median, and mode for READ using the "Statistics" option within the Frequencies procedure. Comment on what these scores suggest about the shape of this distribution.

Exercises

Identify, Define, or Explain

Terms and Concepts

average	mean
measure of central tendency	balance point
mode	algebraic property
modal score	grand mean
bimodal	mathematical tractability
median	sampling stability

Symbols

X Mdn Σ $\overline{X}$ $\overline{\overline{X}}$

Questions and Problems

Note: Answers to starred (*) items are presented in Appendix B.

1. List the physical characteristic of a frequency curve that corresponds to each of the three measures of central tendency.

*2. For each of the following sets of scores, find the mode, the median, and the mean:
   (a) 12, 10, 8, 22, 8
   (b) 14, 12, 25, 17
   (c) 10, 6, 11, 15, 11, 13

3. Which measure of central tendency is most easily estimated from a histogram or frequency polygon? Why?

4. In the following quotation, taken verbatim from a company newsletter, the author was attempting to provide statistical enlightenment:

   One of the most misused words is the word "average." It is often confused with "mean." The difference is this: If five products sell for $2, $3, $5, $8, and $67, *the average price is $17. The median, or mean, price is $5, the $5 price being the middle price—two prices are higher and two are lower. The average of a series may or may not be the middle.*

Your task: Comment on the accuracy of the author's remarks, sentence by sentence.

5. **(a)** What is meant by the "balance point" of a distribution of scores? How is the expression, $\Sigma(X - \bar{X}) = 0$, relevant to this concept?

   (b) Show that $\Sigma(X - \bar{X}) = 0$ for the following sample of scores: 2, 5, 7, 8, 13.

*6. Comment on the probable shape for each of the following distributions:

   (a) $\bar{X} = 52$, $Mdn = 55$, mode $= 60$

   (b) $\bar{X} = 79$, $Mdn = 78$, mode $= 78$

   (c) $\bar{X} = 50$, $Mdn = 50$, mode $= 60, 40$

   (d) $\bar{X} = 28$, $Mdn = 26$, mode $= 20$

*7. State the likely relative positions of the mean, median, and mode for the following distributions:

   (a) family income in a large city

   (b) scores on a very easy exam

   (c) heights of a large group of 25 year-old males

   (d) the number of classes skipped during the year for a large group of under-graduate students

8. A newspaper editor once claimed that *more than half* of American families earned a below-average income. Could this claim possibly be correct? (Explain.)

9. At a local K–6 school, the four K–2 teachers have a mean of 15 students per class, while the five teachers for grades 3–6 have a mean of 18 students per class. What is the mean number of students across the nine teachers in this school?

*10. $\bar{X} = 23$, $Mdn = 28$, mode $= 31$ for a particular distribution of 25 scores. It was subsequently found that a scoring mistake had been made: one score of 43 should have been a 34.

   (a) What is the correct value for $\bar{X}$?

   (b) How would the *Mdn* and mode be affected by this error?

*11. Suppose you were a school psychologist and were interested only in improving the *median* self-esteem score of children in your school. On which of the following students would you work the hardest: (1) those with the lowest self-esteem scores, (2) those with the highest, (3) those just below the median, or (4) those just above the median? (Explain.)

*12. What is the mean, median, and mode for the distribution of scores in Table 2.2?

13. Where must the mode lie in the distribution of GPAs in Table 2.5?

*14. Which measure(s) of central tendency would you be unable to determine from the following data? Why?

Hours of Study per Night	f
5+	6
4	11
3	15
2	13
1 or fewer	8

15. From an article in a local newspaper: "The median price for the houses sold was $125,000. Included in the upper half [of houses sold] are the one or two homes that could sell for more than $1 million, which brings up the median price for the entire market." Comment?

16. If the eventual purpose of a study involves statistical inference, which measure of central tendency is preferable (other things being equal)? (Explain.)

CHAPTER 5

Variability

5.1 Central Tendency Is Not Enough: The Importance of Variability

There is an unhappy story, oft-told and probably untrue, of the general who arrived at a river that separated his troops from their destination. Seeing no bridges and having no boats, he inquired about the depth of the river. Told that "the average depth is only 2 feet," he confidently ordered the army to walk across. Most of the soldiers drowned.

In the words of the late Stephen J. Gould, "central tendency is an abstraction, variation the reality" (Gould, 1996, pp. 48–49). Informative as they are, measures of central tendency do not tell the whole story. To more fully understand a distribution, one also must inquire about the **variability** of scores. The implications of variability go well beyond negotiating rivers. Suppose that you are a high school math teacher and have been assigned two sections of ninth-grade geometry. To get a sense of your students' readiness, you plot their scores from a standardized math test they took at the end of the preceding year. The two distributions appear in Figure 5.1, where you see considerably more variability among students' readiness scores in Section 2. Although the average student (the mean student, if you will) is comparable across the two sections, in Section 2 you will face the additional tasks of remediating the less advanced students and challenging the more advanced. Clearly, the picture is more complex than a comparison of central tendency alone would suggest.

Variability also is of fundamental interest to the education researcher. Indeed, research is nothing if not the study of variability—variability among individuals, variability among experimental conditions, *co*variability among variables, and so on. We consider three measures of variability in this chapter: range, variance, and standard deviation. In its own way, each communicates the *spread* or *dispersion* of scores in a distribution.

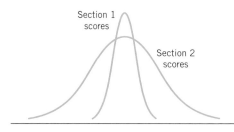

Figure 5.1 Two distributions with same central tendency but different variability.

5.2   *The Range*

You met the **range** earlier when constructing a frequency distribution (Chapter 2). Its definition is simple:

> The range is the difference between the highest and the lowest scores in a distribution.

Like other measures of variability, the range is a *distance*. This is in contrast to measures of central tendency, which reflect *location*. For example, the following sets of scores all have the same range (20 points), even though they fall in very different places along the number scale:

$$3, \ 5, \ 8, \ 14, \ 23$$
$$37, \ 42, \ 48, \ 53, \ 57$$
$$131, \ 140, \ 147, \ 150, \ 151$$

The range is the most straightforward measure of variability and can be quite informative as an initial check on the spread of scores. It also can be helpful for detecting errors in data coding or entry. For example, when statistical software reports a variable's range, the *minimum* and *maximum* values typically are provided. A quick inspection of these values can alert you to implausible data, such as a negative IQ or a percentage that exceeds 100. Although "out of range" values also influence the more sophisticated measures of variability that we will examine shortly, their effects are not as apparent on these measures (and therefore might be missed).

The range, however, has two general limitations. First, because it is based solely on the two extreme scores in a distribution, which can vary widely from sample to sample, the *stability* of the range leaves much to be desired.[1] Second, the range says absolutely nothing about what happens in between the highest and lowest scores. For instance, the three distributions in Figure 5.2 all have the same range, even though the three sets of scores spread out in quite different ways.

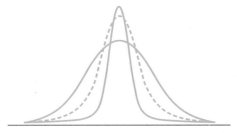

Figure 5.2   Three distributions with same range but different shape.

---

[1]The *interquartile range* provides a somewhat more stable index by relying on two less extreme scores—the score points associated with the first and third quartiles (Q_1 and Q_3, respectively). The *semi-interquartile range* is the interquartile range divided by 2. One rarely encounters either in research, however, so we shall say no more about them here.

Though informative, the range is insufficient as a sole measure of variability. What is needed is a measure that is responsive to every score value in the distribution.

5.3   Variability and Deviations From the Mean

We return to a concept introduced in the preceding chapter, which we call the **deviation score**.

A deviation score, $X - \overline{X}$, indicates the distance of a score from the mean.

You will recall that deviations below the mean are equal in magnitude to deviations above the mean and, as a consequence, deviation scores necessarily sum to zero (see Figure 4.3). Expressed mathematically, $\Sigma(X - \overline{X}) = 0$.

Because deviation scores are distances from the mean, it stands to reason that they can be used to measure variability. That is, the more the raw scores spread out, the farther they will be from the mean, and the larger will be the deviation scores (ignoring algebraic sign). This can be seen by comparing the three distributions in Table 5.1.

For the moment, let's focus on the upper half of this table. Although the three sets of scores have identical ranges (can you see that they do?), these distributions nevertheless differ in the extent to which their scores cluster around the mean. Notice that the three middle scores in distribution A fall directly on the mean. Except for the two extreme scores 1 and 9, there is no variability in this distribution at all. This also is evident from the deviation scores for these three middle values, all of which equal

Table 5.1   Three Distributions with Differing Degrees of Variability

Distribution A		Distribution B		Distribution C	
X	$X - \overline{X}$	X	$X - \overline{X}$	X	$X - \overline{X}$
9	$9 - 5 = +4$	9	$9 - 5 = +4$	9	$9 - 5 = +4$
5	$5 - 5 = 0$	6	$6 - 5 = +1$	8	$8 - 5 = +3$
5	$5 - 5 = 0$	5	$5 - 5 = 0$	5	$5 - 5 = 0$
5	$5 - 5 = 0$	4	$4 - 5 = -1$	2	$2 - 5 = -3$
1	$1 - 5 = -4$	1	$1 - 5 = -4$	1	$1 - 5 = -4$

$$SS = \Sigma(X - \overline{X})^2$$
$$= (+4)^2 + 0^2 + 0^2$$
$$+ 0^2 + (-4)^2$$
$$= 32$$
$$S^2 = 32/5 = 6.4$$

$$SS = (+4)^2 + (+1)^2 + 0^2$$
$$+ (-1)^2 + (-4)^2$$
$$= 34$$
$$S^2 = 34/5 = 6.8$$

$$SS = (+4)^2 + (+3)^2 + 0^2$$
$$+ (-3)^2 + (-4)^2$$
$$= 50$$
$$S^2 = 50/5 = 10.0$$

zero. Distribution B is slightly more variable in this regard. And the raw scores in distribution C cluster around their mean the least, as the deviation scores testify.

How can deviation scores be combined into a *single* measure of variability? Taking the mean deviation score may seem like a logical approach—until you remember that $\Sigma(X - \overline{X})$ always equals zero! You could ignore the minus signs and compute the mean based on the *absolute values* of the deviation scores; however, this approach is problematic from a mathematical standpoint (the details of which we spare you).

The solution lies in squaring each deviation score. It turns out that good things happen when you do this—for example, the negative deviations all become positive. And this operation (squaring) is mathematically more acceptable than simply ignoring the minus signs.

We now turn to two closely related measures of variability based on squared deviation scores. Both are of great importance in statistical analysis.

5.4   The Variance

The **variance**, which we denote with the symbol S^2, is the mean of the squared deviation scores. That is, $S^2 = \Sigma(X - \overline{X})^2/n$. To express this formula more conveniently, we introduce the symbol SS, which stands for **sum of squares**. This important term refers to the sum of squared deviations from the mean, $\Sigma(X - \overline{X})^2$, which serves prominently as the numerator of the variance.

Variance
$$S^2 = \frac{\Sigma(X - \overline{X})^2}{n}$$
$$= \frac{SS}{n}$$

(5.1)

A quick visit back to Table 5.1 will show that the SS and, in turn, the variance, detect differences among these three distributions that the range misses. For example, the SS for distribution A is $(+4)^2 + (0)^2 + (0)^2 + (0)^2 + (-4)^2 = 32$, which, as it should be, is less than the SS for distribution B: $(+4)^2 + (+1)^2 + (0)^2 + (-1)^2 + (-4)^2 = 34$. And both are less than the SS for Distribution C: $(+4)^2 + (+3)^2 + (0)^2 + (-3)^2 + (-4)^2 = 50$. Now divide each SS by the respective n (5 in this case) and you have the three variances: 6.4, 6.8, and 10. Because the variance is responsive to the value of each score in a distribution, the variance uncovers differences in variability that less sophisticated measures of variability (e.g., range) do not.

As you see, the core of the variance—the thing that makes it tick—is SS. A variance is big, small, or somewhere in between only insofar as SS is (big, small, or somewhere in between).

The variance finds its greatest use in more advanced statistical procedures, particularly in statistical inference. But it has a fatal flaw as a descriptive, or interpretive, device: The calculated value of the variance is expressed in *squared* units of measurement. Suppose that the data in Table 5.1 are vocabulary scores. In this case, the mean for distribution A is 5 *words correct* (can you verify this calculation?), but the variance is 6.4 *squared* words correct. Not only is a "squared word" difficult to understand in its own right, but the squaring is problematic on more technical grounds as well: if the scores of one distribution deviate *twice* as far from the mean as those of another, the variance of the first distribution will actually be *four* times as large as that of the second. Because of this, the variance is little used for interpretive purposes.

5.5   *The Standard Deviation*

The remedy for the variance is simple: unsquare it! By taking the square root of the variance, you ensure that the resulting statistic—the **standard deviation**—is expressed in the original units of measurement. For example, if the variance is 6.4 *squared words correct*, then the standard deviation is $\sqrt{6.4} = 2.53$ *words correct*. Thus, the standard deviation, S, simply is the square root of the variance:

Standard deviation[2]
$$S = \sqrt{\frac{\Sigma(X - \overline{X})^2}{n}}$$ (5.2) $$= \sqrt{\frac{SS}{n}}$$

Calculating the Standard Deviation

We now consider the calculation of the standard deviation in more detail. As you will see, however, these calculations are identical to those required for computing the variance—except for the additional step of taking the square root.

Consider the data in Table 5.2. Only five steps are required to calculate the standard deviation using Formula (5.2):

Step 1   *Find $\overline{X}$.* The sum of the 10 scores, ΣX, equals 70 which, when divided by n, yields a mean of 7. This is shown at ❶ in Table 5.2.

Step 2   *Subtract the mean from each score.*
These calculations appear under the column entitled $(X - \overline{X})$. For example, the first value of X (12) results in the difference $12 - 7 = +5$. These deviations sum to zero (❷)—as you should insist they do!

---

[2]In journals that follow the *Publication Manual of the American Psychological Association*, the symbol *SD* is used to represent the standard deviation.

Table 5.2   The Calculation of the Standard Deviation

X	$(X - \overline{X})$	$(X - \overline{X})^2$
12	$12 - 7 = +5$	$(+5)^2 = 25$
11	$11 - 7 = +4$	$(+4)^2 = 16$
9	$9 - 7 = +2$	$(+2)^2 = 4$
8	$8 - 7 = +1$	$(+1)^2 = 1$
7	$7 - 7 = 0$	$(0)^2 = 0$
6	$6 - 7 = -1$	$(-1)^2 = 1$
6	$6 - 7 = -1$	$(-1)^2 = 1$
5	$5 - 7 = -2$	$(-2)^2 = 4$
4	$4 - 7 = -3$	$(-3)^2 = 9$
2	$2 - 7 = -5$	$(-5)^2 = 25$

❶ $\Sigma X = 70$ **❷** $\Sigma(X - \overline{X}) = 0$ **❸** $SS = \Sigma(X - \overline{X})^2$

$\overline{X} = 70/10 = 7$ $= 25 + 16 + \cdots + 25 = 86$

❹ $S = \sqrt{SS/n} = \sqrt{86/10}$

$= \sqrt{8.60} = 2.93$

Step 3 *Square each $(X - \overline{X})$.*
These values are presented in the final column, $(X - \overline{X})^2$, where you see $(+5)^2 = 25$, $(+4)^2 = 16, \ldots, (-5)^2 = 25$. (*Note:* ",...," represents the seven values between 16 and 25 in this column.)

Step 4 *Sum the values of $(X - \overline{X})^2$ to obtain SS.*
As shown at **❸**, $SS = 86$.

Step 5 *Enter SS and n in Formula (5.2) and solve for S.*
Namely: $S = \sqrt{SS/n} = \sqrt{86/10} = \sqrt{8.6} = 2.93$ (**❹**).

The standard deviation of these data, then, is about 3. You may be asking, "3 *what?!*" As with the mean, it depends on what the units of measurement are: 3 errors, 3 fish caught, 3 items correct, 3 books read, 3 dollars earned, 3 loves lost.

Coming to Terms with the Standard Deviation

It can take a while to develop a secure feeling for the meaning of the standard deviation. If you are not feeling at the moment that you "own" this concept, you probably are in good company. Formula (5.2) shows that the standard deviation is the square root of the mean of the squared deviation scores, a definition you may not find terribly comforting at this stage of the game. However, no great harm is done if you think of the standard deviation as being something like the "average dispersion about the mean" in a distribution, expressed in the original units of measurement (e.g., IQ points). Although imprecise and inelegant, this paraphrase may help you get a handle on this important statistic.

Give it time—the meaning of the standard deviation will come. We promise.

5.6   *The Predominance of the Variance and Standard Deviation*

The variance and standard deviation are omnipresent in the analysis of data, more than any other measure of variability. This is for two reasons. First, both measures are more mathematically tractable than the range (and its mathematical relatives). Because they respond to arithmetic and algebraic manipulations, either the variance or standard deviation appears explicitly (or lies embedded) in many descriptive and inferential procedures. Second, the variance and standard deviation have the virtue of greater sampling stability. In repeated random samples, their values tend to jump about less than the range and related indices. That is, there is less sampling variation. As you will see, this property is of great importance in statistical inference.

A word of caution: Both the variance and standard deviation are sensitive to extreme scores (though less so than the range). Because the variance and standard deviation deal with the *squares* of deviation scores, an extreme score that is three times as far from the mean as the next closest score would have a squared deviation *nine* times as large ($3^2 = 9$). Consequently, be careful when interpreting the variance and standard deviation for a distribution that is markedly skewed or contains a few very extreme scores.

5.7   *The Standard Deviation and the Normal Distribution*

We suggested that you think of the standard deviation as something like the average dispersion in a distribution. Insight into the meaning of this statistic also can be gained by learning how the standard deviation works in a variety of contexts. We begin by briefly examining its use as a *distance measure* in that most useful of distribution shapes, the normal curve.

In an ideal normal distribution, the following is found if you start at the mean and go a certain number of standard deviations above and below it:

$\overline{X} \pm 1S$ contains about 68% of the scores.[3]

$\overline{X} \pm 2S$ contains about 95% of the scores.

$\overline{X} \pm 3S$ contains about 99.7% of the scores.

In the next chapter we explore these relationships in considerably greater detail, but let's take a quick look here. Figure 5.3 presents a normal distribution of test scores for a large group of high school students, with $\overline{X} = 69$ and $S = 3$. Given the preceding three statements, you would expect that about 68% of these students have scores between 66 and 72 (69 ± 3), about 95% have scores between 63 and 75 (69 ± 6), and almost all students—99.72%—have scores between 60 and 78 (69 ± 9).

These results are based on the assumption of a normal distribution. But even for skewed distributions, you typically will find that $\overline{X} \pm 1S$ captures the majority of cases, $\overline{X} \pm 2S$ includes an even greater majority, and $\overline{X} \pm 3S$ comprises all but a very few cases.

[3]"$\overline{X} \pm 1S$" translates to "from 1 standard deviation below the mean, to 1 standard deviation above the mean."

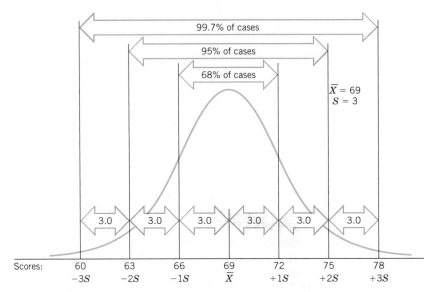

Figure 5.3   Frequency distribution of test scores based on the normal distribution.

5.8   *Comparing Means of Two Distributions: The Relevance of Variability*

Comparing the means of two distributions provides another context for appreciating the use of the standard deviation. Suppose you find a difference of one point between the mean score for two groups: that is, $\overline{X}_1 - \overline{X}_2 = -1.00$. Is this a big difference? It would be if the measure were cumulative college GPA, in which case this difference would represent one *grade point*. If the measure were SAT performance, however, a difference of one *SAT point* would be trivial indeed.

> To adequately appraise a difference between two means, one must take into account the underlying *scale*, or metric, on which the means are based.

The standard deviation is an important frame of reference in this regard. Indeed, the numerical size of a mean difference often is difficult to interpret without taking into account the standard deviation.

For example, SAT scores, which fall on a scale of 200 to 800, have a standard deviation of 100; for a GPA scale of 0 to 4.0, a typical standard deviation is .4. The one-point difference, *when expressed as the corresponding number of standard deviations*, is $-1/.4 = -2.5$ standard deviations for the GPA difference and $-1/100 = -.01$ standard deviations for the SAT difference.

If we were to assume normality for these distributions, the differences would be as shown in Figure 5.4. Note the almost complete overlap of the two SAT distributions $(-.01\,S)$ and the substantial separation between the two GPA distributions

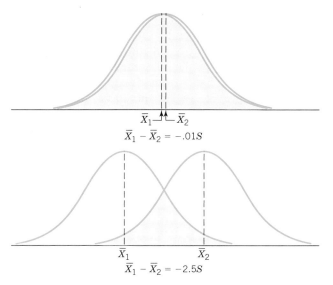

Figure 5.4   Overlap of scores in two distributions whose means differ by varying amounts.

$(-2.5\ S)$. This example illustrates the value of expressing a "raw" difference in terms of standard deviation units.

Effect Size

As you deal with real variables, you will find that the standard deviations of the two distributions to be compared often will be similar, though not identical. In such situations, it is reasonable to somehow combine, or *pool*, the two standard deviations for appraising the magnitude of the difference between the two means. When a mean difference is divided by a "pooled" standard deviation, the resulting index is called an **effect size** (*ES*):

Effect size

$$ES = \frac{\overline{X}_1 - \overline{X}_2}{\sqrt{\dfrac{SS_1 + SS_2}{n_1 + n_2}}}$$

$$= \frac{\overline{X}_1 - \overline{X}_2}{S_{\text{pooled}}}$$

(5.3)

The numerator of Formula (5.3) is straightforward: it is the difference between the two means, $\overline{X}_1$ and $\overline{X}_2$. The denominator, the standard deviation of the two groups combined, is a bit more involved. Of course, it couldn't be as simple as taking the mean of the two standard deviations! Instead, you must work from the sums of squares, SS_1 and SS_2, which are easily derived from their respective standard deviations.

We illustrate the procedure for calculating ES in Table 5.3. In this example, the two means are found to differ by .50 standard deviations. Specifically, the mean of the first group is one-half of a standard deviation lower than the mean of the second ($ES = -.50$). A popular, if somewhat arbitrary, guideline is to consider $ES = .20$ as "small," $ES = .50$ "moderate," and $ES = .80$ "large" (Cohen, 1988). This judgment, however, always should be made in the context of the investigation's variables, instruments, and participants.

The problem of comparing the means of two distributions occurs frequently in both descriptive and inferential statistics. It will prove helpful to get accustomed to thinking about the magnitude of a mean difference in terms of the

Table 5.3   Calculating the Effect Size

	$\overline{X}$	S	n
Group 1	48.00	9.80	20
Group 2	53.00	10.20	20

Follow these steps to calculate the effect size that corresponds to the difference between the two means above:

Step 1   *Determine the difference between the two means.*
$$\overline{X}_1 - \overline{X}_2 = 48.00 - 53.00 = -5.00$$

Step 2   *Calculate each SS from its standard deviation.*

- Begin by recalling Formula (5.2):
$$S = \sqrt{\frac{SS}{n}}$$

- Square each side:
$$S^2 = \frac{SS}{n}$$

- Multiply each side by n:
$$nS^2 = SS$$

- Now you can calculate the SS for each group:
$$SS_1 = n_1 S_1^2 = (20)(96.04) = 1920.80$$
$$SS_2 = n_2 S_2^2 = (20)(104.04) = 2080.80$$

Step 3   *Determine the pooled standard deviation.*
$$S_{\text{pooled}} = \sqrt{\frac{SS_1 + SS_2}{n_1 + n_2}} = \sqrt{\frac{1920.80 + 2080.80}{20 + 20}} = \sqrt{\frac{4001.6}{40}} = \sqrt{100.04} = 10.00$$

Step 4   *Divide the mean difference by the pooled standard deviation.*
$$ES = \frac{\overline{X}_1 - \overline{X}_2}{S_{\text{pooled}}} = \frac{-5.00}{10.00} = -.50$$

Thus, the mean of the first group is half a standard deviation lower than the mean of the second group.

number of standard deviations it represents. We will elaborate on the meaning of this effect size in Chapter 6. In later chapters, you will see that "effect size" in fact is a general term that applies to a variety of research situations (a mean difference being only one).

5.9   In the Denominator: n vs. $n - 1$

If you use computer software or a hand-held calculator to compute either the variance or the standard deviation, you probably will obtain a value that differs from what Formulas (5.1) and (5.2) will give you. This is because computers and calculators tend to insert $(n - 1)$ in the denominator of the variance and standard deviation, unlike the companionless n that appears in Formulas (5.1) and (5.2).

Why the difference? The answer, which we explore in Chapter 13, is found in the distinction between statistical *description* and statistical *inference*. Formulas (5.1) and (5.2) are fine statistically, provided your interests do not go beyond the immediate data at hand. However, if you are using the variance or standard deviation from a *sample* for making inferences about variability in the corresponding *population*, these formulas provide a biased estimate. Specifically, the sample standard deviation (or variance) will tend to be somewhat smaller than the population standard deviation (or variance). (The bias is not great, particularly for large samples.) By replacing the denominator with $(n - 1)$, you arrive at an unbiased estimate. Similar logic explains why you later will see that $(n_1 + n_2 - 2)$ appears in the effect size denominator when the objective is statistical inference. In the meantime, Formulas (5.1), (5.2), and (5.3) are appropriate for our purpose.

5.10   Summary

Measures of variability are important in describing distributions, and they play a particularly vital role in statistical inference. We have considered three measures in this chapter: the range, variance, and standard deviation. Each is a summary figure that describes, in quantitative terms, the spread or dispersion of scores in a distribution. The range gives the distance between the high score and the low score. The variance is the mean of the squared deviations, and the standard deviation is the square root of that quantity. Although important in advanced statistics, the variance is little used in the more practical task of describing the spread of scores because it is expressed in *squared* units.

In comparison to the range, the variance and standard deviation are mathematically more tractable and are more stable from sample to sample. You also saw that the standard deviation is related to the normal curve and, furthermore, that the standard deviation can be used for appraising the magnitude of the difference between two means.

Reading the Research: The Standard Deviation and Effect Size

In Section 5.8 you learned about the value of expressing group differences in standard deviation units. Hanushek (1999) illustrates this approach in his review of the effects of class size reductions in Tennessee. He reported that "the difference between performance in class sizes of 22–25 and 13–17 is 0.17 standard deviations in both math and reading" (p. 155). In other words, $ES = .17$ in both cases. This effect size suggests that the mean achievement of students in small classes was marginally better than that of students in regular-sized classes. If we can assume normality in the two distributions, the average student in small classes scored at roughly the 57th percentile of students in regular-sized classes. (In Section 6.9 of the next chapter, we'll show you how we came up with this last conclusion.)

Source: Hanushek, E. A. (1999). Some findings from an independent investigation of the Tennessee STAR experiment and from other investigations of class size effects. *Educational Evaluation and Policy Analysis, 21*(2), 143–163.

Case Study: (Effect) Sizing Up the Competition

For this case study, we explore sex differences in verbal and mathematical performance using data from a suburban high school located in a northeastern state. Among the data were tenth-grade test scores on the annual state assessment. Students received scores in English language arts (ELA) and mathematics (MATH), and each score fell on a scale of 200–280. These are called scaled scores, which are derived from raw scores. (The choice of scale is largely arbitrary. At the time of this writing, for instance, the scale of the state assessment in New Hampshire was 200–300; in Pennsylvania, 1000–1600, and in Maine, 501–580.)

After examining the frequency distributions for ELA and MATH, we obtained descriptive statistics regarding variability and central tendency (Table 5.4*a*). With a quick inspection of these results, we immediately saw that the maximum ELA score of 2222 (!) fell well beyond the allowable range of scores. We suspected that this was simply a data entry error. Sure enough, a review of the raw data set and school records confirmed that the ELA score for one of the students was mistakenly entered as 2222 rather than the intended score of 222. We corrected the entry and recomputed the descriptive statistics (Table 5.4*b*). Notice that, with the correction, the standard deviation for ELA is considerably lower ($S = 18.61$). With a quick look at Formula (5.2), you easily see why a score of $X = 2222$ had such an inflationary effect on the standard deviation. In short, this single error in data entry resulted in a numerator that was 2000 points larger than it should be! Using similar logic and revisiting Formula (4.1), you also should be able to appreciate why the ELA mean in Table 5.4*b* is considerably lower than that in Table 5.4*a*.

Table 5.4*a*   Statistics for ELA and MATH Scores *before* Correcting Data Entry Error

	n	Range	Minimum	Maximum	$\overline{X}$	S
ELA	194	2022.00	200.00	2222.00	243.47	144.73
MATH	194	80.00	200.00	280.00	230.60	24.17

Table 5.4*b* Statistics for ELA and MATH Scores *after*
Correcting Data Entry Error

	n	Range	Minimum	Maximum	$\overline{X}$	*S*
ELA	194	68.00	200.00	268.00	233.10	18.61
MATH	194	80.00	200.00	280.00	230.60	24.17

The measures of variability in Table 5.4*b* indicate that, compared to scores in MATH, there is less dispersion in ELA scores. In mathematics, students scored across the entire scale range, but in English language arts, no student attained the maximum possible score (in fact, the highest score fell short by 12 points). The lower variability among ELA scores is further substantiated by its relatively smaller standard deviation: $S_{ELA} = 18.61$ vs. $S_{MATH} = 24.17$.

Table 5.5 presents means and standard deviations for ELA and MATH, reported separately by gender. In terms of variability, there is little difference between males and females on both exams; their standard deviations differ by merely fractions of a point. As for central tendency, there appear to be only modest gender differences in mean performance. Females have the edge in English language arts $(\overline{X}_M - \overline{X}_F = -2.49)$, and males the edge in mathematics $(\overline{X}_M - \overline{X}_F = -4.27)$. When expressed in the metric of scaled scores, these differences convey limited meaning. Furthermore, as you have learned in this chapter, measures of central tendency do not tell the whole story about a distribution; variability also should be considered when comparing two distributions. For these reasons, we proceeded to express each mean difference as an effect size.

As you see in Table 5.6, the effect sizes with respect to gender are $ES_{ELA} = -.13$ and $ES_{MATH} = +.18$. Thus, the mean ELA score for males is .13 *SD*s lower than that for females, whereas the mean MATH score for males is .18 *SD*s higher than that for females. The algebraic sign of each ES reflects our arbitrary decision to subtract the female mean from the male mean: $\overline{X}_M - \overline{X}_F$. We just as easily could have gone the other way $(\overline{X}_F - \overline{X}_M)$, in which case the magnitude of each *ES* would remain the same but its algebraic sign would reverse. Regardless of who is subtracted from whom, of course, the substantive meaning of these *ES*s does not change. These data suggest a rather small gender difference favoring males on MATH and an even smaller difference favoring females on ELA. (Recall from Section 5.8 that, according to Cohen's effect size typology, an effect size of .20 is considered "small.")

Table 5.5 ELA and MATH Performance by Gender

	ELA		MATH	
	Males (***n* = 110**)	**Females** (***n* = 84**)	**Males** (***n* = 110**)	**Females** (***n* = 84**)
$\overline{X}$	232.16	234.65	232.54	228.27
S	18.80	18.36	23.64	24.80

Table 5.6   Calculations of Gender Effect Sizes for ELA and MATH

ELA	MATH
1. $\bar{X}_M - \bar{X}_F = 232.16 - 234.65 = -2.49$	1. $\bar{X}_M - \bar{X}_F = 232.54 - 228.27 = -4.27$
2. $nS^2 = SS$	2. $nS^2 = SS$
$\quad SS_M = n_M S_M^2 = (111)(18.80)^2 = 39231.84$	$\quad SS_M = n_M S_M^2 = (111)(23.64)^2 = 62032.30$
$\quad SS_F = n_F S_F^2 = (82)(18.36)^2 = 27641.35$	$\quad SS_F - n_F S_F^2 = (82)(24.80)^2 = 50433.28$
3. $S_{pooled} = 18.61$	3. $S_{pooled} = 24.14$
4. $ES = -2.49/18.61 = -.13$	4. $ES = 4.27/24.14 = +.18$

Suggested Computer Exercises

1. Access the **fourth** data file, which contains student grades from a fourth-grade social studies class.

   (a) Generate the mean, minimum, maximum, and standard deviation for QUIZ and ESSAY. Grading for both assessments is based on 100 points.

   (b) Does one assessment appear more discriminating than the other? That is, do the two assessments differ in their ability to "spread out" students in terms of their performance?

2. Access the **sophomores** data file.

   (a) Compute descriptive statistics for MATH (the score on the state-administered mathematics exam), and report the results separately for the group of students who took algebra in the eighth grade and for those who took general math. (You will need to use the "split file" command, which you will find in the *Data* menu.)

   (b) How do these two groups compare in terms of variability in MATH scores? (How about central tendency?)

Exercises

Identify, Define, or Explain

Terms and Concepts

variability	sum of squares
range	standard deviation
spread	mathematical tractability
dispersion	sampling stability
deviation score	standard deviation as a distance measure
variance	effect size

Symbols

S^2 S SS ES

Note: Answers to starred (*) items are presented in Appendix B.

1. Give three examples, other than those mentioned in this chapter, of an "average" (unaccompanied by a measure of variability) that is either insufficient or downright misleading. For each example, explain why a variability measure is necessary.

2. Each of five raw scores is converted to a deviation score. The values for four of the deviation scores are as follows: -4, $+2$, $+3$, -6. What is the value of the remaining deviation score?

*3. For each set of scores below, compute the range, variance, and standard deviation.

    (a) 3, 8, 2, 6, 0, 5

    (b) 5, 1, 9, 8, 3, 4

    (c) 6, 4, 10, 6, 7, 3

4. Determine the standard deviation for the following set of scores. X: 2.5, 6.9, 3.8, 9.3, 5.1, 8.0

5. Given: $S^2 = 18$ and $SS = 900$. What is n?

*6. For each of the following statistics, what would be the effect of adding one point to every score in a distribution? What generalization do you make from this? (Do this *without* calculations.)

    (a) mode

    (b) median

    (c) mean

    (d) range

    (e) variance

    (f) standard deviation

7. If you wanted to *decrease* variance by adding a point to some (but not all) scores in a distribution, which scores would you modify? What would you do if you wanted to *increase* variance?

*8. After you have computed the mean, median, range, and standard deviation of a set of 40 scores, you discover that the lowest score is in error and should be even lower. Which of the statistics above will be affected by the correction? (Explain.)

9. Why is the variance little used as a descriptive measure?

*10. Imagine that each of the following pairs of means and standard deviations was determined from scores on a 50-item test. With only this information, describe the probable shape of each distribution. (Assume a normal distribution unless you believe the information presented suggests otherwise.)

    (a) $\bar{X} = 29, S = 3$

    (b) $\bar{X} = 29, S = 4$

    (c) $\bar{X} = 48, S = 4$

    (d) $\bar{X} = 50, S = 0$

*11. Consider the four sets of scores:

$$8, \ 8, \ 8, \ 8, \ 8$$
$$6, \ 6, \ 8, \ 10, \ 10$$
$$4, \ 6, \ 8, \ 10, \ 12$$
$$1004, \ 1006, \ 1008, \ 1010, \ 1012$$

(a) Upon inspection, which show(s) the least variability? the most variability?

(b) For each set of scores, compute the mean; compute the variance and standard deviation directly from the deviation scores.

(c) What do the results of Problem 11b suggest about the relationship between central tendency and variability?

12. Determine the sum of squares SS corresponding to each of the following standard deviations ($n = 30$):

(a) 12

(b) 9

(c) 6

(d) 4.5

13. Given: $\overline{X} = 500$ and $S = 100$ for the SAT-CR.

(a) What percentage of scores would you expect to fall between 400 and 600?

(b) between 300 and 700?

(c) between 200 and 800?

*14. The mean is 67 for a large group of students in a college physics class; Duane obtains a score of 73.

(a) From this information only, how would you describe his performance?

(b) Suppose $S = 20$. Now how would you describe his performance?

(c) Suppose $S = 2$. Now how would you describe his performance?

*15. Imagine you obtained the following results in an investigation of sex differences among high school students:

Mathematics Achievement		Verbal Ability	
male ($n = 32$)	female ($n = 34$)	Male ($n = 32$)	female ($n = 34$)
$\overline{X}_M = 48$ $S_M = 9.0$	$\overline{X}_F = 46$ $S_F = 9.2$	$\overline{X}_M = 75$ $S_M = 12.9$	$\overline{X}_F = 78$ $S_F = 13.2$

(a) What is the pooled standard deviation for mathematics achievement?

(b) What is the pooled standard deviation for verbal ability?

(c) Compute the effect size for each of these mean differences.

(d) What is your impression of the magnitude of the two effect sizes?

CHAPTER 6

Normal Distributions and Standard Scores

Frequency distributions, as you know, have many shapes. One of those shapes, the **normal curve**, appears often and in astonishingly diverse corners of inquiry.[1] The weight of harvested sugar beets, the mental ability of children, the crush strength of samples of concrete, the height of cornstalks in July, and the blood count in repeated drawings from a patient—all these and many more tend to follow closely the bell-shaped normal curve.

It was in the nineteenth century that discovery after discovery revealed the wide applicability of the normal curve. In the later years of that century, Sir Francis Galton (cousin of Darwin) began the first serious investigation of "individual differences," an important area of study today in education and psychology. In his research on how people differ from one another on various mental and physical traits, Galton found the normal curve to be a reasonably good description in many instances. He became greatly impressed with its applicability to natural phenomena. Referring to the normal curve as the Law of Frequency of Error, he wrote:

> *I know of scarcely anything so apt to impress the imagination as the wonderful form of cosmic order expressed by the "Law of Frequency of Error." The law would have been personified by the Greeks and deified, if they had known of it. It reigns with serenity and in complete self-effacement amidst the wildest confusion. The huger the mob and the greater the apparent anarchy, the more perfect is its sway. It is the supreme law of Unreason. Whenever a large sample of chaotic elements are taken in hand and marshaled in the order of their magnitude, an unsuspected and most beautiful form of regularity proves to have been latent all along.* (Galton, 1889, p. 66)

Although Galton was a bit overzealous in ascribing such lawful behavior to the normal curve, you probably can understand his enthusiasm in these early days of behavioral science. However, not all variables follow the normal curve. For example, annual income, speed of response, educational attainment, family size, and

---

[1]Because of the seminal work by the nineteenth-century mathematician Karl Friedrich Gauss, the normal curve is also called the *Gaussian distribution* or the *Gaussian curve.*

performance on mastery tests all are characterized by decidedly nonnormal distributions (skewed, in this case). Furthermore, variables that are normally distributed in one context may be nonnormally distributed when the context is changed. For example, spatial reasoning ability is normally distributed among adults as a whole, but among mechanical engineers the distribution would show somewhat of a negative skew.

Nevertheless, the normal curve does offer a convenient and reasonably accurate description of a great number of variables. The normal curve also describes the distribution of many statistics from samples (about which we will have much to say later). For example, if you drew 100 random samples from a population of teenagers and computed the mean weight of each sample, you would find that the distribution of the 100 means approximates the normal curve. In such situations, the fit of the normal curve is often very good indeed. This is a property of paramount importance in statistical inference.

Now we examine the normal curve more closely: what the normal curve is, what its properties are, and how it is useful as a statistical model.

6.2   *Properties of the Normal Curve*

It is important to understand that the normal curve is a *theoretical* invention, a mathematical model, an idealized conception of the form a distribution might take under certain circumstances. No *empirical* distribution—one based on actual data—ever conforms perfectly to the normal curve. But, as we noted earlier, empirical distributions often offer a reasonable approximation of the normal curve. In these instances, it is quite acceptable to say that the data are "normally distributed."

Just as the equation of a circle describes a family of circles—some big, some small—the equation of the normal curve describes a family of distributions. Normal curves may differ from one another with regard to their means and standard deviations, as Figure 6.1 illustrates. However, they are all members of the normal curve family because they share several properties.

What are these properties? First, normal curves are *symmetrical*: the left half of the distribution is a mirror image of the right half. Second, they are *unimodal*. It follows from these first two properties that *the mean, median, and mode all have the same value*. Third, normal curves have that familiar *bell-shaped* form. Starting at the center of the curve and working outward, the height of the curve descends gradually at first, then faster, and finally more slowly. Fourth, a curious and important situation exists at the extremes of the normal curve. Although the curve descends promptly downward, *the tails never actually touch the horizontal axis*—no matter how far out you go.[2] This property alone illustrates why an *empirical* distribution can never be perfectly normal!

---

[2]In this regard, normal curves are said to be *asymptotic*—a term you doubtless will find handy at your next social engagement.

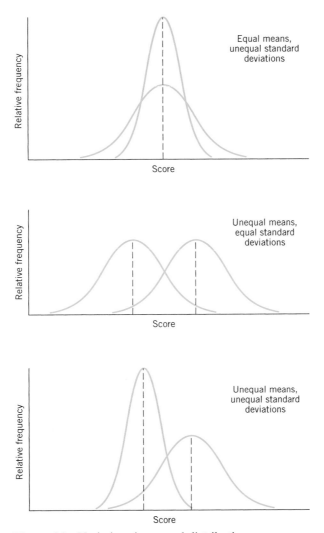

Figure 6.1   Variations in normal distributions.

6.3   More on the Standard Deviation and the Normal Distribution

In Section 3.6, we demonstrated the relationship between relative area and relative frequency of cases. It is an important relationship that we will use again and again. (Before proceeding, you may want to review Section 3.6.)

There also is a precise relationship between the area under the normal curve and units of the standard deviation, which we touched on in Section 5.7. To explore this relationship more fully, let's examine Figure 6.2, which portrays a normal distribution of intelligence test scores ($\overline{X} = 100$, $S = 15$).

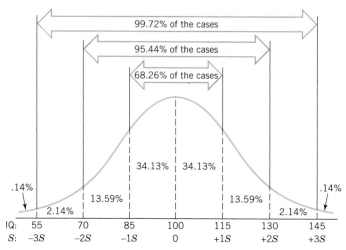

Figure 6.2   Relative frequency of cases contained within standard deviation intervals
($\overline{X} = 100$, $S = 15$).

In a normal distribution, 34.13% of the area is between the mean and one standard deviation above the mean—that is, between $\overline{X}$ and $+1S$. From the discussion in Section 3.6, it follows that 34.13% *of the cases* fall between $\overline{X}$ and $+1S$—or, between IQs 100 and 115.

> The proportion of *area* under any part of a frequency curve is equal to the proportion of *cases* in the same location.

Because the normal curve is symmetrical, 34.13% of the cases also fall between $\overline{X}$ (a score of 100) and $-1S$ (a score of 85). Added together, these two percentages tell you that $\overline{X} \pm 1S$ contains 68.26% of the scores in a normal distribution. That is, a little over two-thirds of IQs are between 85 ($-1S$) and 115 ($+1S$). Given the bell-shaped nature of the normal curve, you should not be surprised to find so many scores falling within only one standard deviation of the mean.

Predictably, the percentages become smaller as the curve makes its way down toward the horizontal axis. Only 13.59% of the cases fall between $+1S$ and $+2S$, with an equal percentage (of course) falling between $-1S$ and $-2S$. A little addition informs you that $\overline{X} \pm 2S$ contains 95.44% of the scores in a normal distribution: 13.59% + 34.13% + 34.13% + 13.59%. Roughly 95% of IQs, then, are between 70 ($-2S$) and 130 ($+2S$).

There are relatively few cases between $+2S$ and $+3S$ (2.14%) and between $-2S$ and $-3S$ (2.14%), and precious few further out (only .14% in either extreme). Almost all the cases in a normal distribution—99.72%—are within ± 3 standard deviations of the mean. Thus, from these data, you can say that almost all IQs are between 55 ($-3S$) and 145 ($+3S$). Indeed, only .28% of IQ scores—about *one-quarter of 1%*—would be either lower than 55 or higher than 145. Individuals with such extreme IQs are exceptional, indeed!

We remind you that these precise figures require the assumption of a perfectly normal distribution. For nonnormal distributions, different figures will obtain. But as we pointed out in Section 5.7, even for skewed distributions one typically finds that $\overline{X} \pm 1S$ captures the majority of cases, $\overline{X} \pm 2S$ includes an even greater majority, and $\overline{X} \pm 3S$ comprises all but a very few cases.

6.4   z Scores

The relationship between the normal curve area and standard deviation units can be put to good use for answering certain questions that are fundamental to statistical reasoning. For example, the following type of question occurs frequently in statistical work: *Given a normal distribution with a mean of 100 and a standard deviation of 15, what proportion of cases fall above the score 115?*

Actually, you can answer this question from the discussion so far. First, you know that a score of 115, with $\overline{X} = 100$ and $S = 15$, is one standard deviation above the mean $(115 - 100 = 15 = 1S)$. Furthermore, you know from Figure 6.2 that 34.13% of the cases fall between 100 and 115, and that another 50% of the cases fall below 100.[3] Thus, 84.13% of the cases fall *below* the score of 115. Subtracting this percentage from 100, you confidently conclude that in a normal distribution with $\overline{X} = 100$ and $S = 15$, roughly 16% (or .16) of the cases fall *above* the score 115.

But what about a score of 120? or 95? You will agree that the precise area falling above (or below) either score is not apparent from Figure 6.2. Fortunately, tables have been constructed that specify the area under the normal curve for specific score points. However, a way must be found to express a score's location in terms that are equivalent for *all* normal curves. The original scores clearly will not do. The score of 115, for example, which is one standard deviation above the mean in Figure 6.2, would have an entirely different location in a normal distribution where $\overline{X} = 135$ and $S = 10$. Indeed, 115 now would be *two* standard deviations *below* the mean.

The solution is to convert the original score to a **standard score** (also called a *standardized* or *derived* score).

> A standard score expresses a score's position in relation to the mean of the distribution, using the standard deviation as the unit of measurement.

Although a mouthful, this statement says nothing more than what you learned two paragraphs ago (as you will see shortly).

---

[3]You can obtain the latter figure by remembering that the normal distribution is *symmetric*, or, if you prefer, you may add the four percentages below the mean in Figure 6.2.

There are many kinds of standard scores. For the moment we will focus on the ***z score***. The idea of a z score is of great importance in statistical reasoning, and we will make much use of it in this and succeeding chapters.

A z score states how many standard deviation units the original score lies above or below the mean of its distribution.

In a distribution where $\overline{X} = 100$ and $S = 15$, the score of 115 corresponds to a z score of +1.00, indicating that the score is one standard deviation above the mean. A z score is convenient because it immediately tells you two things about a score: its algebraic sign indicates whether the score is above or below the mean, and its absolute value tells you by how much (in standard deviation units).

A z score is simply the deviation score divided by the standard deviation, as the following formula illustrates:

z score

$$z = \frac{X - \overline{X}}{S} \qquad (6.1)$$

Consider once again the score 115 from the two different distributions above, one where $\overline{X} = 100$ and $S = 15$ and the other where $\overline{X} = 135$ and $S = 10$. The respective values of z are:

$$z = \frac{115 - 100}{15} = \frac{+15}{15} = +1.00 \quad \text{and} \quad z = \frac{115 - 135}{10} = \frac{-20}{10} = -2.00$$

Even though the original scores are identical, they have different *relative* positions in their respective distributions. This is shown in Figure 6.3, where you see that 16%

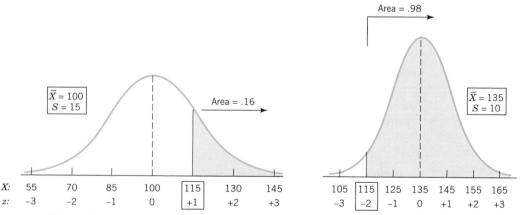

Figure 6.3   Original score and z-score scales for two normal distributions with different means and standard deviations.

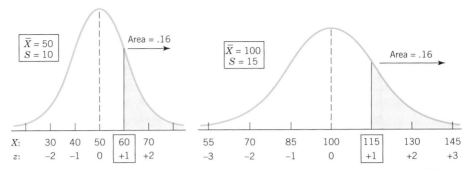

Figure 6.4 Original score and z-score scales for two normal distributions with different means and standard deviations.

of the cases fall above $z = +1.00$ compared with the 98% falling above $z = -2.00$. (Before proceeding further, confirm these percentages from Figure 6.2.)

Now take a normal distribution with $\overline{X} = 50$ and $S = 10$. In this distribution, a score of 60 lies one standard deviation above the mean; consequently, $z = +1.00$. This score, in its distribution, therefore falls at the same relative position as the score of 115 where $\overline{X} = 100$ and $S = 15$. We illustrate this in Figure 6.4, which shows that 16% of the cases exceed the score of 60 in its distribution, just as 16% of cases exceed the score of 115 in its distribution.

Finally, what about those awkward scores of 120 and 95? No problem. If $\overline{X} = 100$ and $S = 15$, then the corresponding z scores are:

$$z = \frac{120 - 100}{15} = \frac{+20}{15} = +1.33 \quad \text{and} \quad z = \frac{95 - 100}{15} = \frac{-5}{15} = -.33$$

The score of 120 is 1.33 standard deviations above the mean, whereas 95 is .33 standard deviations below. (Go back to Figure 6.2 for a moment. Although this figure is insufficient for determining these two z scores from their respective X values, the direction and general magnitude of each z score should agree with your "eyeball" judgment from Figure 6.2 regarding the z score's likely value.)

Now all that is needed is the aforementioned table that specifies the precise area under the normal curve for a particular z score. Enter a z score of, say $+1.33$, and you get the exact proportion of cases falling above (or below) this value. And a whole lot more.

6.5 The Normal Curve Table

In the next two sections, you will learn how to apply the **normal curve table** to common problems involving distributions that follow or can be closely approximated by the normal curve. In Section 6.6, we address the first type of question that was explored above: finding the area under the normal curve, given a specific score. We consider the reverse question in Section 6.7: determining the specific score, given an area.

Table 6.1   Sample Entries from Table A

z	Area between Mean and z	Area beyond z
1	2	3
•	•	•
•	•	•
•	•	•
0.95	.3289	.1711
0.96	.3315	.1685
0.97	.3340	.1660
0.98	.3365	.1635
0.99	.3389	.1611
1.00	.3413	.1587
1.01	.3438	.1562
1.02	.3461	.1539
1.03	.3485	.1515
1.04	.3508	.1492
•	•	•
•	•	•
•	•	•

Let's first examine the format of the normal curve table that appears in Table A in Appendix C. For your convenience, we present a portion of this table in Table 6.1.

Although long, Table A presents only three columns of information. Column 1 contains the values of z. (Table 6.1 includes the z scores 0.95 to 1.04.) You then are told two things about each z score. Column 2 indicates the **area between the mean and the z score**, and column 3 reports the **area beyond the z score**. (Remember, *area* is equivalent to *proportion of cases*.)

Locate $z =$ "1.00" in column 1. You see that .3413 of the area (roughly 34%) lies between the mean and this z score, and .1587 (roughly 16%) of the area lies beyond this point. This, of course, agrees with what you already know from Figure 6.2 and related discussion. What proportion of cases fall beyond, say, $z = 1.03$? Simple: .1515 (or 15%).

Notice that there are no negative z scores in Table 6.1; nor will you find any in Table A. Because the normal curve is symmetric, the area relationships are the same in both halves of the curve. The distinction between positive and negative z scores therefore is not needed; columns 2 and 3 take care of both situations. For example, column 2 in Table 6.1 informs you that .3413 of the area also lies between the mean and $z = -1.00$. When added to the .3413 associated with $z = +1.00$, you obtain a familiar figure—the roughly 68% of the cases falling between $-1S$ and $+1S$ (Figure 6.2).

Now let's see how to use Table A for the kinds of problems one frequently encounters in statistical reasoning.

6.6   Finding Area When the Score Is Known

We present five problems to illustrate this process. Each problem represents a variation on the general question of finding area, given a score.

Problem 1

For a normal distribution with $\overline{X}=100$ and $S=20$, what proportion of cases fall below a score of 80?

This problem is illustrated in Figure 6.5.[4] The first thing you do is convert the score of 80 to a z score:

$$z = \frac{X - \overline{X}}{S} = \frac{80 - 100}{20} = -1.00$$

Now enter Table A with $z = 1.00$ (remember, the symmetry of the normal curve allows you to ignore the negative sign) and look up the area in column 3. Why column 3? "Beyond" always refers to the *tail* of the distribution, so the "area beyond" a *negative* z score is equivalent to the "proportion below" it. The entry in column 3 is .1587, which can be rounded to .16. ***Answer:*** *.16, or 16%, of the cases fall below a score of 80.*

The general language of Problem 1 may sound familiar, for it involves the concept of *percentile rank*—the percentage of cases falling below a given score point (Section 2.9). Thus, Table A can be used for obtaining the percentile rank of a given score, *provided the scores are normally distributed.* By converting $X = 80$ to $z = -1.00$ and then consulting Table A, you are able to determine that the raw score 80 corresponds to the percentile rank of 16, or the 16th percentile. In other words, $P_{16} = 80$.

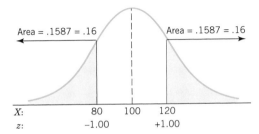

Area = .1587 = .16   Area = .1587 = .16

| X: | 80 | 100 | 120 |
| z: | −1.00 | | +1.00 |

Figure 6.5   Proportion of scores exceeding $X = 120$ and falling below $X = 80$ in a normal distribution ($\overline{X} = 100$, $S = 20$).

[4]In this problem and those that follow, you will find it helpful to draw a sketch—like Figure 6.5—to help keep track of what you are doing.

Problem 2

For a normal distribution with $\overline{X}=100$ and $S=20$, what proportion of cases fall above a score of 120?

The score of 120 corresponds to a z score of $+1.00$:

$$z = \frac{120 - 100}{20} = +1.00$$

Locate $z = 1.00$ in Table A and, as before, go to column 3. (You want column 3 because the "proportion above" a score is synonymous with the "area beyond" it.) The entry is .1587, or .16, which also is illustrated in Figure 6.5. ***Answer: .16, or 16%, of the cases fall above a score of 120.***

Problem 3

For a normal distribution with $\overline{X}=100$ and $S=20$, what proportion of cases fall above a score of 80?

You already know from Problem 1 that the needed z score is -1.00 in this instance. Figure 6.6 shows that you must determine *two* areas to solve this problem: the area between a z of -1.00 and the mean *plus* the area beyond the mean. Column 2 for $z = 1.00$ provides the first area, .3413. Because the normal curve is symmetric, the area above the mean must be half the total area under the curve, or .5000. Consequently, the shaded area in Figure 6.6 represents $.3413 + .5000 = .8413$ of the total area, or .84. ***Answer: .84, or 84%, of the cases fall above a score of 80.***

Problem 4

For a normal distribution with $\overline{X}=100$ and $S=20$, what proportion of cases fall between the values of 90 and 120?

First, you obtain the necessary z scores:

$$z = \frac{90 - 100}{20} = -.50 \quad \text{and} \quad z = \frac{120 - 100}{20} = +1.00$$

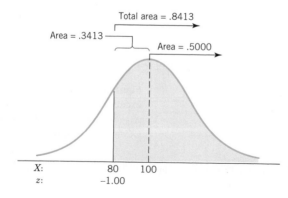

Total area = .8413

Area = .3413

Area = .5000

X: 80   100

z: −1.00

Figure 6.6 Proportion of scores exceeding $X = 80$ in a normal distribution ($\overline{X} = 100$, $S = 20$).

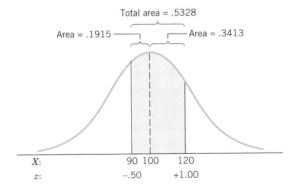

Figure 6.7   Proportion of scores falling between $X = 90$ and $X = 120$ in a normal distribution ($\overline{X} = 100$, $S = 20$).

As Figure 6.7 shows, this problem also requires that you determine and sum two areas. From Table A, find the area between $z = .50$ and the mean (.1915), and the area between the mean and $z = 1.00$ (.3413). Their sum is $.1915 + .3413 = .5328$, or .53. **Answer:** *.53, or 53%, of cases fall between the values of 90 and 120.*

Problem 5

For a normal distribution with $\overline{X} = 100$ and $S = 20$, what proportion of cases fall between the values of 110 and 120?

This problem is similar to Problem 4 except that both scores fall above the mean. Consequently, the solution differs slightly. One approach is to determine the proportion of scores falling above 110 and then subtract the proportion of scores falling above 120. The difference between the two areas isolates the proportion of cases falling between the two scores.[5]

The problem and its solution are illustrated in Figure 6.8. Begin, of course, by converting the original scores to their z equivalents:

$$z = \frac{110 - 100}{20} = +.50 \quad \text{and} \quad z = \frac{120 - 100}{20} = +1.00$$

Determine the two areas from Table A: .3085 beyond $z = +.50$ and .1587 beyond $z = +1.00$. Their difference, and therefore the net area, is $.3085 - .1587 = .1498$, or .15. **Answer:** *.15, or 15%, of the cases fall between the values of 110 and 120.*

What if you want the *number* of cases (or scores) rather than their proportion? Simply multiply the proportion by the n in the distribution. Thus, if $n = 2000$ in Problem 5, then 300 cases fall between the score points 110 and 120. That is, $(.1498)(2000) = 299.6$, or 300.

---

[5]When first solving problems of this kind, some students make the mistake of subtracting one z score from the other and then finding the area corresponding to that difference. This will not work! You want the difference between the two *areas*.

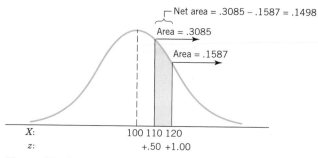

Figure 6.8   Proportion of scores falling between $X = 110$ and $X = 120$ in a normal distribution ($\overline{X} = 100$, $S = 20$).

6.7   *Reversing the Process: Finding Scores When the Area Is Known*

In the last section, you learned how to solve problems where the score is known and you are to find the area. Now the *area* is known, and your task is to find the *score*. This requires the reverse of the process described above, which we illustrate with three general problem types.

Problem 6

For a normal distribution with $\overline{X} = 100$ and $S = 20$, find the score that separates the upper 20% of the cases from the lower 80%.

   To illuminate the process, we divide the solution into several steps.

Step 1   Draw a picture, like Figure 6.9, to help you keep track of the process.

Step 2   Turn to Table A, where you scan the values in column 3, "area beyond z," to find the value closest to .20. It turns out to be .2005. Now look across to column 1, where you see that the value of z associated with it is .84. Because Table A does not distinguish between positive and negative z scores, you must supply that information. Since it is the *top* 20% that is to be distinguished from the remainder, the score you seek is *above* the mean.

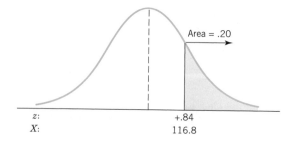

Figure 6.9   The score dividing the upper 20% of observations from the remainder in a normal distribution ($\overline{X} = 100$, $S = 20$).

Therefore, the value of the corresponding z is positive: $z = +.84$. This is the value shown in Figure 6.9.

Step 3   You now convert the z score back to an original score, X. As you know, a z score of $+.84$ states that the score, X, is $+.84$ standard deviations *above* the mean. Remembering that .84 *of* 20 is .84 *times* 20, you determine the value to be $100 + (.84)(20) = 100 + 16.8 = 116.8$. ***Answer:*** *A score of 116.8 separates the upper 20% of the cases from the lower 80%.* This is equivalent to stating that the 80th percentile is a score of 116.8, or $P_{80} = 116.8$.

Problem 7

For a normal distribution with $\overline{X}=100$ and $S=20$, find the score that separates the lower 20% of the cases from the upper 80%.

As before, scan column 3 for the entry closest to .20. Since it is the *lower* 20% that is to be distinguished from the remainder, this time the score you seek is *below* the mean. Therefore, the value of the corresponding z is negative: $z = -.84$. This is shown in Figure 6.10. Now determine X using the same operations as for Problem 6: $100 + (-.84)(20) = 100 - 16.8 = 83.2$. ***Answer:*** *A score of 83.2 separates the lower 20% of the cases from the upper 80%.* This is equivalent to stating that the 20th percentile is a score of 83.2, or $P_{20} = 83.2$.

Problem 8

For a normal distribution with $\overline{X}=100$ and $S=20$, what are the limits within which the central 95% of scores fall?

Figure 6.11 illustrates this problem. If 95% of the cases fall between the two symmetrically located scores, then 2.5% must fall above the upper limit and 2.5% below the lower limit. What is the z score beyond which 2.5% of the cases fall? Scanning column 3 in Table A, you find that .0250 (i.e., 2.5%) of the area falls beyond $z = 1.96$. Remember that, for the present problem, this value of z represents *two* z scores: one for the lower end of the limit, $z_L = -1.96$, and one for the upper

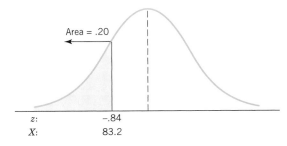

Area = .20

z: −.84
X: 83.2

Figure 6.10   The score dividing the lower 20% of observations from the remainder in a normal distribution ($\overline{X} = 100$, $S = 20$).

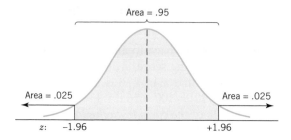

Figure 6.11   The limits that include the central 95% of observations in a normal distribution ($\bar{X} = 100$, $S = 20$).

end, $z_U = +1.96$. (The subscripts refer to lower and upper, respectively.) Your final task, then, is to determine the corresponding values of X_L and X_U:

$$X_L = 100 + (-1.96)(20) = 100 - 39.2 = 60.8$$

$$X_U = 100 + (1.96)(20) = 100 + 39.2 = 139.2$$

Answer: *60.8 and 139.2 are the limits within which the central 95% of scores fall.* This is equivalent to stating that $P_{2.5} = 60.8$ and $P_{97.5} = 139.2$.

At this point, we wish to emphasize that these eight problems require a normal distribution (or a reasonable approximation), as docs *any* statement regarding area and percentage of cases based on Table A. In a negatively skewed distribution, for example, it is not true that 50% of the cases fall below $z = 0$ (or, equivalently, that the mean score is the 50th percentile). As you know from Section 4.5, *fewer* than half of the cases are below the mean ($z = 0$) in a negatively skewed distribution because of the relative positions of the mean and median in such distributions.

6.8   *Comparing Scores from Different Distributions*

You found in Section 6.4 that the z score provides a way of expressing location in terms that are comparable for *all* normal curves. Converting to z scores eliminates the problem of different means and standard deviations because the scale of the original variable has been *standardized*.

> When all scores are converted to z scores, the mean ($\bar{z}$) now is 0 and the standard deviation (S_z) now is 1—*regardless of the distribution's original mean and standard deviation.*

Thus, the tabled values in Table A reflect a normal distribution with a mean of 0 and a standard deviation of 1. This is known as the **standard normal distribution**.

Because $\bar{z} = 0$ and $S_z = 1$ for *any* distribution, z scores and Table A are helpful for comparing scores from different distributions (provided the two distributions approximate normality). Suppose you received a score of 60 on your philosophy midterm exam ($\bar{X} = 40$ and $S = 10$) and a score of 80 on the final ($\bar{X} = 65$ and

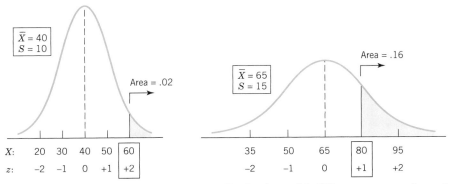

Figure 6.12   Comparing scores from two distributions with different means and standard deviations.

$S = 15$). Which is the better performance? Your higher score on the final exam is misleading, given the different means and standard deviations of the two tests. You can hasten an easy comparison by converting each score to its z-score equivalent: $z = +2.00$ on the midterm and $z = +1.00$ on the final. (Take a moment to check our math.) You clearly did well on both exams relative to your classmates, but you did better in this regard on the midterm exam (see Figure 6.12).

Although standard scores allow you to compare scores from different distributions, the reference groups must be comparable for the comparison of standard scores to be meaningful. There is no difficulty in comparing your two philosophy z scores because both derive from the same group of students. But suppose you obtained a Graduate Record Examination (GRE) score of 550, which is half a standard deviation above the mean ($z = +.50$), and a Stanford-Binet IQ of 116, which is a full standard deviation above the mean ($z = +1.00$). Can you conclude that you did better on the intelligence test than on the GRE? No, because the reference groups are not the same. Whereas the Stanford-Binet test is normed on a representative sample of adults, the GRE norms reflect the more select group of adults who harbor aspirations for graduate school. You would expect to have a *relatively* lower score in the more select group. Again, only with comparable reference groups can standard scores be properly compared.

If this sounds vaguely familiar, it should: it is the same caution you must observe in using percentile ranks (Section 2.9).

6.9   *Interpreting Effect Size*

We introduced the concept of effect size (*ES*) in Section 5.8, where you saw that a difference between two means can be evaluated by expressing it as a proportion of the "pooled" standard deviation. That is,

$$ES = \frac{\overline{X}_1 - \overline{X}_2}{S_{pooled}}$$

An effect size is a lot like a z score. Assuming that each distribution is normally distributed, you can apply Table A to interpret effect size within the context of percentile ranks.

The logic is fairly straightforward. Let's return to Table 5.3, where $\overline{X}_1 = 48$, $\overline{X}_2 = 53$, and ES $= -.50$. Imagine that you placed these two distributions side by side on a single horizontal axis. This effect size indicates that the two means would be offset by .50 of a standard deviation—$\overline{X}_1$ being half a standard deviation to the left of $\overline{X}_2$ (see Figure 6.13a).

Now turn to Table A, where you find the area .1915, or 19%, in column 2 next to $z = .50$. When applied to the concept of effect size, column 2 represents the area between the two means, using the lower group as the reference. Assuming normality, you already know that 50% of the folks in the first group fall below their mean of 48. Column 2 tells you that another 19% fall between this mean and 53, the

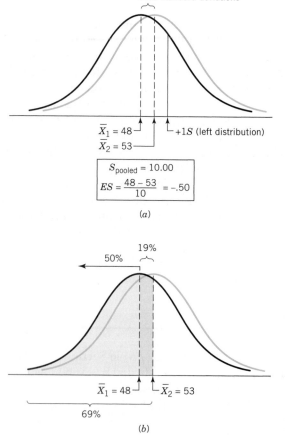

Figure 6.13   Interpreting effect size in light of the normal distribution.

score point corresponding to the mean of the higher group, $\bar{X}_2$. Therefore, 69% of the cases in the first group fall below $\bar{X}_2$, as Figure 6.13b illustrates.

Now, if there were *no* difference between the two means, you would expect only *50%* of the first group to fall below $\bar{X}_2$ (and vice versa). The disparity between the two percentages—50% and 69% in the present case—is a helpful descriptive device for appraising the magnitude of the difference between two means.

Interpreting effect size in this fashion is based on the relationship between area under the normal curve and standard deviation units. As elsewhere in this chapter, interpretations based on Table A will not be accurate where distributions depart markedly from normality.

6.10 *Percentile Ranks and the Normal Distribution*

As demonstrated in Problem 1, percentile ranks can be derived from Table A when the assumption of normality can reasonably be made. Nevertheless, it is important to understand that, as a rule, *percentile ranks do not represent an equal-interval scale.* (This is the third cautionary note regarding percentiles that, in Section 2.9, we promised to describe here.)

Look at Figure 6.14, where we have placed the percentile and z-score scales beneath the normal curve. In contrast to the z-score scale, which is spread out in equal one-standard-deviation units, percentile ranks bunch up in the middle of the distribution and spread out in the tails. This is to be expected: percentile ranks reflect where the cases are, and most of the cases are in the middle of the distribution.[6] But as a consequence of this property, *percentile ranks exaggerate differences between scores near the center of the distribution and underplay differences between scores at the extremes.*

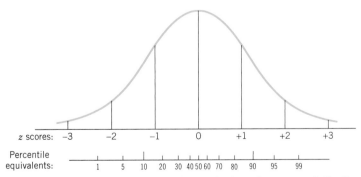

Figure 6.14 z scores and percentile equivalents in a normal distribution. (From the Test Service Bulletin No. 148, January 1955. Copyright © 1955 by The Psychological Corporation. Adapted and reproduced by permission. All rights reserved.)

[6]This assumes a unimodal distribution that is not markedly skewed.

Consider what happens, percentile-wise, with a difference of "one standard deviation" at various places along the horizontal axis. As you go from the mean ($z = 0$) to a position one standard deviation above the mean ($z = +1.00$), the change in percentile rank is a full 34 points: from the 50th percentile to the 84th percentile, or P_{50} to P_{84}.[7] However, the one-standard-deviation difference between $z = +1.00$ and $z = +2.00$ corresponds to only a 14-point change in percentile rank—from P_{84} to P_{98}. And moving one standard deviation from $z = +2.00$ to $z = +3.00$ produces a change of not even 2 percentile points—P_{98} to $P_{99.9}$! There simply are precious few people that far out in the tail of a normal distribution.

Now do the opposite: Compare "standard-deviation-wise" a percentile-rank difference in the middle of the distribution with the identical difference further out in the tail. For example, the 10-percentile-point difference between P_{50} and P_{60} corresponds to a change in z scores from $z = 0$ to $z = .25$—a change of only one-quarter of a standard deviation—whereas the 10-point difference between P_{89} and P_{99} corresponds to a change in z scores from roughly $z = 1.23$ to $z = 2.33$, or a change of 1.10 standard deviations. If these data were Stanford-Binet IQ scores with $S = 16$, the difference between P_{50} and P_{60} would represent only $(.25)(16) = 4$ IQ points. In contrast, more than 17 IQ points is associated with the change from P_{89} and P_{99}: $(1.10)(16) = 17.6$. Clearly, the meaning of a percentile-point difference depends on where in the distribution this difference occurs!

Thus, you see that large differences between percentiles in the middle of a normal distribution correspond to relatively small differences in the underlying scores, and small differences between percentiles in either tail correspond to relatively large differences in underlying scores. It's like driving down a road and seeing *how far you have to go* (difference in underlying scores) *to pass 50 houses* (corresponding differences in percentiles). In a populated area (middle of the normal distribution), you may pass 50 houses in less than half of a mile. But in a rural area (either tail), you could go hundreds of miles before you pass 50 houses!

The advantage of the percentile scale is found in ease of interpretation. However, a considerable disadvantage is its noninterval nature—which you should remain forever mindful of when using percentile ranks.

6.11   *Other Standard Scores*

Using z scores can be inconvenient in several respects. First, you have to contend with both negative and positive values. Second, to be informative, z scores must be reported to at least the nearest tenth, so you also have decimal points to deal with. Third, z scores are awkward for communicating performance to a public unfamiliar with the properties of these scores. Imagine, if you will, a school counselor attempting to explain to two parents that their child's recent performance

---

[7]You should be able to independently arrive at these same numbers using Table A. If you have difficulty doing so, revisit Problem 1.

on a test of moral reasoning, indicated by a score of zero, is actually quite acceptable!

The **T score** is a popular alternative to the z score because it avoids these inconveniences. Like the z score, the T score has been standardized to a fixed mean and standard deviation:

When all scores are converted to T scores, the mean ($\overline{T}$) now is 50 and the standard deviation (S_T) now is 10—*regardless of the distribution's original mean and standard deviation.*

By studying the preceding statement carefully, you can see that any z score can be stated equivalently as a T score. For example, z of $+1.00$ (one standard deviation above the mean) corresponds to a T of 60 (one standard deviation above the mean), just as a z of $-.50$ corresponds to a T of 45. As with the z score, then, a T score locates the original score by stating how many standard deviations it lies above or below the mean.

A T score is easily computed from z using Formula (6.2):

T score

$$T = 50 + 10z \tag{6.2}$$

For instance, the T score that is equivalent to $z = -1.70$ is:

$$T = 50 + (10)(-1.70) = 50 - 17 = 33$$

Figure 6.15 shows the relation between z scores and T scores, along with several other standard score scales. Each standard scale has the common feature of

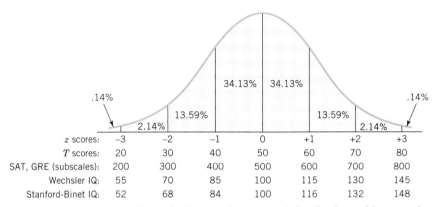

Figure 6.15   Examples of standard scores in a normal distribution, with approximate percentages.

locating the original score *relative to the mean* and *in standard deviation units.* A score that is one standard deviation above the mean corresponds to a GRE or SAT subscale score of 600, a Wechsler IQ of 115, and a Stanford-Binet IQ of 116, as well as a z of $+1.00$ and a T of 60.

Despite their awkward signs and decimal points, we should acknowledge that z scores have the singular merit of giving their meaning *directly* in standard deviation units. A z of -1.50 tells you—with no mental gymnastics required—that the score is *below* the mean by *one and a half* standard deviations. The comparable values for the other standard scores do too, of course, but not as directly.

6.12   Standard Scores Do Not "Normalize" a Distribution

A common misconception of the newcomer to statistics is that converting raw scores to standard scores will transform a nonnormal distribution to a normal one. This isn't true. *The distribution of standard scores is identical in shape to the distribution of original scores—only the values of X, $\overline{X}$, and S have changed.* If you start out with a skewed distribution of raw scores, you will have an equally skewed distribution of z scores.

In technical terms, the conversion of raw scores to standard scores is a "linear transformation." Although there are alternative transformations that indeed will "normalize" a distribution, such transformations go well beyond the scope of this book.

6.13   The Normal Curve and Probability

We have devoted so much attention to the normal curve because of its centrality to statistical reasoning. This is true with respect to descriptive statistics, which is our focus in this chapter.

As you will discover later, the normal curve also is central to many aspects of inferential statistics. This is because the normal curve can be used to answer questions concerning the *probability* of events. For example, by knowing that roughly 16% of adults have a Wechsler IQ greater than 115 ($z = +1.00$), one can state the probability of randomly selecting from the adult population a person whose IQ is greater than 115. (You are correct if you suspect that the probability is .16.) Probability questions also can be asked about means and other statistics, such as the correlation coefficient (which you are about to meet). By answering probability questions, you ultimately are able to arrive at substantive conclusions about your initial research question—which is the point of it all.

As you can see, the import of the normal curve goes well beyond its use descriptively. We will return to this topic beginning with Chapter 9, where we explore the normal curve as a probability distribution.

6.14 Summary

The normal distribution has wide applicability in both descriptive and inferential statistics. Although all normal curves have the same fundamental shape, they differ in mean and standard deviation. To cope with this fact, raw scores can be translated to *z* scores, a process that provides a way of expressing the location of a score in terms that are comparable for all normal curves. A *z* score states how many standard deviations the score's position is above or below the mean. The *z* scores are also called standard scores because they have been standardized to a mean of 0 and a standard deviation of 1. It is important to remember that *z* scores are not necessarily normally distributed. Rather, they are distributed in the same way as the raw scores from which they are derived.

Two fundamental problems involve the normal curve: finding area under the curve (proportion of cases) when the score location is known, and finding score locations when the area is known. The normal curve also can help interpret the difference between two means when this value is expressed as an effect size. Table A is used for these purposes—purposes for which the assumption of normality is critical.

Because *z* scores involve awkward decimals and negative values, standard scores of other kinds have been devised, such as *T* scores which have a mean of 50 and a standard deviation of 10. Standard scores add meaning to raw scores because they provide a frame of reference. Their "standard" properties permit comparison of scores from different distributions. However, it is important always to keep in mind the nature of the reference group from which these scores derive, since it affects interpretation.

Percentile ranks, like standard scores, derive their meaning by comparing an individual performance with that of a known reference group. They are easier to comprehend, but they risk misinterpretation because equal differences in percentile rank do not have the same significance at all points along the scale of scores.

Reading the Research: *z* Scores

Kloosterman and Cougan (1994) used standard scores to separate their research participants into achievement categories.

> *To rank students as high, medium, or low on problem-solving achievement, scores on each of the three process problems were converted to z scores based on grade-level means at the school. Students who had z scores greater than +1 were rated as high achievers on problem solving, those with one or two positive scores or with all scores between +1 and −1 were rated as medium achievers, and those with all three z scores less than −1 were rated as low achievers on problem solving. (p. 379)*

Keep in mind that *z* scores indicate relative performance. Thus, a "low achiever" as defined here is someone who achieved low *relative to the entire group* and is not necessarily a low achiever in an absolute sense. This point applies equally to a "high" or "medium" achiever.

Source: Kloosterman, P., & Cougan, M. C. (1994). Students' beliefs about learning school mathematics. *The Elementary School Journal, 94*(4), 375–388.

Case Study: Making the Grade

Classroom teachers use a variety of assessments to measure their students' achievement. Writing assignments, pop quizzes, and multiple-choice exams are all examples, and each can provide unique and important information about student performance. For assessments that are numerically scored, standardizing these scores can prove beneficial in various ways. For example, standard scores allow teachers to see how a student performed relative to the class. In addition, because of their common metric, standard scores permit comparisons of relative performance *across* various assessments. For instance, a student may perform above the class mean on a writing assignment, below the mean on a lab project, and right around the mean on a multiple-choice exam. Finally—and this is perhaps their greatest utility—standard scores can be combined to form an overall composite score for each student. This case study illustrates the practical uses of standardizing assessment scores.

Mrs. Gort teaches a seventh-grade social studies class at the Wharton-McDonald Community School. At the end of a three-week unit on the U.S. Constitution, all 22 students had completed a pop quiz, essay project, and end-of-unit exam. She standardized the scores from these assessments because she wanted to know how well each student performed relative to the class. She also suspected that many of the parents would be interested in seeing performance expressed in relative terms.

Table 6.2 displays the various raw scores and z scores for each student. Notice that the three z-score variables have a mean of 0 and standard deviation of 1. As you saw in Section 6.8, this is true by definition. A composite also is shown for each student (far right column), which is the mean of the z scores for the pop quiz, essay, and end-of-unit exam: $(z_{\text{popquiz}} + z_{\text{essay}} + z_{\text{exam}})/3$. We can do this because, after standardization, all scores fall on a common scale (mean $= 0$, standard deviation $= 1$). It would be problematic simply to take the mean of the original scores, where means and variances differ across the three variables.[8] Notice, however, that this composite has a standard deviation of .91 rather than 1. This is not an error, for the mean of several z-score variables is not itself a z score. Although the resulting composite will indeed be 0 (as you see here), the standard deviation will not necessarily be 1. The composite, so constructed, is statistically defensible and still useful for making judgments about a student's relative performance. It's just that a composite score of, say, $+1.00$ does not correspond to one standard deviation above the mean (it's a little bit more in this case). If you want your composite to have mean $= 0$ and standard deviation $= 1$, then you must apply the z-score formula to each value in the final column of Table 6.2 (which we do momentarily).

Back to Table 6.2. Look at the z scores for Student 22. This student scored well above average on both the essay assignment and end-of-unit exam but appeared to struggle on the pop quiz. Mrs. Gort knows that this student is one to cram the night

---

[8]The technical basis for this concern goes well beyond our scope. For more detailed discussion, consult an educational measurement and assessment textbook (e.g., Linn & Miller, 2005, ch. 15).

Table 6.2   Raw Scores and z Scores for Mrs. Gort's Social Studies Class ($n = 22$)

ID	Pop quiz (100 pts)	Essay (100 pts)	Exam (25 pts)	z Pop Quiz	z Essay	z Exam	Composite (Mean z)
5	100	97	24	1.41	1.72	1.62	**1.58**
15	100	97	23	1.41	1.72	1.29	**1.47**
6	99	94	25	1.31	1.32	1.94	**1.52**
13	96	92	23	1.02	1.06	1.29	**1.12**
12	92	91	15	.63	.92	−1.27	**.09**
17	92	87	19	.63	.40	.01	**.35**
9	91	86	17	.53	.26	−.63	**.06**
19	90	85	19	.43	.13	.01	**.19**
7	89	85	18	.33	.13	−.31	**.05**
10	89	85	21	.33	.13	.65	**.37**
11	88	84	21	.24	.00	.65	**.30**
21	88	83	16	.24	−.13	−.95	**−.28**
8	86	82	18	.04	−.26	−.31	**−.18**
2	85	81	18	−.06	−.40	−.31	**−.25**
4	83	80	20	−.25	−.53	.33	**−.15**
16	82	80	20	−.35	−.53	.33	**−.18**
22	80	90	21	−.55	.79	.65	**.30**
18	78	78	14	−.74	−.79	−1.59	**−1.04**
3	76	75	15	−.94	−1.19	−1.27	**−1.13**
14	70	74	19	−1.52	−1.32	.01	**−.94**
20	65	72	16	−2.01	−1.58	−.95	**−1.51**
1	64	70	15	−2.11	−1.85	−1.27	**−1.74**
$\overline{X}$	85.59	84.00	18.95	0	0	0	0
S	10.24	7.58	3.12	1	1	1	.91

before a test, which might explain his lack of preparedness for the surprise quiz. (She will have to speak to him about keeping up with class material.)

Examining the z scores for the three assessments can tell us not only about the relative performance of each student, but it also can raise questions about the assessments themselves. Consider the first three z scores for Student 14 ($z_{popquiz} = -1.52$, $z_{essay} = -1.32$, $z_{exam} = .01$). Relative to the class, this student performed poorly on the pop quiz and essay assignment, but scored roughly at the class mean on the end-of-unit exam. This inconsistency caused Mrs. Gort to reflect on the nature of the assessments. She realized that the majority of items on the pop quiz demanded lengthy written responses, whereas the end-of-unit exam comprised largely multiple-choice items. Mrs. Gort wondered: To what extent were these two assessments tapping mere writing ability, in addition to social studies knowledge? An important question indeed.

As you may suspect, the composite scores can inform judgments about each student's overall performance on the unit assessments. Composite scores also can be used to assist teachers in making decisions regarding, say, grading and academic

Table 6.3 z and T Composite Scores ($n = 22$)

ID	z Score Composite	T Score Composite
5	1.73	67.29
6	1.67	66.66
15	1.61	66.12
13	1.23	62.29
10	.41	54.09
17	.38	53.78
22	.33	53.29
11	.32	53.25
19	.21	52.11
12	.10	51.03
9	.06	50.61
7	.06	50.58
4	−.16	48.37
8	−.19	48.07
16	−.20	48.02
2	−.28	47.23
21	−.31	46.93
14	−1.03	39.68
18	−1.14	38.62
3	−1.24	37.63
20	−1.66	33.43
1	−1.91	30.94
$\overline{X}$	0	50
S	1.00	10

grouping. For instance, look at the middle column of Table 6.3 where we present the composite scores in descending order. There appear to be two areas of "natural" separation in the distribution—one occurring between 1.12 and .37 and the other between −.28 and −.94. Conspicuous gaps in the distribution of these overall scores could be indicative of real differences in student achievement, which, again, may inform teacher decision-making.

For the upcoming parent-teacher conferences, Mrs. Gort wants a T-score composite ($T = 50$, $S_T = 10$) for each student as well. She first applies the z-score formula to the last column in Table 6.2, and she then converts the resulting z scores to T scores using Formula (6.2): $T = 50 + 10z$.[9] The result appears in Table 6.3. (Although we present them here to the nearest hundredth of a point, they can be rounded to the nearest whole number for reporting purposes.) Because T scores do away with

[9]If Formula (6.2) had been applied to the last column in Table 6.2 (rather than to z scores), the resulting T scores would not have a standard deviation of 10. This is because, as we pointed out earlier, the composite scores in Table 6.2 are not z scores—which is what Formula (6.2) requires.

negative signs, which have the unfortunate connotation of failure, they are helpful when conveying student achievement data to parents. For the parent of Student 2, for example, doesn't a score of 47 sound more encouraging than a score of $-.28$?

Suggested Computer Exercises

The **assessments** data file contains student assessment results for three eleventh-grade mathematics classes. Among the data are student scores on a teacher-made test (LOCTEST), the eleventh-grade state math assessment (STEXAM), and the Preliminary Scholastic Assessment Test in mathematics (PSATM).

1. Generate histograms for the variables LOCTEST, STEXAM, and PSATM; check the "Display normal curve" option within the histogram procedure. Briefly comment on how close each distribution comes to normality.

2. Use the "Save standardized values as variables" option within the Descriptives procedure to convert the scores on LOCTEST, STEXAM, and PSATM to z scores. Three new variables will automatically be added to your data file (ZLOCTEST, ZSTEXAM, and ZPSATM). Briefly explain how student #40 performed relative to her classmates on each assessment.

3. Assume $\bar{X}_{PSATM} = 49.2$ and $S_{PSATM} = 14.3$ among juniors nationwide. At what percentile does the average (mean) junior at this school score at nationally?

Exercises

Identify, Define, or Explain

Terms and Concepts

normal curve	area between mean and z
theoretical versus empirical distribution	area beyond z
$\bar{X} \pm 1S$	standard normal distribution
standard score	reference group
standardized score	T score
derived score	the normal curve and effect size
z score	the normal curve and percentile ranks
normal curve table	the normal curve and probability

Symbols

z T

Questions and Problems

Note: Answers to starred (*) items are presented in Appendix B.

1. What are the various properties of the normal curve?

*2. $\bar{X} = 82$ and $S = 12$ for the distribution of scores from an "academic self-concept" instrument that is completed by a large group of elementary-level students (high scores reflect a positive academic self-concept). Convert each of the following scores to a z score:

(a) 70

(b) 90

(c) 106

(d) 100

(e) 62

(f) 80

3. Convert the following z scores back to academic self-concept scores from the distribution of Problem 2 (round answers to the nearest whole number):

(a) 0

(b) −2.10

(c) +1.82

(d) −.75

(e) +.25

(f) +3.10

4. Make a careful sketch of the normal curve. For each of the z scores of Problem 3, pinpoint as accurately as you can its location on that distribution.

*5. In a normal distribution, what proportion of cases fall (report to four decimal places):

(a) above $z = +1.00$?

(b) below $z = -2.00$?

(c) above $z = +3.00$?

(d) below $z = 0$?

(e) above $z = -1.28$?

(f) below $z = -1.62$?

6. In a normal distribution, what proportion of cases fall between:

(a) $z = -1.00$ and $z = +1.00$?

(b) $z = -1.50$ and $z = +1.50$?

(c) $z = -2.28$ and $z = 0$?

(d) $z = 0$ and $z = +.50$?

(e) $z = +.75$ and $z = +1.25$?

(f) $z = -.80$ and $z = -1.60$?

*7. In a normal distribution, what proportion of cases fall:

(a) outside the limits $z = -1.00$ and $z = +1.00$?

(b) outside the limits $z = -.50$ and $z = +.50$?

(c) outside the limits $z = -1.26$ and $z = +1.83$?

(d) outside the limits $z = -1.96$ and $z = +1.96$?

*8. In a normal distribution, what z scores:

   (a) enclose the middle 99% of cases?

   (b) enclose the middle 95% of cases?

   (c) enclose the middle 75% of cases?

   (d) enclose the middle 50% of cases?

9. In a normal distribution, what is the z score:

   (a) above which the top 5% of the cases fall?

   (b) above which the top 1% of the cases fall?

   (c) below which the bottom 5% of the cases fall?

   (d) below which the bottom 75% of the cases fall?

10. Given a normal distribution of tests scores, with $\overline{X} = 250$ and $S = 50$:

   (a) What score separates the upper 30% of the cases from the lower 70%?

   (b) What score is the 70th percentile (P_{70})?

   (c) What score corresponds to the 40th percentile (P_{40})?

   (d) Between what two scores do the central 80% of scores fall?

*11. Given a normal distribution with $\overline{X} = 500$ and $S = 100$, find the percentile ranks for scores of:

   (a) 400

   (b) 450

   (c) 380

   (d) 510

   (e) 593

   (f) 678

12. Convert each of the scores in Problem 2 to T scores.

*13. The following five scores were all determined from the same raw score distribution (assume a normal distribution with $\overline{X} = 35$ and $S = 6$). Order these scores from best to worst in terms of the underlying level of performance.

   (a) percentile rank $= 84$

   (b) $X = 23$

   (c) deviation score $= 0$

   (d) $T = 25$

   (e) $z = +1.85$

*14. The mean of a set of z scores is always zero. Does this suggest that half of a set of z scores will always be negative and half always positive? (Explain.)

15. $\overline{X} = 20$ and $S = 5$ on a test of mathematics problem solving (scores reflect number of problems solved correctly). Which represents the greatest difference in problem-solving ability: P_5 vs. P_{25}, or P_{45} vs. P_{65}? Why? (Assume a normal distribution.)

*16. Consider the effect sizes you computed for Problem 15 of Chapter 5. Interpret these within the context of area under the normal curve, as discussed in Section 6.9.

CHAPTER 7

Correlation

7.1   The Concept of Association

Our focus so far has been on **univariate** statistics and procedures, such as those regarding a variable's frequency distribution, central tendency, and variability. You now enter the **bivariate** world, which is concerned with the examination of two variables *simultaneously*.

Is a student's socioeconomic status (SES) related to that student's intelligence? Does a score on a teacher certification test have anything to do with how well one will teach? Is spatial reasoning ability pertinent to solving mathematical problems? What relation exists between per-pupil expenditures and academic achievement? Each of these questions concerns the association between two variables. For example, are lower values of SES associated with lower values of IQ, while higher values of SES are associated with higher values of IQ? Stated more formally, is there a *correlation* between SES and IQ?

This fundamental question cannot be answered from univariate information alone. That is, you cannot tell whether there is an association between two variables by examining the two frequency distributions, means, or variances. You must employ *bivariate* methods.

The **correlation coefficient** is a bivariate statistic that measures the degree of linear association between two quantitative variables, and it enjoys considerable popularity in the behavioral sciences. We will focus on a particular measure of association, the **Pearson product–moment correlation coefficient** because it is so widely used. But first things first: we begin by considering the graphic representation of association.

7.2   Bivariate Distributions and Scatterplots

A problem in correlation begins with a set of **paired scores**. Perhaps the scores are (a) the educational attainment of parents and (b) the educational attainment of their offspring. Or maybe the scores are (a) high school GPA and (b) performance on the high school exit exam. Note that the "pairs" can involve two different groups, as in the first example, or the same individuals, as in the second. But *the data always consist of scores paired in some meaningful way*. The pairing in the first example is based on family membership, and in the second example, on the identity of the individual. If scores are not meaningfully paired, the association between the two variables cannot be examined and a correlation coefficient cannot be calculated.

In Table 7.1, we present hypothetical scores from a spatial reasoning test (X) and a mathematical ability test (which we denote by Y) for 30 college students. Student 1, for instance, has scores of 85 and 133 on these two measures, respectively. After scanning the pairs of scores, you probably agree that this table does not permit a quick and easy determination of whether there is an association between

Table 7.1   Hypothetical Scores on Two Tests: Spatial Reasoning and Mathematical Ability ($n = 30$)

Student	X Spatial Reasoning	Y Mathematical Ability
1	85	133
2	79	106
3	75	113
4	69	105
5	59	88
6	76	107
7	84	124
8	60	76
9	62	88
10	67	112
11	77	90
12	50	70
13	76	99
14	63	96
15	72	103
16	77	124
17	67	93
18	71	96
19	58	99
20	63	101
21	51	78
22	68	97
23	88	115
24	75	101
25	71	112
26	86	76
27	69	110
28	54	89
29	80	112
30	68	87
$n = 30$	$\overline{X} = 70$ $S_X = 9.97$	$\overline{Y} = 100$ $S_Y = 14.83$

these two variables. Do lower values on X tend to be accompanied by lower values on Y? Conversely, are higher values on X generally found with higher values on Y? From tabular data, it is exceedingly difficult to say!

You learned in Chapter 3 that the graphic display of data communicates the nature of a univariate distribution more quickly and vividly. This is equally true when the distribution is bivariate. Figure 7.1 shows these data in the form of a **scatterplot**, arguably the most informative device for illustrating a bivariate distribution.

A scatterplot has two equal-length axes, one for each variable ("*bivariate*"). The horizontal axis of Figure 7.1 represents score values on the spatial reasoning test (X), and the vertical axis represents score values on the test of mathematical ability (Y). Each axis is marked off according to the variable's scale, as shown in this figure, with low values converging where the two axes intersect (45 and 60 in this case). You are correct if you sense from these scales that the two variables have different means and standard deviations: The spatial reasoning scores are generally lower ($\overline{X} = 70.00$ vs. $\overline{Y} = 100.00$) and less spread out ($S_X = 9.97$ vs. $S_Y = 14.83$). (Notice that we just introduced $\overline{Y}$ as the symbol for the mean of Y. Also, we have attached subscripts to the standard deviations to help keep our statistics straight.)

Each dot, or **data point**, represents a student's two scores simultaneously. For example, the data point in the lower left corner of Figure 7.1 is Student 12, who received scores of $X = 50$ and $Y = 70$; you'll find Student 1 in the upper right corner ($X = 85$ and $Y = 133$).

All that is required to construct a scatterplot are graph paper, ruler, pencil, and a close eye on accuracy as you plot each data point. You should consider the

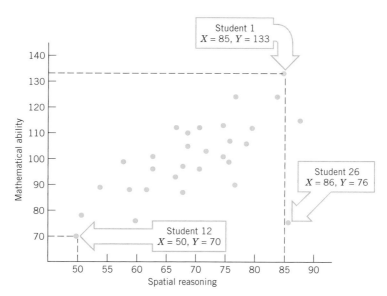

Figure 7.1 Scatterplot for the relationship between spatial reasoning and mathematical ability ($n = 30$).

compulsory

inspection of scatterplots to be a *mandatory* part of correlational work because of the visual information they convey, which we now consider.

Association

First and foremost, a scatterplot reveals the presence of **association** between two variables. The stronger the linear relationship between two variables, the more the data points cluster along an imaginary straight line. The data points in Figure 7.1 collectively take on an **elliptical** form, with the exception of Student 26 (about whom we will have more to say). This suggests that, as a general rule, values of X are indeed "associated with" values of Y; as one goes up, so goes the other. Note how inescapable this visual impression is, particularly in comparison to what little the eye can conclude from Table 7.1. Figures 7.2*b* and 7.2*e* also portray elliptically shaped scatterplots.

If there is *no* association between two variables, data points spread out randomly—like a shotgun blast, as in Figure 7.2*a*. (This scatterplot would characterize the association between, say, adult IQ and shoe size.) If the linear relationship is *perfect*, all data points fall on a straight line (see Figures 7.2*c* and 7.2*d*). In practice, however, one never encounters perfect relationships.

Direction

If there is an association between two variables, a scatterplot also will indicate the *direction* of the relationship. Figure 7.1 illustrates a **positive (direct) association**: the ellipse goes from the lower left corner to the upper right. Higher X values are associated with higher Y values, and lower X values with lower Y values. A positive relationship also is depicted in Figures 7.2*b* and 7.2*c*. In a **negative (inverse) association**, by contrast, the data points go from the upper left corner to the lower right, as shown in Figures 7.2*d* and 7.2*e*. Higher X values are associated with *lower* Y values, and lower X values with *higher* Y values. An example of a negative relationship would be hours without sleep (X) and attentiveness (Y), or days absent from school (X) and grade-point average (Y).

The direction of a relationship is independent of its strength. For example, Figures 7.2*b* and 7.2*e* reflect equally strong relationships; they differ simply in their direction. The same is true for Figures 7.2*c* and 7.2*d*.

Outliers

Just as a quick inspection of a variable's range can reveal dubious data, a scatterplot similarly can alert you to suspicious data points. In Figure 7.1, for example, the data point in the lower right corner stands apart from the pack, which is why such cases are called **outliers**. This is Student 26, who is very low in mathematical ability ($Y = 76$) despite having a relatively high spatial reasoning score ($X = 86$). Such a discrepancy may reflect an error in scoring, an "off day" for Student 26, or an unusual cognitive profile. Only by doing further checking on

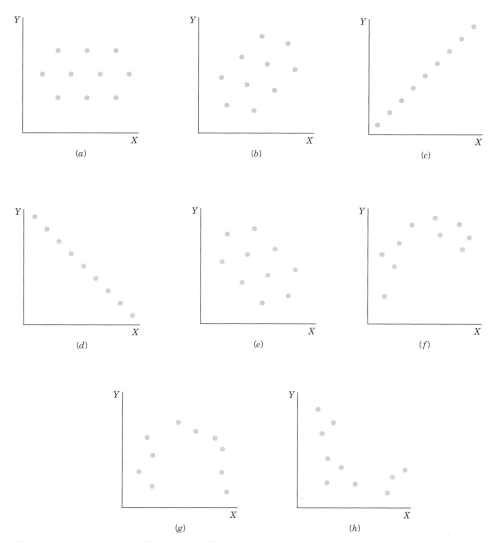

Figure 7.2   Scatterplots illustrating different bivariate distributions.

this case can you narrow the possible explanations and, therefore, take appropriate action.[1]

Notice that Student 26 would not have caught your eye upon simply examining the range of scores for each variable. It is this student's location in *bivariate*, not univariate, space that signals a possible problem. As you will see, outliers can influence the magnitude of the correlation coefficient.

---

[1]For example, you would remove this data point from subsequent analyses if either score turned out to be irrevocably flawed (e.g., misscored).

Nonlinearity

Figure 7.1 shows a **linear** association between spatial reasoning and mathematical ability. This doesn't mean that the data points all fall on a straight line, for in this case they certainly do not. Rather, *a relationship is said to be linear if a straight line accurately represents the constellation of data points*. This indeed is the case in Figure 7.1, where a straight line running from the lower left corner to the upper right corner would capture the nature of this bivariate distribution. (Figures 7.2*b*, 7.2*c*, 7.2*d*, and 7.2*e* also portray linear patterns of data points.)

Now consider Figure 7.2*f*, where the values of X and Y rise together for a while, after which Y begins to drop off with increasingly higher values of X. This illustrates a **curvilinear relationship**, and a *curved line* best captures the constellation of these data points. (Figures 7.2*g* and 7.2*h* also are examples of curvilinear patterns of data points.)

There are at least two reasons for inspecting your scatterplots for departures from linearity. First, the Pearson correlation coefficient, which we will present shortly, is a measure of *linear* association. The use of this statistic is problematic when nonlinearity is present. Second, the presence of nonlinearity could be telling you something very important about the phenomenon you are investigating. Suppose in Figure 7.2*f* that X is *minutes of science instruction per day* for each of 10 classrooms and Y is *mean science achievement* for each classroom at the end of the school year. The curvilinearity in this figure could be suggesting that diminishing returns are associated with more instructional time, a finding that would have important policy implications.

For all these reasons, inspecting scatterplots prior to calculating a correlation coefficient should be considered an essential component of correlational analyses. *Always plot your data!*

7.3   The Covariance

Scatterplots are informative indeed, but they are not enough. Just as a single number can describe the central tendency or variability of a univariate distribution, a single number also can represent the degree and direction of the linear association between two variables. It is important for you to understand how this is so, and for this reason we begin with a close examination of the **covariance**—the mathematical engine of the Pearson correlation coefficient.

Before we introduce the covariance, we should emphasize that our focus is restricted to measuring *linear* relationships. Fortunately, the vast majority of relationships in the behavioral sciences are linear, and over 95% of the correlation coefficients that you will find in the research literature are Pearson correlation coefficients (Glass and Hopkins, 1996, p. 110). Nevertheless, it is always important to inspect scatterplots to verify that *your* data satisfy the assumption of linearity.

Now back to the covariance, the formula for which is:

Covariance

$$\text{Cov} = \frac{\Sigma(X - \overline{X})(Y - \overline{Y})}{n} \qquad (7.1)$$

Formula (7.1), like most formulas, makes more sense once it is broken down and reassembled. Let's begin by calculating the covariance, which involves four steps:

Step 1 Express each X and Y as a deviation score: $X - \overline{X}$ and $Y - \overline{Y}$.

Step 2 Obtain the product of the paired deviation scores for each person. Known as a **crossproduct**, this term appears as $(X - \overline{X})(Y - \overline{Y})$ in the numerator of the covariance.

Step 3 Sum the crossproducts: $\Sigma(X - \overline{X})(Y - \overline{Y})$.

Step 4 Divide this sum by the number of *pairs* of scores, n.

For a quick illustration, we apply Formula (7.1) to the scores of five people:

Person	X	Y	$X - \overline{X}$	$Y - \overline{Y}$	$(X - \overline{X})(Y - \overline{Y})$
A	9	13	+4	+4	+16
B	7	9	+2	0	0
C	5	7	0	−2	0
D	3	11	−2	+2	−4
E	1	5	−4	−4	+16
$n = 5$	$\overline{X} = 5$	$\overline{Y} = 9$			$\Sigma(X - \overline{X})(Y - \overline{Y}) = +28$
					$\text{Cov} = +28/5 = +5.6$

This table shows the five pairs of raw scores, the corresponding deviation scores, and the five crossproducts. For example, the two scores of Person A are $X = 9$ and $Y = 13$, which yield deviation scores of $9 - 5 = +4$ and $13 - 9 = +4$, respectively. The corresponding crossproduct is $(+4)(+4) = +16$. The five crossproducts sum to 28 which, when divided by $n = 5$, produces a covariance of 5.6. Be sure to keep track of algebraic signs when computing and summing the crossproducts. (And remember: Multiplying two numbers with like signs yields a positive product, whereas multiplying numbers having unlike signs gives you a negative product.)

The Logic of the Covariance

What does the covariance accomplish, and why? We begin by rephrasing what it means for two variables to be associated:

> Where there is a *positive* association between two variables, scores above the mean on X tend to be associated with scores above the mean on Y, and scores below the mean on X tend to be accompanied by scores below the mean on Y. Where there is a *negative* association between two variables, scores above the mean on X tend to be associated with scores below the mean on Y, and scores below the mean on X tend to be accompanied by scores above the mean on Y.

For this reason, the familiar deviation score—the difference between a score and its mean—figures prominently in Formula (7.1).

In Figure 7.3, our original scatterplot has been divided into four quadrants by two lines, one located at $\overline{X}$ and one at $\overline{Y}$. Data points located to the right of the vertical line have positive values of $(X - \overline{X})$ and those to the left, negative values of $(X - \overline{X})$. Similarly, data points lying above the horizontal line have positive values of $(Y - \overline{Y})$ and those below, negative values of $(Y - \overline{Y})$. For any data point, the crossproduct will be positive when both $(X - \overline{X})$ and $(Y - \overline{Y})$ have the *same* sign; otherwise the crossproduct will be negative. Consequently, all crossproducts will be *positive* for data points falling in quadrants I and III and *negative* for data points falling in quadrants II and IV.

Now return to Formula (7.1). Since n will always be a positive number, the *algebraic sign* of the covariance must depend on the sign of the numerator, $\Sigma(X - \overline{X})(Y - \overline{Y})$. When the data points are concentrated primarily in the (positive) quadrants I and III, the positive crossproducts will exceed the negative crossproducts

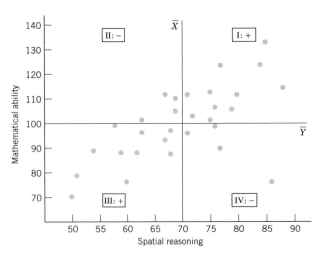

Figure 7.3   The four crossproduct quadrants of a scatterplot.

from quadrants II and IV. Therefore, $\Sigma(X - \bar{X})(Y - \bar{Y})$ will be positive, as will be the covariance. On the other hand, when the data points are concentrated primarily in the (negative) quadrants II and IV, the negative crossproducts will exceed the positive crossproducts from quadrants I and III. Now $\Sigma(X - \bar{X})(Y - \bar{Y})$ will be negative, as will be the covariance.

Furthermore, the *magnitude* of the covariance is determined by the extent to which crossproducts of one sign are outnumbered by crossproducts carrying the other sign. The greater the concentration of data points in just two of the quadrants (either I and III, or II and IV), the greater the magnitude of $\Sigma(X - \bar{X})(Y - \bar{Y})$ and, in turn, the larger the covariance.

From Figure 7.3, you probably are expecting the covariance to be positive. You may even expect it to be of appreciable magnitude—after all, 22 of the 30 data points fall in the positive quadrants I and III. Let's see.

In Table 7.2, we have expanded Table 7.1 to include the deviation scores and crossproduct for each of the 30 students. Notice that 22 of the paired deviation scores in fact are either *both positive* or *both negative* and, accordingly, 22 of the crossproducts are positive. Again, individuals above the mean on spatial reasoning tend to be above the mean on mathematical ability; those below the mean on spatial reasoning tend to be below the mean on mathematical ability. The few negative crossproducts tend to be rather small, with one glaring exception—the aforementioned outlier. (More on Student 26 later.)

We again present the steps for calculating the covariance, this time using the data from Table 7.2:

Step 1 Express each X and Y as a deviation score: $X - \bar{X}$ and $Y - \bar{Y}$. These deviation scores are shown at ❶ and ❷, respectively, in Table 7.2. For Student 1, these values are $85 - 70 = +15$ and $133 - 100 = +33$, respectively.

Step 2 Obtain the crossproduct of the paired deviation scores for each person. (❸). Again for Student 1, the crossproduct is $(15)(33) = 495$.

Step 3 Sum the crossproducts (❹).
Here, $\Sigma(X - \bar{X})(Y - \bar{Y}) = 495 + 54 + \cdots + 26 = +2806$.

Step 4 Divide the sum of the crossproducts by n, the number of paired observations (❺).
Thus, $+2806/30 = +93.53 = \text{Cov}$.

Because the covariance is 93.53, you know that spatial reasoning and mathematical ability are associated to some degree and, furthermore, that this association is positive.

Thus, as promised, the covariance conveys the direction *and* strength of association. We illustrate this further with Table 7.3, which presents data for three (exceedingly simplistic) bivariate distributions along with their scatterplots. First, compare bivariate distributions A and B, which differ only in that distribution A is a perfect *positive* association whereas distribution B is a perfect *negative* association. Note how this important distinction surfaces in the algebraic sign of the deviation scores and crossproducts. In distribution A, the crossproducts are all positive (except for 0)

Table 7.2   Raw Scores, Deviation Scores, Crossproducts, and Covariance

Student	X Spatial Reasoning	Y Mathematical Ability	① $X - \bar{X}$	② $Y - \bar{Y}$	③ $(X - \bar{X})(Y - \bar{Y})$
1	85	133	+15	+33	+495
2	79	106	+9	+6	+54
3	75	113	+5	+13	+65
4	69	105	−1	+5	−5
5	59	88	−11	−12	+132
6	76	107	+6	+7	+42
7	84	124	+14	+24	+336
8	60	76	−10	−24	+240
9	62	88	−8	−12	+96
10	67	112	−3	+12	−36
11	77	90	+7	−10	−70
12	50	70	−20	−30	+600
13	76	99	+6	−1	−6
14	63	96	−7	−4	+28
15	72	103	+2	+3	+6
16	77	124	+7	+24	+168
17	67	93	−3	−7	+21
18	71	96	+1	−4	−4
19	58	99	−12	−1	+12
20	63	101	−7	+1	−7
21	51	78	−19	−22	+418
22	68	97	−2	−3	+6
23	88	115	+18	+15	+270
24	75	101	+5	+1	+5
25	71	112	+1	+12	+12
26	86	76	+16	−24	−384
27	69	110	−1	+10	−10
28	54	89	−16	−11	+176
29	80	112	+10	+12	+120
30	68	87	−2	−13	+26
$n = 30$	$\bar{X} = 70$ $S_X = 9.97$	$\bar{Y} = 100$ $S_Y = 14.83$			④ $\Sigma(X - \bar{X})(Y - \bar{Y}) = +2806$ ⑤ Cov $= +2806/30 = +93.53$

because the two signs for each pair of deviation scores agree. But look what happens in distribution B, where the association is perfectly negative: the signs do not agree within each pair of deviation scores and, consequently, the crossproducts are all negative. As a result, the two covariances have the same absolute value but different algebraic signs: +8 versus −8. When there is *no* association between two variables, as in distribution C, there is no consistent pattern of signs. Positive crossproducts cancel out negative crossproducts, resulting in a covariance of 0—an intuitively satisfying number for the condition of "no association."

Table 7.3 Three Bivariate Distributions Having Different Covariances

(a) Bivariate Distribution A (perfect positive)

Person	X	Y	$X - \bar{X}$	$Y - \bar{Y}$	$(X - \bar{X})(Y - \bar{Y})$
A	9	13	+4	+4	+16
B	7	11	+2	+2	+4
C	5	9	0	0	0
D	3	7	−2	−2	+4
E	1	5	−4	−4	+16
	$\bar{X} = 5$	$\bar{Y} = 9$			$\Sigma(X - \bar{X})(Y - \bar{Y}) = +40$
	$S_X = 2.828$	$S_Y = 2.828$			$\text{Cov} = +40/5 = +8$

(b) Bivariate Distribution B (perfect negative)

Person	X	Y	$X - \bar{X}$	$Y - \bar{Y}$	$(X - \bar{X})(Y - \bar{Y})$
A	9	5	+4	−4	−16
B	7	7	+2	−2	−4
C	5	9	0	0	0
D	3	11	−2	+2	−4
E	1	13	−4	+4	−16
	$\bar{X} = 5$	$\bar{Y} = 9$			$\Sigma(X - \bar{X})(Y - \bar{Y}) = -40$
	$S_X = 2.828$	$S_Y = 2.828$			$\text{Cov} = -40/5 = -8$

(c) Bivariate Distribution C (no linear association)

Person	X	Y	$X - \bar{X}$	$Y - \bar{Y}$	$(X - \bar{X})(Y - \bar{Y})$
A	9	5	+4	−4	−16
B	9	13	+4	+4	+16
C	5	9	0	0	0
D	1	5	−4	−4	+16
E	1	13	−4	+4	−16
	$\bar{X} = 5$	$\bar{Y} = 9$			$\Sigma(X - \bar{X})(Y - \bar{Y}) = 0$
	$S_X = 3.578$	$S_Y = 3.578$			$\text{Cov} = 0/5 = 0$

Table 7.4   The Effect on the Covariance of Multiplying Y by 2 (Compare to Table 7.3a)

Person	X	$Y \times 2$	$X - \bar{X}$	$Y - \bar{Y}$	$(X - \bar{X})(Y - \bar{Y})$
A	9	26	+4	+8	+32
B	7	22	+2	+4	+8
C	5	18	0	0	0
D	3	14	−2	−4	+8
E	1	10	−4	−8	+32

$$\bar{X} = 5 \qquad \bar{Y} = 18 \qquad\qquad \Sigma(X - \bar{X})(Y - \bar{Y}) = +80$$
$$S_X = 2.828 \qquad S_Y = 5.657 \qquad\qquad \text{Cov} = +80/5 = +16$$

Limitations of the Covariance

Although we used three unrealistic sets of numbers in Table 7.3, we hope that they have given you additional insight into the properties of the covariance. The final property of the covariance reveals why this statistic is unsuitable as a general measure of association: *The magnitude of the covariance is dependent on the underlying scales, or metrics, of the variables involved.*

Suppose you returned to bivariate distribution A in Table 7.3 and playfully changed the scale of Y by doubling each value (i.e., $Y \times 2$). This would not alter the *underlying relationship* between X and Y, for there still would be a perfect positive association (which you can confirm by redrawing the scatterplot). However, your mathematical mischief causes an interesting ripple effect that ultimately produces a covariance twice as large as it was before, as Table 7.4 illustrates. This is because doubling each value of Y causes each deviation score $(Y - \bar{Y})$ to double which, in turn, causes each crossproduct to double. Therefore, the sum of these crossproducts, $\Sigma(X - \bar{X})(Y - \bar{Y})$, is doubled, as is the covariance. Has the relationship between X and the doubled Y somehow become *stronger* than the initial relationship between X and Y? Of course not—you can't improve upon a perfect, straight-line relationship!

As you see, then, the covariance is difficult to interpret: Its value depends not only on the direction and strength of association between two variables, but on the *scales* of these variables as well. Clearly, a more useful measure of association is needed. Karl Pearson, with a notable assist from Sir Francis Galton and a few others, came up with a solution in 1896.

7.4   The Pearson r

Karl Pearson, "a man with an unquenchable ambition for scholarly recognition and the kind of drive and determination that had taken Hannibal over the Alps and Marco Polo to China" (Stigler, 1986, p. 266), demonstrated that these effects of scale are nullified if the covariance is divided by the product of the two standard deviations. The result is a scale-independent measure of association, and it is known as the *Pearson product–moment coefficient of correlation* (**Pearson r**, for short).

Pearson r
(defining formula)

$$r = \frac{\Sigma(X - \bar{X})(Y - \bar{Y})/n}{S_X S_Y}$$

$$= \frac{Cov}{S_X S_Y}$$

(7.2)

Again, r simply is the covariance placed over the product of the two standard deviations. When applied to the data in Tables 7.3a and 7.4, Formula (7.2) produces identical correlations: $r = +1.00$ in each case. By comparing the two calculations below, you can appreciate the beauty of Pearson's formulation. As can be seen, the "doubling" in the numerator of the second correlation (40×2) is canceled out by the "doubling" in the denominator of that correlation (2.828×2), so $r = +1.00$ in both instances:

$$r_{(\text{Table 7.3a})} = \frac{+40/5}{(2.828)(2.828)} = \frac{+8}{8} = +1.00 \qquad r_{(\text{Table 7.4})} = \frac{\overbrace{+80/5}^{(40)(2)}}{\underbrace{(2.828)(5.657)}_{(2.828)(2)}} = \frac{\overbrace{+16}^{(8)(2)}}{\underbrace{16}_{(8)(2)}} = +1.00$$

Properties of r

As a simple extension of the covariance, the Pearson r shares several of its basic properties. Most notably, the algebraic sign of r reflects the *direction* of the relationship, and the absolute value of r reflects the *magnitude* of this relationship. The principal difference between the covariance and r is an important one and accounts for the superiority of the Pearson r as a measure of linear association:

The magnitude of r ranges from 0 to ±1.00, regardless of the scales of the two variables.

When no relationship exists, $r = 0$; when a perfect relationship exists, $r = +1.00$ or -1.00; and intermediate degrees of association fall between these two extremes of r. Again, this is true regardless of the variables' scales. If $r = +.35$ between SES and academic achievement when the latter is expressed as z scores, then r will be $+.35$ if the researcher decides to use T scores instead. This is because the Pearson r reflects the degree to which *relative* positions on X match up with relative positions on Y. The *relative* positions of X and Y are completely unaffected by transforming raw scores to percentages or standard scores, by transforming inches to centimeters, or by performing any other *linear transformation* on the data.

A linear transformation is one in which a variable is changed by adding a constant, subtracting a constant, multiplying by a constant, or dividing by a constant. As the scatterplots will testify, the underlying degree of linear association remains the same after such a transformation; consequently, the Pearson r remains the same.

As with the covariance, the algebraic sign of r has nothing to do with its strength. If you obtain a correlation of $r = +.65$ between attentiveness (X) and the

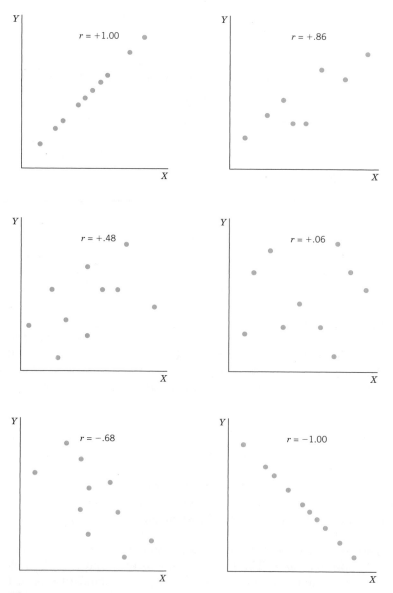

Figure 7.4   Scatterplots illustrating different degrees of correlation.

number of items correct on a final exam (Y), then the correlation between attentiveness and the number of items *incorrect* would be $r = -.65$. The degree of relationship (.65) is identical in both instances; only the sign has changed. *Always consider the algebraic sign of r within the context of the variables being correlated.* We'll have more to say on this in Section 7.7.

With experience, you will be able to judge the general value of r from looking at its scatterplot. Figure 7.4, for example, shows scatterplots corresponding to various degrees of correlation. What about Figure 7.1, you may wonder? The correlation between spatial reasoning and mathematical ability is $r = .63$, which we determined by plugging in the appropriate values from Table 7.2:

$$r = \frac{\text{Cov}}{S_X S_Y} = \frac{+2806/30}{(9.97)(14.83)} = \frac{+93.53}{147.86} = +.63$$

The range of r values you are likely to encounter in practice will depend on the nature of the phenomena in your field of study. In general, correlations greater than $\pm.70$ are rare in the behavioral sciences, unless, say, one is examining correlations among mental tests. And in no discipline will you find r of ±1.00 (unless one engages in the dubious practice of correlating a variable with itself!).

7.5   Computation of r: The Calculating Formula

The Pearson r can be determined by using either a defining formula (Formula 7.2) or an equivalent calculating formula. Although at first glance the calculating formula below may seem a bit complex, it is infinitely easier to use because it does not involve tedious deviation scores.

Pearson r
(calculating formula)

$$r = \frac{\Sigma XY - \dfrac{(\Sigma X)(\Sigma Y)}{n}}{\sqrt{\left(\Sigma X^2 - \dfrac{(\Sigma X)^2}{n}\right)\left(\Sigma Y^2 - \dfrac{(\Sigma Y)^2}{n}\right)}}$$

(7.3)

Let's break it down. The numerator of Formula (7.3) is equivalent to $\Sigma(X - \bar{X})(Y - \bar{Y})$, the sum of the crossproducts. The two expressions in the denominator, sitting under the radical ($\sqrt{}$), are equivalent to SS_X and SS_Y.

This method of calculation is illustrated in Table 7.5, using data you encountered at the beginning of Section 7.3. Although the number of cases is too small for proper use, this table will serve to illustrate the computation of r. First you must find n, ΣX, ΣY, ΣX^2, ΣY^2, and ΣXY. You are already familiar with the first three

Table 7.5   The Necessary Terms to Determine the Pearson r Using the Calculating Formula

Person	X	Y	X^2	Y^2	XY
A	9	13	81	169	117
B	7	9	49	81	63
C	5	7	25	49	35
D	3	11	9	121	33
E	1	5	1	25	5
$n = 5$	$\Sigma X = 25$	$\Sigma Y = 45$	$\Sigma X^2 = 165$	$\Sigma Y^2 = 445$	$\Sigma XY = 253$

terms, and the new terms are nothing to be anxious about. ΣX^2 and ΣY^2 simply tell you to sum the squared values of X and Y, respectively. As for ΣXY, this is the sum of the crossproducts of *raw scores*. For example, we obtained the XY product for person A (117) by multiplying $X = 9$ and $Y = 13$. This crossproduct is added to the other crossproducts to give ΣXY (253 in this case).

The quantities for these six terms appear at the bottom of the columns in Table 7.5. It would be a good idea to calculate these six values yourself, making sure that you obtain the same figures we did. Now carefully plug these values into Formula (7.3) and carry out the operations:

$$r = \frac{\Sigma XY - \dfrac{(\Sigma X)(\Sigma Y)}{n}}{\sqrt{\left(\Sigma X^2 - \dfrac{(\Sigma X)^2}{n}\right)\left(\Sigma Y^2 - \dfrac{(\Sigma Y)^2}{n}\right)}}$$

$$= \frac{253 - \dfrac{(25)(45)}{5}}{\sqrt{\left(165 - \dfrac{(25)^2}{5}\right)\left(445 - \dfrac{(45)^2}{5}\right)}}$$

$$= \frac{253 - 225}{\sqrt{\left(165 - \dfrac{625}{5}\right)\left(445 - \dfrac{2025}{5}\right)}}$$

$$= \frac{28}{\sqrt{(40)(40)}} = \frac{28}{\sqrt{1600}} = \frac{28}{40} = +.70$$

You must take care to distinguish between ΣX^2 and $(\Sigma X)^2$ and between ΣY^2 and $(\Sigma Y)^2$. Here, the first term in each pair tells you to square each value and then take the sum, whereas the second term in each pair tells you to sum all values and then square the sum. It is easy to confuse these symbols, so be careful!

7.6   *Correlation and Causation*

The important refrain here is this: *Correlation does not imply causation.* Never confuse the former with the latter! When a medical researcher experimentally varies drug dosage in a group of patients and then finds a corresponding variation in physiological response, the conclusion is that the differences in dosage *caused* the differences in response. In this instance, attributing a causal relation makes sense. But in the absence of controlled experiments, in which participants are randomly assigned to different treatment groups, causal attribution is far from straightforward.

This is particularly true in the case of correlational research. As Figure 7.5 illustrates, there are three possible explanations (other than chance) for why there is a correlation between X and Y:

1. *X* causes *Y.*
2. *Y* causes *X.*
3. A third factor (Z), or complex of factors (a, b, c, d), causes both X and Y.

For example, teacher enthusiasm (X) has been found to correlate with student achievement (Y) in countless investigations: lower levels of teacher enthusiasm are associated with lower student achievement, and higher levels of enthusiasm with higher student achievement. Does this correlation point to the infectious nature of a teacher's fondness for the subject matter ($X \rightarrow Y$) or, rather, does this correlation suggest that enthusiastic teachers are this way *because* they have a roomful of eager high-achieving students ($Y \rightarrow X$)? Or perhaps teacher enthusiasm and student achievement are both caused by a third factor, Z, such as the level of community support for education. A correlation coefficient is mute with respect to which of the three explanations is the most plausible.

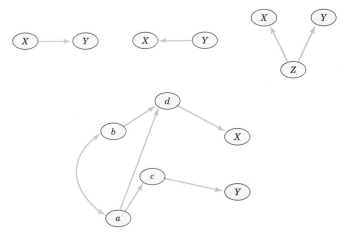

Figure 7.5   Possible reasons for the existence of a correlation between X and Y.

To fully appreciate that the presence of correlation cannot be used to infer causation, one need only consider the many examples of causally ridiculous associations. One of our favorites is the strong positive correlation between the number of churches in a community and the incidence of violent crime. We leave it to your imagination to tease out the possible interpretations of this association, but we trust that you will conclude that a third variable is in play here. (What might it be?)

An obtained correlation between X and Y, then, does not necessarily mean that a causal relationship exists between the two variables. If one is to speak of causation, it must be on logical grounds over and above the statistical demonstration of association. Certain advanced correlational procedures attempt to overcome the limitations of a bivariate correlation coefficient by factoring in additional variables and exercising "statistical control." Partial correlation, multiple regression, and structural equation modeling are examples of such procedures. But no matter how sophisticated the statistical analysis, *the logical argument of cause and effect is always of paramount importance*. There is no substitute for reason in statistical analysis.

7.7   *Factors Influencing Pearson* r

Several major factors influence the magnitude of r, apart from the underlying relationship between the two variables. Consequently, it is important to consider each factor when conducting correlational research and when appraising correlations reported by others.

Linearity

One must never forget that r reflects the magnitude and direction of the *linear* association between two variables. Although a great number of variables tend to exhibit linear relationships, nonlinear relationships do occur. For example, measures of mental ability and psychomotor skill can relate curvilinearly to age if the age range is from, say, 5 to 80 years.

> To the extent that a bivariate distribution departs from linearity, r will underestimate that relationship.

Figures 7.6*a* and 7.6*b* depict equally strong "relationships," the only difference being that Figure 7.6*a* represents a linear relationship and Figure 7.6*b*, a curvilinear one. But note the different values of r (.85 and .54, respectively). The lower r indicates not that there is a weaker relationship in Figure 7.6*b*, but rather that there is a weaker *linear* relationship here. Figure 7.6*c* depicts a *perfect curvilinear* relationship between X and Y—a strong association indeed! In this case, however, $r = 0$: There is absolutely no *linear* association between these variables.

In short, do not misinterpret the absence of *linear* association as the absence of *association*. We are confident that you will not, particularly if you routinely inspect scatterplots when doing correlational work. In any case, it is inappropriate to use the Pearson r when the association between X and Y is markedly curvilinear.

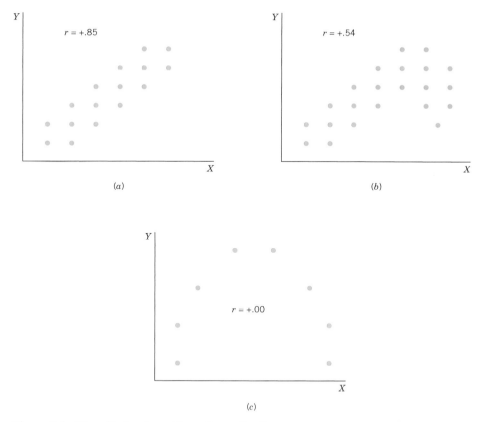

Figure 7.6   The effects of curvilinearity on the Pearson *r*.

Outliers

Discrepant data points, or outliers, can affect the magnitude of the Pearson *r*. The nature of the effect depends on where the outlier is located in the scatterplot.

Consider our friend Student 26, the outlier in the lower right corner of Figure 7.1. Although a single data point, Student 26 clearly detracts from the overall linear trend in these data. You are correct if you suspect that *r* would be larger without this person. Indeed, with Student 26 removed, $r = +.79$ compared to the original $r = +.63$. This increase in *r* should make sense to you *spatially* if you consider the outlier's location in Figure 7.1. Without Student 26, the collective "hug" of the data around the imaginary straight line is a bit tighter. The increase in *r* also should make sense to you *mathematically* if you consider the effect of the outlier's absence on the covariance. The numerator of the covariance becomes larger with the removal of the hefty *negative* crossproduct for Student 26 (-384; Table 7.2), which results in a larger covariance and, in turn, a larger *r*.

Removing an outlier also can reduce a correlation; again, it depends on where the data point is located in the scatterplot. Although well beyond the scope of this book, there are formal statistical criteria for making a decision about an outlier (e.g., Acton, 1959). In short, an improved correlation coefficient is not a sufficient reason for removing (or retaining) an outlier.

Restriction of Range

When we introduced the definition of "variable" back in Chapter 1, we said that a statistical analysis can be sabotaged by a variable that doesn't vary sufficiently. Correlation provides a case in point: Variability is to correlation as oxygen is to fire.

> Other things being equal, restricted variation in either X or Y will result in a lower Pearson r than would be obtained were variability greater.

Consider this example. An ideal way for a university admission's committee to determine the usefulness of standardized test scores for predicting how well students will do at that university is this: record the test scores of all applicants, *admit them all*, and at the end of the first year, determine the correlation between test scores and GPA. In practice, however, correlational research on admissions tests and college GPA typically is based on the far more *select group* of students who survived the screening process, gained admission to the institution, and completed at least one term of studies. In regard to test scores, then, these students represent a generally less variable group than the pool of applicants (many of whom are denied admission). Such **restriction of range** will have an important effect on the size of r.

Look at Figure 7.7*a*, a hypothetical scatterplot based on *all* applicants to a university—that is, the case of admission decisions made without regard to the test scores. This depicts a moderate degree of association between test scores and later GPA. Now suppose that only the applicants with test scores above 60 are admitted. This is the group to the right of the vertical line in Figure 7.7*a*. Figure 7.7*b* shows

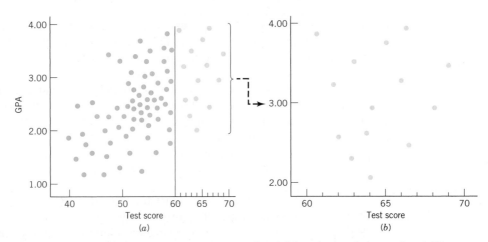

Figure 7.7   Relationship when range is unrestricted (*a*) and when it is restricted (*b*).

the scatterplot that is obtained based only on this more select group of applicants. (The two axes in this figure have been modified so that they are comparable to Figure 7.7*a*.) In Figure 7.7*b*, the evidence for a relationship between test scores and subsequent GPA is much weaker; therefore, the Pearson *r* for these data will be much lower. If members of the admissions committee use only the restricted group to study the effectiveness of this test, they will underestimate its worth as a screening device to be used with *all* applicants.

Thus, the magnitude of *r* depends on the degree of variability in *X* and *Y* as well as on the fundamental relationship between the two variables. This is an important principle to keep in mind as you conceptualize research problems. For example, if your study is limited to eighth-grade students who "did not meet the standard" on the state achievement test, it may make little sense to then correlate their actual scores on this test (which will have restricted variability) with other variables of interest. Similarly, if you are doing research on gifted students, you probably should think twice before calculating correlations that involve measures of general academic achievement. And if you are the admissions officer at a highly selective university, do not be surprised to find that your students' grades bear little relation to their SAT or ACT scores.

A careful inspection of variances and standard deviations, as well as scatterplots, should alert you to the presence of restricted variability in your data. It is a good habit to get into!

Context

We have shown how various factors, alone or in concert, can affect the magnitude of the correlation coefficient. The Pearson *r* also will be affected by the particular instruments that are used. For instance, the correlation between income and "intelligence" will differ depending on how the researcher defines and measures the latter construct. The demographic characteristics of the participants also affect the Pearson *r*. Given the same variables measured by the same instruments, *r* may vary according to age, sex, SES, and other demographic characteristics of the research participants.

Because of the many factors that influence *r*, there is no such thing as *the* correlation between two variables. Rather, the obtained *r* must be interpreted in full view of the factors that affect it and the particular conditions under which it was obtained. That is why good research reports include a careful description of the measures used, the participants studied, and the circumstances under which the correlations were obtained. Do likewise!

7.8 Judging the Strength of Association: r^2

How strong is the association indicated by a coefficient of a particular size? We have already mentioned two ways to judge the strength of association: in terms of the pattern shown by the scatterplot and in terms of *r*'s theoretical range of 0 to ± 1.00.

Reason and prior research provide a third way to judge strength of association. You cannot judge a correlation in isolation. For example, a common way to evaluate the "reliability" of some standardized tests is to give the test to a group of students on two occasions and then correlate the two sets of scores. Within this context, a Pearson r of $+.20$ is exceedingly small. But the same value no doubt would be considered huge if based on, say, reading ability and forearm hair density. Always judge the magnitude of r in full view of what you would *expect* to find, based on reason and prior research.

A fourth way of evaluating the magnitude of r is a bit abstract but very important. Suppose you obtain an $r = +.50$ between SES and reading comprehension for a random sample of fifth-grade students in your state. This r indicates that some of the differences, or variation, in SES among these students are associated with differences, or variation, in their reading comprehension scores. That is, these scores *co*vary: as you move through the range of SES from low to high, reading comprehension scores tend to increase as well. Yet this covariation is far from perfect. The scatterplot for this r would reveal many individual exceptions to the general trend: some low-SES students will have relatively high reading comprehension scores, just as some high-SES students will be relatively low in reading comprehension. These exceptions indicate that variation in SES cannot by itself "account for" all the variation in reading comprehension scores. Indeed, some of the variation in reading comprehension reflects other factors (e.g., motivation, gender, study habits).

Just how much of the variation in reading comprehension is associated with variation in SES and how much is associated with other factors? In other words, what proportion of the variance in SES and reading comprehension is **common variance** shared by the two variables? This question is answered by squaring the correlation coefficient, which provides the **coefficient of determination**.

> The coefficient of determination, r^2, is the proportion of common variance shared by two variables.

In the present example, $r^2 = .50^2 = .25$, indicating that 25% of the variance in reading comprehension is accounted for by variation in SES (and vice versa). That is, 25% of the variance in these two variables is *common* variance. By calculating the difference $1 - r^2$, one sees that 75% of the variance in either variable is associated with factors entirely unrelated to the other variable. This difference, reasonably enough, is called the **coefficient of nondetermination**.

A picture may help to clarify this important concept. If the variance in each variable is represented by a circle, the amount of overlap between two circles corresponds to the proportion of common variance. Because $r^2 = 0$ for the two variables in Figure 7.8a, there is no overlap. Here, there is no common variance between X and Y—variation in one variable has nothing to do with variation in the other. In Figure 7.8b, $r^2 = .25$ and the two variables therefore show a 25% overlap. If X and Y correlate perfectly, as in Figure 7.8c, then $r^2 = 1.00$ and there is perfect overlap.

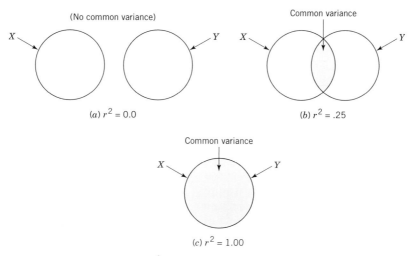

Figure 7.8 Illustrations of r^2 and common variance.

The coefficient of determination throws additional light on the meaning of the Pearson r. *Correlations are not percentages.* For example, a correlation of .50 does not represent a "50% association" or a "50% relationship." Indeed, $r = .50$ is considerably less than "half" the strength of association shown by $r = 1.00$ when both correlations are evaluated as coefficients of determination (.25 vs. 1.00). In fact, a correlation of .71 would be required for half the variance in one variable to be accounted for by variation in the other (i.e., $.71^2 = .50$).

r^2 as "Effect Size"

You learned earlier that a measure of "effect size" can be calculated to evaluate the magnitude of the difference between two means (e.g., see Section 6.9). Actually, effect size is a general term that applies to various research situations, the case of a mean difference being only one (although historically the most prominent). The coefficient of determination also is considered a measure of effect size. By squaring r, we can better communicate the magnitude of association between two variables—as the amount of shared variance between them. For this reason, it is good practice to incorporate r^2 into the presentation of correlational findings.

7.9 Other Correlation Coefficients

The Pearson r, as we indicated earlier, is by far the most frequently used correlation coefficient in the behavioral sciences. But situations sometimes arise that call for other measures of association—for example, when curvilinearity is present or when one or both variables are dichotomous rather than continuous. We leave the treatment of these procedures to more advanced textbooks (e.g., Glass and Hopkins, 1996).

7.10   *Summary*

Determining the extent to which variation in one variable is related to variation in another is important in many fields of inquiry in the behavioral sciences. Pearson r is appropriate when two quantitative variables are linearly related. Its magnitude is determined by the degree to which the data points hug an imaginary straight line, and it varies from $r = 0$ (no linear association) to $r = \pm 1.00$ (all points lie on a straight line). Strength of association depends on the magnitude of r, and its algebraic sign indicates whether the two variables are positively (directly) or negatively (inversely) related. Because Pearson r takes into account the two standard deviations, it is not affected by linear transformations of scores. Thus, r is the same whether raw scores, standard scores, or percentages are used, or whether measurement is in the metric system or the English system.

Many factors influence the magnitude of r. Non-linearity and restricted range each tend to reduce r.

Discrepant cases, or outliers, also can influence r, and the direction of the effect—whether r is weakened or strengthened—is determined by the location of the outlier in the scatterplot. It is important to inspect scatterplots for evidence of nonlinearity and outliers, and to examine the means and standard deviations to ensure adequate variability. Other conditions, such as the specific measures used and the characteristics of the participants, also affect r. Good description of all these factors is therefore an essential part of a research report.

One widely used interpretation of the Pearson r is in terms of r^2 (a measure of effect size), which gives the proportion of variance in one variable that is accounted for by variation in the other. For example, if the correlation between two variables is $-.40$, then there is 16% common variance: 16% of the variance in X is accounted for by variation in Y (and vice versa).

Reading the Research: Restriction of Range

As in many states, teacher candidates in Massachusetts must pass a standardized exam to be certified to teach. In the case of failure, candidates may take the test again. The scatterplot in Figure 7.9 shows the relationship between initial test scores (April) and subsequent test scores (July) on the Massachusetts Teacher Test (MTT) for a sample of candidates who took the test twice (having failed in April). In an independent study of this test, Haney et al. (1999) reported unusually low test-retest correlations. For example, the correlation in Figure 7.9 is a paltry $r = .37$. As these authors explain, this is due in part to restriction of range:

> *This is because people who scored 70 or above "passed" the tests and did not have to retake them in order to be provisionally certified.... [O]ur test-retest data for the MTT are for people who scored below 70 on the April tests. This leads to one possible explanation for the unusually low test-retest correlations, namely attenuation of observed correlation coefficients due to restriction of range.*

In a scatterplot, a tell-tale sign of range restriction is when part of the ellipse looks like it has been "chopped off." This clearly is the case in Figure 7.9, where the upper right end of the ellipse has a clearly definable straight edge—corresponding to the passing score of 70 on the horizontal axis.

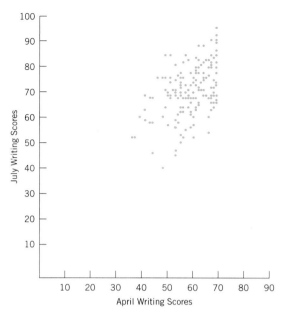

Figure 7.9 Scatterplot of April (horizontal axis) and July (vertical axis) MTT scores in writing ($r = .37$).

Source: Haney, W., Fowler, C., Wheelock, A., Bebell, D., & Malec, N. (1999, February 11). Less truth than error? An independent study of the Massachusetts Teacher Tests. *Education Policy Analysis Archives, 7*(4). Retrieved [April 6, 2002] from http://epaa.asu.edu/epaa/v7n4/.

Case Study: Money Matters

Data from 253 public school districts were obtained from the Office of Superintendent of Public Instruction in the state of Washington. The data consist of various student demographic and performance information, all reported at the school district level. *School district,* then, was the "unit of analysis."

We want to examine the relationship between socioeconomic status and academic achievement in the fourth grade. Socioeconomic status (SES) is defined as the percentage of students in the district who were eligible for free or reduced-priced lunch, a variable we will call LUNCH. Academic achievement is defined as the percentage of fourth graders in the district who performed at or above the "proficient" level in mathematics (MATH), reading (READ), writing (WRITE), and listening (LISTEN) on the fourth-grade exam administered by the state. Our initial focus is on the relationship between LUNCH and MATH.

As we would expect, the scatterplot (Figure 7.10) shows a moderate, negative association between LUNCH and MATH. That is, districts having fewer low-income students tend to have more students scoring proficient or above in fourth-grade mathematics. Of course, the converse is true as well: districts that have more low-income students tend to have fewer proficient students. Inspection of the scatterplot confirms that the relationship is linear, with no evidence of outliers or restriction of range.

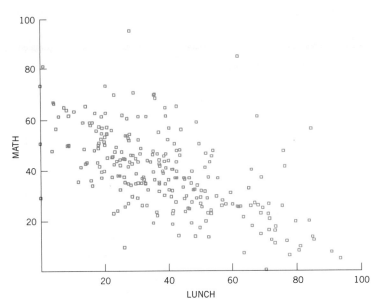

Figure 7.10 Scatterplot of district-level LUNCH and MATH scores.

We calculated $r = -.61$, which is consistent with our visual appraisal. Squaring r produces the coefficient of determination, or the proportion of variance that is shared between MATH and LUNCH: $(-.61)^2 = .37$. Thus, over a third of the variance in MATH scores and LUNCH scores is *shared*, or *common*, variance. Although correlation does not imply causation, this amount of shared variance agrees with the well-known influence that socioeconomic factors have on student achievement.

We also are interested in the relationship between LUNCH and each of the other achievement variables, as well as the relationships among the achievement variables themselves. Table 7.6 displays the correlation matrix for these variables, which presents all possible correlations among LUNCH, MATH, READ, WRITE, and LISTEN. A correlation matrix is "symmetrical," which means that the correlation coefficients in the upper right are a mirror image of those in the lower left. For this reason, only one side is reported (the lower left in this case). The string of 1.00s along the diagonal simply reflects the perfect correlation between a variable with itself—admittedly useless information!

Table 7.6 Correlation Matrix ($n = 255$ districts)

	LUNCH	MATH	READ	WRITE	LISTEN
LUNCH	1.00				
MATH	−.61	1.00			
READ	−.66	.83	1.00		
WRITE	−.53	.76	.73	1.00	
LISTEN	−.58	.63	.78	.57	1.00

The first column of coefficients in Table 7.6 tells us that LUNCH correlates negatively with each measure of achievement, ranging from a low of $r = -.53$ (WRITE) to a high of $r = -.66$ (READ). Again, such relationship between SES and academic achievement is not unique to Washington school districts. There is an accumulation of evidence regarding the strong relationship between community wealth and student achievement.

The rest of Table 7.6 shows the correlations among the achievement measures. As you might expect, these correlations are all positive and fairly strong: A district having a high percentage of proficient students in one subject area (e.g., mathematics) is likely to have a high percentage of proficient students in another subject area (e.g., reading). And the converse holds as well.

We were struck by the somewhat higher correlation between READ and MATH ($r = .83$) in comparison to that between READ and WRITE ($r = .73$). After all, one would expect that reading and writing would have more in common than reading and mathematics. An inspection of the scatterplot for READ and WRITE (Figure 7.11) reveals a suspicious data point in the lower right corner, which, given its location, would lower r. This data point represents a peculiar combination of scores, indeed—a district with 90% of its students proficient in reading (READ $= 90$), yet *no* student proficient in writing (WRITE $= 0$). Was this an error in data entry? Upon inspection of the raw data, we discovered that this district enrolled a mere 118 students, and only 10 of them took the fourth-grade test! The raw data showed that, indeed, 9 students were proficient in reading and none was proficient in writing. Although this result still puzzles us, it is more understandable given the few students tested.

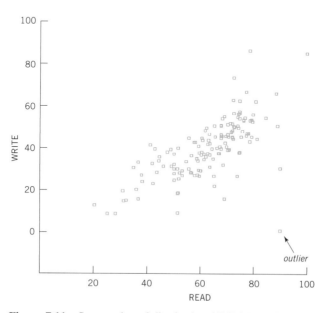

Figure 7.11   Scatterplot of district-level READ and WRITE scores.

To see how this unusually small (and puzzling) district influenced the correlation between READ and WRITE, we eliminated this case and recalculated r. Though higher, the new correlation of $r = .77$ remains lower than that between READ and MATH (i.e., $r = .83$). It is difficult to explain this oddity from the information we have available. For example, the scatterplot does not reveal any restriction of range. Perhaps the answer lies in the reliability of these tests: Writing assessments tend to be less reliable than other subject area tests. Other things being equal, correlations are lower when based on less reliable measures.

As we observed in Section 7.7, it is important to interpret correlations within the context in which they have been obtained. Here, for example, *school district* is the unit of analysis. A different unit of analysis might very well affect the magnitude of these correlations. For example, *student*-level correlations probably would be lower than those obtained above. Also, these correlations could change if SES or academic achievement were defined differently.

Suggested Computer Exercises

Access the **sophomores** data file.

1. Generate a scatterplot for the variables MATH and READ, placing MATH on the Y-axis and READ on the X-axis. Describe the direction and strength of this relationship. (Also, check for any obvious outliers, restriction of range, or evidence of curvilinearity.)

2. Compute the Pearson r for MATH and READ. Does the result coincide with your descriptions in (1) above?

3. Which pair of variables demonstrates the stronger relationship: MATH and GPA, or READ and GPA?

Exercises

Identify, Define, or Explain

Terms and Concepts

univariate
bivariate
correlation coefficient
Pearson product–moment correlation coefficient
correlate
covary
paired scores
scatterplot
bivariate distribution
data point
association
elliptical
positive (direct) association
negative (inverse) association

outlier
linear association
curvilinear relationship
nonlinearity
covariance
crossproduct
Pearson r
correlation vs. causation
factors influencing r
restriction of range
common variance
coefficient of determination
coefficient of nondetermination
effect size

Symbols

X Y r r^2 $1 - r^2$

Note: Answers to starred (*) items are presented in Appendix B.

1. Give examples, other than those mentioned in this chapter, of pairs of variables you would expect to show:

    (a) a positive association

    (b) a negative association

    (c) no association at all

2. Why is it important to inspect scatterplots?

*3. **(a)** Prepare a scatterplot for the data below, following the guidelines presented in this chapter.

X	Y
11	12
9	8
8	10
6	7
4	4
3	6
1	2

    (b) What are your impressions of this scatterplot regarding strength and direction of association?

    (c) Do you detect any outliers or evidence of curvilinearity?

    (d) Based on visual inspection alone and before proceeding to the next problem, estimate Pearson r from this plot.

*4. **(a)** Using the data in Problem 3, determine r from both the defining formula and the calculating formula.

    (b) Interpret r within the context of the coefficient of determination.

*5. What is the covariance for the data in Problem 3?

6. **(a)** Using the data in Problem 3, divide each value of X by 2 and construct a scatterplot showing the relationship between X and Y.

    (b) How do your impressions of the new scatterplot compare with your impressions of the original plot?

    (c) What is the covariance between X and Y?

    (d) How is the covariance affected by this transformation?

    (e) What is the Pearson r between X and Y? How does this compare with the initial r from Problem 4?

(f)   What generalizations do these results permit regarding the effect of linear trans-formations (e.g., halving each score) on the degree of linear association between two variables?

*7.   Suppose you change the data in Problem 3a so that the bottom case is $X = 1$ and $Y = 12$ rather than $X = 1$ and $Y = 2$.

(a)   Without doing any calculations, state how (and why) this change would affect the numerator of the covariance and, in turn, the covariance itself.

(b)   In general, how would this change affect r?

(c)   Estimate the new r (before proceeding to Problem 8).

*8.   Calculate r from Problem 7.

9.   The covariance between X and Y is -72, $S_X = 8$ and $S_Y = 11$. What is the value of r?

10. $r = -.47$, $S_X = 6$, and $S_Y = 4$. What is the covariance between X and Y?

11.   For a particular set of scores, $S_X = 3$ and $S_Y = 5$. What is the largest possible value of the covariance? (Remember that r can be positive *or* negative.)

*12.   An r of $+.60$ was obtained between IQ (X) and number correct on a word-recognition test (Y) in a large sample of adults. For each of the following, indicate whether or not r would be affected, and if so, how (treat each modification as independent of the others):

(a) Y is changed to number of words *incorrect*.

(b)   Each value of IQ is divided by 10.

(c)   Ten points are added to each value of Y.

(d)   You randomly add a point to some IQs and subtract a point from others.

(e)   Ten points are added to each Y score and each value of X is divided by 10.

(f)   Word-recognition scores are converted to z scores.

(g)   Only the scores of adults whose IQs exceed 120 are used in calculating r.

13.   Does a low r necessarily mean that there is little "association" between two variables? (Explain.)

*14.   It is common to find that the correlation between aviation aptitude test scores (X) and pilot proficiency (Y) is higher among aviation cadets than among experienced pilots. How would you explain this?

15.   Some studies have found a strong *negative* correlation between how much parents help their children with homework (X) and student achievement (Y). That is, children who receive more parental help on their homework tend to have lower achievement than kids who receive little or no parental help. Discuss the possible explanations for why these two variables would correlate negatively. Although one cannot infer causality from a correlation, which explanation do you find most persuasive?

CHAPTER 8

Regression and Prediction

A high school student's score on an academic aptitude test, such as the SAT, is related to that student's GPA in college. As a general rule, then, the student who does well on the SAT is a better bet to do well in college than the student who does poorly on the SAT. As a university admissions officer, what GPA would you predict for a student who earns, say, a score of 650 on the SAT critical reading scale (SAT-CR)? And what margin of error should you attach to that prediction? Because the relationship between SAT-CR and college GPA is far from perfect, any prediction from a particular score is only a "good bet"—not a "sure thing." Or as humorist Will Rogers once said, "It's always risky to make predictions, especially about the future."

This scenario illustrates a problem in **prediction**: estimating future performance (e.g., college GPA) from knowledge of current standing on some measure (e.g., SAT-CR score). You may be wondering how this pertains to the subject of the last chapter, correlation. Correlation and prediction indeed are closely related: without a correlation between two variables, there can be no meaningful prediction from one to the other. However, although the size of r is indicative of the predictive potential, the coefficient by itself does not tell you how to make the prediction.

How, then, does one go about the craft of prediction? Let's take as an example the prediction of college grades from academic aptitude scores. Look at the scatterplot in Figure 8.1. The X variable is the SAT-CR score from the senior year of high school, and the Y variable is first-year GPA at Fumone University.[1] Notice that a straight line has been fitted to the data and used to obtain a predicted GPA of 2.78 for an SAT-CR score of 650. This line could be used in similar fashion to obtain a predicted GPA for any other SAT-CR score. When the bivariate trend is reasonably linear, a line of "best fit" easily can be found and used for purposes of predicting values of Y from X. Such a line is called a **regression line**. As shown in Figure 8.1, the prediction is made by noting the Y value (e.g., 2.78) for the point on the line that corresponds to the particular value of X (e.g., 650).

For $r = \pm 1.00$, each case would fall exactly on the regression line, and prediction would be errorless. But when the correlation is not perfect, as in the present instance, there necessarily will be **prediction error**. For example, Katy's and Jane's

---

[1]The exceedingly small sample ($n = 12$) reflects our desire to keep things simple. By no means should 12 be regarded as an appropriate sample size for this kind of analysis.

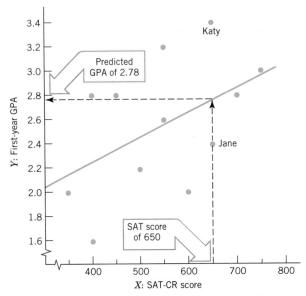

Figure 8.1   The prediction of first-year GPA (Y) from SAT-CR scores (X).

actual GPAs fall considerably above and below the 2.78 that would have been predicted from their SAT-CR score of 650. The lower the correlation, the greater the prediction errors.

There are, then, two tasks now before you: predicting the value on one variable from a value on another, and determining the margin of prediction error. We take up both tasks in the sections that follow.

8.2   *Determining the Line of Best Fit*

It is all very well to speak of finding the straight **line of best fit**, but how do you know when the "best fit" has been achieved? Indeed, "best fit" could be defined in several ways. Here, we show you a common approach when Pearson r is used as the measure of association and when one's purpose is prediction.

First, let's review the relevant symbols. Two are familiar to you, and one is new. As you saw above, X represents the score value of the variable that is doing the predicting. More formally, this variable is called the **independent variable**, and convention dictates that you place it on the horizontal axis. We use Y to represent the *actual* score value of the variable to be predicted, the **dependent variable**, and it is placed on the vertical axis. (Think of the dependent variable as "depending on" the independent variable: College GPA "depends on" academic aptitude, among other things.) Finally, the **predicted score** value of Y is represented by the symbol Y' ("Y prime").

The Least-Squares Criterion

An error of prediction is the difference between the actual and predicted values of Y:

$$\text{error} = (Y - Y')$$

This is shown in Figure 8.2 for Katy and Jane. Both students have the same predicted GPA ($Y' = 2.78$) because they have the same SAT-CR score ($X = 650$), but their actual GPAs (Y) are 3.40 and 2.40, respectively. Thus, their prediction errors are:

$$\text{Katy: error} = (Y - Y') = (3.40 - 2.78) = +.62$$
$$\text{Jane: error} = (Y - Y') = (2.40 - 2.78) = -.38$$

Notice that error is positive for a case above the line and negative for a case that falls below. The regression line is placed in such a way to *minimize* prediction errors—values of $(Y - Y')$—for the scatterplot as a whole.

> With the line of best fit, the sum of the squared prediction errors for all the cases is as small as possible. In other words, $\Sigma(Y - Y')^2$ is at a minimum.

You may recognize $\Sigma(Y - Y')^2$ as a sum of squares, much like the more familiar expressions $\Sigma(X - \bar{X})^2$ and $\Sigma(Y - \bar{Y})^2$. In the present case, it is the **error sum of squares**. Thus, when the regression line is properly fitted, the error sum of squares is smaller than that which would obtain with any other straight line. This is known as the **least-squares criterion** (the *least* amount of error sum of *squares*).

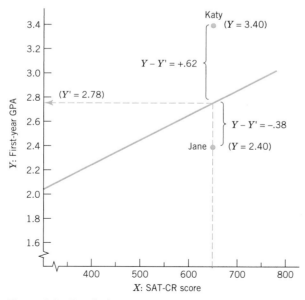

Figure 8.2   Prediction errors for two cases.

The Regression Line as a "Running Mean"

If linearity of regression holds, the regression line may be thought of as a "running mean."

> In a sense, each Y' is an estimate of the mean of Y values corresponding to a particular value of X.

This is illustrated in Figure 8.3. The $\overline{Y}$ of 2.57 is the mean GPA for the entire sample of 12 cases, whose X scores range from 350 to 750. In contrast, the Y' of 2.78 estimates the mean of Y just for those cases where $X = 650$. But, you may point out, only two cases in our sample have an SAT-CR score of 650 (Katy and Jane), and their Y scores (3.40 and 2.40) do not average out to 2.78. True enough; the Y' of 2.78 is only an *estimated* mean. It is what one would *expect* the mean of Y to be for a distribution of many, many cases all having SAT-CR scores of 650 rather than just the two in our sample. Similarly, the Y' of 2.31 is an estimated mean of Y scores where X equals 425. Although our particular sample contains no cases at all with SAT-CR scores of 425, the regression line gives an estimate of the mean GPA

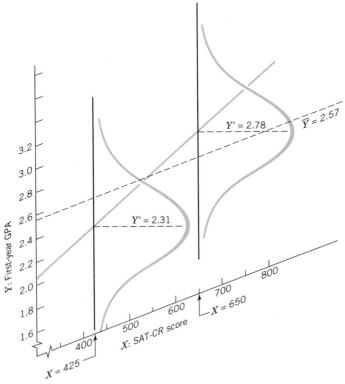

Figure 8.3   The regression line as a "running mean."

that would be expected if there were students with that SAT-CR score. With more realistic sample sizes, of course, there is a greater representation of X values, and therefore you have greater confidence in the corresponding estimates of Y.

Predicting X from Y

There is a *second* straight line of best fit for the data of Figure 8.1. Suppose that you wanted to predict SAT-CR scores from first-year GPA rather than the other way around. The least-squares criterion would then be applied to minimize prediction errors in SAT-CR rather than those in GPA. (To visualize this, simply switch the axes of Figure 8.1.) Unless $S_X = S_Y$, the two regression lines will differ. In practice, interest typically is in predicting in *one* direction, not in both. For example, it makes little sense to predict SAT-CR scores from first-year GPA insofar as SAT-CR *precedes* GPA in time. Rather, the logical prediction is from the "earlier" variable to the "later" variable.

8.3   The Regression Equation in Terms of Raw Scores

Every straight line has an equation. The location of the regression line in a scatterplot is determined by, reasonably enough, the **regression equation**.

You may recall from your earlier school days that a straight line is defined by two terms: **slope** and **intercept**. The slope, symbolized by b, reflects the angle (flat, shallow, or steep) and direction (positive or negative) of the regression line. The intercept, symbolized by a, is the predicted value of Y where $X = 0$.

A predicted value for Y can be obtained for any value of X by using Formula (8.1):

Regression equation:
raw-score formula

$$Y' = a + bX \tag{8.1}$$

where

Slope

$$b = r\left(\frac{S_Y}{S_X}\right) \tag{8.2}$$

and

Intercept

$$a = \overline{Y} - b\overline{X} \tag{8.3}$$

Recasting Formula (8.1) in terms of Formulas (8.2) and (8.3), we can expand the regression equation as:

Regression equation:
expanded raw-score formula

$$Y' = \overline{Y} - r\left(\frac{S_Y}{S_X}\right)\overline{X} + r\left(\frac{S_Y}{S_X}\right)X \qquad (8.4)$$

where the first term is the intercept and the second term is the slope.

Let's see how Formula (8.4) works. We will use it to determine the predicted GPA for students scoring 650 on the SAT-CR, the prediction illustrated in Figure 8.1.

Step 1   Begin with the appropriate summary statistics in Table 8.1, which you insert in Formulas (8.2) and (8.3) as follows:

$$b = r\left(\frac{S_Y}{S_X}\right) = +.50\left(\frac{.52}{123.2}\right) = (+.50)(.0042) = .0021$$

$$a = \overline{Y} - b\overline{X} = 2.57 - .0021(545.8) = 2.57 - 1.15 = 1.42$$

Step 2   In Formula (8.1), insert the slope and intercept values from Step 1 to obtain the regression equation for these data:

$$Y' = a + bX$$
$$= 1.42 + .0021X$$

Step 3   The SAT-CR score of 650 is now substituted for X in the equation at Step 2 to find the predicted GPA for this score:

$$Y' = 1.42 + .0021(650)$$
$$= 2.78$$

Table 8.1   Summary Statistics for Figure 8.1

SAT-CR	GPA
$\overline{X} = 545.80$	$\overline{Y} = 2.57$
$S_X = 123.20$	$S_Y = .52$
$r = +.50$	

If you want to make other predictions, you have only to substitute the appropriate X value in the regression equation. Let's verify the prediction involving $X = 425$ that is shown in Figure 8.3:

$$Y' = 1.42 + .0021X$$
$$= 1.42 + .0021(425)$$
$$= 2.31$$

To find predicted Y values, one normally uses the regression equation as we have done here. Predicted Y values also can be obtained from a graph. Plotting the regression line is easy enough:

Step 1   Find Y' for two values of X (pick a low value and a high value of X). You now have two points: X_1, Y_1' and X_2, Y_2'.

Step 2   Plot these two points on graph paper, using the X and Y axes from the original scatterplot.

Step 3   Draw a straight line through the two points. As a check, the regression line must also go through the point where $\overline{X}$ and $\overline{Y}$ intersect.

Even if you do not intend to derive values of Y' from a graph, you may wish to superimpose the regression line on a scatterplot for illustrative purposes. Figure 8.4 shows the regression line for the association between spatial reasoning

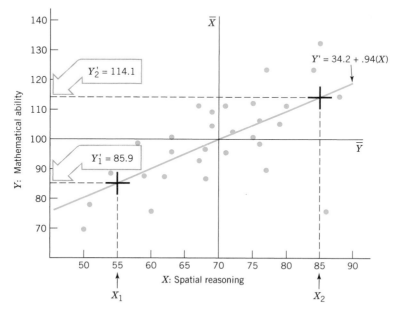

Figure 8.4   Plotting the Y-on-X regression line (from Figure 7.1): Y' values plotted for $X_1 = 55$ and $X_2 = 85$.

and mathematical ability from Chapter 7 (see Figure 7.1). To plot this line, we began with the following summary statistics:

Spatial Reasoning	Mathematical Ability
$\bar{X} = 70$	$\bar{Y} = 100$
$S_X = 9.97$	$S_Y = 14.83$
$r = +.63$	

For these data, the slope is

$$b = r\left(\frac{S_Y}{S_X}\right) = +.63\left(\frac{14.83}{9.97}\right) = (+.63)(1.49) = +.94$$

and the intercept is

$$a = \bar{Y} - b\bar{X} = 100 - .94(70) = 100 - 65.8 = 34.2$$

The regression equation therefore is $Y' = 34.2 + .94X$, which we used for plotting Y' values for $X_1 = 55$ ($Y'_1 = 85.9$) and $X_2 = 85$ ($Y'_2 = 114.1$) in Figure 8.4. The two Y' values, in turn, were connected by a straight line. As it must, this line goes through the point of intersection between $\bar{X}$ and $\bar{Y}$. (*Question:* How do you think the outlier in the lower right corner affects the placement of this line?)

8.4 *Interpreting the Raw-Score Slope*

Let's go back to Formula (8.2) for a moment. From this formula you can see that as r goes, so goes b. If r is positive, b will be positive; if r is negative, so too is b. You also can see that if $r = 0$, b must be zero as well. These similarities aside, r and b typically will have different values—often markedly so. The exception, again as you can reason from Formula (8.2), is where $S_X = S_Y$ (which is highly unlikely with raw-score data).

> Slope always is interpreted in view of the units of X and Y: For each unit increase in X, Y changes b units.

In the case of Figure 8.4, for each one-point increase on the spatial reasoning test, there is a corresponding change of $+.94$ points on the mathematical ability test. The raw-score slope can be, and often is, greater than ± 1.00. Again, it depends on the underlying scale of the two variables. If in the present example we arbitrarily doubled each Y score, then $S_Y = (2)(14.83) = 29.66$ (S_X and r remain the same). The new slope would be:

$$b = +.63\left(\frac{29.66}{9.97}\right) = (+.63)(2.97) = +1.87$$

That is, for every one-point increase on the spatial reasoning test, there now is an increase of 1.87 points on the mathematical ability test—twice the original value of b.

The value of b can look small even when there is an appreciable degree of association between X and Y. In the Fumone University example, you saw that $b = .0021$. This may initially strike you as an infinitesimally small value for a slope, but remember that slope is expressed in terms of the underlying scales of X and Y. That is, for each *SAT-CR point* increase (e.g., from 500 to 501) there is a change of $+.0021$ *grade points* (from 2.47 to 2.4721). Once you acknowledge that SAT-CR scores in this sample range from 350 to 750 and college GPA from 1.6 to 3.4, this value of slope doesn't seem quite as small. For example, a 10-point increase in SAT-CR scores (e.g., from 500 to 510) would correspond to a $(10)(.0021) = .021$ grade-point increase (from 2.47 to 2.49), and a 100-point increase in SAT-CR scores (e.g., from 500 to 600) would correspond to a $(100)(.0021) = .21$ grade-point increase (from 2.47 to 2.68, or from C+ to B−). This degree of covariation is more in line with what you might expect between two variables where $r = .50$.

8.5   The Regression Equation in Terms of z Scores

The regression equation can be stated in z-score form, and when this is done it yields a very simple—and informative—expression. If you transform the original values of X and Y to z scores, the regression equation simplifies to:

Regression equation:
z-score form
$$z_{Y'} = rz_X \tag{8.5}$$

where: $z_{Y'}$ is the predicted value of Y expressed as a z score
r is the correlation between X and Y
z_X is the z score of X

Look carefully at Formula (8.5): It tells you that the predicted value of z_Y is a *proportion* of z_X and that the proportion is equal to r. Data in Table 8.1 permit the calculation of z_X for a student with SAT-CR $= 650$:

$$z_X = (650 - 545.8)/123.2 = +.85.$$

Thus, this person's SAT-CR score falls .85 standard deviations above the SAT-CR mean, $\overline{X}$. With $r = +.50$, you would predict his GPA to be .42 standard deviations above the GPA mean, $\overline{Y}$:

$$z_{Y'} = rz_X = (+.50)(+.85) = +.42.$$

It is easy to demonstrate that this formula gives the same result as Formula (8.4). The value of $z_{Y'}$ that we just calculated can be converted to a predicted GPA of 2.78, the answer obtained earlier:

$$Y' = \bar{Y} + (z_{Y'})(S_Y)$$
$$= 2.57 + (+.42)(.52)$$
$$= 2.78$$

8.6   *Some Insights Regarding Correlation and Prediction*

The z-score approach is not usually convenient for practical work in prediction; Formula (8.4) is much more direct. However, Formula (8.5) is well worth careful inspection because of the valuable insight it provides regarding the nature of correlation and prediction.

Let's begin by noticing the prominent position of r in this formula. The Pearson r is equal to the slope of the regression line when expressed in z-score terms. To see that this is so, consider more closely the formula for slope, $b = r(S_Y/S_X)$. When the data are transformed to z scores, the resulting standard deviations both equal to 1, and therefore $b = r$. The larger the correlation, the steeper the line will slope upward (or downward, if a negative r). The interpretation of the standard score slope is the same as it is for the raw-score slope, except that the "unit" is now a standard deviation:

> For each standard deviation increase in X, Y changes by r standard deviations.

In Figure 8.5 we present four regression lines, corresponding to $r = +1.00$, $+.50$, $+.25$, and 0, respectively. This figure illustrates what happens as you move from a perfect correlation to a correlation of zero.

When r = ±1.00

Consider the case where $r = +1.00$ (Figure 8.5a). Here, the predicted z score on Y is *identical* to the z score on X from which the prediction was made. That is, $z_{Y'} = (+1.00)z_X = z_X$. One's *relative standing* on X is identical to that person's *relative standing* on Y. For each standard deviation increase in X, Y' also increases by one standard deviation. And what if r is perfect but *negative*? Easy: $z_{Y'} = (-1.00)z_X = -z_X$. That is, the predicted value of z_Y has the same absolute value, but opposite algebraic sign, as z_X.

When r ≠ ±1.00

Where r is other than a perfect ± 1.00, the predicted Y scores cluster more closely about the mean of Y. Suppose $r = +.50$ (Figure 8.5b). When predicting from a

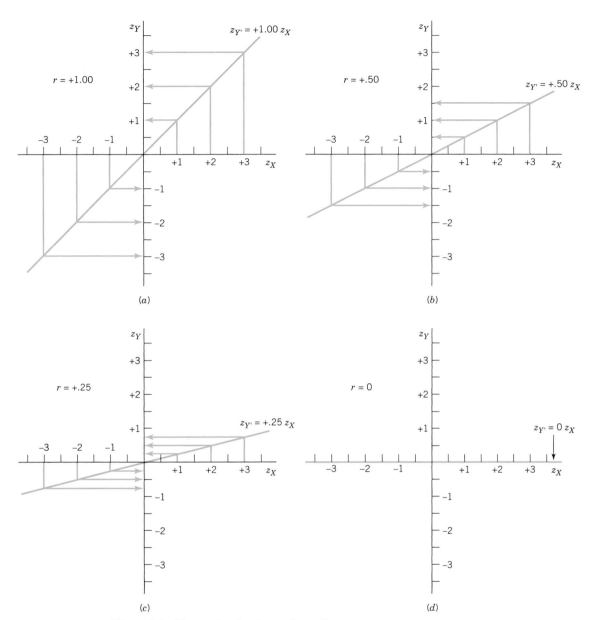

Figure 8.5 Regression for four values of *r*.

value of X that is two standard deviations above the mean (i.e., $z_X = +2.00$), the predicted value of Y is only *one* standard deviation above the mean: $z_{Y'} = (+.50)(+2.00) = +1.00$. Similarly, if $z_X = +1.50$, then $z_{Y'} = (+.50)(+1.50) = +.75$. Thus, when $r = +.50$, the predicted value of Y is *one-half* the value of z_X. When $r = +.25$ (Figure 8.5c), the predicted value of Y is *one-quarter* the value of z_X. For example, when predicting from a value of X that is 1.6 standard deviations below the mean (i.e., $z_X = -1.60$), $z_{Y'} = (+.25)(-1.60) = -.40$.

This same principle holds for *negative* values of r, the only difference being that the algebraic sign of $z_{Y'}$ is opposite that of z_X. If $r = -.50$ and $z_X = +1.50$, for example, then $z_{Y'} = (-.50)(+1.50) = -.75$.

This tendency to move closer to the mean as one goes from X scores to predicted Y scores is known as **regression toward the mean**. Sir Francis Galton generally is given credit for bringing this phenomenon to light. His most celebrated study of the "regression effect" (as it is called today) pertained to human stature, where he observed that tall parents, on average, had offspring shorter than they were (but still tall, mind you) and that short parents tended to have offspring somewhat taller than they were (although still rather short). The height of offspring, Galton demonstrated, "reverted" or "regressed" toward the mean height of the population. (He earlier observed the same tendency with regard to the weight of sweet peas, by the way.)

The regression effect is characteristic of *any* relationship in which the correlation is less than perfect. Regression toward the mean is particularly evident in educational and psychological interventions where (a) participants initially are selected because they score low on a pretest, (b) an intervention of some kind occurs, and (c) a posttest is given to determine the effects of the intervention. Participants—on average—will appear to gain on the posttest *even if there had been no intervention at all.*[2] This is because the correlation between pretest and posttest is less than 1.00 (considerably so, in all likelihood); consequently, participants generally will be less extreme on the posttest than they were on the pretest. Stated more formally, when $r < 1.00$, the value of Y' will be closer to $\overline{Y}$ than the corresponding value of X is to $\overline{X}$. How much closer depends on the magnitude of r, as you can see from Formula (8.5). A key phrase above is "on average." Remember that a predicted value is an estimate of the *mean* value of Y for a particular value of X, not the one and only value of Y. It is still quite possible for tall parents to have a child even taller than they, or for a student low on the pretest to be even lower, relatively speaking, on the posttest.

When r = 0

In the absence of an association between two variables (Figure 8.5*d*), the predicted value of Y will always be the mean of Y:

$$z_{Y'} = (r)(z_X)$$
$$= (0)(z_X)$$
$$= 0$$

(Remember, a z of zero corresponds to the mean.) This says that when X and Y are uncorrelated, you will predict the mean of Y for every case, regardless of the value

---

[2]Our statement assumes that there are no gains due to practice or maturation.

of X. This is sensible: if $r = 0$, then knowing the person's standing on X (e.g., number of freckles) is absolutely irrelevant for predicting that person's standing on Y (e.g., annual income). The mean of Y is an intuitively reasonable "prediction" in this case. Indeed, what more could one say in such a situation?

This also explains why the regression line is *horizontal* when $r = 0$. (When the scatterplot is based on z scores, as in Figure 8.5d, the regression line lies directly on top of the X axis.) No matter what value of X you select, when $r = 0$ the predicted value of Y will always be the mean of Y:

$$
\begin{aligned}
a &= \overline{Y} - b\overline{X} \\
&= \overline{Y} - (0)\overline{X} \\
&= \overline{Y}
\end{aligned}
$$

On a final note, observe in Figure 8.5 that *regardless of r, $Y' = \overline{Y}$ whenever $X = \overline{X}$.* If you are average on X, then the best prediction is that you will be average on Y—regardless of the correlation between X and Y. That is, if $z_X = 0$ (i.e., the mean of X), then $z_{Y'} = rz_X = r(0) = 0$. This is why the regression line always passes through the point where $\overline{X}$ and $\overline{Y}$ intersect.

8.7 Regression and Sums of Squares

The concept of sum of squares, as you saw in Section 8.2, is central to the least-squares criterion for determining the regression line: The best-fitting line minimizes the error sum of squares, $\Sigma(Y - Y')^2$. There actually are *three* sums of squares implicated in regression analysis. By understanding these sums of squares and their interrelationships, you will have a closer and more enduring understanding of regression and prediction.

We begin with $\Sigma(Y - \overline{Y})^2$, the familiar Y sum of squares. Because it centers on the deviation of each Y score from the mean of Y, $\Sigma(Y - \overline{Y})^2$ reflects **total variation** in Y and for this reason is called the **total sum of squares**. $(Y - \overline{Y})$ is illustrated in Figure 8.6a for the prediction of college GPA from SAT-CR scores.

Within the context of bivariate regression, there are only two reasons for variation in Y. The first reason is X. In the present case, total variation in first-year college GPA is explained, in part, by variation in SAT-CR scores. This variation is captured by the sum of squares, $\Sigma(Y' - \overline{Y})^2$, the **explained variation** in Y. The heart of this term is $(Y' - \overline{Y})$, which is the distance between the regression line and $\overline{Y}$ for a given value of X (Figure 8.6b). Whether $\Sigma(Y' - \overline{Y})^2$ is large or small thus reflects the strength of the relationship between X and Y. When r is large (steep slope), many values of Y' depart markedly from $\overline{Y}$, which, when squared and summed, result in a large $\Sigma(Y' - \overline{Y})^2$. But when $r = 0$, the regression line is flat and $Y' = \overline{Y}$ for all values of X. Consequently, $\Sigma(Y' - \overline{Y})^2 = 0$.

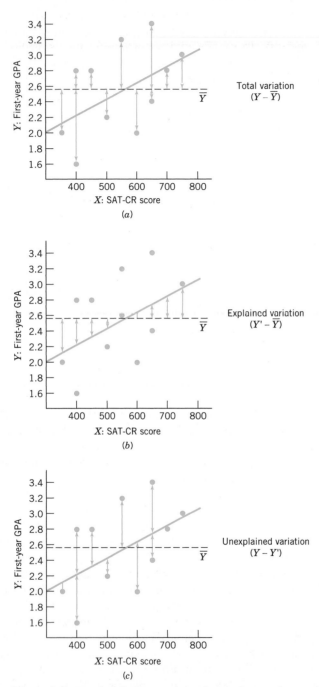

Figure 8.6   Total variation, explained variation, and unexplained variation.

The second reason why Y varies is because of relevant, though unidentified, variables *other* than X. This variation is represented by the familiar error sum of squares, $\Sigma(Y - Y')^2$, which reflects **unexplained variation** in Y (Figure 8.6c). Where $r = \pm 1.00$, prediction is perfect: $(Y - Y') = 0$, as must be $\Sigma(Y - Y')^2$. That is, when $r = \pm 1.00$, there is no *unexplained* variation in Y. X explains it all! When $r = 0$, however, there is considerable discrepancy between the actual and predicted values of Y, which results in a large $\Sigma(Y - Y')^2$.

Total variation in Y, then, reflects both explained and unexplained variation. Stated mathematically:

Total variation in Y

$$\Sigma(Y - \overline{Y})^2 = \Sigma(Y' - \overline{Y})^2 + \Sigma(Y - Y')^2 \qquad (8.6)$$

From this, one can determine the proportion of total variation in Y that is explained variation, which it turns out is equal to r^2, the coefficient of determination (Section 7.8):

$$\frac{explained\ variation}{total\ variation} = \frac{\Sigma(Y' - \overline{Y})^2}{\Sigma(Y - \overline{Y})^2} = r^2$$

It follows, therefore, that the square root of this term is equal to r:

$$\sqrt{\frac{\Sigma(Y' - \overline{Y})^2}{\Sigma(Y - \overline{Y})^2}} = r$$

As we stated at the outset of this chapter, correlation and prediction are closely related indeed!

8.8   Measuring the Margin of Prediction Error: The Standard Error of Estimate

We now return to a question we posed in Section 8.1: How does one determine the margin of error for a particular prediction? Not surprisingly, the error sum of squares, $\Sigma(Y - Y')^2$, is central to this task.

You learned in Chapter 5 that the variance is equal to sum of squares divided by n and that the square root of the variance gives you the standard deviation. This knowledge can be applied to the error sum of squares. Specifically, the *variance* of prediction errors is $\Sigma(Y - Y')^2/n$. The square root of this expression is the *standard deviation* of prediction errors, which is called the **standard error of estimate** and symbolized by $S_{Y \cdot X}$:

Standard error of estimate

$$S_{Y \cdot X} = \sqrt{\frac{\Sigma(Y - Y')^2}{n}}$$

(8.7)

$S_{Y \cdot X}$ can be thought of as the "average dispersion" of data points about the regression line. Stated more formally, $S_{Y \cdot X}$ is the standard deviation of actual Y scores about Y', the predicted value.

$S_{Y \cdot X}$ plays an important role in measuring the margin of prediction error. Let's suppose that the Fumone University sample really consists of several hundred students instead of just the 12 shown in Figure 8.1, but otherwise the results are the same as presented in Table 8.1. The data in Table 8.1 provide the basis for a regression equation that allows you to predict, or estimate, the first-year college GPA of applicants to Fumone.

Take an applicant who scored 650 on the SAT-CR. Although the regression equation predicts a first-year GPA of 2.78,[3] you would not expect this applicant to obtain exactly that GPA. As you saw earlier, the predicted value is only a "best estimate" of the mean of the distribution of GPAs for students with an SAT-CR of 650 (Figure 8.3); some of those students will obtain GPAs higher than predicted, and some lower. If you knew *how much* higher or lower, you would have a basis for attaching a "margin of error" to your prediction for this particular applicant. In short, $S_{Y \cdot X}$ provides this basis.

Although Formula (8.7) provides for important insight into the nature of the standard error of estimate, it is awkward to use in practice. You will find this equivalent formula to be decidedly more convenient:

Standard error of estimate
(alternative formula)

$$S_{Y \cdot X} = S_Y \sqrt{1 - r^2}$$

(8.8)

You can see from Formula (8.8) that the higher the correlation between X and Y, the smaller the standard error of estimate. This makes sense, given our discussion in Section 8.6: when r is low, there will be considerable variation in actual Y values about the predicted values; but when r is high, the actual values cluster more closely about the predicted values. Where $r = \pm 1.00$, there will be no variation at all about the predicted values of Y, and $S_{Y \cdot X}$ will be zero.

[3] $Y' = 1.42 + .0021(650) = 2.78$.

Setting up a Margin of Error

Let's see how to apply $S_{Y \cdot X}$ in setting up a margin of error around the predicted value of 2.78 for the applicant whose SAT-CR score is 650. Formula (8.8) can be used with the data given earlier to obtain the standard error of estimate:

$$S_{Y \cdot X} = S_Y \sqrt{1 - r^2} = .52 \sqrt{1 - (.50)^2} = .52 \sqrt{.75} = (.52)(.87) = .45$$

You now have estimates of both the mean ($Y' = 2.78$) and standard deviation ($S_{Y \cdot X} = .45$) of the distribution of GPAs for students having an SAT-CR score of 650. This distribution is assumed to be normal. You know from Chapter 6 that in a normal distribution, the middle 95% of the cases fall within ± 1.96 standard deviations of the mean.[4] Remembering that $S_{Y \cdot X}$ is a standard deviation (of prediction errors), you therefore would expect that the middle 95% of individuals having a particular X score will obtain Y scores between the limits $Y' = \pm (1.96) S_{Y \cdot X}$. For the present example these limits are:

Lower Limit	Upper Limit
$Y' - 1.96\, S_{Y \cdot X}$	$Y' + 1.96\, S_{Y \cdot X}$
$2.78 - (1.96)(.45) = 1.90$	$2.78 + (1.96)(.45) = 3.66$

The limits are shown in Figure 8.7. For 95% of the students having SAT-CR scores like this applicant's (i.e., 650), you would expect their first-year GPAs at Fumone University to fall between 1.90 and 3.66. In this sense, one can be 95% "confident" that the applicant's GPA will fall between these limits. In practical prediction, it is always desirable to include information about the margin of prediction error. Lacking this information, people often tend to think that performance is "pinpointed" by the predicted value. As our example shows, that view is wrong.

Using what is known about the normal curve, you also could determine the limits that correspond to degrees of confidence other than 95%. For 68%, they would be $Y' \pm (1.00) S_{Y \cdot X}$, and for 99%, $Y' \pm (2.58) S_{Y \cdot X}$. (Can you see from Table A in Appendix C how we got "1.00" and "2.58"?)

The Relation Between r and Prediction Error

Prediction error is at its maximum when $r = 0$, in which case we have $S_{Y \cdot X} = S_Y \sqrt{1 - 0^2} = S_Y \sqrt{1} = S_Y$. That is, when X is entirely unrelated to Y, there is as much variability in prediction error ($S_{Y \cdot X}$) as there is among the Y scores themselves (S_Y). In contrast, the minimum prediction error occurs when $r = \pm 1.00$, in which case $S_{Y \cdot X} = S_Y \sqrt{1 - 1^2} = S_Y \sqrt{0} = 0$. In this situation, of course, there is *no* error in prediction because all data points fall on the regression line.

What happens to prediction error when, say, $r = .50$? The standard error of estimate is $S_{Y \cdot X} = S_Y \sqrt{1 - .50^2} = S_Y \sqrt{.75} = .87 S_Y$. You might have guessed that a coefficient of .50 would mean that prediction error would be reduced by *half*,

---

[4]In case a quick refresher is needed, revisit Problem 8 in Chapter 6.

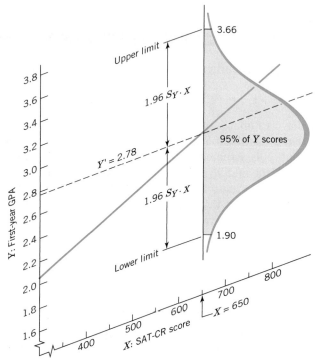

Figure 8.7   95% limits for actual GPAs where $X = 650$.

but in fact it is $.87S_Y$, not $.50S_Y$. If 87% of prediction error remains, then a reduction of only 13% has taken place in going from $r = 0$ to $r = .50$. Table 8.2 presents several values of r, together with the consequences of each for reducing prediction error. This table offers another way, in addition to those described in Section 7.8, of evaluating correlation coefficients of various sizes. If your purpose is prediction, bear in mind that no substantial reduction in prediction error will be achieved unless r is quite high. Table 8.2 also shows that increasing the correlation by any given amount has a more substantial effect for higher values of r than for lower ones.

Table 8.2   Reductions in Prediction Error for Various Values of r

r	Reduction in Prediction Error (%)
1.00	100
.75	34
.50	13
.25	3
.00	0

Assumptions

Several conditions must be met for predictive interpretations of the kind described above to work well:

1. The relationship between the independent variable, X, and the dependent variable, Y, must be essentially linear. One is predicting from the *straight* line of best fit, and those predictions will be off if the relationship is markedly curvilinear.

2. Determining the margin of error requires that the spread of obtained values of Y about Y' be similar for all values of Y'. This requirement is known as the **assumption of homoscedasticity**. Since the value of $S_{Y \cdot X}$ is a single value, determined from the data as a whole, it does not allow for the possibility that variation might be different at different points in the distribution. Figure 8.8 shows two bivariate distributions; one is characterized by homoscedasticity, and the other is not. (Not surprisingly, the term *hetero*scedasticity is used in reference to the latter condition.)

3. The limits of error described above (68%, 95%, 99%) are based on the assumption that Y values are *normally* distributed about Y'.

Fortunately, these assumptions often are close enough to being met that Y' and $S_{Y \cdot X}$ are reasonably accurate. *Significant departures from any one of these conditions can usually be detected by inspecting the scatterplot.* This is yet another reason to plot your data!

We mention one last matter before proceeding: sampling variation. The regression line is determined by the paired values *in a particular sample*. A different selection of participants will produce a similar, *but not identical*, result. A regression line determined from a small sample (like our n of 12) may therefore be rather different from the "true" regression line. There are more complex

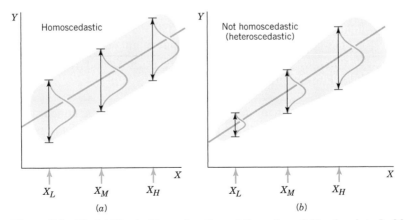

Figure 8.8   Variability in Y as a function of the value of X: subscripts L, M, and H represent low, medium, and high, respectively.

procedures for computing error limits that take sampling variation into account. You are wise to count on the procedures we have described here only when sample size is at least 100.

8.9   *Correlation and Causality (Revisited)*

The dictum that *correlation does not imply causation*, which we introduced in the last chapter (Section 7.6), is just as relevant to the topic of regression and prediction. Arguably more so. Even the seasoned researcher sometimes loses sight of this important principle when surrounded by the language of regression, rich in its causal references: the "*dependent*" variable, which is "*predicted*" from another variable, which "*explains*" variation in the former.

> Never forget that behind every regression equation is a measure of *association* (*r*).

Although *Y* may follow *X* in time (as in our example of college GPA and SAT-CR scores), it is a logical fallacy to conclude that *Y* therefore is caused by *X* when an association between the two is found. Logicians often cite the Latin expression of this fallacy: *post hoc, ergo propter hoc*, or, "after this, therefore because of this."

Consider the negative correlation between how much parents help their children with homework (*X*) and student achievement (*Y*), which we presented as an exercise problem at the end of Chapter 7. You would be committing the **post hoc fallacy**, as it is more conveniently known, if you had reasoned as follows:

- Parents provide some amount of homework assistance to their kids.
- These kids later take an achievement test.
- Homework assistance and achievement scores correlate negatively.
- Therefore, homework assistance must be undermining achievement.

Equally consistent with this negative correlation is the conclusion that parents provide homework assistance *only when their children are doing poorly in school*. Even though the achievement test was given after the parents provided (or didn't provide) homework assistance, kids who did poorly on the test probably were doing poorly in school all along. And when kids do poorly, parents are more likely to assist with the homework. We don't know if our interpretation of this negative correlation is correct, mind you, for only a controlled experiment can disentangle cause and effect. Nevertheless, be careful when drawing conclusions from correlational data, and be critical of the conclusions drawn by others.

8.10   Summary

The equation of the straight line of best fit, $Y' = a + bX$, is used to predict Y from knowledge of X when it can be assumed that the relationship is a linear one. The criterion of "best fit" is that the sum of squares of prediction errors, $\Sigma(Y-Y')^2$, is minimized. Among other things, this "least-squares criterion" means that the resulting regression line can be considered a "running mean," a line that estimates the mean of Y for particular values of X.

The z-score formula for the regression equation reveals several characteristics of regression, including the phenomenon of regression toward the mean. In practical prediction work, the raw-score formula is easier to use.

The predicted value of Y, Y', is but an estimated mean value and is therefore subject to error. On the assumption of linearity of regression and homoscedasticity, the standard error of estimate $S_{Y \cdot X}$—the standard deviation of prediction errors—provides a good measure of prediction error. When it is also possible to assume that the actual scores are normally distributed about Y', it is possible to establish known limits of prediction error about the regression line. The method described in this chapter will be reasonably accurate for large samples ($n \geqslant 100$).

You learned in Chapter 7 that strength of association is not ordinarily interpretable in direct proportion to the magnitude of the correlation coefficient. This is true for the relation between size of the coefficient (r) and magnitude of prediction error ($S_{Y \cdot X}$). As r rises from zero toward one, the standard error of estimate decreases very slowly until r is well above .50.

Finally, regression and prediction do not permit conclusions regarding cause and effect. Just because Y can be predicted from X does not mean that Y is caused by X.

Reading the Research: Regression

Bolon (2001) conducted a regression analysis to show the predictive relationship between community income and mathematics tests scores in Boston-area schools. In the analysis we illustrate here, there were two pieces of data for each school: (a) the per capita income in the school community and (b) the school mean on the tenth-grade mathematics component of the Massachusetts Comprehensive Assessment System (the state test). The predictive relationship between these two variables is illustrated in Figure 8.9 (Bolon, 2001, Figure 2–6). The regression line is superimposed and is defined by the equation $Y' = 197.4 + 1.45(X)$, where Y' is the school's predicted mathematics test score and X is the school community's per capita income.

Each data point in Figure 8.9 represents a different school. As you see, the majority of schools fall close to the regression line, which indicates that there is little unexplained variation in the dependent variable (test scores). In fact, Bolon reports that $r^2 = .84$. That is, a full 84% of the variance in school-level mathematics scores is explained by variation in community income. (From this, we also can determine that $r = .92$.) The raw score slope, $b = 1.45$, means that test scores increase roughly 1½ points with every $1000 in per capita income.

Source: Bolon, C. (2001, October 16). Significance of test-based ratings for metropolitan Boston schools. *Education Policy Analysis Archives, 9*(42). Retrieved [November 10, 2001] from http://epaa.asu.edu/epaa/v9n42/.

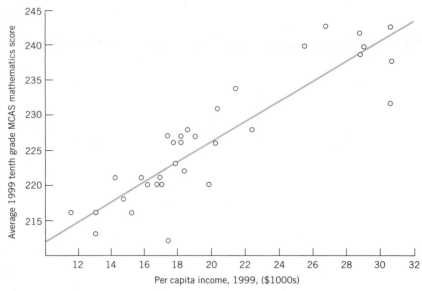

Figure 8.9 Predicting school-level mathematics scores from community income.

Case Study: Regression—It's on the Money

Recall the Chapter 7 case study, where we found negative correlations between the proficiency percentage in a school district—that is, the percentage of students in the district who score at or above the proficient level—and the percentage of students in the district who qualify for free or reduced-priced lunch: $r = -.61$ for MATH and $r = -.66$ for READ. Thus, one would expect wealthier districts to generally have a higher proficiency percentage than their less fortunate counterparts, in part because of reasons beyond the direct control of the district (e.g., more highly educated parents, more college-bound students, larger tax base). As a result, a state sometimes will report a district's proficiency percentage (or mean score) within the context of a "comparison band" involving socioeconomically similar districts. In this sense, a district's achievement is evaluated not only in absolute terms, but also in relation to the range of scores that would be expected among districts of similar socioeconomic status (SES).

Let's use fourth-grade reading as an example. What *is* the "expected" proficiency percentage in a school district with, say, 70% of its students eligible for free or reduced-priced lunch? To answer this question, we began by determining the predictive relationship between the percentage of students in a district who are eligible for free or reduced-priced lunch (LUNCH) and the percentage of students in the district who score at or above the proficient level on the state reading exam

(READ).[5] Using computer software, we regressed READ on LUNCH for the 253 districts in our data set. Having inspected the corresponding scatterplot (Figure 8.10) to check for evidence of nonlinearity and heteroscedasticity, we then turned to the regression equation itself. You learned in Section 8.3 that the raw score regression equation takes the form $Y' = a + bX$. In the present case, Y is READ (the dependent variable) and X is LUNCH (the independent variable). We obtained $a = 81.58$ for the intercept and $b = -.49$ for the slope. Thus, our regression equation is READ$' = 81.58 - .49$(LUNCH). We have superimposed this "line of best fit" in Figure 8.10.

Recall from Section 8.4 that "for each unit increase in X, Y changes b units." Therefore, our raw slope ($b = -.49$) tells us that for each additional 1% of students qualifying for free or reduced-price lunch (a unit increase in LUNCH), the percentage of students who are proficient decreases by roughly half a percentage point (a change of $-.49$ units in READ).

More to our present point, however, this regression equation is used to determine the predicted value of READ for a given value of LUNCH. For example, a district with 70% of its students eligible for free or reduced-price lunch (LUNCH = 70) would have a predicted READ of $a + bX = 81.58 + (-.49)(70) = 81.58 - 34.30 = 47.28$. That is, we would expect, on average, that a district with this SES level would have roughly 47% of its students scoring proficient (or above) in reading. To obtain the desired comparison band, we used the standard error of estimate ($S_{Y \cdot X}$) to establish a 95% margin of error for each value of LUNCH. From our computer output, we were informed that $S_{Y \cdot X} = 11.24$. For LUNCH = 70, the 95%

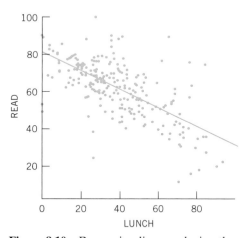

Figure 8.10 Regression line overlaying the scatterplot of READ and LUNCH.

[5]For the purpose of this case study, we will use LUNCH as an indicator of SES. If more data were available, we would include additional variables in our indicator, such as the general level of education and income in the district's community.

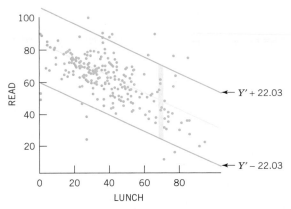

Figure 8.11   95% margin of error for predicting READ from LUNCH with shaded comparison band shown for LUNCH = 70.

margin of error is $Y' = \pm (1.96)(S_{Y \cdot X}) = 47.28 \pm (1.96)(11.24) = 47.28 \pm 22.03 = 25.25$ to 69.31. This is the range of READ values that, theoretically, would capture 95% of all districts having a LUNCH value of 70. Thus, a district with 70% of its students eligible for free or reduced-priced lunch would be expected to have between 25% and 69% of its students scoring proficient or above on the state reading exam.

Such a range can be established for any value of LUNCH, as Figure 8.11 illustrates. School districts that fall outside of these error limits are considered to be performing either markedly worse or markedly better than expected, given their SES composition. Again, a district's achievement is examined *relative to districts of comparable SES.*

Consider Districts A and B, both of which have LUNCH values of approximately 70%. As Figure 8.12 shows, the proficiency percentage for District A (45%) is pretty much what one would expect among districts having this SES level, whereas the proficiency percentage for District B (11%) falls below the expected range. Although low in an absolute sense, the achievement of District B—unlike District A—also is low *relative to similarly impoverished schools.*

Now consider the case of District C, where only one-quarter of the students are eligible for free or reduced-price lunch. The proficiency percentage for this district is almost identical to District A (47% vs. 45%), but the District C proficiency percentage falls below its comparison band. Although District A and District C are comparable in absolute terms (their proficiency percentages are similar), District A's performance is more impressive *relative to expectation.* Because of the advantages that higher-SES districts generally enjoy, one would expect from District C a higher reading proficiency than what was achieved by this district.

Finally, consider District D, where 40% of the students are eligible for free or reduced-price lunch. To be sure, the proficiency percentage for this district (89%) is high in absolute terms. Moreover, this district's performance is high relative to

District A (LUNCH = 70):

District B (LUNCH = 70):

District C (LUNCH = 25):

District D (LUNCH = 40):

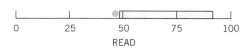

Figure 8.12 READ values presented for four districts, with SES comparison bands.

socioeconomically similar districts. Indeed, the proficiency percentage of District D falls above its comparison band.

Suggested Computer Exercises

Access the **sophomores** data file.

1. Regress READ scores on CGPA.

   (a) Using the regression output, derive the raw-score regression equation that will allow you to predict a READ score for a given value of CGPA. Provide this equation in the form $Y' = a + bX$.

   (b) What proportion of the variance in READ scores is explained by the variance in CGPA? What proportion remains unexplained?

   (c) Use the regression equation to predict a READ score for a student who has a grade-point average of 3.00.

   (d) Construct a 95% margin of error for your answer to (c) and provide a brief interpretation.

Exercises

Identify, Define, or Explain

Terms and Concepts

prediction
correlation and prediction
regression line
prediction error
line of best fit
independent variable
dependent variable
predicted score
error sum of squares
least-squares criterion
regression equation

slope
intercept
regression toward the mean
total variation
total sum of squares
explained variation
unexplained variation
standard error of estimate
assumption of homoscedasticity
post hoc fallacy

Symbols

Y' b a z_X z_Y $z_{Y'}$ $s_{Y \cdot X}$

Questions and Problems

Note: Answers to starred (*) items are presented in Appendix B.

*1.   The scatterplot and least-squares regression line for predicting Y from X is given in the figure below for the following pairs of scores from a pretest and posttest:

	Keith	**Bill**	**Charlie**	**Brian**	**Mick**
Pretest (X)	8	9	4	2	2
Posttest (Y)	10	6	8	5	1

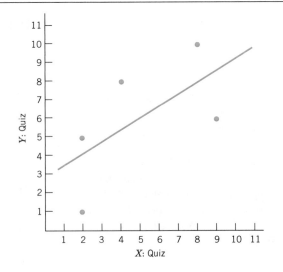

(a) Use a straightedge with the regression line to estimate (to one decimal place) the predicted Y score (Y') of each student.

(b) Use the answers from Problem 1a to determine the error in prediction for each student.

(c) Use the answers from Problem 1b to compute the error sum of squares.

(d) If any other line were used for prediction, how would the error sum of squares compare with your answer to Problem 1c?

2. The relationship between student performance on a state-mandated test administered in the fourth grade and again in the eighth grade has been analyzed for a large group of students in the state. Ellen obtains a score of 540 on the fourth-grade test. From this, her performance on the eighth-grade test is predicted (using the regression line) to be 550.

(a) In what sense can the value 550 be considered an estimated mean?

(b) Why is it an estimated rather than an actual mean?

*3. A physical education teacher, as part of a master's thesis, obtained data on a sizable sample of males for whom heights both at age 10 and as adults were known. The following are the summary statistics for this sample:

Height at Age 10	Adult Height
$\bar{X} = 48.3$	$\bar{Y} = 67.3$
$S_X = 3.1$	$S_Y = 4.1$
$r = +.71$	

(a) Use the values above to compute intercept and slope for predicting adult height from height at age 10 (round to the second decimal place); state the regression equation, using the form of Formula (8.1).

(b) With this regression equation, predict the adult height for the following 10-year-olds: Jean P. (42.5 in.), Albert B. (55.3 in.), and Burrhus S. (50.1 in.).

(c) Consider Jean's predicted adult height. In what sense is that value a mean?

*4. The following are the summary statistics for the scores given in Problem 1:

$$\bar{X} = 5.00, \quad S_X = 2.97, \quad \bar{Y} = 6.00, \quad S_Y = 3.03, \quad r = +.62$$

(a) From these values, compute intercept and slope for the regression equation; state the regression equation.

(b) Obtain predicted scores for Keith, Bill, Charlie, Brian, and Mick. Compare your answers with those obtained in Problem 1a; explain any discrepancies.

(c) Compute the mean of the predicted scores and compare with the summary statistics above. What important generalization (within the limits of rounding error) emerges from this comparison?

(d) Compute the sum of the prediction errors for these five individuals, and state the generalization that this sum illustrates (within the limits of rounding error).

*5. Interpret the slope from Problems 3 and 4.

6. Following are the scores on a teacher certification test administered prior to hiring (X) and the principal's ratings of teacher effectiveness after three months on the job (Y) for a group of six first-year teachers (A–F):

	A	B	C	D	E	F
Test score (X):	14	24	21	38	34	49
Principal rating (Y):	7	4	10	8	13	11

    (a) Compute the summary statistics required for determining the regression equation for predicting principal ratings from teacher certification test scores.

    (b) Using values from Problem 6a, calculate the intercept and slope; state the regression equation.

    (c) Suppose that three teachers apply for positions in this school, obtaining scores of 18, 32, and 42, respectively, on the teacher certification test. Compute their predicted ratings of teacher effectiveness.

    (d) If in fact these data were real, what objections would you have to using the equation from Problem 6b for prediction in a real-life situation?

7. Suppose X in Problem 6 were changed so that there is absolutely no relationship between test scores and principal ratings ($r = 0$).

    (a) What would be the predicted rating for each of the three applicants? (Explain.)

    (b) What would be the intercept and slope of the regression equation for predicting principal ratings from test scores (again, if $r = 0$)?

8. **(a)** On an $8\frac{1}{2}'' \times 11''$ piece of graph paper, construct a scatterplot for the data of Problem 6. Mark off divisions on the two axes so that the plot will be as large as possible and as close to square as possible. Plot the data points accordingly, and draw in the regression line as described in Section 8.3.

    (b) Using a straightedge with the regression line, estimate (accurate to one decimal place) the predicted principal ratings for the three applicants in Problem 6c. Compare these values with the Y' values you calculated earlier from the regression equation.

*9. Gayle falls one standard deviation above the mean of X. What is the correlation between X and Y if her predicted score on Y falls:

    (a) one standard deviation above?

    (b) one-third of a standard deviation below?

    (c) three-quarters of a standard deviation above?

    (d) one-fifth of a standard deviation below?

10. For each condition in Problem 9, state the regression equation in z-score form.

*11. Consider the situation described in Problem 3.

    (a) Convert to z scores the 10-year-old heights of Jean, Albert, and Burrhus.

    (b) Use the standard-score form of the regression equation to obtain their predicted z scores for height as adults.

    (c) Convert the predicted z scores from Problem 11b back to predicted heights in inches and compare with the results of Problem 3b.

12. (No calculations are necessary for this problem.) Suppose the following summary statistics are obtained from a large group of individuals: $\bar{X} = 52.0$, $S_X = 8.7$, $\bar{Y} = 147.3$, $S_Y = 16.9$. Dorothy receives an X score of 52. What is her predicted Y score if:

    (a) $r = 0$?

    (b) $r = -.55$?

    (c) $r = +.38$?

    (d) $r = -1.00$?

    (e) State the principle that emerges from your answers to Problems 12a to 12d.

    (f) Show how Formula (8.5) illustrates this principle.

*13. The following data are for first-year students at Ecalpon Tech:

Aptitude Score	First-year GPA
$\bar{X} = 560.00$	$\bar{Y} = 2.65$
$S_X = 75.00$	$S_Y = .35$
$r = +.50$	

    (a) Calculate the raw-score intercept and slope; state the regression equation.

    (b) Val and Mike score 485 and 710, respectively, on the aptitude test. Predict their first-year GPAs.

    (c) Compute the standard error of estimate.

    (d) Set up the 95% confidence limits around Val's and Mike's predicted GPAs.

    (e) For students with aptitude scores the same as Val's, what proportion would you expect to obtain a GPA better than the first-year mean?

    (f) For students with aptitude scores the same as Val's, what proportion would be expected to obtain a GPA of 2.0 or below?

    (g) For students with aptitude scores the same as Mike's, what proportion would be expected to obtain a GPA of 2.5 or better?

14. **(a)** What assumption(s) underlie the procedure used to answer Problem 13b?

    (b) Explain the role of each assumption underlying the procedures used to answer Problems 13d–13g.

    (c) What is an excellent way to check and see whether the assumptions are being appreciably violated?

15. Consider the situation described in Problem 13. By embarking on a new but *very expensive* testing program, Ecalpon Tech can improve the correlation between the aptitude score and GPA to $r = +.55$. Suppose the primary concern is the accuracy with which GPAs of individuals can be predicted. Would the new testing program be worth it? Perform the calculations necessary to support your answer.

16. At the end of Section 8.3, we asked you to consider how the location of Student 26 would affect the placement of the regression line in Figure 8.4.

    (a) Imagine you deleted this case, recalculated intercept and slope, and drew in the new regression line. Where do you think the new line would lie relative to the original regression line? Why? (Refer to the least-squares criterion.)

(b) How should the removal of Student 26 affect the magnitude of the intercept? the slope?

(c) With Student 26 removed, the relevant summary statistics are $\overline{X} = 69.45$, $S_X = 9.68$, $\overline{Y} = 100.83$, $S_Y = 14.38$, $r = .79$. Calculate the new intercept and slope.

(d) As accurately as possible, draw in the new regression line using the figure below (from which Student 26 has been deleted). How does the result compare with your response to Problems 16a and 16b?

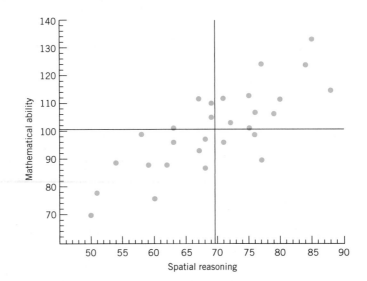

17. At the end of the section on "setting up the margin of error," we asked if you can see from Table A in Appendix C how we got "1.00" and "2.58" for 68% and 99% confidence, respectively. Can you?

PART 2

Inferential Statistics

CHAPTER 9

Probability and Probability Distributions

9.1 Statistical Inference: Accounting for Chance in Sample Results

Suppose the superintendent of your local school district decides to survey taxpayers to see how they feel about renovating the high school, which would be a costly project. From a random sample of 100 taxpayers, the superintendent finds that 70 are in favor of the renovation and the remainder are not. Can the superintendent conclude from these results that 70% of *all* taxpayers favor the renovation? Not necessarily. Random sampling is essentially a lottery-type procedure, where chance factors dictate who is to be included in the sample. Consequently, the percentages that characterize the **sample** of 100 taxpayers are likely to differ somewhat from what characterizes the **population** of all taxpayers in this district. The sample figure of 70% should be close, but you wouldn't expect it to be identical. Therefore, before placing much faith in the observed 70%, it would be important to know how accurate this figure might be. Is it likely to be within one or two percentage points of the true value for the entire population? Or perhaps by chance alone, did this sample overrepresent taxpayers sympathetic to the proposed renovation, thus throwing off the results?

Consider the case of Professor Sartor, who is conducting an experiment on the effects of "test familiarity" on the performance of students on the fourth-grade state achievement test. Using a sample of 50 fourth graders, she randomly forms two groups: an experimental group ($n = 25$) that receives an overview of basic information concerning this test (length, structure, types of questions, and so on), and a control group ($n = 25$) that receives no overview. These students then take the state test during its regular administration. Professor Sartor finds that the performance of experimental-group students, on average, is higher than that of control-group students: $\overline{X}_E = 135$ and $\overline{X}_C = 115$, which she determines is equivalent to an effect size of .25 standard deviations. Should she conclude from these results that test familiarity does in fact improve test performance, at least as examined in this experiment?

Not necessarily. The two groups were formed by "the luck of the draw," and it could be that test familiarity has no effect at all. Just by chance, perhaps more of the "smarter" students ended up in the experimental group than in the control group. If so, Professor Sartor would not expect similar results if the experiment were conducted on a new sample of fourth graders. Certainly she would want to have a strong case for eliminating the possibility of chance before concluding that test familiarity improves test performance.

Both of these examples illustrate the following fundamental principle:

> Chance factors inherent in forming samples always affect sample results, and sample results must be interpreted with this in mind.

Over many years, a variety of techniques and associated theory for dealing with such **sampling variation** have been developed. Consequently, the "error" caused by chance factors can be taken into account when conclusions are drawn about the "true" state of affairs from an examination of sample results. These techniques and the associated theory make up what is commonly referred to as **statistical inference**.

In the parent survey, the superintendent wishes to *infer* the percentage of local taxpayers that would favor the construction of a new high school, based on the opinions of only a subset of taxpayers. In her test-familiarity study, Professor Sartor would like to *infer* what the effect of such familiarity would be, had she tested its efficacy not on just this particular sample, but on many samples of this kind. Hence the name statistical *inference*: in both cases, the problem is to infer what characteristics would remain if the variation due to "the luck of the draw"—sampling variation—were eliminated.

The key to solving problems of statistical inference is to answer the question, *What kind of sample results can be expected on the basis of chance alone*? When samples are selected in a way that allows chance to operate fully, the techniques of statistical inference can provide the answer. Chance is usually examined in terms of probability—the likelihood of a particular event occurring—and the framework for studying chance and its effects is known as **probability theory**. In fact, the procedures of statistical inference that we present in subsequent chapters are nothing more than applications of the laws of probability.

The study of probability can be quite extensive and challenging, as you can quickly see by perusing the probability chapters in any number of statistics textbooks. Our view is that the propositions you need to know to get on with statistical inference are both basic and easily understood. In some cases, these propositions merely formalize what you already know intuitively. In other cases, we will ask you to think in ways that you may not have thought before. In all cases, however, you should find nothing in this material that falls beyond your reach. Bear in mind that if you understand the subject of probability well, the rest of statistical inference will fall into place much more easily.

9.2   *Probability: The Study of Chance*

It is easy to lose sight of the degree to which probabilistic reasoning is used in everyday life. We all live in a world of considerable uncertainty. To make good decisions and function effectively, you must distinguish among events that are likely to occur, those that are not, and those that are in between in likelihood. For example, you carry an umbrella on mornings when the skies are dark and rain is forecast, but you may decide not to lug it around if the morning sky doesn't look particularly ominous and only a 20% chance of rain is reported. You go to class on the assumption that the instructor will show up; you don't drink from a stream because of the possibility that the water will make you ill; and you step into an elevator with strangers on the assumption that they will not assault you. It would seem that practically all decisions involve estimates, conscious or otherwise, of the probability of various events occurring.

In these examples, the probability estimates are *subjective* and consist of little more than general feelings about how likely something is to occur. To build a foundation for statistical inference, however, it is necessary to treat probability in a more objective and precise fashion.

9.3   *Definition of Probability*

You doubtless already have an intuitive feel for how probability works. What is the probability of flipping a coin once and getting heads? Easy, you say: 50/50, or .50. Why? Because (you continue) there are only two possible outcomes when flipping a coin—heads or tails—and one outcome is no more likely than the other. The probability of either, then, is the same and equal to .50. Furthermore, unless you are the object of some cruel hoax, you are unshakable in your certainty that either heads or tails *must* occur (probability of 1.00), just as you are firm in your conviction that it is impossible for both outcomes to occur simultaneously (probability of 0).

Let's build on this understanding. What is meant, in more objective terms, by the probability that a particular **event** will occur? For instance, what is the probability of obtaining a diamond upon drawing a single card from a well-shuffled deck? Consider repeating the exact set of circumstances many, many times: drawing a card from a well-shuffled deck, replacing the card, and reshuffling the deck; drawing a second card, replacing it, and reshuffling; drawing a third card, and so on. The probability of the event—obtaining a diamond—is the proportion of times you would expect to obtain a diamond over the long run if you drew a card many, many times. We will refer to each repetition of the situation—in this case the draw of a card—as a **sampling experiment**.

> The probability of an event is the proportion of times that the event would be expected to occur in an infinitely long series of identical sampling experiments.

In this case, the probability of the event "diamond" is .25. How did we arrive at .25? Obviously not by spending an eternity drawing card after card from a well-shuffled deck! Instead, we used our knowledge that a standard deck contains 13

Table 9.1   Relative Frequency
Distribution of Suits

Suit	f	Relative Frequency
Diamond	13	.25
Heart	13	.25
Club	13	.25
Spade	13	.25
	52	1.00

cards in each of four suits—diamonds, hearts, clubs, and spades—for a total of 52 cards. This knowledge is represented in the relative frequency distribution in Table 9.1. With the assumption that each of the 52 possibilities, or **outcomes**, is equally likely, it is reasonable to expect that a diamond would be selected 25% of the time over the long run: $13/52 = 1/4 = .25$ (or 25%). This illustrates the basic rule for obtaining probabilities in situations where each of the possible outcomes is equally likely:

> If all possible outcomes are equally likely, the probability of the occurrence of an event is equal to the proportion of the possible outcomes favoring the event.

In this case, 13, or .25, of the 52 possible outcomes favor the event "diamond." This rule, of course, also can be applied to the single toss of a coin: one of the two possible outcomes favors the event "heads," and, hence, the probability of obtaining heads is 1/2, or .50.

A probability, then, is a proportion and, as such, is a number between 0 (pigs flying) and 1.00 (death and taxes). It is symbolized by p. Probabilities are usually expressed as decimal fractions (e.g., $p = .25$), although it is sometimes convenient to leave them in ratio form (e.g., $p = 1/4$).

Table 9.1 is a *theoretical* distribution insofar as it is based on what is known about a standard deck of cards. Let's look at an example involving an *empirical* distribution—one based on actual data. Suppose that Dr. Geroski's undergraduate class in introductory psychology has 200 students and that, at the end, she assigns course grades as shown in Table 9.2. If you were to select at random a student from the class, what is the probability that the student will have obtained a grade of B? Or, in terms of our definition, what proportion of times would you expect to obtain a B student over the long run if you selected a student at random from the class, replaced him or her, selected a student at random again, and repeated this process for an unlimited series of sampling experiments? The answer is $p = .30$, since 60 of the 200 equally likely outcomes are characterized by the event B (i.e., relative frequency $= 60/200 = .30$).

Table 9.2   Relative Frequency
Distribution of Grades

Grade	f	Relative Frequency
A	30	.15
B	60	.30
C	80	.40
D	20	.10
F	10	.05
	200	1.00

9.4   Probability Distributions

The relative frequency distributions in Tables 9.1 and 9.2 each can be considered to be **probability distributions**. Each distribution shows all possible outcomes (cards or students) and identifies the event (suit or letter grade) characterizing each outcome. The relative frequencies allow you to state the probability of randomly selecting a card of a particular suit, or a student with a particular grade. *Any relative frequency distribution may be interpreted as a probability distribution.*

As you can see, it is easy to answer a probability question when you know the appropriate probability distribution. And this is equally true with statistical inference, which will become increasingly apparent as you move through subsequent chapters.

> The ability to make statistical inferences is based on knowledge of the probability distribution appropriate to the situation.

Let's return to the familiar case of tossing a coin and explore further the nature of probability and probability distributions, as well as the kinds of questions that can be asked of each. Suppose you toss the coin *four* times. What is the probability of obtaining no heads at all? two heads? three heads? four heads? As with the deck of cards, you need not toss a coin four times over an infinite number of sampling experiments to answer such questions! Rather, because the behavior of an unbiased coin is known—that is, $p_{heads} = p_{tails} = .50$—the **theoretical probability distribution** associated with tossing a coin four times is known. It is known from a mathematical model, called the binomial expansion, which is appropriate for dichotomous (two-value) variables such as heads/tails, correct/incorrect, or present/absent.

When applied to the case of tossing a coin four times where $p_{heads} = p_{tails} = .50$, the binomial expansion identifies the theoretical probability distribution in Table 9.3. The first column in this table shows that five possible *events* are associated with tossing a coin four times: you can obtain no heads, one head, two heads, three heads, or four heads. If n stands for the number of tosses (4), then the number of possible

Table 9.3   The Probability of Tossing a Coin Four Times: 16 Outcomes Distributed Across Five Events

Event: Number of Heads	f	Relative Frequency
0	1	.0625
1	4	.2500
2	6	.3750
3	4	.2500
4	1	.0625
	16	1.0000

events is equal to $n + 1 = 5$. The frequency (f) column reports the number of *outcomes* associated with a particular event, or, stated less formally, the number of different ways the event can occur. The total number of different outcomes is 16.

The distribution of these 16 outcomes across the five events shows that some events are considerably more likely than others. For example, there is only one way of obtaining no heads at all—getting tails on each of the four tosses (i.e., T,T,T,T)—so the probability of the event "0 heads" is $p_{0heads} = 1/16 = .0625$. In other words, over many, many sampling experiments where $n = 4$, you would expect to obtain no heads (i.e., all tails) only about 6% of the time. In contrast, there are six different ways of obtaining two heads: getting two heads and then two tails (H,H,T,T), getting two tails and then two heads (T,T,H,H), and so on. The probability of the event "two heads," then, is $p_{2heads} = 6/16 = .375$. That is, across many sampling experiments of $n = 4$, you would expect to get two heads about 37% of the time. Common sense has long told you that, if you toss a coin four times, you are more likely to obtain two heads than no heads; but the underlying probability distribution clarifies why—there simply are more ways to obtain two heads than no heads.

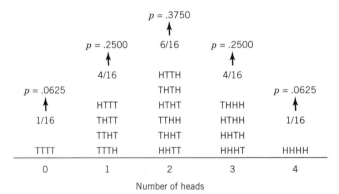

Figure 9.1   The probability distribution of tossing a coin four times: 16 outcomes distributed across 5 events.

Figure 9.1 presents this probability distribution as a histogram, which more vividly displays its underlying shape. Here, the horizontal axis represents the five possible events, and the height of each column corresponds to the number of outcomes associated with the event. We have inserted the actual outcomes (e.g., T,T,T,T) for illustrative purposes. The relative frequency, or probability, of the event appears above each column of outcomes. For instance, Figure 9.1 shows all four outcomes associated with the event, "3 heads," the probability of which is equal to $4/16 = .25$.

9.5 The OR/addition Rule

Our focus so far has been on single events in isolation. You also can ask about the probability of two or more events together. For instance, what is the probability of obtaining no heads *or* four heads upon flipping a coin four times? To obtain the total probability for the occurrence of one event *or* the other, simply add the two separate probabilities indicated in Figure 9.1: $p_{0\text{heads }\underline{\text{or}}\text{ 4heads}} = .0625 + .0625 = .125$. Adding the probabilities of separate events to obtain an overall probability, as in this example, illustrates a useful principle we will call the **OR/addition rule**.

> The probability of occurrence of either one event OR another OR another OR ... is obtained by adding their individual probabilities, provided the events are mutually exclusive.

We must emphasize that the rule as stated applies only to **mutually exclusive events**. That is, if any one of the events occurs, the remaining events cannot occur. For instance, upon tossing a coin four times, you obviously cannot obtain *both* one head and three tails *and* two heads and two tails. This simple stipulation can be easily forgotten in practice, as in the case of the television weather forecaster who, because there was a 50% chance of rain for both Saturday and Sunday, announced that there was 100% chance of rain for the coming weekend (Paulos, 1988, p. 4).

Our example above—the probability of obtaining no heads *or* four heads—is a rather straightforward application of the OR/addition rule. The language of probability typically is more subtle. Let's consider several examples, staying with the probability distribution shown in Figure 9.1.

❶ What is the probability of obtaining *at least three heads*?
The condition of "at least three heads" is satisfied if you obtain *either* three heads *or* four heads. The probability of obtaining at least three heads is therefore $p_{3\text{heads}} + p_{4\text{heads}} = .25 + .0625 = .3125$.

❷ What is the probability of obtaining *no more than one head*?
The reasoning is similar here, although now you are on the other side of the probability distribution. Because *either* no heads *or* one head satisfies this condition, the probability of obtaining no more than one head is $p_{0\text{heads}} + p_{1\text{head}} = .0625 + .25 = .3125$.

❸ What is the probability of an event *as rare as four heads*?

To determine this probability, first you must acknowledge that obtaining *four* heads is just as "rare" as obtaining *no* heads, as the symmetry of Figure 9.1 testifies. Thus, *both sides* of the probability distribution are implicated by the language of this question, and, consequently, you must add the separate probabilities. The probability of an event as rare as four heads is $p_{0heads} + p_{4heads} = .0625 + .0625 + .125$.

❹ What is the probability of an event *as extreme as three heads*?

This question similarly involves both sides of the probability distribution, insofar as no heads is just as "extreme" as four heads, and one head is just as extreme as three heads. (That is, "as rare as" and "as extreme as" are synonymous.) The probability of an event as extreme as three heads is $p_{0heads} + p_{1head} + p_{3heads} + p_{4heads} = .0625 + .25 + .25 + .0625 = .625$.

One-Tailed versus Two-Tailed Probabilities

These four examples illustrate an important distinction in probability. When determined from only one side of the probability distribution, the probability is said to be a **one-tailed probability**, as in ❶ and ❷. But as you saw in ❸ and ❹, the appropriate probability sometimes calls on *both* sides of the probability distribution. In these situations, the probability is said to be a **two-tailed probability**.[1]

The relevance of this distinction goes well beyond tossing coins. As you will learn in chapters to come, the nature of one's research question determines whether a one-tailed or a two-tailed probability is called for.

9.6   *The AND/multiplication Rule*

The **AND/multiplication rule** is applied when you are concerned with the joint occurrence of one event *and* another, rather than one *or* the other. Here, the separate probabilities are *multiplied* rather than added.

You already know, for example, that the probability of tossing a coin four times and obtaining four heads is $p_{H,H,H,H} = .0625$. Slightly rephrased, this is the probability of obtaining heads on the first toss *and* on the second toss *and* on the third toss *and* on the final toss. Since $p(\text{heads}) = .50$ for each toss, the probability of obtaining heads on every toss is $.50 \times .50 \times .50 \times .50 = .0625$.

> The probability of the joint occurrence of one event AND another AND another AND ... is obtained by multiplying their separate probabilities, provided the events are independent.

---

[1]You may also encounter the equivalent distinction, "one-sided" versus "two-sided" probability.

Note that the AND/multiplication rule applies only in the case of **independent events**. Two events are independent if the probability of occurrence of one remains exactly the same regardless of whether the other event has occurred. For instance, obtaining heads on the first toss has no bearing on whether heads is obtained on a subsequent toss.

As another example of the AND/multiplication rule, consider a pop quiz comprising five multiple-choice items, each item having four options. What is the probability that an ill-prepared student will randomly guess the correct answer on all five questions? For any one question, the probability of guessing correctly is $1/4 = .25$. Therefore, the probability of guessing correctly on the first question *and* the second question *and* (etc.) is $.25 \times .25 \times .25 \times .25 \times .25 = .001$. This is unlikely indeed. (To appreciate just how unlikely this event is, imagine the theoretical student who must endure an eternity of five-item pop quizzes, guessing blindly each time. A probability of .001 means that this poor soul would be expected to get all five items correct on only 1 out of every 1000 quizzes!)

Where Both Rules Apply

Sometimes *both* the OR/addition and AND/multiplication rules are needed to determine the probability of an event. There are many examples, some of which go beyond the scope of this book. But you already have encountered one case in which both rules operate, even though we did not present it in this light: the probability of an event that has more than one outcome associated with it. For example, you know from Figure 9.1 that there are four outcomes associated with the event "three heads" and that, consequently, $p_{3heads} = 4/16 = .25$. Within the context of the OR/addition and AND/multiplication rules, you can recast this probability as involving two steps:

Step 1 *Determine the separate probability for each of the four outcomes.*
The AND/multiplication rule is needed here. For example, $p_{H,H,H,T}$ is the probability of obtaining heads on the first toss *and* heads on the second toss *and* heads on the third toss *and* tails on the fourth toss. Because $p_{heads} = p_{tails} = .50$ for each toss, $p_{H,H,H,T} = .50 \times .50 \times .50 \times .50 = .0625$. This also is the probability for the remaining outcomes: $p_{H,H,T,H} = .0625$, $p_{H,T,H,H} = .0625$, and $p_{T,H,H,H} = .0625$.

Step 2 *Determine the total probability of the event "three heads."*
The total probability requires the OR/addition rule: $p_{H,H,H,T} + p_{H,H,T,H} + p_{H,T,H,H} + p_{T,H,H,H} = .0625 + .0625 + .0625 + .0625 = .25$.

9.7 The Normal Curve as a Probability Distribution

You may have noticed that Figure 9.1 somewhat resembles the familiar normal curve, at least in broad brush strokes. In fact, the normal curve can be viewed as a

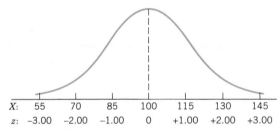

Figure 9.2   The normal distribution of scores for the Peabody Picture Vocabulary Test (PPVT): $\overline{X} = 100$, $S = 15$.

theoretical probability distribution. As you learned in Chapter 6, the normal curve is a mathematical model that specifies the relationship between area and units of standard deviation. The relative frequencies of the normal curve, like those of the binomial expansion, are theoretical values derived rationally by applying the laws of probability. If a frequency distribution can be closely approximated by a normal curve, then the relative frequency, or proportion, of cases falling between any two points can be determined from the normal curve table. Moreover, such a relative frequency is equivalent to a probability, obtained from a table of theoretical values—hence, the normal curve as a theoretical probability distribution.

In the three problems that follow, we illustrate the use of the normal curve for answering questions concerning the probability of events. Although we have changed the context from a dichotomous variable (a coin toss) to a continuous variable (IQ scores), you should find strong parallels in the underlying reasoning.

Imagine that you have a computer disk containing scores on the Peabody Picture Vocabulary Test (PPVT), a measure of receptive vocabulary, for every eighth-grade student in your state. These scores are normally distributed with a mean of 100 and a standard deviation of 15 (see Figure 9.2). Further suppose that you can randomly select a single PPVT score at the stroke of a key. Thus, the chance of being selected is equal for all scores.

Problem 1

What is the probability of randomly selecting a PPVT score of 115 or higher?

This problem is illustrated in Figure 9.3. Because the probability of this event ("a score of 115 or higher") is equivalent to the corresponding area under the normal curve, your first task is to determine the z score for a PPVT score of 115:

$$z = \frac{X - \overline{X}}{S} = \frac{115 - 100}{15} = +1.00$$

Now locate $z = 1.00$ in column 3 of Table A (Appendix C), where you find the entry .1587. Because your interest is only in the upper end of the distribution ("a score 115 or *higher*"), a one-tailed probability is called for. ***Answer:*** *The probability of selecting a PPVT score of 115 or higher is .1587, or .16.* In other words, if you were to randomly select a PPVT score from this distribution over an unlimited

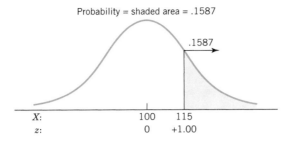

Probability = shaded area = .1587

.1587

X: 100   115
z: 0   +1.00

Figure 9.3   The normal curve as a probability distribution: probability of selecting a student with a PPVT score of 115 or higher.

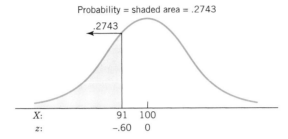

Probability = shaded area = .2743

.2743

X: 91   100
z: −.60   0

Figure 9.4   Probability of selecting a student with a PPVT score of 91 or lower.

number of occasions, you would expect to obtain a score of 115 or higher about 16% of the time.[2]

Problem 2

What is the probability of randomly selecting a PPVT score of 91 or lower?
    Because this question is concerned only with scores in the lower end of the distribution, a one-tailed probability is once again called for. We illustrate this in Figure 9.4. The needed z score is:

$$z = \frac{91 - 100}{15} = -.60$$

Locate $z = .60$ in column 3 of Table A. (Remember, the symmetry of the normal curve allows you to ignore the negative sign.) The entry is .2743. ***Answer:*** *The probability of selecting a PPVT score of 91 or lower is .2743, or .27.*

Problem 3

What is the probability of randomly selecting a PPVT score as extreme as 70?
    The language of this question ("as extreme as") calls for a *two-tailed* probability. First, obtain the z score for a PPVT score of 70:

$$z = \frac{70 - 100}{15} = -2.00$$

[2]This assumes that the selected score is "replaced" on each occasion.

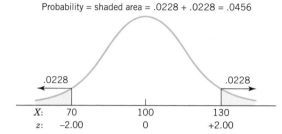

Probability = shaded area = .0228 + .0228 = .0456

.0228   .0228

X: 70   100   130
z: −2.00   0   +2.00

Figure 9.5 Probability of selecting a student with a PPVT score as extreme as 70.

Table A tells you that this score marks the point beyond which .0228 of the area lies, as the left side of Figure 9.5 illustrates. But because a *z of* + 2.00 (a PPVT score of 130) is just as "extreme" as a *z of* − 2.00 (a PPVT score of 70), you must apply the OR/addition rule to obtain the correct, two-tailed probability: .0228 + .0228 = .0456. **Answer:** *The probability of randomly selecting a PPVT score as extreme as 70 is .0456, or .05.*

9.8 *"So What?"—Probability Distributions as the Basis for Statistical Inference*

Fortunately, the substantive questions that you will explore through research are considerably more interesting than coin tossing and card drawing. Nevertheless, behind every substantive conclusion lies a statistical conclusion (Section 1.4), and behind every statistical conclusion is a known probability distribution. For Professor Sartor (Section 9.1) to conclude from her test-familiarity results that there "really" is a difference between experimental and control group subjects in test performance, she must determine the probability of obtaining a difference as large as her sample result *on the basis of chance alone*. She does this by making a few calculations and then consulting the relevant probability distribution. You will see in subsequent chapters how this is done, but the formulas and logic build directly on what you have learned in this chapter.

9.9 *Summary*

Statistical inference is the problem of making conclusions that take into consideration the influence of random sampling variation. Random sampling variation refers to the differences in outcome that characterize results that vary in accordance with the "luck of the draw," where chance factors determine who is to be included in the sample that is obtained. The key to solving problems of statistical inference is to answer the question, "What kind of sample results can be expected from the operation of chance alone?" This, in turn, depends on the study of probability.

Probability expresses the degree of assurance in the face of uncertainty. The probability of an event is the proportion of times you would expect the event to occur in an infinitely long series of identical sampling experiments. If all possible outcomes are equally likely, the probability of an event equals the proportion of possible outcomes that fit, or favor, the event.

A theoretical probability distribution is a relative frequency distribution that shows all possible outcomes and identifies the event characterizing each outcome. A theoretical probability distribution is based on a mathematical model, such as the binomial expansion and the normal curve. Thus, knowing the relevant probability distribution allows you to state the probability of an event—obtaining a certain number of heads upon tossing a coin four times, or randomly selecting from a normal distribution a score as rare as *X*—without having to suffer an unlimited number of sampling experiments.

There are two basic rules of probability: the OR/addition rule and the AND/multiplication rule. The first states that the probability of occurrence of event A *or* B *or* ... is the sum of their individual probabilities, provided that the events are mutually exclusive. The second states that the probability of occurrence of events A *and* B *and* ... is the product of their individual probabilities, provided the events are independent. For some situations there is more than one outcome associated with a particular event, and in such cases both rules are used to arrive at the final probability.

An important distinction is that between a one-tailed and a two-tailed probability. A one-tailed probability is based on only one side of the probability distribution, whereas a two-tailed probability is based on both sides.

Exercises

Identify, Define, or Explain

Terms and Concepts

sample	theoretical probability distribution
population	outcomes versus events
sampling variation	OR/addition rule
statistical inference	mutually exclusive events
probability theory	one-tailed versus two-tailed probability
sampling experiment	AND/multiplication rule
outcomes	independent events
probability distributions	normal curve as a theoretical probability
probability of an event	distribution

Symbols

p

Questions and Problems

Note: Answers to starred (*) items are presented in Appendix B.

*1. In an education experiment, a group of students is randomly divided into two groups. The two groups then receive different instructional treatments and are observed for differences in achievement. Why would the researcher feel it necessary to apply "statistical inference" procedures to the analysis of the observations?

2. Imagine that you toss an unbiased coin five times in a row and heads turns up every time.

   (a) Is it therefore more likely that you will get tails on the sixth toss? (Explain.)

   (b) What *is* the probability of getting tails on the sixth toss?

*3. Six CDs, three portable CD players, and one television are given out as door prizes at a local club. Winners are determined randomly by the number appearing on the patron's admission ticket. Suppose 300 tickets are sold (and there are no no-shows). What is the probability that a particular patron will win (round to four decimal places, where needed):

(a)   a door prize of some kind?

(b)   the television?

(c)   a CD?

(d)   a CD player?

*4.   The following question is asked on a statistics quiz: *If one person is selected at random out of a large group, what is the probability that he or she will have been born in the month beginning with the letter J?* Jack Sprat reasons that since 3 of the 12 months begin with the letter J, the desired probability must be equal to 3/12, or .25. Comment on Jack's reasoning.

5.   A student is selected at random from the group of 200 represented in the table below.

Sex of Student

Course Grade	Male	Female	Total
A	18	12	30
B	30	30	60
C	53	27	80
D	12	8	20
F	7	3	10
f	120	80	200

Using the basic rule given in Section 9.3, determine the probability of selecting:

(a)   an F student

(b)   a female

(c)   a female B student

(d)   a male with a grade below C

*6.   Since a grade of F is one of five possible letter grades, why isn't 1/5, or .20, the answer to Problem 5a?

7.   Suppose you make three consecutive random selections from the group of 200 students in Problem 5. After each selection, you record the grade and sex of the student selected and replace him or her back in the group before making your next selection. First, determine the following three probabilities for a single selection: the probability of a male B student, a male A student, a female student. Now, *apply the appropriate rule(s) to these probabilities* to determine the probability that:

(a)   the first selection is a male with a grade of at least B

(b)   the second selection is a male with a grade of B or a female

(c)   the first selection is a male B student and the second selection is a female

(d)   all three selections are males with a grade of B or better

8.   What is the distinction, if any, between a relative frequency distribution and a probability distribution? (Explain.)

*9. Two fair dice are rolled.

   (a) What is the probability of an even number or a 3 on the first die?

   (b) What is the probability of an even number on the first die and a 3 on the second?

10. In which of the following instances are the events *mutually exclusive*?

   (a) Obtaining heads on the first toss of a coin and tails on the second toss.

   (b) Being a male and being pregnant.

   (c) As an undergraduate student, being an education major and being a psychology major.

   (d) Obtaining a final grade of A and obtaining a final grade of C for your first course in statistics.

   (e) Obtaining three aces in two consecutive hands dealt each time from a complete, well-shuffled deck of playing cards.

   (f) Disliking rock music and attending a rock concert.

   (g) Obtaining a 3 and an even number on a single roll of a die.

   (h) Winning on one play of a slot machine and winning on the very next play.

   (i) Being 15 years old and voting (legally) in the last national election.

11. For each of the instances described in Problem 10, indicate whether the events are independent.

12. Events A and B are *mutually exclusive*. Can they also be *independent*? (Explain.)

*13. A slot machine has three wheels that rotate independently. When the lever is pulled, the wheels rotate and then come to a stop, one by one, in random positions. The circumference of each wheel is divided into 25 equal parts and contains four pictures each of six different fruits and one picture of a jackpot label. What is the probability that the following will appear under the window on the middle wheel:

   (a) a jackpot label?

   (b) an orange?

   (c) any fruit?

14. Suppose you pull the lever on the slot machine described in Problem 13. What is the probability that:

   (a) either an orange or a lemon or a jackpot label will appear on the middle wheel?

   (b) a jackpot label will appear on all three wheels?

   (c) cherries will appear on all three wheels?

*15. You make random guesses on three consecutive true–false items.

   (a) List the way(s) you can guess correctly on exactly two out of the three items.

   (b) What is the probability of guessing correctly on the first two items and guessing incorrectly on the third item?

   (c) What is the probability of guessing correctly on exactly two out of the three items?

   (d) List the way(s) you can guess correctly on all three of the items.

   (e) What is the probability of guessing correctly on *at least* two of the three items?

16. Your statistics instructor administers a test having five multiple-choice items with four options each.

(a) List the ways in which one can guess correctly on exactly four items on this test. What is the probability of:

(b) guessing correctly on any one of the five items?

(c) guessing incorrectly on any one of the five items?

(d) guessing correctly on the first four items and guessing incorrectly on the fifth item?

(e) obtaining a score of exactly four correct by randomly guessing on each item?

(f) randomly guessing and obtaining a perfect score on the test?

(g) obtaining at least four correct by randomly guessing?

(h) missing all five items through random guessing?

17. You're back on the slot machine from Problem 13. What is the probability that:

(a) an orange will appear on exactly two of the wheels?

(b) an orange will appear on *at least* two of the wheels?

(c) a jackpot label will appear on *at least* one of the wheels?

18. The verbal subscale on the SAT (SAT-CR) has a normal distribution with a mean of 500 and a standard deviation of 100. Consider the roughly one million high school seniors who took the SAT last year. If one of these students is selected at random, what is the probability that his or her SAT-CR score will be:

(a) 460 or higher?

(b) between 460 and 540?

(c) 680 or higher?

(d) as extreme as 680?

(e) The probability is .50 that the student's SAT-CR score will be between what two values?

(f) The probability is .10 that the student's SAT-CR score will fall above an SAT-CR score of ____?

(g) The probability is .10 that the student's SAT-CR score will fall below an SAT-CR score of ____?

19. Is the probability in Problem 18d a one- or two-tailed probability? (Explain.)

20. Suppose you randomly select two students from the group in Problem 18. What is the probability that:

(a) the first student falls at least 100 SAT-CR points away from the mean (in either direction)?

(b) both students obtain SAT-CR scores above 700?

(c) the first student obtains a score above 650 and the second student obtains a score below 450?

(d) both students fall above 650 or both students fall below 450?

(e) both students obtain scores as extreme as 650?

CHAPTER 10

Sampling Distributions

10.1   From Coins to Means

Now that you have been introduced to some of the laws of chance, let's consider in greater detail the kinds of results that are likely to obtain from random samples. Remember, a random sample can be thought of, in general terms, as one for which "chance" does the selecting, as in a lottery. Although the concepts introduced in this chapter are highly theoretical, they are a simple extension of what you learned in the preceding chapter. Moreover, they provide the basis for the procedures that researchers employ to take into account the effects of chance on sample results—that is, the procedures of statistical inference. We will develop the various concepts of this chapter within the context of a widely used test, the Stanford-Binet Intelligence Scale.

The Stanford-Binet is normed so that the mean is 100 and the standard deviation is 16. Thus, an IQ of 116 for a 10-year-old falls one standard deviation above the mean of the distribution for all 10-year-olds nationally. Suppose that you randomly select a sample of $n = 64$ from the national population of IQ scores of 10-year-olds and, in turn, calculate the mean IQ. You then "replace" this sample in the population, randomly select a second sample of 64, and again compute the mean. Let's further suppose that you repeat this process many, many times. (Is this sounding familiar?) Chance will be operating here, just as it does when you flip a coin, draw a card, or select an individual score from a pool of scores. As a consequence, your *sample* means will differ by varying amounts from 100, the mean IQ for the *population* of all 10-year-olds in the country. Because each sample was randomly selected from this population, you would expect most of the sample means to be fairly close to 100. But because of random **sampling variation**, some sample means might be considerably above or considerably below this value.

We wish to assure you that in actual practice, you will never have to repeatedly sample a population as outlined here—even for an assignment in your statistics class! But let's pretend that you did. *What sample means would you expect if repeated samples were taken*? What is the probability of obtaining a sample mean IQ of, say, 110 or higher? of 90 or lower? How about a sample mean between 95 and 105? If random sampling can be assumed, such questions are easily answered. These answers provide the key to accounting for sampling variation when making inferences about a larger group from data obtained on a subset of that group.

Before proceeding, notice the parallels between the questions we just posed and those you entertained in Chapter 9. Asking about the probability of obtaining a sample mean of 110 or higher (when you would "expect" a value of 100) is analogous to asking about the probability of obtaining three or more heads upon tossing a coin four times (when you would "expect" only two heads). It also is analogous to asking about the probability of selecting an individual score of 110 or higher (when the mean score is 100). Although we have shifted the focus from coins and individual scores to *sample means*, the underlying logic is the same. Let's now take a closer look at some important concepts associated with random sampling, after which we will return to our 10-year-olds and explore the concept of sampling distributions.

10.2   *Samples and Populations*

We have referred to the terms **sample** and **population**, which now we examine more formally.

> A *population* consists of the complete set of observations or measurements about which conclusions are to be drawn; a *sample* is a part of the population.

Note that for statistical purposes, samples and populations pertain to *observations*, not individuals (although this will not always be clear from the wording used). For instance, if your concern is with measured intelligence, you will consider your sample and the population from which it was selected to consist of *IQ scores* rather than of the children from whom the IQ scores were obtained.

Furthermore, a "population" does not necessarily refer to an entire country, an entire state, or even an entire town. A population simply refers to whatever group you want to draw inferences about, no matter how large or how small. Thus, for the aforementioned superintendent conducting the high school renovation survey, the population is all taxpayers in the community. However, if for some unfathomable reason the superintendent's interest had been limited to taxpayers with blue eyes, then that would have been the population!

Finally, a population may reflect a *theoretical* set of observations rather than a "complete set" of observations as defined above. In her test-familiarity experiment, Professor Sartor (Section 9.1) wishes to make inferences about all students who *potentially* might receive test-familiarity instruction. Theoretical populations are typical in experimental research, where participants are randomly assigned to one of several "treatment" conditions.[1]

---

[1]Such assignment of participants to experimental conditions is referred to as *randomization*, which differs from the process of *randomly selecting* participants from a population. We will discuss randomization in Chapter 14, where we present a statistical test for experimental designs.

Why is there a need to sample at all? Because in many situations it is too expensive, impractical, or even impossible to collect every observation in the entire population. Although the superintendent *could* assess the opinions of all taxpayers in the community, considerable time and money is saved by instead surveying a random sample of 100. And where the researcher's population is theoretical, as in the case of Professor Sartor, there is no choice but to collect observations on samples.

10.3 Statistics and Parameters

Now that the distinction between samples and populations has been made, we also need to distinguish between values determined from sample observations and those determined from the population.

A **statistic** summarizes a characteristic of a sample; a **parameter** summarizes a characteristic of a population.

When you learned that 70% of the polled taxpayers in the local school district favored the proposed renovation, you were being presented with a statistic. It summarizes a characteristic of the sample—how these 100 taxpayers feel about the proposed renovation. This statistic is used as an indicator, or **estimate**, of the corresponding parameter—the percentage of *all* taxpayers in the community who favor the renovation. As you can imagine, a defensible inference from statistic to parameter requires a careful understanding of both the sample and the population about which generalizations are to be made. (More on this in a moment.)

Statistics and parameters are represented by different statistical symbols. The familiar symbol, $\overline{X}$, is actually a statistic—the mean of a sample. The corresponding parameter, the mean of a population, is denoted by the Greek symbol μ (mu, pronounced "mew"). As for variability, lowercase s represents the sample standard deviation and σ (sigma), the standard deviation in the population.[2] Logically enough, s^2 and σ^2 symbolize the sample and population variances, respectively. The Pearson correlation coefficient provides yet another example, where r denotes the sample value and ρ (rho, pronounced "row") the value in the population. Finally, the sample proportion is denoted by P and the proportion in the population, by π (pi).

[2]In earlier chapters, we used (upper-case) S to represent the standard deviation. Now that we must distinguish between sample and population, we will follow common practice and use (lower-case) s to represent the standard deviation of a sample. As you will see in Chapter 13, the formula for s departs slightly from that for S.

In each case, the sample statistic, based on a random sample, is used to estimate the corresponding population parameter:

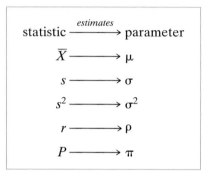

10.4   Random Sampling Model

The **random sampling model** is used to take into account chance factors—sampling variation—when sample results are being interpreted. In this model, you assume that the sample has been randomly selected from the population of interest. The sample is studied in detail, and on the basis of the sample results (statistics) and what is known about how chance affects random samples (probability theory), you make inferences about the characteristics of the population (parameters).

A common problem in statistical inference, which you will encounter in the next chapter, involves making inferences about μ from $\overline{X}$. That is, given a mean that you have determined from a randomly selected sample, what is your best estimate regarding the mean of the corresponding population? Figure 10.1 illustrates the application of the random sampling model to this problem. This figure easily

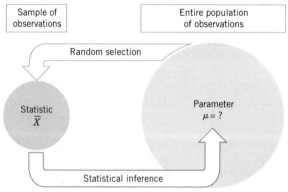

Figure 10.1   The random sampling model for making an inference about μ.

can be modified to represent the process of making inferences about σ from s, σ^2 from s^2, ρ from r, or *any* parameter from the corresponding statistic.

Selecting a Random Sample

Just what is meant by a random sample? The definition of a random sample is quite distinct from popular usage of the term *random*, which tends to suggest a haphazard or poorly conceived process.

> A random sample is a sample drawn from a population such that each possible sample of the specified size has an equal probability of being selected.

This is called **simple random sampling**, which is like a carefully executed lottery. Suppose you need a random sample of workers at a large pulp mill for an investigation of worker morale. You could write the names of all 1000 employees on slips of paper, stuff each slip into a small capsule, mix the capsules thoroughly in a large barrel, and draw out a sample of 50. As you can imagine, such a process is not very practical for most situations. Fortunately, there are easier ways to select a simple random sample, including the use of a table of random numbers or a computer program that generates random numbers.

In random sampling, it is necessarily true that *every observation (or measurement) in the population has an equal opportunity of being included in the sample*, as would be the case in the sampling of mill workers. In fact, if you know that every element of the population has *not* been given an equal chance of inclusion, you also know that, strictly speaking, the sample cannot be a *random* sample. This would be the case in telephone or house-to-house interviews conducted only in the evening, which automatically eliminate people who hold night jobs.

Notice that whether a sample is random depends on how it is selected, not on the results it produces. You cannot determine whether a sample is random by merely examining the results; you must know how the sample was obtained. Although characteristics of random samples *tend* to be representative of the population, characteristics of a particular random sample may not. Again, draw on what you learned in the preceding chapter. If a coin were flipped four times, a perfectly representative "sample" would consist of two heads and two tails. Yet it is possible that chance will return *all* heads. Representative? No. Random? Yes.

Sometimes it is impractical to select a simple random sample, even with the help of a computer. In these instances, shortcut methods such as **systematic sampling** can be used. For example, you could form your sample of 50 mill workers by selecting every twentieth name from an alphabetic list of all 1000 employees. The sample, though not truly random, might well give results close to those obtained by random sampling. There are other variations, such as stratified random sampling, that tend to increase the accuracy of the sample results beyond that expected from a simple random sample (e.g., see Babbie, 1995). To keep things clear and straightforward, we will focus on procedures flowing from simple random sampling.

10.5   *Random Sampling in Practice*

Although we will assume random sampling in the remainder of this book, random sampling in educational research is more ideal than real. When a sample *is* randomly selected from a well-defined population, the inference from sample to population is relatively straightforward. But educational researchers often (perhaps most of the time) rely on samples that are *accessible*, also known as **convenience samples**. Examples include college students in the department's subject pool, members of the community who respond to an advertisement for research volunteers, and students attending a local school.

The use of convenience samples does not necessarily invalidate the researcher's data and statistical analyses, but such samples do call for a more thorough description of the sample so that the **accessible population** is better understood. The accessible population represents the population of individuals like those included in the sample and treated exactly the same way. In a sense, one "pretends" that the convenience sample was randomly selected from a population—even though it really wasn't. This population, admittedly theoretical, is the accessible population. It is to *this* population that statistical inferences or generalizations are to be made.

Unlike random sampling and related methods in which the population is known in advance, convenience samples require the researcher (and reader) to identify the population (i.e., the accessible population) from what is known about the sample. Because this population can be characterized only after careful consideration of the sample, it is the researcher's important responsibility to thoroughly describe the participants and the exact conditions under which the observations were obtained. Then, armed with a clear understanding of the accessible population, researcher and consumer alike are in a position to make judgments about the degree to which inferences to the accessible population may apply in other situations of interest.

10.6   *Sampling Distributions of Means*

We are now ready to return to our 10-year-olds from Section 10.1 and address the fundamental question in statistical inference: *What kinds of sample results are likely to be obtained as a result of random sampling variation?*

You will recall that for the national population of 10-year-olds, the mean Stanford-Binet IQ score is $\mu = 100$ and the standard deviation is $\sigma = 16$. Suppose that your first random sample of size $n = 64$ produces a sample mean of $\overline{X}_1 = 103.70$. (The subscript indicates that this mean is from the first sample). You record this mean, replace the sample in the population, and select a second sample of $n = 64$. This sample mean is $\overline{X}_2 = 98.58$, which you dutifully record. You continue to repeat this exercise again and again, as illustrated in the top half of Figure 10.2. If you were to repeat these sampling experiments *indefinitely* (a theoretical proposition, to be sure), and if all sample means were cast into a relative frequency distribution, you

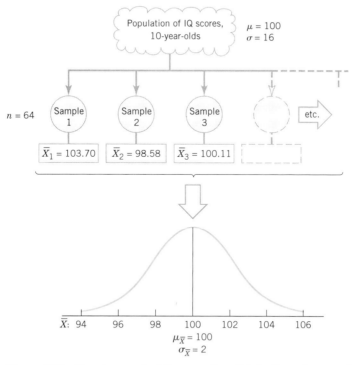

Figure 10.2   Development of the sampling distribution of means for sample size $n = 64$.

would have a **sampling distribution of means**. We show this in the bottom half of Figure 10.2.

> A sampling distribution of means is a probability distribution. It is the relative frequency distribution of means obtained from an unlimited series of sampling experiments, each consisting of a sample of size n randomly selected from the population.

As you see, the sampling distribution of means in Figure 10.2 follows the normal curve, with sample means clustering around the population mean ($\mu = 100$) and tapering off in either direction. We will explore these properties in a moment.

Of course, it is impossible to actually produce the distribution in Figure 10.2 because an infinity of sampling experiments would be necessary. Fortunately for all of us, mathematicians have been able to derive its defining characteristics—mean, standard deviation, and shape—and therefore can state what would happen *if* an infinite series of random sampling experiments were conducted. And by knowing the sampling distribution, you are in a position to answer the fundamental question posed at the beginning of this section: *What kinds of sample results are likely to be obtained as a result of random sampling variation?*

10.7   Characteristics of a Sampling Distribution of Means

Any sampling distribution of means can be characterized by its mean, standard deviation, and shape.

The Mean of a Sampling Distribution of Means

Symbolized by $\mu_{\bar{X}}$, the mean of a sampling distribution of means will be the same as the mean of the population of scores (μ):

> The mean of a sampling
> distribution of means
>
> $$\mu_{\bar{X}} = \mu \qquad (10.1)$$

This perhaps agrees with your intuition. By chance, some of the sample means will fall above μ (perhaps considerably so). But chance plays no favorites. With an infinite number of samples, the sample means falling below μ balance those falling above, resulting in a mean for the entire distribution of means equal to μ.

The Standard Deviation of a Sampling Distribution of Means

The standard deviation of means in a sampling distribution is known as the **standard error of the mean**, symbolized by $\sigma_{\bar{X}}$. It reflects the amount of variability among the sample means—that is, sampling variation. Note that the term *standard error* is used in place of *standard deviation*. This serves notice that $\sigma_{\bar{X}}$ is the standard deviation of a special type of distribution—a sampling distribution.

   Calculating $\sigma_{\bar{X}}$ requires only σ and *n*:

> Standard error of the mean
>
> $$\sigma_{\bar{X}} = \frac{\sigma}{\sqrt{n}} \qquad (10.2)$$

For the example illustrated in the bottom half of Figure 10.2, $\sigma = 16$ and $n = 64$. Therefore, the standard error of the mean is

$$\sigma_{\bar{X}} = \frac{\sigma}{\sqrt{n}} = \frac{16}{\sqrt{64}} = \frac{16}{8} = 2$$

   Several important insights can be gained from a closer look at Formula (10.2).[3] First, $\sigma_{\bar{X}}$ depends on the amount of variability in the population (σ). Because σ is

[3]Strictly speaking, Formula (10.2) is not quite right if the population is limited *and* samples are drawn without replacement (i.e., no individual can appear in a sample more than once). In practice, this is not a problem when *n* is less than 5% of the population—which almost always is the case in behavioral research.

in the numerator, a more variable population will result in a larger standard error of the mean.

Second, $\sigma_{\bar{X}}$ depends on the size of the samples selected. Consequently, there is not just a single sampling distribution of means for a given population; rather, there is a different one for every sample size. That is, there is a *family* of sampling distributions for any given population. We show two members of this family in Figure 10.3, superimposed on the population distribution.

Third, because *n* appears in the denominator of Formula (10.2), the standard error of the mean becomes smaller as *n* is increased. That is, the larger the sample size, the more closely the sample means cluster around μ (see Figure 10.3). This, too, should agree with your intuition. For example, chance factors make it easy for the mean of an extremely small sample of IQs (e.g., *n* = 3) to fall far above or far below the μ of 100. But in a much larger sample, there is considerably more opportunity for chance to operate "democratically" and balance high IQs and lows IQs within the sample, resulting in a sample mean closer to μ. Again the parallel in flipping a coin: you would think nothing of obtaining only heads upon flipping a coin twice (*n* = 2), but you would be highly suspicious if you flipped the coin ten times (*n* = 10) and saw only heads.[4]

The Shape of a Sampling Distribution of Means

According to statistical theory, if the population of observations is normally distributed, a sampling distribution of means that is derived from that population also will be normally distributed. Figure 10.3 illustrates this principle as well.

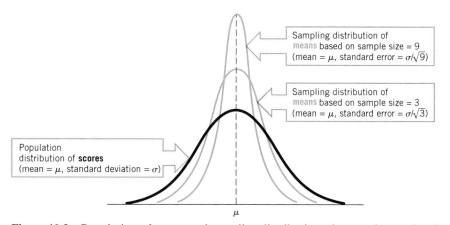

Figure 10.3   Population of scores and sampling distribution of means for *n* = 3 and *n* = 9.

---

[4]You'd probably suspect deceit well before the tenth toss: With only *five* tosses, the probability of obtaining all heads is only $.5 \times .5 \times .5 \times .5 \times .5 = .03$ (right?).

But what if the population distribution doesn't follow the normal curve? A remarkable bit of statistical theory, the **central limit theorem**, comes into play:

> Sampling distributions of means tend toward a normal shape as the sample size increases, *regardless* of the shape of the population distribution from which the samples have been randomly selected.

With many populations, the distribution of scores is sufficiently normal that little assistance from the central limit theorem is needed. But even when the population of observations departs substantially from a normal distribution, the sampling distribution of means may be treated as though it *were* normally distributed if n is reasonably large. What is "reasonably" large? Depending on the degree of nonnormality of the population distribution, 25 to 30 cases is usually sufficient.

Figure 10.4 illustrates the tendency of sampling distributions of means to approach normality as n increases. Two populations of scores are shown in Figure 10.4*a*: one rectangular, the other skewed positively. In Figure 10.4*b*, the sampling distributions appear for samples based on $n = 2$. Notice that the shapes of these

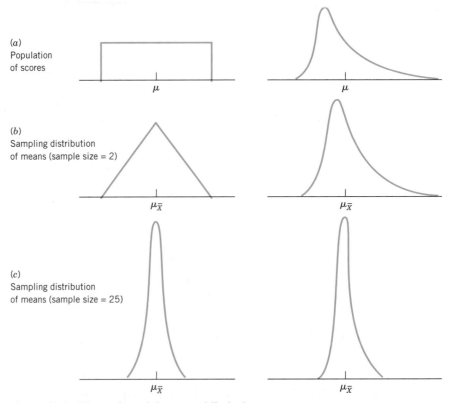

Figure 10.4   Illustration of the central limit theorem.

distributions differ from those of their parent populations of scores and that the difference is in the direction of normality. In Figure 10.4c, where $n = 25$, the sampling distributions bear a remarkable resemblance to the normal distribution.

The importance of the central limit theorem cannot be overstated. Because of the central limit theorem, *the normal curve can be used to approximate the sampling distribution of means* in a wide variety of practical situations. If this were not so, many problems in statistical inference would be very awkward to solve, to say the least.

10.8   *Using a Sampling Distribution of Means to Determine Probabilities*

The relevant sampling distribution of means gives you an idea of how typical or how rare a particular sample mean might be. Inspection of Figure 10.2, for example, reveals that a mean of 101 for a random sample of 64 IQs could easily occur, whereas a sample mean of 106 is highly unlikely. For purposes of statistical inference, however, more precision is required than is afforded by such phrases as "could easily occur" and "is highly unlikely." That is, specific probabilities are needed. These probabilities are readily found in sampling distributions, for all sampling distributions are **probability distributions**: they provide the relative frequencies with which the various sample values occur with repeated sampling over the long run.

The four problems that follow illustrate the use of a sampling distribution of means for answering probability questions fundamental to the kinds that you will encounter in statistical inference. *The logic underlying these problems is identical to the logic behind the eight problems in Chapter 6*, where you used the normal curve to determine area when a score was known (Section 6.6) and to determine a score when area was known (Section 6.7). The only difference is that your earlier concern was with an *individual score*, whereas now it is with a *sample mean*. (We encourage you to take a few minutes and refresh your understanding of the Chapter 6 problems before continuing.)

For each problem that follows, the population is the distribution of Stanford-Binet IQ scores for all 10-year-olds in the United States ($\mu = 100$, $\sigma = 16$). Assume that you have randomly selected a single sample of $n = 64$ from this population of observations.[5]

Problem 1

What is the probability of obtaining a sample mean IQ of 105 or higher?

Let's first clarify this question by recalling that the probability of an event is equal to the proportion of all possible outcomes that favor the event (Section 9.3).

[5]The population of Stanford-Binet IQ scores is reasonably normal. But even if it were not normal, you are assured by the central limit theorem that, with $n = 64$, the underlying sampling distribution *is*—at least enough to use the normal curve as an approximation of the sampling distribution.

The question above, then, can be rephrased as follows: What proportion of all possible samples of $n = 64$ have means of 105 or higher? The sampling distribution of means provides you with the theoretical distribution of all possible samples of $n = 64$. Your task is to determine the area in this sampling distribution above $\overline{X} = 105$. We present the solution to this problem in three steps.

Step 1   Calculate the standard error of the mean:

$$\sigma_{\overline{X}} = \frac{\sigma}{\sqrt{n}} = \frac{16}{\sqrt{64}} = \frac{16}{8} = 2$$

Step 2   Because you will use the normal curve to approximate the sampling distribution of means, you now must restate the location of the sample mean of 105 as a z score. Recall from Formula (6.1) that a z score is obtained by subtracting a mean from a score and dividing by a standard deviation:

$$z = \frac{X - \overline{X}}{S}$$

In a sampling distribution of means, the *sample mean* is the "score," the *population mean* is the "mean," and the *standard error of the mean* is the "standard deviation." That is:

z score for a sample mean

$$z = \frac{\overline{X} - \mu}{\sigma_{\overline{X}}} \tag{10.3}$$

In the present example,

$$z = \frac{\overline{X} - \mu}{\sigma_{\overline{X}}} = \frac{105 - 100}{2} = +2.50$$

This value of z tells you that the sample mean, $\overline{X} = 105$, falls two and a half standard errors above the mean of the population, $\mu = 100$ (see Figure 10.5).

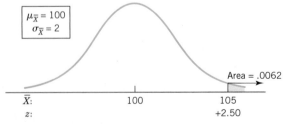

Figure 10.5   Finding the proportion of sample means that differ from the population mean beyond a given value.

Step 3   Locate $z = 2.50$ in column 3 of Table A (Appendix C), where you find that the area beyond this value is .0062. Thus, in repeated random sampling ($n = 64$), the proportion of times you would obtain a sample mean IQ of 105 or higher is .0062. ***Answer:*** *The probability of obtaining a sample mean IQ of 105 or higher is .0062.*

Problem 2

What is the probability of obtaining a sample mean IQ that differs from the population mean by 5 points or more?

This problem, unlike the preceding one, calls for a two-tailed probability because the sample mean can be at least 5 points *below or above* $\mu = 100$. You already know that $z = +2.50$ for an IQ of 105 and that the area beyond 105 is .0062. (Note that because σ and n are the same as in Problem 1, $\sigma_{\bar{X}}$ has not changed.) Because 95 is as far *below* μ as 105 is *above* μ, the z score for 95 is -2.50. And because the normal curve is symmetric, the area beyond 95 also is .0062 (see Figure 10.6). To find the required probability, simply employ the OR/addition rule and double the area beyond 105: $.0062 + .0062 = .0124$. ***Answer:*** *The probability of obtaining a sample mean IQ that differs from the population mean by 5 points or more is .0124.*

Problem 3

What sample mean IQ is so high that the probability is only .05 of obtaining one as high or higher in random sampling?

The process is now reversed: you are given the probability and must determine the sample mean. From Table A, find the z score beyond which only .05 of the area under the normal curve falls. This is a z of 1.65. The algebraic sign is positive because you are interested only in the right-hand side of the sampling distribution— "as high or higher." (As you see from Table A, the precise z value sits somewhere between the two tabled values, 1.64 and 1.65. We go with the larger, more conservative, of the two.)

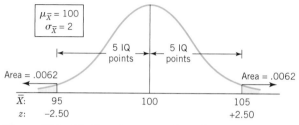

Figure 10.6   Finding the proportion of sample means that differ from the population mean by more than a given amount.

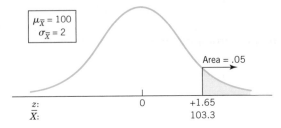

Figure 10.7   Finding the value beyond which a given proportion of sample means will fall.

The desired sample mean, then, must be 1.65 standard errors above $\mu = 100$. Now convert the z score back to a sample mean. From Formula (10.3), it follows that $\overline{X} = \mu + z\sigma_{\overline{X}}$.[6] Therefore:

$$\overline{X} = \mu + z\sigma_{\overline{X}}$$
$$= 100 + (+1.65)(2)$$
$$= 100 + 3.3$$
$$= 103.3$$

Thus, with unlimited random sampling ($n = 64$) of the population of Stanford-Binet IQ scores, you would expect only 5% of the sample means to be 103.3 or higher (see Figure 10.7). **Answer:** *Obtaining a sample mean IQ of 103.3 or higher carries a probability of .05.*

Problem 4

Within what limits would the central 95% of sample means fall?
    If 95% of the sample means are to fall in the center of the sampling distribution, the remaining 5% must be divided equally between the two tails of the distribution. That is, 2.5% must fall above the upper limit and 2.5% below the lower limit (see Figure 10.8). Your first task, then, is to determine the value of z

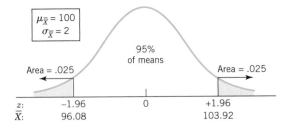

Figure 10.8   Finding the centrally located score limits between which a given proportion of sample means will fall.

[6]Need help? Multiply both sides of Formula (10.3) by $\sigma_{\overline{X}}$, which gives you $z\sigma_{\overline{X}} = \overline{X} - \mu$. Now add μ to both sides (and rearrange the terms) to get $\overline{X} = \mu + z\sigma_{\overline{X}}$.

beyond which .025 of the area under the normal curve is located. From Table A, you find that this value is $z = 1.96$. Now solve for the lower ($\overline{X}_L$) and upper ($\overline{X}_U$) limits:

$$z_L = -1.96 \qquad\qquad z_U = +1.96$$
$$\overline{X}_L = \mu + z_L \sigma_{\overline{X}} \qquad\qquad \overline{X}_U = \mu + z_U \sigma_{\overline{X}}$$
$$= 100 + (-1.96)(2) \qquad\qquad = 100 + (+1.96)(2)$$
$$= 100 - 3.92 \qquad\qquad = 100 + 3.92$$
$$= 96.08 \qquad\qquad = 103.92$$

Answer: *The central 95% of sample means fall between 96.08 and 103.92.* With a single random sample ($n = 64$), the probability therefore is .95 of obtaining a sample mean between these limits. You may not be surprised to learn that the probability is .05 of obtaining a sample mean *beyond* these limits.

10.9 The Importance of Sample Size (n)

As you just saw, the vast majority—95%—of all possible sample means in Problem 4 would be within roughly 4 points of μ when $n = 64$. From Formula (10.2) and Figure 10.3, you know that there would be *greater* spread among sample means when *n* is *smaller*. Let's recompute the lower and upper limits of the central 95% of sample means, but based on an unrealistically small sample size of $n = 4$.

Predictably, the standard error of the mean is much larger with this reduction in *n*:

$$\sigma_{\overline{X}} = \frac{\sigma}{\sqrt{n}} = \frac{16}{\sqrt{4}} = \frac{16}{2} = 8$$

Now plug in the new $\sigma_{\overline{X}}$ to obtain the lower ($\overline{X}_L$) and upper ($\overline{X}_U$) limits:

$$z_L = -1.96 \qquad\qquad z_U = +1.96$$
$$\overline{X}_L = \mu + z_L \sigma_{\overline{X}} \qquad\qquad \overline{X}_U = \mu + z_U \sigma_{\overline{X}}$$
$$= 100 + (-1.96)(8) \qquad\qquad = 100 + (+1.96)(8)$$
$$= 100 - 15.68 \qquad\qquad = 100 + 15.68$$
$$= 84.32 \qquad\qquad = 115.68$$

Rather than falling within roughly four points of μ (Problem 4), 95% of all possible sample means now fall between 84.32 and 115.68—almost 16 (!) points to either side of μ. Again, sample means spread more about μ when sample size is small, and, conversely, they spread less when sample size is large.

Table 10.1 shows the degree of sampling variation for different values of *n* where $\mu = 100$ and $\sigma = 16$. For the largest sample size ($n = 256$), 95% of all possible

Table 10.1 Sampling Variation Among Means for Different Values of n ($\mu = 100$, $\sigma = 16$)

n	$\sigma_{\bar{X}}$	Central 95% of Possible Sample Means
4	$\dfrac{16}{\sqrt{4}} = 8.0$	$84.32 - 115.68$
16	$\dfrac{16}{\sqrt{16}} = 4.0$	$92.16 - 107.84$
25	$\dfrac{16}{\sqrt{25}} = 3.2$	$93.73 - 106.27$
64	$\dfrac{16}{\sqrt{64}} = 2.0$	$96.08 - 103.92$
100	$\dfrac{16}{\sqrt{100}} = 1.6$	$96.86 - 103.14$
256	$\dfrac{16}{\sqrt{256}} = 1.0$	$98.04 - 101.96$

sample means will fall *fewer than 2 points* from μ. This table illustrates an important principle in statistical inference:

> As sample size increases, so does the accuracy of the sample statistic as an estimate of the population parameter.

We will explore this relationship further in subsequent chapters.

10.10 Generality of the Concept of a Sampling Distribution

The focus so far has been on the sampling distribution of *means*. However, the concept of a sampling distribution is general and can apply to any sample statistic. Suppose that you had determined the *median* Stanford-Binet IQ, rather than the mean, from an unlimited number of random samples of 10-year-olds. The relative frequency distribution of sample medians obtained for such a series of sampling experiments would be called, reasonably enough, a *sampling distribution of medians*. And if you were to compute the Pearson r between the same two variables in an infinite series of random samples, you would have a *sampling distribution of correlation coefficients*. In general terms:

> A sampling distribution of a statistic is the relative frequency distribution of that statistic, obtained from an unlimited series of identical sampling experiments.

Of course, for the sampling experiments to be identical, the sample size must remain the same and the samples must be selected (with replacement) from the same population.

For the present, we will continue to develop concepts and procedures of statistical inference as applied to the problems involving single means. When we later turn to inferences about other population parameters, such as the difference between two means or the correlation coefficient, you will find that the general principles now being developed still apply, though the details may differ.

10.11   Summary

The assumption of random sampling underlies most inference procedures used by researchers in the behavioral sciences, and it is the random sampling model that is developed in this book. Even though the samples used in educational research are often not randomly selected, the application of inference procedures that assume random sampling can be very useful, provided the interpretation is done with care.

Three concepts are basic to the random sampling model:

1. *Population*—the set of observations about which the investigator wishes to draw conclusions. Population characteristics are called parameters.

2. *Sample*—a part of the population. Sample characteristics are called statistics.

3. *Random sample*—a sample so chosen that each possible sample of the specified size (n) has an equal probability of selection. When this condition is met, it is also true that each element of the population will have an equal opportunity of being included in the sample.

The key question of statistical inference is, "What are the probabilities of obtaining various sample results under random sampling?" The answer to this question is provided by the relevant sampling distribution. This could be a sampling distribution of sample means, medians, correlations, or any other statistic. All sampling distributions are probability distributions.

The sampling distribution of means is the relative frequency distribution of means of all possible samples of a specified size drawn from a given population. The mean of the sampling distribution of means is symbolized by $\mu_{\bar{X}}$ and is equal to μ. The standard deviation of this distribution (called the standard error of the mean) is symbolized by $\sigma_{\bar{X}}$ and is equal to $\sigma/\sqrt{n}$. The formula for $\sigma_{\bar{X}}$ shows that sampling variation among means will be less for larger samples than for smaller ones. The shape of the distribution will be normal if the population is normal or, because of the central limit theorem, if the sample size is relatively large. Consequently, the normal curve can be used as a mathematical model for determining the probabilities of obtaining sample means of various values.

Reading the Research: Standard Error of the Mean

Baker et al. (2000) reported the mean reading and math scores for subgroups of eighth-grade Hispanic students from across the nation. For each mean (M), these authors also presented the accompanying standard error (SE). As you can see in Table 10.2, larger ns are associated with smaller SEs, and, conversely, smaller ns are found with larger SEs. Consider the relatively small sample of Cuban students ($n = 35$), for whom the reading SE is roughly eight times larger than the SE for the sizable sample of Mexican students ($n = 1571$). There simply is greater "sampling variation" for small samples in comparison to large samples. Consequently, the

Table 10.2 Means and Standard Errors for Subgroups
of Eighth-Grade Hispanic Students

		Reading		Math	
	n	*M*	*SE*	*M*	*SE*
Mexican	1,571	27.8	0.52	34.5	0.52
Cuban	35	33.4	4.05	42.6	3.82
Puerto Rican	148	26.8	1.48	31.2	1.37
Other Hispanic	387	27.2	0.89	34.8	0.95

Source: Table 3 in Baker et al. (2000). (Reprinted by permission of Sage, Inc.)

reading and math means for the smaller sample of Cuban students are less precise estimates of the population means (i.e., the reading and math performance of *all* Cuban eighth graders in the United States) than is the case for the larger sample of Mexican students. You will see the implications of the standard error of the mean more clearly in Chapter 12, where we discuss interval estimation.

Source: Baker, B. D., Keller-Wolff, C., & Wolf-Wendel, L. (2000). Two steps forward, one step back: Race/ethnicity and student achievement in education policy research. *Educational Policy, 14*(4), 511–529.

Case Study: Luck of the Draw

The No Child Left Behind Act (NCLB) requires public schools in each state to administer standardized tests in the core subject areas of reading and mathematics. By the 2007–2008 school year, science exams are to be added to the mix. Many states test in other domains as well. For instance, Missouri and Rhode Island administer assessments in health and physical education, and Kentucky tests in the arts. Several states administer social studies exams. There are, of course, many benefits of state testing programs. But they also can be expensive ventures in terms of both time and money.

What if a state desired to expand its assessment program to include an additional test in, say, the arts? Suppose further that this state, in an effort to minimize costs and inconvenience, decided to test only a *sample* of schools each year. That is, rather than administer this additional test in every school, a random sample of 300 schools is selected to participate in the state arts assessment. The state's interest here is not to hold *every* school (and student) accountable to arts performance standards; rather, it is to track general trends in statewide performance. Such information could be used to identify areas of relative strength and weakness and, in turn, guide state-sponsored reform initiatives. Testing students in a representative sample of schools (rather than every school) is quite consistent with this goal.

Using this approach, would the mean performance, based on this sample of 300 schools, provide a sound basis for making an inference about the performance of *all* schools in the state? What is the likelihood that, by chance, such a sample would include a disproportionate number of high-scoring (or low-scoring) schools, thereby misrepresenting the population of *all* schools?

To explore such questions, we created a data set containing statewide arts as-sessment results for 1574 elementary schools. Data were available on the percentage of students performing at the proficient level or above (a variable we call PROFIC). We then calculated the mean and standard deviation of PROFIC, obtaining $\mu = 78.39$ and $\sigma = 14.07$. That is, the average third-grade school in this state had slightly more than 78% of its third graders scoring proficient or higher, with a standard deviation of about 14 percentage points. Notice our use of μ and σ, since we have population data (i.e., all third-grade schools in this state).

Let's return to our basic question: Is the mean, based on a random sample of $n = 300$ schools, a sound basis for making an inference about the population of schools in this state? Because we know that $\sigma = 14.07$, we can use Formula (10.2) to determine the standard error of the mean:

$$\sigma_{\overline{X}} = \frac{\sigma}{\sqrt{n}} = \frac{14.07}{\sqrt{300}} = \frac{14.07}{17.33} = .81$$

This tells us the amount of sampling variation in means that we would expect, given unlimited random samples of size $n = 300$. Now, because we know that $\mu = 78.39$, we also can determine the central 95% of all sample means that would obtain with repeated sampling of this population:

$$z_{L} = -1.96 \qquad\qquad z_{U} = +1.96$$
$$\overline{X}_{L} = \mu + z_{L}\sigma_{\overline{X}} \qquad\qquad \overline{X}_{U} = \mu + z_{U}\sigma_{\overline{X}}$$
$$= 78.39 + (-1.96)(.81) \qquad = 78.39 + (1.96)(.81)$$
$$= 78.39 - 1.59 \qquad\qquad = 78.39 + 1.59$$
$$= 76.80 \qquad\qquad\qquad = 79.98$$

Thus, we see that the lion's share of random samples—95%—would fall within a mere point and a half (1.59, to be precise) of the population mean. Stated more formally, the probability is .95 that the mean performance of a random sample of 300 schools will fall within 1.59 points of the mean performance of *all* schools. In this case, a mean based on a random sample of 300 schools would tend to esti-mate the population of schools with considerable accuracy!

Imagine that the goal in this state is that the statewide average PROFIC score will be at least 80%. Given $\mu = 78.39$, which falls slightly short of this goal, what is the probability that a random sample of 300 schools nevertheless would result in a mean PROFIC score of 80% or higher? (This outcome, unfortunately, would lead to premature celebration.) The answer is found by applying Formula (10.3):

$$z = \frac{\overline{X} - \mu}{\sigma_{\overline{X}}} = \frac{80.00 - 78.39}{.81} = 1.99$$

Although it is possible to obtain a sample mean of 80% or higher (when $\mu = 78.39$), it is highly unlikely: this outcome corresponds to a z score of 1.99, which carries a probability of only .0233. It is exceedingly unlikely that a random sample of 300 schools would lead to the false conclusion that the statewide goal had been met.

As a final consideration, suppose that a policymaker recommends that only 100 schools are tested, which would save even more money. As you know, reducing n will increase the standard error of the mean: with $n = 100$, the standard error increases to $\sigma_{\bar{X}} = 1.41$, and the central 95% of all possible sample means now extends from 75.63 to 81.15. Witness the tradeoff between precision and cost: with a smaller sample, one gets a wider range of possible means. Similarly, there would be a greater probability (.0793) of wrongly concluding, on the basis of a single sample, that the statewide goal of 80% had been met—a fact you can verify by plugging the new $\sigma_{\bar{X}}$ into Formula (10.3).

We should emphasize that, because we already know μ, this case study is rather unrealistic. In actual practice, the state would have only the random sample of 300 schools and, from this, make a reasoned conclusion about the likely performance of all schools—*had all schools been tested*. But by engaging you in our fantasy, we are able to show you how close such a sample mean would be to the population mean it is intended to estimate.

Suggested Computer Exercises

Access the **sophomores** data file.

1. Compute the mean CGPA score for the entire population of 521 students; generate a histogram for CGPA.

2. Select a random sample of 25 cases from the population of 521 students. To do so, use the *Select Cases* procedure, which is located within the *Data* menu. Calculate the mean for CGPA. Repeat this entire process 19 times and record your results.

3. Open a new (empty) data file in SPSS. Input the 20 sample means in a column, naming the variable S_MEANS. Compute its mean and standard deviation (i.e., the mean and standard deviation of the sample means). Also generate a histogram for S_MEANS and compare it to the histogram of the population of CGPA scores you created in #1 above.

Exercises

Identify, Define, or Explain

Terms and Concepts

sampling variation
sample
population
statistic
parameter
estimate
random sampling model
random sample
simple random sampling

systematic sampling
convenience sample
accessible population
sampling distribution of means
standard error of the mean
central limit theorem
probability distribution
sampling distribution of a statistic

Symbols

$\mu_{\bar{X}}$ $\sigma_{\bar{X}}$ $\bar{X}_L$ $\bar{X}_U$ z_L z_U

Note: Answers to starred (*) items are presented in Appendix B.

*1. "The average person on the street is not happy," or so claimed the newscaster after interviewing patrons of a local sports bar regarding severe sanctions that had been imposed on the state university for NCAA infractions.

(a) What population does the newscaster appear to have in mind?

(b) What is the sample in this instance?

(c) Do you believe this sample is representative of the apparent population? If not, in what ways might this sample be biased?

2. After considering the sampling problems associated with Problem 1, your friend decides to interview people who *literally* are "on the street." That is, he stands on a downtown sidewalk and takes as his population passersby who come near enough that he might buttonhole them for an interview. List four sources of bias that you believe might prevent him from obtaining a truly random sample of interviewees.

*3. A researcher conducting a study on attitudes toward "home schooling" has her assistant select a random sample of ten members from a large suburban church. The sample selected comprises nine women and one man. Upon seeing the uneven distribution of sexes in the sample, the assistant complains, "This sample can't be random—it's almost all women!" How would you respond to the researcher's assistant?

4. A certain population of observations is bimodal (see Figure 3.11*b*).

(a) Suppose you want to obtain a fairly accurate picture of the sampling distribution of means for random samples of size 3 drawn from this population. Suppose also that you have unlimited time and resources. Describe how, through repeated sampling, you could arrive at such a picture.

(b) What would you expect the sampling distribution of means to look like for samples of size 150 selected from this population? State the principle used to arrive at your answer.

*5. Suppose you did not know Formula (10.2) for $\sigma_{\bar{X}}$. If you had unlimited time and resources, how would you go about obtaining an empirical estimate of $\sigma_{\bar{X}}$ for samples of three cases each drawn from the population of Problem 4?

6. Explain on an intuitive basis why the sampling distribution of means for $n = 2$ selected from the "flat" distribution of Figure 10.4*a* has more cases in the middle than at the extremes. (*Hint:* Compare the number of ways an extremely high or an extremely low mean could be obtained with the number of ways a mean toward the center could be obtained.)

7. What are the three defining characteristics of any sampling distribution of means?

*8. What are the key questions to be answered in any statistical inference problem?

*9. Given: $\mu = 100$ and $\sigma = 30$ for a normally distributed population of observations. Suppose you randomly selected from this population a sample of size 36.

(a) Calculate the standard error of the mean.

(b) What is the probability that the sample mean will fall above 92?

(c) What is the probability that the sample mean will fall more than 8 points above the population mean of 100?

(d) What is the probability that the sample mean will differ from the population mean by 4 points or more (in either direction)?

(e) What sample mean has such a high value that the probability is .01 of obtaining one as high or higher?

(f) Within what limits would the central 95% of all possible sample means fall?

*10. Suppose you collected an unlimited number of random samples of size 36 from the population in Problem 9.

(a) What would be the mean of the resulting sample means?

(b) What would be the standard deviation of the sample means?

(c) What would be the shape of the distribution of sample means? (How do you know?)

11. A population of peer ratings of physical attractiveness is approximately normal with $\mu = 5.2$ and $\sigma = 1.6$. A random sample of four ratings is selected from this population.

(a) Calculate $\sigma_{\bar{X}}$.

What is the probability of obtaining a sample mean:

(b) above 6.6?

(c) as extreme as 3.8?

(d) below 4.4?

(e) between the population mean and .5 points below the mean?

(f) no more than .5 points away from the population mean (in either direction)?

(g) What sample mean has such a low value that the probability is .05 of obtaining one as low or lower?

(h) What are the centrally placed limits such that the probability is .95 that the sample mean will fall within those limits?

12. Repeat Problem 11h using a sample of size 100.

(a) What is the effect of this larger sample on the standard error of the mean?

(b) What is the effect of this larger sample on the limits within which the central 95% of sample means fall?

(c) Can you see an advantage of using large samples in attempts to estimate the population mean from the mean of a random sample? (Explain.)

13. Suppose you don't know anything about the shape of the population distribution of ratings used in Problems 11 and 12. Would this lack of knowledge have any implications for solving Problem 11? Problem 12? (Explain.)

*14. Suppose for a normally distributed population of observations you know that $\sigma = 15$, but you don't know the value of μ. You plan to select a random sample ($n = 50$) and use the sample mean to estimate the population mean.

(a) Calculate $\sigma_{\bar{X}}$.

(b) What is the probability that the sample mean will fall within 5 points (in either direction) of the unknown value of μ?

    (c) What is the probability that the sample mean will fall within 2 points of μ (in either direction)?

    (d) The probability is .95 that the sample mean will fall within _____ points of μ (in either direction).

*15. You randomly select a sample ($n = 50$) from the population in Problem 14 and obtain a sample mean of $\overline{X} = 108$. Remember: Although you know that $\sigma = 15$, you don't know the value of μ.

    (a) Would 107 be reasonable as a possible value for μ in light of the sample mean of 108? (Explain in terms of probabilities.)

    (b) In this regard, would 100 be reasonable as a possible value of μ?

16. A population of personality test scores is normal with $\mu = 50$ and $\sigma = 10$.

    (a) Describe the operations you would go through to obtain a fairly accurate picture of the sampling distribution of *medians* for samples of size 25. (Assume you have unlimited time and resources.)

    (b) It is known from statistical theory that if the population distribution is normal, then

$$\sigma_{Mdn} = \frac{1.253\sigma}{\sqrt{n}}$$

    What does σ_{Mdn} stand for (give the name)? In conceptual terms, what is σ_{Mdn}?

    (c) If you randomly select a sample ($n = 25$), what is the probability that the sample median will fall above 55 (assume a normal sampling distribution)?

    (d) For a normal population where μ is unknown, which is likely to be a better estimate of μ: the sample mean or the sample median? (Explain.)

CHAPTER 11

Testing Statistical Hypotheses about μ When σ Is Known: The One-Sample z Test

11.1 Testing a Hypothesis about μ: Does "Homeschooling" Make a Difference?

In the last chapter, you were introduced to sampling theory that is basic to statistical inference. In this chapter, you will learn how to apply that theory to **statistical hypothesis testing**, the statistical inference approach most widely used by educational researchers. It also is known as **significance testing**. We present a very simple example of this approach: testing hypotheses about means of single populations. Specifically, we will focus on testing hypotheses about μ when σ is known.

Since the early 1980s, a growing number of parents across the U.S.A. have opted to teach their children at home. The United States Department of Education estimates that 1.1 million students were being homeschooled in the spring of 2003—up 29% from four years before. Some parents homeschool their children for religious reasons, and others because of dissatisfaction with the local schools. But whatever the reasons, you can imagine the rhetoric surrounding the "homeschooling" movement: Proponents treat its efficacy as a foregone conclusion, and the critics assume the worst.

But *does* homeschooling make a difference—whether good or bad? Marc Meyer, a professor of educational psychology at Puedam College, decides to conduct a study to explore this question. As it turns out, every fourth-grade student attending school in his state takes a standardized test of academic achievement that was developed specifically for that state. Scores are normally distributed with μ = 250 and σ = 50.

Homeschooled children are not required to take this test. Undaunted, Dr. Meyer selects a random sample of 25 homeschooled fourth graders and has each child complete the test. (It clearly would be too expensive and time-consuming to test the *entire* population of homeschooled fourth-grade students in the state.) His general objective is to find out how the mean of the population of achievement scores for homeschooled fourth graders compares with 250, the state value. Specifically, his research question is this: "*Is 250 a reasonable value for the mean of the homeschooled population?*" Notice that the population here is no longer the larger group of fourth graders attending school, but rather the test scores for *homeschooled* fourth graders. This illustrates the notion that it is the concerns and interests of the investigator that determine the population.

Although we will introduce statistical hypothesis testing in the context of this specific, relatively straightforward example, the overall logic to be presented is general. It applies to testing hypotheses in situations far more complex than Dr. Meyer's. In later chapters, you will see how the same logic can be applied to comparing the means of two or more populations, as well as to other parameters such as population correlation coefficients. In all cases—whether here or in subsequent chapters—the statistical tests you will encounter are based on the principles of sampling and probability discussed so far.

11.2   *Dr. Meyer's Problem in a Nutshell*

In the five steps that follow, we summarize the logic and actions by which Dr. Meyer will answer his question. We then provide a more detailed discussion of this process.

Step 1   Dr. Meyer reformulates his question as a statement, or hypothesis: *The mean of the population of achievement scores for homeschooled fourth graders, in fact, is equal to 250. That is,* $\mu = 250$.

Step 2   He then asks, "*If the hypothesis were true,* what sample means would be expected by chance alone—that is, due to sampling variation—if an infinite number of samples of size $n = 25$ were randomly selected from this population (i.e., where $\mu = 250$)?" As you know from Chapter 10, this information is given by the sampling distribution of means. The sampling distribution relevant to this particular situation is shown in Figure 11.1. The mean of this sampling distribution, $\mu_{\overline{X}}$, is equal to the hypothesized value of 250, and the standard error, $\sigma_{\overline{X}}$, is equal to

$$\sigma/\sqrt{n} = 50/\sqrt{25} = 10$$

Step 3   He selects a single random sample from the population of homeschooled fourth-grade students in his state ($n = 25$), administers the achievement test, and computes the mean score, $\overline{X}$.

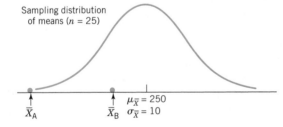

Sampling distribution of means ($n = 25$)

$\mu_{\overline{X}} = 250$
$\sigma_{\overline{X}} = 10$

$\overline{X}_A$ $\overline{X}_B$

Figure 11.1   Two possible locations of the obtained sample mean among all possible sample means when the null hypothesis is true.

Step 4   He then compares his sample mean with all the possible samples of $n = 25$, as revealed by the sampling distribution. This is done in Figure 11.1, where, for illustrative purposes, we have inserted two possible results.

Step 5   On the basis of the comparison in Step 4, Dr. Meyer makes one of two decisions about his hypothesis that $\mu = 250$: It will be either "rejected" or "retained." If he obtains $\overline{X}_A$, he rejects the hypothesis as untenable, for $\overline{X}_A$ is quite unlike the sample means that would be expected *if the hypothesis were true*. That is, the probability is exceedingly low that he would obtain a mean as deviant as $\overline{X}_A$ due to random sampling variation alone, given that $\mu = 250$. It's *possible*, mind you, but not very likely. On the other hand, Dr. Meyer retains the hypothesis as a reasonable statement if he obtains $\overline{X}_B$, for $\overline{X}_B$ is consistent with what would be expected *if the hypothesis were true*. That is, there is sufficient probability that $\overline{X}_B$ could occur by chance alone if, in the population, $\mu = 250$.

The logic above may strike you as being a bit backward. This is because statistical hypothesis testing is a process of **indirect proof**. That is, to test his hypothesis, Dr. Meyer first assumes it to be true. Then he follows the logical implications of this assumption to determine, through the appropriate sampling distribution, all possible sample results that would be expected under this assumption. Finally, he notes whether his actual sample result is contrary to what would be expected. If it is contrary, the hypothesis is rejected as untenable. If the result is not contrary to what would be expected, the hypothesis is retained as reasonably possible.

You may be wondering what Dr. Meyer's decision would be were his sample mean to fall somewhere *between* $\overline{X}_A$ and $\overline{X}_B$. Just how rare must the sample value be to trigger rejection of the hypothesis? How does one decide? As you will soon learn, there are established criteria for making such decisions.

With this general overview of Dr. Meyer's problem, we now present a more detailed account of statistical hypothesis testing.

11.3   *The Statistical Hypotheses:* H_0 *and* H_1

In Step 1 above, Dr. Meyer formulated the hypothesis: *The mean of the population of achievement scores for homeschooled fourth graders is equal to 250.* This is called the **null hypothesis** and is written in symbolic form, H_0: $\mu = 250$.

> The null hypothesis, H_0, plays a central role in statistical hypothesis testing: It is the hypothesis that is assumed to be true and formally tested, it is the hypothesis that determines the sampling distribution to be employed, and it is the hypothesis about which the final decision to "reject" or "retain" is made.

A second hypothesis is formulated at this point: the **alternative hypothesis**, H_1:

> The alternative hypothesis, H_1, specifies the alternative population condition that is "supported" or "asserted" upon rejection of H_0. H_1 typically reflects the underlying research hypothesis of the investigator.

In the present case, the alternative hypothesis specifies a population condition other than $\mu = 250$.

H_1 can take one of two general forms. If Dr. Meyer goes into his investigation without a clear sense of what to expect if H_0 is false, then he is interested in knowing that the actual population value is either higher or lower than 250. He is just as open to the possibility that mean achievement among homeschoolers is above 250 as he is to the possibility that it is below 250. In this case he would specify a **nondirectional alternative hypothesis**: $H_1: \mu \neq 250$.

In contrast, Dr. Meyer would state a **directional alternative hypothesis** if his interest lay primarily in one direction. Perhaps he firmly believes, based on pedagogical theory and prior research, that the more personalized and intensive nature of homeschooling will, if anything, *promote* academic achievement. In this case, he would hypothesize the actual population value to be *greater* than 250 if the null hypothesis is false. Here, the alternative hypothesis would take the form, $H_1: \mu > 250$. If, on the other hand, he posited that the population value was less than 250, then the form of the alternative hypothesis would be $H_1: \mu < 250$.

You see, then, that there are three specific alternative hypotheses from which to choose in the present case:

$$H_1: \mu \neq 250 \text{ (nondirectional)}$$

$$H_1: \mu < 250 \text{ (directional)}$$

$$H_1: \mu > 250 \text{ (directional)}$$

Let's assume that Dr. Meyer has no compelling basis for stating a directional alternative hypothesis. Thus, his two statistical hypotheses are:

$$H_0: \mu = 250$$

$$H_1: \mu \neq 250$$

Notice that both H_0 and H_1 *are statements about populations and parameters, not samples and statistics.* That is, both statistical hypotheses specify the population parameter μ, rather than the sample statistic. Furthermore, both hypotheses are formulated *before* the data are examined. We will further explore the nature of H_0 and H_1 in later sections of this chapter.

11.4 The Test Statistic z

Having stated his null and alternative hypotheses (and collected his data), Dr. Meyer calculates the mean achievement score from his sample of 25 home-schoolers, which he finds to be $\overline{X} = 272$. How likely is this sample mean, if in fact the population mean is 250? In theoretical terms, if repeated samples of $n = 25$ were randomly selected from a population where $\mu = 250$, what proportion of sample means would be as deviant from 250 as 272? To answer this question, Dr. Meyer determines the relative position of his sample mean among all possible sample means that would obtain *if H_0 were true*. He knows that the theoretical sampling distribution has as its mean the value hypothesized under the null hypothesis: 250 (see Figure 11.1). And from his knowledge that $\sigma = 50$, he easily determines the standard error of the mean, $\sigma_{\overline{X}}$, for this sampling distribution:

$$\sigma_{\overline{X}} = \frac{\sigma}{\sqrt{n}} = \frac{50}{\sqrt{25}} = \frac{50}{5} = 10$$

Now Dr. Meyer converts his sample mean of 272 to a z score using Formula (10.3). Within the context of testing statistical hypotheses, the z score is called a **test statistic**: it is the statistic used for testing H_0. The general structure of the z-score formula has not changed from the last time you saw it, although we now replace μ with μ_0 to represent the value of μ that is specified in the *null* hypothesis:

The test statistic z

$$z = \frac{\overline{X} - \mu_0}{\sigma_{\overline{X}}} \qquad (11.1)$$

In the present case,

$$z = \frac{\overline{X} - \mu_0}{\sigma_{\overline{X}}} = \frac{272 - 250}{10} = \frac{22}{10} = +2.20$$

The numerator of this ratio, 22, indicates that the sample mean of 272 is 22 points higher than the population mean under the null hypothesis ($\mu_0 = 250$). When divided by the denominator, 10, this 22-point difference is equivalent to 2.20 standard errors—the value of the z statistic, or **z ratio**. Because it involves data from a single sample, we call this test the **one-sample z test**.

Dr. Meyer, equipped with this z ratio, now locates the relative position of his sample mean in the sampling distribution. Using familiar logic, he then assesses the probability associated with this value of z, as described in the next section.

11.5   *The Probability of the Test Statistic: The* p *Value*

Let's return to the central question: How likely is a sample mean of 272, given a population where $\mu = 250$? More specifically, what is the probability of selecting from this population a random sample for which the mean is as deviant as 272?

From Table A (Appendix C), Dr. Meyer determines that .0139 of the area under the normal curve falls beyond $z = 2.20$, the value of the test statistic for $\overline{X} = 272$. This is shown by the shaded area to the right in Figure 11.2. Is .0139 the probability value he seeks? Not quite. Recall that Dr. Meyer has formulated a *nondirectional* alternative hypothesis, because he is equally interested in either possible result: that is, whether the population mean for homeschoolers is above *or* below the stated value of 250. Even though the actual sample mean will fall on only one side of the sampling distribution (it certainly can't fall on both sides at once!), the language of the probability question nonetheless must honor the nondirectional nature of Dr. Meyer's H_1. (Remember: H_1 was formulated *before* data collection.) This question concerns the probability of selecting a sample mean *as deviant as* 272.

Because a mean of 228 ($z = -2.20$) is just as deviant as 272 ($z = +2.20$), Dr. Meyer uses the OR/addition rule and obtains a *two-tailed* probability value (see Figure 11.2). This is said to be a **two-tailed test**. He combines the probability associated with $z = +2.20$ (shaded area to the right) with the probability associated with $z = -2.20$ (shaded area to the left) to obtain the **exact probability**, or *p* **value**, for his outcome: $p = .0139 + .0139 = .0278$. (In practice, you simply would double the tabled value found in Table A.)

> A *p* value is the probability, if H_0 is true, of observing a sample result as deviant as the result actually obtained (in the direction specified in H_1).

A *p* value, then, is a measure of how rare the sample results would be if H_0 were true. The probability is $p = .0278$ that Dr. Meyer would obtain a mean as deviant as 272, if in fact $\mu = 250$.

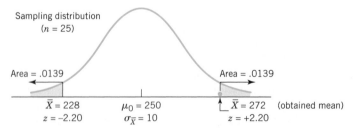

Figure 11.2   Location of Dr. Meyer's sample mean ($\overline{X} = 272$) in the sampling distribution under the null hypothesis ($\mu_0 = 250$).

11.6   The Decision Criterion: Level of Significance (α)

Now that Dr. Meyer knows the probability associated with his outcome, what is his decision regarding H_0? Clearly, a sample mean as deviant as the one he obtained is not very likely *under the null hypothesis* ($\mu = 250$). Indeed, over an infinite number of random samples from a population where $\mu = 250$, fewer than 3% (.0278) of the sample means would deviate this much (or more) from 250. Wouldn't this suggest that H_0 is false?

To make a decision about H_0, Dr. Meyer needs an established criterion. Most educational researchers reject H_0 when $p \leq .05$ (although you often will encounter the lower value .01, and sometimes even .001). Such a decision criterion is called the **level of significance**, and its symbol is the Greek letter α (**alpha**).

> The level of significance, α, specifies how rare the sample result must be in order to reject H_0 as untenable. It is a probability (typically .05, .01, or .001) based on the assumption that H_0 is true.

Let's suppose that Dr. Meyer adopts the .05 level of significance (i.e., $\alpha = .05$). He will reject the null hypothesis that $\mu = 250$ if his sample mean is so far above or below 250 that it falls among the most unlikely 5% of all possible sample means. We illustrate this in Figure 11.3, where the total shaded area in the tails represents the 5% of sample means least likely to occur if H_0 is true. The .05 is split evenly between the two tails—2.5% on each side—because of the nondirectional, two-tailed nature of H_1. The regions defined by the shaded tails are called **regions of rejection**, for if the sample mean falls in either, H_0 is rejected as untenable. They also are known as **critical regions**.

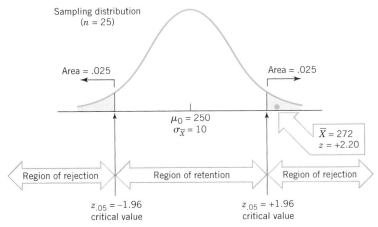

Figure 11.3   Regions of rejection for a two-tailed test ($\alpha = .05$). Dr. Meyer's sample mean ($\overline{X} = 272$) falls in the critical region ($+2.20 > +1.96$); H_0 is rejected and H_1 is asserted.

The **critical values** of z separate the regions of rejection from the middle **region of retention**. In Chapter 10 (Problem 4 of Section 10.8), you learned that the middle 95% of all possible sample means in a sampling distribution fall between $z = \pm 1.96$. This also is illustrated in Figure 11.3, where you see that $z = -1.96$ marks the beginning of the lower critical region (beyond which 2.5% of the area falls) and, symmetrically, $z = +1.96$ marks the beginning of the upper critical region (with 2.5% of the area falling beyond). Thus, the two-tailed critical values of z, where $\alpha = .05$, are $z_{.05} = \pm 1.96$. We attach the subscript ".05" to z, signifying that it is the *critical value* of z ($\alpha = .05$), not the value of z calculated from the data (which we leave unadorned).

Dr. Meyer's test statistic, $z = +2.20$, falls beyond the upper critical value of $+1.96$ (i.e., $+2.20 > +1.96$) and thus in a region of rejection, as shown in Figure 11.3. This indicates that the probability associated with his sample mean is less than α, the level of significance. He therefore rejects H_0: $\mu = 250$ as untenable. Although it is *possible* that this sample of homeschoolers comes from a population where $\mu = 250$, it is so unlikely ($p = .0278$) that Dr. Meyer dismisses the proposition as unreasonable. If his calculated z ratio had been a *negative* 2.20, he would have arrived at the same conclusion (and obtained the same p value). In that case, however, the z ratio would fall in the *lower* rejection region (i.e., $-2.20 < -1.96$).

Notice, then, that there are two ways to evaluate the tenability of H_0. You can compare the p value to α (in this case, $.0278 < .05$), or you can compare the calculated z ratio to its critical value ($+2.20 > +1.96$). Either way, the same conclusion will be reached regarding H_0. This is because both p (i.e., area) and the calculated z reflect the location of the sample mean relative to the region of rejection. The decision rules for a two-tailed test are shown in Table 11.1. The exact probabilities for statistical tests that you will learn about in later chapters cannot be easily determined from hand calculations. With most tests in this book, you therefore will rely on the comparison of calculated and critical values of the test statistic for making decisions about H_0.

Back to Dr. Meyer. The rejection of H_0 implies support for H_1: $\mu \neq 250$. He won't necessarily stop with the conclusion that the mean achievement for the population of homeschooled fourth graders is some value "other than" 250. For if 250 is so far below his obtained sample mean of 272 as to be an untenable value for μ, then any value *below* 250 is even more untenable. Thus, he will follow common practice and conclude that μ must be *above* 250. How far above 250, he cannot say. (You will learn in the next chapter how to make more informative statements about *where* μ probably lies.)

Table 11.1   Decision Rules for a Two-Tailed Test

	Reject H_0	Retain H_0
In terms of p:	if $p \leq \alpha$	if $p > \alpha$
In terms of z:	if $z \leq -z_\alpha$ or $z \geq +z_\alpha$	if $z > -z_\alpha$ or $z < +z_\alpha$

Table 11.2   Summary of the Statistical Hypothesis Testing Conducted by Dr. Meyer

Step 1   *Specify H_0 and H_1, and set the level of significance (α).*

- H_0: $\mu = 250$
- H_1: $\mu \neq 250$
- $\alpha = .05$ (two-tailed)

Step 2   *Select the sample, calculate the necessary sample statistics.*

- Sample mean:

$$\overline{X} = 272$$

- Standard error of the mean, $\sigma_{\overline{X}}$:

$$\sigma_{\overline{X}} = \frac{\sigma}{\sqrt{n}} = \frac{50}{\sqrt{25}} = \frac{50}{5} = 10$$

- Test statistic z:

$$z = \frac{\overline{X} - \mu_0}{\sigma_{\overline{X}}} = \frac{272 - 250}{10} = \frac{22}{10} = +2.20$$

Step 3   *Determine the probability of z under the null hypothesis.*
The two-tailed probability is $p = .0139 + .0139 = .0278$, which is less than .05 (i.e., $p \leq \alpha$). Of course the obtained z ratio also exceeds the critical z value (i.e., $+2.20 > +1.96$) and therefore falls in the rejection region.

Step 4   *Make the decision regarding H_0.*
Because the calculated z ratio falls in the rejection region ($p \leq \alpha$), H_0 is rejected and H_1 is asserted.

In Table 11.2, we summarize the statistical hypothesis testing process that Dr. Meyer followed. We encourage you to review this table before proceeding.

11.7   The Level of Significance and Decision Error

You have just seen that the decision to reject or retain H_0 depends on the announced level of significance, α, and that .05 and .01 are common values in this regard. In one sense these values are arbitrary, but in another they are not. The level of significance, α, is a statement of risk—the risk the researcher is willing to assume in making a decision about H_0. Look at Figure 11.4, which shows how a two-tailed test would be conducted where $\alpha = .05$. When H_0 is true ($\mu_0 = \mu_{\text{true}}$), 5% of all possible sample means nevertheless will lead to the conclusion that H_0 is false. *This is necessarily so*, for 5% of the sample means fall in the "rejection" region of the sampling distribution, even though these extreme means will occur (though rarely) when H_0 is true. Thus, when you adopt $\alpha = .05$, you really are saying that you will accept a probability of .05 that H_0 will be rejected *when it is actually true*. Rejecting a true

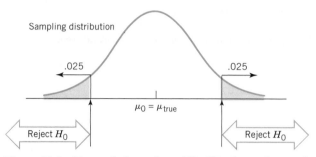

Figure 11.4   Two-tailed test (α = .05); 5% of sample *z* ratios leads incorrectly to the rejection of H_0 *when it is true* (Type I error).

H_0 is a **decision error**, and, barring divine revelation, you have no idea when such an error occurs.

> The level of significance, α, gives the probability of rejecting H_0 when it is actually true. Rejecting H_0 when it is true is known as a **Type I error**.

Stated less elegantly, a Type I error is getting statistically significant results "when you shouldn't."

To reduce the risk of making such an error, the researcher can set α at a lower level. Suppose you set it very low, say at α = .0001. Now suppose you obtain a sample result so deviant that its probability of occurrence is only *p* = .002. According to your criterion, this value is not rare enough to cause you to reject H_0 (i.e., .002 > .0001). Consequently, you retain H_0, even though common sense tells you that it probably is false. Lowering α, then, increases the likelihood of making another kind of error: *retaining H_0 when it is false*. Not surprisingly, this is known as a Type II error:

> A **Type II error** is committed when a false H_0 is retained.

We illustrate the notion of a Type II error in Figure 11.5. Imagine that your null hypothesis, H_0: μ = 150, is tested against a two-tailed alternative with α = .05. You draw a sample and obtain a mean of 152. Now it may be that unbeknown to you, the true mean for this population is 154. In Figure 11.5, the distribution drawn with the solid line is the sampling distribution under the null hypothesis, the one that describes the situation that would exist if H_0 were true ($\mu_0 = 150$). The true distribution, known only to powers above, is drawn with a dashed line and centers on 154, the true population mean ($\mu_{true} = 154$). To test your hypothesis that μ = 150, you evaluate the sample mean of 152 according to its position in the sampling distribution shown by the solid line. Relative to *that* distribution, it is not so deviant (from $\mu_0 = 150$) as to call for the rejection of H_0. Your decision therefore is to retain the null hypothesis, H_0: μ = 150. It is, of course, an erroneous decision—a Type II error

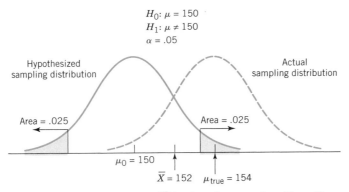

Figure 11.5 H_0 is false, but $\bar{X}$ leads to its retention (Type II error).

has been committed. To put it another way, you failed to claim that a real difference exists when in fact it does (although, again, you could not possibly have known).

Perhaps you now see that $\alpha = .05$ and $\alpha = .01$ are, in a sense, compromise values. These values tend to give reasonable assurance that H_0 will not be rejected when it actually is true (Type I error), yet they are not small enough to raise unnecessarily the likelihood of retaining a false H_0 (Type II error). In special circumstances, however, it makes sense to use a lower, more "conservative," value of α. For example, a lower α (e.g., $\alpha = .001$) is desirable where a Type I error would be costly, as in the case of a medical researcher who wants to be *very* certain that H_0 is indeed false before recommending to the medical profession an expensive and invasive treatment protocol. In contrast, now and then you find researchers adopting a higher, more "liberal," value for α (e.g., .10 or .15), such as investigators conducting exploratory analyses or wishing to detect preliminary trends in their data.

Your reaction to the inevitable tradeoff between a Type I error and a Type II error may well be "darned if I do, darned if I don't" (or a less restrained equivalent). But the possibility of either type of error is simply a fact of life when testing statistical hypotheses. In any one test of a null hypothesis, you just don't know whether a decision error has been made. Although probability usually will be in your corner, there always is the chance that your statistical decision is incorrect. How, then, do you maximize the likelihood of rejecting H_0 when in fact it is false? This question gets at the "power" of a statistical test, which we take up in Chapter 19.

11.8   *The Nature and Role of* H_0 *and* H_1

It is H_0, not H_1, that is tested directly. H_0 is assumed to be true for purposes of the test and then either rejected or retained. Yet, *it is usually H_1 rather than H_0 that follows most directly from the research question.*

Dr. Meyer's problem serves as illustration. His research question is: "How does the mean of the population of achievement scores for homeschooled fourth graders compare with the state value of 250?" Since he is interested in a deviation from 250 in either direction, his research question leads to the alternative hypothesis H_1: $\mu \neq 250$. Or imagine the school superintendent who wants to see whether a random sample of her district's kindergarten students are, on average, lower in reading readiness than the national mean of $\mu = 50$. Her overriding interest, then, necessitates the alternative hypothesis H_1: $\mu < 50$. (And her H_0 would be . . . ?)

If the alternative hypothesis normally reflects the researcher's primary interest, why then is it H_0 that is tested directly? The answer is rather simple:

> H_0 can be tested directly because it provides the specificity necessary to locate the appropriate sampling distribution. H_1 does not.

If you test H_0: $\mu = 250$, statistical theory tells you that the sampling distribution of means will center on 250 (i.e., $\mu_{\bar{X}} = 250$). You then can determine where your sample mean falls in that distribution and, in turn, whether it is sufficiently unlikely to warrant rejection of H_0. In contrast, now suppose you attempt to make a direct test of H_1: $\mu \neq 250$. You assume it to be true, and then identify the corresponding sampling distribution of means. But what *is* the sampling distribution of means, where "$\mu \neq 250$"? Specifically, what would be the *mean* of the sampling distribution of means ($\mu_{\bar{X}}$)? You simply cannot say; the best you can do is acknowledge that it is not 250. Consequently, it is impossible to calculate the test statistic for the sample outcome and determine its probability. The same reasoning applies to the reading readiness example. The null hypothesis, H_0: $\mu = 50$, provides the specific value of 50 for purposes of the test; the alternative hypothesis, H_1: $\mu < 50$, does not.

The approach of testing H_0 rather than H_1 is necessary from a statistical perspective, although it nevertheless may seem rather roundabout—"a ritualized exercise of devil's advocacy," as Abelson (1995, p. 9) put it. You might think of H_0 as a "dummy" hypothesis of sorts, set up to allow you to determine whether the evidence at hand is strong enough to knock it down. It is in this way that the original research question is answered.

11.9   *Rejection versus Retention of* H_0

In some ways, more is learned when H_0 is rejected than when it is retained. Let's look at rejection first. Dr. Meyer rejects H_0: $\mu = 250$ ($\alpha = .05$) because the discrepancy between 250 and his sample mean of 272 is too great to be accounted for by chance sampling variation alone. That is, 250 is too far below 272 to be considered a reasonable value of μ. It appears that μ is not equal to 250 and, furthermore, that it must be above 250. Dr. Meyer has learned something rather definite from his sample results about the value of μ.

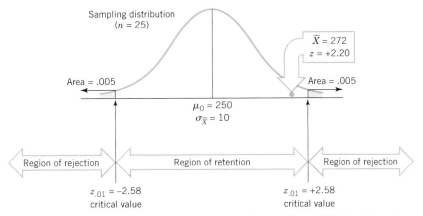

Figure 11.6   Regions of rejection for a two-tailed test ($\alpha = .01$). Dr. Meyer's sample mean ($\overline{X} = 272$) falls in the region of retention ($+2.20 < +2.58$); H_0 is retained.

What is learned when H_0 is retained? Suppose Dr. Meyer uses $\alpha = .01$ as his decision criterion rather than $\alpha = .05$. In this case, the critical values of z mark off the middle 99% of the sampling distribution (with .5%, or .005, in each tail). From Table A, you see that this area of the normal curve is bound by $z = \pm 2.58$. His sample z statistic of $+2.20$ now falls in the region of retention, as shown in Figure 11.6, and H_0 therefore is retained. But this decision will *not* be proof that μ is equal to 250.

> Retention of H_0 merely means that there is insufficient evidence to reject it and thus that it *could* be true. It does not mean that it *must* be true, or even that it *probably* is true.

Dr. Meyer's decision to retain H_0: $\mu = 250$ indicates only that the discrepancy between 250 and his sample mean of 272 is small enough to have resulted from sampling variation alone; 250 is close enough to 272 to be considered a reasonable possibility for μ (under the .01 criterion). If 250 is a reasonable value of μ, then values even *closer* to the sample mean of 272, such as 255, 260, or 265 would also be reasonable. Is H_0: $\mu = 250$ really true? Maybe, maybe not. In this sense, Dr. Meyer hasn't really learned very much from his sample results.

Nonetheless, sometimes something *is* learned from nonsignificant findings. We will return to this issue momentarily.

11.10   *Statistical Significance versus Importance*

If you have followed the preceding logic, you may not be surprised that sample results leading to the rejection of H_0 are referred to as **statistically significant**, suggesting that something has been learned from the sample results. Where $\alpha = .05$, for example, Dr. Meyer would state that his sample mean fell "significantly above" the hypothesized μ of 250, or that the difference between his sample mean and the hypothesized μ was "significant at the .05 level." In contrast, sample results leading to the retention of H_0 are referred to as **statistically nonsignificant**. Here, the language would be that the sample mean "was not significantly above" the hypothesized μ of 250, or that the difference between the sample mean and the hypothesized μ "was not significant at the .05 level."

We wish to emphasize two points about claims regarding the significance and nonsignificance of sample results. First, be very careful not to confuse the statistical term *significant* with the practical terms *important*, *substantial*, *meaningful*, or *consequential*.

> As applied to the results of a statistical analysis, *significant* is a technical term with a precise meaning: H_0 has been tested and rejected according to the decision criterion, α.

It is easy to obtain results that are statistically significant and yet are so trivial that they lack importance in any practical sense. How could this happen? Remember that the fate of H_0 hangs on the calculated value of z:

$$z = \frac{\overline{X} - \mu_0}{\sigma_{\overline{X}}}$$

As this formula demonstrates, the magnitude of z depends not only on the size of the difference between $\overline{X}$ and μ_0 (the numerator), but also on the size of $\sigma_{\overline{X}}$ (the denominator). You will recall that $\sigma_{\overline{X}}$ is equal to $\sigma/\sqrt{n}$, which means that if you have a very large sample, $\sigma_{\overline{X}}$ will be very small (because σ is divided by a big number). And if $\sigma_{\overline{X}}$ is very small, then z could be large—even if the actual difference between $\overline{X}$ and μ_0 is rather trivial.

For example, imagine that Dr. Meyer obtained a sample mean of $\overline{X} = 253$— merely three points different from μ_0—but his sample size was $n = 1200$. The corresponding z ratio would now be:

$$z = \frac{\overline{X} - \mu_0}{\sigma_{\overline{X}}} = \frac{253 - 250}{50/\sqrt{1200}} = \frac{3}{50/34.64} = \frac{3}{1.46} = +2.05$$

Although *statistically* significant ($\alpha = .05$), this z ratio nonetheless corresponds to a rather inconsequential sample result. Indeed, of what *practical* significance is it to learn that the population mean for homeschoolers in fact may be closer to 253 than 250? In short, *statistical* significance does not imply *practical* significance. Although we have illustrated this point in the context of the z statistic, you will see in subsequent chapters that n influences the magnitude of other test statistics in precisely the same manner.

Our second point is that sometimes something *is* learned when H_0 is retained. This is particularly true when the null hypothesis reflects the underlying research question, which occasionally it does. For example, a researcher may hypothesize that the known difference between adolescent boys and girls in mathematics problem-solving ability will disappear when the comparison is based on boys and girls who have experienced similar socialization practices at home. (You will learn of the statistical test for the difference between two sample means in Chapter 14.) Here, H_0 would reflect the *absence of a difference* between boys and girls on average—which in this case is what the researcher is hypothesizing will happen. If in fact this particular H_0 were tested and retained, something important arguably *is* learned about the phenomenon of sex-based differences in learning.

11.11   *Directional and Nondirectional Alternative Hypotheses*

Dr. Meyer wanted to know if his population mean differed from 250 *regardless of direction*, which led to a nondirectional H_1 and a two-tailed test. On some occasions, the research question calls for a directional H_1 and therefore a **one-tailed test**.

Let's go back and revise Dr. Meyer's intentions. Suppose instead that he believes, on a firm foundation of reason and prior research, that the homeschooling experience will *foster* academic achievement. His null hypothesis remains H_0: $\mu = 250$, but he now adopts a *directional* alternative hypothesis, H_1: $\mu > 250$. The null hypothesis will be rejected only if the evidence points with sufficient strength to the likelihood that μ is *greater* than 250. Only sample means greater than 250 would offer that kind of evidence, so the entire region of rejection is placed in the *upper* tail of the sampling distribution.

The regions of rejection and retention are as shown in Figure 11.7 ($\alpha = .05$). Note that the entire rejection region—all 5% of it—is confined to *one* tail (in this

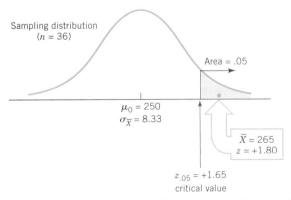

Figure 11.7   Region of rejection for a one-tailed test ($\alpha = .05$). Dr. Meyer's sample mean ($\bar{X} = 265$) falls in the critical region ($+1.80 > +1.65$); H_0 is rejected and H_1 is asserted.

case, the upper tail). This calls for a critical value of z that marks off the upper 5% of the sampling distribution. Table A discloses that +1.65 is the needed value. (If his alternative hypothesis had been H_1: $\mu < 250$, Dr. Meyer would test H_0 by comparing the sample z ratio to $z_{.05} = -1.65$, rejecting H_0 where $z \leq -1.65$.)

To conduct a one-tailed test, Dr. Meyer would proceed in the same general fashion as he did before:

Step 1 *Specify H_0, H_1, and α.*
- H_0: $\mu = 250$
- H_1: $\mu > 250$
- $\alpha = .05$ (one-tailed)

Step 2 *Select the sample, calculate the necessary sample statistics.*
(To get some new numbers on the table, let's change his sample size and mean.)
- $\overline{X} = 265$
- $\sigma_{\overline{X}} = \sigma/\sqrt{n} = 50/\sqrt{36} - 50/6 = 8.33$
- $z = \dfrac{\overline{X} - \mu_0}{\sigma_{\overline{X}}} = \dfrac{265 - 250}{8.33} = \dfrac{15}{8.33} = +1.80$

Step 3 *Determine the probability of z under the null hypothesis.*
Table A shows that a z of +1.80 corresponds to a one-tailed probability of $p = .0359$, which is less than .05 (i.e., $p \leq \alpha$). This p value, of course, is consistent with the fact that the obtained z ratio exceeds the critical z value (i.e., +1.80 > +1.65) and therefore falls in the region of rejection, as shown in Figure 11.7.

Step 4 *Make the decision regarding H_0.*
Because the calculated z ratio falls in the region of rejection ($p \leq \alpha$), H_0 is rejected and H_1 is asserted. Dr. Meyer thus concludes that the mean of the population of homeschooled fourth graders is greater than 250. The decision rules for a one-tailed test are shown in Table 11.3.

Table 11.3   Decision Rules for a One-Tailed Test

	Reject H_0	**Retain H_0**
In terms of p:	if $p \leq \alpha$	if $p > \alpha$
In terms of z:	if $z \leq -z_\alpha$ (H_1: $\mu < \mu_0$)	if $z > -z_\alpha$ (H_1: $\mu < \mu_0$)
	if $z \geq +z_\alpha$ (H_1: $\mu > \mu_0$)	if $z < +z_\alpha$ (H_1: $\mu > \mu_0$)

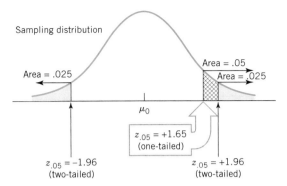

Figure 11.8   One-tailed versus two-tailed rejection regions: the statistical advantage of correctly advancing a directional H_1.

There is an advantage in stating a directional H_1 *if there is sufficient basis—prior to data collection—for doing so.* By conducting a one-tailed test and having the entire rejection region at one end of the sampling distribution, you are assigned a *lower* critical value for testing H_0. Consequently, it is "easier" to reject H_0—*provided you were justified in stating a directional H_1.* Look at Figure 11.8, which shows the rejection regions for both a two-tailed test ($z = \pm1.96$) and a one-tailed test ($z = +1.65$). If you state a directional H_1 *and* your sample mean subsequently falls in the hypothesized direction relative to μ_0, you will be able to reject H_0 with smaller values of z (i.e., smaller differences between $\overline{X}$ and μ_0) than would be needed to allow rejection with a nondirectional H_1. Calculated values of z falling in the cross-hatched area in Figure 11.8 will be statistically significant under a one-tailed test ($z_{.05} = +1.65$) but not under a two-tailed test ($z_{.05} = \pm1.96$). Dr. Meyer's latest finding is a case in point: his z of $+1.80$ falls only in the critical region of a one-tailed test ($\alpha = .05$). In a sense, statistical "credit" is given to the researcher who is able to correctly advance a directional H_1.

11.12   *Prologue: The Substantive versus the Statistical*

As you begin to cope with more and more statistical details, it is easy to lose the broader perspective concerning the role of significance tests in educational research. Let's revisit the model that we presented in Section 1.4 of Chapter 1:

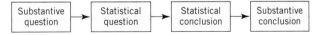

Significance tests occur in the middle of the process. First, the substantive question is raised. Here, one is concerned with the "substance" or larger context of the investigation: academic achievement among homeschooled children, a drug's effect on attention-deficit disorder, how rewards influence motivation, and so on. (The substantive question also is called the research question.) Then the substantive

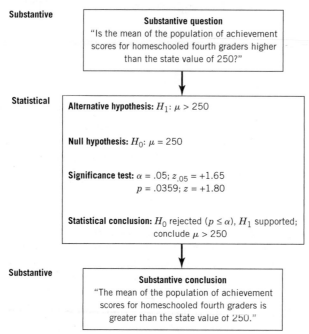

Figure 11.9   Substantive and statistical aspects of an investigation.

question is translated into the statistical hypotheses H_0 and H_1, data are collected, significance tests are conducted, and statistical conclusions are reached. Now you are in the realm of means, standard errors, levels of significance, test statistics, critical values, probabilities, and decisions to reject or retain H_0. But these are only a means to an end, which is to arrive at a substantive conclusion about the initial research question. Through his statistical reasoning and calculations, Dr. Meyer reached the substantive conclusion that the average academic achievement among homeschooled fourth graders is higher than that for fourth graders as a whole.[1]

Thus, a substantive question precedes the statistical work, and a substantive conclusion follows the statistical work. We illustrate this in Figure 11.9, using Dr. Meyer's directional alternative hypothesis from Section 11.11 as an example. Even though we have separated the substantive from the statistical in this figure, you should know that statistical considerations interact with substantive considerations from the very beginning of the research process. They have important implications for such matters as sample size and use of the same or different individuals

---

[1]Notice that the statistical analysis does not allow conclusions regarding *why* the significant difference was obtained—only that it did. Do these results speak to the positive effects of homeschooling, or do these results perhaps indicate that parents of academically excelling children are more inclined to adopt homeschooling?

under different treatment conditions. These and related matters are discussed in succeeding chapters.

11.13   Summary

This chapter introduced the general logic of statistical hypothesis testing (or, significance testing) in the context of testing a hypothesis about a single population mean using the one-sample z test. The process begins by translating the research question into two statistical hypotheses about the mean of a population of observations, μ. The null hypothesis, H_0, is a very specific hypothesis that μ equals some particular value; the alternative hypothesis, H_1, is much broader and describes the alternative population condition that the researcher is interested in discovering if, in fact, H_0 is not true. H_0 is tested by assuming it to be true and then comparing the sample results with those that would be expected under the null hypothesis. The value for μ specified in H_0 provides the mean of the sampling distribution, and $\sigma/\sqrt{n}$ gives the standard error of the mean, $\sigma_{\bar{X}}$. These combine to form the z statistic used for testing H_0.

If the sample results would occur with a probability (p) smaller than the level of significance (α), then H_0 is rejected as untenable, H_1 is supported, and the results are considered "statistically significant"

(i.e., $p \leq \alpha$). In this case, the calculated value of z falls beyond the critical z value. On the other hand, if $p > \alpha$, then H_0 is retained as a reasonable possibility, H_1 is unsupported, and the sample results are "statistically nonsignificant." Here, the calculated z falls in the region of retention. A Type I error is committed when a true H_0 is rejected, whereas retaining a false H_0 is called a Type II error.

Typically, H_1 follows most directly from the research question. However, H_1 cannot be tested directly because it lacks specificity; support or nonsupport of H_1 comes as a result of a direct test of H_0. A research question that implies an interest in one direction leads to a directional H_1 and a one-tailed test. In the absence of compelling reasons for hypothesizing direction, a nondirectional H_1 and a two-tailed test are appropriate. The decision to use a directional H_1 must occur prior to any inspection or analysis of the sample results. In the course of an investigation, a substantive question precedes the application of statistical hypothesis testing, which is followed by substantive conclusions.

Reading the Research: z Tests

Kessler-Sklar and Baker (2000) examined parent-involvement policies using a sample of 173 school districts. Prior to drawing inferences about the population of districts ($n = 15,050$), the researchers compared the demographic characteristics between their sample and the national population. They conducted z tests on five of these demographic variables, the results of which are shown in Table 11.4 (Kessler-Sklar & Baker, 2000, Table 1). The authors obtained statistically significant differences between their sample's characteristics and those of the population. They concluded that their sample was "overrepresentative of larger districts, ... districts with greater median income and cultural diversity, and districts with higher student/teacher ratios" (p. 107).

Source: Kessler-Sklar, S. L., & Baker, A. J. L. (2000). School district parent involvement policies and programs. *The Elementary School Journal, 101*(1), 101–118.

Table 11.4 Demographic Characteristics of Responding Districts and the National Population of Districts

Demographic Characteristics	Respondents	National Population
District size	$N = 173$	$N = 15,050$
M	2,847	7,523
SD	2,599	4,342
Z	-14.16***	
Student/teacher ratio	$N = 156$	$N = 14,407$
M	17.55	15.9
SD	3.35	5.47
Z	3.77***	
Minority children in catchment		
area (%)	$N = 173$	$N = 14,228$
M	16.70	11.4
SD	16.70	17.66
Z	3.95***	
Children who do not speak		
English well in catchment area (%)	$N = 173$	$N = 14,458$
M	1.86	1.05
SD	2.6	2.6
Z	4.10***	
Median income of households		
w/children	$N = 173$	$N = 14,227$
M	$49,730	$33,800
SD	$20,100	$13,072
Z	16.03***	

**$p < .01$.
***$p < .001$.
Source: Table 1 in Kessler-Sklar & Baker (2000). © 2000 by the University of Chicago. All rights reserved.

Case Study: Smarter Than Your Average Joe

For this case study, we analyzed a nationally representative sample of beginning schoolteachers from the Baccalaureate and Beyond longitudinal data set (B&B). The B&B is a randomly selected sample of adults who received a baccalaureate degree in 1993. It contains pre-graduation information (e.g., college admission exam scores) as well as data collected in the years following graduation.

Some of the B&B participants entered the teaching force upon graduation. We were interested in seeing how these teachers scored, relative to the national norms, on two college admissions exams: the SAT and the ACT. The national mean for the SAT mathematics and verbal exams is set at $\mu = 500$ (with $\sigma = 100$). The ACT has a national mean of $\mu = 20$ (with $\sigma = 5$). How do the teachers' means compare to these national figures?

Table 11.5   Means, Standard Deviations, and
Ranges for SAT-M, SAT-V, and the ACT

	n	$\overline{X}$	s	range
SAT-M	476	511.01	89.50	280–800
SAT-V	476	517.65	94.54	230–800
ACT	506	21.18	4.63	2–31

Table 11.5 provides the means, standard deviations, and ranges for 476 teachers who took the SAT exams and the 506 teachers taking the ACT. Armed with these statistics, we conducted the hypothesis tests below.

SAT-M

Step 1   *Specify H_0, H_1, and α.*

$$H_0: \mu_{SAT-M} = 500$$

$$H_1: \mu_{SAT-M} \neq 500$$

$$\alpha = .05 \text{ (two-tailed)}$$

Notice our nondirectional alternative hypothesis. Despite our prejudice in favor of teachers and their profession, we nevertheless believe that should the null hypothesis be rejected, the outcome arguably could go in either direction. (Although the sample means in Table 11.5 are all *greater* than their respective national mean, we make our decision regarding the form of H_1 *prior* to looking at the data.)

Step 2   *Select the sample, calculate the necessary sample statistics.*

$$\overline{X}_{SAT-M} = 511.01$$

$$\sigma_{\overline{X}} = \frac{\sigma}{\sqrt{n}} = \frac{100}{\sqrt{476}} = \frac{100}{21.82} = 4.58$$

$$z = \frac{\overline{X} - \mu_0}{\sigma_{\overline{X}}} = \frac{511.01 - 500}{4.58} = +2.40$$

Step 3   *Determine the probability of z under the null hypothesis.*
Table A (Appendix C) shows that a z of $+2.40$ corresponds to a one-tailed probability $p = .0082$. This tells us the (two-tailed) probability is .0164 for obtaining a sample mean as extreme as 511.01 if, in the population, $\mu = 500$.

Step 4   *Make the decision regarding H_0.*
Given the unlikelihood of such an occurrence, we can conclude with a reasonable degree of confidence that H_0 is false and that H_1 is tenable. Substantively, this suggests that the math aptitude of *all* teachers (not just those in the B&B sample) is different from the national average; in all likelihood, it is greater.

SAT-V

Step 1   *Specify H_0, H_1, and α.*

$$H_0: \mu_{SAT\text{-}V} = 500$$

$$H_1: \mu_{SAT\text{-}V} \neq 500$$

$$\alpha = .05 \text{ (two-tailed)}$$

(We again have specified a nondirectional H_1.)

Step 2   *Select the sample, calculate the necessary sample statistics.*

$$\overline{X}_{SAT\text{-}V} = 517.65$$

$$\sigma_{\overline{X}} = \frac{\sigma}{\sqrt{n}} = \frac{100}{\sqrt{476}} = \frac{100}{21.82} = 4.58$$

$$z = \frac{\overline{X} - \mu_0}{\sigma_{\overline{X}}} = \frac{517.65 - 500}{4.58} = +3.85$$

Step 3   *Determine the probability of z under the null hypothesis.*
Because Table A does not show *z* scores beyond 3.70, we do not know the exact probability of our *z* ratio of +3.85. However, we do know that the two-tailed probability is considerably less than .05! This suggests there is an exceedingly small chance of obtaining an SAT-V sample mean as extreme as what was observed ($\overline{X} = 517.65$) if, in the population, $\mu = 500$.

Step 4   *Make the decision regarding H_0.*
We reject our null hypothesis and conclude that the alternative hypothesis is tenable. Indeed, our results suggest that the verbal aptitude of teachers is higher than the national average.

ACT

Step 1   *Specify H_0, H_1, and α.*

$$H_0: \mu_{ACT} = 20$$
$$H_1: \mu_{ACT} \neq 20$$
$$\alpha = .05 \text{ (two-tailed)}$$

(We again have specified a nondirectional H_1.)

Step 2   *Select the sample, calculate the necessary sample statistics.*

$$\overline{X}_{ACT} = 21.18$$

$$\sigma_{\overline{X}} = \frac{\sigma}{\sqrt{n}} = \frac{5}{\sqrt{506}} = \frac{5}{22.49} = .22$$

$$z = \frac{\overline{X} - \mu_0}{\sigma_{\overline{X}}} = \frac{21.18 - 20}{.22} = +5.36$$

Step 3   *Determine the probability of z under the null hypothesis.*
Once again, our z ratio ($+5.36$) is, quite literally, off the charts. There is only the slightest probability of obtaining an ACT sample mean as extreme as 21.18 if, in the population, $\mu = 20$.

Step 4   *Make the decision regarding H_0.*
Given the rarity of observing such a sample mean, H_0 is rejected and H_1 is asserted. Substantively, we conclude that teachers have higher academic achievement than the national average.

School teachers—at least this sample of beginning teachers—indeed appear to be smarter than the average Joe! (Whether the differences obtained here are *important* differences is another matter.)

Suggested Computer Exercises

Access the **seniors** data file, which contains a range of information from a random sample of 120 high school seniors.

1. Use *SPSS* to generate the mean for the variable GPA. GPA represents the grade-point averages of courses taken in math, English language arts, science, and social studies.

2. Test the hypothesis that the GPAs among seniors are, on average, different from those of juniors. Assume that for juniors, $\mu = 2.70$ and $\sigma = .75$.

3. Test the hypothesis that seniors who reported spending at least 5 1/2 hours on homework per week score higher than the national average on READ, MATH, and SCIENCE. READ, MATH, and SCIENCE represent standardized test scores measured in *T*-score units ($\mu = 50$, $\sigma = 10$).

4. Test the hypothesis that seniors who reported spending fewer than three hours of homework per week score below average on READ.

Exercises

Identify, Define, or Explain

Terms and Concepts

statistical hypothesis testing	level of significance
significance testing	alpha
indirect proof	region(s) of rejection
null hypothesis	critical region(s)
nondirectional alternative hypothesis	critical value(s)
directional alternative hypothesis	region of retention
test statistic	decision error
z ratio	Type I error Type II error
one-sample z test	statistically significant
one- versus two-tailed test	statistically nonsignificant
exact probability (p value)	statistical significance versus importance

Symbols

H_0 H_1 μ_0 p α z

z_α $z_{.05}$ $z_{.01}$ μ_{true}

Questions and Problems

Note: Answers to starred (*) items are presented in Appendix B.

*1. The personnel director of a large corporation determines the keyboarding speeds, on certain standard materials, of a random sample of secretaries from her company. She wishes to test the hypothesis that the mean for *her* population is equal to 50 words per minute, the national norm for secretaries on these materials. Explain in general terms the logic and procedures for testing her hypothesis. (Revisit Figure 11.1 as you think about this problem.)

2. The personnel director in Problem 1 finds her sample results to be highly inconsistent with the hypothesis that $\mu = 50$ words per minute. Does this indicate that something is wrong with her sample and that she should draw another? (Explain.)

*3. Suppose that the personnel director in Problem 1 wants to know whether the keyboarding speed of secretaries at her company is different from the national mean of 50.

(a) State H_0.

(b) Which form of H_1 is appropriate in this instance—directional or nondirectional? (Explain.)

(c) State H_1.

(d) Specify the critical values, $z_{.05}$ and $z_{.01}$.

*4. Let's say the personnel director in Problem 1 obtained $\bar{X} = 48$ based on a sample of size 36. Further suppose that $\sigma = 10$, $\alpha = .05$, and a two-tailed test is conducted.

   (a) Calculate $\sigma_{\bar{X}}$.

   (b) Calculate z.

   (c) What is the probability associated with this test statistic?

   (d) What statistical decision does the personnel director make? (Explain.)

   (e) What is her substantive conclusion?

*5. Repeat Problems 4a–4e, but with $n = 100$.

*6. Compare the results from Problem 5 with those of Problem 4. What generalization does this comparison illustrate regarding the role of n in significance testing? (Explain.)

*7. Consider the generalization from Problem 6. What does this generalization mean for the distinction between a *statistically significant* result and an *important* result?

8. Mrs. Grant wishes to compare the performance of sixth-grade students in her district with the national norm of 100 on a widely used aptitude test. The results for a random sample of her sixth graders lead her to retain H_0: $\mu = 100$ ($\alpha = .01$) for her population. She concludes, "My research proves that the average sixth grader in our district falls right on the national norm of 100." What is your reaction to such a claim?

9. State the critical values for testing H_0: $\mu = 500$ against H_1: $\mu < 500$, where

   (a) $\alpha = .01$

   (b) $\alpha = .05$

   (c) $\alpha = .10$

*10. Repeat Problems 9a–9c, but for H_1: $\neq 500$.

   (d) Compare these results with those of Problem 9; explain why the two sets of results are different.

   (e) What does this suggest about which is more likely to give significant results: a two-tailed test or a one-tailed test (*provided the direction specified in H_1 is correct*)?

*11. Explain in general terms the roles of H_0 and H_1 in hypothesis testing.

12. Can you make a direct test of, say, $H_0 \neq 75$? (Explain.)

13. To which hypothesis, H_0 or H_1, do we restrict the use of the terms *retain* and *reject*?

14. Under what conditions is a directional H_1 appropriate? (Provide several examples.)

*15. Given: $\mu = 60$, $\sigma = 12$. For each of the following scenarios, report z_α, the sample z ratio, its p value, and the corresponding statistical decision. (*Note:* For a one-tailed test, assume that the sample result is consistent with the form of H_1.)

   (a) $\bar{X} = 53$, $n = 25$, $\alpha = .05$ (two-tailed)

   (b) $\bar{X} = 62$, $n = 30$, $\alpha = .01$ (one-tailed)

   (c) $\bar{X} = 65$, $n = 9$, $\alpha = .05$ (two-tailed)

   (d) $\bar{X} = 59$, $n = 1000$, $\alpha = .05$ (two-tailed)

    (e) $\bar{X} = 54$, $n = 50$, $\alpha = .001$ (two-tailed)

    (f) Why is the 1-point difference in Problem 15d statistically significant, whereas the 5-point difference in Problem 15c is not?

*16. A researcher plans to test H_0: $\mu = 3.50$. His alternative hypothesis is H_1: $\neq 3.50$. Complete the following sentences:

    (a) A Type I error is possible only if the population mean is _____.

    (b) A Type II error is possible only if the population mean is _____.

17. On the basis of her statistical analysis, a researcher retains the hypothesis, $H_0 : \mu = 250$. What is the probability that she has committed a Type I error? (Explain.)

18. What is the relationship between the level of significance and the probability of a Type I error?

*19. Josh wants to be almost certain that he does not commit a Type I error, so he plans to set α at .00001. What advice would you give Josh?

20. Suppose a researcher wishes to test H_0: $\mu = 100$ against H_1: $\mu > 100$ using the .05 level of significance; however, if she obtains a sample mean far enough *below* 100 to suggest that H_0 is unreasonable, she will switch her alternative hypothesis to H_1: $\neq 100$ ($\alpha = .05$) with the same sample data. Assume H_0 to be true. What is the probability that this decision strategy will result in a Type I error?(*Hint:* Sketch the sampling distribution and put in the regions of rejection.)

CHAPTER 12

Estimation

12.1   *Hypothesis Testing versus Estimation*

Statistical inference is the process of making inferences from random samples to populations. In educational research, the dominant approach to statistical inference traditionally has been hypothesis testing, which we introduced in the preceding chapter and which will continue to be our focus in this book. But there is another approach to statistical inference: **estimation**. Although less widely used by educational researchers, estimation procedures are equally valid and are enjoying greater use—increasingly so—than in decades past. Let's see how estimation differs from conventional hypothesis testing.

In testing a null hypothesis, you are asking whether a specific condition holds in the population. For example, Dr. Meyer tested his sample mean against the null hypothesis that $H_0 = 250$. Having obtained a mean of 272, he rejected H_0, asserted $H_1: \mu \neq 250$, and concluded that μ in all likelihood is above 250. But questions linger. *How much* above 250 might μ be? For example, is 251 a plausible value for μ? After all, it is "above" 250. How about 260, 272 (the obtained mean), or any other value above 250? Given this sample result, *what is a reasonable estimate of μ? Within what range of values might μ reasonably lie*? Answers to these questions throw additional light on Dr. Meyer's research question beyond what is known from a simple rejection of H_0. Estimation addresses such questions.

Most substantive questions for which hypothesis testing might be useful can also be approached through estimation. This is the case with Dr. Meyer's problem, as we will show in sections that follow. For some kinds of problems, however, hypothesis testing is inappropriate and estimation is the only relevant approach. Suppose the manager of your university bookstore would like to know how much money the student body, on average, has available for textbook purchases this term. Toward this end, she polls a random sample of all students. Estimation procedures are exactly suited to this problem, whereas hypothesis testing would be useless. For example, try to think of a meaningful H_0 that the bookstore manager might specify. $H_0: \mu = \$50$? $H_0: \mu = \$250$? Indeed, *no specific H_0 immediately presents itself*. The bookstore manager's interest clearly is more exploratory: she wishes to *estimate* μ from the sample results, not test a specific value of μ as indicated by a null hypothesis.

In this chapter we examine the logic of estimation, present the procedures for estimating μ, and discuss the relative merits of estimation and hypothesis testing.

Although we restrict our discussion to estimating the mean of a single population for which σ is known, the same logic is used in subsequent chapters for more complex situations and for parameters other than μ.

12.2   *Point Estimation versus Interval Estimation*

An estimate of a parameter may take one of two forms.

> A **point estimate** is a single value—a "point"—taken from a sample and used to estimate the corresponding parameter in the population.

You may recall from Chapter 10 (Section 10.3) our statement that a statistic is an estimate of a parameter: $\overline{X}$ estimates μ, s estimates σ, s^2 estimates σ^2, r estimates ρ, and P estimates π. Although we didn't use the term *point estimate*, you now see what we technically had in mind. Opinion polls offer the most familiar example of a point estimate. When, on the eve of a presidential election, you hear on CNN that 55% of voters prefer Candidate X (based on a random sample of likely voters), you have been given a point estimate of voter preference in the population. In terms of Dr. Meyer's undertaking, his sample mean of $\overline{X} = 272$ is a point estimate of μ—his single best bet regarding the mean achievement of all homeschooled fourth graders in his state. In the next chapter, you will learn how to test hypotheses about μ when σ is *not* known, which requires use of the sample standard deviation, s, as a point estimate of σ.

Point estimates should not be stated alone. That is, they should not be reported without some allowance for error due to sampling variation. It is a statistical fact of life that sampling variation will cause any point estimate to be in error—but by how much? Without additional information, it cannot be known whether a point estimate is likely to be fairly close to the mark (the parameter) or has a good chance of being far off. Dr. Meyer knows that 272 is only an *estimate* of μ, and therefore the actual μ doubtless falls to one side of 272 or the other. But *how far* to either side might μ fall? Similarly, the pollster's pronouncement regarding how 55% of the voters feel is also subject to error and, therefore, in need of qualification.

This is where the second form of estimation can help.

> An **interval estimate** is a range of values—an "interval"—within which it can be stated with reasonable confidence the population parameter lies.

In providing an interval estimate of μ, Dr. Meyer might state that the mean achievement of homeschooled fourth graders in his state is between 252 and 292 (i.e., $272 \pm$ 20 points), just as the pollster might state that between 52% and 58% of all voters prefer Candidate X (i.e., 55% $\pm$ 3 percentage points).

Of course, both Dr. Meyer and the pollster could be wrong in supposing that the parameters they seek lie within the reported intervals. Other things being equal, if wide limits are set, the likelihood is high that the interval will include the population value; when narrow limits are set, there is a greater chance the parameter falls outside the interval. For instance, the pollster would be unshakably confident that between 0% and 100% of all voters in the population prefer Candidate X, but rather doubtful that between 54.99% and 55.01% do. An interval estimate therefore is accompanied by a statement of the degree of confidence, or **confidence level**, that the population parameter falls within the interval. Like the level of significance in Chapter 11, the confidence level is decided beforehand and is usually 95% or 99%—that is, $(1 - \alpha)(100)$ percent. The interval itself is known as a **confidence interval**, and its limits are called **confidence limits**.

12.3   *Constructing an Interval Estimate of μ*

Recall from Chapter 6 that in a normal distribution of individual scores, 95% of the observations are no farther away from the mean than 1.96 standard deviations (Section 6.7, Problem 8). In other words, the mean plus or minus 1.96 standard deviations—or, $\overline{X} \pm 1.96S$—captures 95% of all scores in a normal distribution. Similarly, in a sampling distribution of means, 95% of the means are no farther away from μ than 1.96 standard errors of the mean (Section 10.8, Problem 4). That is, $\mu \pm 1.96\sigma_{\overline{X}}$ encompasses 95% of all possible sample means in a sampling distribution (see Figure 12.1). So far, nothing new.

Now, if 95% of means in a sampling distribution are no farther away from μ than $1.96\sigma_{\overline{X}}$, it is equally true that for 95% of sample means, μ is no farther away than $1.96\sigma_{\overline{X}}$. That is, μ will fall in the interval, $\overline{X} \pm 1.96\sigma_{\overline{X}}$, for 95% of the means. Suppose for each sample mean in Figure 12.1 the statement is made that μ lies within the range $\overline{X} \pm 1.96\sigma_{\overline{X}}$. For 95% of the means this statement would be

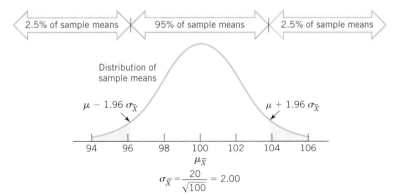

Figure 12.1 Distribution of sample means based on $n = 100$, drawn from a population where $\mu = 100$ and $\sigma = 20$; 95% of all sample means fall in the interval $\mu \pm 1.96 \sigma_{\overline{X}}$.

correct (those falling in the nonshaded area), and for 5% it would not (those falling in the shaded area). We illustrate this in Figure 12.2, which displays the interval, $\overline{X} \pm 1.96\sigma_{\overline{X}}$, for each of 20 random samples ($n = 100$) from the population on which Figure 12.1 is based. With $\sigma = 20$, the standard error is $\sigma_{\overline{X}} = \sigma/\sqrt{n} = 20/10 = 2.0$, which results in the interval $\overline{X} \pm 1.96(2.0)$, or $\overline{X} \pm 3.92$. For example, the mean of the first sample is $\overline{X}_1 = 102$, for which the interval is 102 ± 3.92, or 98.08 to 105.92. Notice that although the 20 sample means in Figure 12.2 vary about the population mean ($\mu = 100$)—some means below, some above—μ falls within the interval

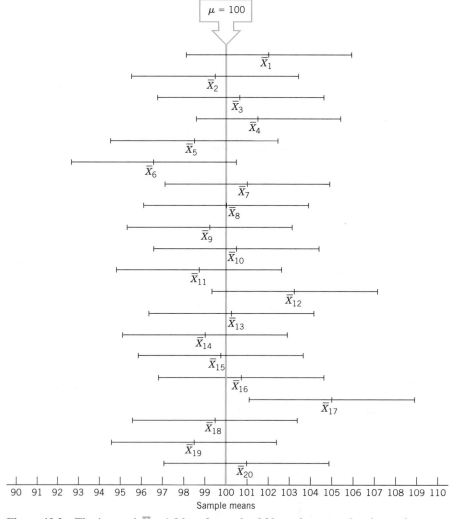

Figure 12.2   The interval $\overline{X} \pm 1.96\sigma_{\overline{X}}$ for each of 20 random samples drawn from a population with $\mu = 100$. The population mean, μ, falls in the interval for 19 of the 20 samples.

$\overline{X} \pm 1.96\sigma_{\overline{X}}$ for 19 of the 20 samples. For only one sample does the interval fail to capture μ: sample 17 gives an interval of 105 ± 3.92, or 101.08 to 108.92 (which, you'll observe, does not include 100).

All of this leads to an important principle:

In drawing samples at random, the probability is .95 that an interval constructed with the rule, $\overline{X} \pm 1.96\sigma_{\overline{X}}$, will include μ.

This fact makes it possible to construct a confidence interval for estimating μ—an interval within which the researcher is "95% confident" μ falls. This interval, you might suspect, is $\overline{X} \pm 1.96\sigma_{\overline{X}}$:

Rule for a 95% confidence
interval (σ known)

$$\overline{X} \pm 1.96\sigma_{\overline{X}} \qquad (12.1)$$

For an illustration of interval estimation, let's return to Dr. Meyer and his mean of 272, which he derived from a random sample of 25 homeschooled fourth graders. From the perspective of interval estimation, his question is, *"What is the range of values within which I am 95% confident μ lies?"* He proceeds as follows:

Step 1   *$\sigma_{\overline{X}}$ is determined:*

$$\sigma_{\overline{X}} = \sigma/\sqrt{n} = 50/5 = 10 \text{ (remember, } n = 25 \text{ and } \sigma = 50)$$

Step 2   *$\overline{X}$ and $\sigma_{\overline{X}}$ are entered in Formula (12.1):*

$$\overline{X} \pm 1.96\sigma_{\overline{X}} = 272 \pm (1.96)(10) = 272 \pm 19.6$$

Step 3   *The interval limits are identified:*

$$252.4 \text{ (lower limit) and } 291.6 \text{ (upper limit)}$$

Dr. Meyer therefore is 95% confident that μ lies in the interval 272 ± 19.6, or between 252.4 and 291.6. He knows that if he selected many, many random samples from the population of homeschoolers, intervals constructed using the rule in Formula (12.1) would vary from sample to sample, as would the values of $\overline{X}$. On the average, however, 95 of every 100 intervals so constructed would include μ—hence Dr. Meyer's confidence that *his* interval contains μ. From his single sample, then, he is reasonably confident that the mean achievement score of *all* homeschooled fourth graders in his state is somewhere roughly between 252 and 292.

A note on interpretation. When intervals are constructed according to the rule $\overline{X} \pm 1.96$, one says that the probability is .95 that an interval *so constructed* will include μ. However, once the specific limits have been established from a given sample, the obtained interval either *does* or *does not* include μ. At this point, then, the probability is either 0 or 1.00 that the sample interval includes μ. Consequently, it would be incorrect for Dr. Meyer to say that the probability is .95 that μ is between 252.4 and 291.6. It is for this reason that the term *confidence*, not probability, is preferred when one is speaking of a specific interval.

12.4   *Interval Width and Level of Confidence*

Suppose that one prefers a greater degree of confidence than is provided by the 95% interval. To construct a 99% confidence interval, for example, the only change is to insert the value of z that represents the middle 99% of the underlying sampling distribution. You know from Chapter 11 that this value is $z = 2.58$, the value of z beyond which .005 of the area falls in either tail (for a combined area of .01). Hence:

Rule for a 99% confidence
interval (σ known)

$$\overline{X} \pm 2.58\sigma_{\overline{X}} \qquad\qquad (12.2)$$

Dr. Meyer is 99% confident that the mean achievement score of homeschooled fourth graders in his state falls in the interval,

$$\overline{X} \pm 2.58\sigma_{\overline{X}} = 272 \pm (2.58)(10) = 272 \pm 25.8,$$

or between 246.2 and 297.8.

Notice that this interval is considerably wider than his 95% confidence interval. In short, *with greater confidence comes a wider interval*. This stands to reason, for a wider interval includes more candidates for μ. Of course Dr. Meyer is more confident that his interval has captured μ! But there is a tradeoff between confidence and specificity: if a 99% confidence interval is chosen over a 95% interval, the increase in confidence must be paid for by accepting a wider—and less informative—interval.

This discussion points to the more general expression of the rule for constructing a confidence interval:

General rule for a confidence
interval (σ known)

$$\overline{X} \pm z_{\alpha}\sigma_{\overline{X}} \qquad\qquad (12.3)$$

Here, z_{α} is the value of z that bounds the middle area of the sampling distribution that corresponds to the level of confidence. As you saw earlier, $z_{\alpha} = 1.96$ for a 95% confidence interval (because this value marks off the middle 95% of the sampling distribution). Similarly, $z_{\alpha} = 2.58$ for a 99% confidence interval because it bounds the middle 99%.

Thus, there is a close relationship between the level of significance (α) and the level of confidence. Indeed, as we pointed out earlier, the level of confidence is equal to $(1 - \alpha)(100)$ percent. Sometimes the terms *level of confidence* and *level of significance* are used interchangeably. It is best to reserve the former for interval estimation and confidence intervals, and the latter for hypothesis testing.

12.5   Interval Width and Sample Size

Sample size is a second influence on the width of confidence intervals: a larger n will result in a narrower interval. Dr. Meyer's 95% confidence limits of 252.4 and 291.6 were based on a sample size of $n = 25$. Suppose that his sample size instead had been $n = 100$. How would this produce a narrower confidence interval?

The answer is found in the effect of n on the standard error of the mean: because $\sigma_{\bar{X}} = \sigma/\sqrt{n}$, a larger n will result in a smaller standard error. (You may recall that this observation was made earlier in Section 11.10, where we discussed the effect of sample size on statistical significance.) With $n = 100$, the standard error is reduced from 10 to $\sigma_{\bar{X}} = 50/10 = 5$. The 95% confidence interval is now $\bar{X} \pm 1.96\sigma_{\bar{X}} = 272 \pm (1.96)(5) = 272 \pm 9.8$, resulting in confidence limits of 262.2 and 281.8. By estimating μ from a larger sample, Dr. Meyer reduces the interval width considerably and, therefore, provides a narrower—and more informative—estimate of μ. The relationship between n and interval width follows directly from what you learned in Chapter 10, where we introduced the standard error of the mean (Section 10.7). Specifically, the larger the sample size, the more closely the means in a sampling distribution cluster around μ (see Figure 10.3).

The relationship between interval width and n suggests an important way to pin down estimates within a desired margin of error: Use a large sample! We will return to this observation in subsequent chapters when we consider interval estimation in other contexts.

12.6   Interval Estimation and Hypothesis Testing

Interval estimation and hypothesis testing are two sides of the same coin. Suppose that for a particular set of data you conducted a two-tailed test ($\alpha = .05$) of a null hypothesis concerning μ *and* you constructed a 95% confidence interval for μ. You would learn two things from this exercise.

First, you would find that if H_0 was *rejected*, the value specified in H_0 would fall *outside* the confidence interval. Let's once again return to Dr. Meyer. His statistical hypotheses were H_0: $\mu = 250$ and the two-tailed H_1: $\mu \neq 250$. His sample mean, $\bar{X} = 272$, corresponded to a z statistic of $+2.20$, which led to the rejection of H_0 (Section 11.6). Now compare his decision about H_0 to the 95% confidence interval, 272 ± 19.6 (Section 12.3). Notice that the resulting interval, 252.4 to 291.6, does *not*

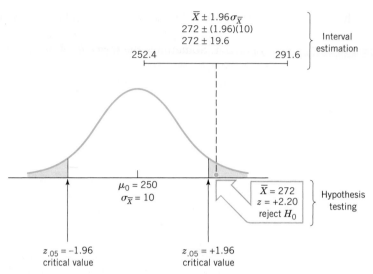

Figure 12.3   Hypothesis testing and interval estimation: the null hypothesis, H_0: $\mu = 250$, is *rejected* ($\alpha = .05$, two-tailed), and the value specified in H_0 falls *outside* the 95% confidence interval for μ.

include 250 (the population mean under the null hypothesis). Testing H_0 and constructing a 95% confidence interval thus lead to the same conclusion: 250 is not a reasonable value for μ (see Figure 12.3). This holds for any value falling outside the confidence interval.

Second, you would find that if H_0 was *retained*, the value specified in H_0 would fall *within* the confidence interval. Consider the value, 255. Because it falls within Dr. Meyer's 95% confidence interval, 252.4 to 291.6, 255 is a reasonable value for μ (as is *any* value within the interval). Now imagine that Dr. Meyer tests his sample mean, $\overline{X} = 272$, against the null hypothesis, H_0: $\mu = 255$ (we'll continue to assume that $\sigma = 50$). The corresponding z statistic would be:

$$z = \frac{\overline{X} - \mu_0}{\sigma_{\overline{X}}} = \frac{272 - 255}{10} = \frac{17}{10} = +1.70$$

Because $+1.70 < +1.96$, H_0 is retained. That is, 272 is not significantly different from 255, and 255 therefore is taken to be a reasonable value for μ (see Figure 12.4). Again you see that conducting a two-tailed test of H_0 and constructing a 95% confidence interval lead to the same conclusion. This would be the fate of *any* H_0 that specifies a value falling within Dr. Meyer's confidence interval, because any value within the interval is a reasonable candidate for μ.

> A 95% confidence interval contains all values of μ that, had they been specified in H_0, would have led to retaining H_0 at the 5% level of significance (two-tailed).

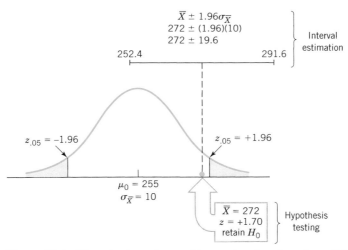

Figure 12.4   Hypothesis testing and interval estimation: the null hypothesis, H_0: $\mu = 255$, is *retained* ($\alpha = .05$, two-tailed), and the value specified in H_0 falls *within* the 95% confidence interval for μ.

Naturally enough, the relationships that we have described in this section also hold for the 99% level of confidence and the .01 level of significance. That is, any H_0 involving a value of μ falling outside the 99% confidence limits would have been rejected in a two-tailed test ($\alpha = .01$), and, conversely, any H_0 involving a value of μ falling within the 99% confidence limits would have been retained.

The equivalence between interval estimation and hypothesis testing holds *exactly* only for two-tailed tests. For example, if you conduct a *one*-tailed test ($\alpha = .05$) and H_0 is just barely rejected (e.g., $z = +1.66$), a 95% confidence interval for μ will *include* the value of μ specified in the rejected H_0. Although there are procedures for constructing "one-tailed" confidence intervals (e.g., Kirk, 1990, p. 431), such confidence intervals seldom are encountered in research reports.

12.7   *Advantages of Interval Estimation*

Which approach should be used—hypothesis testing or interval estimation? Although hypothesis testing historically has been the favored method among educational researchers, interval estimation has a number of advantages.

First, once you have the interval estimate for, say, a 95% level of confidence, you automatically know the results of a two-tailed test of any H_0 (at $\alpha = .05$). You can think of a 95% confidence interval as simultaneously testing your sample mean against all possible null hypotheses: H_0's based on values within the interval would be retained, and H_0's based on values outside the interval would be rejected. In contrast, a significance test gives only the result for the one H_0 tested.

Second, an interval estimate displays in a straightforward manner the influence of sampling variation and, in particular, sample size. Remember that for a given level of confidence, large samples give narrow limits and thus more precise estimates, whereas small samples give wide limits and relatively imprecise estimates. Inspecting the interval width gives the investigator (and reader) a direct indication of whether the estimate is sufficiently precise, and therefore useful, for the purpose at hand.

Third, in hypothesis testing, it is easy to confuse "significance" and "importance" (see Section 11.10). This hazard essentially disappears with interval estimation. Suppose an investigator obtains a mean of 102 from an extraordinarily large sample and subsequently rejects the null hypothesis, H_0: $\mu = 100$, at the .000001 level of significance. Impressive indeed! But let's say the 95% confidence interval places μ somewhere between 101.2 and 102.8, which is unimpressively close to 100. Interval estimation, arguably more than hypothesis testing, forces researchers to come to terms with the importance of their findings.

Fourth, as we mentioned at the outset, interval estimation is the logical approach when there is no meaningful basis for specifying H_0. Indeed, hypothesis testing is useless in such instances.

The advantages of interval estimation notwithstanding, hypothesis testing is the more widely used approach in the behavioral sciences. Insofar as the dominance of this tradition is likely to continue, researchers should at least be encouraged to add confidence intervals to their hypothesis testing results. Indeed, this is consistent with current guidelines for research journals in both education (American Educational Research Association, 2006) and psychology (Wilkinson, 1999). For this reason, as we present tests of statistical hypotheses in the chapters that follow, we also will fold in procedures for constructing confidence intervals.

12.8   *Summary*

Estimation is introduced as a second approach to statistical inference. Rather than test a null hypothesis regarding a specific condition in the population (e.g., "Does $\mu = 250$?"), the researcher asks the more general question, "What is the population value?"

Either point estimates or interval estimates can be obtained from sample data. A point estimate is a single sample value used as an estimate of the parameter (e.g., as an estimate of μ). Because of chance sampling variation, point estimates inevitably are in error—by an unknown amount. Interval estimates, on the other hand, incorporate sampling variation into the estimate and give a range within which the population value is estimated to lie.

Interval estimates are provided with a specified level of confidence, equal to $(1 - \alpha)(100)$ percent

(usually 95% or 99%). A 95% confidence interval is constructed according to the rule, $\overline{X} \pm 1.96\sigma_{\overline{X}}$, whereas a 99% confidence interval derives from the rule, $\overline{X} \pm 2.58\sigma_{\overline{X}}$. Once an interval has been constructed, it either will or will not include the population value; you do not know which condition holds. But in the long run, 95% (or 99%) of intervals so constructed will contain the parameter estimated. In general, the higher the level of confidence selected, the wider the interval and the less precise the estimate. Greater precision can be achieved at a given level of confidence by increasing sample size.

Hypothesis testing and interval estimation are closely related. A 95% confidence interval, for example, gives the range of null hypotheses that would be retained at the .05 level of significance (two-tailed).

Interval estimation also offers the advantage of directly exhibiting the influence of sample size and sampling variation, whereas the calculated z associated with hypothesis testing does not. Interval estimation also eliminates the confusion between a statistically significant finding and an important one. Although many researchers in the behavioral sciences appear to favor hypothesis testing, the advantages of interval estimation suggest that the latter approach should be much more widely used. Toward that end, you are encouraged to report confidence intervals to accompany the results of hypothesis testing.

Reading the Research: Confidence Intervals

Using a procedure called meta-analysis, Gersten and Baker (2001) synthesized the research literature on writing interventions for students with learning disabilities. Gersten and Baker first calculated the mean effect size across the 13 studies they examined. (Recall our discussion of effect size in Section 5.8, and the corresponding case study.) The mean effect size was .81. This indicated that, across the 13 studies, there was a performance difference of roughly eight-tenths of a standard deviation between students receiving the writing intervention and students in the comparison group.

These researchers then constructed a 95% confidence interval to estimate the mean effect size in the population. (This population, an admittedly theoretical entity, would reflect all potential studies examining the effect of this particular intervention.) Gersten and Baker concluded: "The 95% confidence interval was 0.65–0.97, providing clear evidence that the writing interventions had a significant positive effect on the quality of students' writing" (p. 257).

Note that the mean effect size (.81) is located, as it should be, halfway between the lower and upper limits of the confidence interval. The *actual* effect size in the population could be as small as .65 or as large as .97 (with 95% confidence). Nevertheless, this range is consistent with the researchers' statement that there is "clear evidence" of a "positive effect."

Source: Gersten, R., & Baker, S. (2001). Teaching expressive writing to students with learning disabilities: A meta-analysis. *The Elementary School Journal, 101*(3), 251–272.

Case Study: Could You Give Me an Estimate?

Recall from the Chapter 11 case study that beginning teachers scored significantly better on college admissions exams than the average test-taker. We determined this using the one-sample z test. Hypothesis testing, however, does not determine *how much* better these nascent educators did. For the present case study, we used confidence intervals to achieve greater precision in characterizing this population of beginning teachers with respect to performance on the college admissions exams.

In the previous chapter, Table 11.5 showed that the 476 teachers taking the SAT-M and SAT-V obtained mean scores of 511.01 and 517.65, respectively. Because the SATs are designed to have a national standard deviation of 100, we know $\sigma = 100$ for each exam. From this, we proceeded to calculate the standard error of the mean:

$$\sigma_{\overline{X}} = \frac{\sigma}{\sqrt{n}} = \frac{100}{\sqrt{476}} = \frac{10}{21.82} = 4.58$$

We then used Formula (12.1) to construct a 95% confidence interval for each mean. For $\mu_{SAT\text{-}M}$: $511.01 \pm 1.96(4.58)$, or 502.03 to 519.99. And for $\mu_{SAT\text{-}V}$: $517.65 \pm 1.96(4.58)$, or 508.67 to 526.63.

Each interval was constructed in such a manner that 95% of the intervals so constructed would contain the corresponding mean (either $\mu_{SAT\text{-}M}$ or $\mu_{SAT\text{-}V}$) for the population of teachers. Stated less formally, we are 95% confident that the mean SAT-M score for this population lies between 502 and 520 and, similarly, that the mean SAT-V score for this population lies between roughly 509 and 527. (Notice that neither confidence interval includes the national average of 500. This is consistent with our statistical decision, in the Chapter 11 case study, to reject H_0: $\mu = 500$ for both SAT-M and SAT-V. In either case, "500" is not a plausible value of μ for this population of teachers.)

We proceeded to obtain the 95% confidence interval for μ_{ACT}. You saw earlier that the ACT mean was $\overline{X} = 21.18$ for these beginning teachers (Table 11.5). Knowing that $\sigma - 5$ and $n = 506$, we determined that

$$\sigma_{\overline{X}} = \frac{\sigma}{\sqrt{n}} = \frac{5}{\sqrt{506}} = \frac{5}{22.49} = .22$$

and then applied Formula (12.1) to our sample mean: $21.18 \pm 1.96(.22)$, or 20.75 to 21.61. Stated informally, we are 95% "confident" that μ_{ACT} for the population of beginning teachers falls between 20.75 and 21.61. (Again, note that this confidence interval does not include the value 20, which is consistent with our earlier decision to reject H_0: $\mu = 20$.)

What if we desired more assurance—more than "95% confidence"—that each interval, in fact, captured the population mean? Toward this end, we might decide to construct a 99% confidence interval. This additional confidence has a price, however: By increasing our level of confidence, we must accept a wider interval. Table 12.1 shows the three 99% confidence intervals, each of which was constructed using Formula (12.2): $\overline{X} \pm 2.58\sigma_{\overline{X}}$. For comparison purposes, we also include the 95% confidence intervals. As you can see, the increase in interval width is rather minor,

Table 12.1   Comparisons of 95% and 99% Confidence Intervals

Measure	95% Confidence Interval	99% Confidence Interval
SAT-M	502 to 520	499 to 523
SAT-V	508 to 527	505 to 529
ACT	20.75 to 21.61	20.61 to 21.75

given the gain in confidence obtained. This is because the standard errors are relatively small, due in good part to the large ns.

There is an interesting sidebar here. In contrast to the 95% confidence interval for SAT-V, the 99% confidence interval for this measure *includes* the national average of 500. That is, we would conclude with 99% confidence that "500" is a plausible value for μ_{SAT-V} (as is any other value in this interval). The implication? Were we to conduct a two-tailed hypothesis test using the .01 level of significance, the results would *not* be statistically significant (although they were at the .05 level).

Suggested Computer Exercises

Access the **sophomores** data file.

1. Compute the mean READ score for the entire population of 521 students. Record it in the top row of the table below.

2. Select a random sample of 25 cases from the population of 521 students. (Use the *Select Cases* procedure, which is located within the *Data* menu.) Calculate the mean and standard error for READ. Repeat this entire process nine times and record your results.

3. Use the information above to construct ten 68% confidence intervals. Record them in the table below. How many confidence intervals did you expect would capture the actual population mean? How many of your intervals captured μ?

68% Confidence Intervals

note μ: _____

		READ		
sample	lower limit	sample mean	upper limit	captures μ?
1				
2				
3				
4				
5				
6				
7				
8				
9				
10				

4. Using the *Explore* function in *SPSS*, construct 95% and 99% confidence intervals for MATH.

Exercises

Terms and Concepts

estimation	confidence interval
point estimate	confidence limits
interval estimate	95% confidence interval
confidence level	99% confidence interval

Questions and Problems

Note: Answers to starred (*) items are presented in Appendix B.

*1. The national norm for third graders on a standardized test of reading achievement is a mean score of 27 ($\sigma = 4$). Rachel determines the mean score on this test for a random sample of third graders from her school district.

   (a) Phrase a question about her population mean that could be answered by testing a hypothesis.

   (b) Phrase a question for which an estimation approach would be appropriate.

*2. The results for Rachel's sample in Problem 1 is $\overline{X} = 33.10$ ($n = 36$).

   (a) Calculate $\sigma_{\overline{X}}$.

   (b) Construct the 95% confidence interval for her population mean score.

   (c) Construct the 99% confidence interval for her population mean score.

   (d) What generalization is illustrated by a comparison of your answers to Problems 2b and 2c?

*3. Explain in precise terms the meaning of the interval you calculated in Problem 2b. Exactly what does "95% confidence" refer to?

4. Repeat Problems 2a and 2b with $n = 9$ and then with $n = 100$. What generalization is illustrated by a comparison of the two sets of answers (i.e., $n = 9$ versus $n = 100$)?

5. Consider Problem 4 in Chapter 11, where $\overline{X} = 48$, $n = 36$, and $\sigma = 10$.

   (a) Construct a 95% confidence interval for μ.

   (b) Construct a 99% confidence interval for μ.

6. Construct a confidence interval for μ that corresponds to each scenario in Problems 15a and 15c–15e in Chapter 11.

7. The interval width is much wider in Problem 6a than in Problem 6d. What is the principal reason for this discrepancy? Explain by referring to the calculations that Formula (12.1) entails.

*8. The 99% confidence interval for μ is computed from a random sample. It runs from 43.7 to 51.2.

   (a) Suppose for the same set of sample results H_0: $\mu = 48$ were tested using $\alpha = .01$ (two-tailed). What would the outcome be?

    (b) What would the outcome be for a test of H_0: $\mu = 60$?

    (c) Explain your answers to Problems 8a and 8b.

*9. **(a)** If a hypothesized value of μ falls outside a 99% confidence interval, will it also fall outside the 95% confidence interval for the same sample results?

    (b) If a hypothesized value of μ falls outside a 95% confidence interval, will it also fall outside the 99% confidence interval for the same sample results?

    (c) Explain your answers to Problems 9a and 9b.

10. For a random sample, $\overline{X} = 83$ and $n = 625$; assume $\sigma = 15$.

    (a) Test H_0: $\mu = 80$ against H_1: $\neq 80$ ($\alpha = .05$). What does this tell you about μ?

    (b) Construct the 95% confidence interval for μ. What does this tell you about μ?

    (c) Which approach gives you more information about μ? (Explain.)

CHAPTER 13

Testing Statistical Hypotheses about μ When σ Is Not Known: The One-Sample t Test

13.1 Reality: σ Often Is Unknown

We introduced hypothesis testing (Chapter 11) and estimation (Chapter 12) by considering the simple case in which the population standard deviation, σ, is known. This case is simple (which is why we began there), but it also is unrealistic. As it turns out, σ often is not known in educational research. That's the bad news. The good news is that the general logic of hypothesis testing (and estimation) remains the same. Although the statistical details change somewhat when σ is not known, you shouldn't find these changes difficult to accommodate. In short, the general sequence of events is similar to what transpires when σ is known (Table 11.2):

- Specify H_0 and H_1, and set the level of significance (α).
- Select the sample and calculate the necessary sample statistics.
- Determine the probability of the test statistic.
- Make the decision regarding H_0.

In this chapter, we describe the process of testing statistical hypotheses about μ when σ is unknown. Data from the following scenario will be used to illustrate the various concepts and procedures that we introduce.

Suppose that Professor Coffey learns from a national survey that the average high school student in the United States spends 6.75 hours each week on the Internet—composing and reading e-mail, exploring Web sites, and so forth. The professor is interested in knowing how Internet use among students at the local high school compares with this national average. Is local use more than, or less than, this average? Her statistical hypotheses are H_0: $\mu = 6.75$ and H_1: $\mu \neq 6.75$, and she sets her level of significance at $\alpha = .05$. Given her tight budget for research, Professor Coffey randomly selects a sample of only 10 students.[1] Each student is asked to report the number of hours he or she spends on the Internet

---

[1] This small n merely reflects our desire to simplify the presentation of data and calculations. Professor Coffey, of course, would use a larger sample for a real study of this kind.

Table 13.1   Data from Professor Coffey's Survey on Internet Use

Student	Number of Hours in Typical Week (X)	$(X-\overline{X})^2$
A	6	15.21
B	9	.81
C	12	4.41
D	3	47.61
E	11	1.21
F	10	.01
G	18	65.61
H	9	.81
I	13	9.61
J	8	3.61
$n = 10$	$\overline{X} = 9.90$	$SS = \Sigma(X - \overline{X})^2 = 148.90$

$$s = \sqrt{SS/(n-1)}$$
$$= \sqrt{148.90/9}$$
$$= \sqrt{16.54}$$
$$= 4.07$$

in a typical week during the school year. The data appear in Table 13.1, from which you can determine the sample mean to be $\overline{X} = \Sigma X/n = 99/10 = 9.90$ hours of Internet use per week.

13.2   *Estimating the Standard Error of the Mean*

Now, if σ *were* known, Professor Coffey simply would proceed with the one-sample *z* test. That is, she would make her decision about H_0 based on the probability associated with the test statistic *z* (Formula 11.1)

$$z = \frac{\overline{X} - \mu_0}{\sigma_{\overline{X}}}$$

But because σ is *not* known, Professor Coffey cannot compute $\sigma_{\overline{X}}$ (which you will recall is equal to $\sigma/\sqrt{n}$). And because she cannot compute $\sigma_{\overline{X}}$, she cannot compute *z*. However, she can *estimate* σ from her sample data. The estimated σ, in turn, can be used for estimating $\sigma_{\overline{X}}$, which then can be used for calculating the appropriate test statistic. As you will soon learn, this test statistic is very similar to the *z* ratio.

First, the matter of estimating σ. You might think that Formula (5.2)

$$S = \sqrt{\frac{\Sigma(X - \bar{X})^2}{n}}$$

would be the best estimate of the population standard deviation, σ. In fact, S tends to be slightly too small as an estimate of σ. But by replacing n with $n - 1$ in the denominator, a better estimate is obtained. We use lower-case s to denote this estimate:

Estimate of the population
standard deviation

$$s = \sqrt{\frac{\Sigma(X - \bar{X})^2}{n - 1}}$$

$$= \sqrt{\frac{SS}{n - 1}} \qquad (13.1)$$

Because of its smaller denominator, s (Formula 13.1) will be slightly larger than S (Formula 5.2). Although the difference in the computed values of s and S often will be quite small—particularly when n is large—*we will use s in all inference problems to follow.*[2]

The final column of Table 13.1 shows the calculation of s from Professor Coffey's data ($s = 4.07$). The standard error of the mean now can be estimated by substituting s for σ. That is:

Estimated standard
error of the mean

$$s_{\bar{X}} = \frac{s}{\sqrt{n}} \qquad (13.2)$$

Applied to Professor Coffey's sample values, $s_{\bar{X}}$ is:

$$s_{\bar{X}} = \frac{s}{\sqrt{n}} = \frac{4.07}{\sqrt{10}} = \frac{4.07}{3.16} = 1.29$$

The standard error of the mean, $s_{\bar{X}}$, is the estimated standard deviation of all possible sample means, based on samples of size $n = 10$ randomly drawn from this population. Notice that we use the symbol $s_{\bar{X}}$ (not $\sigma_{\bar{X}}$) for the standard error of the mean, just as we use s (not σ) for the standard deviation. This convention

---

[2]If S is already at hand, you can find s by calculating $s = S\sqrt{n/(n - 1)}$.

serves as an important reminder that both s and $s_{\overline{X}}$ are *estimates*, not the "true" or population values.

13.3   *The Test Statistic* t

When σ is not known, a test statistic other than z must be used. The test statistic in this case is t, and its formula bears a striking resemblance to z:

> The test statistic t
>
> $$t = \frac{\overline{X} - \mu_0}{s_{\overline{X}}}$$
>
> (13.3)

Calculated from Professor Coffey's sample values, the test statistic t, or **t ratio**,[3] is:

$$t = \frac{\overline{X} - \mu_0}{s_{\overline{X}}} = \frac{9.90 - 6.75}{1.29} = \frac{3.15}{1.29} = +2.44$$

The only difference between the computation of t and z is that $s_{\overline{X}}$ is substituted for $\sigma_{\overline{X}}$ in Formula (13.3). Conceptually, the two formulas also are quite similar: each represents the difference between the sample mean ($\overline{X}$) and the population value under the null hypothesis (μ_0), in units of the standard error of the mean ($s_{\overline{X}}$ or $\sigma_{\overline{X}}$). Thus, the difference between Professor Coffey's sample mean and μ_0 is almost 2.5 standard errors.

Conceptual similarity aside, the aforementioned difference between t and z—the substitution of $s_{\overline{X}}$ for $\sigma_{\overline{X}}$—is statistically an important one. The t ratio requires *two* statistics from the sample data ($\overline{X}$ and $s_{\overline{X}}$), whereas z requires only one ($\overline{X}$). With repeated random samples of size n, the sample-to-sample variability of t will therefore reflect sampling variation with respect to both $\overline{X}$ and $s_{\overline{X}}$. In contrast, sampling variation of z reflects variability with respect only to $\overline{X}$.

What all this means is that *the sampling distribution of t departs from the normally distributed z, particularly for small samples.* Consequently, the familiar critical values of z, such as ± 1.96, are generally inappropriate for evaluating the magnitude of a t ratio. That is, the rejection regions that these normal curve values mark off, when applied to the sampling distribution of t, do not generally correspond to the announced level of significance (e.g., $\alpha = .05$). Although no great harm will be done when samples are large (say, $n \geq 30$), the inaccuracy will be substantial when samples are relatively small, as in the case of Professor Coffey.

How, then, are critical values for t obtained? The basis for the solution to this problem was provided in the early 1900s by William Sealy Gosset, whose contribution to statistical theory "might well be taken as the dawn of modern inferential statistical methods" (Glass & Hopkins, 1996, p. 271). Gosset, a statistician who worked

---

[3]The t ratio is unrelated to the "T score," the standard score you encountered in Chapter 6.

for the Guinness Brewery of Dublin, demonstrated that the sampling distribution of *t* actually is a "family" of probability distributions, as we will show in Section 13.5. Because Gosset wrote under the pseudonym "Student," this family of distributions is known as **Student's *t* distribution**. Gosset's work ultimately led to the identification of critical values of *t*, which, as you will soon learn, are summarized in an easy-to-use table. For samples of size *n*, you simply read off the correct critical value, compare it to the calculated *t* ratio, and then make your decision regarding H_0.

13.4 Degrees of Freedom

Before continuing with the discussion of Student's *t* distribution, we must introduce an important notion—that of **degrees of freedom**.

> Degrees of freedom, *df*, is a value indicating the number of independent pieces of information a sample of observations can provide for purposes of statistical inference.

In calculating *t*, you must use information from the sample to compute *s* (the estimate of σ) and, in turn, $s_{\overline{X}}$ (the estimate of $\sigma_{\overline{X}}$). How many *independent* pieces of information does the sample provide for this purpose?

The answer is found in the fact that *s* and thus $s_{\overline{X}}$ are based on the deviations of sample observations about the sample mean. This is confirmed by looking back on Formula (13.1):

$$s = \sqrt{\frac{\Sigma(X - \overline{X})^2}{n - 1}}$$

Suppose you have a sample of three observations: 2, 2, 5. The sample mean equals 3, and the deviations about the mean are -1, -1, and $+2$. Are these three deviations—the basic information on which *s* is based—independent of one another? No, for there is a restriction on the deviation scores: *They must always sum to zero*. That is, $\Sigma(X - \overline{X}) = 0$. So, if you know that two of the deviation scores are -1 and -1, the third deviation score gives you no new independent information—it has to be $+2$ for all three deviations to sum to 0. No matter what order you take them in, the last deviation score is always completely determined by, and thus completely dependent on, the other deviation scores. For your sample of three scores, then, you have only two independent pieces of information—or *degrees of freedom*—on which to base your estimates *s* and $s_{\overline{X}}$. Similarly, for a sample of 20 observations there would be only 19 degrees of freedom available for calculating *s* and $s_{\overline{X}}$—the 20th deviation score would be completely determined by the other 19.

In general terms, the degrees of freedom available from a single sample for calculating *s* and $s_{\overline{X}}$ is $n - 1$. In Professor Coffey's case, where $n = 10$, there are $10 - 1 = 9$ degrees of freedom (i.e., $df = 9$). Situations in subsequent chapters feature estimates based on more than one sample or involving more than one restriction. In such situations, this rule for determining degrees of freedom is modified.

13.5   *The Sampling Distribution of Student's* t

What is the nature of Student's *t* distribution, and how are critical values obtained? Let's begin with the first part of this question.

When random samples are large, *s* is a fairly accurate estimate of σ. Therefore, $s_{\bar{X}}$ will be close to $σ_{\bar{X}}$, and *t* consequently will be much like *z*. In this case, the distribution of *t* is very nearly normal.[4] On the other hand, when *n* is small, values of $s_{\bar{X}}$ vary substantially from $σ_{\bar{X}}$. The distribution of *t* may then depart importantly from that of normally distributed *z*. Figure 13.1 shows how. Note especially that when *df* is small (i.e., small sample size), the curve describing *t* has considerably more area, or "lift," in the tails. As we will show, this additional lift has an important consequence:

> To find the critical values of *t* corresponding to the level of significance (e.g., .05), you must move farther out in the distribution than would be necessary in the distribution of the normally distributed *z*.

Figure 13.1 also illustrates that the *t* distribution is a *family* of distributions, one member for every value of *df*. The amount by which the *t* distribution differs from the normal curve depends on how much *s* varies from sample to sample, and this in turn depends on the degrees of freedom (i.e., amount of information) used to calculate *s*. For very small samples of *n* = 5, chance sampling variation will result in values of *s* that may vary considerably from σ. Thus, the *t* distribution for *df* = 5 − 1 = 4 differs considerably from the normal curve. On the other hand, the larger the sample, the more the degrees of freedom, and the more accurately *s* estimates σ. Figure 13.1

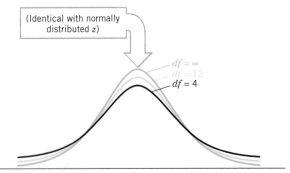

Figure 13.1   The distribution of Student's *t* for three levels of degrees of freedom.

[4]The sampling distribution of means is assumed to follow the normal curve.

shows that even for samples as small as 13 (*df* = 12), the *t* distribution roughly approximates the normal curve. For very large samples, say *n* ≥ 200, the *t* distribution is practically indistinguishable from the normal curve. Indeed, for infinitely large samples (*df* = ∞), the *t* distribution and the normal curve are one and the same.

Obtaining Critical Values of t

A table of Student's *t* distribution appears in Table B (Appendix C), which is used for determining the **critical values of *t***. We have reproduced a portion of this table in Table 13.2 for the present discussion.

The format of Table B is different from that of the normal curve (Table A). The normal curve table reports areas for every value of *z* between 0 and 3.70, from which you can determine exact probabilities (see Sections 11.5 and 11.6). In contrast, Table B reports only critical values and for selected areas (i.e., rejection regions). Furthermore, there are separate entries according to *df*. Let's take a closer look.

The figures across the top two rows of Table 13.2 give, respectively, the area in *one tail* of the distribution (for a directional H_1) and in *both tails combined* (for a non-directional H_1). The figures in the body of the table are the critical values of *t*, each

Table 13.2   Portions of Table B: Student's *t* Distribution

	Area in *Both* Tails					
	.50	.20	.10	.05	.02	.01
	Area in *One* Tail					
df	.25	.10	.05	.025	.01	.005
1	1.000	3.078	6.314	12.706	31.821	63.657
2	0.816	1.886	2.920	4.303	6.965	9.925
•	•	•	•	•	•	•
•	•	•	•	•	•	•
•	•	•	•	•	•	•
9	0.703	1.383	1.833	2.262	2.821	3.250
•	•	•	•	•	•	•
•	•	•	•	•	•	•
•	•	•	•	•	•	•
60	0.679	1.296	1.671	2.000	2.390	2.660
•	•	•	•	•	•	•
•	•	•	•	•	•	•
•	•	•	•	•	•	•
120	0.677	1.289	1.658	1.980	2.358	2.617
•	•	•	•	•	•	•
•	•	•	•	•	•	•
•	•	•	•	•	•	•
∞	0.674	1.282	1.645	1.960	2.326	2.576

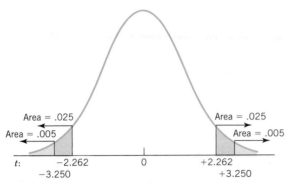

Area = .025

Area = .005

Area = .025

Area = .005

t: −2.262   0   +2.262
     −3.250   +3.250

Figure 13.2   Areas under Student's *t* distribution when $df = 9$.

row corresponding to the degrees of freedom listed in the leftmost column. For instance, each of the values in the row for $df = 9$ is the value of *t* beyond which fall the areas listed at the top of the respective column. This is shown in Figure 13.2 for the two shaded entries in that row. You see that .025 of the area falls beyond a *t* of 2.262 (either + or −) in *one tail* of the sampling distribution, and thus .05 of the area falls outside of the area bounded by $t = -2.262$ and $+2.262$ in the *two tails combined* (i.e., .025 + .025 = .05). Similarly, .005 falls beyond a *t* of 3.250 (either + or −) in one tail, and .01 therefore falls beyond *t* values of −3.250 and +3.250 in both tails combined.

The critical *t* value, or t_α, that is appropriate for testing a particular hypothesis about μ thus depends on the form of H_1, level of significance, and degrees of freedom. Consider these examples, referring back to Table 13.2 as necessary:

- H_1 = nondirectional, $\alpha = .05$, and $df = 60$ → $t_{.05} = \pm 2.000$
- H_1 = nondirectional, $\alpha = .01$, and $df = 120$ → $t_{.01} = \pm 2.617$
- H_1 = directional, $\alpha = .05$, and $df = 9$ → $t_{.05} = -1.833$ (if $H_1: \mu < \mu_0$)
      → $t_{.05} = +1.833$ (if $H_1: \mu > \mu_0$)
- H_1 = directional, $\alpha = .01$, and $df = 9$ → $t_{.01} = -2.821$ (if $H_1: \mu < \mu_0$)
      → $t_{.01} = +2.821$ (if $H_1: \mu > \mu_0$)

(In Table 13.2, what is t_α for Professor Coffey?)

You will notice that Table B does not list values of *t* for every possible value of *df*. If the correct number of degrees of freedom does not appear in this appendix, the conservative practice is to use the closest *smaller* value that is listed. For example, if you have 33 *df*, go with the tabled value of $df = 30$ (not $df = 40$).

13.6   *An Application of Student's* t

Let's now apply the **one-sample *t* test**, as it is often called, to Professor Coffey's problem. To clarify this process, we present her actions in a series of steps, some of which reiterate what you have encountered in this chapter so far.

Step 1   *Specify H_0 and H_1, and set the level of significance (α).*
Professor Coffey's null hypothesis is H_0: $\mu = 6.75$, her alternative hypothesis is H_1: $\mu \neq 6.75$, and she has set $\alpha = .05$. She will conduct a *two-tailed* test because she is interested in knowing whether Internet use at the local high school deviates from the national average in *either* direction (i.e., her H_1 is nondirectional).

Step 2   *Select the sample, calculate the necessary sample statistics.*
There are three sample statistics: the mean, $\overline{X} = 9.90$; the estimated standard error of the mean, $s_{\overline{X}} = 1.29$; and the *t* ratio, $t = +2.44$.

Step 3   *Determine the critical values of t.*
With a nondirectional H_1, an alpha level of .05, and 9 degrees of freedom, the critical values of *t* are ± 2.262 (see Table 13.2). These values mark off the combined region of rejection in the two tails of Student's *t* distribution ($df = 9$). We illustrate this in Figure 13.3, where the shaded portions represent 5% of the area of this sampling distribution.

Step 4   *Make the decision regarding H_0.*
The calculated *t* falls in the region of rejection (i.e., $+2.44 > +2.262$), also illustrated in Figure 13.3. Consequently, Professor Coffey rejects the null hypothesis that $\mu = 6.75$ for her population (all high school students at the local high school), concluding that Internet use appears to exceed 6.75 hours per week for this population.

Suppose Professor Coffey had instead formulated the directional alternative hypothesis, H_1: $\mu > 6.75$. In this case, the entire 5% of the rejection region would

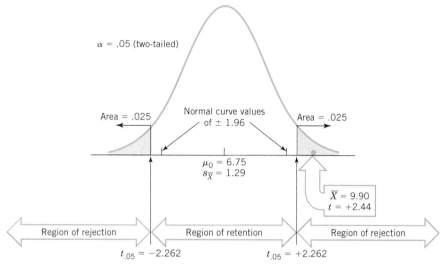

Figure 13.3   Professor Coffey's problem: two-tailed decision strategy based on Student's *t* distribution when *df* = 9.

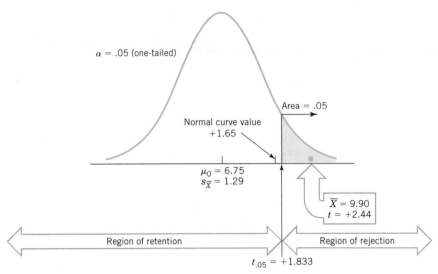

Figure 13.4   One-tailed decision strategy based on Student's *t* distribution when *df* = 9.

be placed in the right-hand tail of the sampling distribution, and the correct critical value would be $t_{.05} = +1.833$ ($df = 9$). This is shown in Figure 13.4. Because $+2.262 > +1.833$, Professor Coffey would reject H_0 here as well. (Perhaps you were expecting this. If *t* falls beyond a two-tailed critical value, surely this same *t* will fall above the smaller *one-tailed* critical value!)

For comparison, we also include in Figure 13.3 the location of the normal curve critical values ($z_{.05}$) of ± 1.96; similarly, Figure 13.4 includes the normal curve critical value of $+1.65$. Notice that these values do *not* mark off the region of rejection in a *t* distribution with 9 degrees of freedom. As we noted earlier, the critical *t* values will always be more extreme (numerically larger) than critical *z* values, since you must go farther out in the tails of the *t* distribution to cut off the same area. Again, this is because of the greater "lift," or area, in the tails of Student's *t*. For Professor Coffey's data, the critical *t* values (± 2.262) are substantially larger than those obtained from the normal curve (± 1.96). This is to be expected from such a small sample. However, if you compare the values in the rows for 60 and 120 *df* in Table 13.2 with those in the bottom row for $df = \infty$ (i.e., the normal curve), you see little difference. This is consistent with our earlier point that when large samples are used, normal curve values are close approximations of the correct *t* values.

13.7   *Assumption of Population Normality*

It's easy to think that it is the sampling distribution of *means* that departs from normality and takes on the shape of Student's *t* distribution when *s* is used to estimate σ.

This is not so. It is not the sample mean you look up in Table B; rather, the position of the sample mean is evaluated indirectly through use of the *t* statistic. It is the position of *t* that is evaluated directly by looking in Table B, and *it is the sampling distribution of t*—which is determined only in part by $\overline{X}$—*that follows Student's distribution*. In fact, sample *t* ratios follow Student's *t* distribution exactly *only* when the sampling distribution of means itself is perfectly normal. That is:

> Sample *t* ratios follow Student's *t* distribution exactly only if the samples have been randomly selected from a population of observations that itself has the normal shape.

If a sample is drawn from a population that is *not* normal, values from Table B will, to some degree, be incorrect. As you might suspect, however, the central limit theorem (Section 10.7) will help out here. Remember that as sample size is increased, the sampling distribution of means approaches normality even for nonnormal populations. As a consequence, the sampling distribution of *t* approaches Student's *t* distribution. As a practical matter, the values in Table B will be fairly accurate even for populations that deviate considerably from normality *if the sample size is reasonably large*, say $n \geq 30$. However, when samples are small (e.g., $n < 15$), you are well advised to examine the sample data for evidence that the population departs markedly from a unimodal, symmetrical shape. If it does, a *t* test should not be used. Fortunately, there are a variety of alternative techniques that make few or no assumptions about the nature of the population (see Minium, Clarke, & Coladarci, 1999, ch. 21).

13.8   *Levels of Significance versus* p *Values*

In the one-sample *z* test (Chapter 11), the exact probability of the *z* ratio is obtained from the normal curve table. For instance, if $z = -2.15$, Table A (Appendix C) informs you that the two-tailed probability is $p = .0158 + .0158 = .0316$. In contrast, exact probabilities are not obtained when you conduct a *t* test (at least by hand)—although you do have a pretty good idea of the general magnitude of *p*. Suppose you are testing $H_0: \mu = 100$ and, for a sample of 25 observations, you obtain $t = +1.83$. The *t* distribution for 24 *df* reveals that a *t* of $+1.83$ falls between the tabled values of 1.711 and 2.064. This is shown in Figure 13.5, where both one-tailed and two-tailed (in parentheses) areas are indicated. Thus, if you had adopted $H_1: \mu > 100$, the *p* value would be somewhere between .025 and .05; for $H_1: \mu \neq 100$, the *p* value would be between .05 and .10. Following this logic, Professor Coffey knows that because her *t* ratio falls between 2.262 and 2.821, the two-tailed *p* value is between .02 and .05.

Exact probabilities are easily obtained if you use computer software packages for conducting *t* tests (and other statistical tests). Nonetheless, investigators often

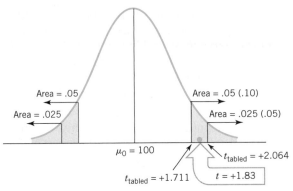

Figure 13.5   Determining the _p_ value for a _t_ ratio when $df = 24$.

do not report their sample _p_ values as exact figures. Instead, they may report them relative to the landmarks of .05 and .01—and sometimes .10 and .001. If a result is statistically significant (i.e., H_0 is rejected), the _p_ value typically is reported as falling below the landmark, whereas if the result is nonsignificant it is reported as falling above the landmark. Several examples are provided in Table 13.3.

The terminology used by some researchers in describing their results can be quite confusing, tending to blur the distinction between _p_ value and level of significance. For instance, an investigator may report that one set of results was "significant at the .05 level," a second set was "significant at the .001 level," and a third "did not reach significance at the .10 level." Does this mean that $\alpha = .05$, $\alpha = .001$, and $\alpha = .10$, respectively, were used for evaluating the three sets of results? Almost assuredly not. This is just a way of reporting three _p_ values: $p < .05$, $p < .001$, and $p > .10$. Chances are that the level of significance the investigator had in mind, though not explicitly stated, would be the same for evaluating all three sets of results, say $\alpha = .05$. Of course, any ambiguity is removed simply by stating α at the outset.

Table 13.3   Exact versus Reported Probability Values

	Reported _p_ Value	
	Investigator Considers the Results to Be:	
Exact _p_ Value	**"Statistically Significant"**	**"Not Statistically Significant"**
.003	$p < .01$	$p > .001$
.02	$p < .05$	$p > .01$
.08	$p < .10$	$p > .05$
.15	—	$p > .10$

13.9 Constructing a Confidence Interval for μ When σ Is Not Known

You have learned that when σ is known, a confidence interval for μ is constructed by using Formula (12.3): $\overline{X} \pm z_\alpha \sigma_{\overline{X}}$. For a 95% confidence interval, $z_\alpha = 1.96$, whereas $z_\alpha = 2.58$ for a 99% confidence interval. (Remember, $\sigma_{\overline{X}}$ is the standard error of the mean and is computed directly from σ.)

Formula (12.3) requires two modifications for use when σ is not known: $s_{\overline{X}}$ is substituted for $\sigma_{\overline{X}}$, and t_α for z_α.

General rule for a confidence interval for μ (σ not known)		
	$\overline{X} \pm t_\alpha s_{\overline{X}}$	(13.4)

Recall that the level of confidence, expressed as a percentage, is equal to $(1 - \alpha)(100)$. In Formula (13.4), t_α is the tabled value of t that includes the middle $(1 - \alpha)(100)$ percent of the area of Student's distribution for $df = n - 1$. For example, let's say $\alpha = .05$ and $df = 60$. Table 13.2 informs you that 2.000 is the value of t beyond which lies 5% of the area *in the two tails combined*. Thus, with 60 df, the middle 95% of Student's distribution falls in the range of $t_{.05} = \pm 2.000$.

Suppose that Professor Coffey wishes to construct a 95% confidence interval for μ, given her sample mean. (Again, this is good practice.) Professor Coffey's question now is, "*What is the range of values within which I am 95% confident μ lies?*" She inserts the appropriate values for $\overline{X}$, $t_{.05}$, and $s_{\overline{X}}$ into Formula (13.4):

$$\overline{X} \pm t_\alpha s_{\overline{X}} = 9.90 \pm (2.262)(1.29) = 9.90 \pm 2.92$$

Professor Coffey is 95% confident that μ falls in the interval, 9.90 ± 2.92. In terms of her initial question, she is reasonably confident that the average high school student at the local high school spends between 6.98 hours (lower limit) and 12.82 hours (upper limit) on the Internet each week. (The width of this interval—almost 6 hours—reflects the exceedingly small size of Professor Coffey's sample.)

Notice that the lower limit of this 95% confidence interval does not include 6.75, the value that Professor Coffey earlier had specified in her null hypothesis and subsequently rejected at the .05 level of significance (Section 13.6). This illustrates that interval estimation and hypothesis testing are "two sides of the same coin," as we pointed out in Section 12.6.

13.10 Summary

When σ is not known, the t statistic is used in place of the z statistic for testing hypotheses about μ. The two look quite similar, except that $s_{\overline{X}}$ is substituted for $\sigma_{\overline{X}}$ in the formula for $t = (\overline{X} - \mu_0)/s_{\overline{X}}$: The denominator, $s_{\overline{X}}$, is an *estimate* of the standard error of the mean, $\sigma_{\overline{X}}$. Because t involves the calculation of *two* statistics from the sample data—both $\overline{X}$ and $s_{\overline{X}}$—the sampling distribution of t is not precisely normal, particularly for small samples. Consequently, normal curve critical values, such as ± 1.96, are generally inappropriate for evaluating calculated values of t.

A proper evaluation can be made by using Table B, a special table of t values that makes allowance for the fact of estimation. Development of this table is owed to the contribution of William Gosset, a statistician who published under the pseudonym "Student." You enter this table with the number of degrees of freedom (df) associated with the estimated quantity. The df is determined by the number of independent pieces of information the sample of observations can provide for purposes of statistical inference. For inference involving single means, $df = n - 1$. The consequence of using this table is that the critical values of t will lie in a more extreme position than the corresponding values of normally distributed z. How much more depends on the degrees of freedom (hence

on n): the smaller the df, the more extreme the critical values of t. Student's distribution of t therefore is not one distribution but a family of distributions, each member corresponding to a specific number of degrees of freedom. Using Student's distribution does not relieve the researcher of the requirement that the sampling distribution of means is close to normal in shape. If sample size is large enough, the central limit theorem will help out here, but for small n's the sample data should be inspected for marked nonnormality.

In research practice, it is not uncommon to find that no explicit α level has been stated. Many researchers choose instead to report p values relative to traditional landmark values, such as .05 and .01.

A confidence interval for μ can be constructed with the rule, $\overline{X} \pm t_{\alpha}s_{\overline{X}}$, where t_{α} marks off the middle area of the t distribution (with $df = n - 1$) that corresponds to the level of confidence. As in the formula for the t statistic, $s_{\overline{X}}$ is substituted for $\sigma_{\overline{X}}$.

Reading the Research: One-Sample t *Test*

In an evaluative study of its curriculum, the Psychology Department at Ursuline College compared the performance of its graduates against the national norm on a standardized test in psychology. The researchers used a one-sample t test to evaluate the null hypothesis that the mean performance of their graduates was not significantly different from the nationwide average of 156.5. "The analysis revealed that our departmental mean ($M = 156.11$, $SD = 13.02$) did not significantly differ from the national mean ($t(96) = -.292$, $p = .771$)" (Frazier & Edmonds, 2002, p. 31). As is often the case in published studies, the authors reported the exact probability (.771) rather than α. Clearly, the p value is far greater than either .05 or .01. (Accordingly, the t ratio fails to exceed the critical t values for either level of significance: $t_{.05} = \pm 1.98$ or $t_{.01} = \pm 2.62$.) Thus, there was insufficient evidence to reject the null hypothesis of no difference. In other words, the test performance of graduates from this department, on average, does not appear to differ from that of the national norm.

Source: Frazier, T. W., & Edmonds, C. L. (2002). Curriculum predictors of performance on the Major Field Test in Psychology II. *Journal of Instructional Psychology* 29(1), 29–32.

Case Study: Like Grapes on the Vine

David Berliner, education researcher at Arizona State University, once maintained that it can take up to eight years for teachers to fully develop expertise in teaching

Table 13.4   Years of Experience

n	$\bar{X}$	s	$s_{\bar{X}}$
628	8.35	8.80	.35

(Scherer, 2001). For this case study, we examined how a sample of 628 public school teachers from the western United States stacked up in this regard. Specifically, does the average teacher stay in the profession that long? The data are courtesy of the National Center for Education Statistics *Schools and Staffing Survey*.[5] The information for this particular sample was collected in the mid-1990s.

We tested whether the mean experience in this sample of teachers was significantly greater than eight years. In other words, was there evidence that the average teacher in the western United States had taught long enough, given Berliner's criterion, to fully develop expertise in teaching? Accordingly, our null hypothesis was H_0: $\mu_{YEARS} = 8$. (Although Berliner specified "up to" eight years, our H_0 reflected the more conservative premise of "at least" eight years.) Because we wanted to know whether the mean was *greater* than eight years, we adopted the directional alternative hypothesis, H_1: $\mu_{YEARS} > 8$. We set alpha at .05. From Table B in Appendix C, we determined the one-tailed critical value ($df = 627$): $t_{.05} = +1.658$.

If the mean experience of this sample of teachers was greater than eight years *for reasons likely not due to random sampling variation*, this would be evidence that the corresponding population of teachers, on average, had indeed mastered their craft (given Berliner's criterion). In the absence of a statistically significant difference, we would conclude that this population of teachers on average had insufficient time in the field to fully develop expertise in teaching (again, given Berliner's criterion).

The mean years of experience for this sample of teachers was $\bar{X} = 8.35$, which is modestly higher than the criterion value of eight years (Table 13.4). However, the results from a one-sample *t* test indicate that random sampling variation can account for this difference (Table 13.5): the obtained *t* ratio of +1.003 fell short of the critical value (+1.658), and, consequently, the null hypothesis was retained. The experience level of this sample of teachers was not significantly greater than eight years. According to Berliner, then, this population of teachers (teachers in the western United States at the time of this survey) on average had not been in the field long enough to fully develop expertise in teaching.

Table 13.5   One-Sample *t* Test (H_0: $\mu_{YEARS} = 8$)

Mean Difference	t	df	p value (one-tailed)
+.35	1.003	627	.158

[5]National Center for Education Statistics, U.S. Department of Education (http://nces.ed.gov).

Table 13.6   Years of Experience Among
Elementary and Secondary Teachers

	n	$\overline{X}$	s	$s_{\overline{X}}$
Elementary	325	8.83	8.79	.49
Secondary	303	7.84	8.78	.51

You will notice that Table 13.5 also reports the one-tailed exact *p* value (.158) provided by the statistical software we used. Of course, we reach the same decision regarding H_0 if we compare this *p* value to alpha. Specifically, because $p > \alpha$ (i.e., .158 > .05), there is insufficient evidence to reject the null hypothesis. (When using a computer to conduct statistical analyses, you will find that the decision to reject or retain H_0 requires only that you compare the reported *p* value to alpha. No comparison between the test statistic and critical value is necessary.)

We decided to repeat this statistical test, but separately for teachers at the elementary (K–8) and secondary (9–12) levels. The particulars remained the same. That is, H_0: $\mu_{\text{YEARS}} = 8$, H_1: $\mu_{\text{YEARS}} > 8$, $\alpha = 0.5$ and $t_{.05} = 1.658$ (one-tailed). Table 13.6 shows that the mean experience for elementary teachers (8.83 years) was greater than that for secondary educators (7.84 years). Although this is an intriguing comparison, our purpose here is not to compare elementary and secondary teachers. Rather, it is to compare each sample mean to the single value specified in the null hypothesis: 8 years. (Methods for testing the significance of the difference between two sample means are addressed in Chapters 14 and 15.)

The analysis of secondary teachers resulted in statistical nonsignificance (Table 13.7): the obtained *t* ratio (−.314) is less than the critical value (1.658), and, therefore, the exact *p* value (.377) is greater than alpha (.05). H_0 was retained. This outcome should not surprise you, insofar as the secondary teachers' sample mean was actually *less* than the value under the null hypothesis. With the one-tailed alternative hypothesis, H_1: $\mu_{\text{YEARS}} > 8$, the result would *have* to be statistically nonsignificant.

In contrast, the elementary teachers' mean of 8.83 was significantly higher than eight years ($t = 1.697$, $p = .046$). From our analyses, then, it would appear that the population of elementary teachers, on average, had sufficient time in the field to fully develop expertise, whereas secondary teachers had not.

Table 13.7   One-Sample *t* Tests (H_0: $\mu_{\text{YEARS}} = 8$),
Separately for Elementary and Secondary Teachers

	Mean Difference	t	df	*p* value (one-tailed)
Elementary	+.83	1.697	324	.046
Secondary	−.16	−.314	302	.377

Suggested Computer Exercises

1. Access **gosset**, a data set used by W. S. Gosset circa 1908. The file contains one variable, ADDHRS, which represents the additional hours of sleep gained by 10 patients after exposure to laevohysocyamine hydrobromide. Using the one-sample t test, determine whether the experimental treatment improved the amount of sleep time—that is, whether the mean ADDHRS score is significantly greater than zero. Use an α of .01.

2. Access the **fiscal** data file, which contains average teacher salaries and per-pupil expenditures from 60 school districts in a southeastern state. Use the one-sample t test to conduct the following tasks.

   (a) Determine whether mean teacher salary is significantly different from $32,000.

   (b) Determine whether mean per-pupil expenditure is significantly different from $5500.

   Use an α of .05 for both analyses.

Exercises

Identify, Define, or Explain

Terms and Concepts

estimated standard deviation
estimated standard error of the mean
t ratio
Student's t distribution
degrees of freedom
family of distributions

critical values of t
one-sample t test
t distribution versus z distribution
normality assumption
"landmark" p values
confidence intervals for μ

Symbols

s $\quad s_{\overline{X}}$ $\quad t$ $\quad t_\alpha$ $\quad t_{.05}$ $\quad df$

Questions and Problems

Note: Answers to starred (*) items are presented in Appendix B.

*1. Ben knows that the standard deviation of a particular population of scores equals 16. However, he does not know the value of the population mean and wishes to test the hypothesis H_0: $\mu = 100$. He selects a random sample, computes $\overline{X}$, s, and $s_{\overline{X}}$, and proceeds with a t test. Comment?

2. When would S (Formula 5.2) and s (Formula 13.1) be very similar? very different? (Explain.)

*3. A random sample of five observations is selected. The deviation scores for the first four observations are -5, 3, 1, and -2.

   (a) What is the fifth deviation score?

   (b) Compute SS and $s_{\overline{X}}$ for the sample of all five observations.

4. You select a random sample of ten observations and compute s, the estimate of σ. Even though there are ten observations, s is really based on only nine independent pieces of information. (Explain.)

5. Why is the *t* distribution a whole family rather than a single distribution?

*6. Suppose that $df = 3$. How do the tails of the corresponding *t* distribution compare with the tails of the normal curve? Support your answer by referring to Tables A and B in Appendix C (assume $\alpha = .10$, two-tailed).

7. Comment on the following statement: For small samples selected from a normal population, the sampling distribution of means follows Student's *t* distribution.

*8. Compute the best estimate of σ and $\sigma_{\bar{X}}$ for each of the following samples:

(a) percentage correct on a multiple-choice exam: 72, 86, 75, 66, 90

(b) number of points on a performance assessment: 2, 7, 8, 6, 6, 11, 3

9. From Table B, identify the value of *t* that for $df = 15$:

(a) is so high that only 1% of the *t* values would be higher

(b) is so low that only 10% of the *t* values would be lower

*10. From Table B, identify the centrally located limits, for $df = 8$, that would include:

(a) 90% of *t* values

(b) 95% of *t* values

(c) 99% of *t* values

11. From Table B and for $df = 25$, find the proportion of *t* values that would be:

(a) less than $t = -1.316$

(b) less than $t = +1.316$

(c) between $t = -2.060$ and $t = +2.060$

(d) between $t = -1.708$ and $t = +2.060$

*12. For each of the following instances, locate the regions of rejection and the sample results on a rough distribution sketch; perform the test; and give final conclusions about the value of μ.

(a) $H_0: \mu = 10$, $H_1: \mu \neq 10$, $\alpha = .10$, sample: 15, 13, 12, 8, 15, 12

(b) Same as Problem 12a except $\alpha = .05$

(c) $H_0: \mu = 50$, $H_1: \mu \neq 50$, $\alpha = 0.5$, sample: 49, 48, 54, 44, 46

(d) $H_0: \mu = 20$, $H_1: \mu < 20$, $\alpha = .01$, sample: 11, 19, 17, 15, 13, 22, 12, 22, 10, 17

13. The task in a particular concept-formation experiment is to discover, through trial and error, the correct sequence in which to press a row of buttons. It is determined from the nature of the task that the average score obtained by random guessing alone would be 20 correct out of a standard series of trials. The following are the scores for a sample of volunteer college students: 31, 24, 21, 25, 32. You wish to determine whether such subjects do better, on the average, than expected by just guessing.

(a) Set up H_0 and H_1.

(b) Determine $t_{.05}$.

(c) Perform the statistical test.

(d) Draw final conclusions.

*14. Consider the data in Problem 8a above. Suppose the researcher wants to test the hypothesis that the population mean is equal to 72; she is interested in sample departures from this mean in either direction.

  (a) Set up H_0 and H_1.

  (b) Determine $t_{.05}$.

  (c) Perform the statistical test.

  (d) Draw final conclusions.

15. Using the data in Problem 8b, an investigator tests H_0: $\mu = 11.25$ against H_1: $\mu \neq 11.25$.

  (a) Determine $t_{.01}$.

  (b) Perform the statistical test.

  (c) Draw final conclusions.

*16. The following are the times (in seconds) that a sample of five 8-year-olds took to complete a particular item on a spatial reasoning test: $\overline{X} = 12.3$ and $s = 9.8$. The investigator wishes to use these results in performing a t test of H_0: $\mu = 8$.

  (a) From the sample results, what makes you think that the proposed t test may be inappropriate?

  (b) If any other sample were drawn, what should be done differently so that a t test would be appropriate?

*17. For each of the following sample t ratios, report the p value relative to a suitable "landmark" (as discussed in Section 13.8). Select among the landmarks .10, .05, and .01, and assume that the investigator in each case has in mind $\alpha = .05$.

  (a) H_1: $\mu < 100$, $n = 8$, $t = -2.01$

  (b) H_1: $\mu \neq 60$, $n = 23$, $t = +1.63$

  (c) H_1: $\mu > 50$, $n = 16$, $t = +2.71$

  (d) H_1: $\mu > 50$, $n = 16$, $t = -2.71$

  (e) H_1: $\mu \neq 2.5$, $n = 29$, $t = -2.33$

  (f) H_1: $\mu \neq 100$, $n = 4$, $t = +7.33$

18. Repeat Problem 17, this time assuming that the investigator has in mind $\alpha = .01$.

19. Translate each of the following statements into symbolic form involving a p value:

  (a) "The results did not reach significance at the .05 level."

  (b) "The sample mean fell significantly below 50 at the .01 level."

  (c) "The results were significant at the .001 level."

  (d) "The difference between the sample mean and the hypothesized μ was not statistically significant ($\alpha = .05$)."

*20. Suppose $\alpha = 0.5$ and the researcher reports that the sample mean "approached significance."

  (a) What do you think is meant by this expression?

  (b) Translate the researcher's statement into symbolic form involving a p value.

21. The expression "$p < .001$" occurs in the results section of a journal article. Does this indicate that the investigator used the very conservative level of significance $\alpha = .001$ to test the null hypothesis? (Explain.)

*22. Fifteen years ago, a complete survey of all undergraduate students at a large university indicated that the average student smoked $\overline{X} = 8.3$ cigarettes per day. The director of the student health center wishes to determine whether the incidence of cigarette smoking at his university has decreased over the 15-year period. He obtains the following results (in cigarettes smoked per day) from a recently selected random sample of undergraduate students: $\overline{X} = 4.6$, $s = 3.2$, $n = 100$.

    (a) Set up H_0 and H_1.

    (b) Perform the statistical test ($\alpha = .05$).

    (c) Draw the final conclusions.

23. Suppose the director in Problem 22 is criticized for conducting a *t* test in which there is evidence of nonnormality in the population.

    (a) How do these sample results suggest population nonnormality?

    (b) What is your response to this critic?

*24. From the data in Problems 8a and 8b, determine and interpret the respective 95% confidence intervals for μ.

25. How do you explain the considerable width of the resulting confidence intervals in Problem 24?

CHAPTER 14

Comparing the Means of Two Populations: Independent Samples

Do children in phonics-based reading programs become better readers than children in "whole-language" programs? Do male and female high school students differ in mathematics ability? Do students who received training in test-taking strategies obtain higher scores on a statewide assessment than students who did not receive such training? These questions lead to an important way of increasing knowledge: studying the difference between two groups of observations. In each case you obtain two samples, and your concern is with comparing the two populations from which the samples were selected. This is in contrast to making inferences about a single population from a single sample, as has been our focus so far. Nonetheless, you soon will be comforted by discovering that even though we have moved from one μ to two, the general logic of hypothesis testing has not changed. In the immortal words of Yogi Berra, it's like *déjà vu* all over again.

Before we proceed, we should clarify what is meant by the phrase **independent samples**. Two samples are said to be independent when none of the observations in one group is in any way related to observations in the other group. This will be true, for example, when the samples are selected at random from their populations or when a pool of volunteers is divided at random into two "treatment" groups. In contrast, the research design in which an investigator uses the *same* individuals in both groups, as in a before-after comparison, provides a common example of **dependent samples**. (We will deal with dependent samples in Chapter 15.)

Let's look at an experiment designed to study the effect of scent on memory, which Gregory is conducting as part of his undergraduate honors thesis. He selects 18 volunteers and randomly divides them into two groups. Participants in Group 1 read a 1500-word passage describing a person's experience of hiking the Appalachian Trail. The paper on which the passage appears has been treated with a pleasant, unfamiliar fragrance so that there is a noticeable scent as Group 1 participants read about the hiker's adventure. One week later, Gregory tests their recall by having them write down all that they can remember from the passage.

They do so on a sheet of paper noticeably scented with the same fragrance. Group 2 participants are subjected to exactly the same conditions, except that there is no noticeable fragrance at any time during the experiment. Finally, Gregory determines for each participant the number of facts that have been correctly recalled from the passage (e.g., the weather was uncharacteristically cooperative, there was a close encounter with a mother bear and her cubs) and then computes the mean for each group:

$$\text{Group 1 (scent present): } \overline{X}_1 = 23$$

$$\text{Group 2 (scent absent): } \overline{X}_2 = 18$$

On average, participants in Group 1 recalled five more facts from the passage than did participants in Group 2. Does this sample difference necessarily mean that there is a "true" difference between the two conditions—that is, a difference between the means, μ_1 and μ_2, of the two theoretical populations of observations? (These two populations would comprise all individuals, similar in characteristics to those studied here, who potentially could participate in the two conditions of this experiment.) If so, it would support the substantive conclusion that memory is facilitated by scent. But you cannot be sure simply by inspecting $\overline{X}_1$ and $\overline{X}_2$, for you know that both sample means are affected by random sampling variation. You would expect a difference between these sample means on the basis of chance alone *even if scent had no effect on memory at all*. As always in statistical inference, the important question is not about samples, but rather about the populations that the samples represent.

To determine whether the difference between two sample means, $\overline{X}_1 - \overline{X}_2$, is large enough to indicate a difference in the population, $\mu_1 - \mu_2$, you use the same general logic as for testing hypotheses about means of single populations. The application of this logic to the problem of comparing the means of two populations is the main concern of this chapter, and we will use Gregory's experiment as illustration.

14.2   *Statistical Hypotheses*

Gregory's interest in the influence of scent on memory leads to the research question, *Does the presence of a noticeable scent, both while reading a passage and later while recalling what had been read, affect the amount of information recalled?* If it does, the mean of the population of scores obtained under the Group 1 condition (scent present) should differ from that obtained under the Group 2 condition (scent absent). This becomes the alternative hypothesis, $H_1: \mu_1 - \mu_2 \neq 0$. Although Gregory wants to know if there *is* a difference, he will formally test the null hypothesis that there is *no* difference ($\mu_1 - \mu_2 = 0$). As you saw in Chapter 11, he does this because the null hypothesis has the specificity that makes a statistical test possible. Thus Gregory's statistical hypotheses are:

$$H_0: \mu_1 - \mu_2 = 0 \text{ (scent } has\ no\ effect \text{ on recall)}$$

$$H_1: \mu_1 - \mu_2 \neq 0 \text{ (scent } has\ an\ effect \text{ on recall)}$$

In comparisons of two populations, the specific hypothesis to be tested typically is that of no difference, or $H_0: \mu_1 - \mu_2 = 0$. The nondirectional alternative, $H_1: \mu_1 - \mu_2 \neq 0$, is appropriate in Gregory's case, for he is interested in knowing whether the difference in treatment made *any* difference in the response variable (scores on the recall test).[1] That is, an effect of scent in either direction is of interest to him. If he were interested in only one direction, the alternative hypothesis would take one of two forms:

$$H_1: \mu_1 - \mu_2 > 0 \text{ (interested in only a } positive \text{ effect of scent)}$$

or

$$H_1: \mu_1 - \mu_2 < 0 \text{ (interested in only a } negative \text{ effect of scent)}$$

From here on, the test of $H_0: \mu_1 - \mu_2 = 0$ follows the same logic and general procedure described in Chapters 11 and 13 for testing hypotheses about single means. Gregory adopts a level of significance, decides on sample size, and selects the sample. He then compares his obtained sample difference, $\overline{X}_1 - \overline{X}_2$, with the sample differences that would be expected *if there were no difference between the population means*—that is, if $H_0: \mu_1 - \mu_2 = 0$ were true. This comparison is accomplished with a *t* test, modified to accommodate a difference between two sample means. If the sample difference is so great that it falls among the very rare outcomes (under the null hypothesis), then Gregory rejects H_0 in favor of H_1; if not, H_0 is retained.

14.3   The Sampling Distribution of Differences Between Means

The general notion of the sampling distribution of *differences* between means is similar to the familiar sampling distribution of means, which provides the basis for the one-sample tests described in Chapters 11 and 13. Suppose that the presence of scent has *absolutely no effect* on recall ($\mu_1 - \mu_2 = 0$) and that, just for perverse fun, you repeat Gregory's experiment many, many times. For the pair of samples described earlier, Gregory obtained $\overline{X}_1 = 23$ and $\overline{X}_2 = 18$, giving a difference between means of +5. The experiment is repeated in an identical manner but with a new random selection of participants. Again the two means are calculated, and the difference between them is determined. Let's say this time the mean score for the scent-present group is *lower* than that for the scent-absent group: $\overline{X}_1 - \overline{X}_2 = -2$. A third pair of samples yields the sample difference, $\overline{X}_1 - \overline{X}_2 = +0.18$ (barely any difference at all). If this procedure were repeated for an unlimited number of sampling

---

[1]The response variable also is called the dependent variable.

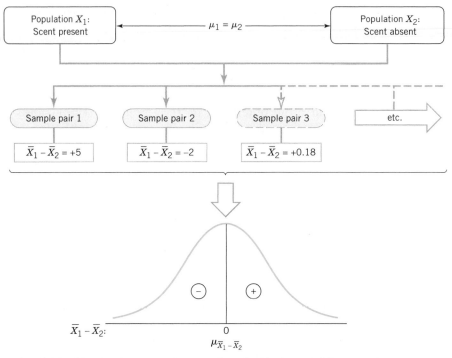

Figure 14.1   The development of a sampling distribution of differences between means of independent populations.

experiments, the sample differences thus generated form the **sampling distribution of differences between means**. This is illustrated in Figure 14.1. To summarize:

> A sampling distribution of differences between means is the relative frequency distribution of $\overline{X}_1 - \overline{X}_2$ obtained from an unlimited series of sampling experiments, each consisting of a pair of samples of given size randomly selected from the two populations.

Properties of the Sampling Distribution of Differences Between Means

When we introduced the sampling distribution of means in Chapter 10, you saw that such a distribution is characterized by its mean, standard deviation, and shape (Section 10.7). This is equally true with a sampling distribution of *differences* between means, as we now will show.

The sampling distribution in Figure 14.1 describes the differences between $\overline{X}_1$ and $\overline{X}_2$ that would be expected, with repeated sampling, if $H_0: \mu_1 - \mu_2 = 0$ were true. Now, if the means of the two populations are the same and pairs of samples are drawn at random, sometimes $\overline{X}_1$ will be larger than $\overline{X}_2$ (leading to a positive value for $\overline{X}_1 - \overline{X}_2$) and sometimes $\overline{X}_2$ will be larger than $\overline{X}_1$ (leading to a negative value for $\overline{X}_1 - \overline{X}_2$). This, of course, is because of sampling variation. But over the long run, the positive differences will be balanced by the negative differences, and the mean of all the differences will be zero. We will use $\mu_{\overline{X}_1 - \overline{X}_2}$ to signify the mean of this sampling distribution. Thus:

> Mean of a sampling distribution
> of differences between means
> when H_0: $\mu_1 - \mu_2 = 0$ is true
>
> $$\mu_{\overline{X}_1 - \overline{X}_2} = 0 \qquad\qquad (14.1)$$

This is shown at the bottom of Figure 14.1.

   The standard deviation of this sampling distribution is called the **standard error of the difference between means**. This standard error reflects the amount of variability that would be expected among all possible sample differences. It is given in the following formula:

> Standard error of the
> difference between means
>
> $$\sigma_{\overline{X}_1 - \overline{X}_2} = \sqrt{\sigma^2_{\overline{X}_1} + \sigma^2_{\overline{X}_2}} \qquad\qquad (14.2)$$

Formula (14.2) shows that the standard error of the difference between two sample means depends on the (squared) standard error of each sample mean involved— that is, $\sigma_{\overline{X}_1}$ and $\sigma_{\overline{X}_2}$. Now, remember that $\sigma_{\overline{X}} = \sigma/\sqrt{n}$ (Formula 10.2). By squaring each side of this expression, you see that $\sigma^2_{\overline{X}} = \sigma^2/n$. Formula (14.2) therefore can be expressed in terms of the two **population variances**, σ^2_1 and σ^2_2:

> Standard error of the
> difference between means
> (using population variances)
>
> $$\sigma_{\overline{X}_1 - \overline{X}_2} = \sqrt{\frac{\sigma^2_1}{n_1} + \frac{\sigma^2_2}{n_2}} \qquad\qquad (14.3)$$

Formula (14.3) shows that $\sigma_{\overline{X}_1 - \overline{X}_2}$ is affected by the amount of variability in each population (σ^2_1 and σ^2_2) and by the size of each sample (n_1 and n_2). Because of the location of these terms in the formula, more variable populations lead to larger standard errors, and larger sample sizes lead to smaller standard errors.

   Finally, the sampling distribution will be normal in shape if the distribution of observations for each population is normal. However, the central limit theorem applies here, just as it did earlier for the sampling distributions of single means. Unless the population shapes are most unusual, sampling distributions of differences between means will tend toward a normal shape if n_1 and n_2 are each at least 20 to 30 cases (there is no sharp dividing line).

14.4   *Estimating $\sigma_{\overline{X}_1 - \overline{X}_2}$*

As you will recall, the population standard deviation (σ) in one-sample studies is seldom known, and consequently you must compute an estimated standard error of the mean ($s_{\overline{X}}$) from the sample results. Not surprisingly, the situation is similar when two samples are involved: the population standard deviations, σ_1 and σ_2, frequently are unknown, so you must obtain an *estimated* standard error of the difference between means, $s_{\overline{X}_1 - \overline{X}_2}$.

How is this done? An important assumption underlying the test of a difference between two means is that the population variances are equal: $\sigma_1^2 = \sigma_2^2$. This is called the **assumption of homogeneity of variance**. A logical extension of this assumption is the use of a combined, or "pooled," variance estimate to represent *both* σ_1^2 and σ_2^2, rather than making separate estimates from each sample. It is the **pooled variance estimate**, s_{pooled}^2, that you use to determine $s_{\overline{X}_1 - \overline{X}_2}$. The first task, then, is to calculate s_{pooled}^2.

Calculating s_{pooled}^2

To understand how to combine the two sample variances (s_1^2 and s_2^2) as one (s_{pooled}^2), let's first examine the nature of a variance estimate. Remember: the variance is the square of the standard deviation. You calculate it just like a standard deviation except that the last step—taking the square root—is omitted. You saw in Formula (13.1) that the sample standard deviation is:

$$s = \sqrt{\frac{SS}{n-1}}$$

Square each side and you have the variance estimate:

$$s^2 = \frac{SS}{n-1}$$

In the present situation, you have *two* variance estimates (s_1^2 and s_2^2), and a *single* variance estimate is required (s_{pooled}^2). To obtain this single estimate, simply combine the sums of squares from both samples and divide by the total degrees of freedom:

Pooled variance estimate of σ_1^2 and σ_2^2 $$s_{pooled}^2 = \frac{SS_1 + SS_2}{n_1 + n_2 - 2} \qquad (14.4)$$

The pooled variance is an "average" of the two sample variances, where each variance is weighted by its *df*. This can be seen most easily from the following formula, which is equivalent to Formula (14.4) (and particularly convenient if s_1^2 and s_2^2 already are at hand):

$$s_{pooled}^2 = \frac{(n_1 - 1)s_1^2 + (n_2 - 1)s_2^2}{n_1 + n_2 - 2}$$

Notice that each variance is weighted by $n - 1$ degrees of freedom, and the sum of the two weighted variances is then divided by the total degrees of freedom. The total df shows that one degree of freedom is "lost" for each sample variance. This is more easily seen by the equality, $n_1 + n_2 - 2 = (n_1 - 1) + (n_2 - 1)$.

Calculating $s_{\overline{X}_1 - \overline{X}_2}$

If you replace s_{pooled}^2 for each of the population variances in Formula (14.3), you have a formula for $s_{\overline{X}_1 - \overline{X}_2}$:

$$s_{\overline{X}_1 - \overline{X}_2} = \sqrt{\frac{s_{pooled}^2}{n_1} + \frac{s_{pooled}^2}{n_2}}$$

which is equivalent to:

$$s_{\overline{X}_1 - \overline{X}_2} = \sqrt{s_{pooled}^2 \left(\frac{1}{n_1} + \frac{1}{n_2}\right)}$$

Now substitute Formula (14.4) for s_{pooled}^2:

Estimate of $\sigma_{\overline{X}_1 - \overline{X}_2}$

$$s_{\overline{X}_1 - \overline{X}_2} = \sqrt{\frac{SS_1 + SS_2}{n_1 + n_2 - 2} \left(\frac{1}{n_1} + \frac{1}{n_2}\right)} \qquad (14.5)$$

It is now time to introduce the t test for independent samples, which we will then apply to the data from Gregory's experiment.

14.5   The t Test for Two Independent Samples

Recall the structure of the one-sample t test: it is the difference between the sample result ($\overline{X}$) and the condition specified in the null hypothesis (μ_0), divided by the standard error ($s_{\overline{X}}$):

$$t = \frac{\overline{X} - \mu_0}{s_{\overline{X}}}$$

The t test for independent samples has the same general structure. It, too, compares the sample result ($\overline{X}_1 - \overline{X}_2$) with the condition specified under the null hypothesis

$(\mu_1 - \mu_2)$, dividing the difference by the standard error $(s_{\overline{X}_1 - \overline{X}_2})$. Expressed formally:

$$t = \frac{(\overline{X}_1 - \overline{X}_2) - (\mu_1 - \mu_2)}{s_{\overline{X}_1 - \overline{X}_2}}$$

Because the null hypothesis typically specifies that $\mu_1 - \mu_2 = 0$, the formula above simplifies to:

<table>
<tr><td>

t test for two
independent samples

</td><td>

$$t = \frac{\overline{X}_1 - \overline{X}_2}{s_{\overline{X}_1 - \overline{X}_2}}$$

</td><td>(14.6)</td></tr>
</table>

This t ratio will follow Student's t distribution with $df = n_1 + n_2 - 2$, provided several assumptions are met. We have alluded to these assumptions, but it is helpful to reiterate them at this point.

The first assumption is that the two samples are independent. That is, none of the observations in one group is in any way related to observations in the other group. (As you will learn in Chapter 15, the *dependent*-samples t test has a slightly different standard error.)

The second assumption is that each of the two populations of observations is normally distributed. Here, of course, the central limit theorem helps out, as it did when we were making inferences about single means (Chapter 13). Consequently, when each sample is larger than 20 to 30 cases, considerable departure from population normality can be tolerated.

Finally, it is assumed that the two populations of observations are equally variable $(\sigma_1^2 = \sigma_2^2)$. Earlier we referred to this as the assumption of homogeneity of variance, out of which arises the calculation of a pooled variance estimate (s_{pooled}^2). Research has shown that violation of this assumption is not problematic unless the population variances are quite different, the two sample sizes also are quite different, *and* either n_1 or n_2 is small. Therefore, when samples are small, you should look carefully at the data for skewness or large differences in variability. Here, the eyeball is a powerful tool. If you cannot see a problem by such inspection, then it probably won't matter. But if sample size is small and departure from the conditions specified seems to be substantial, you should consider "nonparametric" or "distribution-free" techniques that involve few or no assumptions about the population distributions (e.g., see Minium, Clarke, & Coladarci, 1999, ch. 21).

14.6 Testing Hypotheses about Two Independent Means: An Example

Now let's carry through on Gregory's problem. *Does the presence of a noticeable scent, both while reading a passage and later while recalling what had been read, affect the amount of information recalled?* Again, we emphasize that the overall logic involved in testing H_0: $\mu_1 - \mu_2 = 0$ is the same as that for all significance tests in this text. You assume H_0 to be true and then determine whether the obtained sample result is sufficiently rare—in the direction(s) specified in H_1—to cast doubt on H_0. To do this, you express the sample result as a test statistic (t, in the present case), which you then locate in the theoretical sampling distribution. If the test statistic falls in a region of rejection, H_0 is rejected; if not, H_0 is retained. With this in mind, we now proceed with Gregory's test.

Step 1   *Formulate the statistical hypotheses and select a level of significance.*
Gregory's statistical hypotheses are:

$$H_0: \mu_1 - \mu_2 = 0$$

$$H_1: \mu_1 - \mu_2 \neq 0$$

He must now select his decision criterion, which we will assume is $\alpha = .05$.

Step 2   *Determine the desired sample size and select the sample.*
To simplify computational illustrations, we limited Gregory's samples to nine participants each. In practice, one must decide what sample size is needed. Too few participants makes it difficult to discover a difference where one exists, which increases the chances of a Type II error; too many is wasteful and costly. (You will learn more about how to choose sample size in Chapter 19.)

Step 3   *Calculate the necessary sample statistics.*
The raw data and all calculations are given in Table 14.1. Gregory begins by computing the mean and sum of squares for each group (the row at ❶). The pooled variance estimate, s^2_{pooled}, is calculated at ❷, which is followed by the calculation of $s_{\bar{X}_1 - \bar{X}_2}$ (❸). Finally, Gregory computes the t ratio, obtaining $t = +2.19$ (❹) which has $9 + 9 - 2 = 16$ degrees of freedom (❺).
Notice that we also presented the sample variance and standard deviation for each group at ❷ (in brackets), even though neither is required for subsequent calculations. We did this for three reasons. First, good practice requires reporting s_1 and s_2 along with the outcome of the test, so you'll need these later. Second, knowing the separate variances—s^2_1 and s^2_2—allows you to easily confirm the reasonableness of the value you obtained for s^2_{pooled}. Because it is a weighted average of s^2_1 and s^2_2, s^2_{pooled} must fall between these two values (right in the middle, if $n_1 = n_2$). If it does not, then a calculation error has been made. Gregory's s^2_{pooled} (23.50) happily rests between 22.25 and 24.75, the values for s^2_1 and s^2_2, respectively. Third, extreme differences between s^2_1 and s^2_2 might suggest differences between the population variances, σ^2_1 and σ^2_2, thereby casting doubt on the assumption of homogeneous variances. (Gregory's sample variances seem fine in this regard.)

Step 4   *Identify the region(s) of rejection.*
To identify the rejection region(s), you first identify the critical t value(s), t_α. Remember that there are three things to consider when selecting critical values from Table B (Appendix C): H_1, α, and df (see Section 13.5). With a

Table 14.1   Test of the Difference Between Means of Two Independent Samples

Group 1 (scent present) n = 9		Group 2 (scent absent) n = 9	
X	$(X - \bar{X}_1)^2$	X	$(X - \bar{X}_2)^2$
25	4	20	4
23	0	10	64
30	49	25	49
14	81	13	25
22	1	21	9
28	25	15	9
18	25	19	1
21	4	22	16
26	9	17	1

① $\bar{X}_1 = 209/9$ $SS_1 = \Sigma(X - \bar{X}_1)^2$ $\bar{X}_2 = 162/9$ $SS_2 = \Sigma(X - \bar{X}_2)^2$

      $= 23$ $= 198$ $= 18$ $= 178$

② $s^2_{pooled} = \dfrac{SS_1 + SS_2}{n_1 + n_2 - 2} = \dfrac{198 + 178}{9 + 9 - 2} = \dfrac{376}{16} = 23.50$

$\begin{cases} s^2_1 = \dfrac{SS_1}{n_1 - 1} = \dfrac{198}{9 - 1} = 24.75 \quad s_1 = \sqrt{24.75} = 4.97 \\[3mm] s^2_2 = \dfrac{SS_2}{n_2 - 1} = \dfrac{178}{9 - 1} = 22.25 \quad s_2 = \sqrt{22.25} = 4.72 \end{cases}$

③ $s_{\bar{X}_1 - \bar{X}_2} = \sqrt{s^2_{pooled}\left(\dfrac{1}{n_1} + \dfrac{1}{n_2}\right)} = \sqrt{23.50\left(\dfrac{1}{9} + \dfrac{1}{9}\right)} = \sqrt{23.50\left(\dfrac{2}{9}\right)} = \sqrt{\dfrac{47}{9}} = 2.28$

④ $t = \dfrac{\bar{X}_1 - \bar{X}_2}{s_{\bar{X}_1 - \bar{X}_2}} = \dfrac{23 - 18}{2.28} = \dfrac{+5}{2.28} = +2.19$

⑤ $df = n_1 + n_2 - 2 = 9 + 9 - 2 = 16$

⑥ $t_{.05} = \pm 2.12$

⑦   Statistical decision: reject H_0: $\mu_1 - \mu_2 = 0$

      Substantive conclusion: The presence of scent improves memory.

two-tailed H_1, $\alpha = .05$, and $df = 16$, Gregory has all the information he needs for finding t_α. He locates $df = 16$ in the first column of Table B and moves over to the column under ".05" (in *both* tails), where he finds the entry 2.120. Thus, $t_{.05} = \pm 2.12$ (**⑥**)—the values of t beyond which the most extreme 5% of all possible sample outcomes fall (in both tails combined) if H_0 is true. The regions of rejection and the obtained sample t ratio are shown in Figure 14.2.

Step 5   *Make statistical decision and form conclusion.*

Because the obtained t ratio falls in a rejection region (i.e., $+2.19 >$ $+2.12$), Gregory rejects the H_0 of no difference (**⑦**). The difference

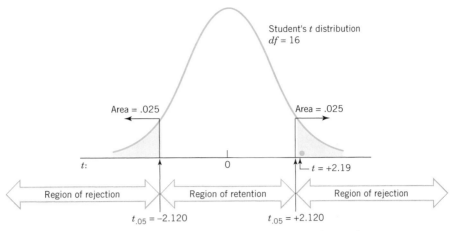

Student's t distribution
$df = 16$

Area = .025

Area = .025

t:

0

$t = +2.19$

Region of rejection

Region of retention

Region of rejection

$t_{.05} = -2.120$

$t_{.05} = +2.120$

Figure 14.2   Testing H_0: $\mu_1 - \mu_2 = 0$ against H_1: $\mu_1 - \mu_2 \neq 0$ ($\alpha = .05$).

between the two means is statistically significant ($\alpha = .05$). Because the mean recall score for Group 1 (scent-present) is higher than the mean for Group 2 (scent-absent), Gregory draws the substantive conclusion that, under these conditions, scent would appear to improve memory (**❼**).

14.7   Interval Estimation of $\mu_1 - \mu_2$

The logic underlying interval estimation of $\mu_1 - \mu_2$ is basically the same as that for estimation of μ. The form of the estimate for independent samples is:

> Rule for a confidence
> interval for $\mu_1 - \mu_2$
>
> $$(\bar{X}_1 - \bar{X}_2) \pm t_{\alpha} s_{\bar{X}_1 - \bar{X}_2} \tag{14.7}$$

Formula (14.7) is structurally equivalent to $\bar{X} \pm t_{\alpha} s_{\bar{X}}$ (Formula 13.4), the confidence interval for μ presented in Section 13.9. We're simply replacing $\bar{X}$ with $\bar{X}_1 - \bar{X}_2$ and $s_{\bar{X}}$ with $s_{\bar{X}_1 - \bar{X}_2}$. As before, t_{α} is the tabled value of t for which the middle $(1 - \alpha)(100)$ percent of the area of Student's distribution is included within the limits $-t$ to $+t$. Now, however, $df = n_1 + n_2 - 2$ rather than $n - 1$.

Suppose Gregory, consistent with good practice, followed up his test of H_0: $\mu_1 - \mu_2 = 0$ by constructing a 95% confidence interval for $\mu_1 - \mu_2$. His question is, "What is the range of values within which I am 95% confident $\mu_1 - \mu_2$ lies?" He already has all the ingredients:

- $\bar{X}_1 - \bar{X}_2 = 23 - 18 = 5$
- $s_{\bar{X}_1 - \bar{X}_2} = 2.28$
- $t_{.05} = 2.12$

He now substitutes these in Formula (14.7):

$$5 \pm (2.12)(2.28) = 5 \pm 4.83$$

Gregory is 95% confident that $\mu_1 - \mu_2$ falls in the interval, 5 ± 4.83. That is, he is reasonably confident that the effect of scent on memory in the population—the "true" effect—is somewhere between 0.17 (lower limit) and 9.83 (upper limit) additional facts recalled. He doesn't know for sure, of course. But he does know that if his experiment were repeated many times and an interval was constructed each time using Formula (14.7), 95% of such intervals would include $\mu_1 - \mu_2$.

Note that Gregory's 95% confidence interval does not span zero, the value he specified in H_0 and then rejected in a two-tailed test. Whether approached through hypothesis testing or interval estimation, zero (no difference) would not appear to be a reasonable value for $\mu_1 - \mu_2$ in this instance.

Also note the large width of this confidence interval. This should be expected, given the small values for n_1 and n_2. The "true" effect of scent on memory could be anywhere between negligible (less than one additional fact recalled) and substantial (almost 10 additional facts). As you saw in Section 12.5, one simply needs larger samples to pin down effects.

With a 99% confidence interval, of course, the interval is wider still—so wide, in fact, that the interval now spans zero. This confidence interval, which requires $t_{.01} = 2.921$, is:

$$5 \pm (2.921)(2.28) = 5 \pm 6.66$$

$$- 1.66 \text{ (lower limit) to } + 11.66 \text{ (upper limit)}$$

Thus, with 99% confidence, Gregory concludes that the true effect of scent on memory is somewhere between (a) small and *negative* and (b) much larger and *positive*—including the possibility that there is no effect of scent whatsoever. This is shown in Figure 14.3.

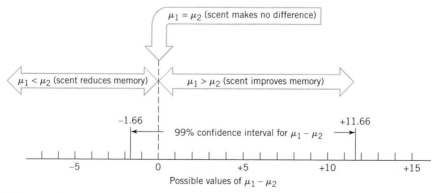

Figure 14.3 The 99% confidence interval for the true difference in mean recall scores in the scent experiment.

Consistent with this 99% confidence interval, Gregory would have retained H_0: $\mu_1 - \mu_2 = 0$ had he adopted $\alpha = .01$ (two-tailed). That is, the sample t ratio is less than $t_{.01}$, and, thus, zero is a reasonable possibility for $\mu_1 - \mu_2$ (at the .01 level of significance).

14.8   Appraising the Magnitude of a Difference: Measures of Effect Size for $\overline{X}_1 - \overline{X}_2$

When you reject the null hypothesis regarding a difference between two means, you are concluding that you have a "true" difference. *But how large is it?* Unfortunately, "statistically significant" frequently is mistaken for "important," "substantial," "meaningful," or "consequential," as you first saw in Section 11.10. But even a small (and therefore possibly unimportant) difference between two means can result in rejection of H_0 when samples are large. This is because of the effect that sample size has on reducing the standard error, $s_{\overline{X}_1 - \overline{X}_2}$. Recall the location of n_1 and n_2 in the standard error:

$$s_{\overline{X}_1 - \overline{X}_2} = \sqrt{s_{\text{pooled}}^2 \left(\frac{1}{n_1} + \frac{1}{n_2} \right)}$$

When sample sizes are humongous, the term $(1/n_1 + 1/n_2)$ is a very small proportion indeed. Consequently, the product of s_{pooled}^2 and $(1/n_1 + 1/n_2)$—hence $s_{\overline{X}_1 - \overline{X}_2}$—is much smaller than when sample sizes are meager (in which case the aforementioned proportion is relatively large). Now, because $s_{\overline{X}_1 - \overline{X}_2}$ is the *denominator* of the t ratio, a smaller standard error for a given mean difference will result in a larger value of t (unless $\overline{X}_1 - \overline{X}_2$ is zero). Other things being equal, then, larger samples are more likely to give statistically significant results.

Let's consider a quick illustration. Recall from the preceding section that Gregory's obtained t ratio, with $df = 16$, would fail to reach statistical significance at $\alpha = .01$. Suppose that we somehow cloned each participant in Gregory's sample so that each score now appears *twice*: that is, $df = 18 + 18 - 2 = 34$. As Table 14.2 shows,

Table 14.2   The Effects of Doubling the Number of Observations: 16 df versus 34 df

	$df = 9 + 9 - 2 = 16$	$df = 18 + 18 - 2 = 34$
$\overline{X}_1$	23	23
$\overline{X}_2$	18	18
$\overline{X}_1 - \overline{X}_2$	5	5
s_{pooled}^2	23.50	22.12
$s_{\overline{X}_1 - \overline{X}_2}$	2.28	1.57
t	$5/2.28 = +2.19$	$5/1.57 = +3.18$
$t_{.01}$	± 2.921	± 2.750
decision	retain H_0	reject H_0

this act of mischief does not change either mean, and $\overline{X}_1 - \overline{X}_2$ therefore remains +5. You also see that the pooled variance changes only slightly. But doubling the number of cases reduces $s_{\overline{X}_1 - \overline{X}_2}$ by almost one-third: from 2.28 to 1.57. As a consequence, the sample t ratio *increases* from +2.19 to +3.18. With 34 df, the critical t values are ± 2.750 ($\alpha = .01$), putting the new t ratio comfortably in the region of rejection. The difference between means is now statistically significant at the .01 level, whereas with 16 df the same difference was not.

> With large enough samples, *any* obtained difference (other than zero) can be "statistically significant." Such an outcome does not imply that the difference is large or important. Rather, it means that the difference in the population probably is not zero.

Our advice to you is simple: *look at the results carefully*. Upon rejecting H_0, note how much difference there is between the two sample means. This is important to do in any case, but particularly when samples are large and even trivial differences can be statistically significant.

The magnitude of a difference is not always self-evident. Probably no one will disagree that "40 points" is substantial if it represents the difference between two cities in mean summer temperature (40° Fahrenheit), and that this same figure is negligible if it represents the difference between men and women in mean annual income ($40). But unlike temperature and dollars, many variables in educational research lack the familiar meaning necessary to conclude whether, statistical significance aside, a given difference between means is large, small, or somewhere in between. For instance, what is your opinion of the 5-point difference that Gregory obtained? We offer two measures of effect size for a difference between means, the first of which you encountered earlier.

Expressing a Mean Difference Relative to the Pooled Standard Deviation: d

In Sections 5.8 and 6.9, you saw that a difference between two means can be evaluated by expressing it relative to the pooled standard deviation. This is a popular measure of effect size for a difference between means.

Following common practice, we use the symbol d when estimating this effect size from sample data:

Effect size: d

$$d = \frac{\overline{X}_1 - \overline{X}_2}{\sqrt{\dfrac{SS_1 + SS_2}{n_1 + n_2 - 2}}} = \frac{\overline{X}_1 - \overline{X}_2}{s_{\text{pooled}}} \tag{14.8}$$

The pooled standard deviation in the denominator, s_{pooled}, is simply the square root of s^2_{pooled}, the familiar pooled variance estimate (Formula 14.4). For Gregory's data, $s_{pooled} = \sqrt{23.50} = 4.85$. Thus,

$$d = \frac{\overline{X}_1 - \overline{X}_2}{s_{pooled}} = \frac{+5}{4.85} = +1.03$$

The difference between these two means corresponds to 1.03 standard deviations. In other words, the mean number of facts recalled in Group 1 is roughly one standard deviation higher than the mean in Group 2. A difference of $d = +1.03$ is illustrated in Figure 14.4a, where you see a substantial offset between the two distributions. Indeed, if normal distributions are assumed in the population, it is estimated that the average scent-present subject falls at the 85th percentile of the scent-absent distribution—35 percentile points beyond what would be expected if there were no effect of scent on memory whatsoever. We show this in Figure 14.4b. (You may find it helpful to review Section 6.9 for the logic and calculations underlying Figure 14.4b.)

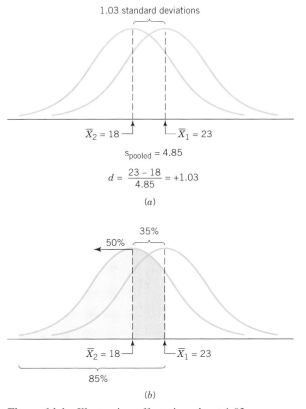

Figure 14.4   Illustrating effect size: $d = +1.03$.

As you saw in Section 5.8, one convention is to consider $d = .20$ as small, $d = .50$ as moderate, and $d = .80$ as large (Cohen, 1988). In this light, too, the present finding is impressive. Again, however, always take into account the methodological and substantive context of the investigation when making a judgment about effect size. And remember, any sample difference is subject to sampling variation. When sample size is small (as in the present case), d could be appreciably different were the investigation to be repeated.

Expressing a Mean Difference in Terms of Explained Variance ($\hat{\omega}^2$)

A second measure of effect size for Gregory's obtained difference is expressed as the proportion of variation in recall scores that is accounted for, or explained, by "variation" in group membership (i.e., whether a participant is in Group 1 or Group 2). This follows the general logic of association that we introduced in Chapter 7, where you saw that the proportion of "common variance" between two variables is equal to r^2 (see Section 7.8). In the case of a difference between two means, one variable—group membership—is dichotomous rather than continuous. Here, $\hat{\omega}^2$ ("omega squared") is analogous to r^2 and is calculated from Formula (14.9):

Effect size: $\hat{\omega}^2$

$$\hat{\omega}^2 = \frac{t^2 - 1}{t^2 + n_1 + n_2 - 1} \tag{14.9}$$

For Gregory, $t = +2.19$ and $n_1 = n_2 = 9$. Now enter these values in Formula (14.9):

$$\hat{\omega}^2 = \frac{t^2 - 1}{t^2 + n_1 + n_2 - 1} = \frac{2.19^2 - 1}{2.19^2 + 9 + 9 - 1} = \frac{4.80 - 1}{4.80 + 17} = \frac{3.80}{21.80} = .17$$

Thus, Gregory estimates that 17% of the variation in recall scores is accounted for by variation in group membership. In other words, the experimental manipulation of scent explains 17% of the variance in recall scores.[2]

In summary, there are various ways to appraise the magnitude of a difference between two means. Hypothesis testing and interval estimation address the inferential question regarding the corresponding difference in the population, but both can fall short of providing meaningful information about whether the obtained difference is large or important. In contrast, d and $\hat{\omega}^2$ can be quite helpful in this regard. For this reason, we recommend that you consider one or both effect sizes in your own work.

---

[2]Where the absolute value of t is less than one, $\hat{\omega}^2$ is negative and therefore meaningless. In such situations, $\hat{\omega}^2$ is set to zero. By the way, the "hat" ($\wedge$) over this term signifies it as an *estimate* of the population parameter, ω^2.

14.9   How Were Groups Formed? The Role of Randomization

Gregory had randomly divided his 18 volunteers into two groups of nine each, perhaps by flipping a coin or using a table of random numbers. The random assignment of participants to treatment conditions is called **randomization**:

> Randomization is a method for dividing an available pool of research participants into two or more groups. It refers to any set of procedures that allows "chance" to determine who is included in what group.

Randomization provides two important benefits. The first is a statistical benefit: in a randomized sample, you can apply the rules that govern sampling variation and thus determine the magnitude of difference that is more than can reasonably be attributed to chance. This, as you know, is of vital importance for making statistical inferences.

The second benefit of randomization is that it provides **experimental control** over extraneous factors that can bias the results. Where experimental control is high, a researcher can more confidently attribute an obtained difference to the experimental manipulation. In short, the "why" of one's results is much clearer when participants have been randomly assigned to treatment conditions.

Imagine that Gregory had assigned to the scent-present condition the nine participants who volunteered first, the remainder being assigned to Group 2. The two groups might well differ with regard to, say, their interest in the topic of memory, their eagerness to participate in a research investigation, or perhaps even an underlying need to be needed. Any one of these factors could affect motivation to perform, which in turn could influence the results Gregory subsequently obtains. The effect of the factor he is studying—the presence or absence of scent—would be hopelessly confounded with the effects of the uncontrolled, extraneous factors associated with group assignment.

In contrast, randomization results in the *chance* assignment of extraneous influences among the groups to be compared. Eager versus reluctant, able versus less able, interested versus bored, rich versus poor—the participants in the various groups will tend to be comparable where randomization has been employed. Indeed, the beauty of randomization is that it affords this type of experimental control over extraneous influences *regardless of whether they are known by the researcher to exist*. As a result, the investigator can be much more confident that the manipulated factor (e.g., scent) is the only factor that differentiates one group from another and, therefore, the only factor that reasonably explains any group difference subsequently obtained. We emphasize that the random assignment of participants to treatment groups does not *guarantee* equality with regard to extraneous factors, any more than 50 heads are guaranteed if you toss a coin 100 times. But randomization *tends* toward equality, particularly as sample size increases.

When Randomization Is Not Possible

In many instances, randomization is either logically impossible or highly unrealistic. Suppose you wish to compare groups differing on such characteristics as sex, political party, social class, ethnicity, or religious denomination. Or perhaps your interest is in comparing bottle-fed and breast-fed infants (say, on a measure of maternal attachment). You certainly cannot randomly assign participants to the "treatment condition" male or female, Democrat or Republican, and so on. And it is highly unlikely that mothers will agree to be randomly assigned to a particular method of feeding their newborns. Rather, you take individuals "as they are."

In such cases, you lose a considerable degree of control of extraneous factors, and determining the "why" of the results is not easy. This is because when groups are formed in this fashion, they necessarily bring along other characteristics as well. For example, males and females differ in physiology *and* socialization; Democrats and Republicans differ in political ideology *and* economic/demographic characteristics; and the two groups of mothers likely differ in beliefs and behaviors regarding motherhood beyond the decision to breast-feed or bottle-feed their children. In each instance, then, the announced comparison is confounded with uncontrolled, extraneous factors.

Field-based educational research typically involves already formed groups, as can be found in achievement comparisons of schools that have adopted different instructional programs. Randomization can be unfeasible in such research, and the investigator must be sensitive to extraneous influences here too. For example, perhaps the schools that adopted an innovative curriculum also have more talented teachers, higher levels of parent involvement, or more students from higher socioeconomic backgrounds. Any one of these factors can influence achievement—beyond any effect that the innovative curriculum may have.

Separating out the relative influence of confounding factors requires great care, and when it can be done, procedures are required that go beyond those offered in an introductory course in statistics. None of this is to say that only studies that permit randomization should be conducted. Quite the contrary, for such a restriction would rule out the investigation of many important and interesting research questions. Nevertheless, in the absence of randomization, one must use considerable care in the design, analysis, and interpretation of such studies.

14.10 Statistical Inferences and Nonstatistical Generalizations

Most statistical inference procedures, including those covered in this text, are based on the random sampling model described in Section 10.4. That is, they assume that the sample observations have been randomly selected from the population of interest. If the sample has been selected in this way, the procedures permit inferences about characteristics (such as means) of the defined population. These inferences are *statistical inferences*, based directly on the laws of probability and statistics, and their function is to take chance sampling variation into account.

The investigator, however, usually wishes to generalize beyond the original population that was sampled. Thus, when you have at hand the results of a particular investigation performed at a particular time under particular conditions using participants of a particular type who were selected in a particular way, you attempt to apply the outcome more broadly. As we showed in Section 10.5, this involves a close analysis of the participants and conditions of the investigation, and a reasoned argument regarding the characteristics of the accessible population and broader populations to which your results may apply. Generalizations of this sort are *nonstatistical* in nature; insofar as they involve judgment and interpretation, they go beyond what statistics can show.

What are the implications of this for educational research? In effect, although statistical inference procedures can account for random sampling variation in the sample results, they do not provide any mathematically based way of generalizing from, or making inferences beyond, the type of participants used and the exact set of conditions at the time. This does not mean that broader generalizations cannot properly be made; indeed, they should be made. Rather, it means that *statistics* does not provide a sufficient basis for making them. This type of generalization must also be based on knowledge and understanding of the substantive area, as well as on judgment of the similarity of new circumstances to those that characterized the original study. Statistical inference is a necessary first step toward the broader generalization.

14.11   *Summary*

This chapter is concerned with examining a difference between the means of two independent groups. Two groups are independent if none of the observations in one group is related in any way to observations in the other group. The general logic and procedure of a two-sample test are quite similar to those characterizing tests of hypotheses about single means: the investigator formulates the statistical hypotheses, sets the level of significance, collects data, calculates the test statistic, compares it to the critical value(s), and then makes a decision about the null hypothesis.

The test statistic t is given in the formula, $t = \overline{X}_1 - \overline{X}_2 / s_{\overline{X}_1 - \overline{X}_2}$. An important assumption is that the population distributions are normal in shape. But because of the central limit theorem, the sampling distribution of differences between means can be considered to be reasonably close to a normal distribution except when samples are small and the two distributions are substantially nonnormal. An additional assumption is that the population variances are equal ($\sigma_1^2 = \sigma_2^2$), which leads to the calculation of a pooled variance estimate (s_{pooled}^2) used for calculating the

standard error ($s_{\overline{X}_1 - \overline{X}_2}$). Once calculated, the t ratio is evaluated by reference to Student's t distribution, using $df = n_1 + n_2 - 2$. A $(1 - \alpha)(100)$ percent confidence interval for $\mu_1 - \mu_2$ can be estimated with the rule, $\overline{X}_1 - \overline{X}_2 \pm t_\alpha s_{\overline{X}_1 - \overline{X}_2}$.

When a statistically significant difference between two means is found, you should ask whether it is large enough to be important. The simplest way to do this is to examine the size of the difference between $\overline{X}_1$ and $\overline{X}_2$, although measures of effect size often are more helpful in this regard. One measure, d, expresses a difference in terms of (pooled) standard deviation units. A second measure, $\hat{\omega}^2$, estimates the proportion of variance in the dependent variable that is explained by group membership.

Randomization is a procedure whereby an available group of research participants is randomly assigned to two or more treatment conditions. Randomization not only furnishes a statistical basis for evaluating obtained sample differences but also provides an effective means of controlling factors extraneous to the study. Such controls make interpretation of significant differences between means considerably easier than when the groups are already formed on the basis of some characteristic of the participants (e.g., sex, ethnicity).

The assumption of random sampling underlies nearly all the statistical inference techniques used by educational researchers, including the t test and other procedures described in this book. Inferences to populations from which the samples have been randomly selected are directly backed by the laws of probability and statistics and are known as statistical inferences; inferences or generalizations to all other groups are nonstatistical in nature and involve judgment and interpretation.

Reading the Research: Independent-Samples t *Test*

Santa and Hoien (1999, p. 65) examined the effects of an early-intervention program on a sample of students at risk for reading failure:

> *A t-test analysis showed that the post-intervention spelling performance in the experimental group (M = 59.6, SD = 5.95) was statistically significantly higher than in the control group (M = 53.7, SD = 12.4), t(47) = 2.067, p < .05.*

Notice that an exact p value is not reported; rather, probability is reported relative to the significance level of .05. The result of this independent-samples t test is therefore deemed significant at the .05 level.

Source: Santa, C. M. & Hoien, T. (1999). An assessment of early steps: A program for early intervention of reading problems. *Reading Research Quarterly, 34*(1), 54–79.

Case Study: Doing Our Homework

This case study demonstrates the application of the independent-samples t test. We compared the academic achievement of students who, on average, spend two hours a day on homework to students who spend about half that amount of time on homework. Does that extra hour of homework—in this case, double the time—translate into a corresponding difference in achievement?

The sample of nearly 500 students was randomly selected from a population of seniors enrolled in public schools located in the northeastern United States. (The data are courtesy of the National Center for Education Statistics' *National Education Longitudinal Study of 1988.*) We compared two groups of students: those reporting 4–6 hours of homework per week (Group 1) and those reporting 10–12 hours per week (Group 2). The criterion measures were reading achievement, mathematics achievement, and grade-point average.

One could reasonably expect that students who did more homework would score higher on measures of academic performance. We therefore chose the directional alternative hypothesis, $H_1: \mu_1 - \mu_2 < 0$, for each of the three t tests below. (The "less than" symbol simply reflects the fact that we are subtracting the hypothetically larger mean from the smaller mean.) For all three tests, the null hypothesis stated no difference, $H_0: \mu_1 - \mu_2 = 0$. The level of significance was set at .05.

Table 14.3   Statistics for Reading, Mathematics, and GPA

	n	$\overline{X}$	s	$s_{\overline{X}}$
READ				
Group 1	332	52.41	9.17	.50
Group 2	163	54.34	9.08	.71
MATH				
Group 1	332	52.44	9.57	.53
Group 2	163	55.34	8.81	.69
GPA				
Group 1	336	2.46	.58	.03
Group 2	166	2.54	.58	.05

Our first test examined the mean difference between the two groups in reading performance. Scores on the reading exam are represented by T scores, which, you may recall from Chapter 6, have a mean of 50 and a standard deviation of 10. (Remember not to confuse T scores, which are standard scores, with t ratios, which make up the t distribution and are used for significance testing.) The mean scores are shown in Table 14.3. As expected, the mean reading achievement of Group 2 ($\overline{X}_2 = 54.34$) exceeded that of Group 1 ($\overline{X}_1 = 52.41$). An independent-samples t test revealed that this mean difference was statistically significant at the .05 level (see Table 14.4). Because large sample sizes can produce statistical significance for small (and possibly trivial) differences, we also determined the effect size in order to capture the magnitude of this mean difference. From Table 14.4, we see that the raw mean difference of −1.93 points corresponds to an effect size of −.21. Remember, we are subtracting $\overline{X}_2$ from $\overline{X}_1$ (hence the negative signs). This effect size indicates that the mean reading achievement of Group 1 students was roughly one-fifth of a standard deviation below that of Group 2 students—a rather small effect.

We obtained similar results on the mathematics measure. The difference again was statistically significant—in this case, satisfying the more stringent .001 significance level. The effect size, $d = -.31$, suggests that the difference between the two groups in mathematics performance is roughly one-third of a standard deviation. (It is tempting to conclude that the mathematics difference is larger than the reading difference, but this would require an additional analysis—testing the

Table 14.4   Independent-Samples t Tests and Effect Sizes

	$\overline{X}_1 - \overline{X}_2$	t	df	p **(one-tailed)**	d
READ	−1.93	−2.21	493	.014	−.21
MATH	−2.90	−3.24	493	.001	−.31
GPA	−.08	−1.56	500	.059	−.14

statistical significance of the difference between two differences. We have not done that here.)

Finally, the mean difference in GPA was $\overline{X}_1 - \overline{X}_2 = -.08$, with a corresponding effect size of $-.14$. This difference was not statistically significant ($p = .059$). Even if it were, its magnitude is rather small ($d = -.14$) and arguably of little *practical* significance. Nevertheless, the obtained p value of .059 raises an important point. Although, strictly speaking, this p value failed to meet the .05 criterion, it is important to remember that ".05" (or any other value) is entirely arbitrary. Should this result, $p = .059$, be declared "statistically significant"? Absolutely not. But nor should it be dismissed entirely. When a p value is tantalizingly close to α but nonetheless fails to meet this criterion, researchers sometimes use the term *marginally significant*. Although no convention exists (that we know of) for deciding between a "marginally significant" result and one that is patently nonsignificant, we believe that it is important to not categorically dismiss results that, though exceeding the announced level of significance, nonetheless are highly improbable. (In the present case, for example, the decision to retain the null hypothesis rests on the difference in probability between 50/1000 and 59/1000.) This also is a good reason for reporting exact p values in one's research: it allows readers to make their own judgments regarding statistical significance. By considering the exact probability *in conjunction with effect size*, readers draw a more informed conclusion about the importance of the reported result.

Suggested Computer Exercises

1. Access the **students** data set, which contains grade-point averages (GPA) and television viewing information (TVHRSWK) for a random sample of 75 tenth-grade students. Test whether there is a statistically significant difference in GPA between students who watch less than two hours of television per weekday and those who watch two or more hours of television. In doing so,

    (a) set up the appropriate statistical hypotheses,

    (b) perform the test ($\alpha = .05$), and

    (c) draw final conclusions.

2. Repeat the process above, but instead of GPA as the dependent variable, use performance on the reading and mathematics exams.

Exercises

Identify, Define, or Explain

Terms and Concepts

independent samples
dependent samples
sampling distribution of differences between means
standard error of the difference between means
population variance

assumption of homogeneity of variance
variance estimate
pooled variance estimate
assumption of population normality

interval estimation of $\mu_1 - \mu_2$
sample size and statistical significance
effect size
explained variance

randomization
experimental control
statistical inferences vs.
nonstatistical generalizations

Symbols

$\overline{X}_1$ and $\overline{X}_2$ n_1 and n_2 σ_1^2 and σ_2^2 $\mu_{\overline{X}_1 - \overline{X}_2}$ $\sigma_{\overline{X}_1 - \overline{X}_2}$ $s_{\overline{X}_1 - \overline{X}_2}$

s_{pooled}^2 t df d $\hat{\omega}^2$

Questions and Problems

Note: Answers to starred (*) items are presented in Appendix B.

*1. Translate each of the following into words, and then express each in symbols in terms of a difference between means relative to zero:

   (a) $\mu_A > \mu_B$

   (b) $\mu_A < \mu_B$

   (c) $\mu_A = \mu_B$

   (d) $\mu_A \neq \mu_B$

2. A graduate student wishes to compare the high school grade-point averages (GPAs) of males and females. He identifies 50 brother/sister pairs, obtains the GPA for each individual, and proceeds to test H_0: $\mu_{males} - \mu_{females} = 0$. Are the methods discussed in this chapter appropriate for such a test? (Explain.)

*3. Consider two large populations of observations, A and B. Suppose you have unlimited time and resources.

   (a) Describe how, through a series of sampling experiments, you could construct a fairly accurate picture of the sampling distribution of $\overline{X}_A - \overline{X}_B$ for samples of size $n_A = 5$ and $n_B = 5$.

   (b) Describe how the results used to construct the sampling distribution could be used to obtain an estimate of $\sigma_{\overline{X}_A - \overline{X}_B}$.

4. Assume H_0: $\mu_1 - \mu_2 = 0$ is true. What are the three defining characteristics of the sampling distribution of differences between means?

*5. The following results are for two samples, one from Population 1 and the other from Population 2:

$$\text{from Population 1 : } 3, \ 5, \ 7, \ 5$$
$$\text{from Population 2 : } 8, \ 9, \ 6, \ 5, \ 12$$

   (a) Compute SS_1 and SS_2.

   (b) Using the results from Problem 5a, compute the pooled variance estimate.

   (c) Using the result from Problem 5b, obtain $s_{\overline{X}_1 - \overline{X}_2}$.

   (d) Test H_0: $\mu_1 - \mu_2 = 0$ against H_1: $\mu_1 - \mu_2 < 0$ ($\alpha = .05$).

   (e) Draw final conclusions.

*6. From the data given in Problem 5:

(a) Compute and interpret the effect size, d; evaluate its magnitude in terms of Cohen's criteria and in terms of the normal curve.

(b) Calculate and interpret the effect size, $\hat{\omega}^2$

*7. For each of the following cases, give the critical value(s) of t:

(a) $H_1: \mu_1 - \mu_2 > 0$, $n_1 = 6, n_2 = 12, \alpha = .05$

(b) $H_1: \mu_1 - \mu_2 \neq 0$, $n_1 = 12, n_2 = 14, \alpha = .01$

(c) $H_1: \mu_1 - \mu_2 < 0$, $n_1 = 14, n_2 = 16, \alpha = .05$

(d) $H_1: \mu_1 - \mu_2 \neq 0$, $n_1 = 19, n_2 = 18, \alpha = .01$

8. Does familiarity with an assessment increase test scores? You hypothesize that it does. You identify 11 fifth-grade students to take a writing assessment that they had not experienced before. Six of these students are selected at random and, before taking the assessment, are provided with a general overview of its rationale, length, question format, and so on. The remaining five students are not given this overview. The following are the scores (number of points) for students in each group:

$$\text{overview provided}: 20, 18, 14, 22, 16, 16$$
$$\text{no overview provided}: 11, 15, 16, 13, 9$$

(a) Set up H_0 and H_1.

(b) Perform the test ($\alpha = .01$).

(c) Draw your final conclusions.

9. An educational psychologist is interested in knowing whether the experience of attending preschool is related to subsequent sociability. She identifies two groups of first graders: those who had attended preschool and those who had not. Then each child is assigned a sociability score on the basis of observations made in the classroom and on the playground. The following sociability results are obtained:

Attended preschool	Did not attend preschool
$n_1 = 12, \ \Sigma X_1 = 204, \ SS_1 = 192$	$n_2 = 16, \ \Sigma X_2 = 248, \ SS_2 = 154$

(a) Set up the appropriate statistical hypotheses.

(b) Perform the test ($\alpha = .05$).

(c) Draw final conclusions.

*10. You are investigating the possible differences between eighth-grade boys and girls regarding their perceptions of the usefulness and relevance of science for the roles they see themselves assuming as adults. Your research hypothesis is that boys hold more positive perceptions in this regard. Using an appropriate instrument, you obtain the following results (higher scores reflect more positive perceptions):

Male	Female
$n_1 = 26, \ \overline{X}_1 = 65.0, \ s_1 = 10.2$	$n_2 = 24, \ \overline{X}_2 = 57.5, \ s_2 = 9.7$

(a) Set up the appropriate statistical hypotheses.

(b) Perform the test ($\alpha = .05$).

(c) Draw final conclusions.

11. From the data given in Problem 10:

(a) Compute and interpret the effect size, d; evaluate its magnitude in terms of Cohen's criteria and in terms of the normal curve.

(b) Calculate and interpret the effect size, $\hat{\omega}^2$.

12. *Parametric* statistical tests are tests that are based on one or more assumptions about the nature of the populations from which the samples are selected. What assumptions are required in the t test of H_0: $\mu_1 - \mu_2 = 0$?

*13. You read the following in a popular magazine: "A group of college women scored *significantly higher*, on average, than a group of college men on a test of emotional intelligence." (Limit your answers to statistical matters covered in this chapter.)

(a) How is the statistically unsophisticated person likely to interpret this statement (particularly the italicized phrase)?

(b) What does this statement really mean?

(c) Is it possible that the difference between the average woman and the average man was in fact quite small? If so, how could a *significant* difference be observed?

(d) What additional statistical information would you want in order to evaluate the actual difference between these women and men?

*14. A high school social studies teacher decides to conduct action research in her classroom by investigating the effects of immediate testing on memory. She randomly divides her class into two groups. Group 1 studies a short essay for 20 minutes, whereas Group 2 studies the essay for 20 minutes and immediately following takes a 10-minute test on the essay. The results below are from a final exam on the essay, taken one month later:

Group 1 (studied only)	Group 2 (studied and tested)
$n_1 = 15$, $\Sigma X_1 = 300$, $SS_1 = 171$	$n_2 = 15$, $\Sigma X_2 = 330$, $SS_2 = 192$

(a) Set up the appropriate statistical hypotheses.

(b) Perform the test ($\alpha = .05$).

(c) Draw final conclusions.

*15. (a) Suppose you constructed a 95% confidence interval for $\mu_1 - \mu_2$, given the data in Problem 14. What one value do you already know will reside in that interval? (Explain.)

(b) Now construct a 95% confidence interval for $\mu_1 - \mu_2$, given the data in Problem 14. Any surprises?

(c) Without performing any calculations, comment on whether a 99% confidence interval estimated from the same data would include zero.

(d) Now construct a 99% confidence interval for $\mu_1 - \mu_2$, given the data in Problem 14. Any surprises?

16. The director of Academic Support Services wants to test the efficacy of a possible intervention for undergraduate students who are placed on academic probation. She randomly assigns 28 such students to two groups. During the first week of the semester, students in Group 1 receive daily instruction on specific strategies for learning and studying. Group 2 students spend the same time engaged in general discussion about the importance of doing well in college and the support services that are available on campus. At the end of the semester, the director determines the mean GPA for each group:

Group 1 (strategy instruction)	**Group 2 (general discussion)**
$n_1 = 14, \quad \bar{X}_1 = 2.83, \quad s_1 = .41$	$n_2 = 14, \quad \bar{X}_2 = 2.26, \quad s_2 = .39$

   (a) Set up the appropriate statistical hypotheses.

   (b) Perform the test ($\alpha = .05$).

   (c) Draw final conclusions.

17. From the data given in Problem 16:

   (a) Compute and interpret the effect size, d; evaluate its magnitude in terms of Cohen's criteria and in terms of the normal curve.

   (b) Calculate and interpret the effect size, $\hat{\omega}^2$.

18. Compare the investigation described in Problem 9 with that in Problem 14. Suppose a significant difference had been found in both—in favor of the children who attended preschool in Problem 9 and in favor of Group 2 in Problem 14.

   (a) For which investigation would it be easier to clarify the relationship between cause and effect? (Explain.)

   (b) What are some other possible explanations—other than whether a child attended preschool—for a significant difference in sociability in Problem 9?

*19. Examine Problems 8, 9, 10, 14, and 16. In which would it be easiest to clarify causal relationships? (Explain.)

20. Is randomization the same as random sampling? (Explain.)

21. Suppose the following statement were made on the basis of the significant difference reported in Problem 13: "Statistics show that women are higher in emotional intelligence than men."

   (a) Is the statement a statistical or nonstatistical inference? (Explain.)

   (b) Describe some of the limits to any statistical inferences based on the study.

CHAPTER 15

Comparing the Means of Dependent Samples

15.1 The Meaning of "Dependent"

You just learned about assessing the difference between means obtained from two independent samples, where observations from the samples are in no way related. Sometimes the substantive question or research design involves **dependent samples**. Here, observations from one sample are related in some way to those from the other. In this chapter, we examine the statistical procedures for analyzing the difference between means that derive from such samples. As you will see, the general logic of testing a null hypothesis involving dependent samples is identical to that used when samples are independent.

There are two basic ways in which samples can be dependent. In the first case, the two means, $\overline{X}_1$ and $\overline{X}_2$, are based on the *same individuals*. This is known as a **repeated-measures design**. The "before-after" scenario is an example: a sample is selected, all participants complete a pretest, an intervention occurs, and then the same individuals complete a posttest. The researcher's interest is in the difference between the pretest mean ($\overline{X}_1$) and the posttest mean ($\overline{X}_2$). Suppose you wish to test the effectiveness of a weight-reduction intervention for young adolescents. You select 30 volunteers, recording their weights before the intervention and again afterward. Presumably, the heavier children at the initial weigh-in (X_1) generally will be taller and have bigger frames and, therefore, will also tend to be among the heavier children at the final weigh-in (X_2)—regardless of any effect the intervention may have. Similarly, you would expect the children who were lighter at the outset (smaller frames, shorter) to be among the lighter children at the end. That is, if you were to calculate the Pearson correlation coefficient (r) between the 10 pairs of X_1 and X_2 weights, you would expect to find a positive correlation. (For this reason, dependent samples also are called "paired" or "correlated" samples.) In short, X_1 and X_2 are not independent. This differs from the independent-samples design described in the last chapter, where there is no basis whatever for pairing the X_1 and X_2 scores.

In experiments, sometimes one group of participants experiences both treatment conditions; this is another example of a repeated-measures design. For instance, you ask each individual to recall items from a word list presented under two conditions—auditorily in one, visually in the other. Thus, each participant has a pair of scores: the number of words recalled from the auditory presentation of words (X_1) and the number of words recalled from the visual presentation (X_2). Your interest is in the difference between the two means, $\overline{X}_1$ and $\overline{X}_2$. In what sense are these two means "dependent"? Well, individuals with high verbal ability and word knowledge will tend to have better recall under *either* condition (i.e., higher X_1 and X_2 scores on both) than individuals low in verbal ability and word knowledge, thus creating a positive correlation between the paired scores. When the same individuals are used in both conditions of an experiment, each person in a sense is serving as his or her own control group.

Samples can be dependent in a second way. Here, different individuals are used for the two conditions of a study, but, prior to forming the groups, the investigator *matches* them person-for-person on some characteristic related to the response variable. Known as a **matched-subjects design**, this procedure increases the equivalence of the two groups (on the matching variable) over and above that effected by random assignment alone. Imagine that you want to investigate the relative effectiveness of two first-grade reading interventions. Before randomly assigning the 60 beginning first graders to one intervention or the other, you match the children on reading readiness. Specifically, you form 30 pairs of children such that in each pair the two children have equal (or nearly equal) scores on a recently administered reading-readiness assessment. Taking each pair in turn, you flip a coin to assign one of the children to intervention A and the other to intervention B. At the end of the intervention, you administer a reading achievement test to all and then compare the mean score of children in intervention A $(\overline{X}_A)$ with that of children in intervention B $(\overline{X}_B)$. To the extent that the test used for matching is an adequate measure of a child's readiness to profit from reading instruction, you would expect relatively high X_A and X_B scores from a matched pair high in reading readiness and relatively low X_A and X_B scores from a matched pair low in reading readiness. That is, if you consider the two achievement scores for each matched pair, you would expect a tendency for a high X_A score to go with a high X_B score and a low X_A score to go with a low X_B score. Again, there would be a positive correlation between pairs of scores; consequently, the two samples are not independent.[1]

15.2   *Standard Error of the Difference Between Dependent Means*

When samples are dependent, the standard error of the difference between means is modified to take into account the degree of correlation between the

---

[1]Sometimes the nonindependence of samples is the result of "natural" matching, as in studies of identical twins, siblings, spouses, or, in research involving animals, littermates.

paired scores. The estimated standard error for dependent means is shown in Formula (15.1):

Standard error of the
difference between means:
Dependent samples

$$s_{\overline{X}_1 - \overline{X}_2} = \sqrt{\frac{s_1^2 + s_2^2 - 2r_{12}s_1s_2}{n}} \tag{15.1}$$

At first glance, this formula may appear to be quite a handful! Let's first identify the terms, all of which you have seen before: s_1^2 and s_2^2 are estimates of the population variances, r_{12} is the sample correlation between X_1 and X_2, s_1 and s_2 are estimates of the population standard deviations, and n is the number of pairs of observations. If you divide the fraction under the square root into three parts, each with the common denominator n, Formula (15.1) can be compared with the estimated standard error for independent samples (Section 14.4):

Dependent Samples	**Independent Samples**
$s_{\overline{X}_1 - \overline{X}_2} = \sqrt{\dfrac{s_1^2}{n} + \dfrac{s_2^2}{n} - \dfrac{2r_{12}s_1s_2}{n}}$	$s_{\overline{X}_1 - \overline{X}_2} = \sqrt{\dfrac{s_{pooled}^2}{n_1} + \dfrac{s_{pooled}^2}{n_2}}$

If $n_1 = n_2 = n$, these formulas appear to differ in just two ways. First, for dependent samples, the two variance estimates (s_1^2 and s_2^2) are used separately to estimate their respective population variances, whereas for independent samples the pooled variance estimate (s_{pooled}^2) is used for both. But when $n_1 = n_2 = n$, as is the case with paired samples, this proves to be no difference at all. That is, it can be shown that

$$\left(\frac{s_1^2}{n} + \frac{s_2^2}{n} \right) = \left(\frac{s_{pooled}^2}{n_1} + \frac{s_{pooled}^2}{n_2} \right)$$

when $n_1 = n_2$. The remaining difference between the two formulas above—and therefore the *only* difference—is the term involving r_{12}, which is *subtracted* in the formula for dependent samples. Thus,

When samples are dependent, the standard error of the difference between means normally will be *smaller* than when samples are independent. This is because of the positive correlation between X_1 and X_2 scores.

Look again at the numerator of Formula (15.1). The amount of reduction in the standard error depends mainly on the size of the correlation coefficient, r_{12}: the larger the positive correlation, the smaller the standard error. Using the same people under both conditions almost always forces a positive correlation between the X_1 and X_2 scores (the size of which depends on the particular variable being measured and the particular conditions imposed).

As for the matched-subjects design, the reduction in the standard error brought about by matching depends largely on the relevance of the matching variable. It makes sense to match on reading-readiness scores in studies of the effect of two reading interventions because those high in reading readiness will most likely do well in either condition relative to their low-readiness peers. In contrast, it would be silly to match kids on, say, freckle density, for freckle density has no relation to reading achievement (that we're aware of, at least). Consequently, there would be no reduction in the standard error.

The reduction in the standard error is the major statistical advantage of using dependent samples: the smaller the standard error, the more the sample results will reflect the extent of the "true" or population difference. In this sense, a smaller standard error gives you a more statistically powerful test. That is, it is more likely that you will reject a false H_0. (Chapter 19 is devoted to the subject of statistical power.)

15.3   *Degrees of Freedom*

When samples are dependent, the degrees of freedom associated with the standard error is $n - 1$, where n is the number of *pairs*. Note that here the *df* is just half of the $(n - 1) + (n - 1)$ *df* for two independent samples having the same number of observations. To see why this is so, recall that *df* reflects the number of *independent* pieces of information that the sample results provide for estimating the standard error. With independent samples, you have $n - 1$ *df* for the sample of X_1 scores and $n - 1$ *df* for the sample of X_2 scores. With dependent samples, however, every X_1 score is in some way and to some degree related to an X_2 score, so you get no additional *independent* pieces of information when you use both the X_1 and X_2 scores in the estimated standard error.

Giving up degrees of freedom for a smaller standard error is a statistical tradeoff in using dependent samples—a tradeoff that should be thought through carefully. If r_{12} is low, the reduction in *df* could be the difference between rejecting and retaining a false null hypothesis, particularly when n is small. As a quick glance at Table B (Appendix C) will confirm, this is because the critical value of t is *larger* as *df* decreases, thereby making it more difficult to reject H_0. Consequently, when matching the participants, you should not match on a variable that "might help," but only on one you are reasonably sure has a strong association with the response variable.

15.4   *The* t *Test for Two Dependent Samples*

The structure of the t test for dependent samples is identical to that of the independent-samples t test:

$$t = \frac{(\overline{X}_1 - \overline{X}_2) - (\mu_1 - \mu_2)}{s_{\overline{X}_1 - \overline{X}_2}}$$

In the numerator, you see that the difference between the two (dependent) sample means, $\overline{X}_1 - \overline{X}_2$, is compared with the condition specified in the null hypothesis, $\mu_1 - \mu_2$. The denominator is the standard error as given in Formula (15.1). Because the null hypothesis typically specifies that $\mu_1 - \mu_2 = 0$, the formula for the dependent-samples *t* test simplifies to:

t test for two dependent samples

$$t = \frac{\overline{X}_1 - \overline{X}_2}{s_{\overline{X}_1 - \overline{X}_2}}$$

(15.2)

The *t* ratio will follow Student's *t* distribution with $df = n - 1$ (where, again, *n* is the number of *paired* observations). Although an assumption of normality underlies the use of *t* when samples are dependent, it is not necessary to assume homogeneity of variance.

   Formula (15.2) can be rather burdensome in practice, particularly because of the need to calculate r_{12} for the standard error. Consequently, we offer you the popular alternative for calculating *t*, the **direct-difference method**. It is equivalent to Formula (15.2) and easier to use.

The Direct-Difference Method

The method of Formula (15.2) deals explicitly with the characteristics of two distributions—that of the X_1 scores and that of the X_2 scores. In contrast, the direct-difference method focuses on the characteristics of a single distribution, the distribution of *differences* between the paired X_1 and X_2 scores.

   Look at Table 15.1, which shows a subset of data from a dependent-samples design. By subtracting each X_2 score from its paired X_1 score, you obtain the difference score *D* (❶) for each pair. For example, the first pair of scores corresponds to $D = X_1 - X_2 = 24 - 37 = -13$, indicating that the first score in this pair is 13 points

Table 15.1   Data from a Dependent-Samples Design

Pair	X_1	X_2	❶ $\overline{X}_1 - \overline{X}_2 = D$
1	24	37	−13
2	16	21	−5
3	20	18	+2
•	•	•	•
•	•	•	•
•	•	•	•
n	12	20	−8

$$❷ \;\; \overline{D} = \frac{\Sigma D}{n}$$

lower than the second. Now consider the null hypothesis that $\mu_1 - \mu_2 = 0$. If this hypothesis is true, then the mean of the population of differences between the paired values, μ_D, is equal to zero as well. That is, H_0: $\mu_1 - \mu_2 = 0$, which is stated in terms of two populations, can be restated in terms of a single population of difference scores as H_0: $\mu_D = 0$. With the direct-difference method, you find $\bar{D}$ ("d-bar"), the mean of the sample of difference scores (❷). You then inquire whether this mean differs significantly from the hypothesized mean (zero) of the population of difference scores.

The standard error of the difference scores, symbolized by $s_{\bar{D}}$, is calculated as follows:

> Standard error:
> Direct-difference method
>
> $$s_{\bar{D}} = \frac{s_D}{\sqrt{n}}$$
>
> $$= \sqrt{\frac{SS_D}{n(n-1)}} \qquad (15.3)$$

SS_D is the sum of squares based on difference scores. As we will show momentarily, it is obtained by summing $(D - \bar{D})^2$ across all values of D (much like you do in calculating the X sum of squares).

The resulting test statistic takes on the familiar form: it is the difference between the sample result ($\bar{D}$) and the condition specified in the null hypothesis (μ_D), divided by the standard error ($s_{\bar{D}}$):

$$t = \frac{\bar{D} - \mu_D}{s_{\bar{D}}}$$

Because the null hypothesis typically takes the form $\mu_D = 0$, the numerator simplifies to $\bar{D}$. Thus:

> *t* test for two dependent samples:
> Direct-difference method
>
> $$t = \frac{\bar{D}}{s_{\bar{D}}}$$
>
> $$= \frac{\bar{D}}{\sqrt{\dfrac{SS_D}{n(n-1)}}} \qquad (15.4)$$

15.5   Testing Hypotheses about Two Dependent Means: An Example

Suppose that strong claims, with weak evidence, have been made about the efficacy of an herbal treatment for attention deficit disorder (ADD). You decide to empirically test the validity of these claims. You locate 10 fifth-grade students, in 10 different classrooms, who have been diagnosed with ADD. Sitting unobtrusively at the back of each classroom with stopwatch in hand, you record the number of seconds that the child with ADD is out of seat during a 20-minute period of silent reading (X_1). Each of the 10 children is then given daily doses of the herbal treatment for one month, after which you return to the classrooms to again record out-of-seat behavior during silent reading (X_2). Thus, you end up with 10 pairs of observations: a pre-treatment score and post-treatment score for each child. These data appear in the first two columns of Table 15.2 (which, for your convenience, we have rounded to the nearest minute).

Are the claims about the herbal treatment's efficacy valid? That is, do children with ADD show less distractibility and off-task behavior after receiving the herbal antidote? If so, then you expect a *positive* mean difference, $\bar{D}$. That is, the X_1 score

Table 15.2   The Number of Out-of-Seat Minutes in a Sample of Children with Attention Deficit Disorder, before (X_1) and after (X_2) Herbal Treatment

Pair	X_1	X_2	① D	③ $(D - \bar{D})^2$
1	11	8	3	4
2	4	5	−1	4
3	19	15	4	9
4	7	7	0	1
5	9	11	−2	9
6	3	0	3	4
7	13	9	4	9
8	5	4	1	0
9	8	13	−5	36
10	6	3	3	4

$n = 10$ $\bar{X}_1 = 8.5$ $\bar{X}_2 = 7.5$ ② $\bar{D} = \Sigma D/n$ ④ $SS_D = \Sigma(D - \bar{D})^2$
$= 10/10$ $= 80$
$= +1$

⑤ $s_{\bar{D}} = \sqrt{\dfrac{SS_D}{n(n-1)}} = \sqrt{\dfrac{80}{10(9)}} = \sqrt{\dfrac{80}{90}} = \sqrt{.89} = .94$

⑥ $t = \dfrac{\bar{D}}{s_{\bar{D}}} = \dfrac{1}{.94} = +1.06$

⑦ $df = n - 1 = 10 - 1 = 9$

⑧ $t_{.05}(\text{one-tailed}) = +1.833$

⑨ Decision: Retain H_0

in a pair should tend to be *higher* than the corresponding X_2 score. The inferential question is whether $\bar{D}$ is large enough to reject the null hypothesis of no difference— that in the population the mean difference is zero ($\mu_D = 0$). Let's walk through the steps of testing this hypothesis, which you will find to parallel the argument of significance testing in earlier chapters.

Step 1 *Formulate the statistical hypotheses and select a level of significance.*
Your statistical hypotheses are:

$$H_0: \mu_D = 0$$

$$H_1: \mu_D > 0$$

You formulated a *directional* alternative hypothesis because the publicized claims about the herbal treatment are valid only if the children show *less* distractibility (in the form of out-of-seat time) after one month of receiving the herbal treatment. You decide to set the level of significance at $\alpha = .05$.

Step 2 *Determine the desired sample size and select the sample.*
In this illustration, we use 10 pairs of subjects (so that all computations may be easily demonstrated).

Step 3 *Calculate the necessary sample statistics.*
First, determine D for each pair of scores, which we show at ❶ in Table 15.2. For example, $D = 11 - 8 = 3$ for the first case. Then calculate the mean of the D values: $\bar{D} = +1.00$ (❷). Notice that $\bar{D}$ is equivalent to the difference between $\bar{X}_1$ and $\bar{X}_2$: $\bar{D} = \bar{X}_1 - \bar{X}_2 = 8.5 - 7.5 = +1.00$. For this sample of children with ADD, then, the average out-of-seat time was one minute less after a month of the herbal treatment.

Now obtain the squared deviation for each D score (❸), which you then sum to obtain $SS_D = 80$ (❹). Plug this figure into Formula (15.3) and you have the standard error, $s_{\bar{D}} = .94$(❺). Step back for a moment: As the standard error, this value represents the amount of variability in the underlying sampling distribution of differences. That is, .94 is your estimate of the standard deviation of all possible values of $\bar{D}$, had you conducted an unlimited number of sampling experiments of this kind. As with any standard error, it is used to evaluate the discrepancy between your sample result ($\bar{D}$ in the present case) and the condition stated in the null hypothesis ($\mu_D = 0$). That is, how large is this discrepancy, given what you would expect from random sampling variation alone? This question is answered by the final calculation, the t ratio (❻): $t = +1.06$.

Step 4 *Identify the region(s) of rejection.*
The sample t ratio follows Student's t distribution with $df = 10 - 1 = 9$ (❼). Consult Table B to find the critical t value for a one-tailed test at $\alpha = .05$ with 9 df. This value is $t_{.05} = +1.833$ (❽), the value of t beyond which the most extreme 5% of all possible samples fall (in the upper tail only) if H_0 is true. The region of rejection and the obtained sample t ratio are shown in Figure 15.1.

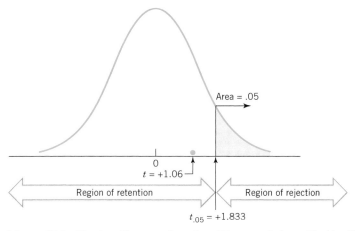

Figure 15.1   Testing H_0: $\mu_D = 0$ against H_1: $\mu_D > 0$ ($\alpha = .05$, df = 9).

Step 5   *Make the statistical decision and form conclusion.*
The sample t ratio of $+1.06$ falls in the region of retention, so H_0 is re-tained (❾). It very well could be true that $\mu_D = 0$ (although you have in no way *proven* that this is the case). As is often said in this situation, there is "no significant difference" between the two means. This leads you to the substantive conclusion that, after one month of herbal treatment, children with ADD are no less distractible than they were before treatment, which calls into question the popular claims regarding the treatment's efficacy.

The outcome would be identical had you instead used Formula (15.2) to test H_0. Although the direct-difference method is easier to use than Formula (15.2), we should acknowledge that the direct-difference method yields less information. When you are done, you know the size of the difference between the two sample means ($\overline{D}$) and its statistical significance. In most research, however, you also will want to know—and will be obliged to report—the two means and standard deviations. And if you are curious about how much correlation was induced by the pairing, you will want to know r_{12} as well ($r_{12} = +.80$ in the present case). But the direct-difference method yields none of that information. If these quantities are desired, you must re-turn to the data and compute them (in which case you may conclude that the total amount of work is about the same between the two methods).

15.6   *Interval Estimation of* μ_D

The logic of interval estimation with dependent samples is identical to that in which samples are independent. The only procedural difference is found in the determination of *df* and the standard error, each of which takes into account the paired nature of the observations. The form of the interval estimate for dependent samples is:

Rule for a confidence interval for μ_D		
	$$\overline{D} \pm t_\alpha s_{\overline{D}}$$	(15.5)

Let's determine the 95% confidence interval for μ_D from the herbal treatment study, where $\overline{D} = +1.00$ and $s_{\overline{D}} = .94$. To do this, you need the *two*-tailed critical value, 2.262 ($\alpha = .05$, $df = 9$). Now insert $\overline{D}$, $s_{\overline{D}}$, and the two-tailed critical value into Formula (15.5):

$$1.00 \pm (2.262)(.94) = 1.00 \pm 2.13$$

$$-1.13 \text{ (lower limit) to } +3.13 \text{ (upper limit)}$$

Thus, you are 95% confident that the true difference is anywhere from a slight *increase* in out-of-seat time (-1.13 minutes) to a somewhat larger *decrease* in such behavior ($+3.13$ minutes). Any value within this interval is a reasonable candidate for μ_D—including no difference at all. Given these results, claims regarding the efficacy of the herbal treatment of ADD would appear to be suspect.

Because $\overline{D} = \overline{X}_1 - \overline{X}_2$, $\mu_D = \mu_1 - \mu_2$, and $s_{\overline{D}} = s_{\overline{X}_1 - \overline{X}_2}$, Formula (15.5) can be presented equivalently in terms of $\overline{X}_1 - \overline{X}_2$, $\mu_1 - \mu_2$, and $s_{\overline{X}_1 - \overline{X}_2}$:

Rule for a confidence interval for $\mu_1 - \mu_2$		
	$$\overline{X}_1 - \overline{X}_2 \pm t_\alpha s_{\overline{X}_1 - \overline{X}_2}$$	(15.6)

Formula (15.6) provides a $(1 - \alpha)(100)$ percent confidence interval for $\mu_1 - \mu_2$, which is identical to the interval resulting from Formula (15.5).

15.7 *Summary*

The test of the difference between two means can be conducted with dependent samples as well as with independent samples. There are two common ways of forming dependent samples. In the repeated-measures design, $\overline{X}_1$ and $\overline{X}_2$ are based on the same individuals—for example, participants may be tested before and after an intervention, or they may receive both treatment conditions of an experiment. In contrast, different individuals are used in the matched-subjects design, but they are matched on some relevant characteristic before being randomly assigned to treatment conditions.

The statistical benefit of using dependent samples is a smaller standard error, which means that there will be a higher probability of detecting a difference between the two populations when a difference actually exists. This benefit depends on the size of the positive correlation induced by pairing: the higher the correlation, the greater the advantage. The experimental benefit is that it is possible to exert greater control over extraneous factors that could affect the outcome by holding them constant through the pairing process.

In the matched-subjects design, the statistical advantage of matching is lost if individuals are matched on a characteristic that is weakly related to the response variable. Because there are fewer degrees of freedom in this design, the ability to reject a false H_0 can be undermined, particularly when n is small. The experimental advantage is lost as well.

The sample t ratio, calculated either by $t = (\overline{X}_1 - \overline{X}_2)/s_{\overline{X}_1 - \overline{X}_2}$ or $t = \overline{D}/s_{\overline{D}}$, follows the Student's distribution with $n - 1$ degrees of freedom, where n is the number of pairs of observations. A $(1 - \alpha)(100)$ percent confidence interval is estimated using the rule, $\overline{D} \pm t_\alpha s_{\overline{D}}$, which is equivalent to $\overline{X}_1 - \overline{X}_2 \pm t_\alpha s_{\overline{X}_1 - \overline{X}_2}$.

Reading the Research: Dependent-Samples t Test

Wyver and Spence (1999) studied the effects of a specialized training program on the divergent problem-solving skills of 28 preschool children. Children in the experimental group received training, while control-group children did not. These researchers administered a pretest (before training) and a posttest (after training), and they then examined the amount of gain made by each group:

> When pre- to post-training changes were examined for statistical significance, only the experimental group demonstrated a significant change $(t(13) = -2.04, p < .05)$.

The result of this dependent-samples t test was significant at the .05 level.

Source: Wyver, S. R., & Spence, S. H. (1999). Play and divergent problem solving: Evidence supporting a reciprocal relationship. *Early Education and Development, 10*(4), 419–444.

Case Study: Mirror, Mirror, on the Wall

Self-concept has long been of interest to practitioners and researchers in education. Beyond its inherent value, positive self-concept is regarded by some theorists to be a precursor to high academic achievement. For this case study, we evaluated the "stability" of this construct during the formative high school years. Specifically, does self-concept tend to improve, decline, or stay the same between the eighth and twelfth grades?

A random sample of 2056 urban, public school students was obtained from the *National Education Longitudinal Study of 1988* (National Center for Education Statistics, U.S. Department of Education, http://nces.ed.gov). We applied the dependent-samples t test to assess change in self-concept from the eighth to twelfth grades, first for the entire sample and then separately for males and females.

We established the following statistical hypotheses:

$$H_0: \mu_D = 0$$

$$H_1: \mu_D \neq 0$$

Table 15.3   Statistics for Eighth- and Twelfth-Grade Self-Concept Scores

	$\overline{X}$	n	s	$s_{\overline{X}}$
SELF-CONCEPT 8th				
Overall	3.163	2056	.405	.009
Males	3.223	945	.394	.013
Females	3.110	1097	.408	.012
SELF-CONCEPT 12th				
Overall	3.156	2056	.422	.009
Males	3.184	945	.408	.013
Females	3.132	1097	.432	.013

(*Note:* Because some respondents did not report their gender, the sum of males and females does not quite equal the "entire sample" figure of 2056.)

In this case, a nondirectional alternative hypothesis makes sense because we are uncertain how self-concept behaves over time. Aware that large samples can more easily produce statistically significant results, we chose the more stringent .01 level of significance.

We constructed the self-concept variables, SELFC8 and SELFC12, from several individual items in the database (e.g., "I feel good about myself," "I am able to do things as well as others"). Students responded to these statements by providing their level of agreement on a Likert-type scale. Scores on SELFC8 and SELFC12 range from 1 to 4, with higher scores indicating greater levels of self-concept (Table 15.3).

Before we get to the meaty part of the t test results, let's briefly explore the degree of association between the paired samples. Most statistical software packages provide the "paired-samples correlation" as part of the t test output. This correlation is nothing more than the familiar Pearson r, and it tells us the magnitude of association between the pairs of scores. In the present case, $r = .43$, suggesting a moderate, positive relationship between eighth- and twelfth-grade self-concept scores. Now on to the final t test results.

Table 15.4 shows that there was negligible change in self-concept among the overall sample of students (i.e., $\overline{D} = -.007$). The statistically nonsignificant ($p = .468$) outcome of the dependent-samples t test directs us to retain the null hypothesis of no change in self-concept among urban public school students in the population.

Table 15.4   Dependent-Samples t Test Results

	$\overline{D}$	s	$s_{\overline{D}}$	t	df	p (two-tailed)
Overall	.007	.443	.010	.726	2055	.468
Males	.039	.447	.015	2.654	944	.008
Females	-.022	.438	.013	-1.633	1096	.103

The difference for females, $\overline{D} = -.022$, also was statistically nonsignificant ($p = .103$). In contrast, the self-concept of males on average decreased from the eighth grade to the twelfth grade by a statistically significant .039 points ($p < .01$). Statistical significance notwithstanding, this difference is of questionable *practical* significance. To appreciate just how small this statistically significant result is, consider that the effect size corresponding to this difference is a paltry .09—roughly one-tenth of a standard deviation! This is a vivid illustration of why statistically significant results, particularly those deriving from large samples, should also be interpreted in terms of their practical import.

We also can evaluate change in self-concept by interval estimation. Using the male group as an example, our statistical software produced a 95% confidence interval with a lower limit of +.010 and an upper limit of +.067. (Remember: The positive algebraic sign indicates that the eighth-grade mean is larger than the twelfth-grade mean.) Self-concept appears to diminish for males in the population, a conclusion entirely consistent with the results of the dependent-samples t test above. Like effect size, the 95% confidence interval highlights the generally small magnitude of this decline in the population: somewhere between 1/10 to 7/10 of a point (on a 4-point scale).

Suggested Computer Exercises

Access the **technology** data file, which is from a study that examined the effects of a technology curriculum on students' computer skills. Fifty-six fifth graders were tested before and after the three-week unit.

1. Use a dependent-samples t test to assess whether the technology unit has a significant effect ($\alpha = .01$) on students' computer skills. In doing so,

   (a) formulate the statistical hypotheses,

   (b) compute the necessary sample statistics, and

   (c) draw your final conclusions.

2. Use interval estimation to capture the mean difference in test performance. (Construct both 95% and 99% confidence intervals.)

Exercises

Identify, Define, or Explain

Terms and Concepts

dependent samples   matched-subjects design
repeated-measures design   direct-difference method

Symbols

X_1, X_2 $\overline{X}_1, \overline{X}_2$ s_1^2, s_2^2 n r_{12} D $\overline{D}$ μ_D SS_D $s_{\overline{D}}$

Questions and Problems

Note: Answers to starred (*) items are presented in Appendix B.

*1. Suppose you wish to use high school seniors for an investigation concerning the relative efficacy of two treatment conditions for reducing test anxiety. You draw a random sample of seniors from a local high school, randomly assign subjects to treatments, and then conduct the statistical test. Should you consider these to be *dependent* groups because they are "matched" on year in school—that is, both groups are high school seniors? (Explain.)

2. (a) How can the use of matched pairs be of help statistically?

(b) What *one single value* can you compute from the results of a matched-pairs investigation that will tell you the degree to which the matching has helped?

*3. The following are scores for five participants in an investigation having a pretest–posttest design:

Participant

	A	B	C	D	E
Pretest	12	6	8	5	9
Posttest	9	8	6	1	6

(a) Compute SS_{pre}, SS_{post}, and $r_{\text{pre,post}}$.

(b) From SS_{pre} and SS_{post}, determine s^2_{pre} and s^2_{post}.

(c) Compute $s_{\bar{X}_{\text{pre}} - \bar{X}_{\text{post}}}$

(d) Test $H_0: \mu_{\text{pre}} - \mu_{\text{post}} = 0$ against $H_1: \mu_{\text{pre}} - \mu_{\text{post}} > 0$ ($\alpha = .05$)

(e) Draw final conclusions.

4. Repeat Problem 3c, except use the direct-difference method.

(a) What are the statistical hypotheses?

(b) Compute $\bar{D}$, SS_D, and $s_{\bar{D}}$.

(c) Test H_0.

(d) Draw final conclusions.

(e) Give the symbols for the quantities from Problem 3 that correspond to μ_D, $\bar{D}$, and $s_{\bar{D}}$.

(f) Compare your results to those for Problem 3.

*5. Professor Civiello wishes to investigate problem-solving skills under two conditions: solving a problem with and without background music. In a carefully controlled experiment involving six research participants, Dr. Civiello records the time it takes each participant to solve a problem when background music is being played and the time required to solve a second problem in the presence of "white noise." (Half of the participants receive the music condition first, half the white noise condition first.) The following are the results, in milliseconds:

Participant	Background Music	White Noise
A	39	35
B	37	37
C	44	38
D	42	41
E	43	39
F	41	40

Using the direct-difference method:

(a) Set up the statistical hypotheses.

(b) Compute $\bar{D}$, SS_D, and $s_{\bar{D}}$.

(c) Perform the test ($\alpha = .05$).

(d) Draw final conclusions.

*6. The sales manager of a large educational software company compares two training programs offered by competing firms. She forms eight matched pairs of sales trainees on the basis of their verbal aptitude scores obtained at the time of initial employment; she randomly assigns one member of each pair to program 1 and the other to program 2. The following are the results for the two groups after six months on the job (sales in thousands of dollars):

Training Program 1: $\bar{X}_1 = 56.3$ $SS_1 = 538$

Training Program 2: $\bar{X}_2 = 44.3$ $SS_2 = 354$

$$r_{12} = +.04$$

(a) Compute $s_{\bar{X}_1 - \bar{X}_2}$.

(b) Specify the statistical hypotheses.

(c) Perform the test ($\alpha = .01$).

(d) Draw final conclusions.

(e) Do you believe that the magnitude of this particular $r_{pre,post}$ is sufficient? (Explain.)

7. Consider Problem 6:

(a) Without performing any calculations, what one value do you know for certain would fall in a 99% confidence interval for $\mu_1 - \mu_2$? (Explain.)

(b) Construct and interpret a 99% confidence interval for $\mu_1 - \mu_2$.

(c) What two factors contribute to the width of the confidence interval in Problem 7b?

(d) Construct and interpret a 95% confidence interval for $\mu_1 - \mu_2$.

*8. Consider Problem 5:

(a) Without performing any calculations, what one value do you know for certain would *not* fall in a 95% confidence interval for $\mu_1 - \mu_2$? (Explain.)

(b) Construct and interpret a 95% confidence interval for $\mu_1 - \mu_2$.

*9. Is one Internet search engine more efficient than another? You ask each of seven student volunteers to find information on a specific topic using one search engine (search 1) and then to find information on the same topic using a competing search engine (search 2). Four of the students use search 1 first, whereas the remaining three use search 2 first. The results (in seconds) are as follows:

Student	Search 1	Search 2
A	25	26
B	53	55
C	67	71
D	74	80
E	94	93
F	93	105
G	110	120

Using the direct-difference method:

(a) Set up the statistical hypotheses.

(b) Compute $\overline{D}$, SS_D, and $s_{\overline{D}}$.

(c) Perform the test ($\alpha = .05$).

(d) Draw final conclusions.

10. A psychological testing firm wishes to determine whether college applicants can improve their college aptitude test scores by taking the test twice. To investigate this question, a sample of 40 high school juniors takes the test on two occasions, three weeks apart. The following are the results:

$$\text{First testing: } \overline{X}_1 = 48.3 \qquad s_1 = 9.2$$
$$\text{Second testing: } \overline{X}_2 = 50.1 \qquad s_2 = 11.1$$
$$r_{12} = +.81$$

(a) Compute $s_{\overline{X}_1 - \overline{X}_2}$.

(b) Specify the statistical hypotheses.

(c) Perform the test ($\alpha = .05$).

(d) Draw final conclusions.

11. An exercise physiologist compares two cardiovascular fitness programs. Ten matched pairs of out-of-shape adult volunteers are formed on the basis of a variety of factors such as sex, age, weight, blood pressure, exercise, and eating habits. In each pair, one individual is randomly assigned to program 1 and the other to program 2. After four months, the individuals in the two programs are compared on several measures. The following are the results for resting pulse rate:

$$\text{Program 1: } \Sigma X_1 = 762 \qquad SS_1 = 150.6$$
$$\text{Program 2: } \Sigma X_2 = 721 \qquad SS_2 = 129.9$$
$$r_{12} = +.46$$

   (a) Compute $s_{\bar{X}_1 - \bar{X}_2}$.

   (b) Specify the statistical hypotheses.

   (c) Perform the test ($\alpha = .05$).

   (d) Draw final conclusions.

12. You wish to see whether students perform differently on essay tests and on multiple-choice tests. You select a sample of eight students enrolled in an introductory biology course and have each student take an essay test and a multiple-choice test. Both tests cover the same unit of instruction and are designed to assess mastery of factual knowledge. (Half the students take the essay test first; the remaining half take the multiple-choice test first.) The results are as follows:

Student

	A	B	C	D	E	F	G	H
Essay:	43	39	44	47	30	46	34	41
Multiple choice:	45	33	46	49	28	43	36	37

   Using the direct-difference method:

   (a) Set up the statistical hypotheses.

   (b) Compute $\bar{D}$, SS_D, and $s_{\bar{D}}$.

   (c) Perform the test ($\alpha = .05$).

   (d) Draw final conclusions.

*13. Parents of 14 entering first graders eagerly volunteer their children for the tryout of a new experimental reading program announced at a PTA meeting. To obtain an "equivalent" group for comparison purposes, each experimental child is matched with a child in the regular program on the basis of sex and reading-readiness scores from kindergarten. At the end of the first grade, a dependent-samples t test shows those in the experimental program to have significantly higher reading achievement scores than their matched counterparts in the regular program.

   (a) What is the essential difference between this research design and the design described in Problems 6 and 11?

   (b) Explain any important advantage(s) either design might have over the other.

   (c) Provide an alternative possible explanation (other than the experimental reading program itself) for the significantly better scores of the experimental children.

14. The correlation calculated in Problem 3a ($r_{\text{pre,post}} = +.68$) indicates a considerable advantage to using the same participants under both conditions rather than two independent groups of five participants each. To see this advantage more directly, reanalyze the data in Problem 3 as if the scores were from *independent* groups (of five participants each). Compare the two sets of results with respect to $s_{\bar{X}_1 - \bar{X}_2}$ and the sample t ratio.

15. Recall the very low correlation between matched pairs in Problem 6 ($r_{12} = +.04$). Reanalyze these data as if the scores were from two *independent* groups of eight participants each.

   (a) Compare the two sets of results with respect to $s_{\bar{X}_1 - \bar{X}_2}$, the sample t ratio, and the appropriate statistical decision.

   (b) What important principle, in addition to that illustrated in Problem 14, derives from this exercise?

CHAPTER 16

Comparing the Means of Three or More Independent Samples: One-Way Analysis of Variance

16.1 *Comparing More Than Two Groups: Why Not Multiple t Tests?*

In Chapter 14, you learned how to test the hypothesis of no difference between the means of two independent samples. This, you will recall, is accomplished with the test statistic t:

$$t = \frac{\overline{X}_1 - \overline{X}_2}{s_{\overline{X}_1 - \overline{X}_2}}$$

What if your research question entails more than two independent groups? For example, each of the following questions easily could involve three or more groups: Does reading comprehension differ according to *how a passage is organized*? Do educational aspirations differ by *student ethnicity*? Does the *decision-making style of school principals* make a difference in teacher morale? Do SAT scores differ by *college major*?

You may be wondering why you can't continue to use the conventional t test. If there are three means to compare, why not just compute separate t ratios for $\overline{X}_1 - \overline{X}_2$, $\overline{X}_1 - \overline{X}_3$, and $\overline{X}_2 - \overline{X}_3$? It turns out that this method is inadequate in several ways. Let's say you are comparing the SAT scores of college students from five different majors:

1. There are $k(k-1)/2$ comparisons possible, where k is the number of groups. With $k = 5$ college majors, then, there must be $5(4)/2 = 10$ separate comparisons if each major is to be compared with each of the others.

2. In any one comparison, you are using only information provided by the two groups involved. The remaining groups contain information that could make the tests more sensitive, or statistically powerful.

3. When the 10 tests are completed, there are 10 bits of information rather than a single, direct answer as to whether there is evidence of test performance differences among the five majors.

4. Last and by no means least, *the probability of a Type I error is increased* when so many tests are conducted. That is, there is a greater likelihood that "significant

differences" will be claimed when, in fact, no true difference exists. When there are only two means and therefore only one test, this probability is equal to α, say .05. With 10 tests, however, the probability that there will be *at least one* Type I error among them is considerably higher. If these 10 tests were independent of each another, the probability of at least one Type I error is .40—quite a bit larger than the announced α! But to make matters worse, these 10 tests are *not* independent: If $\overline{X}_1$ is significantly greater than $\overline{X}_4$ and $\overline{X}_4$ is significantly greater than $\overline{X}_5$, then $\overline{X}_1$ *must* be significantly greater than $\overline{X}_5$. When tests are not independent, the probability of at least one Type I error is even *larger* (although it is impossible to provide a precise figure).

The solution to this general problem is found in **analysis of variance**. Sir Ronald Aylmer Fisher, who was elected a Fellow of the Royal Society in 1929 and knighted by the queen for his statistical accomplishments, is to be thanked for this important development in statistics. Fisher's contributions to mathematical statistics (and experimental design) are legendary and certainly too numerous and profound to adequately summarize here. Let us simply echo the words of Maurice Kendall, himself a prominent figure in the history of statistics, who had this to say about Fisher: "Not to refer to some of his work in any theoretical paper written [between 1920 and 1940] was almost a mark of retarded development" (quoted in Tankard, 1984, p. 112). High praise, indeed!

One-Way ANOVA

In research literature and informal conversations alike, analysis of variance often is referred to by its acronym **ANOVA (an**alysis **o**f **va**riance). ANOVA actually is a class of techniques, about which entire volumes have been written (e.g., Kirk, 1982; Winer, Brown, & Michels, 1991). We will concentrate on **one-way ANOVA**, which is used when the research question involves only one factor, or independent variable. The research questions we posed above at the end of our opening paragraph are of this kind, the individual factors being passage organization, ethnicity, decision-making style, and college major.

Although one-way ANOVA typically is considered when there are more than three independent groups, this procedure in fact can be used to compare the means of *two or more* groups. For the special case of two groups and a nondirectional H_1, one-way ANOVA and the independent samples t test lead to identical conclusions. The t test, therefore, may be thought of as a special case of one-way ANOVA, or, if you like, one-way ANOVA may be regarded as an extension of the t test to problems involving more than two groups.

16.2   *The Statistical Hypotheses in One-Way ANOVA*

There are k groups in one-way ANOVA, where k may be 2 or more. We will identify the various groups as Group 1, Group 2,..., Group k; their sample means as

$\overline{X}_1, \overline{X}_2, \ldots, \overline{X}_k$; and the corresponding population means as $\mu_1, \mu_2, \ldots, \mu_k$. To inquire as to whether there are differences among the population means, you test the overall hypothesis:

$$H_0: \mu_1 = \mu_2 = \ldots = \mu_k$$

If $k = 4$, for example, the null hypothesis would be $H_0: \mu_1 = \mu_2 = \mu_3 = \mu_4$. The alternative hypothesis is that the population means are unequal "in some way." Although there is no single convention for stating H_1 when there are more than two means, the following form will suffice for our purposes:

$$H_1: \text{not } H_0$$

In testing the hypothesis of no difference between two means ($k = 2$), we made the distinction between directional and nondirectional alternative hypotheses. Such a distinction does not make sense when $k > 2$. This is because H_0 may be false in any one of a number of ways: two means may be alike while the others differ, all may be different, and so on.

16.3   The Logic of One-Way ANOVA: An Overview

As with the independent-samples t test, participants are either randomly assigned to k treatment conditions (e.g., passage organization) or selected from k populations (e.g., college major). The general logic of ANOVA is the same regardless of how the groups have been formed. For the purposes of this overview, let's assume a true experimental design in which you have randomly assigned participants to one of three different treatment conditions ($k = 3$).

If the various treatments in fact have no differential effect, then $\mu_1 = \mu_2 = \mu_3$, H_0 is true, and the three distributions of sample observations might appear as in Figure 16.1a. As you see, differences among the three sample means ($\overline{X}_1$, $\overline{X}_2$ and $\overline{X}_3$) are minor and consistent with what you would expect from random sampling variation alone. In contrast, if there *is* a treatment effect such that μ_1, μ_2, and μ_3 have different values, then H_0 is false and the three groups might be as in Figure 16.1b. Note the greater separation among the three sample means (although each $\overline{X}$ is not far from its μ).

Let's examine Figures 16.1a and 16.1b more closely. In particular, let's compare these figures with regard to two types of variation: *within-groups* and *between-groups* variation.

Within-Groups Variation

Within each group, individual observations vary about their sample mean. This phenomenon is called **within-groups variation**, and it is a direct reflection of the **inherent variation** among individuals given the same treatment. You can present an identically organized passage to everyone in a group and still observe variation in reading comprehension. *It is inevitable that even under identical conditions, individuals will*

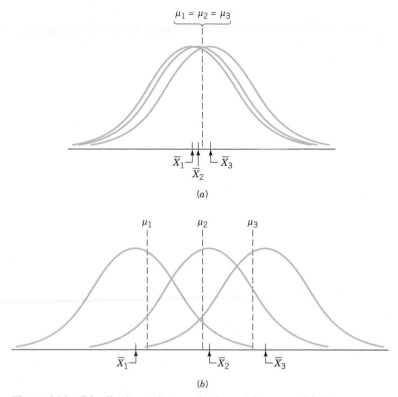

Figure 16.1   Distributions of scores in three subgroups: (*a*) H_0: $\mu_1 = \mu_2 = \mu_3$ is true (no treatment effect) and (*b*) H_0: $\mu_1 = \mu_2 = \mu_3$ is false (treatment effect is present).

vary in performance. This point also holds in designs for which random assignment is impossible or impractical. For example, there is considerable variation in SAT scores within a single college major.

Each of the three distributions in Figures 16.1*a* and 16.1*b* represents within-groups variation. Note that in both figures, scores vary around their group means to about the same extent in Groups 1, 2, and 3. Note particularly that the amount of within-groups variation is about the same whether the three population means are identical (H_0 true) or different (H_0 false). Thus:

Within-groups variation reflects only inherent variation. It does not reflect differences caused by differential treatment.

The logic is simple: because each participant *within* a particular treatment group gets the *same* treatment, differences among observations in that group cannot be attributed to differential treatment.

You may be wondering how "variance" enters into this discussion. True to its name, ANOVA is concerned with *variance* as the basic measure of variation. The sample variance for a particular group, say Group 1, is used as an estimate of the inherent variance for that particular treatment in the population. That is, s_1^2 estimates σ_1^2. If you make the assumption that the inherent variance is the same for all treatments ($\sigma_1^2 = \sigma_2^2 = \sigma_3^2$), then *inherent variance, free from the influence of treatment effects, can be represented by the single symbol* σ^2. As with the pooled variance estimate that you used in the independent-samples t test (s_{pooled}^2), the best estimate of σ^2 is found by averaging, or pooling, the three sample variances to provide the **within-groups variance estimate**, s_{within}^2. Thus,

$$s_{within}^2 \xrightarrow{\text{estimates}} \sigma^2$$

We'll fill in the computational details later. At the moment, the important point is that s_{within}^2 reflects *only* inherent variance—whether H_0 is true (Figure 16.1a) or H_0 is false (Figure 16.1b).

Between-Groups Variation

You can also see in Figures 16.1a and 16.1b that the sample means vary among themselves, which is called **between-groups variation**.[1] When the hypothesis H_0: $\mu_1 = \mu_2 = \mu_3$ is true (Figure 16.1a), the differences among the three sample means are in accord with what you have learned about random sampling. That is, when $\mu_1 = \mu_2 = \mu_3$, you nonetheless expect differences among $\overline{X}_1$, $\overline{X}_2$, and $\overline{X}_3$ because of sampling variation. Even though it reflects variation among sample means, *between-groups variation is also a reflection of the inherent variation of individuals.* How so, you ask? Consider for a moment what would happen if $\mu_1 = \mu_2 = \mu_3$ and there were *no* inherent variation: all individuals in the three populations would obtain the *same* score, and thus the three sample means could not vary from each other. On the other hand, the greater the inherent variation among individuals, the greater the opportunity for chance to produce sample means that vary from one another (even though $\mu_1 = \mu_2 = \mu_3$).

Now, notice the substantially greater variation among the sample means in Figure 16.1b, where μ_1, μ_2, and μ_3 have different values. When H_0 is false, as it is here, the variation among $\overline{X}_1$, $\overline{X}_2$, and $\overline{X}_3$ consequently is greater than what is expected from inherent variation alone. In short:

> Between-groups variation reflects inherent variation *plus* any differential treatment effect.

Like variation within groups, between-groups variation can be expressed as a *variance estimate*. This is called the **between-groups variance estimate**, which we will symbolize by $s_{between}^2$. When H_0 is true, $s_{between}^2$ simply provides a second and

---

[1]Perhaps you protest our use of "between" in this context. Although "among" is proper English when referring to more than two things, "*between*-groups" is the (grammatically incorrect) convention in statistics. We shall follow suit.

independent estimate of inherent variance, σ^2. That is, the variance of sample means, $s^2_{between}$, is no greater than what you would expect from repeatedly sampling the same population. When H_0 is false, however, $s^2_{between}$ reflects both inherent variance *and* the differential treatment effect. That is, when H_0 is false:

$$s^2_{between} \xrightarrow{\textit{estimates}} \sigma^2 + \text{treatment effect}$$

The F Ratio

The ratio $s^2_{between}/s^2_{within}$ is called the ***F ratio***,[2] and it provides the basis for testing the null hypothesis that $\mu_1 = \mu_2 = \mu_3$. Like z and t before it, F is a *test statistic*. When H_0 is true, s^2_{within} and $s^2_{between}$ will be of similar magnitude because both are estimates of inherent variance only (σ^2); consequently, the F ratio will be approximately 1.00. When H_0 is false, however, F will tend to be greater than 1.00 because the numerator, $s^2_{between}$, reflects the treatment effect in addition to inherent variance (while s^2_{within} continues to estimate only inherent variance). If the F ratio is so much larger than 1.00 that sampling variation cannot reasonably account for it, H_0 is rejected.

You see, then, that although our focus is on between-groups and within-groups *variances*, these variances ultimately permit decisions about null hypotheses regarding differences among *means*. Before we turn to the computational details for determining within- and between-groups variation, we briefly describe a research scenario that will serve as a context for that discussion.

16.4   Alison's Reply to Gregory

Gregory, you will recall from Chapter 14, compared two treatment conditions to examine the effect of scent on memory. Before reading on, you might review the details of his investigation (Section 14.1).

Imagine that Alison, a fellow student, reads Gregory's research report and attempts to "replicate" his finding that scent improves memory. If, using the same procedures that Gregory employed, she were to obtain a comparable outcome, Gregory's substantive conclusion would receive additional credence. But Alison decides to add a third treatment condition: for participants in Group 3, a pleasant, unfamiliar fragrance is present only during the reading phase of the investigation. Thus, her three groups are as follows:

Group 1:   Scent is present during passage reading *and* passage recall
              (equivalent to Gregory's Group 1)
Group 2:   No scent is present on either occasion
              (equivalent to Gregory's Group 2)
Group 3:   Scent is present during passage reading *only*
              (new group)

---

[2]Lest you accuse Fisher of immodestly naming a statistic after himself, you should know that it was George W. Snedecor who named the F ratio (in Fisher's honor).

Table 16.1   Alison's Data: Raw Scores,
Group Means, and Grand Mean

Group 1 ($n_1 = 3$)	Group 2 ($n_2 = 3$)	Group 3 ($n_3 = 3$)
32	23	22
29	20	17
26	14	15
$\overline{X}_1 = 29$	$\overline{X}_2 = 19$	$\overline{X}_3 = 18$

$$\overline{\overline{X}} = 22$$
$$(n_{\text{total}} = 9)$$

Alison randomly assigns each of nine volunteers to the three treatment conditions.[3] Except for the addition of Group 3 (and smaller n's), her investigation is identical to Gregory's in all respects. Thus, each participant reads the 1500-word passage and, one week later, is asked to recall as much information from the passage as possible. Alison then determines a score for each participant, representing the number of facts that have been correctly recalled. Her null hypothesis is H_0: $\mu_1 = \mu_2 = \mu_3$; for the alternative hypothesis, she simply states "not H_0."

We present Alison's data in Table 16.1, along with each sample group mean and the grand mean, $\overline{\overline{X}}$. The basic elements in any one-way ANOVA problem are the sums of squares that reflect within-groups and between-groups variation in the sample results. It is to these sums of squares that we now turn.

16.5   Partitioning the Sums of Squares

In one-way ANOVA, the total variation in the data is "partitioned," or separated, into its within-groups and between-groups components.

Any variance estimate is equal to a sum of squares divided by the corresponding degrees of freedom. You saw this with the variance estimate based on a single sample,

$$s^2 = \frac{\Sigma(X - \overline{X})^2}{n - 1} = \frac{SS}{n - 1},$$

and you saw this again with the pooled variance estimate used in the independent-samples t test,

$$s^2_{\text{pooled}} = \frac{\Sigma(X - \overline{X}_1)^2 + \Sigma(X - \overline{X}_2)^2}{n_1 + n_2 - 2} = \frac{SS_1 + SS_2}{n_1 + n_2 - 2}.$$

[3]As in previous chapters, the small n reflects our desire to minimize computations. To have adequate statistical power, an actual study of this kind doubtless would require larger n's.

Naturally enough, s^2_{within} and $s^2_{between}$ are derived in the same fashion as these earlier variance estimates. That is,

$$s^2_{within} = \frac{SS_{within}}{df_{within}} \quad \text{and} \quad s^2_{between} = \frac{SS_{between}}{df_{between}}$$

To calculate s^2_{within} and $s^2_{between}$, then, you must first determine the **within-groups sum of squares** (SS_{within}) and the **between-groups sum of squares** ($SS_{between}$). Once the corresponding degrees of freedom have been identified, you are one press of the calculator keypad away from s^2_{within} and $s^2_{between}$.

We'll now consider each sum of squares and its associated degrees of freedom.

Within-Groups Sum of Squares (SS_within)

You obtain the within-groups sum of squares, SS_{within}, by first expressing each score as a squared deviation from its group mean: $(X - \overline{X})^2$. The squared deviation score is $(X - \overline{X}_1)^2$ for each member of Group 1; $(X - \overline{X}_2)^2$ for each Group 2 member; and $(X - \overline{X}_3)^2$ for each Group 3 member. The first three columns of Table 16.2 show these calculations for Alison's data. For example, the first member of Group 1 has a score of $X = 32$ (shown at ❶). With $\overline{X}_1 = 29$, the squared deviation for this individual is $(32 - 29)^2$ (❷), which results in a value of $3^2 = 9$ (❸). The within-groups squared deviations are obtained for the remaining eight participants following the same procedure, as you can see by scanning down the first three

Table 16.2 Determining the Within-Groups, Between-Groups, and Total Sums of Squares

		Within			Between			Total	
	❶	❷	❸		❺	❻		❽	❾
	X	$(X - \overline{X})^2$			$(\overline{X} - \overline{\overline{X}})^2$			$(X - \overline{\overline{X}})^2$	
Group 1	32	$(32 - 29)^2$	$= 9$		$(29 - 22)^2$	$= 49$		$(32 - 22)^2$	$= 100$
($\overline{X}_1 = 29$)	29	$(29 - 29)^2$	$= 0$		$(29 - 22)^2$	$= 49$		$(29 - 22)^2$	$= 49$
	26	$(26 - 29)^2$	$= 9$		$(29 - 22)^2$	$= 49$		$(26 - 22)^2$	$= 16$
Group 2	23	$(23 - 19)^2$	$= 16$		$(19 - 22)^2$	$= 9$		$(23 - 22)^2$	$= 1$
($\overline{X}_2 = 19$)	20	$(20 - 19)^2$	$= 1$		$(19 - 22)^2$	$= 9$		$(20 - 22)^2$	$= 4$
	14	$(14 - 19)^2$	$= 25$		$(19 - 22)^2$	$= 9$		$(14 - 22)^2$	$= 64$
Group 3	22	$(22 - 18)^2$	$= 16$		$(18 - 22)^2$	$= 16$		$(22 - 22)^2$	$= 0$
($\overline{X}_3 = 18$)	17	$(17 - 18)^2$	$= 1$		$(18 - 22)^2$	$= 16$		$(17 - 22)^2$	$= 25$
	15	$(15 - 18)^2$	$= 9$		$(18 - 22)^2$	$= 16$		$(15 - 22)^2$	$= 49$
($\overline{\overline{X}} = 22$)		❹ $\Sigma(X - \overline{X})^2 = 86$			❼ $\Sigma(\overline{X} - \overline{\overline{X}})^2 = 222$			❿ $\Sigma(X - \overline{\overline{X}})^2 = 308$	
		$= SS_{within}$			$= SS_{between}$			$= SS_{total}$	

columns of Table 16.2. The within-groups sum of squares is the sum of these squared deviations, as shown at ❹. That is:

> **Within-groups sum of squares**
>
> $$SS_{within} = \overset{\substack{\text{all} \\ \text{scores}}}{\Sigma}(X - \bar{X})^2 \qquad\qquad (16.1)$$

Thus, for Alison's data, $SS_{within} = 9 + 0 + \ldots + 9 = 86$. Remember: SS_{within} reflects only *inherent variation*, free from the influence of any differential treatment effect.

There are $n - 1$ degrees of freedom associated with the deviations about a sample mean. Because there are *three* sample means in the present case, $df_{within} = (n_1 - 1) + (n_2 - 1) + (n_3 - 1) = 6$. In general, then:

> **Within-groups degrees of freedom**
>
> $$df_{within} = n_{total} - k \qquad\qquad (16.2)$$

In Formula (16.2), n_{total} is the total number of cases in the investigation, and k is the number of groups.

Between-Groups Sum of Squares (SS_between)

As a measure of variation among the sample means, $SS_{between}$ is based on the squared deviation of each participant's group mean from the grand mean: $(\bar{X} - \bar{\bar{X}})^2$. The squared deviation for each member of Group 1 is $(\bar{X}_1 - \bar{\bar{X}})^2 = (29 - 22)^2$ (❺), resulting in a value of $7^2 = 49$ (❻). The calculation for Group 2 participants is $(\bar{X}_2 - \bar{\bar{X}})^2 = (19 - 22)^2 = 9$, and for Group 3 participants $(\bar{X}_3 - \bar{\bar{X}})^2 = (18 - 22)^2 = 16$. As shown at ❼, the between-groups sum of squares, $SS_{between}$, is the sum of these squared deviations:

> **Between-groups sum of squares**
>
> $$SS_{betweeen} = \overset{\substack{\text{all} \\ \text{scores}}}{\Sigma}(\bar{X} - \bar{\bar{X}})^2 \qquad\qquad (16.3)$$

Given the data at hand, $SS_{between} = 49 + 49 + \ldots + 16 = 222$. Remember: $SS_{between}$ is influenced by inherent variation *plus* any differential treatment effect.

As for degrees of freedom, the three sample means contain only two independent pieces of information. No matter how often each sample mean is used in Formula (16.3), you essentially have the deviations of three sample means about $\bar{\bar{X}}$. Once you know $\bar{X} - \bar{\bar{X}}$ for two of the three means, the third $\bar{X} - \bar{\bar{X}}$ is completely determined. Thus, $df_{between} = 3 - 1 = 2$. In general:

Between-groups
degrees of freedom

$$df_{between} = k - 1 \tag{16.4}$$

Total Sum of Squares (SS$_{total}$)

The **total sum of squares**, SS_{total}, is a measure of total variation in the data *without regard to group membership*. SS_{total} is not used to obtain a variance estimate, but this sum is helpful to consider here because it "completes" the picture. Let us explain.

As a measure of total variation, SS_{total} is based on the deviations of each score from the grand mean: $(X - \bar{\bar{X}})^2$. These squared deviations are presented in columns **❽** and **❾** of Table 16.2 for each of the nine participants. SS_{total} is the sum:

Total sum of squares

$$SS_{total} = \overset{\text{all scores}}{\Sigma}(X - \bar{\bar{X}})^2 \tag{16.5}$$

For these data, then, $SS_{total} = 100 + 49 + \ldots + 49 = 308$ (**❿**). Because SS_{total} is based on the deviations of the nine scores about the mean of the nine, you have $9 - 1 = 8$ degrees of freedom. In general:

Total degrees of freedom

$$df_{total} = n - 1 \tag{16.6}$$

In our example, $SS_{within} = 86$, $SS_{between} = 222$, and $SS_{total} = 308$. Notice that SS_{total} is the sum of the first two values. This relationship holds in any analysis of variance:

The composition
of SS_{total}

$$SS_{total} = SS_{within} + SS_{between} \tag{16.7}$$

Thus, the total sum of squares—the total variation in the data—is partitioned into within-groups and between-groups components. It also holds that $df_{total} = df_{within} + df_{between}$. For instance, in our example $df_{within} = 6$, $df_{between} = 2$, and $df_{total} = 8$—the last value being the sum of the first two.

16.6   *Within-Groups and Between-Groups Variance Estimates*

If you divide SS_{within} and $SS_{between}$ by their respective degrees of freedom, you have the two variance estimates needed to test H_0: $\mu_1 = \mu_2 = \mu_3$, Alison's null hypothesis. These variance estimates, along with what they estimate, are:

Within-groups
variance estimate

$$s^2_{within} = \frac{SS_{within}}{n_{total} - k} \xrightarrow{\text{estimates}} \sigma^2 \text{ (inherent variance)} \qquad (16.8)$$

and

Between-groups
variance estimate

$$s^2_{between} = \frac{SS_{between}}{k - 1} \xrightarrow{\text{estimates}} \sigma^2 + \text{treatment effect} \qquad (16.9)$$

A "total" variance estimate is not calculated in analysis of variance because the test of H_0 requires the two variance estimates to be *independent* of one another. Since $SS_{total} = SS_{within} + SS_{between}$, a variance estimate based on SS_{total} obviously would not be independent of either s^2_{within} or $s^2_{between}$.

For Alison, $s^2_{within} = 86/6 = 14.33$ and $s^2_{between} = 222/2 = 111$. Remember: If H_0 is true, there is no differential treatment effect, and both s^2_{within} and $s^2_{between}$ will estimate the same thing—inherent variance (σ^2). In this case, s^2_{within} and $s^2_{between}$ should be equal, within the limits of sampling variation. On the other hand, if H_0 is false (differential treatment effect present), then $s^2_{between}$ will tend to be larger than s^2_{within}. As you saw earlier, the test statistic *F* is used for comparing s^2_{within} and $s^2_{between}$. Let's look at the *F* test more closely.

16.7   *The F Test*

The *F* statistic is formed by the ratio of two independent variance estimates:

F ratio for one-way ANOVA

$$F = \frac{s^2_{between}}{s^2_{within}} \qquad (16.10)$$

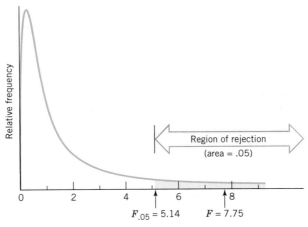

Figure 16.2   Distribution of F for 2 and 6 degrees of freedom.

If H_0 is true and certain other population conditions hold (which we take up in Section 16.12), then F ratios will follow the theoretical **F distribution** presented in Table C (Appendix C).

Like the t distribution, the F distribution is actually a family of curves depending on degrees of freedom. Here, however, you must consider *two* values for degrees of freedom: $df_{between}$ is associated with the numerator of F, and df_{within} with the denominator. The theoretical F distribution for $df_{between} = 2$ and $df_{within} = 6$ is presented in Figure 16.2. Notice that the distribution does not extend below 0. Indeed, it cannot do so, for variance estimates are never negative.

Alison's sample F is:

$$F = \frac{s^2_{between}}{s^2_{within}} = \frac{111.00}{14.33} = 7.75$$

If H_0: $\mu_1 = \mu_2 = \mu_3$ is true, both $s^2_{between}$ and s^2_{within} are estimates of inherent variance (σ^2), and sample F ratios will follow the tabled F distribution for 2 and 6 degrees of freedom (between and within, respectively). However, if there *is* a differential treatment effect (H_0 is false), $s^2_{between}$ will estimate inherent variance plus differential treatment effect and will tend to be too large. Now, since $s^2_{between}$ is always placed in the numerator of F, evidence that H_0 is false will be reflected by a sample F that is *larger* than expected when H_0 is true. Consequently, the region of rejection is placed entirely in the *upper* tail of the F distribution, as in Figure 16.2.

Using Table C

To obtain the critical value of F, turn to Table C and locate the entries at the intersection of 2 df for the numerator and 6 df for the denominator. (Be careful not to switch these values—the critical value of F will *not* be the same!) Let's assume that Alison has set $\alpha = .05$, in which case the critical value is $F_{.05} = 5.14$. (For $\alpha = .01$, the critical value is $F_{.01} = 10.92$ and appears in boldface type.) *If H_0 were true, a*

Table 16.3   One-Way ANOVA Summary Table

Source	SS	df	s^2 (mean square)	F	p
Between-groups	222	2	111.00	7.75	$p < .05$
Within-groups	86	6	14.33		
Total	308	8			

sample F ratio greater than 5.14 would be obtained only 5% of the time through random sampling variation. Because the obtained $F = 7.75$ falls beyond the critical value, Alison rejects the overall hypothesis that all differences among the population means are equal to zero (H_0: $\mu_1 = \mu_2 = \mu_3$) in favor of the alternative hypothesis that the population means differ in some way. That is, she concludes that there are real differences among the treatment conditions with regard to their effects on recall. The overall F test of H_0: $\mu_1 = \mu_2 = \mu_3 = \ldots = \mu_k$ often is referred to as the **omnibus F test**.

The ANOVA Summary Table

It is convenient to present an **ANOVA summary table** that indicates the sources of variation, sums of squares, degrees of freedom, variance estimates, calculated F ratio, and p value. The summary table for Alison's problem is presented in Table 16.3. As you might imagine, this summary table can be extremely helpful as a "worksheet" for recording the various values as you proceed through ANOVA calculations.

Why the parenthetical *mean square* in Table 16.3? In this book, we symbolize the within-groups variance estimate by s^2_{within} and the between-groups variance estimate by $s^2_{between}$ to emphasize their character as *variance* estimates. In research literature, you will find that a variance estimate is typically represented by the symbol MS, for "mean square" (e.g., "MS_{within}" and "$MS_{between}$").

16.8   Tukey's "HSD" Test

Suppose that Alison's sample F ratio turned out to be *smaller* than the critical value of 5.14. She would conclude that her data do not support a claim of differential treatment effects associated with the presence or absence of scent, and she would call it a day. There would be no need for further statistical work.

But this is not the case with Alison's results: the overall F ratio of 7.75 leads her to reject H_0: $\mu_1 = \mu_2 = \mu_3$ in favor of the very broad alternative hypothesis that the three population means differ "in some way." But *where* is the real difference (or differences)—between μ_1 and μ_2? between μ_2 and μ_3? between μ_1 and μ_3? all of the above? two of the three? To answer this general question, Alison proceeds with further statistical comparisons involving the group means. We illustrate only one of the many procedures developed for this purpose: **Tukey's HSD Test**.

The HSD ("honestly significant difference") test is used for making all possible pairwise comparisons among the means of groups. *Tukey's test is conducted only after a significant overall F has been found*—no significant *F*, no Tukey. Such comparisons therefore are known as **post hoc comparisons**.[4] Post hoc ("after the fact") comparisons are designed to protect against the inflated Type I error probability that would result from conducting a conventional *t* test on each pair of means (Section 16.1). Post hoc tests, such as Tukey's, provide this protection by demanding a *larger* difference for any one comparison before statistical significance can be claimed. Thus, across the entire set of $k(k-1)/2$ comparisons, the probability of at least one Type I error remains equal to α.

Tukey's test requires that you determine a critical HSD value for your data. The hypothesis of equal population means is then rejected for any pair of groups for which the absolute value of the difference between sample means is as large as (or larger than) the critical value. The test is two-tailed because of the exploratory nature of post hoc comparisons, and either the 5% or 1% significance level may be used.

The critical HSD is calculated from the following formula:

Critical HSD for Tukey's test

$$HSD = q\sqrt{\frac{s^2_{within}}{n_{group}}} \qquad (16.11)$$

Here, q is the value of the **Studentized range statistic** that is obtained from Table D (given the level of significance, within-groups *df*, and number of groups), s^2_{within} is the familiar within-groups variance estimate, and n_{group} is the number of cases *within each group* (e.g., $n_{group} = 3$ in Alison's study).

Let's apply Tukey's HSD test to Alison's data. She obtained a significant overall *F* and now wishes to test each of the differences between her group means. She accomplishes this in four easy steps:

Step 1   *Find q.*

Using Table D, Alison locates the point of intersection between the column corresponding to $k = 3$ and the row corresponding to $df_{within} = 6$. She determines that $q = 4.34$ ($\alpha = .05$). (Had she set α at .01, q would be 6.33.)

Step 2   *Calculate the critical HSD.*

With $s^2_{within} = 14.33$ and $n = 3$, the critical HSD is:

$$HSD = 4.34\sqrt{\frac{14.33}{3}} = 9.48$$

---

[4]Sometimes the investigator has a rationale, based on the logic of the study, for examining only a *subset* of all possible comparisons. In this case, one is making "planned comparisons" (see Kirk, 1982).

Thus, the absolute value of the difference between any two sample means must be at least 9.48 for it to be deemed statistically significant.

Step 3   *Determine the differences for all possible pairs of sample means.*
All pairwise differences are displayed in the table below. Each entry is the difference between the mean listed at the side and that listed at the top (e.g., $10 = \overline{X}_1 - \overline{X}_2$).

	$\overline{X}_1 = 29$	$\overline{X}_2 = 19$	$\overline{X}_3 = 18$
$\overline{X}_1 = 29$	–	10	11
$\overline{X}_2 = 19$		–	1
$\overline{X}_3 = 18$			–

Step 4   *Compare each obtained difference with the critical HSD value and draw conclusions.*
Two of three pairwise differences, $\overline{X}_1 - \overline{X}_2$ and $\overline{X}_1 - \overline{X}_3$, exceed a magnitude of 9.48 and thus are significant at the .05 level. That is to say, Alison rejects the two null hypotheses, $\mu_1 - \mu_2 = 0$ and $\mu_1 - \mu_3 = 0$. She therefore concludes that the presence of scent during passage reading and passage recall (Group 1) results in greater recall than when no scent is present on either occasion (Group 2) or when scent is present during passage reading only (Group 3). However, she cannot reject H_0: $\mu_2 - \mu_3 = 0$, and she concludes that there is no difference between these two treatment conditions.

Suppose that Alison's design instead had *four* groups with three participants per group ($n_{total} = 12$). Thus, $k = 4$, $df_{within} = 12 - 4 = 8$, and $q = 4.53$ ($\alpha = .05$). Let's assume that the additional group does not change the within-groups variance estimate (14.33). The critical HSD value would now be:

$$\text{HSD} = 4.53\sqrt{\frac{14.33}{3}} = 9.90$$

Thus, for each of her $k(k - 1)/2 = 4(3)/2 = 6$ comparisons, Alison now would need a difference of 9.90 to claim statistical significance. The larger critical value—9.90 versus 9.48—is the statistical cost she must bear for making three additional comparisons. That is, it is slightly more difficult to attain statistical significance for any one comparison when $k = 4$ than when $k = 3$. This illustrates how Tukey's HSD test protects against an inflated Type I error probability across all pairwise comparisons.

Unequal n's

If the n's are not the same across the k groups, HSD can be approximated by substituting the *harmonic mean*, $\tilde{n}$, for n in Formula (16.11):

Averaging n:
The harmonic mean

$$\tilde{n} = \frac{k}{\dfrac{1}{n_1} + \dfrac{1}{n_2} + \dots + \dfrac{1}{n_k}} \qquad (16.12)$$

Suppose Alison's third group had *four* members instead of three (and s^2_{within} remained the same). The harmonic mean and HSD ($\alpha = .05$), respectively, are

$$\tilde{n} = \frac{3}{\dfrac{1}{3} + \dfrac{1}{3} + \dfrac{1}{4}} = \frac{3}{.917} = 3.27$$

$$\text{HSD} = 4.34\sqrt{\frac{14.33}{3.27}} = 9.09$$

16.9   *Interval Estimation of* $\mu_i - \mu_j$

When there are more than two groups ($k > 2$), the general logic for constructing a confidence interval for the difference between any two means is the same as when there are only two groups in an investigation. However, we need to introduce new notation for stating the general rule. When $k > 2$, it is common practice to use the expression, $\bar{X}_i - \bar{X}_j$, for the difference between any two sample means, and $\mu_i - \mu_j$ for the difference between any two population means. Here, the subscript i simply denotes the first group in the comparison, and j the second. For example, if you are comparing Group 1 and Group 3, then $i = 1$ and $j = 3$.

When all pairwise comparisons are made, the form of the interval estimate for the difference between any two of the k population means is:

Rule for a confidence
interval for $\mu_i - \mu_j$

$$\bar{X}_i - \bar{X}_j \pm \text{HSD} \qquad (16.13)$$

If HSD is based on $\alpha = .05$, then Formula (16.13) gives a 95% confidence interval. For Alison's data, the 95% confidence interval is $\bar{X}_i - \bar{X}_j \pm 9.48$. That is:

$\bar{X}_1 - \bar{X}_2$:	$29 - 19 \pm 9.48$	$=$	10 ± 9.48	$=$	$.52$ to 19.48
$\bar{X}_1 - \bar{X}_3$:	$29 - 18 \pm 9.48$	$=$	11 ± 9.48	$=$	1.52 to 20.48
$\bar{X}_2 - \bar{X}_3$:	$19 - 18 \pm 9.48$	$=$	1 ± 9.48	$=$	-8.48 to 10.48

Alison is 95% confident that $\mu_1 - \mu_2$ falls somewhere between .52 and 19.48 and that $\mu_1 - \mu_3$ resides somewhere between 1.52 and 20.48. (The considerable width of these intervals reflects her exceedingly small sample sizes.) You may not be surprised to find that the confidence interval for $\mu_2 - \mu_3$ includes zero. This is consistent with the outcome of the Tukey test, which resulted in a statistically nonsignificant difference between $\overline{X}_2$ and $\overline{X}_3$.

To construct a 99% confidence interval, Alison would find in Table D the value of q corresponding to $\alpha = .01$ (6.33), recompute HSD, and enter the new HSD in Formula (16.13):

- $q = 6.33$ ($\alpha = .01$, $k = 3$, $df_{within} = 6$)
- $\text{HSD} = 6.33\sqrt{\dfrac{14.33}{3}} = 13.83$
- 99% confidence interval: $\overline{X}_i - \overline{X}_j \pm 13.83$

Each of the 99% confidence intervals includes zero. (Within the context of hypothesis testing, this is to say that none of the pairwise comparisons would be statistically significant at the .01 level.)

16.10   One-Way ANOVA: Summarizing the Steps

We have thrown quite a bit at you in this chapter. Let's summarize the process so far, using Alison's experiment as context. The steps below should help you better see the proverbial forest for the trees and, at the same time, reaffirm that the general logic of analysis of variance is the same as that of significance tests you have already encountered. That is, you assume H_0 to be true and then determine whether the obtained sample result is rare enough to raise doubts about H_0. To do this, you convert the sample result into a test statistic (F, in this case), which you then locate in the theoretical sampling distribution (the F distribution). If the test statistic falls in the region of rejection, H_0 is rejected; if not, H_0 is retained. The only new twist is that if H_0 is rejected, follow-up testing is required to identify the specific source(s) of significance.

Step 1   *Formulate the statistical hypotheses and select a level of significance.*
Alison's statistical hypotheses are:

$$H_0: \mu_1 = \mu_2 = \mu_3$$
$$H_1: \text{not } H_0$$

She selects $\alpha = .05$ as her level of significance.

Step 2   *Determine the desired sample size and select the sample.*
We limited Alison's sample sizes to simplify computational illustrations.

Step 3   *Calculate the necessary sample statistics.*
- sample means and grand mean:

$$\overline{X}_1 = 29, \quad \overline{X}_2 = 19, \quad \overline{X}_3 = 18, \quad \overline{\overline{X}} = 22$$

- within-groups sum of squares, degrees of freedom, and variance estimate:

$$SS_{within} = 86$$

$$df_{within} = n_{total} - k = 9 - 3 = 6$$

$$s^2_{within} = 86/6 = 14.33$$

- between-groups sum of squares, degrees of freedom, and variance estimate:

$$SS_{between} = 222$$

$$df_{between} = k - 1 = 3 - 1 = 2$$

$$s^2_{between} = 222/2 = 111$$

- total sum of squares and degrees of freedom:

$$SS_{total} = 308$$

$$df_{total} = n_{total} - 1 = 9 - 1 = 8$$

(check: $308 = 86 + 222$ and $8 = 6 + 2$)

- *F* ratio:

$$F = \frac{s^2_{between}}{s^2_{within}} = \frac{111}{14.33} = 7.75$$

Step 4   *Identify the region of rejection.*
With $df_{between} = 2$ and $df_{within} = 6$, the critical value of F is 5.14 (Table C). This is the value of F beyond which the most extreme 5% of sample outcomes will fall when H_0 is true.

Step 5   *Make the statistical decision and form conclusions.*
Because the sample F ratio falls in the rejection region (i.e., $7.75 > 5.14$), Alison rejects H_0: $\mu_1 = \mu_2 = \mu_3$. The overall F ratio is statistically significant ($\alpha = .05$), and she concludes that the population means differ in some way. Scent would appear to affect recall (again, in some way). She therefore proceeds to conduct post hoc comparisons to determine the specific source(s) of the statistical significance.

Step 6   *Conduct Tukey's HSD test.*
- Calculate HSD:

$$HSD = q\sqrt{\frac{s^2_{within}}{n_{group}}} = 4.34\sqrt{\frac{14.33}{3}} = 9.48$$

- Compare HSD with each difference between sample means:

$$\bar{X}_1 - \bar{X}_2 = 29 - 19 = 10 \text{ (greater than HSD)}$$
$$\bar{X}_1 - \bar{X}_3 = 29 - 18 = 11 \text{ (greater than HSD)}$$
$$\bar{X}_2 - \bar{X}_3 = 19 - 18 = 1 \text{ (less than HSD)}$$

- Make the statistical decisions and form conclusions:

    Group 1 is significantly different from Groups 2 and 3; the difference between Groups 2 and 3 is not significant. Alison concludes that the presence of scent during passage reading and passage recall leads to greater recall than when no scent is present on either occasion or when scent is present only during passage reading.

16.11   Estimating the Strength of the Treatment Effect: Effect Size ($\hat{\omega}^2$)

The magnitude of F, just like t, depends in part on sample size. You can see this by examining the full expression of the F ratio:

$$F = \frac{s^2_{between}}{s^2_{within}} = \frac{SS_{between}/df_{between}}{SS_{within}/df_{within}}$$

Remember, $df_{within} = n_{total} - k$. In most investigations (unlike the simplified examples in a statistics book), n_{total} typically is quite a bit larger than k. That is, df_{within} typically reflects total sample size more than anything else. Because of the location of df_{within} in the formula for F, a larger sample will result in a *smaller* value for s^2_{within} and therefore a *larger* F ratio (other things being equal). While a statistically significant F ratio certainly is not bad news, it does not necessarily speak to the strength or importance of the treatment effect.

In the case of the independent-samples t test, you saw in Section 14.8 that $\hat{\omega}^2$, a measure of effect size, can be used to estimate the proportion of variation in scores that is explained by variation in group membership. In Gregory's experiment, for example, 21% of the variation in recall scores was explained by whether a participant had been assigned to Group 1 or to Group 2. Importantly, $\hat{\omega}^2$ can also be applied to designs involving more than two groups. Within the context of one-way ANOVA, $\hat{\omega}^2$ is an estimate of the amount of variation in scores that is accounted for by the k levels of the factor, or independent variable, in the population. It is calculated from Formula (16.14) and relies on terms familiar to you by now:

Explained variance:
One-way ANOVA

$$\hat{\omega}^2 = \frac{SS_{between} - (k - 1)s^2_{within}}{SS_{total} + s^2_{within}} \qquad (16.14)[5]$$

---

[5]$\hat{\omega}^2$ is negative when F is less than one, in which case $\hat{\omega}^2$ is set to zero.

To apply $\hat{\omega}^2$ to Alison's data, you therefore need the following values: $SS_{between} = 222$, $k = 3$, $s^2_{within} = 14.33$, and $SS_{total} = 308$. Now insert these figures into Formula (16.14):

$$\hat{\omega}^2 = \frac{SS_{between} - (k-1)s^2_{within}}{SS_{total} + s^2_{within}} = \frac{222 - (3-1)14.33}{308 + 14.33} = \frac{222 - 28.66}{322.33} = .60$$

Alison estimates that fully 60% of the variance in recall scores is explained by the three levels of her independent variable (whether participants had been assigned to Group 1, Group 2, or Group 3).

Arguably more is learned about the strength and potential importance of this differential treatment effect by knowing that $\hat{\omega}^2 = .60$ than by knowing that the F ratio of 7.75 is "statistically significant at the .05 level." For this reason, it is good practice to report $\hat{\omega}^2$ along with the statistical significance of F.

16.12   *ANOVA Assumptions (and Other Considerations)*

The assumptions underlying the F test are the same as those for the independent-samples t test:

1. *The k samples are independent.* Just as with the t test for dependent samples, a different procedure must be employed when the k samples are not independent (e.g., when the groups comprise either matched participants or the same participants).[6]

2. *Each of the k populations of observations is normally distributed.* As in the case of the t test, this becomes important only when samples are small. The larger the samples, the greater the departure from normality that can be tolerated without unduly distorting the outcome of the test. "Nonparametric" or "distribution-free" alternatives to ANOVA should be considered when population normality cannot be assumed (e.g., see Minium et al., 1999, ch. 21).

3. *The k populations of observations are equally variable.* That is, it must be assumed that $\sigma^2_1 = \sigma^2_2 = \sigma^2_3 = \ldots = \sigma^2_k$. This, you may recall, is the assumption of homogeneity of variance. Here, too, violations generally can be tolerated when samples are large. However, when samples are small—particularly if attended by unequal n's—markedly different sample variances should not be casually dismissed. A general rule of thumb is that unequal variances are tolerable unless the ratio of the largest group n to the smallest group n exceeds 1.5, in which case alternative procedures should be considered.[7]

Also remember that samples that are too small tend to give nonsignificant results: a Type II error may result, and an opportunity to uncover important effects in

[6]The procedure for analyzing differences among three or more means from dependent samples is called *repeated measures analysis of variance* (see King & Minium, 2003, pp. 413–418).

[7]The Welch procedure is an example of such an alternative; another is the Brown-Forsythe procedure. Both are fairly straightforward extensions of the formulas we present here. (For details, see Glass & Hopkins, 1996, pp. 405–406.)

the population may be missed. On the other hand, samples can be too large: they can be wasteful, and they may indicate statistical significance in cases of population effects so small that they are in fact unimportant. There are tables you can consult for selecting an appropriate sample size in an ANOVA problem. (See Chapter 19 for discussion of the principles involved and a reference to those tables.)

Finally, we remind you to be particularly cautious in interpreting results where research participants have not been randomly assigned to treatment conditions. As we indicated in Section 14.9 in the case of the independent-samples t test, the "why" of your results is considerably less straightforward when random assignment has not been (or cannot be) employed. We encourage you to carefully revisit Section 14.9, for that discussion is just as relevant here.

16.13   *Summary*

Despite its name, analysis of variance (in the forms presented here) is a test about *means*. You can think of one-way ANOVA as an extension of the independent-samples t test to more than two groups, or conversely, you can consider the t test as a special case of one-way ANOVA.

Two types of variation are compared in one-way ANOVA: the within-groups variation of individual scores and the between-groups variation of sample means. When H_0 is true, both types of variation reflect inherent variation—the variation in performance of individuals subjected to identical conditions. When H_0 is false, the within-groups variation is unaffected, but the between-groups variation now reflects inherent variation *plus* differential treatment effect.

True to its name, analysis of variance is concerned with the *variance* as the basic measure of variation. Consequently, inherent variation becomes inherent variance, which, if you make the assumption of homogeneity of variance, can be represented by the single symbol, σ^2. To estimate σ^2, you use the familiar form for a variance estimate: SS/df, the sum of squares divided by degrees of freedom. You can compute three sums of squares from the sample results: SS_{within} (variation of individuals *within* sample groups about the sample mean), $SS_{between}$ (variation *among* the sample means), and SS_{total} (*total* variation in the sample data). In one-way ANOVA, the total sum of squares (SS_{total}) and the associated degrees of freedom (df_{total}) can be partitioned into within- and between-groups components. That is, $SS_{total} = SS_{within} + SS_{between}$, and $df_{total} = df_{within} + df_{between}$.

The two variance estimates, s^2_{within} and $s^2_{between}$, are used in the test of H_0. When H_0 is true, both s^2_{within} and $s^2_{between}$ are independent estimates of σ^2 and should be equal within the limits of random sampling variation. When H_0 is false, $s^2_{between}$ will tend to be larger than s^2_{within} because of the added influence of differential treatment effect. The F ratio, $s^2_{between}/s^2_{within}$, is used to compare $s^2_{between}$ and s^2_{within}. If H_0 is true, calculated F ratios will follow the theoretical F distribution with $k - 1$ and $n_{total} - k$ degrees of freedom. H_0 is rejected if the sample F ratio is equal to or larger than the critical value of F. The effect size omega squared ($\hat{\omega}^2$), which estimates the amount of variation in scores that is explained by variation in treatment levels, is a useful statistic for characterizing the magnitude or importance of the treatment effect.

The F test for one-way analysis of variance shares the basic assumptions of the independent-samples t test: independent groups, normality, and homogeneity of variance. The last two assumptions become important only when samples are small.

The overall F test examines the question of whether the population values of the treatment group means are all equal against the broad alternative that they are unequal in some (any) way. Tukey's HSD test is a useful post hoc test that, following a significant overall F ratio, examines all pairwise comparisons between group means. It protects against the inflated Type I error probability that results from conducting multiple t tests. An interval estimate can be obtained for the difference between any two of the k population means.

Reading the Research: One-Way ANOVA

Wiest et al. (2001, p. 120) compared the mean grade-point averages of students placed into regular education, special education, and alternative education programs.

> *An analysis of variance indicated that there was a significant main effect of educational placement, F(2, 245) = 70.31, p < .001. Post hoc comparisons, employing Tukey's HSD test, were then conducted to examine specific group differences. . . . Regular education students had a significantly higher mean GPA (2.86) than did special education students (2.17) and alternative education students (1.88). In addition, the difference in GPA between special education and alternative education was significant.*

The significant overall *F* value prompted the researchers to conduct post hoc comparisons, which revealed significant differences in GPA among all three pairs. Following common practice, these authors included the degrees of freedom in parentheses when reporting the *F* ratio: 2 between-group *df* and 245 within-group *df*. (Question: How large is the sample on which this analysis was based?)

Source: Wiest, D. J., Wong, E. H., Cervantes, J. M., Craik, L., & Kreil, D. A. (2001). Intrinsic motivation among regular, special, and alternative education high school students. *Adolescence, 36*(141), 111–126.

Case Study: "Been There, Done That"

Using a sample of teachers from a rural high school in New England, we explored the relationship between level of experience and ratings of two professional development activities. Fifty-four teachers were categorized into one of three experience levels. Those teaching fewer than 4 years were labeled "novice," those teaching between 4 and 10 years were deemed "experienced," and those teaching more than 10 years were considered "vintage." Teachers used a five-point scale from 0 (no effect) to 4 (strong positive effect) to indicate how *district-sponsored workshops* and *classroom observations of peers* contributed to their professional growth (see Table 16.4).

Figures 16.3*a* and 16.3*b* illustrate the mean comparisons in the form of "means plots." In contrast to Figure 16.3*b*, Figure 16.3*a* shows differences in teacher ratings across experience levels. Novice teachers rated district workshops higher than experienced teachers, who, in turn, rated them higher than vintage educators. But are these differences statistically significant?

Our first one-way ANOVA[8] tested the overall null hypothesis that teacher perceptions of district workshops are unrelated to level of experience (i.e., H_0: $\mu_{novice} = \mu_{experienced} = \mu_{vintage}$). The alternative hypothesis was that the population means were unequal "in some way." For instance, one might speculate that teachers early in

---

[8]As explained in Section 16.1, "one-way" refers to the testing of one factor. In this case, the factor is "level of experience" (or EXPER).

Table 16.4 Statistics for Teacher Ratings of District
Workshops and Peer Observations

	$\overline{X}$	s	$s_{\overline{X}}$
WORKSHOP			
Novice ($n = 16$)	2.81	.83	.21
Experienced ($n = 18$)	2.33	1.03	.24
Vintage ($n = 20$)	1.60	.99	.22
PEEROBSV			
Novice ($n = 16$)	2.44	1.21	.30
Experienced ($n = 18$)	2.44	1.04	.25
Vintage ($n = 20$)	2.40	1.14	.26

their career would get more out of in-service programs than experienced teachers who believe that they have "been there, done that." We used an α of .05.

The ANOVA results indicated that there was a significant difference among group means ($p < .01$; see Table 16.5). Consequently, we proceeded to conduct post hoc comparisons using the Tukey HSD test: novice vs. experienced, novice vs. vintage, and experienced vs. vintage. Only the difference between novice and vintage teachers, $\overline{X}_{\text{novice}} - \overline{X}_{\text{vintage}} = 1.21$, was statistically significant ($p < .01$). Thus, novice

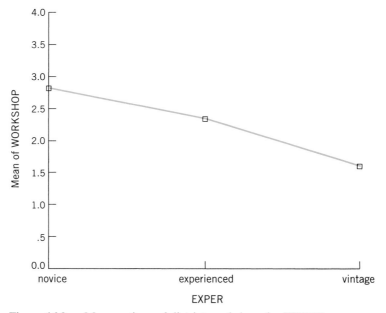

Figure 16.3a Mean ratings of district workshops by EXPER.

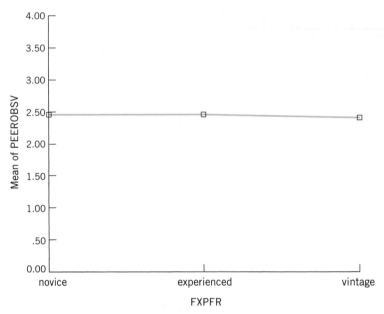

Figure 16.3b   Mean ratings of peer observations by EXPER.

teachers tended to rate the value of district workshops significantly higher (more positive) than did vintage teachers. This difference corresponded to an impressive effect size of $d = +1.31$. The difference between experienced and vintage teachers, $\overline{X}_{experienced} - \overline{X}_{vintage} = .73$, fell just short of statistical significance ($p = .059$).

We conducted a second one-way ANOVA to test for differences in teacher ratings of peer classroom observations. (Given the flat line in Figure 16.3b, however, we were not expecting statistical significance.) As above, EXPER was the independent variable or factor. The results indeed were not statistically significant: $F(2, 51) = .01$, $p > .05$.[9] Because the omnibus F ratio was not statistically significant, no subsequent tests were conducted.

Table 16.5   Results from the One-Way ANOVA on WORKSHOP

Source	SS	df	MS	F	p
Between-groups	13.52	2	6.76	7.30	.002
Within-groups	47.24	51	.93		
Total	60.76	53			

[9]The numbers in parentheses following F represent the between-groups df and within-groups df, respectively.

As with any sample, this sample of teachers does not necessarily represent the perceptions of high school teachers elsewhere. That is, it may not be the case universally that novice teachers (as defined here) derive more from district workshops than do vintage teachers (again, as defined here). Nor is it necessarily true that there are no differences, due to experience level, regarding the perceived value of peer classroom observations. The political, financial, and cultural characteristics of this particular school no doubt influence the perceptions of its teachers. Although we are confident that our sample results generalize to the population of teachers at this high school (and even to high schools very similar to this one), subsequent research is required to determine whether our findings hold up in diverse settings.

Suggested Computer Exercises

Access the **hswriting** data file, which is from a study that examined the influence of teacher feedback on student writing performance. Students taking a sophomore creative writing course randomly received one of three types of feedback (TREATMT) on their weekly writing assignments: oral feedback provided during regularly scheduled student-teacher conferences, written feedback provided directly on student papers, and feedback in the form of a letter grade only (e.g., B+). A standardized writing exam (WRITING) was administered to students toward the end of the course.

1. Conduct a one-way ANOVA to test the hypothesis that the three types of feedback are equal in their effects on test performance. In doing so, formulate the statistical hypotheses and use an α of .05. When executing the ANOVA, request descriptive statistics, a means plot, and the Tukey HSD test.

Exercises

Identify, Define, or Explain

Terms and Concepts

analysis of variance (ANOVA)
one-way ANOVA
factor, independent variable
H_0 and H_1 for one-way ANOVA
within-groups variation
inherent variation
within-groups variance estimate
between-groups variation
between-groups variance estimate
F ratio
within-groups sum of squares
between-groups sum of squares

total sum of squares
partitioning the sums of squares
F distribution (Table C)
omnibus F test
ANOVA summary table
mean square
Tukey's HSD test
post hoc comparisons
Studentized range statistic (Table D)
harmonic mean
explained variance
ANOVA assumptions

Symbols

k

$\mu_1, \mu_2, \ldots, \mu_k$

$\overline{X}_1, \overline{X}_2, \ldots, \overline{X}_k$

$n_1, n_2, \ldots, n_k,$

$\overline{\overline{X}}$

$SS_1, SS_2, \ldots, SS_k$

MS

q

$\overline{X}_i - \overline{X}_j$

$\mu_i - \mu_j$

$\hat{\omega}^2$

Questions and Problems

Note: Answers to starred (*) items are presented in Appendix B.

1. Using the formula $k(k-1)/2$, determine the number of t tests required to make all possible pairwise comparisons for each of the following conditions:

   (a) $k = 2$

   (b) $k = 4$

   (c) $k = 6$

   (d) $k = 7$

2. List all the possible comparisons in Problem 1c (e.g., "1 vs. 2," "1 vs. 3," ...).

*3. You have designed an investigation involving the comparison of four groups.

   (a) Express H_0 in symbolic form.

   (b) Why can't H_1 be expressed in symbolic form?

   (c) List several possible ways in which H_0 can be false.

   (d) What's wrong with expressing the alternative hypothesis as H_1: $\mu_1 \neq \mu_2 \neq \mu_3 \neq \mu_4$?

*4. A researcher randomly assigns six students with behavioral problems to three treatment conditions (this, of course, would be far too few participants for practical study). At the end of three months, each student is rated on the "normality" of his or her behavior, as determined by classroom observations. The results are as follows:

	Behavior Ratings for Each of Six Students
Treatment 1:	3, 7
Treatment 2:	4, 10
Treatment 3:	6, 12

   (a) State H_0 in symbolic form; express H_1 in words.

   (b) Calculate SS_{within}, $SS_{between}$, and SS_{total}.

   (c) What are the values for df_{within}, $df_{between}$, and df_{total}?

(d) Compute s^2_{within}, $s^2_{between}$, and F.

(e) What is the statistical decision ($\alpha = .05$) and final conclusion?

5. Consider s^2_{within} and $s^2_{between}$ in Problem 4d.

(a) Which is an estimate of inherent variation, and which is an estimate of differential treatment effects?

(b) Explain, within the context of this problem, what is meant by "inherent variation" and "differential treatment effects."

*6. Determine $F_{.05}$ and $F_{.01}$ from Table C for each situation below:

	Total Sample Size	Number of Groups
(a)	82	3
(b)	25	5
(c)	120	4
(d)	44	3

7. Study the following ANOVA summary, and then provide the missing information for the cells designated a–f:

Source	SS	df	MS	F	p
Between-groups	(a)	3	(b)	(c)	(d)
Within-groups	64	(e)	(f)		
Total	349	19			

*8. Study the following ANOVA summary, and then provide the missing information for the cells designated a–f:

Source	SS	df	MS	F	p
Between-groups	1104	(a)	(b)	3.00	(c)
Within-groups	(d)	(e)	184		
Total	4416	(f)			

9. (a) How many groups are there in Problem 7? (How do you know?)

(b) What is the total sample size in Problem 7? (How do you know?)

(c) How many groups are there in Problem 8? (How do you know?)

(d) What is the total sample size in Problem 8? (How do you know?)

10. Which case, Problem 7 or Problem 8, calls for the application of Tukey's HSD test? (Explain.)

*11. Consider the assumptions underlying the F test for one-way analysis of variance (Section 16.12). Given the following data, do you believe the F test is defensible? (Explain.)

	$\overline{X}$	s	n
Group 1:	75	21	36
Group 2:	58	16	37
Group 3:	60	10	18

*12. Professor Loomis selects a sample of second-grade students from each of three schools offering different instructional programs in reading. He wishes to determine whether there are corresponding differences between these schools in the "phonological aware-ness" of their students. Professor Loomis has each child complete a phonological awareness inventory and obtains these results:

	Phonological Awareness Scores
Program 1:	17, 13, 14, 10
Program 2:	7, 5, 12, 8
Program 3:	16, 9, 15, 18

(a) Give H_0.

(b) Compute SS_{within}, $SS_{between}$, and SS_{total}.

(c) What are the values for df_{within}, $df_{between}$, and df_{total}?

(d) Conduct the F test ($\alpha = .05$) and present your results in an ANOVA summary table.

(e) What is your statistical decision regarding H_0?

(f) Compute and interpret $\hat{\omega}^2$ from these data.

(g) What is your substantive conclusion from this analysis? (Is your analysis complete?)

13. (a) Apply Tukey's HSD test ($\alpha = .05$) to the results of Problem 12.

(b) State your conclusions.

14. (a) Construct a 95% confidence interval for each of the mean differences in Problem 12.

(b) How do these confidence intervals compare with the answers to Problem 13?

(c) Interpret the confidence interval for $\mu_2 - \mu_3$.

15. Suppose you obtained a significant F ratio and now wish to apply the Tukey test. However, you have unequal n's : $n_1 = 15$, $n_2 = 18$, and $n_3 = 14$. Compute the harmonic mean.

16. A study is performed using observations from five samples of 20 cases each. The following are partial results from a one-way analysis of variance: $SS_{between} = 717$ and $SS_{total} = 6861$.

(a) Compute s^2_{within} and $s^2_{between}$.

(b) Complete the F test ($\alpha = .01$), state your statistical decision regarding H_0, and present the results in a summary table.

*17. A one-way ANOVA is carried out using the performance scores from five different treatment groups of nine cases each. A significant F is obtained. For this analysis $s^2_{within} = 20.5$, and the treatment group means are as follows:

$$\overline{X}_1 = 20.3, \qquad \overline{X}_2 = 12.2, \qquad \overline{X}_3 = 15.3, \qquad \overline{X}_4 = 13.6, \quad \text{and} \quad \overline{X}_5 = 19.1$$

(a) Use the formula $k(k-1)/2$ to determine the number of all possible pairs of means.

(b) Display the differences between the means for all possible pairs of samples as illustrated in Section 16.8 (step 3).

(c) Apply the Tukey test ($\alpha = .05$) to all possible pairwise comparisons between means and draw final conclusions.

(d) Repeat Problem 17c using $\alpha = .01$.

*18. You wish to compare the effectiveness of four methods for teaching metacognitive strategies to elementary school children. A group of 40 fifth graders is randomly divided into four subgroups, each of which is taught according to one of the different methods. You then individually engage each child in a "think aloud" problem-solving task, during which you record the number of metacognitive strategies the child invokes. The results are as follows:

Teaching Method

1	2	3	4
$n_1 = 10$	$n_2 = 10$	$n_3 = 10$	$n_4 = 10$
$\Sigma X_1 = 242$	$\Sigma X_2 = 295$	$\Sigma X_3 = 331$	$\Sigma X_4 = 264$
$\Sigma(X - \overline{X}_1)^2 = 527.6$	$\Sigma(X - \overline{X}_2)^2 = 361.5$	$\Sigma(X - \overline{X}_3)^2 = 438.9$	$\Sigma(X - \overline{X}_4)^2 = 300.4$

(a) Give H_0.

(b) Calculate $\overline{X}_1, \overline{X}_2, \overline{X}_3, \overline{X}_4$, and $\overline{\overline{X}}$.

(c) Compute SS_{within}, $SS_{between}$, and SS_{total}.

(d) Complete the F test ($\alpha = .05$), state your statistical decision regarding H_0, and present your results in a summary table.

(e) If appropriate, apply the Tukey test ($\alpha = .05$).

(f) Compute and interpret $\hat{\omega}^2$ from these data.

(g) Draw your final conclusions from these analyses.

*19. (a) Construct a 95% confidence interval for each mean difference in Problem 18.

20. Compare the investigation described in Problem 12 with that in Problem 18.

(a) For which investigation is it more difficult to argue a cause-and-effect relationship? (Explain.)

(b) What are possible explanations—other than instructional program—for the significant F ratio in Problem 12?

CHAPTER 17

Inferences about the Pearson Correlation Coefficient

17.1 From μ to ρ

Our focus so far has been on inferences involving population *means*. You are about to see that the general logic of statistical inference does not change when one's objective is to make inferences about a population *correlation coefficient*. That is, the Pearson *r*, like a mean, will vary from sample to sample because of random sampling variation. Given the particular sample correlation that you have calculated, you wish to know what the coefficient would be if the effects of sampling variation were removed—that is, what the "true" or *population* correlation is. The population correlation, you may recall from Section 10.3, is symbolized by the Greek letter ρ (rho). Thus, *r* is used for making inferences about ρ.

In this chapter, we focus on inferences about single coefficients. As before, we will consider making statistical inferences from the two perspectives of hypothesis testing and interval estimation.

17.2 The Sampling Distribution of r When ρ = 0

The most common null hypothesis for testing a single correlation coefficient is H_0: ρ = 0. That is, there is no linear association between X and Y. Think of two variables that you are certain are absolutely unrelated to each other (ρ = 0). How about the correlation between, say, visual acuity (X) and neck size (Y) among adults in your community? Now suppose you repeatedly select random samples of size $n = 10$ from this population, each time calculating the correlation coefficient between X and Y and replacing the sample in the population. Even though ρ = 0, you nonetheless would expect sampling variation in the values of r. Sometimes r will be positive, sometimes negative. Although the values of r tend to be small (because ρ = 0), some are moderate and, indeed, every now and then a relatively large r surfaces. Let's say your first three samples yield $r = +.08$, $r = -.15$, and $r = -.02$, respectively. If you calculated an *unlimited* number of sample coefficients in this fashion and plotted them in a relative frequency distribution, you would have a **sampling distribution of *r*** (see Figure 17.1).

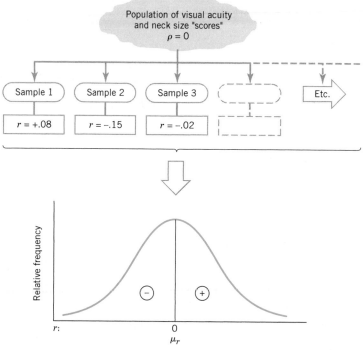

Figure 17.1   The development of a sampling distribution of sample values of r ($n = 10$).

When $\rho = 0$, the sampling distribution of r is similar to the other sampling distributions you have encountered so far. First, because positive values of r are balanced by negative values, the mean of this sampling distribution (μ_r) is zero.

The mean of a sampling
distribution of r ($\rho = 0$)

$$\mu_r = 0 \tag{17.1}$$

We have noted this in Figure 17.1. Second, the standard deviation of the sampling distribution of r, known (not surprisingly) as the **standard error of r (s_r)**, is given in the following formula:

Standard error of r
($\rho = 0$)

$$s_r = \sqrt{\frac{1 - r^2}{n - 2}} \tag{17.2}$$

As with any standard error, s_r is smaller when n is larger. That is, there is less sample-to-sample variation in r when calculated from large samples. In such situations, r therefore is a more precise estimate of ρ. (We explore the implications of this in Section 17.6.) Third, when $\rho = 0$, the sampling distribution of r is approximately normal in shape.

17.3   Testing the Statistical Hypothesis That $\rho = 0$

In testing the hypothesis of no linear association, H_0: $\rho = 0$, you are asking whether the sample Pearson r is significantly different from zero. You can test this null hypothesis by applying the t test. The t ratio for a correlation coefficient takes on the familiar structure of any t test:

$$t = \frac{r - \rho_0}{s_r}$$

Except for a few symbols, there is nothing new here: the sample result (r in this case) is compared with the condition specified under the null hypothesis (symbolized by ρ_0), and the difference is divided by the standard error (s_r). Because H_0: $\rho = 0$, this formula simplifies to:

t ratio for r
$$t = \frac{r}{s_r} \qquad (17.3)$$

The t ratio will follow Student's t distribution with $df = 2$. Here, n reflects the number of *pairs* of scores. A basic assumption is that the population of observations has a **normal bivariate distribution**. Evidence of marked *heteroscedasticity*, where the spread of Y values is dissimilar across values of X, would suggest that this assumption is questionable (see Section 8.8). In this case, you should consider a "nonparametric" or "distribution-free" alternative (e.g., see Minium et al., 1999, ch. 21).

17.4   An Example

Consider the correlation that we presented in Chapter 7 between spatial reasoning and mathematical ability, $r = +.63$. (You may wish to refresh your memory by revisiting the scatterplot in Figure 7.1.) Imagine that you calculated this coefficient from sample data after reviewing the literature on cognitive aptitudes and their interrelationships. You proceed to test the hypothesis H_0: $\rho = 0$. Let's walk through the steps:

Step 1 *Formulate the statistical hypotheses and select a level of significance.*
Your statistical hypotheses are:

$$H_0: \rho = 0$$
$$H_1: \rho > 0$$

Guided by logic and theory, you formulated a *directional* alternative hypothesis because you believe that the only reasonable expectation, if H_0 is false, is that spatial reasoning and mathematical ability are *positively* related (i.e., $\rho > 0$). You set the level of significance at $\alpha = .05$.

Step 2 *Determine the desired sample size and select the sample.*
You may recall that this sample comprised 30 decidedly fictitious college students.

Step 3 *Calculate the necessary sample statistics.*
- You must calculate r, of course. We describe the procedure for doing so in Chapter 7, which you may wish to review before proceeding. Again, here $r = +.63$.
- The standard error of r easily follows:

$$s_r = \sqrt{\frac{1 - r^2}{n - 2}} = \sqrt{\frac{1 - (+.63)^2}{30 - 2}} = \sqrt{\frac{.60}{28}} = .146$$

That is, .146 is your estimate of the standard deviation of all possible values of r had you conducted an unlimited number of sampling experiments of this nature.

- Now use Formula (17.3) to obtain the sample t ratio:

$$t = \frac{r}{s_r} = \frac{+.63}{.146} = +4.32$$

We shouldn't get ahead of ourselves, but notice how large this t ratio is. If you think of t as being an "approximate z," particularly for large samples, then you can see that this value is off the charts! (This is true *literally*—Table A does not extend to $z = 4.32$.) As you may suspect, such a discrepant t would seem to portend statistical significance.

Step 4 *Identify the region(s) of rejection.*
The critical t value for a one-tailed test ($\alpha = .05$, 28 df) is $t_{.05} = +1.701$ (see Table B). The region of rejection and the obtained t ratio are shown in Figure 17.2.

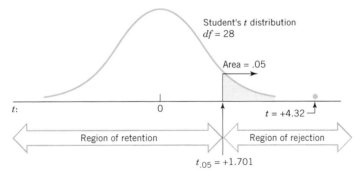

Figure 17.2   Testing H_0: $\rho = 0$ against H_1: $\rho > 0$ ($\alpha = .05$) using the t test. Because $+4.32 > +1.701$, H_0 is rejected.

Step 5   *Make the statistical decision and form conclusion.*
The sample t ratio of $+4.32$ easily falls in the region of rejection ($+4.32 > +1.701$), and, therefore, H_0 is rejected. Your sample correlation coefficient is statistically significant; or in equivalent terms, it is significantly different from zero. You draw the substantive conclusion that there is a positive relationship between the two constructs, spatial reasoning and mathematical ability, as examined under the specific conditions of this investigation.

17.5   Table E

We have shown you Formula (17.3) and the five steps above so you can see that the general logic of testing hypotheses about correlation coefficients is the same as that for testing hypotheses about means. As it turns out, however, you can conveniently sidestep the calculation of t altogether by taking advantage of Table E in Appendix C. This table shows the **critical values of r (r_α)**—the minimum values of r necessary to reject H_0. These values are presented for both $\alpha = .05$ and $\alpha = .01$, and for both one- and two-tailed tests. In short, to test H_0: $\rho = 0$, all you do is compare your r with the appropriate r_α.

Let's stay with the example in Section 17.4, where H_1: $\rho > 0$, $\alpha = .05$, $df = 28$, and r is found to be $+.63$. To locate the critical value of r, first look down the left-hand column of Table E until you come to 28 df. Now look across to find the entry in the column for a one-tailed test at $\alpha = .05$, which you see is .306. H_0 is rejected when the sample correlation coefficient *equals or surpasses* the one-tailed critical value *and is in the direction stated in the alternative hypothesis.* Because your r is positive and surpasses the critical value (i.e., $+.63 > +.306$), H_0 is rejected. (In this one-tailed test, any r less than $+.306$, such as $r = +.20$ or $r = -.45$, would have resulted in the retention of H_0.) Figure 17.3 shows the region of rejection and sample correlation.

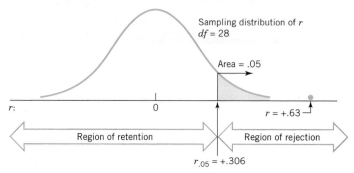

Figure 17.3   Testing H_0: $\rho = 0$ against H_1: $\rho > 0$ ($\alpha = .05$) using Table E. Because $+.63 > +.306$, H_0 is rejected.

What if your directional alternative hypothesis had taken the *opposite* form— H_1: $\rho < 0$? In this case, the critical value of r is $r_{.05} = -.306$, and H_0 is rejected only if the sample correlation falls at or beyond this value (e.g., $r = -.35$). Thus, your r of $+.63$ in this one-tailed test would lead to the *retention* of H_0 (see Figure 17.4).

Where the alternative hypothesis is nondirectional (H_1: $\rho \neq 0$), the null hypothesis is rejected if the sample correlation is of equal or greater size than the critical value, *whether negative or positive*. With $\alpha = .05$ and $df = 28$, the two-tailed critical value of r is $\pm.361$. Consequently, $r = +.63$ would result in the rejection of H_0 (see Figure 17.5).

A note before we move on. The directional alternative hypothesis, H_0: $\rho < 0$, would be difficult to justify in the present context, given the two aptitudes involved. As you can see from Figure 17.4, a possible consequence of positing a one-tailed H_1 in the *wrong* direction is the obligation to retain H_0 in the face of a substantial correlation. This is why it is important to formulate a directional alternative hypothesis *only when you have a strong rationale for doing so*; otherwise, employ the more cautious two-tailed H_1.

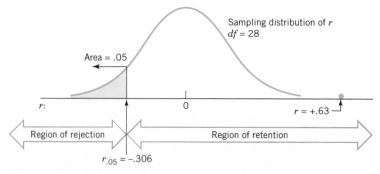

Figure 17.4   Regions of rejection and retention for H_1: $\rho < 0$ ($df = 28$).

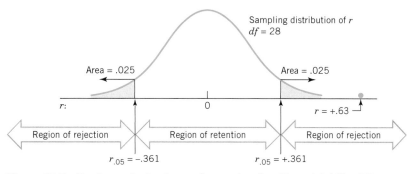

Figure 17.5 Regions of rejection and retention for H_1: $\rho \neq 0$ ($df = 28$).

17.6 *The Role of n in the Statistical Significance of r*

As with each of the standard error terms considered in previous chapters, the standard error of *r* is influenced by sample size. You can easily see this by considering the location of *n* in Formula (17.2):

$$s_r = \sqrt{\frac{1 - r^2}{n - 2}}$$

Thus, for a given value of *r*, a larger *n* in the denominator of s_r results in a smaller standard error, and, conversely, a smaller *n* results in a larger standard error. This principle has two important consequences for hypothesis testing.

First, because s_r serves as the *denominator* of the *t* test, a larger *n* ultimately results in a larger *t* ratio. Specifically, a larger *n* produces a smaller s_r which, given the location of s_r in Formula (17.3), makes for a larger *t*. Thus, for a given value of *r* (other than zero), there is a greater likelihood of statistical significance with larger values of *n*. We illustrate this in the following comparison, where *r* = .50 in both cases but sample size is quite different:

$$r = .50 \ \text{and} \ \ n = 10 \ \ \rightarrow \ \ t = \frac{.50}{\sqrt{\dfrac{1 - .25}{10 - 2}}} = \frac{.50}{.306} = 1.63$$

$$r = .50 \ \text{and} \ \ n = 30 \ \ \rightarrow \ \ t = \frac{.50}{\sqrt{\dfrac{1 - .25}{30 - 2}}} = \frac{.50}{.164} = 3.05$$

Notice that the error term for *n* = 30 is roughly *half* the error term for *n* = 10 (.164 vs. .306). Consequently, the *t* ratio is almost *twice* as large (3.05 vs. 1.63). Furthermore, this larger *t* ratio is statistically significant by any conventional criterion, whereas the smaller value is not (see Table B). Thus, even though *r* is the same in both cases, the difference in sample size will result in a different statistical decision—and a different substantive conclusion.

The second consequence of the relationship between n and s_r is that smaller samples require *larger* critical values to reject H_0 and, conversely, larger samples enjoy *smaller* critical values. Remember that s_r reflects the amount of variation in r that would be expected in an unlimited number of sampling experiments. When n is small (large s_r), r is subject to greater sampling variation and therefore is a less precise estimate of ρ than when n is large (small s_r). For this reason, an r calculated from a small sample must satisfy a more stringent condition—a higher critical value—before the researcher can reject the hypothesis that $\rho = 0$. You can see this most directly in Table E, where the critical values are expressed in terms of r. With $\alpha = .01$ (two-tailed), a sample correlation based on 1 *df* would have to be at least .9999 (!) to be declared statistically significant, but a correlation of only .081 is required where $df = 1000$.

17.7   *Statistical Significance versus Importance (Again)*

We have raised the distinction between statistical significance and practical (or theoretical) importance several times in earlier chapters. This distinction is equally relevant to the significance testing of correlation coefficients.

> The expression "statistically significant correlation" means that H_0: $\rho = 0$ has been tested and rejected according to a given decision criterion (α).

In other words, "statistical significance" is a conclusion that ρ does not fall *precisely on the point 0*. Statistical significance says nothing about the importance of the result. Indeed, as you saw in the previous section, a very large sample can result in a significant r that, while not precisely on the point 0, comes pretty darn close! And in such samples, as r goes, so (probably) goes ρ.

The measure of effect size, r^2 (coefficient of determination), is helpful for making judgments about the importance of a sample correlation coefficient. (We discussed r^2 in Section 7.8, which you may wish to quickly review before proceeding.)

17.8   *Testing Hypotheses Other Than $\rho = 0$*

For values of ρ other than zero, the sampling distribution of r is skewed—increasingly so as ρ approaches ± 1.00. Look at Figure 17.6, which shows the sampling distributions for three values of ρ. Take $\rho = -.80$. Because r cannot exceed -1.00, there simply isn't enough "room" to the left of $-.80$ to allow sample values of r to fall symmetrically about ρ. But there is ample room to the right, which explains why the sampling distribution of r is positively skewed in this instance. Similar logic applies

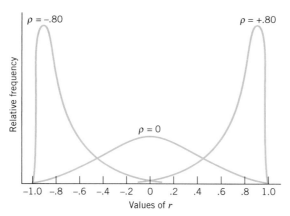

Figure 17.6   Sampling distribution of *r* for three values of ρ (*n* = 8). (From *Statistical Reasoning in Psychology and Education*, B. M. King & E. W. Minium. Copyright © 2003 by John Wiley & Sons, Inc., p. 332. Reprinted by permission of John Wiley & Sons, Inc.)

to ρ = +.80, although the resulting skew is now *negative*. One implication of this is that a "normalizing" transformation of *r* is required when testing a null hypothesis other than ρ = 0 (for details, see Glass & Hopkins, 1996).

17.9   *Interval Estimation of* ρ

Rather than (or in addition to) testing the hypothesis H_0: ρ = 0, you may wish to provide an interval estimate of ρ corresponding to the selected level of confidence. The basic logic of interval estimation applies here as well. However, because the sampling distribution of *r* is not symmetric for values of ρ other than zero, the confidence intervals are not symmetrically placed about the sample *r* (other than *r* = 0). As a result, the aforementioned normalizing transformation is necessary for locating those limits. If you intend to make a formal presentation of an interval estimate for ρ in a research report or publication, it is advisable to use this transformation. However, if your primary concern is to interpret a sample *r*, reasonably accurate limits corresponding to the 95% level of confidence can be obtained directly from Figure 17.7.

Let's determine the confidence limits for the correlation *r* = +.63 (*n* = 30) between spatial reasoning and mathematical ability. For the purpose of illustration, we will work from the simplified Figure 17.8. First, move along the horizontal axis of this figure to the approximate location of *r* = +.63 and place a straightedge vertically through that point. Now find where the straightedge intersects the upper and lower curves for *n* = 30. (For a sample size falling between the sizes indicated in Figure 17.7, you must estimate by eye where the curves would be located.) Move horizontally from these points of intersection to the vertical axis on the left and read off the 95% confidence limits for ρ on the vertical scale. The lower limit (ρ_L) is

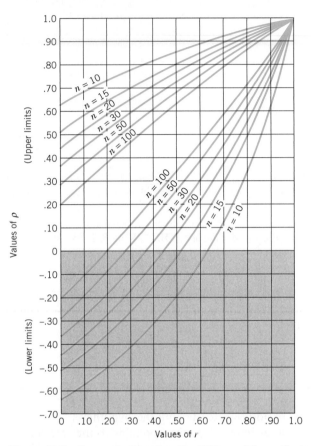

Values of ρ (Upper limits) / (Lower limits)

Values of r

Figure 17.7   Curves for locating the 95% confidence limits for ρ.

roughly $+.35$ and the upper limit (ρ_U), $+.80$. In the present example, then, you can be 95% confident that the population correlation, ρ, falls between about $+.35$ and $+.80$.[1]

The effect of sample size on the confidence limits is easily seen from close inspection of Figure 17.7. Notice that for a given r, the limits become narrower and narrower as n is increased. This reflects the smaller standard error that a larger sample entails and, therefore, the greater precision of r as an estimate of ρ. If your sample size had been only $n = 10$, the confidence limits would be considerably wider indeed: extending from approximately $.00$ to $+.90$! You can also see that for higher values of r, the limits become narrower.

Figure 17.7 will work just as well for negative values of r. Suppose, for instance, that $r = -.63$ ($n = 30$). Simply treat r as though it were positive and reverse the signs of the obtained limits. Thus, the 95% confidence limits for $r = -.63$ are $-.35$ and $-.80$.

---

[1] Although such "eyeball approximation" may seem uncharacteristically imprecise, our result is remarkably close to what would have obtained if we had used the normalizing transformation for estimating the confidence limits: $\rho_L = +.34$ and $\rho_U = +.81$. (Details can be found in Glass & Hopkins, 1996, pp. 357–358.)

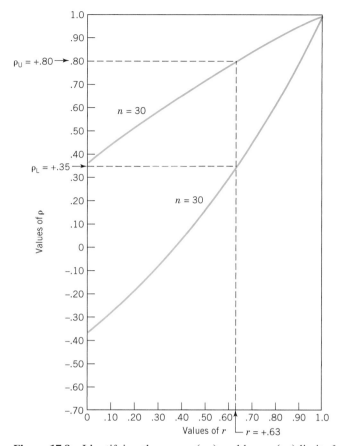

Figure 17.8   Identifying the upper (ρ_U) and lower (ρ_L) limits for $r = +.63$ ($n = 30$).

17.10   Summary

The correlation coefficients calculated in practice typically are sample values, and therefore are subject to sampling variation. Thus, statistical inference techniques become useful here as well. The most common application is the test of the hypothesis that there is no linear association between the two variables. A t test of H_0: $\rho = 0$ can be performed, or the chore of calculating t can be bypassed by using critical values of r (Table E).

   One must be careful to distinguish between statistical significance and practical or theoretical importance when dealing with correlation. The statistical significance of a sample correlation refers to the outcome of a test of the hypothesis that the population coefficient (ρ) is zero, and whether significance is reached depends importantly on the size of the sample. The coefficient of determination (r^2), more than its significance, should be considered when interpreting sample correlations obtained from large samples. A normalizing transformation is required for testing hypotheses other than $\rho = 0$. This transformation is used for constructing an interval estimate of ρ, or approximate confidence limits can be determined directly from the curves of Figure 17.7. Whether samples are large or small, the use of interval estimation techniques helps to put the influence of sampling variation in proper perspective.

Reading the Research: Inferences about ρ

Bruno (2002) examined the bivariate relationships between teacher absenteeism and various environmental indicators from 49 large, urban high schools (see the following table). He found that schools with higher rates of teacher absenteeism also tended to have more uncredentialed teachers ($r = .37$), a higher dropout rate ($r = .40$), more teaching positions unfilled ($r = .52$), and lower academic performance ($r = -.54$), to mention four indicators.

Intercorrelation of All Variables with Teacher
Absenteeism Rates (** = $p < .01$)

Variable	Correlation
Number w/o credential	.37**
Number < 2 years experience	.24
Substitute teacher requests	−.01
Substitute requests unfilled	.45**
Dropout rate	.40**
Transiency percent	.50**
Number of suspensions	−.04
Opportunity transfers	.19
Crimes against property	.44**
Crimes against people	.64**
Number of unfilled teaching positions	.52**
Academic Performance Index	−.54**

Notice that the lowest significant correlation is $r = .37$ and that the highest non-significant correlation is $r = .24$. This is consistent with the critical value obtained from Table E in Appendix C. That is, for samples of roughly this size ($df = 50$), correlations having an absolute value of at least .354 are significant at the .01 level (two-tailed).

Source: Bruno, J. E. (2002, July 26). The geographical distribution of teacher absenteeism in large urban school district settings: Implications for school reform efforts aimed at promoting equity and excellence in education. *Education Policy Analysis Archives, 10*(32). Retrieved [August 23, 2002] from http://epaa.asu.edu/epaa/v10n32/.

Case Study: Mind over Math

Students of all ages tend to have strong and varied feelings about mathematics. Some students are rather interested in math, while others try to avoid it at all costs. The same holds for self-perceived ability: while some students are confident in their math skills, others cower at the mere thought of, say, "solving for an unknown." Educational psychologists refer to self-perceived ability as *self-efficacy*. For this case study, we explored the correlations among student interest, self-efficacy, and performance in math.

We obtained data from several fifth-grade math classes in a medium-sized suburban school district in Virginia. Interest in math (INTEREST) was measured by students' responses to various statements about math (e.g., "I like learning about math"). We measured self-efficacy in math (EFFICACY) in a similar fashion (e.g., "Even if the work in math is hard, I can learn it"). For both INTEREST and EFFICACY, higher scores reflected higher levels of the attribute. Finally, the Virginia Standards of Learning fifth-grade math exam (GR5TEST) served as the measure of math performance.

We visually inspected each scatterplot before obtaining the Pearson rs, looking for evidence of outliers, nonlinearity, and restriction of range. A restriction of range was apparent in two of the scatterplots, with EFFICACY looking like the culprit. Indeed, the histogram for this variable revealed a decidedly negative skew (i.e., scores bunching up at the high end of the scale). As you saw in Chapter 7, such restriction in variability tends to underestimate Pearson r. We acknowledged this limitation and pressed on.

The bivariate correlations are presented in Table 17.1. We directed our statistical software to report one-tailed probabilities for each of the three correlations. We believed that if the null hypothesis were false for any ρ, the relationship would be *positive* (i.e., H_1: $\rho > 0$). Students who like math or have confidence in their math ability should, if anything, perform *better* than students who dislike math or harbor self-doubts. A similar justification can be made for the relationship between interest and self-efficacy in math: if you like it, chances are you will do well at it; if you do well in it, chances are you will like it.

The correlation between INTEREST and GR5TEST was statistically nonsignificant ($r = .097$, $p = .095$). The null hypothesis, $\rho = 0$, was retained. In contrast, EFFICACY and GR5TEST demonstrated a significant, positive relationship ($r = .365$, $p = .000$).[2] The coefficient of determination, $r^2 = .133$, shows that roughly 13% of the variation in test scores is accounted for by variation in self-efficacy. While self-efficacy appears to be related to math performance, other variables

Table 17.1   Bivariate Correlations ($n = 185$)

	GR5TEST	**INTEREST**	**EFFICACY**
GR5TEST	—		
INTEREST	.097 ($p = .095$)	—	
EFFICACY	.365 ($p = .000$)	.455 ($p = .000$)	—

[2]Reported p values of ".000" do not, of course, indicate zero probability! Rather, our statistical software (like most) simply rounds any p value to three places beyond the decimal point.

account for differences in test scores as well. Finally, the strongest correlation was found between INTEREST and EFFICACY ($r = .455$, $p = .000$). Roughly one-fifth ($.455^2 = .21$) of the variation in self-efficacy is accounted for by variation among students in terms of the interest they have in math.

We went a step further and, using Figure 17.7, estimated the 95% confidence interval for the two significant correlations. For the correlation between INTEREST and EFFICACY, we estimate that ρ could be as small as .30 or as large as .60. For the EFFICACY-GR5TEST correlation, ρ falls somewhere between .19 and .52.

In conclusion, then, interest in mathematics was unrelated to test performance, whereas math self-efficacy correlated significantly with both test performance and interest in math. With this (nonrandom) sample of convenience, we must be particularly careful in making nonstatistical generalizations from these sample results. Such generalizations can be made only after thoughtful consideration of the characteristics of the sample and the setting from which it was drawn.

Suggested Computer Exercises

1. Access the **ch17** data file, which contains information on a nonrandom sample ($n = 64$) of eighth-grade students from a rural school district in the Midwest. The data include science test scores from state and district assessments, as well as two self-report measures: science self-efficacy and classroom support in science.

   (a) Compute the Pearson r between classroom support and performance on the district

   exam, and determine its statistical significance ($\alpha = .05$). (Decide whether you wish to conduct a one-tailed or a two-tailed test.) If significant, interpret the magnitude of r in terms of the coefficient of determination.

   (b) Repeat 1a, but with respect to the relationship between science self-efficacy and performance on the state exam.

Exercises

Identify, Define, or Explain

Terms and Concepts

linear association
sampling distribution of r
standard error of r
normal bivariate distribution

heteroscedasticity
critical values of r
coefficient of determination

Symbols

ρ μ_r s_r ρ_0 r_α r^2 ρ_L ρ_U

Note: Answers to starred (*) items are presented in Appendix B.

*1. Suppose that a friend wishes to test H_0: $\rho = .25$ and asks for your assistance in using the procedures described in this chapter. What would be your response?

*2. For each situation below, provide the following: s_r, sample t ratio, critical t value, and the statistical decision regarding H_0: $\rho = 0$. (Assume that the obtained correlation is in the direction of H_1.)

    (a) $r = -.38$, $n = 30$, $\alpha = .05$, two-tailed test

    (b) $r = +.60$, $n = 10$, $\alpha = .05$, two-tailed test

    (c) $r = -.17$, $n = 62$, $\alpha = .01$, two-tailed test

    (d) $r = +.69$, $n = 122$, $\alpha = .05$, one-tailed test

    (e) $r = -.43$, $n = 140$, $\alpha = .01$, one-tailed test

*3. For the five situations in Problem 2, provide the critical r value and the statistical decision regarding H_0: $\rho = 0$. (Do the statistical decisions agree across the two problems?)

4. Using a sample of 26 twelve-year-olds from diverse backgrounds, a researcher conducts an exploratory study of the relationship between self-esteem and socioeconomic status. She obtains a sample correlation of $r = -.12$.

    (a) Specify the statistical hypotheses.

    (b) Specify the critical r value and statistical decision ($\alpha = .05$).

    (c) Draw final conclusions.

5. Suppose that the researcher in Problem 4, while presenting her results at a conference, said the following: "Interestingly, the obtained correlation was *negative*. That is, there is a slight tendency for children of higher socioeconomic backgrounds to be lower in self-esteem." What would be your response to this interpretation?

6. For each of the following cases, give the size of the sample r required for statistical significance:

    (a) $n = 5$, $\alpha = .05$, one-tailed test

    (b) $n = 24$, $\alpha = .05$, two-tailed test

    (c) $n = 42$, $\alpha = .01$, two-tailed test

    (d) $n = 125$, $\alpha = .05$, two-tailed test

    (e) $n = 1500$, $\alpha = .05$, one-tailed test

    (f) $n = 3$, $\alpha = .01$, two-tailed test

7. You read in a review article: "A researcher found a significant positive correlation between popularity and IQ for a large sample of college students."

    (a) How might such a statement be misinterpreted by the statistically unsophisticated?

    (b) What does the statement really mean? (Be precise; use appropriate symbols and statistical terminology.)

    (c) What single piece of additional information would be most necessary for adequately interpreting the result claimed?

*8. An education professor has 15 college seniors who are doing their student teaching. They also recently took a teacher certification test required by the state. The professor obtains a correlation of +.40 between these test scores and ratings of student-teaching performance that were provided by the field supervisor at the end of the semester.

   (a) Use a significance testing approach (Table E) to evaluate the sample result ($\alpha = .05$).

   (b) Use an interval estimation approach to evaluate the sample results (95% level of confidence).

   (c) What particular weakness of the personnel director's study is illustrated by your answer to Problem 8b?

*9. Use Figure 17.7 to determine (as accurately as you can) the 95% confidence interval for ρ in each of the following instances:

   (a) $r = +.90, n = 10$

   (b) $r = +.50, n = 10$

   (c) $r = +.20, n = 10$

   (d) $r = +.20, n = 30$

   (e) $r = +.20, n = 100$

*10. (a) Compare the widths of the intervals obtained in Problems 9a–9c. What generalization concerning the sampling variation of the correlation coefficient is suggested by this comparison?

   (b) Now compare the widths of the intervals obtained in Problems 9c–9e. What is the corresponding generalization concerning the sampling variation of the correlation coefficient?

11. Use Figure 17.7 to determine (as accurately as you can) the 95% confidence interval for ρ in each of the following instances:

   (a) $r = +.35, n = 50$

   (b) $r = -.45, n = 15$

   (c) $r = +.78, n = 10$

   (d) $r = -.52, n = 100$

12. Consider the confidence intervals you estimated in Problems 9 and 11. If in each of those cases you instead had tested H_0: $\rho = 0$ ($\alpha = .05$, two-tailed), which sample correlation coefficients would have resulted in nonsignificance? (Explain.) (*Note:* Answer this question simply by examining the confidence intervals.)

13. (a) Suppose the correlation between two variables is reported as "not significant" for a sample of 1000 cases. Is it possible, without knowing the actual value of r, to make an adequate interpretation concerning the true degree of relationship from this information alone? (Explain.)

   (b) Suppose the correlation between two variables is reported as "significant" for a sample of 1000 cases. Is it possible, without knowing the actual value of r, to make an adequate interpretation concerning the true degree of relationship from this information alone? (Explain.)

*14. Why is the sample r alone sufficient for adequate interpretation when the sample size is quite large (say over 300 or 400 cases), whereas an interval estimate is recommended for smaller samples?

*15. For a sample of her 10 students, an instructor correlates "test anxiety" (X) with "percent correct" (Y) on the recent midterm. The data are as follows:

Student

	A	B	C	D	E	F	G	H	I	J
percent correct:	73	92	55	84	64	88	69	96	59	77
test anxiety:	35	26	48	21	10	30	42	25	4	16

(a) Would the Pearson r be an appropriate measure of association for these data? (Explain.) (*Hint:* Construct a scatterplot.)

(b) What would be the statistical consequence of computing Pearson r from these data? (No calculations necessary.)

16. Using a sample of 120 high schools, a researcher obtains a correlation of $r = -.52$ ($p < .05$) between average teacher salary (X) and the proportion of students who drop out (Y). Considering the earlier discussion of correlation and causation (Section 7.6), what do you believe is the most likely explanation of why these two variables correlate?

*17. A researcher believes that the ability to identify constellations of stars in the night sky is related to spatial reasoning ability. She obtains the correlation between scores on a spatial reasoning test (X) and the number of constellations correctly identified (Y). She calculates this correlation for each of two samples: one is based on a random sample of adults in her community, and the other is drawn from members of a local astronomy club. Which correlation would you expect to be larger? (Explain.)

CHAPTER 18

Making Inferences from Frequency Data

18.1 *Frequency Data versus Score Data*

Up to this point, our treatment of statistical inference has been concerned with scores on one or more variables, such as spatial ability, mathematics achievement, hours spent on the computer, and number of facts recalled. These scores have been used to make inferences about population means and correlations. To be sure, not all research questions involve *score* data. In this chapter, the data to be analyzed consist of *frequencies*—that is, the *numbers of observations* falling into the categories of a variable. Here, your task is to make inferences about the population frequency distribution. In particular, your goal is to draw conclusions about the relative frequencies, or proportions of cases, in the population that fall into the various categories of interest.

Typically, the variables here are qualitative. That is, they fall on a nominal scale where the underlying categories differ only "in kind" (Section 1.5). Ethnicity, sex, subject matter, and political party are examples of qualitative variables. However, the procedures we discuss in this chapter can also be applied to frequencies associated with quantitative variables, and in Section 18.15 we show how this is done.

Although the general form of the data under consideration has changed from scores to frequencies, the overall logic of statistical inference has not. One begins with a null hypothesis concerning the population proportions. (For example, "Equal proportions of male and female high school students are proficient in science.") Then the obtained, or *observed*, sample frequencies are compared with those *expected* under the null hypothesis. If the observed frequencies deviate sufficiently from those expected, then H_0 is rejected. Sound familiar? Whereas z, t, and F ratios are used for testing hypotheses about population means and correlation coefficients, the test statistic for frequency data is **chi-square**, χ^2. ("Chi" rhymes with "tie.") Specifically, the magnitude of χ^2 reflects the amount of discrepancy between observed and expected frequencies and, therefore, the tenability of H_0.

We will consider two applications of χ^2. We begin with the **one-variable case**, where responses are categorized on a single variable. For reasons that soon will be clear, this is also known as the **χ^2 goodness-of-fit test**. We then take up the **two-variable case**, or the **χ^2 test of independence**, where responses are categorized according to two variables simultaneously.

18.2   *A Problem Involving Frequencies: The One-Variable Case*

Suppose there are four candidates for a vacant seat on the local school board: Martzial, Breece, Dunton, and Artesani. You poll a random sample of 200 registered voters regarding their candidate of choice. *Do differences exist among the proportions of registered voters preferring each school board candidate?*

Here you have a single variable (school board candidate) comprising four categories (Martzial, Breece, Dunton, and Artesani). The **observed frequencies** are the number of registered voters preferring each candidate, as shown in Table 18.1. Note that there is an observed frequency, f_o, for each category. For example, 40 voters declare their preference for Martzial ($f_o = 40$), whereas 62 voters appear to be particularly fond of Breece ($f_o = 62$). The observed frequencies of all four candidates, naturally enough, sum to n: $\Sigma f_o = 200 = n$.

To answer the question posed, you first hypothesize that the four candidates do *not* differ in regard to voter preference. In other words, in the population, each candidate will be chosen as the preferred candidate one-fourth of the time. This is your null hypothesis, and it is expressed as follows:

$$H_0: \pi_{Martzial} = \pi_{Breece} = \pi_{Dunton} = \pi_{Artesani} = .25$$

Table 18.1   Expected and Observed Frequency of Voter Preference for Four School-Board Candidates, and the Calculation of χ^2 ($n = 200$)

	Voter Preference				
	Martzial	**Breece**	**Dunton**	**Artesani**	
Observed frequency	$f_o = 40$	$f_o = 62$	$f_o = 56$	$f_o = 42$	$\Sigma f_o = 200$
Expected frequency	$f_e = 50$	$f_e = 50$	$f_e = 50$	$f_e = 50$	$\Sigma f_e = 200$
	①	②	③	④	
$\dfrac{(f_o - f_e)^2}{f_e}$	$\dfrac{(40 - 50)^2}{50}$	$\dfrac{(62 - 50)^2}{50}$	$\dfrac{(56 - 50)^2}{50}$	$\dfrac{(42 - 50)^2}{50}$	
	$= \dfrac{(-10)^2}{50}$	$= \dfrac{(12)^2}{50}$	$= \dfrac{(6)^2}{50}$	$= \dfrac{(-8)^2}{50}$	
	$= 2.00$	$= 2.88$	$= .72$	$= 1.28$	

⑤ $\chi^2 = \Sigma \left[\dfrac{(f_o - f_e)^2}{f_e} \right]$

$= 2.00 + 2.88 + .72 + 1.28$

$= 6.88$

Following convention, we use the Greek symbol π (pi) to represent the population proportion. Thus, π_{Martzial} is the proportion of *all* registered voters who prefer Martzial, π_{Breece} is the corresponding value regarding Breece, and so on.

The alternative hypothesis cannot be expressed so simply. It states that the proportions *do* differ and therefore are not all equal to .25. This state of affairs could occur in many ways: π_{Martzial} and π_{Breece} could be alike but different from π_{Dunton} and π_{Artesani}, all four could be different, and so on. Thus, the H_1 in this case is nondirectional.

> H_0 states that the population proportions falling into the various categories are equal to certain predetermined values; H_1 includes all other possibilities.

The **expected frequencies** (f_e) of voter preference under the null hypothesis also are shown in Table 18.1. Each f_e is calculated by multiplying the hypothesized proportion ($\pi = .25$) by the total sample size, n. For example, the expected frequency for Martzial is:

$$f_e = (\pi_{\text{Martzial}})(n) = (.25)(200) = 50$$

The expected frequencies are those that would, *on average*, occur in an infinite number of repetitions of such a study where all population proportions equal .25. As with the observed frequencies, the expected frequencies sum to n: $\Sigma f_e = 200 = n$.

If H_0 were true, then you would expect to find a good fit between the observed and expected frequencies—hence, the χ^2 "goodness-of-fit" test. That is, under the null hypothesis, f_o and f_e should be similar for each category. Of course, you would be surprised if the observed and expected frequencies were *identical*, because sampling variation operates here just as it does in the analogous situations discussed in earlier chapters. But how much difference is reasonable if H_0 is true? A measure of discrepancy between observed and expected frequencies is needed, as well as a procedure for testing whether that discrepancy is larger than what would be anticipated on the basis of chance alone.

18.3 χ^2: A Measure of Discrepancy Between Expected and Observed Frequencies

Invented by Karl Pearson, the χ^2 statistic provides the needed measure of discrepancy between expected and observed frequencies:

> Chi-Square
>
> $$\chi^2 = \Sigma \left[\frac{(f_o - f_e)^2}{f_e} \right]$$
>
> (18.1)

This formula instructs you to do the following:

Step 1   Obtain the discrepancy, $f_o - f_e$, for each category.

Step 2   Divide the *squared* discrepancy by its f_e.

Step 3   Sum these values across the number of discrepancies for the given problem.

If you are wondering why you simply can't add up the unsquared discrepancies, $\Sigma(f_o - f_e)$, it is because you will get zero every time! Remember, both the sum of observed frequencies and the sum of expected frequencies are equal to n. That is, $\Sigma f_o = \Sigma f_e = n$. Therefore,

$$\Sigma(f_o - f_e)$$
$$= \Sigma f_o - \Sigma f_e$$
$$= n - n$$
$$= 0$$

Squaring each discrepancy takes care of this problem. By then dividing each squared discrepancy by f_e prior to summing, you are "weighting" each discrepancy by its expected frequency. This is shown in Table 18.1 at ❶, ❷, ❸, and ❹. The sample χ^2 is the sum of these four values (❺). That is:

$$\chi^2 = \frac{(40 - 50)^2}{50} + \frac{(62 - 50)^2}{50} + \frac{(56 - 50)^2}{50} + \frac{(42 - 50)^2}{50}$$

$$= 2.00 + 2.88 + .72 + 1.28$$

$$= 6.88$$

Examination of Formula (18.1) and the illustrated calculation reveals several points of interest about χ^2. First, because all discrepancies are squared, χ^2 cannot be negative. That is, discrepancies *in either direction* make a positive contribution to the value of χ^2. Second, the larger the discrepancies (relative to the f_e's), the larger the χ^2. Third, χ^2 will be zero only in the highly unusual event that each f_o is *identical* to the corresponding f_e.

A fourth point of interest concerns the degrees of freedom for the one-variable χ^2. Note that the value of χ^2 also depends on the number of discrepancies, or categories, involved in its calculation. For example, if there were only three candidates (i.e., three categories) in the study, there would be only three discrepancies to contribute to χ^2. As a consequence, the degrees of freedom in the one-variable case will be $C - 1$, where C is the number of categories.

Degrees of freedom: One-variable χ^2	
$$df = C - 1$$	(18.2)

For the survey of prospective voters, then, $df = 4 - 1 = 3$.

18.4 The Sampling Distribution of χ^2

The obtained χ^2 of 6.88 reflects the discrepancies between observed frequencies and those expected under the null hypothesis. What kinds of χ^2 values would be reasonably anticipated for this situation as a result of sampling variation alone? With 3 *df*, what minimum value of χ^2 would be required for rejecting the null hypothesis? Where does the obtained χ^2 of 6.88 fall relative to this value? These questions, as you may recognize, are analogous to those encountered in earlier chapters in relation to *z*, *t*, and *F*. To answer these questions, you must consider the **sampling distribution of χ^2**.

Suppose the null hypothesis, $\pi_{\text{Martzial}} = \pi_{\text{Breece}} = \pi_{\text{Dunton}} = \pi_{\text{Artesani}} = .25$, is true. Suppose also that you repeat the study many, many times under identical circumstances. That is, you select a random sample of 200 registered voters, ask each voter to indicate his or her preferred candidate, and compute χ^2 as described above. You would expect the value of χ^2 to vary from sample to sample because of the chance factors involved in random sampling. The distribution of sample χ^2 values, if H_0 were true, would follow the theoretical χ^2 distribution for 3 *df*, shown in Figure 18.1. Just as with the *t* distribution, the theoretical χ^2 distribution is a family of distributions, one for every value of *df*. If, for instance, only three candidates had been on the ballot, a different χ^2 distribution would be appropriate—that for $3 - 1 = 2$ *df*. The theoretical χ^2 distributions for various degrees of freedom are summarized in Table F of Appendix C, which we discuss in the next section.

Notice that the distribution of Figure 18.1 is positively skewed. This you might expect, for although the value of χ^2 has a lower limit of zero (no discrepancies between f_o and f_e), it theoretically has no upper limit. Larger and larger discrepancies, regardless of direction, result in larger and larger χ^2 values. Of course, larger and larger discrepancies become less and less probable if H_0 is true, which gives the distribution in Figure 18.1 its long tail to the right. As you can see from Figure 18.2, however, the positive skew of the χ^2 sampling distribution becomes less pronounced

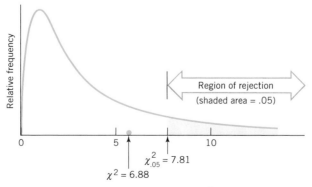

Figure 18.1 Sampling distribution of χ^2 distribution for 3 *df*, showing the calculated and critical values for the voter survey problem.

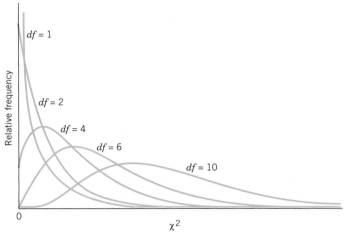

Figure 18.2 Sampling distribution of χ^2 for $df = 1, 2, 4, 6$ and 10.

with increased degrees of freedom. In any case, only large values of χ^2 can be taken as evidence against H_0; thus, *the region of rejection lies entirely in the upper tail* (as shown in Figure 18.1).

18.5 Completion of the Voter Survey Problem: The χ^2 Goodness-of-Fit Test

We are now ready to complete the χ^2 goodness-of-fit test for the voter survey problem. The test procedure is summarized in the following steps:

Step 1 *Formulate the statistical hypotheses and select a level of significance.*

H_0: $\pi_{Martzial} = \pi_{Breece} = \pi_{Dunton} = \pi_{Artesani} = .25$

H_1: any state of affairs other than that specified in H_0 (nondirectional)

$\alpha = .05$.

Step 2 *Determine the desired sample size and select the sample.*
A sample of 200 registered voters is selected.

Step 3 *Calculate the necessary sample statistics.*
The expected and observed frequencies are summarized in Table 18.1, from which a sample χ^2 value of 6.88 is obtained (see calculations in Table 18.1).

Step 4 *Identify the critical χ^2 value.*
If H_0 is true, sample χ^2 values for the one-variable case follow the sampling distribution of χ^2 with $C - 1$ degrees of freedom. In the present example,

$df = 4 - 1 = 3$. To find the critical χ^2 value, locate in Table F the intersection of the row for 3 df and the column for area $(\alpha) = .05$. With $df = 3$ and $\alpha = .05$, the critical value is $\chi^2_{.05} = 7.81$.

Step 5   *Make the statistical decision and form conclusion.*
The χ^2 sample of 6.88 falls short of $\chi^2_{.05}$. This also is shown in Figure 18.1, where you see that the sample χ^2 lies outside the region of rejection. Thus, H_0 is retained as a reasonable possibility: although there are discrepancies between the observed and expected frequencies, they are of a magnitude small enough to be expected if H_0 were true. That is, the preferences of the 200 registered voters in the sample do not deviate significantly from what would be expected if the candidates were equally popular. You conclude that, in the population, there are no differences among the four candidates in terms of voter preference (i.e., $\pi_{\text{Martzial}} = \pi_{\text{Breece}} = \pi_{\text{Dunton}} = \pi_{\text{Artesani}} = .25$).

If you had obtained a sample χ^2 larger than the critical value of 7.81, you would reject H_0 and conclude that some candidates are preferred over others. Which ones? You cannot tell from the χ^2 value alone, because the alternative hypothesis is simply that H_0 is untrue in some (any) way, and there are many ways in which that could occur. However, remember that the sample χ^2 is the sum of the C discrepancy terms (e.g., $6.88 = 2.00 + 2.88 + .72 + 1.28$). By inspecting the relative magnitude of these terms when a statistically significant χ^2 is obtained, you often can get a sense of which discrepancies are contributing most to the sample χ^2.

You may be wondering whether the proportions specified under the null hypothesis are always equal to each other, as they are in the present example. Absolutely not! *The substantive question determines the proportions that are hypothesized under H_0* (although they must sum to 1.00). For example, if the substantive question had called for it, you could have stated the hypothesis,

$$H_0\text{: } \pi_{\text{Martzial}} = .10, \ \pi_{\text{Breece}} = .30, \ \pi_{\text{Dunton}} = .20, \ \pi_{\text{Artesani}} = .40$$

Perhaps these proportions correspond to the amount of television and radio air time each candidate has relative to the four candidates combined (Martzial has 10% of the total air time, Breece 30%, etc.). Here, the substantive question would be whether voter preferences simply reflect how much media exposure each candidate has. In practice, of course, only one H_0 will be tested with the data from a given sample.

18.6   The χ^2 Test of a Single Proportion

When the variable has only two categories, the one-variable case is equivalent to a test of a single proportion. Suppose that you want to know whether students prefer one exam format over another. You design a study in which a sample of students receives instruction on some topic, after which a comprehension test is administered. Each student is allowed to take either an essay exam or a multiple-choice exam. To answer your research question, you test the hypothesis that, in the population, the proportion of students selecting the essay exam format is .5. (You just as easily could have specified the multiple-choice exam—it doesn't matter.) Now translate this to a null hypothesis with a nondirectional alternative hypothesis:

$$H_0: \pi_{essay} = .5$$

$$H_1: \pi_{essay} \neq .5$$

You select a sample of 50 students, observe which of the two exam formats each chooses, and obtain these frequencies:

essay: $f_o = 15$ multiple choice: $f_o = 35$

If the two formats do not differ in popularity, the proportionate preference for the essay exam should be .5, as specified in the null hypothesis. Under H_0, the expected frequencies therefore are:

essay: $f_e = (.5)(50) = 25$ multiple choice: $f_e = (.5)(50) = 25$

Now apply Formula (18.1):

$$\chi^2 = \frac{(15 - 25)^2}{25} + \frac{(35 - 25)^2}{25}$$

$$= \frac{(-10)^2}{25} + \frac{(10)^2}{25}$$

$$= 4 + 4$$

$$= 8.00$$

With two categories, this problem has $C - 1 = 2 - 1 = 1$ *df* and a critical χ^2 value of $\chi^2_{.05} = 3.84$. Since the sample χ^2 exceeds this value, H_0 is rejected. You conclude that the two exam formats *do* differ with respect to student choice, noting that the multiple-choice exam is preferred.

When—and *only* when—$df = 1$, a directional test is possible because there are only two ways in which H_0 can be wrong. In the present problem, for example, π_{essay} could be less than .5 or it could be greater. For a directional test with one degree of freedom, it can be shown that $\chi^2_{.05} = 2.71$ and $\chi^2_{.01} = 5.41$. Of course, with a directional test the null hypothesis should be rejected *only* for a difference in the direction specified in the alternative hypothesis. Suppose you had hypothesized that students would be *less* likely to choose the essay exam. First, note that the evidence from the sample shows a smaller proportion of students selecting the essay exam (if it did not, there would be no point in pursuing the matter further). If the test is conducted at the 5% significance level, H_0 is rejected because the sample χ^2 of 8.00 is greater than the one-tailed $\chi^2_{.05} = 2.71$.

18.7   *Interval Estimate of a Single Proportion*

In addition to (or rather than) testing the null hypothesis of a single proportion, π, you may use Formulas (18.3) and (18.4) to construct a **95% confidence interval for π.**

Rule for a 95% confidence
interval for π

$$\pi_L = \frac{n}{n + 3.84}\left[P + \frac{1.92}{n} - 1.96\sqrt{\frac{P(1 - P)}{n} + \frac{.96}{n^2}}\right] \qquad (18.3)$$

$$\pi_U = \frac{n}{n + 3.84}\left[P + \frac{1.92}{n} + 1.96\sqrt{\frac{P(1 - P)}{n} + \frac{.96}{n^2}}\right] \qquad (18.4)$$

In Formulas (18.3) and (18.4), P is the sample proportion, π_L and π_U are the lower and upper limits of the population proportion, and n is sample size.[1] Returning to the preceding scenario, let's apply these two formulas to the obtained proportion of students selecting the essay exam, $P = 15/50 = .30$:

$$\pi_L = \frac{50}{50 + 3.84}\left[\left(.30 + \frac{1.92}{50}\right) - 1.96\sqrt{\frac{.30(1 - .30)}{50} - \frac{.96}{50^2}}\right]$$

$$= .9287[.3384 - .1327]$$

$$= .19$$

$$\pi_U = \frac{50}{50 + 3.84}\left[\left(.30 + \frac{1.92}{50}\right) + 1.96\sqrt{\frac{.30(1 - .30)}{50} + \frac{.96}{50^2}}\right]$$

$$= .9287[.3384 + .1327]$$

$$= .44$$

You can state with 95% confidence that the population proportion falls between .19 and .44. (The procedure is identical for constructing a confidence interval based on $P = .70$, the sample proportion of students selecting the multiple choice exam. All that is required is the substitution of .70 for .30 in the calculations above.)

Perhaps you noticed that this particular confidence interval is not symmetric around the sample proportion. That is, the sample proportion (.30) is a bit closer to the interval's lower limit (.19) than upper limit (.44). (If we instead had constructed a confidence interval for $P = .70$, the sample proportion would be somewhat closer to

[1]Some authors use the lower case p to denote the sample proportion, which also is the symbol for the probability value. To avoid any confusion between the two, we prefer upper case P to symbolize the sample proportion.

the *upper* limit of the interval.) This is because the sampling distribution of a proportion, unless *n* is large, is increasingly skewed as π approaches either 0 or 1.00. The exception is where π = .50, in which case the sampling distribution is perfectly
symmetrical. As a consequence, statistics textbooks historically have specified minimum values for *n* and *P* to ensure accurate interval estimates. However, it turns out

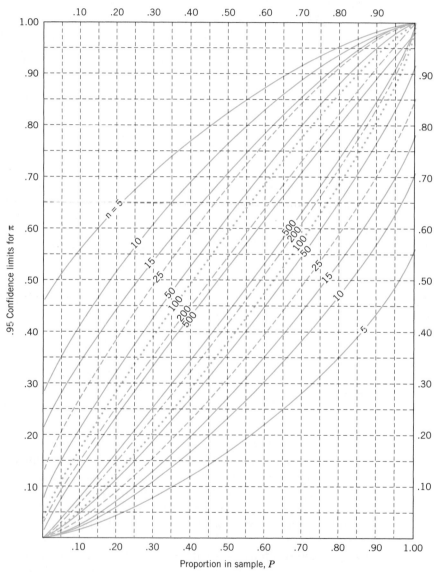

Figure 18.3   Curves for locating the 95% confidence limits for π. (*Source:* Glass, G. V &
Hopkins, K. D. *Statistical Methods in Education and Psychology* (3rd ed.). Copyright © 1996
by Pearson Education. Reprinted by permission of the publisher.)

that those practices are unnecessarily conservative, producing confidence intervals that tend to be too wide. In contrast, Formulas (18.3) and (18.4) provide accurate interval estimates regardless of the magnitude of n or P (Glass & Hopkins, 1996, p. 326).

Formulas (18.3) and (18.4) can be a bit cumbersome, to be sure. Figure 18.3 is convenient when a reasonable approximation of the confidence interval will suffice. Let's determine the confidence limits for the above sample proportion of .30 ($n = 50$). First, move along the horizontal axis of this figure to the location of .30 and place a straightedge vertically through that point. Now find where the straightedge intersects the upper and lower curves for $n = 50$. (For a sample size falling between the sizes indicated in Figure 18.3, you must estimate by eye where the curves would be located.) Move horizontally from these points of intersection to the vertical axis on the left and read off the 95% confidence limits for π on the vertical scale. The lower limit (π_L) is roughly .19 and the upper limit (π_U), .44—in this case, the same values we obtained by hand calculation.

18.8   *When There Are Two Variables: The χ^2 Test of Independence*

So far, we have limited the application of chi-square to the one-variable case. Chi-square also can be applied to the analysis of *bivariate* frequency distributions. Here, the categories are formed by the possible combinations of outcomes for *two* variables.

In the voter survey, suppose you had also recorded the respondent's sex and now wish to know whether males and females differ in their preferences for the four school board candidates. In other words, is voter preference dependent, or *contingent*, on sex? To study this question, you prepare a **contingency table** as shown in Table 18.2. This contingency table is really a bivariate frequency distribution, or **crosstabulation**, with rows representing the categories of one variable (sex in this case) and columns representing the categories of the second variable (preferred candidate). As you see from the row frequencies (f_{row}), 106 of the 200 prospective voters are female and 94 are male. The column frequencies (f_{col}) correspond to the total number of voters who prefer each of the four candidates: 40, 62, 56, and 42, respectively, for Martzial, Breece, Dunton, and Artesani. (Note that the column frequencies agree with the observed frequencies in our one-variable case.) Each of the

Table 18.2   Contingency Table: Classifying Voter Preference by Sex of Respondent

		Voter Preference				
		Martzial	**Breece**	**Dunton**	**Artesani**	f_{row}
Sex of	**Female**	$f_o = 10$	$f_o = 30$	$f_o = 42$	$f_o = 24$	106
Respondent	**Male**	$f_o = 30$	$f_o = 32$	$f_o = 14$	$f_o = 18$	94
	f_{col}	40	62	56	42	$n = 200$

eight cells contains the observed frequency (f_o) corresponding to the intersection of a particular row and column. For example, 30 of the 106 female respondents prefer Breece; Artesani is preferred by 18 of the 94 males.

18.9   *Finding Expected Frequencies in the Two-Variable Case*

As in the one-variable case, the expected frequencies in a contingency table reflect what is expected *if the null hypothesis were true*. Here, the null hypothesis is that there is no association between the two variables—that they are independent of one another. In the present scenario, this means that whether the prospective voter is male or female has nothing to do with which candidate is preferred. The null hypothesis in the two-variable case is called, perhaps not surprisingly, the **null hypothesis of independence**. The alternative hypothesis, the hypothesis of dependence, includes many possibilities. Clearly, there are innumerable ways in which the observed and expected frequencies can differ in any contingency table.

In the two-variable case, the calculation of f_e for any cell requires f_{row}, f_{col}, and n:

Expected frequency
(contingency table)

$$f_e = \frac{(f_{row})(f_{col})}{n} \tag{18.5}$$

Table 18.3 shows the expected frequencies for our contingency table. For example, the expected frequency for the first cell (females, Martzial) is:

$$\frac{(f_{row})(f_{col})}{n} = \frac{(106)(40)}{200} = \frac{4240}{200} = 21.20$$

Table 18.3   Expected Frequencies in a Contingency Table (Data from Table 18.2)

		Voter Preference				
		Martzial	**Breece**	**Dunton**	**Artesani**	f_{row}
Sex of Respondent	**Female**	$f_e = \frac{(106)(40)}{200}$ $= 21.20$	$f_e = \frac{(106)(62)}{200}$ $= 32.86$	$f_e = \frac{(106)(56)}{200}$ $= 29.68$	$f_e = \frac{(106)(42)}{200}$ $= 22.26$	106
	Male	$f_e = \frac{(94)(40)}{200}$ $= 18.80$	$f_e = \frac{(94)(62)}{200}$ $= 29.14$	$f_e = \frac{(94)(56)}{200}$ $= 26.32$	$f_e = \frac{(94)(42)}{200}$ $= 19.74$	94
	f_{col}	40	62	56	42	$n = 200$

Let's examine this particular value more closely so that you fully understand the meaning of a two-variable f_e.

If sex and voter preference were independent (i.e., H_0 is true), you would expect 21.20 of the 40 fans of Martzial—53% of them—to be female. Notice that 53% also is the percentage of female respondents in the sample as a whole ($f_{row}/n = 106/200 = .53$). Thus, under H_0, the expected number of Martzial fans who are female is proportionate to the overall number of females in the sample: if 53% of the sample are female, then 53% of the 40 respondents preferring Martzial should be female as well. You can more readily see this with a slight modification of Formula (18.5):

$$\frac{(f_{row})(f_{col})}{n} = \left(\frac{f_{row}}{n}\right)f_{col} = \left(\frac{106}{200}\right)40 = (.53)(40) = 21.20$$

It must be equally true, of course, that the expected number of females who prefer Martzial is proportionate to the overall number of Martzial fans in the sample. That is, because 20% of all respondents prefer Martzial ($f_{col}/n = 40/200 = .20$), you expect 20% of the 106 females to prefer Martzial as well. Again, a slight modification of Formula (18.5):

$$\frac{(f_{row})(f_{col})}{n} = \left(\frac{f_{col}}{n}\right)f_{row} = \left(\frac{40}{200}\right)106 = (.20)(106) = 21.20$$

Although Formula (18.5) is convenient to use and easy to remember, you will have a better understanding of the two-variable expected frequency by comprehending the equivalency of these various expressions. Toward this end, we encourage you to apply the reasoning behind this particular f_e to other cells in Table 18.3.

As you probably suspect, Formula (18.5) works for any number of rows and columns. Regardless, always verify that the total of the expected frequencies in any row or column equals the total of the observed frequencies for that row or column. (For instance, note that the expected frequencies for females sum to 106, and the expected frequencies for Breece sum to 62.) If not, there is a calculation error.

18.10   Calculating the Two-Variable χ^2

To test the null hypothesis of independence, you use χ^2 to compare the observed frequencies with the frequencies you would expect under H_0. As in the one-variable case, the test of H_0 therefore amounts to an inquiry as to whether the observed frequencies differ significantly from the expected frequencies. If the $(f_o - f_e)$ discrepancies are large, χ^2 will be large, suggesting a relationship between the two variables—that one variable (voter preference) is dependent on the other (sex). On the other hand, independence is retained as a reasonable possibility if χ^2 is small and nonsignificant—hence, the χ^2 "test of independence."

Table 18.4   Calculating a Two-Variable χ^2 (Observed and Expected Frequencies from Table 18.3)

		Martzial	Breece	Dunton	Artesani
		Voter Preference			
Sex of Respondent	**Female**	$\dfrac{(f_o - f_e)^2}{f_e} =$ $\dfrac{(10-21.20)^2}{21.20} =$ $\dfrac{125.44}{21.20} = 5.92$	$\dfrac{(f_o - f_e)^2}{f_e} =$ $\dfrac{(30-32.86)^2}{32.86} =$ $\dfrac{8.18}{32.86} = .25$	$\dfrac{(f_o - f_e)^2}{f_e} =$ $\dfrac{(42-29.68)^2}{29.68} =$ $\dfrac{151.78}{29.68} = 5.11$	$\dfrac{(f_o - f_e)^2}{f_e} =$ $\dfrac{(24-22.26)^2}{22.26} =$ $\dfrac{3.03}{22.26} = .14$
	Male	$\dfrac{(f_o - f_e)^2}{f_e} =$ $\dfrac{(30-18.80)^2}{18.80} =$ $\dfrac{125.44}{18.80} = 6.67$	$\dfrac{(f_o - f_e)^2}{f_e} =$ $\dfrac{(32-29.14)^2}{29.14} =$ $\dfrac{8.18}{29.14} = .28$	$\dfrac{(f_o - f_e)^2}{f_e} =$ $\dfrac{(14-26.32)^2}{26.32} =$ $\dfrac{151.78}{26.32} = 5.77$	$\dfrac{(f_o - f_e)^2}{f_e} =$ $\dfrac{(18-19.74)^2}{19.74} =$ $\dfrac{3.03}{19.74} = .15$

$$\chi^2 = \Sigma \left[\frac{(f_o - f_e)^2}{f_e} \right]$$
$$= 5.92 + .25 + 5.11 + .14 + 6.67 + .28 + 5.77 + .15$$
$$= 24.29$$

Now let's calculate χ^2. Apply Formula (18.1) to the observed and expected frequencies in Table 18.3, as shown in Table 18.4:

$$\chi^2 = \Sigma \left[\frac{(f_o - f_e)^2}{f_e} \right]$$

$$= 5.92 + .25 + 5.11 + .14 + 6.67 + .28 + 5.77 + .15$$

$$= 24.29$$

Under the null hypothesis, sample χ^2 values for tests of independence follow the sampling distribution of χ^2 with $(R-1)(C-1)$ degrees of freedom, where R is the number of rows and C is the number of columns.[2]

[2]"Columns" in the two-variable case is equivalent to "categories" in the one-variable case.

Degrees of freedom:
Two-variable χ^2

$$df = (R-1)(C-1) \qquad (18.6)$$

For the present problem, $df = (2-1)(4-1) = 3$.

If H_0 is false, the sample χ^2 will tend to be larger according to the degree of dependence in the population. As before, the region of rejection is therefore placed in the upper tail of the χ^2 distribution. For $df = 3$, Table F shows the critical value to be $\chi^2_{.05} = 7.81$. Because the sample χ^2 of 24.29 exceeds this critical value, H_0 is rejected. You conclude that voter preference is dependent to some degree on sex of the respondent.

18.11   The χ^2 Test of Independence: Summarizing the Steps

We can now summarize the two-variable χ^2 test of independence for the current example.

Step 1   *Formulate the statistical hypotheses and select a level of significance.*
The statistical hypotheses are:

H_0: Independence in the population of the row and column variables (in this case, voter preference and sex of respondent)
H_1: Any state of affairs other than that specified in H_0

The level of significance is $\alpha = .05$.

Step 2   *Determine the desired sample size and select the sample.*
A sample of 200 registered voters is selected.

Step 3   *Calculate the necessary sample statistics.*

- Construct a contingency table and, as described in Section 18.9 and shown in Table 18.3, calculate the expected frequency for each cell.
- Use Formula (18.1) to compute χ^2 from the observed and expected frequencies, as shown in Table 18.4. Here, $\chi^2 = 24.29$.

Step 4   *Identify the critical χ^2 value.*
With $df = (R-1)(C-1) = 3$, $\chi^2_{.05} = 7.81$ (Table F).

Step 5   *Make the statistical decision and form conclusion.*
The sample χ^2 of 24.29 falls beyond the critical value, and the null hypothesis of independence is rejected. You conclude that voter preference is dependent to some degree on sex of the respondent.

As in the one-variable case, the alternative hypothesis includes many possibilities. Clearly, dependence can occur in various ways—more so as the number of rows and columns increases. When a significant χ^2 is obtained, comparing the magnitude of the various cell discrepancies that make up the sample χ^2 often can throw light on the source(s) of "dependence" between the two variables. In the present case, for example, you see that the largest contributions to χ^2 are associated with the cells for Martzial (5.92, 6.67) and Dunton (5.11, 5.77). By also noting the relative value of the f_o's and f_e's for these two candidates, you conclude that Martzial appears to be more popular among males, whereas Dunton is more popular among females.

18.12   The 2 × 2 Contingency Table

There is a shortcut for calculating χ^2 when a contingency table has only two rows and two columns:

Chi-square for a
2 × 2 table

$$\chi^2 = \frac{n(AD - BC)^2}{(A + B)(C + D)(A + C)(B + D)} \tag{18.7}$$

where: n is the total number cases; A, B, C, and D are the *obtained* frequencies in the four cells of the contingency table (as shown in Table 18.5).

The data in Table 18.5 are from a fictitious study in which a sample of fourth-grade students with reading difficulties received either an innovative reading program or the reading program presently used in their school district. Suppose that a researcher subsequently noted, for each student, whether or not the student scored

Table 18.5   A 2 × 2 Contingency Table: The Incidence of End-of-Year Reading Proficiency among Students in an "Innovative" versus "Standard" Reading Program

		Is Student Proficient?		
		Yes	No	f_{row}
Reading Program	**Innovative**	A 46	B 15	61 (A+B)
	Standard	C 10	D 49	59 (C+D)
	f_{col}	56 (A + C)	64 (B + D)	$n = 120$

"proficient" on the reading portion of the state test administered at the end of the school year. Let's apply Formula (18.7) to these data:

$$\chi^2 = \frac{120\big[(46)(49) - (15)(10)\big]^2}{(46+15)(10+49)(46+10)(15+49)}$$

$$= \frac{120\big[2{,}254 - 150\big]^2}{(61)(59)(56)(64)}$$

$$= \frac{120\big[4{,}426{,}816\big]}{12{,}898{,}816}$$

$$= 41.18$$

With $(2-1)(2-1) = 1$ *df*, the critical χ^2 value is 6.63 ($\alpha = .01$). The sample χ^2 easily exceeds $\chi^2_{.01}$, and the null hypothesis of independence is rejected. The conclusion is that, in the population sampled, students who receive the innovative reading program are more likely to become proficient readers than students receiving the standard program.

18.13   Testing a Difference Between Two Proportions

Recall from Section 18.6 that when $df = 1$, the one-variable χ^2 is equivalent to testing a hypothesis about a single proportion. Similarly, the application of χ^2 to a 2×2 table ($df = 1$) is equivalent to **testing a difference between two proportions** from independent samples. For the data in Table 18.5, the null and alternative hypotheses could be written as follows:

$$H_0\!: \pi_{\text{innovative}} - \pi_{\text{standard}} = 0$$

$$H_1\!: \pi_{\text{innovative}} - \pi_{\text{standard}} \neq 0$$

$\pi_{\text{innovative}}$ is the proportion of innovative-group students in the population who subsequently show reading proficiency; π_{standard} is the same figure for students receiving the standard reading program. The *sample* proportions are $46/61 = .75$ for innovative-group students and $10/59 = .17$ for standard-group students, resulting in a sample difference of $.75 - .17 = .58$. The sample χ^2 of 41.18 supports the rejection of $H_0\!: \pi_{\text{innovative}} - \pi_{\text{standard}} = 0$.

Because χ^2 has one degree of freedom, a one-tailed test is possible. Had this researcher advanced a directional alternative hypothesis, say, $H_0\!: \pi_{\text{innovative}} - \pi_{\text{standard}} > 0$, the (one-tailed) critical χ^2 value would have been $\chi^2_{.01} = 5.41$.

18.14   The Independence of Observations

The chi-square test statistic requires the assumption that the observed frequencies are independent of one another. For the one- and two-variable cases alike, each respondent must be represented by one—and only one—observed frequency. In Table 18.2, for example, each individual is represented in only one of the four cells: a respondent is classified as either male *or* female, and his or her preferred candidate is limited to *one* of the four choices. In general, the set of observations will not be completely independent when their number exceeds the number of respondents. For example, imagine that in a sample of 50 you determine the number of people who are either "for" or "against" a controversial issue, and you do this *before* they view a video on the topic and then again *after* they view the video. This sample of 50 individuals consequently yields a 2×2 contingency table comprising $(50)(2) = 100$ observations: 50 before the video, 50 after. In this case, the χ^2 test statistic is not appropriate, and other procedures should be used.[3]

18.15 χ^2 *and Quantitative Variables*

The χ^2 examples in this chapter have all involved *qualitative* variables—that is, variables having nominal scales where observations differ "in kind" (e.g., school board candidate, sex of respondent). As we indicated at the outset, the one- and two-variable χ^2 tests apply equally to quantitative variables, where observations differ "in magnitude."[4]

Consider the following survey item, which is an example of an ordinal scale:

Students Should Be Required to Wear School Uniforms				
A	B	C	D	E
strongly disagree	disagree	undecided	agree	strongly agree

Let's say you give a survey containing this item to a random sample of 60 students at your local high school. The observed frequencies for this item are 5, 9, 19, 17, and 10. Each observed frequency is the number of students selecting a particular response option (e.g., 5 students selected "A"), which you then compare with the frequency expected under the null hypothesis. (For example, perhaps H_0 is $\pi_A = \pi_B = \pi_C = \pi_D = \pi_E$, in which case $f_e = 12$ for each of the five options.) Using Formula (18.1), you calculate χ^2 ($df = 5 - 1 = 4$), compare the sample χ^2 with the appropriate critical χ^2 value ($\chi^2_{.05} = 9.49$, $\chi^2_{.01} = 13.28$), and make your statistical decision regarding H_0.

What if a variable rests on an interval or ratio scale? For example, maybe one of your variables is a test score. Here, you can group the scores into a smaller number of class intervals as described in Chapter 2 and treat the class intervals as categories. The sample χ^2 is then calculated in the usual manner.

---

[3]For example, an appropriate test for this design would be McNemar's test for correlated proportions (see Glass & Hopkins, 1996, pp. 339–340).

[4]You may wish to revisit Section 1.5, where we discuss qualitative and quantitative variables and scales of measurement.

For qualitative and quantitative variables alike, remember that the observations to be analyzed in a χ^2 problem are *frequencies* (rather than scores, ratings, or rankings).

18.16   Other Considerations

Small Expected Frequencies

Sampling distributions of χ^2 begin to depart from the theoretical distributions in Table F as the *expected* frequencies approach small size. How small is too small? For many years, a conservative rule of thumb has been that each expected cell frequency should be at least 5 where $df > 1$ and at least 10 where $df = 1$. In addition, researchers were encouraged to use the "Yates correction for continuity" for χ^2 applications involving 2×2 tables, particularly if any expected frequency fell below 5. This advice now appears to be unnecessarily conservative. For example, it has been shown that χ^2 will give accurate results when the average expected frequency is as low as 2 (e.g., Glass & Hopkins, 1996, p. 335).

Sample Size

Although it may not be readily apparent, the magnitude of χ^2 depends directly on n. If you use samples 10 times as large and the proportion of cases in each cell remains the same, you will expect χ^2 statistics 10 times as large—even though the number of categories, and thus df, remain the same. Here again, you run into the problem of sample size and the distinction between significance and importance. In short, very large samples will tend to give significant χ^2 values even when the discrepancies between observed and expected frequencies appear to be unimportant. This caveat applies equally to the χ^2 goodness-of-fit test and the χ^2 test of independence.

18.17   Summary

The sample data analyzed in earlier chapters consisted primarily of *score* data. In this chapter, our concern is with *frequency* data—that is, the numbers of individuals falling into various categories. In the one-variable case, the χ^2 goodness-of-fit test, the categories are based on a single variable. In the two-variable case, the χ^2 test of independence, the categories (cells) are based on the possible combinations of outcomes for two variables. Both tests can be applied to variables that are either qualitative (nominal scale) or quantitative (ordinal, interval, or ratio scales)—as long as the observations to be analyzed are in the form of *frequencies*.

In the one-variable case, the null hypothesis to be tested can be formulated in terms of the proportions of cases in the population that fall into each of the categories. The alternative hypothesis is very broad and encompasses every state of affairs other than that specified in the null hypothesis. The overall scheme for the test involves determining whether the discrepancies between the observed frequencies (f_o's) and the frequencies expected under H_0 (f_e's) are greater than would be anticipated on the basis of sampling variation alone. The expected frequencies are computed by multiplying the hypothesized proportions by n, sample size. The discrepancies between observed and expected frequencies are summarized in a sample χ^2 statistic. If H_0 is true, the sample χ^2 values follow the theoretical sampling distribution of χ^2 with $C - 1$ degrees of freedom, where C is the number of categories. Since larger discrepancies, regardless of direction, result in larger χ^2 values, a single region of rejection to the right is used for the test, although the test by its nature is nondirectional. When $df > 1$ and H_0 is rejected, adequate interpretation usually requires inspection of the relative value of the various discrepancies that make up the sample χ^2. In the one-variable case, where there are just two categories, the null hypothesis can be formulated as a test of a single proportion. This test can be directional or nondirectional, as desired.

In the two-variable case, the frequencies are crosstabulated in a bivariate frequency distribution called a contingency table. Here, the usual null hypothesis is that the two variables are independent. The alternative hypothesis is again very broad; it is that the two variables are related in some (any) way. If two variables are independent in the population, the proportional distributions of frequencies are the same for each row—or equivalently, for each column. This translates to a convenient formula for calculating each cell's expected frequency: $f_e = (f_{row})(f_{col})/n$. A χ^2 statistic, comparing observed frequencies with expected frequencies, is then computed. A χ^2 larger than the critical value for $(R - 1)(C - 1)$ degrees of freedom leads to rejection of H_0 and to the conclusion that the two variables are dependent in some way. When $df > 1$, adequate interpretation of a significant χ^2 in the two-variable case requires further inspection of the observed and expected proportions. For a 2×2 contingency table, the null hypothesis can be stated as a test of the difference between two proportions, and the alternative hypothesis can be either directional or nondirectional. A shortcut computational procedure is available for the 2×2 table.

A critical assumption when one is conducting a χ^2 analysis is that the observations are independent of one another. That is, each individual must be represented by one—and only one—observed frequency.

Reading the Research: χ^2 Goodness-of-Fit Test

Apodaca-Tucker and Slate (2002) used a series of χ^2 goodness-of-fit tests to compare the perceptions of public and private elementary school principals regarding decision-making authority. Both groups of principals were asked whether they felt each of several stakeholders (e.g., administrators, parents, teachers) had "no influence," "some influence," or "major influence" with respect to a variety of policy issues. For example, the vast majority (88.6%) of private school principals reported that administrators have a "major influence" on the setting of curricular guidelines and standards, whereas roughly half (54.1%) of the public school principals held this sentiment. Almost four times as many public school principals believed that administrators had only "some influence" in this policy area (39.4%), compared to the 10.4% of private school principals who felt this way. The authors reported that a "chi-square revealed the presence of a statistically significant difference in the degree of principal influence in the setting of curricular guidelines and standards, $\chi^2(2) = 72.07, p < .0001.$"

Source: Apodaca-Tucker, M. T., & Slate, J. R. (2002, April 28). School-based management: Views from public and private elementary school principals. *Education Policy Analysis Archives, 10*(23). Retrieved [September 2, 2002] from http://epaa.asu.edu/epaa/v10n23.html.

Case Study: Great Expectations

We use data from the Wyoming eleventh-grade state assessment to illustrate applications of the χ^2 goodness-of-fit test, χ^2 test of a single proportion, and χ^2 test of independence.

In Wyoming, four performance levels are used for reporting student performance on the state assessment: novice, partially proficient, proficient, and advanced. Table 18.6 presents the frequency and proportion of eleventh-grade students falling in each performance level on the reading and math portions of this assessment. For example, of the 6711 eleventh graders in Wyoming, 896 (13%) were advanced in reading and 820 (12%) were advanced in math. Table 18.7 displays the results for a single school district, which we have given the pseudonym SFM #1. As you see, the SFM #1 results depart to some extent from the statewide profiles in this particular year. But are these differences statistically significant?[5]

Our first goal was to test, separately for each content area, whether the performance-level proportions in SFM #1 are significantly different from the respective statewide proportions. Each null hypothesis is that the district and statewide proportions are identical. Thus, for reading, H_0: $\pi_{nov} = .18$, $\pi_{partprof} = .32$, $\pi_{prof} = .37$, $\pi_{adv} = .13$; and for math, H_0: $\pi_{nov} = .20$, $\pi_{partprof} = .40$, $\pi_{prof} = .28$, $\pi_{adv} = .12$. Each H_1 is any condition other than that specified in H_0.

We obtained $\chi^2 = 8.46$ for reading and $\chi^2 = 16.97$ for math. Because both calculated χ^2 values exceed $\chi^2_{.05} = 7.81$ ($df = 3$; see Table F in Appendix C), we

Table 18.6   Wyoming Statewide Results on the Eleventh-Grade Reading and Mathematics Assessments ($n = 6711$)

	Reading		Mathematics	
	f	π	f	π
Novice	1242	.18	1353	.20
Partially Proficient	2122	.32	2650	.40
Proficient	2451	.37	1886	.28
Advanced	896	.13	820	.12

[5]Perhaps you find it odd that we regard district data—based on *all* students in SFM #1—as a "sample." We subscribe to the view that district data can be treated as a sample of a larger, decidedly theoretical, population of observations. This argument applies to school-level data as well. Referring to the latter, Cronbach, Linn, Brennan, and Haertel (1997) perhaps said it best: "an infinite population could be assumed to exist for each school, and the pupils tested could be conceived of as a random sample from the population associated with the school" (p. 391). Furthermore, "[t]o conclude on the basis of an assessment that a school is effective as an institution requires the assumption, implicit or explicit, that the positive outcome would appear with a student body other than the present one, drawn from the same population" (p. 393). Thus, school- or district-level data arguably can be regarded as a random sample, drawn from the theoretical universe of students that the particular school or district represents.

Table 18.7   SFM #1 District Results on the Eleventh-Grade
Reading and Mathematics Assessments ($n = 266$)

	Reading		Mathematics	
	f	P	f	P
Novice	38	.14	46	.17
Partially Proficient	89	.34	104	.39
Proficient	90	.34	64	.24
Advanced	49	.18	52	.20

rejected the null hypothesis that SFM #1 performance-level proportions are equal to the statewide proportions. Compared to the statewide proportions in both content areas, SFM #1 appears to have a smaller proportion of eleventh graders at the novice level and a larger proportion at the advanced level.

What would happen if we collapsed the four performance levels into the simple dichotomy *proficient* (combining proficient and advanced) vs. *not proficient* (combining novice and partially proficient)? As you saw in this chapter, the one-variable case is equivalent to testing a single proportion when the variable has only two categories (1 *df*). Here, we chose to focus on the proportion of students who are *proficient*. (Of course, we could have just as easily focused on the proportion of *not proficient* students.)

We used the χ^2 test of a single proportion to determine whether the SFM #1 proportions for reading, $P_{prof} = .52$ (i.e., $.34 + .18$), and math, $P_{prof} = .44$ (i.e., $.24 + .20$), are significantly different from their respective statewide proportions: .50 and .40. We obtained $\chi^2 = 0.43$ for reading and $\chi^2 = 1.77$ for math, neither of which exceeded $\chi^2_{.05} = 3.84$ (1 *df*, two-tailed). The null hypothesis was thus retained, and we concluded that the proportion of eleventh-grade students who are proficient in reading and math in SFM #1 does not differ from statewide results. The 95% confidence interval for reading extends from .46 to .58 and, for math, from .38 to .50. Naturally, each confidence interval includes the value of π that had been specified in the retained null hypothesis (.50 and .40, respectively).

Finally, we determined whether the SFM #1 reading and math proficiency rates are the same for boys and girls (using the dichotomous proportions). This calls for a χ^2 test of independence. Both null hypotheses are that sex and proficiency are independent: Whether or not an eleventh-grade student is proficient (in reading or in math) is unrelated to whether that student is male or female. The alternative hypothesis is that proficiency and sex are associated in some way.[6]

---

[6]Because there are only two categories for each variable (i.e., *df* = 1), this analysis is equivalent to testing the difference between two proportions (e.g., the proportion of proficient males vs. the proportion of proficient females). Further, a directional H_1 may be formulated if deemed appropriate. For example, perhaps SFM #1 has a history of higher reading proficiency for females than for males. In this case, district officials may want to know whether there is evidence of this trend in the present data. Toward this end, they would formulate the directional alternative hypothesis that the reading proficiency proportion for females is higher than that for males (i.e., H_1: $\pi_{females} - \pi_{males} > 0$).

Table 18.8   SFM #1 District Results on the Eleventh-Grade State Reading Assessment: Proficiency × Sex Contingency Table ($\chi^2 = 3.68$, $p = .055$)

	Not Proficient	Proficient	f_{row}
Female	$f_o = 60$ $f_e = 67.8$	$f_o = 82$ $f_e = 74.2$	142
Male	$f_o = 67$ $f_e = 59.2$	$f_o = 57$ $f_e = 64.8$	124
f_{col}	127	139	$n = 266$

The data appear in Tables 18.8 and 18.9, which, for illustrative purposes, also include expected frequencies. For example, you can see that more females, and fewer males, are proficient in reading than would be expected, whereas in math, the discrepancies between observed and expected frequencies are negligible. What about statistical significance? We obtained $\chi^2 = .00034$ ($p = .985$) for math, which is about as statistically nonsignificant as a result can get! Among eleventh graders in SFM #1, then, math proficiency and sex appear to be unrelated indeed. For reading, $\chi^2 = 3.68$ ($p = .055$), which falls just short of statistical significance at the .05 level. However, because the p-value (.055) is so close to the arbitrary level of significance (.05), we are not inclined to dismiss this "marginally significant" finding altogether.[7] Analyses in subsequent years should clarify this possible relationship between sex and reading proficiency in SFM #1.

Table 18.9   SFM #1 District Results on the Eleventh-Grade State Mathematics Assessment: Proficiency × Sex Contingency Table ($\chi^2 = .00034$, $p = .985$)

	Not Proficient	Proficient	f_{row}
Female	$f_o = 80$ $f_e = 80.1$	$f_o = 62$ $f_e = 61.9$	142
Male	$f_o = 70$ $f_e = 69.9$	$f_o = 54$ $f_e = 54.1$	124
f_{col}	150	116	$n = 266$

[7]Indeed, if a *directional* H_1 had been deemed appropriate, this sample χ^2 would have exceeded the one-tailed critical value ($\chi^2_{.05} = 2.71$) and been declared statistically significant.

Suggested Computer Exercises

Access the **sophomores** data file.

1. Use this sample of students to test whether eighth graders are equally likely to take either algebra or general math (i.e., .50 take algebra, .50 take general math).

   (a) provide H_0;

   (b) compute χ^2;

   (c) complete the test at $\alpha = .05$.

2. Repeat the test above, this time testing the observed proportions against .33 algebra and .67 general math.

3. Examine whether there is a relationship between gender and eighth-grade math course selection. In doing so,

   (a) construct a contingency table that includes both observed and expected frequency counts;

   (b) compute the necessary tests at $\alpha = .05$;

   (c) draw final conclusions.

Exercises

Identify, Define, or Explain

Terms and Concepts

frequency data versus score data
chi-square
one-variable case
χ^2 goodness-of-fit test
two-variable case
χ^2 test of independence
observed frequencies
expected frequencies
sampling distribution of χ^2
test of a single proportion

confidence interval for π
contingency table
crosstabulation
null hypothesis of independence
expected frequencies in a contingency table
test of independence
testing a difference between two proportions
the independence of observations
quantitative variables

Symbols

χ^2 f_o f_e π P C R

Questions and Problems

Note: Answers to starred (*) items are presented in Appendix B.

*1. Give the critical χ^2 values and df for testing each of the following null hypotheses for one-variable problems at $\alpha = .05$ and $\alpha = .01$.

   (a) H_0: $\pi_1 = \pi_2 = \pi_3 = \pi_4$

   (b) H_0: $\pi_1 = .10,\ \pi_2 = .10,\ \pi_3 = .80$

   (c) H_0: $\pi_1 = .25,\ \pi_2 = .75$

   (d) H_0: $\pi_1 = \pi_2$

   (e) H_0: $\pi_1 = .50,\ \pi_2 = \pi_3 = \pi_4 = \pi_5 = \pi_6 = .10$

2. (a) For which H_0 in Problem 1 would a directional H_1 be possible? (Explain.)

(b) What is the *one-tailed* value for $\chi^2_{.05}$ and for $\chi^2_{.01}$?

***3.** A researcher wishes to determine whether four commercially available standardized achievement tests differ in their popularity. He obtains a random sample of 60 school districts in his region of the country and asks each superintendent which standardized achievement test is used. (Assume that each district uses such a test, and only four tests exist.) The researcher has no basis for hypothesizing which test, if any, is preferred by school districts. The results are as follows:

Test:	A	B	C	D
frequency of selection:	18	6	12	24

(a) Give, in symbolic form, two equivalent statements of H_0 for this situation.

(b) Can H_1 be written in a single symbolic statement? (Explain.)

(c) Compute the expected frequencies under H_0. (Do they sum to n?)

(d) Compute χ^2 and test H_0 at $\alpha = .01$.

(e) From this χ^2, what is your general conclusion? That is, do the four achievement tests appear to differ in popularity?

4. In the χ^2 test, why is it that only the area in the upper tail of the χ^2 distribution is of interest?

***5.** Suppose it is known in a large urban school district that four out of five teenagers who join a gang subsequently drop out of high school. A "stay in school" intervention is instituted for a sample of 45 gang members. It is later found that 30 of these students have remained in school and 15 dropped out. Is the intervention effective?

(a) Give H_0 and H_1 in terms of the proportion of gang members who drop out of high school.

(b) Compute χ^2 and perform the test at $\alpha = .05$.

(c) Draw final conclusions.

***6.** Regarding Problem 5:

(a) Calculate the proportion of gang members who dropped out of high school.

(b) Use Formulas (18.3) and (18.4) to construct and interpret a 95% confidence interval for π.

(c) Use Figure 18.3 to obtain an approximate confidence interval for π. How does this compare to what you obtained in Problem 6b?

7. The 72 college students in an educational psychology class take a multiple-choice midterm exam. The professor wishes to test the hypothesis that students guessed at random on the options for question 36. The frequency of responses for that item was as follows:

Option:	A	B	C	D
Frequency:	15	40	5	12

(a) Give H_0.

(b) Compute χ^2 and complete the test at $\alpha = .01$.

(c) Draw final conclusions.

8. You wish to determine whether a friend's die is "loaded." You roll the die 120 times and obtain the following results:

Side coming up:	1	2	3	4	5	6
Number observed:	16	16	10	20	28	30

(a) Give H_0 for this situation (use fractions).

(b) Can a single H_1 be written? (Explain.)

(c) Compute χ^2, complete the test ($\alpha = .05$), and draw your conclusion regarding this die.

(d) Do these results prove the die is loaded and thus unfair? (Explain.)

9. Give the critical χ^2 values for testing the null hypothesis of independence at $\alpha = .05$ and $\alpha = .01$ for each of the following contingency tables:

(a) 2 × 3 table

(b) 2 × 6 table

(c) 3 × 5 table

(d) 2 × 2 table

*10. A sample of 163 prospective voters is identified from both rural and urban communities. Each voter is asked for his or her position on the upcoming "gay rights" state refer endum. The results are as follows:

	In favor	Opposed
Rural	35	55
Urban	53	20

(a) Given this situation, state (in words) the null hypothesis of independence in terms of proportions.

(b) Determine f_o and f_e for each of the four cells of this 2 × 2 contingency table. Present this information in a 2 × 2 table that includes row totals, column totals, and the grand total. (For each row, does $\Sigma f_e = f_{row}$?)

(c) Compute χ^2 (using Formula [18.1]) and complete the test at $\alpha = .05$ and at $\alpha = .01$ (two-tailed).

(d) What is your general conclusion from this χ^2?

(e) What is your general interpretation of this finding, based on a comparison of the f_o's and f_e's?

11. (a) Why is a directional H_1 possible in the Problem 10 scenario?

(b) Offer an example of a directional H_1 (in words).

*12. Using the data given in Problem 10, calculate χ^2 from Formula (18.7).

*13. Forty volunteers participate in an experiment on attitude change. An attitude item is completed by these individuals both before and after they watch a spirited debate on the topic. The following data are obtained:

	Response to Attitude Statement		
	Agree	**Undecided**	**Disagree**
Before	8	20	12
After	18	12	10

The researcher calculates $\chi^2 = 6.03$ and, because $\chi^2_{.05} = 5.99$, rejects the null hypothesis of independence. After calculating the obtained proportions within each of the six cells in this 2×3 contingency table (i.e., $f_o \div$ row total), the researcher concludes that watching the debate seems to have shifted many of the "undecided" individuals into the "agree" category. What critical mistake did this researcher make?

14. Is sexual activity among adolescent females related to whether one is a smoker or non-smoker? Harriet Imrey, in an article appearing in *The Journal of Irreproducible Results* (Imrey, 1983), provided the following data from a sample of 508 girls between the ages of 14 and 17:

	Sexually Active	**Sexually Inactive**
Smokers	24	122
Nonsmokers	11	351

(a) Given this situation, state two equivalent expressions (in words) for the null hypothesis of independence in terms of proportions.

(b) State H_1 (nondirectional) in words for each H_0 in Problem 14a.

(c) Determine f_o and f_e for each of the four cells of this 2×2 contingency table. Present this information in a 2×2 table that includes row totals, column totals, and the grand total.

(d) Compute χ^2 (using Formula [18.1]) and complete the test at $\alpha = .05$.

(e) What is your general conclusion from this significant χ^2?

(f) Translate each obtained frequency into a proportion based on its row frequency. What interpretation seems likely?

15. Using the data given in Problem 14, calculate χ^2 from Formula (18.7).

*16. In a particular county, a random sample of 225 adults are asked for their preferences among three individuals who wish to be the state's next commissioner of education. Respondents also are asked to report their annual household income. The results:

	Candidate		
Household Income	**Jadallah**	**Yung**	**Pandiscio**
less than $20,000	8	11	6
$20,000–$39,999	23	17	18
$40,000–$59,999	20	22	20
$60,000 or more	25	33	22

(a) Stated very generally, what is the null hypothesis of independence in this situation?

(b) Determine f_o and f_e for each of the 12 cells of this 3×4 contingency table. Present this information in a 3×4 table that includes row totals, column totals, and the grand total. (For each row, does $\Sigma f_e = f_{row}$?)

(c) Compute χ^2 (using Formula [18.1]) and complete the test at $\alpha = .05$.

(d) What is your general conclusion from this χ^2?

*17. Consider the data given in Problem 16. Test the null hypothesis that all candidates are equally popular ($\alpha = .05$).

18. In any χ^2 problem, what is the relationship between the row frequency and that row's expected frequencies?

CHAPTER 19

Statistical "Power" (and How to Increase It)

19.1 The Power of a Statistical Test

A research team is investigating the relative effectiveness of two instructional programs for teaching early literacy skills to preschool students. With the cooperation of school officials in volunteer schools, the team randomly divides the schools into two groups. One group of schools will use Program A for preschool literacy instruction, and the other group will use Program B. At the end of the school year, first-grade students in both groups complete an assessment of early literacy skills, and the team then compares mean scores by testing H_0: $\mu_1 - \mu_2 = 0$ against the two-tailed H_1: $\mu_1 - \mu_2 \neq 0$.

Suppose that the null hypothesis *is actually false* and, in fact, students who receive Program A instruction tend to acquire more advanced literacy skills than Program B students do. This would mean that μ_1 is higher than μ_2 and thus $\mu_1 - \mu_2 > 0$. (Our scenario is utterly fanciful, of course, for the research team would not "know" that H_0 is false. If they did, there would be no need to perform the research in the first place!)

Continuing in this hypothetical vein, suppose that the team repeated the experiment many times under exactly the same conditions. Would you expect *every* repetition to result in the rejection of H_0? We trust that your answer is a resounding "no!" Because random sampling variation will lead to somewhat different values of $\overline{X}_1 - \overline{X}_2$ from experiment to experiment, some of the time H_0 will be rejected but at other times it will be retained—even though it is actually false. Imagine the team keeps a record and finds that 33%, or .33, of the repetitions result in the decision to reject H_0 and 67%, or .67, lead to the decision to retain H_0. You say, then, that the **power** of the test of H_0 equals .33. That is:

> The power of a statistical test is the probability, given that H_0 is false, of obtaining sample results that will lead to the rejection of H_0.

"Power of a test" clearly is an important concept. To put it in other words, a powerful test is one that has a high probability of claiming that a difference or an association exists when it really does.

The procedures for calculating power from sample results fall outside our purpose in writing this book. Instead, we will concentrate on the general concept of power, the factors that affect it, and what this all means for selecting sample size. We focus mostly on the test of the difference between two independent means, because it provides a relatively straightforward context for developing some rather abstract notions. However, the principles that we discuss are general and apply to a wide variety of research situations and statistical tests.

19.2   *Power and Type II Error*

As you learned in Section 11.7, two types of errors can occur in making the decision about a null hypothesis: in a Type I error you reject an H_0 that is true, and in a Type II error you retain an H_0 that is false. (You may wish to review that section before reading on.)

Power and the probability of committing a Type II error stand in opposition to each other. The probability of a Type II error is the probability of *retaining* the null hypothesis when it is false. Statisticians call this probability β (beta). In contrast, power is the probability of *rejecting* the null hypothesis when it is false. Power, then, is equal to 1 minus the probability of a Type II error, or $1 - \beta$.

To illustrate the relationship between power and Type II error, let's return to the research team, for whom $\beta = .67$ and power is $1 - .67 = .33$. Look at Figure 19.1, which presents two sampling distributions of differences between means. The distribution drawn with the dashed line is the sampling distribution under the null hypothesis, $H_0: \mu_1 - \mu_2 = 0$, which, in our fanciful scenario, is known to be false. Note the regions of rejection and retention for this sampling distribution ($\alpha = .05$,

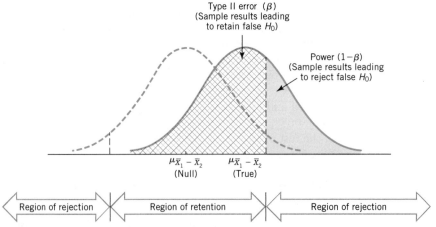

Figure 19.1   Power and Type II error: the sampling distribution of a difference between two means under the null hypothesis (drawn with dashed line) versus the true sampling distribution (solid line).

two-tailed). The *true* sampling distribution is shown with a solid line. Because in reality there are higher literacy skills among Program A recipients ($\mu_1 - \mu_2 > 0$), this distribution sits somewhat to the right of the H_0 distribution. Bear in mind that the actual sample results come from the true sampling distribution, *not* the sampling distribution under the (false) null hypothesis. Thus the cross-hatched area of the true distribution is the proportion of all sample results, across unlimited repetitions, that lead to *retaining* the false H_0. This proportion, $\beta = .67$, is the probability of a Type II error. The shaded area is the proportion of all sample results that lead to *rejecting* the false H_0. This corresponds to .33 of the area $(1 - \beta)$, which, as you know, is the power of the research team's statistical test.

You probably are not alone if you are concerned about the low power of this test. After all, power equal to .33 means that there is only one chance in three that the investigator will uncover a difference *when one actually exists.* Two related questions immediately come to mind: What are the factors that affect power? How can you set up your research to ensure that your statistical test is adequately powerful? We will deal with these questions shortly. First, however, there is a preliminary matter we must consider.

19.3   *Effect Size (Revisited)*

Again, statistical power is the probability of rejecting H_0 when H_0 is false. But *when H_0 is false, it is false by some degree*—that is, the true parameter value can differ by a small or large amount from what has been hypothesized in H_0. It is much easier to uncover a difference between μ_1 and μ_2 when $\mu_1 - \mu_2$ is large than when it is small. To illustrate this, we first need a way to characterize the magnitude of the difference between μ_1 and μ_2. The convention is to use the familiar **effect size**.

As you saw in Section 14.8, the effect size, d, is used to capture the magnitude of a difference between two sample means. We will follow convention by using the Greek letter δ (delta) to symbolize a difference between two means in the *population* (Hedges & Olkin, 1985):

> Population effect size
> (mean difference)
>
> $$\delta = \frac{\mu_1 - \mu_2}{\sigma}$$
>
> Formula (19.1)

That is, δ is the difference between the population means relative to the population standard deviation.[1] Consider Figure 19.2, which shows pairs of population distributions that are separated by various degrees.[2] In Figure 19.2*a* there is no separation between μ_1 and μ_2; H_0: $\mu_1 - \mu_2 = 0$ is true and thus $d = 0$. In Figures 19.2*b* through

---

[1]This formula assumes homogeneity of variance ($\sigma_1^2 = \sigma_2^2 = \sigma^2$).

[2]We should emphasize that Figures 19.2*a–f* are *population distributions* of individual observations, unlike the *sampling distributions* of differences between two means in Figure 19.1.

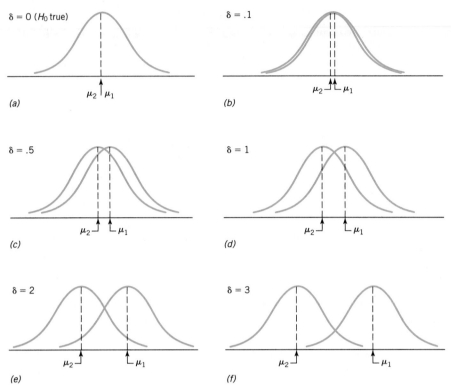

Figure 19.2   Separation between population distributions for various values of $\delta = (\mu_1 - \mu_2)/\sigma$.

19.2f, H_0 is false and the two populations show a progressively greater separation. For instance, the null hypothesis is only slightly off the mark in Figure 19.2b ($\delta = .1$); the two means are only one-tenth of a standard deviation apart, and the research team would most likely consider such a population difference as negligible. On the other hand, suppose that the true difference is as shown in, say, Figure 19.2e ($\delta = 2$). A population difference that large—two standard deviations—would surely be worthy of note.

19.4   *Factors Affecting Power: The Effect Size*

How is the size of the actual difference in the population, δ, related to the power of a statistical test? Let's assume that the research team tests $H_0: \mu_1 - \mu_2 = 0$ against the nondirectional alternative $H_1: \mu_1 - \mu_2 \neq 0$. The decision concerning H_0, you well know, will depend on the magnitude of the sample t ratio:

$$t = \frac{\overline{X}_1 - \overline{X}_2}{s_{\overline{X}_1 - \overline{X}_2}}$$

Consider for a moment the numerator, $\overline{X}_1 - \overline{X}_2$. The larger this difference, the larger the value of t and the more likely you will reject the hypothesis of no difference between μ_1 and μ_2. Now look again at the several situations in Figure 19.2. If you were to select a pair of random samples of a given size from the two populations, in which case would you be most likely to obtain a large difference between $\overline{X}_1 - \overline{X}_2$? Where $\delta = 3$, of course! Sample means *tend* to reflect the population means, particularly where n is large. Thus the greater the separation between μ_1 and μ_2, the more likely you are to obtain a large difference between $\overline{X}_1 - \overline{X}_2$, and thus a t ratio large enough to reject H_0. In summary:

> The larger the effect size, δ, the greater the power of a test of H_0: $\mu_1 - \mu_2 = 0$ against the nondirectional alternative H_1: $\mu_1 - \mu_2 \neq 0$.

The same principle holds for a one-tailed test as well, but with the qualification that the true difference, $\mu_1 - \mu_2$, must be in the direction specified in H_1.

Let's apply the principle above to the literacy study: the more the two instructional programs "truly" differ in their ability to develop literacy skills in preschool students, the more likely it is that the hypothesis of no difference will be rejected. And this is as it should be! You certainly want to have greater chance of rejecting the null hypothesis for differences that are large enough to be important than for those so small as to be negligible.

Effect size is a general concept and applies to situations other than the difference between two population means. In a correlational study, for instance, ρ typically serves as the measure of effect size—the degree to which two variables are correlated in the population of observations. The same principle applies to ρ as to δ: the larger the effect size, ρ, the greater the power of a test of H_0: $\rho = 0$. That is, you are much more likely to reject the hypothesis of no correlation when ρ is large (e.g., $\rho = .75$) than when ρ is small (e.g., $\rho = .15$).

19.5 Factors Affecting Power: Sample Size

The effect size is determined by the specific set of conditions under which the investigation is carried out. Given these conditions, there is no way of altering effect size for purposes of increasing power. You wouldn't want to anyway, because the resulting "effect" is the object of your investigation in the first place! However, there are other factors affecting power over which you can exercise control. *The most important of these is sample size.*

Actually, you already know this from earlier chapters, even though we did not use the term *power*. That is, you have learned that as sample size *increases*, the standard error *decreases*. You saw this with respect to both the standard error of the difference between means ($s_{\overline{X}_1 - \overline{X}_2}$; Section 14.8) and the standard error of r (s_r; Section 17.6). Other things being equal, a smaller standard error results in a larger t ratio and therefore in a greater likelihood of rejecting a false H_0. In other words:

> For any given effect size (other than zero), the larger the sample size, the greater the power of the statistical test.

In short, investigators who use large samples are much more likely to uncover effects in the population than are those who use small samples (assuming comparable effect sizes). This can be taken to an extreme, however. With very large samples, even the most trivial—and therefore unimportant—effect in the population can be detected by a statistical test. Or perhaps the effect is important, but the researcher uses a sample size twice as large as that necessary to detect such an effect. In either case, research resources are wasted.

The opposite is true as well. Because smaller samples lead to a larger standard error and less power, there is a greater chance of committing a Type II error as sample size is decreased. With insufficient sample size, then, the investigator may conclude "no effect" when, in fact, there is one.

Effect size and sample size indeed are important factors affecting the power of a statistical test. We will return to them after brief consideration of several additional factors.

19.6   *Additional Factors Affecting Power*

Level of Significance

Suppose the research team decides to use 20 cases in each of the two groups for purposes of testing $H_0: \mu_1 - \mu_2 = 0$ against $H_1: \mu_1 - \mu_2 \neq 0$. The resulting regions of rejection for $\alpha = .05$ are compared with those for $\alpha = .001$ in Figure 19.3. You can see that the regions for $\alpha = .05$ cover more territory than do the regions for $\alpha = .001$. This of course is true *by definition*, for the level of significance (α) specifies the *area* of the sampling distribution that will constitute the rejection region. As a consequence, if the research team uses $\alpha = .05$ rather than $\alpha = .001$, their obtained t ratio is more likely to fall in a region of rejection. This illustrates the following principle:

> The larger the value of α, the larger the regions of rejection and thus the greater the power. Inversely, the smaller the value of α, the less the power.

This is why a level of significance as low as .001 is seldom used by educational researchers. Such a "conservative" α increases the chances of committing a Type II error (retaining a false H_0). The added protection against a Type I error (rejecting a true H_0) that is afforded by $\alpha = .001$ typically is unnecessary in educational research, given the relatively benign consequences of Type I errors (compared, say, to medical research).

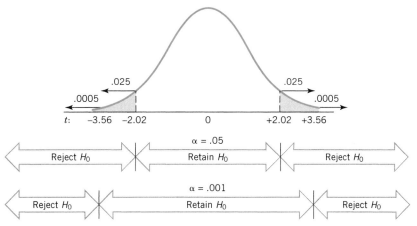

Figure 19.3 Comparison of the regions of rejection for $\alpha = .05$ and $\alpha = .001$ (two-tailed test), with 38 *df*.

One-Tailed Versus Two-Tailed Tests

As we showed in Section 11.11, you have a statistical advantage by correctly specifying a directional alternative hypothesis. That is, if you state a one-tailed H_1 *and you are correct*, then you have a larger critical region to work with and a greater likelihood of rejecting H_0 (see Figure 11.8). In such situations, then, the one-tailed test is more powerful than the two-tailed test. But always remember that the choice of the alternative hypothesis should flow from the logic of the investigation. If that logic forcefully leads to a one-tailed test, then you may welcome the increased power as a statistical bonus.

Use of Dependent Samples

Recall that the standard error of the difference between means is expected to be smaller for dependent samples than for independent samples (Section 15.2). The amount of reduction will depend on the similarity between the paired observations as specified by the size of r_{12} in Formula (15.1). Consequently, using dependent samples has an effect like that of increasing sample size. That is, the standard errors tend to be smaller; thus when the null hypothesis is false, the *t* ratios tend to be larger. This in turn leads to a greater chance of rejecting H_0.

> The use of dependent samples will normally increase the power of a test of H_0: $\mu_1 - \mu_2 = 0$. The amount of increase depends on the degree of dependence.

However, remember that you give up degrees of freedom by using dependent samples (Section 15.3). If you have a small sample, the increased power resulting from a smaller standard error may be offset by fewer *df* and, therefore, a larger critical value of *t* for testing H_0.

Other Considerations

We should acknowledge, if only in passing, the influence of research design and measurement considerations on the power of statistical tests. Other things being equal, you will have greater power by fashioning sound treatment conditions, using instruments and scoring procedures high in reliability, making valid interpretations of the data, and otherwise adhering to established principles of research design and measurement.

19.7   Significance versus Importance

The distinction between a statistically significant finding and an important one is a recurring theme in this book. As you well know by now, it is possible to have a "statistically significant" but "practically unimportant" sample result.

How great an effect (e.g., mean difference, correlation) in the population is large enough to be important? No statistician can tell you the answer. It is a question for the subject matter expert, and the answer will differ depending on the circumstances and values that characterize the particular setting. For example, a small effect may be important if it involves the risk of loss of life, but a larger effect may be relatively unimportant if it concerns only the presence or absence of an inconvenience. Thus an effect size of $\delta = .2$ could be important in one setting, whereas in another a δ of .5 might be of only moderate importance.

Cohen (1988), an authoritative source for the subject of effect size and power, suggested that in the absence of information to the contrary, it may be useful to consider $\delta = .2$ as small, $\delta = .5$ moderate, and $\delta = .8$ large. (You may recall this from Section 14.8). This suggestion has some value in cases that are difficult to decide. But fundamentally, the issue of importance must be resolved by the researcher in consideration of the substantive and methodological context of the investigation.

19.8   Selecting an Appropriate Sample Size

Clearly, you should select samples that are large enough to have a good chance of detecting an important effect in the population. Yet they should not be so large as to be wasteful of time and effort or to result in statistical significance when the effect is small and unimportant. How then do you determine the appropriate sample size?

Fortunately, there are tables to help you make this important judgment. Cohen (1988) provides sample size tables for a multitude of statistical tests, and we encourage you to consult this valuable source as the need arises. We will focus on two of these tables: one for tests of the difference between two independent means (H_0: $\mu_1 - \mu_2 = 0$) and one for tests of a single correlation coefficient (H_0: $\rho = 0$).

Whether you wish to test H_0: $\mu_1 - \mu_2 = 0$ or H_0: $\rho = 0$, follow these steps to determine the sample size appropriate for your investigation:

Step 1   *Specify the smallest effect size—either δ or ρ—that you want to be reasonably certain of detecting.* This is the minimum effect that, in your best judgment, is large enough to be considered "important." (This arguably is the most challenging step!)

Step 2   *Set the desired level of power*—the probability that your test will detect the effect specified in step 1. Cohen (1988) proposed the convention of setting power at .80, unless the investigator has a rationale for an alternative value.

Step 3   *Enter the values for effect size and power in Table 19.1 (for δ) or Table 19.2 (for ρ) and read off the desired sample size.* Both tables assume a level of significance of $\alpha = .05$ and include sample sizes for either one- or two-tailed tests.

Let's take a closer look, beginning with Table 19.1. Suppose that the research team investigating the effects of the two instructional programs decides that it would be important to know a population difference of $\delta = .30$ or larger. (The researchers believe that a difference this large would have implications for recommending one program over the other, whereas a smaller difference would not.) They set power at .80—that is, they want a probability of at least .80 of detecting a difference of $\delta = .30$ in the population. Finally, they adopt the 5% level of significance (two-tailed). Thus, they go to Table 19.1 with the following information:

$$\delta = .30$$
$$\text{power} = .80$$
$$\alpha = .05 \text{ (two-tailed)}$$

Table 19.1 provides the sample size—*in each group*—necessary to detect a given δ at the specified level of power. Its structure is fairly simple: possible values of δ are listed across the top, various levels of power are along the left side, and the necessary sample size appears where a row and column intersect. The upper half of Table 19.1 is for two-tailed tests, the lower half for one-tailed tests ($\alpha = .05$). For our scenario, a sample size of 175 appears where the row and column intersect. To detect, with a probability of .80, a difference as large as $\delta = .30$, the research team therefore needs 175 cases in each group.

You would follow the same general logic if you were planning a correlational study, except your interest would be in ρ and Table 19.2. This table is organized like

Table 19.1   Sample-Size Table for the t Test of H_0: $\mu_1 - \mu_2 = 0$ (Independent Samples, $\alpha = .05$): The Needed n (in Each Group) to Detect the Specified Effect, δ, at the Designated Power

						For Two-Tailed Tests ($\alpha=.05$) δ					
Power	**.10**	**.20**	**.30**	**.40**	**.50**	**.60**	**.70**	**.80**	**1.00**	**1.20**	**1.40**
.25	332	84	38	22	14	10	8	6	5	4	3
.50	769	193	86	49	32	22	17	13	9	7	5
.60	981	246	110	62	40	28	21	16	11	8	6
.70	1235	310	138	78	50	35	26	20	13	10	7
.75	1389	348	155	88	57	40	29	23	15	11	8
.80	1571	393	175	99	64	45	33	26	17	12	9
.85	1797	450	201	113	73	51	38	29	19	14	10
.90	2102	526	234	132	85	59	44	34	22	16	12
.95	2600	651	290	163	105	73	54	42	27	19	14
.99	3675	920	409	231	148	103	76	58	38	27	20

						For One-Tailed Tests ($\alpha=.05$) δ					
Power	**.10**	**.20**	**.30**	**.40**	**.50**	**.60**	**.70**	**.80**	**1.00**	**1.20**	**1.40**
.25	189	48	21	12	8	6	5	4	3	2	2
.50	542	136	61	35	22	16	12	9	6	5	4
.60	721	181	81	46	30	21	15	12	8	6	5
.70	942	236	105	60	38	27	20	15	10	7	6
.75	1076	270	120	68	44	31	23	18	11	8	6
.80	1237	310	138	78	50	35	26	20	13	9	7
.85	1438	360	160	91	58	41	30	23	15	11	8
.90	1713	429	191	108	69	48	36	27	18	13	10
.95	2165	542	241	136	87	61	45	35	22	16	12
.99	3155	789	351	198	127	88	65	50	32	23	17

Source: From *Statistical Power Analysis for the Behavioral Sciences* (Table 2.4.1, pp. 54–55) by J. Cohen, 1988, Hillsdale, NJ; Erlbaum. Copyright 1988 by Lawrence Erlbaum Associates. Adapted with permission.

Table 19.1 except that ρ, not δ, appears across the top. Let's go back to the correlation between spatial reasoning and mathematical ability (Section 17.4). Suppose that, having reviewed the literature on the relationships among cognitive aptitudes, you decide that you want to detect an effect of at least $\rho = .40$. You also decide to set power at .80. Thus,

$$\rho = .40$$
$$\text{power} = .80$$
$$\alpha = .05 \text{ (one-tailed)}$$

Table 19.2   Sample-Size Table for the *t* Test of H_0: $\rho = 0$ ($\alpha = .05$): The Needed *n* to Detect the Specified Effect, ρ, at the Designated Power

For Two-Tailed Tests ($\alpha = .05$)

ρ

Power	.10	.20	.30	.40	.50	.60	.70	.80	.90
.25	167	42	20	12	8	6	5	4	3
.50	385	96	42	24	15	10	7	6	4
.60	490	122	53	29	18	12	9	6	5
.70	616	153	67	37	23	15	10	7	5
.75	692	172	75	41	25	17	11	8	6
.80	783	194	85	46	28	18	12	9	6
.85	895	221	97	52	32	21	14	10	6
.90	1047	259	113	62	37	24	16	11	7
.95	1294	319	139	75	46	30	19	13	8
.99	1828	450	195	105	64	40	27	18	11

For One-Tailed Tests ($\alpha = .05$)

ρ

Power	.10	.20	.30	.40	.50	.60	.70	.80	.90
.25	97	24	12	8	6	4	4	3	3
.50	272	69	30	17	11	8	6	5	4
.60	361	91	40	22	14	10	7	5	4
.70	470	117	52	28	18	12	8	6	4
.75	537	134	59	32	20	13	9	7	5
.80	617	153	68	37	22	15	10	7	5
.85	717	178	78	43	26	17	12	8	6
.90	854	211	92	50	31	20	13	9	6
.95	1078	266	116	63	39	25	16	11	7
.99	1570	387	168	91	55	35	23	15	10

Source: From *Statistical Power Analysis for the Behavioral Sciences* (Table 3.4.1, pp. 101–102), by J. Cohen. 1988, Hillsdale. NJ: Erlbaum. Copyright 1988 by Lawrence Erlbaum Associates. Adapted with permission.

From Table 19.2, you find that a sample size of 37 is needed to uncover such an effect in the population.

By scanning down a particular *column* of either Table 19.1 or Table 19.2, you can see how sample size and power are related for a given effect size: more powerful tests require larger samples. Similarly, by moving across a particular *row* of either table, you see the relationship between sample size and effect size for a given level of power: smaller effects in the population require larger samples. Finally, by putting these two observations together, you see that small effects *and* high power demand very large samples (lower left corner). These insights, we hope you agree, confirm points made earlier in this chapter.

19.9   Summary

This chapter introduced an important concept for modern statistical practice: the power of a statistical test. Power is the probability of rejecting H_0 when in truth it is false. Power is inversely related to the probability of committing a Type II error (β): as power increases, the probability of a Type II error decreases. Stated mathematically, power $= 1 - \beta$.

In any given situation, the probability of rejecting the null hypothesis depends on a number of factors, one of which is the difference between what is hypothesized and what is true. This difference is known as the effect size. For the test of H_0: $\mu_1 - \mu_2 = 0$, a useful measure of effect size is the index $\delta = (\mu_1 - \mu_2)/\sigma$, which expresses the size of the difference between the two population means in relation to the population standard deviation. For the test of H_0: $\rho = 0$, the measure of effect size is ρ—the degree of correlation in the population of observations. Effect size is related to power: the larger the effect size, the greater the power. However, the effect size is not under the control of the investigator. But the investigator *can* increase or decrease the power of the test in the following ways:

1. *Sample size*—the larger the sample, the greater the power.
2. *Level of significance*—the higher the level (e.g., .05 vs. .01), the greater the power.
3. *One- versus two-tailed tests*—one-tailed tests have greater power than two-tailed tests, provided the direction of H_1 is correct.
4. *Dependent samples*—the greater the degree of dependence, the greater the power.

Samples that are very large have a high probability of giving statistical significance for unimportant effects, and samples that are too small can fail to show significance for important effects. "Significance" is a statistical matter, where the "importance" of any given effect size can be determined only by careful attention to a variety of substantive and value concerns.

Once a minimum effect size has been established and the desired power selected, the appropriate sample size can be determined through the use of available tables. These tables also show the relationships among power, effect size, and sample size. For example, large samples are required where effect size is small and power is high.

For illustrative purposes, the discussion of this chapter was limited to the test of H_0: $\mu_1 - \mu_2 = 0$ and the test of H_0: $\rho = 0$. However, power and effect size, along with the associated concepts and principles, are general and apply to all statistical hypothesis testing.

Reading the Research: Power Considerations

Below, a research team comments on the lack of power in their experimental study regarding a new reading strategy.

The small sample size (N = 20) provided limited statistical power to detect changes resulting from the interventions. It was thought that the differences in the two interventions were significant enough to produce large effects. Only one of the between-group comparisons resulted in a statistically significant finding. Two others approached statistical significance. The inclusion of a larger sample would have increased the study's power to detect smaller between-group differences. (Nelson & Manset-Williamson, 2006, p. 227)

Source: Nelson, J. M., & Manset-Williamson, G. (2006). The impact of explicit, self-regulatory reading comprehension strategy instruction on the reading-specific self-efficacy, attributions, and affect of students with reading disabilities. *Learning Disability Quarterly, 29*(3), 213–230.

Case Study: Power in Numbers

A team of early childhood researchers set out to examine the relationship between the use of manipulatives in the classroom and students' spatial abilities. Manipulatives are physical representations of abstract concepts and, when used in hands-on activities, are thought to enhance spatial reasoning skills. To test this hypothesis, the researchers designed a correlational study. They planned to observe a sample of first-grade classrooms to determine the percentage of the school day that students typically used manipulatives. At the end of the year, students would be given a standardized assessment measuring spatial ability. The data would be analyzed by correlating time spent using manipulatives with the average classroom score on the spatial reasoning assessment.

Before going forward, the investigators conducted a power analysis to determine an appropriate sample size for their study. They did not want to inconvenience any more classrooms than necessary, nor did they want to incur needless expenses associated with data collection (e.g., travel to additional schools, salaries for extra graduate assistants).

The researchers first specified the smallest population effect size—in this case, ρ—that they wanted to be able to detect (in the event of a false null hypothesis). Using relevant research and theory as a guide, the investigators presumed a low-to-moderate effect size: $\rho = .30$. The next step was to set the desired level of power. This is the probability that the statistical test will detect an effect size of $\rho = .30$ or larger. The investigators chose .80 per Cohen's (1988) proposed convention. The investigators then turned to Table 19.2 to determine the needed sample size. The more conservative two-tailed test in this table calls for a sample size of $n = 85$ ($\alpha = .05$).

Equipped with this information, the researchers set off to collect their data. However, as they approached schools to participate in the study, they were coming up short of volunteers: instead of the desired 85 classrooms, the researchers could only obtain data from 22. Looking back at Table 19.2, you can see what the *effective* power of the analysis would have been had the researchers stayed with this smaller sample—somewhere around .25. That is, the probability is only .25—one in four—that the researchers' statistical tests would uncover a population effect size of $\rho = .30$ or larger. Finding this unacceptable, the researchers continued to recruit participants until the desired sample size was achieved.

Exercises

Identify, Define, or Explain

Terms and Concepts

power   significance versus importance
effect size   sample size tables
factors affecting power

Symbols

β $1-\beta$ δ ρ

Questions and Problems

Note: Answers to starred (*) items are presented in Appendix B.

*1. Consider a hypothetical situation in which an experiment to compare the effects of treatment A with those of treatment B is repeated 500 times under identical circumstances. A two-tailed test of H_0: $\mu_A - \mu_B = 0$ is performed each time, and nonsignificant results are obtained 400 times.

   (a) If the *true* value $\mu_A - \mu_B$ is 2.4, what is your best estimate of the power of the test?

   (b) If, in truth, the effects of treatments A and B are *identical*, what is the power of the test? (Before responding, revisit the definition of power.)

2. If the power of your test is .62 and you perform a particular experiment 50 times under identical circumstances, how many times would you expect to obtain statistically nonsignificant results?

*3. You wish to determine the effects of a preschool enrichment program on verbal intelligence. Using a standardized instrument with $\mu = 100$ and $\sigma = 15$, you intend to compare a group of children participating in the enrichment program with a matched group of nonparticipating children; α is set at .05 (one-tailed). How large a sample size (for each group) would be needed to ensure a .90 probability of detecting a true difference of:

   (a) 3 IQ points?

   (b) 9 IQ points?

    (c) 15 IQ points?

    (d) 21 IQ points?

4. Repeat Problem 3 with power = .50.

*5. In Problem 3, suppose you were interested in detecting a true difference of 9 IQ points but you ended up with only 6 children in each group.

    (a) From Table 19.1, what would be your best estimate of the power of your test?

    (b) Imagine that the enrichment program, in truth, has an impact on the verbal intelligence of children. Given the estimate in Problem 5a, what proportion of such experiments—conducted repeatedly under identical conditions—would you expect to result in statistical significance?

6. A novice researcher is unable to recruit very many volunteers for his study. To increase his power, he decides to specify a larger effect size. What's wrong with this approach?

7. The researcher in Problem 6, after examining his results, decides to increase his power by using a one-tailed test in the direction of the results. What is your response to this strategy?

*8. You are planning an experiment. You set power at .85 and wish to detect an effect of at least $\delta = .30$ ($\alpha = .05$, two-tailed).

    (a) What is the required sample size?

    (b) If you were to use dependent samples, is the n in Problem 8a *larger* or *smaller* than it needs to be? (Explain.)

    (c) If you decided to adopt $\alpha = .01$, is the n in Problem 8a *larger* or *smaller* than it needs to be? (Explain.)

*9. You wish to correlate the number of errors committed on a problem-solving task with scores on a measure of impulsivity administered to a sample of college students. Your hypothesis is that students higher in impulsivity will tend to make more errors. You wish to detect an effect of $\rho = .40$ and have set power equal to .80.

    (a) What are your statistical hypotheses?

    (b) What is the required sample size to detect the specified effect at the desired level of power?

    (c) Assuming a false H_0, what proportion of such investigations—conducted repeatedly under identical conditions—would you nonetheless expect to result in nonsignificance?

    (d) Suppose you were able to recruit only 22 volunteers for your investigation. From Table 19.2, what would be your best estimate of the power of your test?

    (e) Given the situation in Problem 9d and assuming a false H_0, what proportion of such investigations—conducted repeatedly under identical conditions—would you expect to result in nonsignificance?

*10. Determine the required sample size for each situation below:

	Effect Size (ρ)	Desired Power	Form of H_1
(a)	.10	.80	Two-tailed
(b)	.60	.85	One-tailed
(c)	.70	.80	Two-tailed
(d)	.40	.99	One-tailed
(e)	.50	.75	Two-tailed
(f)	.40	.25	One-tailed

11. **(a)** What generalization is illustrated by the comparison of Problems 10a and 10c?

(b) What generalization is illustrated by the comparison of Problems 10d and 10f?

12. Are the generalizations stated in Problem 11 limited to testing hypotheses about population correlation coefficients? (Use Table 19.1 to support your answer.)

REFERENCES

Abelson, R. P. (1995). *Statistics as principled argument*. Hillsdale, NJ: Erlbaum.

Acton, F. S. (1959). *Analysis of straight-line data*. New York: Wiley.

American Educational Research Association (2006, June). *Standards for reporting empirical social science research in AERA publications*. Washington, DC: Author. (Available online at http://www.aera.net/)

Babbie, E. R. (1995). *The practice of social research* (7th ed.). Belmont, CA: Wadsworth.

Cohen, J. (1988). *Statistical power analysis for the behavioral sciences* (2nd ed.). Hillsdale, NJ: Erlbaum.

Cronbach, L. J., Linn, R. L., Brennan, R. L., & Haertel, E. H. (1997). Generalizability analysis for performance assessments of student achievement or school effectiveness. *Educational & Psychological Measurement, 57*(3), 373–399.

Gaito, J. (1980). Measurement scales and statistics: Resurgence of an old misconception. *Psychological Bulletin, 87*, 564–567.

Galton, F. (1889). *Natural inheritance*. London: Macmillan.

Glass, G. V, & Hopkins, K. D. (1996). *Statistical methods in education and psychology* (3rd ed.). Boston: Allyn & Bacon.

Gould, S. J. (1996). *Full house: The spread of excellence from Plato to Darwin*. New York: Harmony Books.

Hedges, L. V., & Olkin, I. (1985). *Statistical methods for meta-analysis*. New York: Academic Press.

Huff, H. H. (1954). *How to lie with statistics*. New York: Norton.

Imrey, H. H. (1983). Smoking cigarettes: A risk factor for sexual activity among adolescent girls. *Journal of Irreproducible Results, 28*(4), 11.

King, B. M., & Minium, E. W. (2003). *Statistical reasoning in psychology and education* (4th ed.). New York: Wiley.

Kirk, R. E. (1982). *Experimental design: Procedures for the behavioral sciences* (2nd ed.). Monterey, CA: Brooks/Cole.

Kirk, R. E. (1990). *Statistics: An introduction* (3rd ed.). Fort Worth, TX: Holt, Rinehart & Winston.

Linn, R. L., & Miller, M. D. (2005). *Measurement and assessment in teaching* (9th ed.). Upper Saddle River, NJ: Merrill.

Minium, E. W., Clarke, R. B., & Coladarci, T. (1999). *Elements of statistical reasoning* (2nd ed.). New York: Wiley.

Paulos, J. A. (1988). *Innumeracy: Mathematical illiteracy and its consequences*. New York: Vintage Books.

Scherer, M. (2001). Improving the quality of the teaching force: A conversation with David C. Berliner. *Educational Leadership, 58*(8), 7.

Shavelson, R. J. (1996). *Statistical reasoning for the behavioral sciences* (3rd ed.). Boston: Allyn & Bacon.

Stigler, S. M. (1986). *The history of statistics: The measurement of uncertainty before 1900*. Cambridge, MA: The Belknap Press of Harvard University Press.

Stine, W. W. (1989). Meaningful inference: The role of measurement in statistics. *Psychological Bulletin, 105*, 147–155.

Tankard, J. W. (1984). *The statistical pioneers*. Cambridge, MA: Schenkman.

Wilkinson, L., and Task Force on Statistical Inference (1999). Statistical methods in psychology journals: Guidelines and explanations. *American Psychologist, 54*, 594–604.

Winer, B. J., Brown, D. R., & Michels, K. M. (1991). *Statistical principles in experimental design* (3rd ed.). New York: McGraw-Hill.

APPENDIX A

Review of Basic Mathematics

A.1   Introduction

This appendix offers information about basic skills that is useful in an introductory course in statistics. It is not intended to be a comprehensive compendium, nor should it be considered an initial unit of instruction for those who have no knowledge of the subject. It is intended primarily as a reminder of principles formerly learned, albeit possibly covered with mental cobwebs.

A.2   Symbols and Their Meaning

Symbol	Meaning
$X \neq Y$	X is not equal to Y.
$X \approx Y$	X is approximately equal to Y.
$X > Y$	X is greater than Y.
$X \geq Y$	X is greater than or equal to Y.
$X < Y$	X is less than Y.
$X \leq Y$	X is less than or equal to Y.
$X \pm Y$	As used in this book, it always identifies two limits: $X + Y$ and $X - Y$.
XY	The product of X and Y; X times Y.
$\dfrac{X}{Y}$ or X/Y	Alternative ways of indicating X divided by Y.
Y/X	The reciprocal of X/Y.
$1/Y$	The reciprocal of $Y/1$.
$(X)\left(\dfrac{1}{Y}\right)$	The product of X and the reciprocal of $Y/1$; an alternative way of writing X/Y.
$(XY)^2$	The square of the product of X and Y.
$X^2 Y^2$	The product of X^2 and Y^2; it is the same as $(XY)^2$.
XY^2	The product of X and Y^2; the "square" sign modifies Y but not X.
∞	Infinity; a number indefinitely large.
4 or +4	When a *specific* number is written without a sign in front of it, a positive number is intended. Negative numbers are so indicated, for example, -4.

A.3   *Arithmetic Operations Involving Positive and Negative Numbers*

Problem	Comment
$3 - 12 = -9$	To subtract a large number from a smaller one, subtract the smaller from the larger and reverse the sign.
$3 + (-12) = -9$	Adding a negative number is the same as subtracting that number.
$3 - (-12) = 15$	Subtracting a negative number is the same as adding it.
$-3 - 12 = -15$	The sum of two negative numbers is the negative sum of the two numbers.
$(3)(-12) = -36$	The product of two numbers is negative when *one* of the two is negative.
$(-3)(-12) = 36$	The product of two numbers is positive when *both* are negative.
$(-2)^2 = 4$	The square of a negative number is positive, since to square is to multiply a number by itself.
$(-2)(3)(-4) = 24$	The product of more than two numbers is obtained by finding the product of any two of them, multiplying that product by one of the remaining numbers, and continuing this process as needed. Thus: $(-2)(3) = -6$, and $(-6)(-4) = 24$.
$(2)(0)(4) = 0$	The product of several terms is zero if any one of them is zero.
$2 + 3(-4) = 2 - 12 = -10$	In an additive sequence, reduce each term before summing. In the example, obtain the product *first*, then add it to the other term.
$\dfrac{-4}{2} = -2$	When *one* of the numbers in a fraction is negative, the quotient is negative.

A.4   *Squares and Square Roots*

Problem	Comment
$[(2)(3)(4)]^2 = (2^2)(3^2)(4^2)$ $24^2 = (4)(9)(16)$ $576 = 576$	The square of a product equals the product of the squares.
$(2 + 3 + 4)^2 \neq 2^2 + 3^2 + 4^2$ $9^2 \neq 4 + 9 + 16$ $81 \neq 29$	The square of a sum does *not* equal the sum of the squares.
$\left(\dfrac{4}{16}\right)^2 = \dfrac{4^2}{16^2}$ $\left(\dfrac{1}{4}\right)^2 = \dfrac{16}{256}$ $\dfrac{1}{16} = \dfrac{1}{16}$	The square of a fraction equals the fraction of the squares.

$$\sqrt{(4)(9)(16)} = \sqrt{4}\sqrt{9}\sqrt{16}$$

$$\sqrt{576} = (2)(3)(4)$$

$$24 = 24$$

The square root of a product equals the product of the square roots.

$$\sqrt{9 + 16} \neq \sqrt{9} + \sqrt{16}$$

$$\sqrt{25} \neq 3 + 4$$

$$5 \neq 7$$

The square root of a sum does *not* equal the sum of the square roots.

$$\sqrt{\frac{4}{6}} = \frac{\sqrt{4}}{\sqrt{16}}$$

$$\sqrt{\frac{1}{4}} = \frac{2}{4}$$

$$\frac{1}{2} = \frac{1}{2}$$

The square root of a fraction equals the fraction of the square roots.

$$(\sqrt{4})^2 = 4$$

$$2^2 = 4$$

$$4 = 4$$

The square of a square root is the same quantity found under the square root sign.

A.5 Fractions

Problem	**Comment**
$\dfrac{1}{4} = .25$	To convert the ratios of two numbers to a decimal fraction, divide the numerator by the denominator.
$.25 = 100(.25)\%$ $\;\;\;\; = 25\%$	To convert a decimal fraction to percent, multiply by 100.
$\dfrac{1}{10} + \dfrac{1}{25} = .10 + .04$ $\quad\quad\quad = .14$	To add two fractions, convert both to decimal fractions, and then add.
$\left(\dfrac{3}{5}\right)(16) = \dfrac{(3)(16)}{5}$ $\quad\quad = \dfrac{48}{5}$ $\quad\quad = 9.6$	To multiply a quantity by a fraction, multiply the quantity by the *numerator* of the fraction, and divide that product by the denominator of the fraction.
$\dfrac{16}{4} = \left(\dfrac{1}{4}\right)(16)$	To divide by a number, multiply by its reciprocal.
$\dfrac{16}{4/5} = \left(\dfrac{5}{4}\right)(16)$ $\quad = \dfrac{(5)(16)}{4}$ $\quad = 20$	To divide by a fraction, multiply by its reciprocal.
$\dfrac{3 + 4 - 2}{8} = \dfrac{3}{8} + \dfrac{4}{8} - \dfrac{2}{8}$ $\quad\quad\quad = \dfrac{5}{8}$	When the numerator of a fraction is a sum, the numerator may be separated into component additive parts, each divided by the denominator.

$$\frac{3}{8} + \frac{4}{8} - \frac{2}{8} = \frac{3+4-2}{8}$$

$$= \frac{5}{8}$$

When the several terms of a sum are fractions having a common denominator, the sum may be expressed as the sum of the numerators, divided by the common denominator.

$$\frac{(3)(15)}{5} = \frac{(3)(3)(5)}{5}$$

$$= (3)(3)$$

$$= 9$$

When the numerator and/or denominator of a fraction is the product of two or more terms, identical terms appearing in the numerator and denominator may be canceled.

$$\left(\frac{1}{5}\right)\left(\frac{2}{7}\right)\left(\frac{3}{11}\right) = \frac{(1)(2)(3)}{(5)(7)(11)}$$

$$= \frac{6}{385}$$

The product of several fractions equals the product of the numerators divided by the product of the denominators.

A.6   *Operations Involving Parentheses*

Problem

Comment

$2 + (4 - 3 + 2) =$

$2 + 4 - 3 + 2 = 5$

When a positive sign precedes parentheses, the parentheses may be removed without changing the signs of the terms within.

$2 - (4 - 3 + 2) =$

$2 - 4 + 3 - 2 = -1$

When a negative sign precedes parentheses, they may be removed if signs of the terms within are reversed.

$a(b + c) = ab + ac$

A numerical example:

$2(3 + 4) = (2)(3) + (2)(4)$

$2(7) = 6 + 8$

$14 = 14$

When a quantity within parentheses is to be multiplied by a number, *each* term within the parentheses must be so multiplied.

$2a + 4ab^2 = (2a)(1) + (2a)(2b^2)$

$= 2a(1 + 2b^2)$

A numerical example:

$6 + 8 = (2)(3) + (2)(4)$

$14 = 2(3 + 4)$

$14 = (2)(7) = 14$

When all terms of a sum contain a common multiplier, that multiplier may be factored out as a multiplier of the remaining sum.

$3 + (1 + 2)^2 = 3 + 3^2$

$= 3 + 9$

$= 12$

When parentheses are modified by squaring or some other function, take account of the modifier before combining with other terms.

$$\left[100 - 40\left(\frac{20}{10}\right)\right] + \left[\frac{20}{10} + (40 - 30)\right] =$$

$[100 - 40(2)] + [2 + (40 - 30)] =$

$[100 - 80] + [12] =$

$20 + 12 = 3$

When an expression contains nested parentheses, *perform those operations required to remove the most interior parentheses first.* Simplify the expression by working outward.

A.7   Approximate Numbers, Computational Accuracy, and Rounding

Some numbers are **exact numbers**. If you discover that there are 3 children in a family, you may speak of 3 as being an exact number, since it contains *no* margin of error. Numbers lacking this kind of accuracy are known as **approximate numbers**. Numbers resulting from the act of measurement are usually approximate numbers. For example, if you measure weight to the nearest pound, a weight of 52 pounds means that the object is closer to 52 pounds than it is to 51 pounds or 53 pounds. Therefore, the actual weight is somewhere between 51.5 pounds and 52.5 pounds.

In computations involving both exact and approximate numbers, the accuracy of the answer is limited by the accuracy of the approximate numbers involved. In such computations you are faced with the question, "How many decimal places should I keep?" The best answer we can give is "Whatever seems sensible." If weight is measured to the nearest pound and the total weight of three objects is 67 pounds, it seems reasonable to report the "average" weight as 22.3 pounds or possibly 22 pounds. To report it as 22.333333 (which may appear on the display of your hand calculator) is both unnecessary and downright misleading in view of the initial inaccuracy in the numbers. On the other hand, to round the answer to the nearest 10 pounds (i.e., a weight of 20 pounds) gives up accuracy to which you are entitled.

Most of the exercises you encounter in this book require a sequence of calculations that result in a single answer. Here, inaccuracy can easily compound. However, this is not a problem if you use a hand calculator. Take advantage of your calculator's memory capability by storing the intermediate calculations, which the calculator will carry out well beyond the decimal point. Then combine these calculations for determining the final answer, which can be rounded back to a figure that seems sensible.[1] In the interest of being consistent across the many problems in the chapters of this book, we almost always round the final answer to the nearest hundredth.

Rounding typically is a straightforward process, as the following examples illustrate:

to the nearest whole number:	5.4	→	5
	10.73	→	11
	−12.6	→	−13
to the nearest tenth:	46.28	→	46.3
	158.639	→	158.6
	.05732	→	.1
to the nearest hundredth:	2.50193	→	2.50
	−3.08399	→	−3.08
	74.359	→	74.36

But how do you round, say, 109.500000 to the nearest whole number? Is it 109 or 110? How about 90.250000 rounded to the nearest tenth (90.2 or 90.3?), .865000 rounded to the nearest hundredth (.86 or .87?), or 7.421500 rounded to the nearest thousandth (7.421 or 7.422?)? Here we follow the popular, if arbitrary, convention of rounding to *the nearest even number*: 110, 90.2, .86, and 7.422. This practice results in sometimes rounding up and other times rounding down, thus avoiding the introduction of systematic bias into one's calculations.

[1] If you do not follow this practice, you periodically will find minor (but nonetheless frustrating) discrepancies between your answers and ours, particularly on the more involved problems having intermediate calculations.

APPENDIX B

Answers to Selected End-of-Chapter Problems

Chapter 1

1. **(a)** ratio
   (b) ordinal
   (c) nominal
   (d) interval
   (e) nominal
   (f) ordinal
   (g) ratio
   (h) nominal
   (i) ordinal
   (j) nominal
   (k) ratio

4. **(a)** 9, −43, 123, 0
   (b) 27.3, 1.9, −.4, 5.0
   (c) −31.52, 76.00, .83, 40.74

Chapter 2

1. The intervals are not all of the same width, intervals overlap (e.g., 30 appears in two intervals), intervals are not continuous (score values of 45–50 omitted), there are too few intervals, higher scores are toward the bottom.

3. **(a)** 46, 3, 24–26, 69–71
   (b) 74, 5, 25–29, 100–104 (4 or 6 also are satisfactory interval widths, although even)
   (c) 13, 1, 56, 69
   (d) 634, 50, 150–199, 800–849 (30, 40, or 60 also satisfactory interval widths)
   (e) 15.6, 1.0, 6.0–6.9, 21.0–21.9
   (f) 2.20, .20, 1.20–1.39, 3.40–3.59 (perhaps .10 or .15 would be satisfactory interval sizes as well)
   (g) 26, 2.0, 36–37, 62–63

5. **(a)** 26%

  (b) 5%

  (c) .4%

  (d) 55.5%

  (e) 79%

7. **(a)** The range divided by 10 is 3.2, which is rounded to 3; the range divided by 20 is 1.6, which is rounded to 2.

(b)

Score Limits	Exact Limits	f	%	Cum. f	Cum. %
96–98	95.5–98.5	1	3	30	100
93–95	92.5–95.5	0	0	29	97
90–92	89.5–92.5	3	10	29	97
87–89	86.5–89.5	4	13	26	87
84–86	83.5–86.5	3	10	22	73
81–83	80.5–83.5	7	23	19	63
78–80	77.5–80.5	5	17	12	40
75–77	74.5–77.5	2	7	7	23
72–74	71.5–74.5	3	10	5	17
69–71	68.5–71.5	1	3	2	7
66–68	65.5–68.5	0	0	1	3
63–65	62.5–65.5	1	3	1	3

$n = 30$

(c)

Score Limits	Exact Limits	f	%	Cum. f	Cum. %
96–97	95.5–97.5	1	3	30	100
94–95	93.5–95.5	0	0	29	97
92–93	91.5–93.5	1	3	29	97
90–91	89.5–91.5	2	7	28	93
88–89	87.5–89.5	2	7	26	87
86–87	85.5–87.5	3	10	24	80
84–85	83.5–85.5	2	7	21	70
82–83	81.5–83.5	5	17	19	63
80–81	79.5–81.5	4	13	14	47
78–79	77.5–79.5	3	10	10	33
76–77	75.5–77.5	1	3	7	23
74–75	73.5–75.5	2	7	6	20
72–73	71.5–73.5	2	7	4	13
70–71	69.5–71.5	1	3	2	7
68–69	67.5–69.5	0	0	1	3
66–67	65.5–67.5	0	0	1	3
64–65	63.5–65.5	1	3	1	3

$n = 30$

(d) If you are like us, you probably prefer the frequency distribution where $i = 3$. Notice that, with the larger interval width, there are fewer intervals containing a frequency of zero or one, and the underlying shape of the distribution is more apparent.

10. You would concentrate on the relative frequencies, for the absolute frequencies are not comparable when the total n's differ for the groups being compared. Suppose that there are 200 females and 50 males and, further, a particular score interval has a frequency of 4 (i.e., $f = 4$) in both distributions. This is 2% of the female distribution, whereas it is 8%—four times greater—of the male distribution. (This general point is illustrated in Figure 3.7.)

12.

Score Limits	f	Proportion
3.90–4.19	3	.05
3.60–3.89	5	.08
3.30–3.59	8	.13
3.00–3.29	16	.27
2.70–2.99	10	.17
2.40–2.69	7	.12
2.10–2.39	5	.08
1.80–2.09	3	.05
1.50–1.79	1	.02
1.20–1.49	1	.02
.90–1.19	1	.02
	$n = 60$	

14.

Score Limits	f	Proportion
50–54	3	.04
45–49	11	.14
40–44	12	.15
35–39	19	.24
30–34	17	.21
25–29	8	.10
20–24	8	.10
5–19	2	.02
	$n = 80$	

Irregularities tend to be smoothed out, and one can see the characteristic shape of the distribution better. For example, the zero frequency for 51–53 and dips in frequency at 42–44 and 36–38 are eliminated.

Chapter 3

1. Because graphs of widely differing appearance may be constructed from the same distribution, under some circumstances the graphic representation may be misleading.

However, salient features of the data may be more apparent in graphic representation (e.g., distributional shape). Clearly, it is important to inspect the frequency distribution *and* a graphic representation of the data.

3. **(a)** 12
   (b) 299.5
   (c) 2.62
   (d) 3.095
   (e) 35

4.

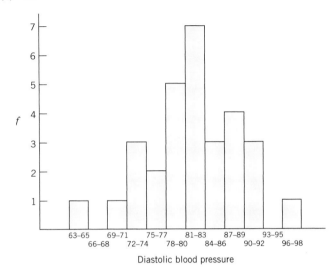

8. Did you find the midpoints in the frequency polygon slightly awkward to work with (because the interval width was an even number)?

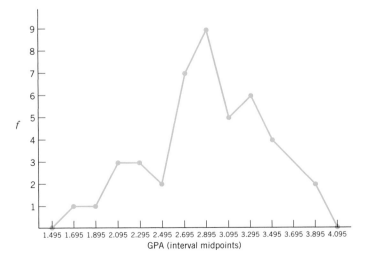

11. **(a)** somewhat bimodal (sex difference in height)
    (b) markedly bimodal
    (c) normal
    (d) negatively skewed
    (e) positively skewed
    (f) reverse J-curve

13. A large graph is better if values are to be read from it; it is easier to construct with accuracy, and it is easier to read. A small graph would be acceptable if used to show pertinent features of the distribution, not to display values.

Chapter 4

2. **(a)** mode $= 8, Mdn = 10, \bar{X} = 12$
   (b) no mode, $Mdn = 15.5, \bar{X} = 17$
   (c) mode $= 11, Mdn = 11, \bar{X} = 11$

6. **(a)** negative skew
   (b) normal
   (c) bimodal
   (d) positive skew

7. **(a)** mode $< Mdn < \bar{X}$
   (b) mode $> Mdn > \bar{X}$
   (c) mode $= Mdn = \bar{X}$
   (d) mode $< Mdn < \bar{X}$

10. **(a)** First determine the original ΣX, which is equal to $(n)(\bar{X}) = (25)(23) = 575$. Reduce ΣX by nine points (i.e., $43 - 34 = 9$) and divide by 25 to obtain the correct $\bar{X} = 22.64$.
    (b) The Mdn and mode would not be affected by this error. (Although technically the mode *could* change because of this error, it is rather unlikely.)

11. Those just below the median. If they improve sufficiently to pass the median, the median must increase to maintain an equal number of scores above and below.

12. $\bar{X} = 3964/50 = 79.28$; $Mdn = 80.5$; mode $= 86$

14. The mean, because you must know each score to compute its value.

Chapter 5

3. **(a)** range $= 8, S^2 = 7.00, S = 2.65$
   (b) range $= 8, S^2 = 7.67, S = 2.77$
   (c) range $= 7, S^2 = 5.00, S = 2.24$

6. Mode, median, and mean each go up a point, whereas range, variance, and standard deviation are unaffected. Measures of central tendency, but not variability, are affected by adding a constant to each score in a distribution.

8. $\overline{X}$ and S are affected because both depend on the value of every score. Because it depends on the two extreme scores, the range also is affected. The median does not change because it is unaffected by extreme scores—the "middle" value remains the same.

10. Distributions (a) and (b) both will be normal about a mean of 29, although distribution (b) will be slightly more variable. Distribution (c) will evidence considerable negative skew, and distribution (d) will have no variability whatsoever—everyone received a score of 50.

11. **(a)** (1) shows the least; (3) and (4) show the most

    (b) for (1) $\overline{X} = 8, S^2 = 0, S = 0$; for (2) $\overline{X} = 8, S^2 = 3.2, S = 1.79$; for (3) $\overline{X} = 8, S^2 = 8, S = 2.83$; for (4) $\overline{X} = 1008, S^2 = 8, S = 2.83$

    (c) Samples may have the same mean but show different degrees of variability, or samples may have very different means but show the same degree of variability.

14. **(a)** above the mean

    (b) "average"; although above the mean, his score falls toward the center of the distribution.

    (c) very high; his score falls between $\overline{X} + 2S$ and $\overline{X} + 3S$.

15. **(a)** 9.10

    (b) 13.06

    (c) $+.22$ and $-.23$, respectively

    (d) In both cases, the difference between means is between one-fifth and one-quarter of a standard deviation. According to Cohen's classification, these are "small" effect sizes.

Chapter 6

(When the precise value required was not listed in Table A, we took the *nearest* tabled value.)

2. **(a)** -1.00

   (b) $+0.67$

   (c) $+2.00$

   (d) $+1.50$

   (e) -1.67

   (f) -0.17

5. **(a)** .1587

   (b) .0228

   (c) .0013

   (d) .5000

   (e) .8997

   (f) .0526

7. **(a)**   .3174
    (b)   .6170
    (c)   .1374
    (d)   .0500

8. **(a)**   ±2.58
    (b)   ±1.96
    (c)   ±1.15
    (d)   ±.67

11. **(a)**   .1587
    (b)   .3085
    (c)   .1151
    (d)   .5398
    (e)   .8238
    (f)   .9625

13. By expressing all scores as z scores, you find the following order from best to worst: e, a, c, b, d.

14. No. This will be true only in a *symmetric* distribution; in a skewed distribution, the mean ($z = 0$) and the median will not be the same. Where skew is positive, less than half the z scores in a distribution will be positive; where skew is negative, less than half the z scores will be negative. (If this puzzles you, draw a picture of the two distributions along with the relative positions of the mean and median.)

16. Mathematics achievement: if both distributions are normal, then approximately 59% (58.71%, to be precise) of the female scores fall below the mean for males. Verbal ability: assuming normality, roughly 59% (59.10%) of the male scores fall below the female mean.

Chapter 7

3. **(a)**

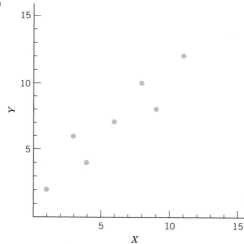

(b) This scatterplot shows a strong positive association between these two variables.

(c) No outliers are present, nor is there any evidence of curvilinearity.

(d) We estimate Pearson r to be roughly $+.90$.

4. (a) $r = +.93$

(b) $r^2 = .93^2 = .86$; a large portion of the variance in X and Y—86%—is shared, or common, variance; that is, 86% of the variation in X is associated with variation in Y.

5. 9.71

7. (a) The numerator of the covariance would be smaller owing to the *negative* cross-product for this pair of scores; consequently, the covariance would be smaller as well.

(b) r also would be smaller.

(c) We'd estimate that r would drop to $+.30$ or so.

8. $+.28$

12. (a) $-.60$

(b) no change

(c) no change

(d) r would be smaller

(e) no change

(f) no change

(g) r would be smaller

14. There is less variability in X and Y among experienced pilots than among cadets. Restriction of range reduces r.

Chapter 8

1. (a) Keith: 7.9, Bill: 8.5, Charlie: 5.4, Brian: 4.1, Mick: 4.1

(b) $+2.1, -2.5, +2.6, -3.1$

(c) 27.8

(d) It would be larger.

3. (a) $a = 21.94$[1], $b = +.94$, $Y' = 21.94 + .94(X)$

(b) Jean: 61.89 in., Albert: 73.92 in., Burrhus: 69.03 in.

(c) Y' for 10-year-old Jean is an estimate of the mean adult height for a large group of 10-year-olds, all of whom are 42.5 in. tall.

4. (a) $a = 2.84$, $b = +.63$, $Y' = 2.84 + .63(X)$

(b) Keith: 7.9, Bill: 8.5, Charlie: 5.4, Brian: 4.1, Mick: 4.1; any discrepancies would be due to errors, rounding or otherwise.

---

[1]To calculate this value, we entered the unrounded $b = .9390322$ (rather than .94) to minimize cumulative rounding error. If you used $b = .94$, you probably obtained an intercept of 21.90.

(c)　$\overline{Y}' = 6.00$; the mean of the predicted Y scores will equal the mean of the actual Y scores.

(d)　$\Sigma(Y - Y') = 0$; the sum of the deviations about the regression line equals 0.

5.　Problem 3: For every inch increase in height at age 10, there is a corresponding increase of .94 inches in adult height. Problem 4: For every point increase in quiz 1 performance, there is a corresponding increase of .63 points in quiz 2 performance.

7.　(a)　8.83 (i.e., $\overline{Y}$); given any value of X, the best prediction of Y is $\overline{Y}$ when $r = 0$.

　　(b)　$Y' = 8.83 + 0(X)$

9.　(a)　$+1.00$

　　(b)　$-.33$

　　(c)　$+.75$

　　(d)　$-.20$

11.　(a)　Jean: -1.87, Albert: $+2.26$, Burrhus: $+.58$

　　(b)　Jean: -1.33, Albert: $+1.60$, Burrhus: $+.41$

　　(c)　Jean: $67.3 + (-1.33)(4.1) = 61.8$, Albert: $67.3 + (1.60)(4.1) = 73.9$, Burrhus: $67.3 + (.41)(4.1) = 69.0$

13.　(a)　$a = 1.34, b = .0023, Y' = 1.34 + .0023(X)$

　　(b)　Val: 2.46, Mike: 2.97

　　(c)　.30

　　(d)　Val: 1.87 to 3.05, Mike: 2.38 to 3.56

　　(e)　$z = (2.65 - 2.46)/.30 = +.63$, so proportion $= .26$

　　(f)　$z = (2.00 - 2.46)/.30 = -1.53$, so proportion $= .06$

　　(g)　$z = (2.50 - 2.97)/.30 = -1.57$, so proportion $= .94$

Chapter 9

1.　To account for the effects of chance factors; sample differences will reflect both "chance" and any effects associated with the different instructional treatments.

3.　(a)　.0333

　　(b)　.0033

　　(c)　.02

　　(d)　.01

4.　It turns out that his reasoning is faulty: each of the 12 months is *not equally likely*, for there are more births in some months than in others.

6.　Each of the grades is *not* equally likely.

9.　(a)　$1/2 + 1/6 = .67$

　　(b)　$(1/2)(1/6) = .083$

11. **(a)** yes
    (b) no
    (c) no
    (d) no
    (e) yes
    (f) no
    (g) no
    (h) yes
    (i) no

13. **(a)** .04
    (b) .16
    (c) .96

15. **(a)** RRW, RWR, WRR
    (b) .125
    (c) $(.125)(3) = .375$
    (d) RRR
    (e) $.375 + .125 = .50$

18. **(a)** $.50 + .1554 = .66$
    (b) $.6554 - .3446 = .31$
    (c) .04
    (d) .07
    (e) 433 and 567
    (f) 628
    (g) 372

19. Two-tailed. An SAT-CR score of 320 ($z = -1.80$) is just as extreme as a score of 680 ($z = +1.80$), and the area beyond each score must therefore be considered in determining the corresponding probability.

Chapter 10

1. **(a)** the proverbial "person on the street" (i.e., people in general)
   (b) patrons at a local sports bar
   (c) No. Relative to the population, the sample undoubtedly overrepresents people who are interested in sports and frequent sports bars; other possible sources of bias are sex and age.

3. Whether a sample is random depends on how it was selected, not on its composition. The chance factors involved in random sampling (sampling variation) occasionally lead to very atypical samples.

5. Treat the sample means obtained in Problem 4 as scores and calculate their standard deviation according to the procedures of Chapter 5.

8. What sample values would be expected to occur in repeated random sampling and with what relative frequencies?

9. **(a)** 5
   (b) .95
   (c) .05
   (d) .42
   (e) 111.65
   (f) $\bar{X}_L = 90.2$, $\bar{X}_U = 109.8$

10. **(a)** 100
    (b) 5
    (c) normal (central limit theorem)

14. **(a)** 2.12
    (b) $z = \pm 5/2.12 = \pm 2.36$, $p = .98$
    (c) .65
    (d) $(1.96)(2.12) = 4.16$

15. **(a)** $z = (108 - 107)/2.12 = .47$; yes, because the probability is $(.32)(2) = .64$ of obtaining a sample mean as far away (or farther) from $\mu = 107$ as $\bar{X} = 108$.
    (b) $z = (108 - 100)/2.12 = 3.77$; no, because the probability is less than $(.0001)(2) = .0002$ of obtaining a sample mean as far away (or farther) from $\mu = 100$ as $\bar{X} = 108$.

Chapter 11

1. She would compare $\bar{X}$ with sample means expected through random sampling if the hypothesis $\mu = 50$ were true. If $\bar{X}$ is typical, she retains this hypothesis as a reasonable possibility; if $\bar{X}$ is very atypical, she rejects this hypothesis as unreasonable.

3. **(a)** $\mu = 50$
   (b) Nondirectional; the personnel director wants to know if there is a difference in *either* direction.
   (c) $\mu \neq 50$
   (d) $z_{.05} = \pm 1.96$, $z_{.01} = \pm 2.58$.

4. **(a)** 1.67
   (b) -1.20
   (c) $(.1151)(2) = .23$
   (d) H_0 is retained because the sample z falls short of the critical value (similarly, $p > \alpha$).
   (e) The keyboarding speed of secretaries at her company is comparable to the national average.

5. **(a)** 1.00
   (b) -2.00
   (c) $(.0228)(2) = .05$

(d) H_0 is rejected because the sample z falls in the critical region (similarly, $p \leq \alpha$).

(e) The keyboarding speed of secretaries at her company is lower than the national average.

6. A larger n results in a smaller standard error of the mean, which in turn produces a larger z ratio (unless $\overline{X} - \mu = 0$) and therefore a smaller p value. A larger sample thus can give statistical significance where a smaller sample would not.

7. With a large enough n, even the most trivial and inconsequential difference between $\overline{X}$ and μ nonetheless can be "statistically significant." Statistical significance aside, such a difference typically lacks "importance."

10. **(a)** ± 2.58

(b) ± 1.96

(c) ± 1.65

(d) Critical values for the two-tailed alternative hypothesis ($H_1 \neq 500$) are larger than those for the one-tailed alternative hypotheses of Problem 9. This is because in a two-tailed test, the region of rejection is divided between the two tails (.025 in each tail, if $\alpha = .05$), which requires a normal curve value farther out (in each tail) than is the case when the entire rejection region lies in one tail.

(e) a one-tailed test, *provided the direction specified in H_1 is correct.*

11. Usually, H_1 follows most directly from the research question, whereas H_0 provides specificity to allow for the test. Retention or rejection of H_0 leads to conclusions concerning H_1 and the research question.

15. **(a)** $z_{.05} = \pm 1.96$, $z = -2.92$, $p = (.0018)(2) = .004$, reject H_0

(b) $z_{.01} = +2.33$, $z = +.91$, $p = .18$, retain H_0

(c) $z_{.05} = \pm 1.96$, $z = +1.25$, $p = (.1056)(2) = .21$, retain H_0

(d) $z_{.05} = \pm 1.96$, $z = -2.64$, $p = (.0041)(2) = .01$, reject H_0

(e) $z_{.001} = \pm 3.30$, $z = -3.54$, $p = (.0002)(2) = .0004$, reject H_0

(f) The sample sizes are markedly different: $n = 1000$ for the former and $n = 9$ for the latter. (See Problem 6 above.)

16. **(a)** 3.50

(b) not 3.50

19. While there indeed is little chance that he will reject a true null hypothesis, Josh is taking on an unacceptably high probability of a Type II error—that is, the probability of retaining a false H_0. He would be well advised to adopt a more conventional level of significance (in this instance, perhaps .01 or .001).

Chapter 12

1. **(a)** Does her school district mean differ from 27, and if so in what direction?

(b) What is the value of her school district mean?

2. **(a)** .67

(b) 33.10 ± 1.31, or 31.79 to 34.41

(c) 33.10 ± 1.73, or 31.37 to 34.83

(d) The higher the level of confidence, the wider the interval.

3. The interval 31.79 to 34.41 may or may not include the school district (population) mean. If many, many random samples of size 36 were obtained, 95% of the intervals constructed in the same way would include μ. Thus, one can be 95% confident that μ falls somewhere between 31.79 and 34.41.

8. **(a)** Retain H_0.
   (b) Reject H_0.
   (c) If the value specified in H_0 falls within the 99% confidence interval, H_0 would be retained at the .01 level (two-tailed test) for the same sample results; if it falls outside the interval, H_0 would be rejected.

9. **(a)** Yes.
   (b) Maybe.
   (c) Because a 99% confidence interval is wider than a 95% confidence interval calculated from the same data, a value falling outside the former will necessarily fall outside the latter. However, a value falling outside a 95% confidence interval may or may not fall outside the corresponding 99% confidence interval.

Chapter 13

1. With the value of σ known, Ben should compute $\sigma_{\bar{X}}$ and proceed with a one-sample z test (using the normal curve).

3. **(a)** +3
   (b) $SS = 48$, $s_{\bar{X}} = 1.55$

6. The tails of the t distribution ($df = 3$) are "fatter" than those of the normal curve. That is, there is more area in the former. For example, .10 of the area in the t distribution ($df = 3$) falls beyond a t of ± 2.353 (Table B), whereas the corresponding z is only ± 1.65 (Table A).

8. **(a)** $s = 9.96$, $s_{\bar{X}} = 4.45$
   (b) $s = 3.02$, $s_{\bar{X}} = 1.14$

10. **(a)** ± 1.860
    (b) ± 2.306
    (c) ± 3.355

12. **(a)** $\bar{X} = 12.50$, $s_{\bar{X}} = 1.06$, $t = +2.36$, $t_{.10} = \pm 2.015$; reject H_0; conclude $\mu > 10$.
    (b) $t = +2.36$, $t_{.05} = \pm 2.571$; retain H_0; conclude 10 is not an unreasonable value for μ.
    (c) $\bar{X} = 48.20$, $s_{\bar{X}} = 1.69$, $t = -1.07$, $t_{.05} = \pm 2.776$; retain H_0; conclude 50 is not an unreasonable value for μ.
    (d) $\bar{X} = 15.80$, $s_{\bar{X}} = 1.37$, $t = -3.07$, $t_{.01} = -2.821$; reject H_0; conclude $\mu < 20$.

14. **(a)** $H_0: \mu = 72$, $H_1: \mu \neq 72$
    (b) $t_{.05} = \pm 2.776$
    (c) $\bar{X} = 77.80$, $s_{\bar{X}} = 4.45$, $t = +1.30$, retain H_0.
    (d) 72 is a reasonable possibility for the population mean.

16. **(a)** Since the lowest possible score is 0 seconds, this $\overline{X}$ and s suggest a highly positively skewed distribution. With a sample size of only five observations, such skewness violates the normality assumption of the t test.

    (b) Use a much larger sample.

17. **(a)** $p < .05$
    (b) $p > .05$ (or perhaps $p > .10$)
    (c) $p < .05$ (or perhaps $p < .01$)
    (d) $p > .05$ (or perhaps $p > .10$)
    (e) $p < .05$
    (f) $p < .05$ (or perhaps $p < .01$)

20. **(a)** The result was almost, but not quite, significant at the .05 level.
    (b) $p > .05$ (or $p < .10$)

22. **(a)** $H_0: \mu = 8.3$, $H_1: \mu < 8.3$
    (b) $s_{\overline{X}} = .32$, $t = -11.56$, $t_{.05} = -1.658$; reject H_0 in favor of H_1.
    (c) There is less cigarette smoking at the university than there was 15 years ago.

24. **(a)** 77.80 ± 12.35, or 65.45 to 90.15; one can be 95% confident that the mean score in the population falls between 65.45 and 90.15.
    (b) 6.14 ± 2.79, or 3.35 to 8.93; one can be 95% confident that the mean score in the population falls between 3.35 and 8.93.

Chapter 14

1. **(a)** μ_A is greater than μ_B; $\mu_A - \mu_B > 0$
    (b) μ_A is less than μ_B; $\mu_A - \mu_B < 0$
    (c) μ_A equals μ_B; $\mu_A - \mu_B = 0$
    (d) μ_A doesn't equal μ_B; $\mu_A - \mu_B \neq 0$

3. **(a)** Select repeated pairs of random samples of size $n_A = 5$ and $n_B = 5$ from the two populations and compute the sample difference $\overline{X}_A - \overline{X}_B$ for each pair; group the sample differences into a frequency distribution and construct a frequency polygon.
    (b) Compute the standard deviation of the sample differences obtained in Problem 3a.

5. **(a)** $SS_1 = 8$, $SS_2 = 30$
    (b) 5.43
    (c) 1.56
    (d) $\overline{X}_1 - \overline{X}_2 = -3$, $t = -1.92$, $t_{.05} = -1.895$, reject H_0 in favor of H_1
    (e) conclude $\mu_1 < \mu_2$

6. **(a)** $d = -1.29$; the mean of sample 1 is 1.29 standard deviations below the mean of sample 2, which is a "large" effect by Cohen's criteria. Because .40 of the area in a normal distribution falls between the mean and $z = 1.29$ (Table A), this effect size

indicates that the average person in Population 2 falls at the 90th percentile of the Population 1 distribution (assuming population normality).

(b) $\hat{\omega}^2 = .23$, meaning that 23% of the variance in scores is accounted for, or explained, by group membership (i.e., whether participants are drawn from the first population or the second population).

7. (a) $+1.746$
   (b) ± 2.797
   (c) -1.701
   (d) ± 2.750

10. (a) $H_0: \mu_1 - \mu_2 = 0$, $H_1: \mu_1 - \mu_2 > 0$
    (b) $\bar{X}_1 - \bar{X}_2 = +7.5$, $SS_1 = 2601$, $SS_2 = 2164.07$, $s_{\bar{X}_1 - \bar{X}_2} = 2.82$, $t = +2.66$, $t_{.05} = +1.684$, reject H_0 in favor of H_1.
    (c) Eighth-grade boys, on average, hold more positive views regarding the usefulness and relevance of science for adult life.

13. (a) The differences between women and men are large and important.
    (b) $H_0: \mu_{women} - \mu_{men} = 0$ was tested and rejected; the conclusion is that $\mu_{women} - \mu_{men} > 0$.
    (c) Yes. Very large samples would result in a very small standard error $(s_{\bar{X}_1 - \bar{X}_2})$ and, therefore, a large t ratio.
    (d) You would want to see $\bar{X}_{women}$, $\bar{X}_{men}$, and s_{pooled}, along with the estimated effect size, d.

14. (a) $H_0: \mu_1 - \mu_2 = 0$, $H_1: \mu_1 - \mu_2 \neq 0$
    (b) $\bar{X}_1 - \bar{X}_2 = -2$, $s_{\bar{X}_1 - \bar{X}_2} = 1.31$, $t = -1.52$, $t_{.05} = \pm 2.048$, retain H_0.
    (c) There appears to be no effect of immediate testing on memory.

15. (a) Zero. From the retention of $H_0: \mu_1 - \mu_2 = 0$ in Problem 14, you know that zero is a reasonable possibility for $\mu_1 - \mu_2$ ($\alpha = .05$). Consequently, zero will fall in the 95% confidence interval for $\mu_1 - \mu_2$.
    (b) $-2 \pm (2.048)(1.31) = -2 \pm 2.68$, or -4.68 to $+0.68$. No surprises—the 95% confidence interval indeed includes zero.
    (c) It will include zero in this instance. Because a 99% confidence interval is *wider* than a 95% confidence interval (given the same data), the former will include zero whenever the latter does.
    (d) $-2 \pm (2.763)(1.31) = -2 \pm 3.62$, or -5.62 to $+1.62$. No surprises here either: The 99% confidence interval indeed is wider and includes zero.

19. In Problems 8, 14, and 16 because randomization was used; it was not used in Problems 9 and 10.

Chapter 15

1. No. "Matching" involves forming pairs according to a characteristic that varies across individuals; grade in school has been held constant for all individuals.

3. (a) $SS_{pre} = 30$, $SS_{post} = 38$, $r_{pre,post} = +.68$
   (b) $s_{pre}^2 = 7.5$, $s_{post}^2 = 9.5$

(c) $s_{\bar{X}_1 - \bar{X}_2} = \sqrt{\dfrac{7.5 + 9.5 - 2(.68)(2.74)(3.08)}{5}} = 1.05$

(d) $t = +2/1.05 = +1.90$, $t_{.05} = +2.132$, retain H_0.

(e) There is insufficient evidence to conclude an effect from pretest to posttest.

5. (a) $H_0: \mu_D = 0$, $H_1: \mu_D \neq 0$
   (b) $\bar{D} = +2.67$, $SS_D = 27.33$, $s_{\bar{D}} = .95$
   (c) $t = +2.67/.95 = +2.81$, $t_{.05} = \pm 2.571$; reject H_0.
   (d) Conclude $\mu_D > 0$ (i.e., $\mu_{music} - \mu_{white\ noise} > 0$): Problem solving is faster with white noise than with background music.

6. (a) $s_{\bar{X}_1 - \bar{X}_2} = \sqrt{\dfrac{76.86 + 50.57 - 2(.04)(8.77)(7.11)}{8}} = 3.91$

   (b) $H_0: \mu_1 - \mu_2 = 0$, $H_1: \mu_1 - \mu_2 \neq 0$
   (c) $t = +12.00/3.91 = +3.07$, $t_{.01} = \pm 3.499$; retain H_0.
   (d) The sample difference is insufficient to permit the conclusion that a real difference exists between the two training programs.
   (e) Such a low correlation ($r_{12} = .04$) will not appreciably reduce the standard error, thus negating the statistical advantage of forming matched pairs.

8. (a) Because $H_0: \mu_1 - \mu_2 = 0$ was earlier rejected ($\alpha = .05$, two-tailed), you know that a 95% confidence interval would not include zero.
   (b) $2.67 \pm (2.571)(.95)$, or $+.23$ to $+5.11$. With 95% confidence, you conclude that the "true" treatment effect is between .23 and 5.11 milliseconds in favor of the white-noise condition.

9. (a) $H_0: \mu_D = 0$, $H_1: \mu_D \neq 0$
   (b) $\bar{D} = -4.86$, $SS_D = 136.86$, $s_{\bar{D}} = 1.81$
   (c) $t = -4.86/1.81 = -2.69$, $t_{.05} = \pm 2.447$, reject H_0.
   (d) Conclude $\mu_D < 0$ (i.e., $\mu_{browser1} - \mu_{browser2} < 0$): Finding the desired information on the Internet is faster when using browser 1.

13. (a) Unlike Problems 6 and 11, here there is no random assignment within pairs.
    (b) With random assignment, it is much easier to clarify cause-and-effect relationships.
    (c) Volunteer parents are more likely to provide academic assistance and encouragement to their children.

Chapter 16

3. (a) $H_0: \mu_1 = \mu_2 = \mu_3 = \mu_4$
   (b) There are many ways in which H_0 can be incorrect.

(c) e.g., $\mu_1 = \mu_2 \neq \mu_3 = \mu_4$; every μ is unequal to every other μ; $\mu_1 \neq \mu_2 = \mu_3 = \mu_4$.

(d) As written, this H_1 states that *adjacent* μ's are unequal (e.g., μ_1 could still equal μ_3). This H_1 includes only part of the possible ways H_0 could be incorrect.

4. **(a)** H_0: $\mu_1 = \mu_2 = \mu_3$; H_1: the entire set of possibilities other than equality of the three population means

(b) $SS_{within} = 44$, $SS_{between} = 16$, $SS_{total} = 60$.

(c) $df_{within} = 3$, $df_{between} = 2$, $df_{total} = 5$.

(d) $s^2_{within} = 14.67$, $s^2_{between} = 8$, $F = .55$

(e) H_0 is retained ($F_{.05} = 9.55$): there is no evidence that the three treatment conditions differentially affect student behavior.

6. **(a)** $F_{.05} = 3.13$, $F_{.01} = 4.92$

(b) $F_{.05} = 2.87$, $F_{.01} = 4.43$

(c) $F_{.05} = 2.70$, $F_{.01} = 3.98$

(d) $F_{.05} = 3.23$, $F_{.01} = 5.18$

8. **(a)** 2

(b) 552

(c) $p > .05$ ($F_{.05} = 3.55$)

(d) 3312

(e) 18

(f) 20

11. Because the variances (obtained here by squaring the standard deviations) are appreciably different *and* the ns are markedly unequal, the F test would be inappropriate in this case.

12. **(a)** H_0: $\mu_1 = \mu_2 = \mu_3$

(b) $SS_{within} = 96$, $SS_{between} = 98$, $SS_{total} = 194$

(c) $df_{within} = 9$, $df_{between} = 2$, $df_{total} = 11$

(d) Summary table:

Source	SS	df	MS	F	p
Between-groups	98	2	49	4.59	$p < .05$
Within-groups	96	9	10.67		
Total	194	11			

(e) Reject H_0 ($F_{.05} = 4.26$)

(f) $\hat{\omega}^2 = .37$, or 37% of the variance in phonological awareness scores is explained by the independent variable, reading program.

(g) In the population, the mean phonological awareness of students differs across the reading programs. A post hoc test (e.g., Tukey) now must be conducted to determine which of the three possible comparisons—$\overline{X}_1$ vs. $\overline{X}_2$, $\overline{X}_1$ vs. $\overline{X}_3$, $\overline{X}_2$ vs. $\overline{X}_3$—is (are) statistically significant.

17. **(a)** 10

(b)

	$\overline{X}_1 = 20.3$	$\overline{X}_2 = 12.2$	$\overline{X}_3 = 15.3$	$\overline{X}_4 = 13.6$	$\overline{X}_5 = 19.1$
$\overline{X}_1 = 20.3$	—	8.1	5.0	6.7	1.2
$\overline{X}_2 = 12.2$		—	−3.1	−1.4	−6.9
$\overline{X}_3 = 15.3$			—	1.7	−3.8
$\overline{X}_4 = 13.6$				—	−5.5
$\overline{X}_5 = 19.1$					—

(c) $HSD = 4.04\sqrt{20.5/9} = 6.10$; $\mu_1 > \mu_2$, $\mu_1 > \mu_4$, $\mu_2 < \mu_5$

(d) $HSD = 4.93\sqrt{20.5/9} = 7.44$; $\mu_1 > \mu_2$

18. **(a)** $H_0: \mu_1 = \mu_2 = \mu_3 = \mu_4$

(b) $\overline{X}_1 = 24.2$, $\overline{X}_2 = 29.5$, $\overline{X}_3 = 33.1$, $\overline{X}_4 = 26.4$, $\overline{\overline{X}} = 28.3$

(c) $SS_{within} = 1628.4$, $SS_{between} = 449$, $SS_{total} = 1628.4 + 449 = 2077.4$

(d) $F = 3.31$, reject H_0 ($F_{.05} = 2.86$). Summary table:

Source	SS	df	MS	F	p
Between-groups	449	3	149.67	3.31	$p < .05$
Within-groups	1628.4	36	45.23		
Total	2077.4	39			

(e) $HSD = 3.85\sqrt{45.23/10} = 8.19$; only the difference between $\overline{X}_1$ and $\overline{X}_3$ (-8.9) exceeds this value.

(f) $\hat{\omega}^2 = .15$, or 15% of the variance in the response variable (number of metacognitive strategies invoked by the child) is explained by the independent variable, teaching method.

(g) $\mu_3 > \mu_1$: Method 3 is superior to Method 1 for teaching metacognitive strategies to fifth graders.

19. **(a)** $\mu_1 - \mu_2$: -5.3 ± 8.19, or -13.49 to $+2.89$
$\mu_1 - \mu_3$: -8.9 ± 8.19, or -17.09 to $-.71$
$\mu_1 - \mu_4$: -2.2 ± 8.19, or -10.39 to $+5.99$
$\mu_2 - \mu_3$: -3.6 ± 8.19, or -11.79 to $+4.59$
$\mu_2 - \mu_4$: 3.1 ± 8.19, or -5.09 to $+11.29$
$\mu_3 - \mu_4$: 6.7 ± 8.19, or -1.49 to $+14.89$

(b) They agree, of course: where H_0 had been retained, the 95% confidence interval includes 0; where H_0 had been rejected ($\mu_1 - \mu_3$), 0 falls outside the 95% confidence interval.

20. **(a)** Problem 12: because students were not *randomly assigned* to the instructional programs, it is difficult to conclude that a causal relationship exists between the instructional program and the phonological awareness of students.

(b) The three schools may also differ in the socioeconomic status of the community they serve, the teacher-student ratio, or the level of experience and ability of the teaching staff.

Chapter 17

1. You would point out, we trust, that these procedures are appropriate only for testing $H_0: \rho = 0$. A "normalizing" procedure is required where H_0 specifies a value for ρ other than 0.

2. **(a)** $s_r = .175$, $t = -2.17$, $t_{.05} = \pm 2.048$, reject H_0.
   (b) $s_r = .283$, $t = +2.12$, $t_{.05} = \pm 2.306$, retain H_0.
   (c) $s_r = .127$, $t = -1.34$, $t_{.01} = \pm 2.660$, retain H_0.
   (d) $s_r = .066$, $t = +10.45$, $t_{.05} = +1.658$, reject H_0.
   (e) $s_r = .077$, $t = -5.58$, $t_{.01} = -2.358$, reject H_0.

3. **(a)** $r_{.05} = \pm .361$, reject H_0.
   (b) $r_{.05} = \pm .632$, retain H_0.
   (c) $r_{.01} = \pm .325$, retain H_0.
   (d) $r_{.05} = + .150$, reject H_0.
   (e) $r_{.01} = - .210$, reject H_0.
   (The statistical decisions, of course, necessarily agree across the two problems.)

8. **(a)** $r_{.05} = .441$ (one-tailed); retain H_0.
   (b) approximate interval: $-.14$ to $+.76$
   (c) The very wide interval indicates that the sample was far too small to allow for estimating ρ with satisfactory precision.

9. **(a)** $+.62$ to $+.98$
   (b) $-.19$ to $+.86$
   (c) $-.49$ to $+.74$
   (d) $-.17$ to $+.52$
   (e) $+.01$ to $+.38$

10. **(a)** Intervals are narrower for higher values of r: for samples of a given size, the higher the correlation the less the sampling error.
    (b) Intervals are narrower for larger values of n: for a given sample r, the larger the sample size the less the sampling error.

14. For large samples, the sampling error is sufficiently small that r alone can be taken as a fairly accurate estimate of ρ. For small samples, sampling error can be substantial and should be taken into account by means of an interval estimate.

15. **(a)** No, because the scatterplot reveals considerable curvilinearity.
    (b) Because Pearson r is a measure of *linear* association, r will underestimate the degree of relationship between these two variables (see Section 7.7).

17. The correlation based on the second sample probably would be larger because of less variability—that is, a restriction of range—in one or both variables (see Section 7.7).

1. **(a)** $\chi^2_{.05} = 7.81$, $\chi^2_{.01} = 11.34$ $(df = 3)$
   (b) $\chi^2_{.05} = 5.99$, $\chi^2_{.01} = 9.21$ $(df = 2)$
   (c) $\chi^2_{.05} = 3.84$, $\chi^2_{.01} = 6.63$ $(df = 1)$
   (d) $\chi^2_{.05} = 3.84$, $\chi^2_{.01} = 6.63$ $(df = 1)$
   (e) $\chi^2_{.05} = 11.07$, $\chi^2_{.01} = 15.09$ $(df = 5)$

3. **(a)** H_0: $\pi_A = .25$, $\pi_B = .25$, $\pi_C = .25$, $\pi_D = .25$; H_0: $\pi_A = \pi_B = \pi_C = \pi_D$
   (b) No, because there are many ways H_0 can be false.
   (c) $f_e = 60/4 = 15$ for each test. (Yes, they sum to 60.)
   (d) $\chi^2 = 12.00$, $\chi^2_{.01} = 11.34$, reject H_0.
   (e) The four tests differ in popularity. Test D is chosen more, and Test B less, than chance would dictate.

5. **(a)** H_0: $\pi_{\text{dropout}} = .80$, H_1: $\pi_{\text{dropout}} < .80$
   (b) $\chi^2 = 61.25$, $\chi^2_{.05} = 3.84$, reject H_0.
   (c) The intervention is effective in decreasing dropout.

6. **(a)** .36

   (b) $$\pi_L = \frac{45}{48.84}\left[.36 + \frac{1.92}{45} - 1.96\sqrt{\frac{.36(.64)}{45} + \frac{.96}{2025}}\right] = .24$$

   $$\pi_U = \frac{45}{48.84}\left[.36 + \frac{1.92}{45} + 1.96\sqrt{\frac{.36(.64)}{45} + \frac{.96}{2025}}\right] = .51$$

   With 95% confidence, we can conclude that the dropout rate in the population is between 24% and 51%. (The population is all gang members in this high school who potentially could participate in the stay-in-school intervention.)

   (c) $\pi_L = .23$, $\pi_U = .50$. Figure 18.3, of course, provides only values for π_L and π_U. Furthermore, this figure has no explicit reference to either $P = .36$ or $n = 45$, which results in even greater approximation. Nevertheless, $\pi_L = .23$ and $\pi_U = .50$ are almost identical to the hand-calculated values obtained in Problem 6b.

10. **(a)** The proportion of rural citizens who are in favor of (or, who oppose) the referendum is equal to the proportion of urban citizens who are in favor of (or, who oppose) the referendum.

    (b)

	In favor	Opposed	f_{row}
Rural	$f_o = 35$ $f_e = 48.59$	$f_o = 55$ $f_e = 41.41$	90
Urban	$f_o = 53$ $f_e = 39.41$	$f_o = 20$ $f_e = 33.59$	73
f_{col}	88	75	163

(c) $\chi^2 = 18.45$, $\chi^2_{.05} = 3.84$ and $\chi^2_{.01} = 6.63$, reject H_0 at either level. (In actual practice, of course, you would specify only one level of significance.)

(d) One's position on the gay rights referendum is dependent on whether one resides in an urban or rural community.

(e) Rural: .39 in favor and .61 opposed; urban: .73 in favor and .27 opposed. More people from urban communities are in favor of the referendum in comparison to people from rural communities.

12. $\chi^2 = 18.44$ (which, allowing for rounding, is the same as that obtained for Problem 9c).

13. Because the *before* and *after* responses are based on the same individuals, these observations are not independent of one another. Consequently, the χ^2 test of independence is inappropriate in this instance.

16. (a) The two variables are independent: choice of candidate is unrelated to the respondent's household income.

(b)

	Jadallah	**Yung**	**Pandiscio**	f_{row}
less than $20,000	$f_o = 8$ $f_c = 8.44$	$f_o = 11$ $f_e = 9.22$	$f_o = 6$ $f_e = 7.33$	25
$20,000– $39,999	$f_o = 23$ $f_e = 19.59$	$f_o = 17$ $f_e = 21.40$	$f_o = 18$ $f_e = 17.01$	58
$40,000– $59,999	$f_o = 20$ $f_e = 20.94$	$f_o = 22$ $f_e = 22.87$	$f_o = 20$ $f_e = 18.19$	62
$60,000 or more	$f_o = 25$ $f_c = 27.02$	$f_o = 33$ $f_e = 29.51$	$f_o = 22$ $f_e = 23.47$	80
f_{col}	76	83	66	225

(c) $\chi^2 = 3.07$, $\chi^2_{.05} = 12.59$, retain H_0.

(d) Candidate choice is unrelated to the respondent's household income.

17. To answer this question, a one-variable χ^2 is carried out on the column frequencies. $\chi^2 = 1.95$, $\chi^2_{.05} = 5.99$, retain H_0.

Chapter 19

1. (a) .20

(b) This question makes no sense: power is the probability of rejecting H_0 *given that it is false.*

3. (a) 429

(b) 48

(c) 18

(d) 10

5. **(a)** .25, or only one in four
   (b) one in four

8. **(a)** 201 in each group
   (b) larger
   (c) smaller

9. **(a)** $H_0: \rho = 0$, $H_1: \rho > 0$ **(d)** .60
   (b) 37   **(e)** .40
   (c) .20

10. **(a)** 783   **(d)** 91
    (b) 17   **(e)** 25
    (c) 12   **(f)** 8

APPENDIX C

Statistical Tables

Table A   Areas under the Normal Curve

Column 2 gives the proportion of the area under the entire curve that is between the mean ($z = 0$) and the positive value of z. Areas for negative values of z are the same as for positive values, since the curve is symmetrical.

Column 3 gives the proportion of the area under the entire curve that falls beyond the stated positive value of z. Areas for negative values of z are the same, since the curve is symmetrical.

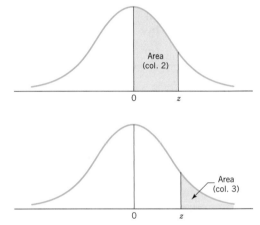

z	Area Between Mean and z	Area Beyond z	z	Area Between Mean and z	Area Beyond z	z	Area Between Mean and z	Area Beyond z
1	**2**	**3**	**1**	**2**	**3**	**1**	**2**	**3**
0.00	.0000	.5000	0.15	.0596	.4404	0.30	.1179	.3821
0.01	.0040	.4960	0.16	.0636	.4364	0.31	.1217	.3783
0.02	.0080	.4920	0.17	.0675	.4325	0.32	.1255	.3745
0.03	.0120	.4880	0.18	.0714	.4286	0.33	.1293	.3707
0.04	.0160	.4840	0.19	.0753	.4247	0.34	.1331	.3669
0.05	.0199	.4801	0.20	.0793	.4207	0.35	.1368	.3632
0.06	.0239	.4761	0.21	.0832	.4168	0.36	.1406	.3594
0.07	.0279	.4721	0.22	.0871	.4129	0.37	.1443	.3557
0.08	.0319	.4681	0.23	.0910	.4090	0.38	.1480	.3520
0.09	.0359	.4641	0.24	.0948	.4052	0.39	.1517	.3483
0.10	.0398	.4602	0.25	.0987	.4013	0.40	.1554	.3446
0.11	.0438	.4562	0.26	.1026	.3974	0.41	.1591	.3409
0.12	.0478	.4522	0.27	.1064	.3936	0.42	.1628	.3372
0.13	.0517	.4483	0.28	.1103	.3897	0.43	.1664	.3336
0.14	.0557	.4443	0.29	.1141	.3859	0.44	.1700	.3300

(Table continues on next page)

Table A   (Continued)

z	Area Between Mean and z	Area Beyond z	z	Area Between Mean and z	Area Beyond z	z	Area Between Mean and z	Area Beyond z
1	2	3	1	2	3	1	2	3
0.45	.1736	.3264	0.80	.2881	.2119	1.15	.3749	.1251
0.46	.1772	.3228	0.81	.2910	.2090	1.16	.3770	.1230
0.47	.1808	.3192	0.82	.2939	.2061	1.17	.3790	.1210
0.48	.1844	.3156	0.83	.2967	.2033	1.18	.3810	.1190
0.49	.1879	.3121	0.84	.2995	.2005	1.19	.3830	.1170
0.50	.1915	.3085	0.85	.3023	.1977	1.20	.3849	.1151
0.51	.1950	.3050	0.86	.3051	.1949	1.21	.3869	.1131
0.52	.1985	.3015	0.87	.3078	.1922	1.22	.3888	.1112
0.53	.2019	.2981	0.88	.3106	.1894	1.23	.3907	.1093
0.54	.2054	.2946	0.89	.3133	.1867	1.24	.3925	.1075
0.55	.2088	.2912	0.90	.3159	.1841	1.25	.3944	.1056
0.56	.2123	.2877	0.91	.3186	.1814	1.26	.3962	.1038
0.57	.2157	.2843	0.92	.3212	.1788	1.27	.3980	.1020
0.58	.2190	.2810	0.93	.3238	.1762	1.28	.3997	.1003
0.59	.2224	.2776	0.94	.3264	.1736	1.29	.4015	.0985
0.60	.2257	.2743	0.95	.3289	.1711	1.30	.4032	.0968
0.61	.2291	.2709	0.96	.3315	.1685	1.31	.4049	.0951
0.62	.2324	.2676	0.97	.3340	.1660	1.32	.4066	.0934
0.63	.2357	.2643	0.98	.3365	.1635	1.33	.4082	.0918
0.64	.2389	.2611	0.99	.3389	.1611	1.34	.4099	.0901
0.65	.2422	.2578	1.00	.3413	.1587	1.35	.4115	.0885
0.66	.2454	.2546	1.01	.3438	.1562	1.36	.4131	.0869
0.67	.2486	.2514	1.02	.3461	.1539	1.37	.4147	.0853
0.68	.2517	.2483	1.03	.3485	.1515	1.38	.4162	.0838
0.69	.2549	.2451	1.04	.3508	.1492	1.39	.4177	.0823
0.70	.2580	.2420	1.05	.3531	.1469	1.40	.4192	.0808
0.71	.2611	.2389	1.06	.3554	.1446	1.41	.4207	.0793
0.72	.2642	.2358	1.07	.3577	.1423	1.42	.4222	.0778
0.73	.2673	.2327	1.08	.3599	.1401	1.43	.4236	.0764
0.74	.2704	.2296	1.09	.3621	.1379	1.44	.4251	.0749
0.75	.2734	.2266	1.10	.3643	.1357	1.45	.4265	.0735
0.76	.2764	.2236	1.11	.3665	.1335	1.46	.4279	.0721
0.77	.2794	.2206	1.12	.3686	.1314	1.47	.4292	.0708
0.78	.2823	.2177	1.13	.3708	.1292	1.48	.4306	.0694
0.79	.2852	.2148	1.14	.3729	.1271	1.49	.4319	.0681

(*Table continues on next page*)

Table A   *(Continued)*

z	Area Between Mean and z	Area Beyond z	z	Area Between Mean and z	Area Beyond z	z	Area Between Mean and z	Area Beyond z
1	**2**	**3**	**1**	**2**	**3**	**1**	**2**	**3**
1.50	.4332	.0668	1.85	.4678	.0322	2.20	.4861	.0139
1.51	4345	.0655	1.86	.4686	.0314	2.21	.4864	.0136
1.52	.4357	.0643	1.87	.4693	.0307	2.22	.4868	.0132
1.53	.4370	.0630	1.88	.4699	.0301	2.23	.4871	.0129
1.54	.4382	.0618	1.89	.4706	.0294	2.24	.4875	.0125
1.55	.4394	.0606	1.90	.4713	.0287	2.25	.4878	.0122
1.56	.4406	.0594	1.91	.4719	.0281	2.26	.4881	.0119
1.57	.4418	.0582	1.92	.4726	.0274	2.27	.4884	.0116
1.58	.4429	.0571	1.93	.4732	.0268	2.28	.4887	.0113
1.59	.4441	.0559	1.94	.4738	.0262	2.29	.4890	.0110
1.60	.4452	.0548	1.95	.4744	.0256	2.30	.4893	.0107
1.61	.4463	.0537	1.96	.4750	.0250	2.31	.4896	.0104
1.62	.4474	.0526	1.97	.4756	.0244	2.32	.4898	.0102
1.63	.4484	.0516	1.98	.4761	.0239	2.33	.4901	.0099
1.64	.4495	.0505	1.99	.4767	.0233	2.34	.4904	.0096
1.65	.4505	.0495	2.00	.4772	.0228	2.35	.4906	.0094
1.66	.4515	.0485	2.01	.4778	.0222	2.36	.4909	.0091
1.67	.4525	.0475	2.02	.4783	.0217	2.37	.4911	.0089
1.68	.4535	.0465	2.03	.4788	.0212	2.38	.4913	.0087
1.69	.4545	.0455	2.04	.4793	.0207	2.39	.4916	.0084
1.70	.4554	.0446	2.05	.4798	.0202	2.40	.4918	.0082
1.71	.4564	.0436	2.06	.4803	.0197	2.41	.4920	.0080
1.72	.4573	.0427	2.07	.4808	.0192	2.42	.4922	.0078
1.73	.4582	.0418	2.08	.4812	.0188	2.43	.4925	.0075
1.74	.4591	.0409	2.09	.4817	.0183	2.44	.4927	.0073
1.75	.4599	.0401	2.10	.4821	.0179	2.45	.4929	.0071
1.76	.4608	.0392	2.11	.4826	.0174	2.46	.4931	.0069
1.77	.4616	.0384	2.12	.4830	.0170	2.47	.4932	.0068
1.78	.4625	.0375	2.13	.4834	.0166	2.48	.4934	.0066
1.79	.4633	.0367	2.14	.4838	.0162	2.49	.4936	.0064
1.80	.4641	.0359	2.15	.4842	.0158	2.50	.4938	.0062
1.81	.4649	.0351	2.16	.4846	.0154	2.51	.4940	.0060
1.82	.4656	.0344	2.17	.4850	.0150	2.52	.4941	.0059
1.83	.4664	.0336	2.18	.4854	.0146	2.53	.4943	.0057
1.84	.4671	.0329	2.19	.4857	.0143	2.54	.4945	.0055

(Table continues on next page)

Table A   *(Continued)*

z	Area Between Mean and z	Area Beyond z	z	Area Between Mean and z	Area Beyond z	z	Area Between Mean and z	Area Beyond z
1	**2**	**3**	**1**	**2**	**3**	**1**	**2**	**3**
2.55	.4946	.0054	2.80	.4974	.0026	3.05	.4989	.0011
2.56	.4948	.0052	2.81	.4975	.0025	3.06	.4989	.0011
2.57	.4949	.0051	2.82	.4976	.0024	3.07	.4989	.0011
2.58	.4951	.0049	2.83	.4977	.0023	3.08	.4990	.0010
2.59	.4952	.0048	2.84	.4977	.0023	3.09	.4990	.0010
2.60	.4953	.0047	2.85	.4978	.0022	3.10	.4990	.0010
2.61	.4955	.0045	2.86	.4979	.0021	3.11	.4991	.0009
2.62	.4956	.0044	2.87	.4979	.0021	3.12	.4991	.0009
2.63	.4957	.0043	2.88	.4980	.0020	3.13	.4991	.0009
2.64	.4959	.0041	2.89	.4981	.0019	3.14	.4992	.0008
2.65	.4960	.0040	2.90	.4981	.0019	3.15	.4992	.0008
2.66	.4961	.0039	2.91	.4982	.0018	3.16	.4992	.0008
2.67	.4962	.0038	2.92	.4982	.0018	3.17	.4992	.0008
2.68	.4963	.0037	2.93	.4983	.0017	3.18	.4993	.0007
2.69	.4964	.0036	2.94	.4984	.0016	3.19	.4993	.0007
2.70	.4965	.0035	2.95	.4984	.0016	3.20	.4993	.0007
2.71	.4966	.0034	2.96	.4985	.0015	3.21	.4993	.0007
2.72	.4967	.0033	2.97	.4985	.0015	3.22	.4994	.0006
2.73	.4968	.0032	2.98	.4986	.0014	3.23	.4994	.0006
2.74	.4969	.0031	2.99	.4986	.0014	3.24	.4994	.0006
2.75	.4970	.0030	3.00	.4987	.0013	3.30	.4995	.0005
2.76	.4971	.0029	3.01	.4987	.0013	3.40	.4997	.0003
2.77	.4972	.0028	3.02	.4987	.0013	3.50	.4998	.0002
2.78	.4973	.0027	3.03	.4988	.0012	3.60	.4998	.0002
2.79	.4974	.0026	3.04	.4988	.0012	3.70	.4999	.0001

Table B Student's *t* Distribution

The first column identifies the specific *t* distribution according to its degrees of freedom. Other columns give the value of *t* that corresponds to the *area beyond t* in one or both tails, according to the particular column heading. Areas beyond negative values of *t* are the same as those beyond positive values, since the curve is symmetrical.

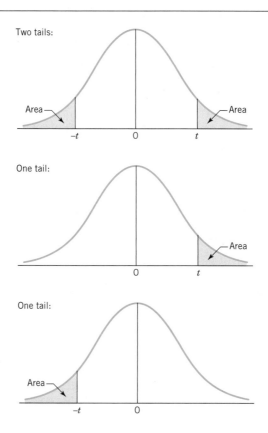

Two tails:

Area —

Area

−*t*   0   *t*

One tail:

Area

0   *t*

One tail:

Area —

−*t*   0

			Area in *Both* Tails			
	.50	.20	.10	.05	.02	.01
			Area in *Both* Tails			
df	.25	.10	.05	.025	.01	.005
1	1.000	3.078	6.314	12.706	31.821	63.657
2	0.816	1.886	2.920	4.303	6.965	9.925
3	0.765	1.638	2.353	3.182	4.541	5.841
4	0.741	1.533	2.132	2.776	3.747	4.604
5	0.727	1.476	2.015	2.571	3.365	4.032
6	0.718	1.440	1.943	2.447	3.143	3.707
7	0.711	1.415	1.895	2.365	2.998	3.499
8	0.706	1.397	1.860	2.306	2.896	3.355
9	0.703	1.383	1.833	2.262	2.821	3.250
10	0.700	1.372	1.812	2.228	2.764	3.169
11	0.697	1.363	1.796	2.201	2.718	3.106
12	0.695	1.356	1.782	2.179	2.681	3.055
13	0.694	1.350	1.771	2.160	2.650	3.012
14	0.692	1.345	1.761	2.145	2.624	2.977
15	0.691	1.341	1.753	2.132	2.602	2.947
16	0.690	1.337	1.746	2.120	2.583	2.921
17	0.689	1.333	1.740	2.110	2.567	2.898
18	0.688	1.330	1.734	2.101	2.552	2.878
19	0.688	1.328	1.729	2.093	2.539	2.861
20	0.687	1.325	1.725	2.086	2.528	2.845
21	0.686	1.323	1.721	2.080	2.518	2.831
22	0.686	1.321	1.717	2.074	2.508	2.819
23	0.685	1.319	1.714	2.069	2.500	2.807
24	0.685	1.318	1.711	2.064	2.492	2.797
25	0.684	1.316	1.708	2.060	2.485	2.787
26	0.684	1.315	1.706	2.056	2.479	2.779
27	0.684	1.314	1.703	2.052	2.473	2.771
28	0.683	1.313	1.701	2.048	2.467	2.763
29	0.683	1.311	1.699	2.045	2.462	2.756
30	0.683	1.310	1.697	2.042	2.457	2.750
40	0.681	1.303	1.684	2.021	2.423	2.704
60	0.679	1.296	1.671	2.000	2.390	2.660
120	0.677	1.289	1.658	1.980	2.358	2.617
∞	0.674	1.282	1.645	1.960	2.326	2.576

Source: © 1963 R. A. Fisher and F. Yates, reprinted by permission of Pearson Education Limited.

Table C   The *F* Distribution

The values of *F* are those corresponding to
5% (Roman type) and 1% (**boldface** type)
of the area in the upper tail of the distribution.
The specific *F* distribution must be identified
by the number of degrees of freedom
characterizing the numerator and the
denominator of *F*.

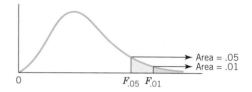

Degrees of Freedom: Denominator	Degrees of Freedom: Numerator														
	1	2	3	4	5	6	7	8	9	10	11	12	14	16	20
1	161	200	216	225	230	234	237	239	241	242	243	244	245	246	248
	4,052	**4,999**	**5,403**	**5,625**	**5,764**	**5,859**	**5,928**	**5,981**	**6,022**	**6,056**	**6,082**	**6,106**	**6,142**	**6,169**	**6,208**
2	18.51	19.00	19.16	19.25	19.30	19.33	19.36	19.37	19.38	19.39	19.40	19.41	19.42	19.43	19.44
	98.49	**99.00**	**99.17**	**99.25**	**99.30**	**99.33**	**99.34**	**99.36**	**99.38**	**99.40**	**99.41**	**99.42**	**99.43**	**99.44**	**99.45**
3	10.13	9.55	9.28	9.12	9.01	8.94	8.88	8.84	8.81	8.78	8.76	8.74	8.71	8.69	8.66
	34.12	**30.82**	**29.46**	**28.71**	**28.24**	**27.91**	**27.67**	**27.49**	**27.34**	**27.23**	**27.13**	**27.05**	**26.92**	**26.83**	**26.69**
4	7.71	6.94	6.59	6.39	6.26	6.16	6.09	6.04	6.00	5.96	5.93	5.91	5.87	5.84	5.80
	21.20	**18.00**	**16.69**	**15.98**	**15.52**	**15.21**	**14.98**	**14.80**	**14.66**	**14.54**	**14.45**	**14.37**	**14.24**	**14.15**	**14.02**
5	6.61	5.79	5.41	5.19	5.05	4.95	4.88	4.82	4.78	4.74	4.70	4.68	4.64	4.60	4.56
	16.26	**13.27**	**12.06**	**11.39**	**10.97**	**10.67**	**10.45**	**10.27**	**10.15**	**10.05**	**9.96**	**9.89**	**9.77**	**9.68**	**9.55**
6	5.99	5.14	4.76	4.53	4.39	4.28	4.21	4.15	4.10	4.06	4.03	4.00	3.96	3.92	3.87
	13.74	**10.92**	**9.78**	**9.15**	**8.75**	**8.47**	**8.26**	**8.10**	**7.98**	**7.87**	**7.79**	**7.72**	**7.60**	**7.52**	**7.39**
7	5.59	4.47	4.35	4.12	3.97	3.87	3.79	3.73	3.68	3.63	3.60	3.57	3.52	3.49	3.44
	12.25	**9.55**	**8.45**	**7.85**	**7.46**	**7.19**	**7.00**	**6.84**	**6.71**	**6.62**	**6.54**	**6.47**	**6.35**	**6.27**	**6.15**
8	5.32	4.46	4.07	3.84	3.69	3.58	3.50	3.44	3.39	3.34	3.31	3.28	3.23	3.20	3.15
	11.26	**8.65**	**7.59**	**7.01**	**6.63**	**6.37**	**6.19**	**6.03**	**5.91**	**5.82**	**5.74**	**5.67**	**5.56**	**5.48**	**5.36**
9	5.12	4.26	3.86	3.63	3.48	3.37	3.29	3.23	3.18	3.13	3.10	3.07	3.02	2.98	2.93
	10.56	**8.02**	**6.99**	**6.42**	**6.06**	**5.80**	**5.62**	**5.47**	**5.35**	**5.26**	**5.18**	**5.11**	**5.00**	**4.92**	**4.80**
10	4.96	4.10	3.71	3.48	3.33	3.22	3.14	3.07	3.02	2.97	2.94	2.91	2.86	2.82	2.77
	10.04	**7.56**	**6.55**	**5.99**	**5.64**	**5.39**	**5.21**	**5.06**	**4.95**	**4.85**	**4.78**	**4.71**	**4.60**	**4.52**	**4.41**
11	4.84	3.98	3.59	3.36	3.20	3.09	3.01	2.95	2.90	2.86	2.82	2.79	2.74	2.70	2.65
	9.65	**7.20**	**6.22**	**5.67**	**5.32**	**5.07**	**4.88**	**4.74**	**4.63**	**4.54**	**4.46**	**4.40**	**4.29**	**4.21**	**4.10**
12	4.75	3.88	3.49	3.26	3.11	3.00	2.92	2.85	2.80	2.76	2.72	2.69	2.64	2.60	2.54
	9.33	**6.93**	**5.95**	**5.41**	**5.06**	**4.82**	**4.65**	**4.50**	**4.39**	**4.30**	**4.22**	**4.16**	**4.05**	**3.98**	**3.86**
13	4.67	3.80	3.41	3.18	3.02	2.92	2.84	2.77	2.72	2.67	2.63	2.60	2.55	2.51	2.46
	9.07	**6.70**	**5.74**	**5.20**	**4.86**	**4.62**	**4.44**	**4.30**	**4.19**	**4.10**	**4.02**	**3.96**	**3.85**	**3.78**	**3.67**
14	4.60	3.74	3.34	3.11	2.96	2.85	2.77	2.70	2.65	2.60	2.56	2.53	2.48	2.44	2.39
	8.86	**6.51**	**5.56**	**5.03**	**4.69**	**4.46**	**4.28**	**4.14**	**4.03**	**3.94**	**3.86**	**3.80**	**3.70**	**3.62**	**3.51**
15	4.54	3.68	3.29	3.06	2.90	2.79	2.70	2.64	2.59	2.55	2.51	2.48	2.43	2.39	2.33
	8.68	**6.36**	**5.42**	**4.89**	**4.56**	**4.32**	**4.14**	**4.00**	**3.89**	**3.80**	**3.73**	**3.67**	**3.56**	**3.48**	**3.36**

Source: From *Statistical Methods*, Eighth Edition, G. W. Snedecor and W. G. Cochran © 1989 by Iowa State University Press.

(Table continues on next page)

Table C   *(Continued)*

Degrees of Freedom: Denominator	Degrees of Freedom: Numerator														
---	1	2	3	4	5	6	7	8	9	10	11	12	14	16	20
16	4.49	3.63	3.24	3.01	2.85	2.74	2.66	2.59	2.54	2.49	2.45	2.42	2.37	2.33	2.28
	8.53	**6.23**	**5.29**	**4.77**	**4.44**	**4.20**	**4.03**	**3.89**	**3.78**	**3.69**	**3.61**	**3.55**	**3.45**	**3.37**	**3.25**
17	4.45	3.59	3.20	2.96	2.81	2.70	2.62	2.55	2.50	2.45	2.41	2.38	2.33	2.29	2.23
	8.40	**6.11**	**5.18**	**4.67**	**4.34**	**4.10**	**3.93**	**3.79**	**3.68**	**3.59**	**3.52**	**3.45**	**3.35**	**3.27**	**3.16**
18	4.41	3.55	3.16	2.93	2.77	2.66	2.58	2.51	2.46	2.41	2.37	2.34	2.29	2.25	2.19
	8.28	**6.01**	**5.09**	**4.58**	**4.25**	**4.01**	**3.85**	**3.71**	**3.60**	**3.51**	**3.44**	**3.37**	**3.27**	**3.19**	**3.07**
19	4.38	3.52	3.13	2.90	2.74	2.63	2.55	2.48	2.43	2.38	2.34	2.31	2.26	2.21	2.15
	8.18	**5.93**	**5.01**	**4.50**	**4.17**	**3.94**	**3.77**	**3.63**	**3.52**	**3.43**	**3.36**	**3.30**	**3.19**	**3.12**	**3.00**
20	4.35	3.49	3.10	2.87	2.71	2.60	2.52	2.45	2.40	2.35	2.31	2.28	2.23	2.18	2.12
	8.10	**5.85**	**4.94**	**4.43**	**4.10**	**3.87**	**3.71**	**3.56**	**3.45**	**3.37**	**3.30**	**3.23**	**3.13**	**3.05**	**2.94**
21	4.32	3.47	3.07	2.84	2.68	2.57	2.49	2.42	2.37	2.32	2.28	2.25	2.20	2.15	2.09
	8.02	**5.78**	**4.87**	**4.37**	**4.04**	**3.81**	**3.65**	**3.51**	**3.40**	**3.31**	**3.24**	**3.17**	**3.07**	**2.99**	**2.88**
22	4.30	3.44	3.05	2.82	2.66	2.55	2.47	2.40	2.35	2.30	2.26	2.23	2.18	2.13	2.07
	7.94	**5.72**	**4.82**	**4.31**	**3.99**	**3.76**	**3.59**	**3.45**	**3.35**	**3.26**	**3.18**	**3.12**	**3.02**	**2.94**	**2.83**
23	4.28	3.42	3.03	2.80	2.64	2.53	2.45	2.38	2.32	2.28	2.24	2.20	2.14	2.10	2.04
	7.88	**5.66**	**4.76**	**4.26**	**3.94**	**3.71**	**3.54**	**3.41**	**3.30**	**3.21**	**3.14**	**3.07**	**2.97**	**2.89**	**2.78**
24	4.26	3.40	3.01	2.78	2.62	2.51	2.43	2.36	2.30	2.26	2.22	2.18	2.13	2.09	2.02
	7.82	**5.61**	**4.72**	**4.22**	**3.90**	**3.67**	**3.50**	**3.36**	**3.25**	**3.17**	**3.09**	**3.03**	**2.93**	**2.85**	**2.74**
25	4.24	3.38	2.99	2.76	2.60	2.49	2.41	2.34	2.28	2.24	2.20	2.16	2.11	2.06	2.00
	7.77	**5.57**	**4.68**	**4.18**	**3.86**	**3.63**	**3.46**	**3.32**	**3.21**	**3.13**	**3.05**	**2.99**	**2.89**	**2.81**	**2.70**
26	4.22	3.37	2.98	2.74	2.59	2.47	2.39	2.32	2.27	2.22	2.18	2.15	2.10	2.05	1.99
	7.72	**5.53**	**4.64**	**4.14**	**3.82**	**3.59**	**3.42**	**3.29**	**3.17**	**3.09**	**3.02**	**2.96**	**2.86**	**2.77**	**2.66**
27	4.21	3.35	2.96	2.73	2.57	2.46	2.37	2.30	2.25	2.20	2.16	2.13	2.08	2.03	1.97
	7.68	**5.49**	**4.60**	**4.11**	**3.79**	**3.56**	**3.39**	**3.26**	**3.14**	**3.06**	**2.98**	**2.93**	**2.83**	**2.74**	**2.63**
28	4.20	3.34	2.95	2.71	2.56	2.44	2.36	2.29	2.24	2.19	2.15	2.12	2.06	2.02	1.96
	7.64	**5.45**	**4.57**	**4.07**	**3.76**	**3.53**	**3.36**	**3.23**	**3.11**	**3.03**	**2.95**	**2.90**	**2.80**	**2.71**	**2.60**
29	4.18	3.33	2.93	2.70	2.54	2.43	2.35	2.28	2.22	2.18	2.14	2.10	2.05	2.00	1.94
	7.60	**5.42**	**4.54**	**4.04**	**3.73**	**3.50**	**3.33**	**3.20**	**3.08**	**3.00**	**2.92**	**2.87**	**2.77**	**2.68**	**2.57**
30	4.17	3.32	2.92	2.69	2.53	2.42	2.34	2.27	2.21	2.16	2.12	2.09	2.04	1.99	1.93
	7.56	**5.39**	**4.51**	**4.02**	**3.70**	**3.47**	**3.30**	**3.17**	**3.06**	**2.98**	**2.90**	**2.84**	**2.74**	**2.66**	**2.55**
32	4.15	3.30	2.90	2.67	2.51	2.40	2.32	2.25	2.19	2.14	2.10	2.07	2.02	1.97	1.91
	7.50	**5.34**	**4.46**	**3.97**	**3.66**	**3.42**	**3.25**	**3.12**	**3.01**	**2.94**	**2.86**	**2.80**	**2.70**	**2.62**	**2.51**
34	4.13	3.28	2.88	2.65	2.49	2.38	2.30	2.23	2.17	2.12	2.08	2.05	2.00	1.95	1.89
	7.44	**5.29**	**4.42**	**3.93**	**3.61**	**3.38**	**3.21**	**3.08**	**2.97**	**2.89**	**2.82**	**2.76**	**2.66**	**2.58**	**2.47**
36	4.11	3.26	2.86	2.63	2.48	2.36	2.28	2.21	2.15	2.10	2.06	2.03	1.98	1.93	1.87
	7.39	**5.25**	**4.38**	**3.89**	**3.58**	**3.35**	**3.18**	**3.04**	**2.94**	**2.86**	**2.78**	**2.72**	**2.62**	**2.54**	**2.43**
38	4.10	3.25	2.85	2.62	2.46	2.35	2.26	2.19	2.14	2.09	2.05	2.02	1.96	1.92	1.85
	7.35	**5.21**	**4.34**	**3.86**	**3.54**	**3.32**	**3.15**	**3.02**	**2.91**	**2.82**	**2.75**	**2.69**	**2.59**	**2.51**	**2.40**
40	4.08	3.23	2.84	2.61	2.45	2.34	2.25	2.18	2.12	2.07	2.04	2.00	1.95	1.90	1.84
	7.31	**5.18**	**4.31**	**3.83**	**3.51**	**3.29**	**3.12**	**2.99**	**2.88**	**2.80**	**2.73**	**2.66**	**2.56**	**2.49**	**2.37**

(Table continues on next page)

Table C   *(Continued)*

Degrees of Freedom: Denominator	Degrees of Freedom: Numerator														
	1	2	3	4	5	6	7	8	9	10	11	12	14	16	20
42	4.07	3.22	2.83	2.59	2.44	2.32	2.24	2.17	2.11	2.06	2.02	1.99	1.94	1.89	1.82
	7.27	**5.15**	**4.29**	**3.80**	**3.49**	**3.26**	**3.10**	**2.96**	**2.86**	**2.77**	**2.70**	**2.64**	**2.54**	**2.46**	**2.35**
44	4.06	3.21	2.82	2.58	2.43	2.31	2.23	2.16	2.10	2.05	2.01	1.98	1.92	1.88	1.81
	7.24	**5.12**	**4.26**	**3.78**	**3.46**	**3.24**	**3.07**	**2.94**	**2.84**	**2.75**	**2.68**	**2.62**	**2.52**	**2.44**	**2.32**
46	4.05	3.20	2.81	2.57	2.42	2.30	2.22	2.14	2.09	2.04	2.00	1.97	1.91	1.87	1.80
	7.21	**5.10**	**4.24**	**3.76**	**3.44**	**3.22**	**3.05**	**2.92**	**2.82**	**2.73**	**2.66**	**2.60**	**2.50**	**2.42**	**2.30**
48	4.04	3.19	2.80	2.56	2.41	2.30	2.21	2.14	2.08	2.03	1.99	1.96	1.90	1.86	1.79
	7.19	**5.08**	**4.22**	**3.74**	**3.42**	**3.20**	**3.04**	**2.90**	**2.80**	**2.71**	**2.64**	**2.58**	**2.48**	**2.40**	**2.28**
50	4.03	3.18	2.79	2.56	2.40	2.29	2.20	2.13	2.07	2.02	1.98	1.95	1.90	1.85	1.78
	7.17	**5.06**	**4.20**	**3.72**	**3.41**	**3.18**	**3.02**	**2.88**	**2.78**	**2.70**	**2.62**	**2.56**	**2.46**	**2.39**	**2.26**
55	4.02	3.17	2.78	2.54	2.38	2.27	2.18	2.11	2.05	2.00	1.97	1.93	1.88	1.83	1.76
	7.12	**5.01**	**4.16**	**3.68**	**3.37**	**3.15**	**2.98**	**2.85**	**2.75**	**2.66**	**2.59**	**2.53**	**2.43**	**2.35**	**2.23**
60	4.00	3.15	2.76	2.52	2.37	2.25	2.17	2.10	2.04	1.99	1.95	1.92	1.86	1.81	1.75
	7.08	**4.98**	**4.13**	**3.65**	**3.34**	**3.12**	**2.95**	**2.82**	**2.72**	**2.63**	**2.56**	**2.50**	**2.40**	**2.32**	**2.20**
65	3.99	3.14	2.75	2.51	2.36	2.24	2.15	2.08	2.02	1.98	1.94	1.90	1.85	1.80	1.73
	7.04	**4.95**	**4.10**	**3.62**	**3.31**	**3.09**	**2.93**	**2.79**	**2.70**	**2.61**	**2.54**	**2.47**	**2.37**	**2.30**	**2.18**
70	3.98	3.13	2.74	2.50	2.35	2.23	2.14	2.07	2.01	1.97	1.93	1.89	1.84	1.79	1.72
	7.01	**4.92**	**4.08**	**3.60**	**3.29**	**3.07**	**2.91**	**2.77**	**2.67**	**2.59**	**2.51**	**2.45**	**2.35**	**2.28**	**2.15**
80	3.96	3.11	2.72	2.48	2.33	2.21	2.12	2.05	1.99	1.95	1.91	1.88	1.82	1.77	1.70
	6.96	**4.88**	**4.04**	**3.56**	**3.25**	**3.04**	**2.87**	**2.74**	**2.64**	**2.55**	**2.48**	**2.41**	**2.32**	**2.24**	**2.11**
100	3.94	3.09	2.70	2.46	2.30	2.19	2.10	2.03	1.97	1.92	1.88	1.85	1.79	1.75	1.68
	6.90	**4.82**	**3.98**	**3.51**	**3.20**	**2.99**	**2.82**	**2.69**	**2.59**	**2.51**	**2.43**	**2.36**	**2.26**	**2.19**	**2.06**
125	3.92	3.07	2.68	2.44	2.29	2.17	2.08	2.01	1.95	1.90	1.86	1.83	1.77	1.72	1.65
	6.84	**4.78**	**3.94**	**3.47**	**3.17**	**2.95**	**2.79**	**2.65**	**2.56**	**2.47**	**2.40**	**2.33**	**2.23**	**2.15**	**2.03**
150	3.91	3.06	2.67	2.43	2.27	2.16	2.07	2.00	1.94	1.89	1.85	1.82	1.76	1.71	1.64
	6.81	**4.75**	**3.91**	**3.44**	**3.14**	**2.92**	**2.76**	**2.62**	**2.53**	**2.44**	**2.37**	**2.30**	**2.20**	**2.12**	**2.00**
200	3.89	3.04	2.65	2.41	2.26	2.14	2.05	1.98	1.92	1.87	1.83	1.80	1.74	1.69	1.62
	6.76	**4.71**	**3.88**	**3.41**	**3.11**	**2.90**	**2.73**	**2.60**	**2.50**	**2.41**	**2.34**	**2.28**	**2.17**	**2.09**	**1.97**
400	3.86	3.02	2.62	2.39	2.23	2.12	2.03	1.96	1.90	1.85	1.81	1.78	1.72	1.67	1.60
	6.70	**4.66**	**3.83**	**3.36**	**3.06**	**2.85**	**2.69**	**2.55**	**2.46**	**2.37**	**2.29**	**2.23**	**2.12**	**2.04**	**1.92**
1000	3.85	3.00	2.61	2.38	2.22	2.10	2.02	1.95	1.89	1.84	1.80	1.76	1.70	1.65	1.58
	6.66	**4.62**	**3.80**	**3.34**	**3.04**	**2.82**	**2.66**	**2.53**	**2.43**	**2.34**	**2.26**	**2.20**	**2.09**	**2.01**	**1.89**
∞	3.84	2.99	2.60	2.37	2.21	2.09	2.01	1.94	1.88	1.83	1.79	1.75	1.69	1.64	1.57
	6.64	**4.60**	**3.78**	**3.32**	**3.02**	**2.80**	**2.64**	**2.51**	**2.41**	**2.32**	**2.24**	**2.18**	**2.07**	**1.99**	**1.87**

Table D   The Studentized Range Statistic

| df_w | α | \multicolumn{9}{c}{k = Number of Groups} |
		2	3	4	5	6	7	8	9	10
5	.05	3.64	4.60	5.22	5.67	6.03	6.33	6.58	6.80	6.99
	.01	5.70	6.98	7.80	8.42	8.91	9.32	9.67	9.97	10.24
6	.05	3.46	4.34	4.90	5.30	5.63	5.90	6.12	6.32	6.49
	.01	5.24	6.33	7.03	7.56	7.97	8.32	8.61	8.87	9.10
7	.05	3.34	4.16	4.68	5.06	5.36	5.61	5.82	6.00	6.16
	.01	4.95	5.92	6.54	7.01	7.37	7.68	7.94	8.17	8.37
8	.05	3.26	4.04	4.53	4.89	5.17	5.40	5.60	5.77	5.92
	.01	4.75	5.64	6.20	6.62	6.96	7.24	7.47	7.68	7.86
9	.05	3.20	3.95	4.41	4.76	5.02	5.24	5.43	5.59	5.74
	.01	4.60	5.43	5.96	6.35	6.66	6.91	7.13	7.33	7.49
10	.05	3.15	3.88	4.33	4.65	4.91	5.12	5.30	5.46	5.60
	.01	4.48	5.27	5.77	6.14	6.43	6.67	6.87	7.05	7.21
11	.05	3.11	3.82	4.26	4.57	4.82	5.03	5.20	5.35	5.49
	.01	4.39	5.15	5.62	5.97	6.25	6.48	6.67	6.84	6.99
12	.05	3.08	3.77	4.20	4.51	4.75	4.95	5.12	5.27	5.39
	.01	4.32	5.05	5.50	5.84	6.10	6.32	6.51	6.67	6.81
13	.05	3.06	3.73	4.15	4.45	4.69	4.88	5.05	5.19	5.32
	.01	4.26	4.96	5.40	5.73	5.98	6.19	6.37	6.53	6.67
14	.05	3.03	3.70	4.11	4.41	4.64	4.83	4.99	5.13	5.25
	.01	4.21	4.89	5.32	5.63	5.88	6.08	6.26	6.41	6.54
15	.05	3.01	3.67	4.08	4.37	4.59	4.78	4.94	5.08	5.20
	.01	4.17	4.84	5.25	5.56	5.80	5.99	6.16	6.31	6.44
16	.05	3.00	3.65	4.05	4.33	4.56	4.74	4.90	5.03	5.15
	.01	4.13	4.79	5.19	5.49	5.72	5.92	6.08	6.22	6.35
17	.05	2.98	3.63	4.02	4.30	4.52	4.70	4.86	4.99	5.11
	.01	4.10	4.74	5.14	5.43	5.66	5.85	6.01	6.15	6.27
18	.05	2.97	3.61	4.00	4.28	4.49	4.67	4.82	4.96	5.07
	.01	4.07	4.70	5.09	5.38	5.60	5.79	5.94	6.08	6.20
19	.05	2.96	3.59	3.98	4.25	4.47	4.65	4.79	4.92	5.04
	.01	4.05	4.67	5.05	5.33	5.55	5.73	5.89	6.02	6.14
20	.05	2.95	3.58	3.96	4.23	4.45	4.62	4.77	4.90	5.01
	.01	4.02	4.64	5.02	5.29	5.51	5.69	5.84	5.97	6.09

Source: From *Biometrika Tables for Statisticians*, E. Pearson and H. Hartley. (Copyright © 1976 by the Oxford University Press, Table 29. Adapted by permission of the Oxford University Press on behalf of the Biometrika Trust.)

(*Table continues on next page*)

Table D   *(Continued)*

df_w	α	2	3	4	5	6	7	8	9	10
					k = Number of Groups					
24	.05	2.92	3.53	3.90	4.17	4.37	4.54	4.68	4.81	4.92
	.01	3.96	4.55	4.91	5.17	5.37	5.54	5.69	5.81	5.92
30	.05	2.89	3.49	3.85	4.10	4.30	4.46	4.60	4.72	4.82
	.01	3.89	4.45	4.80	5.05	5.24	5.40	5.54	5.65	5.76
40	.05	2.86	3.44	3.79	4.04	4.23	4.39	4.52	4.63	4.73
	.01	3.82	4.37	4.70	4.93	5.11	5.26	5.39	5.50	5.60
60	.05	2.83	3.40	3.74	3.98	4.16	4.31	4.44	4.55	4.65
	.01	3.76	4.28	4.59	4.82	4.99	5.13	5.25	5.36	5.45
120	.05	2.80	3.36	3.68	3.92	4.10	4.24	4.36	4.47	4.56
	.01	3.70	4.20	4.50	4.71	4.87	5.01	5.12	5.21	5.30
∞	.05	2.77	3.31	3.63	3.86	4.03	4.17	4.29	4.39	4.47
	.01	3.64	4.12	4.40	4.60	4.76	4.88	4.99	5.08	5.16

Table E Critical Values of r

	Levels of Significance for a One-Tailed Test			
	.05	.025	.01	.005
	Levels of Significance for a Two-Tailed Test			
df	**.10**	**.05**	**.02**	**.01**
1	.988	.997	.9995	.9999
2	.900	.950	.980	.990
3	.805	.878	.934	.959
4	.729	.811	.882	.917
5	.669	.755	.833	.875
6	.622	.707	.789	.834
7	.582	.666	.750	.798
8	.549	.632	.716	.765
9	.521	.602	.685	.735
10	.497	.576	.658	.708
11	.476	.553	.634	.684
12	.458	.532	.612	.661
13	.441	.514	.592	.641
14	.426	.497	.574	.623
15	.412	.482	.558	.606
16	.400	.468	.542	.590
17	.389	.456	.529	.575
18	.378	.444	.516	.561
19	.369	.433	.503	.549
20	.360	.423	.492	.537
22	.344	.404	.472	.515

(*Continued in next column*)

	Levels of Significance for a One-Tailed Test			
	.05	.025	.01	.005
	Levels of Significance for a Two-Tailed Test			
df	**.10**	**.05**	**.02**	**.01**
24	.330	.388	.453	.496
26	.317	.374	.437	.479
28	.306	.361	.423	.463
30	.296	.349	.409	.449
35	.275	.325	.381	.418
40	.257	.304	.358	.393
45	.243	.288	.338	.372
50	.231	.273	.322	.354
55	.220	.261	.307	.339
60	.211	.250	.295	.325
70	.195	.232	.274	.302
80	.183	.217	.256	.283
90	.173	.205	.242	.267
100	.164	.195	.230	.254
120	.150	.178	.210	.232
150	.134	.159	.189	.208
200	.116	.138	.164	.181
300	.095	.113	.134	.148
400	.082	.098	.116	.128
500	.073	.088	.104	.115
1000	.052	.062	.073	.081

Source: © 1963 R. A. Fisher and F. Yates, reprinted by permission of Pearson Education Limited.

Table F   The χ^2 Statistic

The first column identifies the specific χ^2 distribution according to its number of degrees of freedom. Other columns give the proportion of the area under the entire curve that falls above the tabled value of χ^2.

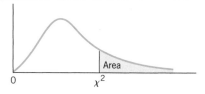

	Area in the Upper Tail				
df	**.10**	**.05**	**.025**	**.01**	**.005**
1	2.71	3.84	5.02	6.63	7.78
2	4.61	5.99	7.38	9.21	10.60
3	6.25	7.81	9.35	11.34	12.84
4	7.78	9.49	11.14	13.28	14.86
5	9.24	11.07	12.83	15.09	16.75
6	10.64	12.59	14.45	16.81	18.55
7	12.02	14.07	16.01	18.48	20.28
8	13.36	15.51	17.53	20.09	21.96
9	14.68	16.92	19.02	21.67	23.59
10	15.99	18.31	20.48	23.21	25.19
11	17.28	19.68	21.92	24.72	26.76
12	18.55	21.03	23.34	26.22	28.30
13	19.81	22.36	24.74	27.69	29.82
14	21.06	23.68	26.12	29.14	31.32
15	22.31	25.00	27.49	30.58	32.80
16	23.54	26.30	28.85	32.00	34.27
17	24.77	27.59	30.19	33.41	35.72
18	25.99	28.87	31.53	34.81	37.16
19	27.20	30.14	32.85	36.19	38.58
20	28.41	31.41	34.17	37.57	40.00
21	29.62	32.67	35.48	38.93	41.40
22	30.81	33.92	36.78	40.29	42.80
23	32.01	35.17	38.08	41.64	44.18
24	33.20	36.42	39.36	42.98	45.56
25	34.38	37.65	40.65	44.31	46.93
26	35.56	38.89	41.92	45.64	48.29
27	36.74	40.11	43.19	46.96	49.64
28	37.92	41.34	44.46	48.28	50.99
29	39.09	42.56	45.72	49.59	52.34
30	40.26	43.77	46.98	50.89	53.67
40	51.81	55.76	59.34	63.69	66.77
50	63.17	67.50	71.42	76.15	79.49
60	74.40	79.08	83.30	88.38	91.95
70	85.53	90.53	95.02	100.42	104.22
80	96.58	101.88	106.63	112.33	116.32
90	107.56	113.14	118.14	124.12	128.30
100	118.50	124.34	129.56	135.81	140.17

Source: From *Biometrika Tables for Statisticians*, E. Pearson and H. Hartley. (Copyright © 1976 by the Oxford University Press, Table 8. Adapted by permission of the Oxford University Press on behalf of the Biometrika Trust.)

INDEX

USEFUL FORMULAS

Percentile rank (ungrouped frequency distribution)	$P = \left(\dfrac{f/2 + \textit{Cum. } f(\textit{below})}{n} \right) 100$	Formula (2.1)
Arithmetic mean	$\overline{X} = \dfrac{\Sigma X}{n}$	Formula (4.1)
Grand mean	$\overline{\overline{X}} = \dfrac{(n_1 \overline{X}_1) + (n_2 \overline{X}_2)}{n_1 + n_2}$	Formula (4.2)
Variance (descriptive statistic)	$S^2 = \dfrac{\Sigma(X - \overline{X})^2}{n} = \dfrac{SS}{n}$	Formula (5.1)
Standard deviation (descriptive statistic)	$S = \sqrt{\dfrac{\Sigma(X - \overline{X})^2}{n}} = \sqrt{\dfrac{SS}{n}}$	Formula (5.2)
z score	$z = \dfrac{X - \overline{X}}{S}$	Formula (6.1)
T score	$T = 50 + 10z$	Formula (6.2)
Covariance	$\text{Cov} = \dfrac{\Sigma(X - \overline{X})(Y - \overline{Y})}{n}$	Formula (7.1)
Pearson r (defining formula)	$r = \dfrac{\text{Cov}}{S_X S_Y}$	Formula (7.2)
Regression equation (expanded raw-score formula)	$Y' = \overbrace{\overline{Y} - r\left(\dfrac{S_Y}{S_X}\right)\overline{X}}^{\text{intercept}} + \overbrace{r\left(\dfrac{S_Y}{S_X}\right)X}^{\text{slope}}$	Formula (8.4)
Regression equation (z-score form)	$z_{Y'} = r z_X$	Formula (8.5)
Standard error of estimate	$S_{Y \cdot X} = \sqrt{\dfrac{\Sigma(Y - Y')^2}{n}}$	Formula (8.7)
Standard error of estimate (alternate formula)	$S_{Y \cdot X} = S_Y \sqrt{1 - r^2}$	Formula (8.8)

Standard error of the mean	$\sigma_{\overline{X}} = \dfrac{\sigma}{\sqrt{n}}$	Formula (10.2)
One-sample z test	$z = \dfrac{\overline{X} - \mu_0}{\sigma_{\overline{X}}}$	Formula (11.1)
General rule for a confidence interval for μ (σ known)	$\overline{X} \pm z_\alpha \sigma_{\overline{X}}$	Formula (12.3)
Standard deviation (inferential statistic)	$s = \sqrt{\dfrac{\Sigma(X - \overline{X})^2}{n-1}} = \sqrt{\dfrac{SS}{n-1}}$	Formula (13.1)
Standard error of the mean (estimated)	$s_{\overline{X}} = \dfrac{s}{\sqrt{n}}$	Formula (13.2)
One-sample t test	$t = \dfrac{\overline{X} - \mu_0}{s_{\overline{X}}}$	Formula (13.3)
General rule for a confidence interval for μ (σ not known)	$\overline{X} \pm t_\alpha s_{\overline{X}}$	Formula (13.4)
Pooled variance estimate of σ_1^2 and σ_2^2	$s^2_{\text{pooled}} = \dfrac{SS_1 + SS_2}{n_1 + n_2 - 2}$	Formula (14.4)
Estimate of $\sigma_{\overline{X}_1 - \overline{X}_2}$	$s_{\overline{X}_1 - \overline{X}_2} = \sqrt{\dfrac{SS_1 + SS_2}{n_1 + n_2 - 2}\left(\dfrac{1}{n_1} + \dfrac{1}{n_2}\right)}$	Formula (14.5)
t test for two independent samples	$t = \dfrac{\overline{X}_1 - \overline{X}_2}{s_{\overline{X}_1 - \overline{X}_2}}$	Formula (14.6)
General rule for a confidence interval for $\mu_1 - \mu_2$	$(\overline{X}_1 - \overline{X}_2) \pm t_\alpha s_{\overline{X}_1 - \overline{X}_2}$	Formula (14.7)
Effect size, d	$d = \dfrac{\overline{X}_1 - \overline{X}_2}{\sqrt{\dfrac{SS_1 + SS_2}{n_1 + n_2 - 2}}} = \dfrac{\overline{X}_1 - \overline{X}_2}{s_{\text{pooled}}}$	Formula (14.8)
Effect size, $\hat{\omega}^2$ (independent-samples t test)	$\hat{\omega}^2 = \dfrac{t^2 - 1}{t^2 + n_1 + n_2 - 1}$	Formula (14.9)

Standard error of the difference between means (dependent samples)	$s_{\overline{X}_1 - \overline{X}_2} = \sqrt{\dfrac{s_1^2 + s_2^2 - 2r_{12}s_1s_2}{n}}$	Formula (15.1)
t test for two dependent samples: direct-difference method	$t = \dfrac{\overline{D}}{s_{\overline{D}}} = \dfrac{\overline{D}}{\sqrt{\dfrac{SS_D}{n(n-1)}}}$	Formula (15.4)
General rule for confidence interval for μ_D	$\overline{D} \pm t_\alpha s_{\overline{D}}$	Formula (15.6)
Within-groups sum of squares	$SS_{\text{within}} = \overset{\text{all scores}}{\Sigma}(X - \overline{X})^2$	Formula (16.1)
Between-groups sum of squares	$SS_{\text{between}} = \overset{\text{all scores}}{\Sigma}(\overline{X} - \overline{\overline{X}})^2$	Formula (16.3)
Within-groups variance estimate	$s_{\text{within}}^2 = \dfrac{SS_{\text{within}}}{n_{\text{total}} - k}$	Formula (16.8)
Between-groups variance estimate	$s_{\text{between}}^2 = \dfrac{SS_{\text{between}}}{k - 1}$	Formula (16.9)
F-ratio for one-way analysis of variance	$F = \dfrac{s_{\text{between}}^2}{s_{\text{within}}^2}$	Formula (16.10)
Critical HSD for Tukey's test	$HSD = q\sqrt{\dfrac{s_{\text{within}}^2}{n_{\text{group}}}}$	Formula (16.14)
General rule for a confidence interval for $\mu_i - \mu_j$	$\overline{X}_i - \overline{X}_j \pm HSD$	Formula (16.16)
Effect size, $\hat{\omega}^2$ (one-way analysis of variance)	$\hat{\omega}^2 = \dfrac{SS_{\text{between}} - (k-1)s_{\text{within}}^2}{SS_{\text{total}} + s_{\text{within}}^2}$	Formula (16.17)
Standard error of r ($\rho = 0$)	$s_r = \sqrt{\dfrac{1 - r^2}{n - 2}}$	Formula (17.2)
t ratio for r	$t = \dfrac{r}{s_r}$	Formula (17.3)

Chi-square

$$\chi^2 = \sum \left[\frac{(f_o - f_e)^2}{f_e} \right]$$

Formula (18.1)

General rule for a
confidence interval for π

$$\pi_L = \frac{n}{n + 3.84} \left[P + \frac{1.92}{n} - 1.96\sqrt{\frac{P(1 - P)}{n} + \frac{.96}{n^2}} \right]$$

Formulas (18.3)
and (18.4)

$$\pi_U = \frac{n}{n + 3.84} \left[P + \frac{1.92}{n} + 1.96\sqrt{\frac{P(1 - P)}{n} + \frac{.96}{n^2}} \right]$$

Chi-square for a 2×2 table

$$\chi^2 = \frac{n(AD - BC)^2}{(A + B)(C + D)(A + C)(B + D)}$$

Formula (18.9)

Population effect size
(mean difference)

$$\delta = \frac{\mu_1 - \mu_2}{\sigma}$$

Formula (19.1)